Dictionary of Literary Biography

Documentary Series

Yearbooks

1980 edited by Karen L. Rood, Jean W. Ross, and Richard Ziegfeld (1981)

1981 edited by Karen L. Rood, Jean W. Ross, and Richard Ziegfeld (1982)

1982 edited by Richard Ziegfeld; associate editors: Jean W. Ross and Lynne C. Zeigler (1983)

1983 edited by Mary Bruccoli and Jean W. Ross; associate editor: Richard Ziegfeld (1984)

1984 edited by Jean W. Ross (1985)

1985 edited by Jean W. Ross (1986)

1986 edited by J. M. Brook (1987)

1987 edited by J. M. Brook (1988)

1988 edited by J. M. Brook (1989)

1989 edited by J. M. Brook (1990)

1990 edited by James W. Hipp (1991)

1991 edited by James W. Hipp (1992)

1992 edited by James W. Hipp (1993)

1993 edited by James W. Hipp, contributing editor George Garrett (1994)

1994 edited by James W. Hipp, contributing editor George Garrett (1995)

1995 edited by James W. Hipp, contributing editor George Garrett (1996)

1996 edited by Samuel W. Bruce and L. Kay Webster, contributing editor George Garrett (1997)

1997 edited by Matthew J. Bruccoli and George Garrett, with the assistance of L. Kay Webster (1998)

1998 edited by Matthew J. Bruccoli, contributing editor George Garrett, with the assistance of D. W. Thomas (1999)

Concise Series

Concise Dictionary of American Literary Biography, 6 volumes (1988-1989): *The New Consciousness, 1941-1968; Colonization to the American Renaissance, 1640-1865; Realism, Naturalism, and Local Color, 1865-1917; The Twenties, 1917-1929; The Age of Maturity, 1929-1941; Broadening Views, 1968-1988.*

Concise Dictionary of British Literary Biography, 8 volumes (1991-1992): *Writers of the Middle Ages and Renaissance Before 1660; Writers of the Restoration and Eighteenth Century, 1660-1789; Writers of the Romantic Period, 1789-1832; Victorian Writers, 1832-1890; Late-Victorian and Edwardian Writers, 1890-1914; Modern Writers, 1914-1945; Writers After World War II, 1945-1960; Contemporary Writers, 1960 to Present.*

Dictionary of Literary Biography
Yearbook: 1998

Dictionary of Literary Biography
Yearbook: 1998

Edited by
Matthew J. Bruccoli

George Garrett, Contributing Editor

With the Assistance of D. W. Thomas

A Bruccoli Clark Layman Book
The Gale Group
Detroit, Washington, D.C., London

Printed in the United States of America

The paper used in this publication meets the minimum requirements
of American National Standard for Information Sciences–Permanence
Paper for Printed Library Materials, ANSI Z39.48-1984. ⊚™

ISBN 0-7876-2520-5
ISSN 0731-7867

"Nobel Lecture 1998" by José Saramago

Copyright © 1998 by the Nobel Foundation

10 9 8 7 6 5 4 3 2 1

Contents

Contents

Plan of the Series

The advisory board, the editors, and the publisher of the *Dictionary of Literary Biography* are joined in endorsing Mark Twain's declaration. The literature of a nation provides an inexhaustible resource of permanent worth. We intend to make literature and its creators better understood and more accessible to students and the reading public, while satisfying the standards of teachers and scholars.

To meet these requirements, *literary biography* has been construed in terms of the author's achievement. The most important thing about a writer is his writing. Accordingly, the entries in *DLB* are career biographies, tracing the development of the author's canon and the evolution of his reputation.

The purpose of *DLB* is not only to provide reliable information in a convenient format but also to place the figures in the larger perspective of literary history and to offer appraisals of their accomplishments by qualified scholars.

The publication plan for *DLB* resulted from two years of preparation. The project was proposed to Bruccoli Clark by Frederick C. Ruffner, president of the Gale Research Company, in November 1975. After specimen entries were prepared and typeset, an advisory board was formed to refine the entry format and develop the series rationale. In meetings held during 1976, the publisher, series editors, and advisory board approved the scheme for a comprehensive biographical dictionary of persons who contributed to North American literature. Editorial work on the first volume began in January 1977, and it was published in 1978. In order to make *DLB* more than a reference tool and to compile volumes that individually have claim to status as literary history, it was decided to organize volumes by

topic, period, or genre. Each of these freestanding volumes provides a biographical-bibliographical guide and overview for a particular area of literature. We are convinced that this organization—as opposed to a single alphabet method—constitutes a valuable innovation in the presentation of reference material. The volume plan necessarily requires many decisions for the placement and treatment of authors who might properly be included in two or three volumes. In some instances a major figure will be included in separate volumes, but with different entries emphasizing the aspect of his career appropriate to each volume. Ernest Hemingway, for example, is represented in *American Writers in Paris, 1920–1939* by an entry focusing on his expatriate apprenticeship; he is also in *American Novelists, 1910–1945* with an entry surveying his entire career, as well as in *American Short-Story Writers, 1910–1945, Second Series* with an entry concentrating on his short stories. Each volume includes a cumulative index of the subject authors and articles. Comprehensive indexes to the entire series are planned.

Since 1981 the series has been further augmented by the *DLB Yearbooks*, which update published entries and add new entries to keep the *DLB* current with contemporary activity. There have also been *DLB Documentary Series* volumes which provide biographical and critical source materials for figures whose work is judged to have particular interest for students. One of these companion volumes is entirely devoted to Tennessee Williams.

We define literature as the *intellectual commerce of a nation*: not merely as belles lettres but as that ample and complex process by which ideas are generated, shaped, and transmitted. *DLB* entries are not limited to "creative writers" but extend to other figures who in their time and in their way influenced the mind of a people. Thus the series encompasses historians, journalists, publishers, book collectors, and screenwriters. By this means readers of *DLB* may be aided to perceive literature not as cult scripture in the keeping of intellectual high priests but firmly positioned at the center of a nation's life.

DLB includes the major writers appropriate to each volume and those standing in the ranks behind them. Scholarly and critical counsel has been sought in deciding which minor figures to include and how full their entries should be. Wherever possible, useful references are made to figures who do not warrant separate entries.

Each *DLB* volume has an expert volume editor responsible for planning the volume, selecting the figures for inclusion, and assigning the entries. Volume editors are also responsible for preparing, where appropriate, appendices surveying the major periodicals and literary and intellectual movements for their volumes, as well as lists of further readings. Work on the series as a whole is coordinated at the Bruccoli Clark Layman editorial center in Columbia, South Carolina, where the editorial staff is responsible for accuracy and utility of the published volumes.

One feature that distinguishes *DLB* is the illustration policy–its concern with the iconography of literature. Just as an author is influenced by his surroundings, so is the reader's understanding of the author enhanced by a knowledge of his environment. Therefore *DLB* volumes include not only drawings, paintings, and photographs of authors, often depicting them at various stages in their careers, but also illustrations of their families and places where they lived. Title pages are regularly reproduced in facsimile along with dust jackets for modern authors. The dust jackets are a special feature of *DLB* because they often document better than anything else the way in which an author's work was perceived in its own time. Specimens of the writers' manuscripts and letters are included when feasible.

Samuel Johnson rightly decreed that "The chief glory of every people arises from its authors." The purpose of the *Dictionary of Literary Biography* is to compile literary history in the surest way available to us–by accurate and comprehensive treatment of the lives and work of those who contributed to it.

The *DLB* Advisory Board

Foreword

The *Dictionary of Literary Biography Yearbook* adheres to the same principles that have provided the basic rationale for the entire *DLB* series: 1) the literature of a nation represents an inexhaustible resource of permanent worth; 2) the surest way to trace the outlines of literary history is by a comprehensive treatment of our lives and works of those who contributed to it; and 3) the greatest service the series can provide is to make literary achievements better understood and more accessible to students and the literate public, while serving the needs of scholars. In keeping with those principles, the *Yearbook* has been planned to augment *DLB* by reflecting the vitality of contemporary literature and summarizing current literary activity. The librarian, scholar, or student attempting to stay informed of literary developments is faced with an endless task. The purpose of the *DLB Yearbook* is to serve those readers while at the same time enlarging the scope of the *DLB*.

The *Yearbook* includes articles about the past year's literary events or topics, as well as obituaries and tributes. Each *Yearbook* also includes a list of literary prizes and awards, a necrology, and a checklist of literary histories and biographies published during the year. This *Yearbook* continues the *Dictionary of Literary Biography Yearbook* Awards for the novel, first novel, poetry, children's book, and literary biography.

From the outset, the *DLB* series has undertaken to compile literary history as it is revealed in the lives and works of authors. The *Yearbook* supports the commitment, providing a useful and necessary current record.

Acknowledgments

This book was produced by Bruccoli Clark Layman, Inc. Karen L. Rood is senior editor for the *Dictionary of Literary Biography* series. D. W. Thomas was the in-house editor.

Production manager is Philip B. Dematteis.

Administrative support was provided by Ann M. Cheschi, Tenesha S. Lee, and Angi Pleasant.

Accountant is Neil Senol.

Copyediting supervisor is Phyllis A. Avant. The copyediting staff includes Ronald D. Aiken II, Brenda Carol Blanton, Thom Harman, Melissa D. Hinton, Beth Peters, Raegan E. Quinn, and Audra Rouse. Freelance copyeditors are Brenda Cabra, Rebecca Mayo, Nicole M. Nichols, and Jennie Williamson.

Layout and graphics staff includes Janet E. Hill and John F. Henson.

Office manager is Kathy Lawler Merlette.

Photography editors are Margo Dowling, Charles Mims, Scott Nemzek, Alison Smith, and Paul Talbot. Digital photographic copy work was performed by Joseph M. Bruccoli.

SGML supervisor is Cory McNair. The SGML staff includes Tim Bedford, Linda Drake, Frank Graham, Joann Whittaker, and Alex Snead.

Systems manager is Marie L. Parker.

Database manager is Javed Nurani. Kimberly Kelly performed data entry.

Typesetting supervisor is Kathleen M. Flanagan. The typesetting staff includes Karla Corley Brown, Mark J. McEwan, Patricia Flanagan Salisbury, and Kathy F. Wooldridge. Freelance typesetters include Deidre Murphy and Delores Plastow.

Walter W. Ross and Steven Gross did library research. They were assisted by the following librarians at the Thomas Cooper Library of the University of South Carolina: Linda Holderfield and the interlibrary-loan staff; reference-department head Virginia Weathers; reference librarians Marilee Birchfield, Stefanie Buck, Stefanie DuBose, Rebecca Feind, Karen Joseph, Donna Lehman, Charlene Loope, Anthony McKissick, Jean Rhyne, and Kwamine Simpson; circulation-department head Caroline Taylor; and acquisitions-searching supervisor David Haggard.

Dictionary of Literary Biography
Yearbook: 1998

Dictionary of Literary Biography

The 1998 Nobel Prize in Literature
José Saramago
(16 November 1922 –)

Celso Lemos de Oliveira
University of South Carolina

BOOKS: *Terra do Pecado* (Lisbon: Editorial Minserva, 1947);

Os Poemas Possíveis (Lisbon: Portugália, 1966);

Provavelmente Alegria (Lisbon: Livros Horizonte, 1970);

Deste Mundo e do Outro (Lisbon: Arcadia, 1971);

A Bagagem do Viajante (Lisbon: Futura, 1973);

As Opiniões Que o DL Teve (Lisbon: Futura, 1974);

O Ano de 1993 (Lisbon: Futura, 1975);

Os Apontamentos (Lisbon: Seara Nova, 1976);

Manual de Pintura e Caligrafia (Lisbon: Moraes Editores, 1977);

Objecto Quase (Lisbon: Moraes Editores, 1978);

A Noite (Lisbon: Caminho, 1979);

Poética dos Cinco Sentidos–Ouvido (Lisbon: Bertrand, 1979);

Que Farei com Este Livro? (Lisbon: Caminho, 1980);

Levantado do Chão (Lisbon: Caminho, 1980);

Viagem a Portugal (Lisbon: Circulo de Leitores, 1981);

Memorial do Convento (Lisbon: Caminho, 1982);

O Ano da Morte de Ricardo Reis (Lisbon: Caminho, 1984);

A Jangada de Pedra (Lisbon: Caminho, 1986);

A Segunda Vida de Francisco de Assis (Lisbon: Caminho, 1989);

História do Cerco de Lisboa (Lisbon: Caminho, 1989);

O Evangelho Segundo Jesus Cristo (Lisbon: Caminho, 1991);

In Nomine Dei (Lisbon: Caminho, 1993);

Cadernos de Lanzarote I (Lisbon: Caminho, 1994);

Ensaio Sobre a Cegueira (Lisbon: Caminho, 1995);

Cadernos de Lanzarote II (Lisbon: Caminho, 1995);

Cadernos de Lanzarote III (Lisbon: Caminho, 1996);

Todos os Nomes (Lisbon: Caminho, 1997);

Cadernos de Lanzarote IV (Lisbon: Caminho, 1997);

José Saramago, from the dust jacket of Blindness *(1998)*

Cadernos de Lanzarote V (Lisbon: Caminho, 1998).

Editions in English: *Baltasar and Blimunda* (New York: Harcourt Brace, 1987);

The Year of the Death of Ricardo Reis (New York: Harcourt Brace, 1990);

Manual of Painting and Calligraphy (Manchester: Carcanet Press, 1994);

The Gospel According to Jesus Christ (New York: Harcourt Brace Jovanovich, 1994);

The Stone Raft (New York: Harcourt Brace, 1995);

The History of the Siege of Lisbon (New York: Harcourt Brace Jovanovich, 1997);

Blindness (New York: Harcourt Brace, 1998).

When José Saramago received the Nobel Prize in Literature on 8 October 1998, President Jorge Sampaio of Portugal described the award as a "recognition of Portuguese culture." The headline on the story in *USA Today* read, "Writer, his language are Nobel winners," and other journalistic accounts suggested that more than a single literary figure was being honored. As the first Portuguese writer to win the award, Saramago said, "The Portuguese language had to wait 100 years for this," and "Portuguese will become more visible and more audible." When he heard the news he was at the Frankfurt airport, en route to Madrid, after having attended the Book Fair; he immediately returned to receive congratulations and champagne from his many admirers. He has been translated into more than twenty languages, and the Frankfurt Book Fair, with its international clientele, was an appropriate place for him to be recognized.

Although Portugal has a long cultural tradition, it is small, with a population of only ten million, many of whom have lived in modest circumstances, at least until recently. It has sometimes been overshadowed by neighboring Spain. But, like Spain, it had a Golden Age and an empire during the late Renaissance, and from time to time important writers have emerged. Saramago is very much aware of his country's history, and several of his novels are concerned with some of its major events. Three Portuguese writers might be mentioned as being in the background of his work. Luis de Camões (1524?–1580), who is still considered by some as the greatest figure in Portuguese literature, wrote the epic poem *Os Lusíadas* (The Portuguese), published in 1572. Modeled on Virgil's *Aeneid* and influenced in its technique by Ariosto's *Orlando Furioso,* it is a national poem whose central character is the explorer Vasco da Gama (1469?–1524), the first European to reach India. It was published at a high moment in Portugal's history and stands as a kind of monument to national achievement. Portugal was not touched in a decisive way by the Enlightenment of the eighteenth century or the Romantic movement, but in the late nineteenth century a first-rate novelist appeared. This was Eça de Queiroz (1845–1900), whose work was influenced by Gustave Flaubert. Living in Paris after 1888 as the Portuguese consul, he knew well the British and French traditions

in novel writing. As the eminent British critic V. S. Pritchett remarked, Eça "was responsive to the intellectual forces that were bringing the European novel to the height of its powers." His finest novel, *Os Maias* (The Maias) was published in 1888. This chronicle of a great Portuguese family in decline might rank as one of the best European novels of its period.

Finally there is the poet Fernando Pessoa (1888–1935), a modernist figure born in the same year as T. S. Eliot. Although he is only now, during the 1990s, becoming well known in English, he is increasingly considered a writer of international importance. The critic Harold Bloom recently devoted part of a chapter to him in *The Western Canon;* Bloom sees him as an heir to Walt Whitman. Saramago considers him one of this century's three greatest writers—the other two are Franz Kafka and Jorge Luis Borges. One of Saramago's finest novels, *The Year of the Death of Ricardo Reis* (1984) is an homage to Pessoa, who appears in the novel as a ghost.

Saramago was born in 1922 in Azinhaga, a small farming community in the province of Ribatejo; his family members were poor laborers. According to an account of his career in the Brazilian magazine *Veja,* his real name was José de Souza. *Saramago* (meaning a wild radish) was his father's nickname, no doubt well known in the community, and when the child's birth was registered, he was called José de Souza Saramago, which has been his name ever since. When he was only two years old the family moved to Lisbon, where he had an education of a sort. His family was so poor that he had to attend a trade school, but he was forced to drop out and become an automobile mechanic. His real literary education came by way of the public library, where he read at night. Despite these adverse circumstances, Saramago acquired a first-rate knowledge of literary history, and not just Portuguese. In a recent essay, published in translation in the London *Times Literary Supplement,* he shows his familiarity with great works from the Homeric poems to the novels of such contemporaries as Gabriel García Márquez.

Those nights in the public library must have inspired him to try his hand at being a writer, and in 1947 he managed to publish a novel called *Terra do Pecado* (Land of Sin). He was only twenty-five. This conventional novel, a tale of peasant life which may have been suggested by his family background, sold poorly, but at least it introduced him to the literary world of Lisbon. It has never been republished, and indeed some bibliographies of Saramago's work do not even mention it, as though the author were ashamed of it. He did not publish another novel for thirty years. Meanwhile he wrote poetry in his youth, like so many novelists from Sir Walter Scott to William Faulkner. In his recent essay he mentions the historical movement from poetry to the novel, from Homer to Marcel Proust and James Joyce, and he seems to suggest that individual writers often re-create this movement in their careers. At any rate, he published three collections of poetry (in 1966, 1970, and 1975) before he turned to the novel in 1977.

What of his life outside his books? He was married and had a daughter, but his private life has never been publicized, and as of 1998, despite his literary fame, he does not appear in *Who's Who* or *International Who's Who*. It is known that he had various jobs, in a publishing house, an insurance agency, and the government; none of these ever became a real vocation. He did frequently write *crónicas* (short essays on political and literary subjects) for the newspapers, and four volumes of these were published during the 1970s. During much of Saramago's lifetime Portugal was under the authoritarian (some say the fascist) rule of António Salazar, the prime minister beginning in 1932, and Saramago, like many others, actively opposed his regime. In 1969 he joined the Communist Party, then illegal; he is still a member, although he has often been critical of the Party. After the death of Salazar in 1970 and the Revolution of April 1974, he was an editor of a major Lisbon newspaper, *Diário de Notícias,* but in November 1975 he was forced from this position by anticommunist factions in the government and left without a job. He then began translating French texts into Portuguese, and at last he turned to fiction.

His debut as a novelist (if one disregards the youthful *Terra do Pecado,* as Saramago would prefer) came with *Manual de Pintura e Caligrafia* in 1977. This translates as *Manual of Painting and Calligraphy* and was published in England in 1994 following the fame that Saramago was rapidly attaining with two later novels. He was already fifty-five years old in 1977. This novel is a kind of parable of his own situation as an artist. The central character is an undistinguished painter who gradually "finds himself" as a writer. He is involved with two women, one of whom is the mistress of a prominent political figure in the post-Salazar regime; this man is sitting for his portrait being painted by our artist. The other woman is the sister of a political prisoner. Obviously the extremities of the political situation in Portugal during the early 1970s gave Saramago the framework for his novel. His hero abandons the portrait of the authoritarian politician and discovers his real vocation as a writer. This is a theme that has been used by a number of authors, for instance Proust at the end of *Remembrance of Things Past* and Joyce in *A Portrait of the Artist as a Young Man.* But Saramago has given the situation a political dimension, and his novel ends with the Revolution of April 1974, which happens just as his hero "finds himself" as a writer. Composing this novel a year or so later, Saramago is taking a rather ironic view

Dust jacket for a Saramago novel about the lives of the rural poor of his native province

of his own situation, somewhat like Herman Melville in his "Bartleby the Scrivener." Richard Zenith, a critic writing from Lisbon soon after Saramago won the Nobel Prize, comments that this novel "was a kind of blueprint, too schematic to make a truly good novel, but serving as an enduring statement of intent: art in alliance with ideas, ideals and the verbalized expression of experience." Although it has not been published in the United States, it has been available in the British edition and of course remains in print in Portuguese.

Saramago soon became a professional writer who published plays, a travel book called *Viagem a Portugal* (Journey to Portugal, 1981), and short stories as well as novels. His next novel, *Levantado do Chão* (Raised from the Ground, 1980), has not yet been translated into English, but a brief account of the Portuguese edition is of some interest. The author returns to the subject of his earliest novel, the forgotten *Terra do Pecado* of 1947. Again he takes up the life of the poor agricultural workers of Alentejo, his native province, but the scale of this novel is much larger than that of *Terra do Pecado,* and it moves through several generations. Since Saramago's novels to date, taken together, form a kind of history of Portugal over several centuries, this account of rural poverty in the twentieth century has some importance in his work. It is relatively conventional in technique; that is perhaps why critics in Portugal and elsewhere have not paid much attention to it.

By this time Saramago's momentum as a novelist was well under way; he was sixty years old and just moving into his full creativity in 1982. In that year he published *Memorial do Convento* (literally Memoir of the Convent but translated as *Baltasar and Blimunda* in 1987). This novel had international success, and indeed the Swedish Academy, in its citation for the Nobel Prize, noted that "This is a rich, multifaceted and polysemous text that at the same time has a historical, a social and an individual perspective." It is set in Portugal during the eighteenth century, when the Inquisition lingered and life could be very grim for those caught in its operations. At this time King João V decreed that the enormous Convent of Mafra, near Lisbon, be created as a monument to Church and monarchy. It required the labor of thousands of peasants—an event reminiscent of the construction of St. Petersburg in Russia earlier in the eighteenth century. Saramago uses historical figures in his re-creation of this little world. The most important is Padre Bartolomeu de Gusmão, a Brazilian-born priest who conceived a flying machine, the *passarola,* and actually carried out experiments with hot-air balloons. If he were successful, he could be brought before the Inquisition.

Richard A. Preto-Rodas, an American scholar, points out that Saramago "contrasts these two enterprises throughout his novel, so that the convent becomes the expression of the dead weight of reactionary absolutism while the flying machine embodies the aspiration of a few to soar above the limitations of their time." Saramago uses two fictional characters at the center of his story: Baltasar Mateus, a soldier who has lost a hand in the recent wars; and Blimunda, an attractive young woman who is clairvoyant. These two seem to have some immediate affinity for each other; they meet at an auto-da-fé, where they also encounter Bartolomeu de Gusmão. So there is a love story set within the historical situation, and Saramago elaborates it by having Domenico Scarlatti (1685–1757), the Italian composer, as a kindred spirit. Scarlatti, the most famous of composers for the harpsichord, actually was attached to the court at Lisbon at this time, but he is not known to have had any political opinions. Obviously, as a musician he also represents the aspiration "to soar above the limitations of their time," as figured by the

auto-da-fé, described in graphic and horrifying detail. Saramago's main episode involves the *passarola* that is successfully fabricated by Padre Bartolomeu (with background music provided by Scarlatti). The priest, however, fears the Inquisition and flees, and Scarlatti leaves. The two lovers, as they have become, keep the *passarola* hidden. At the climax of the novel Baltazar is accidentally lifted towards the sun in his flying machine and disappears from sight. For nine years Blimunda searches for him in vain, but she suddenly comes upon his remains at an auto-da-fé in Lisbon; he has been burned at the stake. The novelist has combined a remarkable synthesis of historical and fictional elements here; what was only potential (for instance, the priest's flying machine) becomes actual, and only a reader who insisted on separating historical details from Saramago's fable would have any problem in accepting the result.

Some readers have referred to the "baroque" features of Saramago's work. Richard Preto-Rodas draws attention to the way in which the novelist paraphrases Camões's *Os Lusíadas* at certain points in a parody of the epic style, just as British and American writers have often referred to John Milton's *Paradise Lost.* Another stylistic source for Saramago is the baroque writer Padre António Vieira (1608–1697), who was born in Portugal but taken to Brazil when he was six years old and spent much of his life there. This Jesuit priest was the founder of a school of religious eloquence, and the fifteen volumes of his sermons are still reprinted and admired for their qualities of style. A somewhat parallel case in English would be the sermons of John Donne, which have been taken up by a number of twentieth-century writers. At any rate, *Memorial do Convento* was Saramago's "breakthrough" as a novelist. He was soon being translated into almost every European language, and an Italian composer, Azio Corgi, inspired by this novel, wrote a three-act opera, "Blimunda," which was performed at La Scala in Milan in 1990. Corgi was perhaps attracted to the idea of a famous Italian predecessor having some part, however fictional, in Portuguese history.

O Ano da Morte de Ricardo Reis (1984) is said to be Saramago's favorite among his novels; it was published in the United States as *The Year of the Death of Ricardo Reis* in 1990. *The Year of the Death of Ricardo Reis* alludes directly to Fernanco Pessoa, Portugal's great modernist poet, who died in 1935. Pessoa was, according to the British poet-critic Michael Hamburger, "the most extreme case of multiple personality and self-division in modern poetry." He divided his poetic self into four authors, each of whom writes his own style of poetry. Many modern poets (for instance Eliot in "The Love Song of J. Alfred Prufrock") have written with *personae,* but not in the thoroughgoing way that Pessoa did. One of his heteronyms or disguises is Ricardo Reis, who writes "classical" poems in traditional stanzas. In the novel Saramago makes him into the principal character, who in fact survives Pessoa.

The novel is set in 1936, the year after Pessoa actually died, early in the Salazar dictatorship. Ricardo Reis, a doctor, has been living for sixteen years in Brazil, and he returns at the end of 1935 to a Europe in which Hitler is already a threat; the Spanish Civil War will soon break out. He is forty-eight, a bachelor evidently without any family, and indeed he is not even sure where he is going to stay. But he remembers a hotel overlooking the river, the Bragança, and that is where some of the action takes place. Bragança is the name of the Portuguese royal family that ruled until 1910, when a republic was established. The point about the name is that Reis fled to Brazil in 1919 because of his monarchist sympathies.

Reis heard about the death of Fernando Pessoa from Álvaro de Campos, who is another of Pessoa's *personae,* a poet influenced by Walt Whitman in his irregular rhapsodic style. Although Reis thinks about setting up his medical practice in Lisbon, he spends much of the time walking the streets and reciting his poetry, which of course was composed by Pessoa. Pessoa himself visits the doctor as a ghostly presence who engages him in dialogues, usually on the state of public events in 1936. Saramago writes very long paragraphs that sometimes run to several pages, and part of his fictional technique is to blend dialogue into the narrative. Here is a typical passage:

> Fernando Pessoa rose from the sofa, buttoned his jacket, and adjusted the knot in his tie, going by the natural order of things he would have done just the opposite, Well, I'm off now, I'll see you one of these days, and thanks for being so patient, the world is in even worse shape than when I left it, and Spain is almost certainly heading for civil war. Do you think so. If the best prophets are those who are already dead, then at least I have that advantage. Try not to make any noise when you go downstairs, on account of the neighbors. I shall descend like a feather. And don't bang the front door, Don't worry, the lid of the tomb makes no echo. Good night Fernando, Sleep well, Ricardo.

If Fernando Pessoa uses Ricardo Reis as one of the spokesmen to express his complex poetic personality, then one can say that Saramago in turn uses Pessoa for his meditations on politics and art. In a sense this novel is a kind of high comedy on the nature of reality and illusion, and one can understand why Saramago is a great admirer of Borges, his Argentine predecessor.

The novel is not altogether meditation, because Ricardo Reis is involved in affairs with two women at

Cover for the translation of the Saramago novel that the author regards as his favorite

the Hotel Bragança. One is Lydia, the chambermaid who brings his breakfast; she soon moves to his bed and becomes his lover. At the same time he is attracted to Marcenda, a rich young girl, the daughter of another guest in the hotel. She is afflicted with a withered arm, and the doctor is perhaps drawn to her out of pity as much as love. But these two relationships are not as important as his visitations from Fernando Pessoa, and on his last appearance they leave the world together; hence the title of the novel, whose first sentence is, "Here the sea ends and the earth begins." The final sentence is, "Here, where the sea ends and the earth awaits."

By this time Saramago was writing a novel every other year. *A Jangada de Pedra* was published in 1986; the English translation, *The Stone Raft,* came out in the United States in 1995. This novel is based on a kind of conceit—the possibility that the Iberian Peninsula could be separated from the rest of Europe. In 1937, during the Spanish Civil War, the English poet W. H. Auden wrote a meditation on history called "Spain," which contains these lines:

> On that arid square, that fragment nipped off from hot Africa, soldered so crudely to inventive Europe;

And Saramago supposes the reverse process, with the peninsula drifting toward the Azores in the direction of the New World; Gilbraltar, still a British colony, is left behind. The novel could be taking place in 1986, the date of its publication in Lisbon, which is also the year when Portugal and Spain joined the European Community. The irony of this coincidence may be deliberate.

Saramago builds up his fable, with its obvious political overtones, through a group of five characters who are introduced in the opening chapter, strangers who are gradually involved with each other. There is also a dog called Ardent who has a considerable part in the story. The geological cataclysm is actually very gradual. The first crack appears in the Pyrenees, but, as the inhabitants of the peninsula begin to realize what is happening, they flee from the coastal cities (Lisbon and Oporto) that would get the first impact of the collision if the Stone Raft hit the Azores. The tourists have already gone back to France as all Europe has begun to realize what has happened. The three men of the quintet, one of them a Spaniard named Pedro Orce, start a trip round the peninsula in a small car called the Deux Chevaux, whose advantage is that it uses very little fuel at a time when there is a gasoline shortage. They evidently are headed for a town in Ribatejo, the province of which Saramago is a native. Along the way they pass through the tourist resorts of Spain and Portugal. In the Algarve the homeless are moving into the deserted fashionable hotels. When they reach Lisbon, they take rooms in the Hotel Bragança, where Ricardo Reis stayed long ago. At this point one of the women, Joana Carda, turns up; she stays at the Hotel Borges, which could be an allusion to the Argentine writer whom Saramago admires, even though the name is fairly common in Portuguese. Joana Carda actually opened the novel by scratching the ground with an elm branch, portending the more serious breach in the Pyrenees that soon emerges. But she hasn't been seen for one hundred pages. At any rate, the affair that she has with José Anaico, one of the trio of travelers, repeats some of the action of *The Year of the Death of Ricardo Reis*.

Saramago covers a lot of territory in *The Stone Raft*, a novel about the Iberian world and its place in history. We move, through the narrative voice, from contemporary Lisbon to Paris to London, finally to the United States and Canada, because the Stone Raft will evidently settle somewhere closer to North America than to Europe. Despite the large theme, which might be given various political interpretations, the texture of the novel is as vivid as anything that Saramago has written, and the narrative voice is witty and ironic. As Richard Zenith has observed, Saramago has "reinvigorated the Continental tradition of novels founded on ideas. . . ." At the end of the twentieth century the inhabitants of the Iberian Peninsula are indeed preoccupied with their place in the global civilization dominated by the United States. Saramago "interprets" his fable of the Stone Raft in the language of a Henry Kissinger:

> From the standpoint of realpolitik, discussion of the problem in European and American foreign ministries centered on spheres of influence, that is to say on whether, ignoring the question of distance, the peninsula or island should preserve its natural ties with Europe, or whether, without entirely severing them, it should orient itself rather toward the ideal and destiny of the great American nation.

His next novel, *História do Cerco de Lisboa* (1989; translated as *The History of the Siege of Lisbon* in 1996), is also a witty exploration of Portugal's history and destiny. In this case the principal character, Raimundo Silva, is a proofreader at a publishing house in present-day Lisbon. One day he impulsively changes the meaning of a text (*The History of the Siege of Lisbon*, in fact) by inserting the word "not" in a crucial passage of historiography. This concerns the first Portuguese king, Afonso I, who in 1147 sought the assistance of the Crusaders in expelling the Moors from Lisbon. Raimundo's little change in the text now in effect rewrites history; the Crusaders, according to his revision, will *not* help Afonso to conquer Lisbon, an important event in the national saga. Twelve days later Raimundo's subversive act is discovered. It could be the end of his career at this publishing house, but a new supervisor, Maria Sara, is rather captivated by the consequences, and she urges him to write a revisionist history based on his impulsive change. So now we have a book being rewritten within a book of the same title.

Giovanni Pontiero, Saramago's translator, has a short "Afterword" at the end of the Harcourt Brace edition. As he observes,

> The book operates on two planes of action: one set in the twelfth century, packed with key episodes of the alternative history of the siege of Lisbon the proofreader Raimundo Silva feels compelled to write; the other in the twentieth century, dealing with the routine existence of the proofreader's daily life. . . .

The parallels suggested by this narrative structure are very intricate. The proofreader falls in love with Maria

Sara, who in turn is intrigued by him and his fanciful historiography. His revisionist account of the siege of Lisbon introduces a Portuguese hero's love for a concubine, Ouroana; this suggests a blending of the Catholic religion of the twelfth century with Islam. At one point Raimundo Silva, writing his history, thinks of Fernando Pessoa as a kind of role model, and indeed there are resemblances between the great poet and the timid withdrawn proofreader.

The religious issue, which has been more than hinted at in some of the earlier novels, becomes central in *O Evangelho Segundo Jesus Christo* (1991; translated as *The Gospel According to Jesus Christ* in 1994). This is Saramago's most controversial novel, especially in Portugal. Like Nikos Kazantzakis's *The Last Temptation of Christ* (1951: translation in 1960) and Norman Mailer's *The Gospel According to the Son* (1997), its interpretation of Jesus is decidedly unconventional. He is the son of Joseph, not of God, and thus is completely human. Indeed Saramago directs his criticism against God for using Jesus as the center of a religion that has produced intolerance and bloodshed; the God of this novel is a despot. The human Jesus may be fallible, but not in the way that God is. Jesus even argues with God over these matters:

> "Being God, You must know everything, Up to a certain point, What point is that, the point where it starts to become interesting to pretend that I know nothing. . . ."

For many Christian readers the most blasphemous episode may be the meeting and lovemaking between Jesus and Mary Magdalene; like all erotic scenes in Saramago's novels, it is discreet but powerful. Although the novelist adds little to the Gospel story, he does make rather more out of Joseph, as the father of Jesus. Joseph has accidentally heard about the massacre of the innocents that Herod plans for Bethlehem, and he flees with his wife and son, as in the traditional account. But he fails to warn the other parents and consequently suffers from his guilt in this matter. Later he is mistakenly accused of treachery by the Romans and crucified on a hill at the age of thirty-three. So the son will eventually repeat the fate of his father, and Saramago clearly implies that Jesus is sacrificed for his father's sins; ultimately the evil originates with God. The presentation of this story is done in a beautiful austere style that has reminded some readers of Franz Kafka in *The Castle* and *The Trial.* It is quite different from the pseudobiblical style of Mailer in *The Gospel According to the Son,* which was published three years after Saramago's novel appeared in translation. Saramago, unlike Mailer, was harshly criticized by the Vatican and the then-conservative government of Portugal.

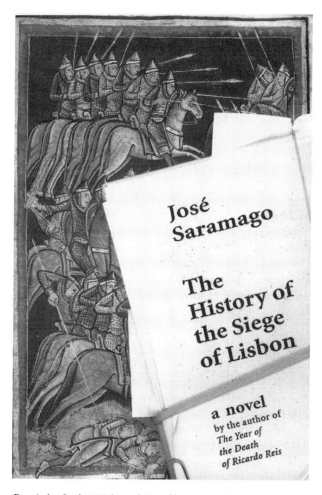

Dust jacket for the 1996 translation of Saramago's historical novel set in twelfth-century Portugal

Nevertheless, the novel has had its greatest success in Brazil, the world's largest Roman Catholic country.

Ensaio Sobre a Cegueira (1995; translated as *Blindness,* 1998) is even more Kafkaesque. It is an allegory set in a nameless country at no particular date; here the author seems to depart from his usual preoccupation with Portuguese history, but the physical details indicate that it is a subject of our time. The characters have no names; they are distinguished by their professional roles as much as anything else. A number of readers have mentioned Albert Camus's *The Plague* (1947) as a predecessor, and there are certainly some similarities, but Saramago has his own style that links this novel with his others.

In brief, it concerns an entire population that loses its sight—all but the wife of an ophthamologist, and she pretends to go blind. The victims are at first kept in an abandoned mental asylum, but their number increases and they take to the streets. The social system breaks down and unbelievable filth clutters the city. Although the blind are capable of occasional generosity, even they are violent.

Out of this human chaos seven characters emerge. All of them have some association with blindness or seeing: for example, a cross-eyed boy, a young lady who always wears sunglasses, and the ophthamologist. His wife is the central figure. She leads the little group as best as she can, and at a certain point she reveals that she has only feigned blindness, perhaps out of guilt that she has been so fortunate. At the end an incredible light takes over the scene, anticipated at the beginning of the novel when a driver, sitting in his car waiting for a traffic light to change, suddenly is struck blind as if he "had fallen into a milky sea." Saramago's own comment on his novel is worth quoting: "This blindness isn't a real blindness, it's a blindness of rationality. We're rational beings but we don't behave rationally. If we did, there would be no starvation in the world."

In his recent essay in the *Times Literary Supplement* Saramago proposes that the literary genre we call the novel is gradually returning to the condition of poetry. Certainly he is not the first modern writer to hold such a view, but it does seem to describe the evolution of his work to date, and perhaps it describes the movement of any one of his mature books. His most recent novel, *Todos os Nomes* (All the Names, 1997) concerns a clerk in a public records office in Lisbon. He chances on a woman in the records. Who was she? What was her name? This obsession leads him on an endless search that in its way is a love story. And at the end of 1998 Saramago is writing another novel to be called *A Caverna* (The Cave), which starts with the famous allegory of the cave in Plato's *Republic,* in which humankind confuses shadows with reality.

At the age of seventy-six Saramago stands at the peak of a brilliant career that started late. He has been publishing his diaries under the title of *Cadernos de Lanzarote,* five volumes of which are as yet untranslated, like his other work aside from the novels. Lanzarote is one of the Canary Islands; it has been his home since 1992, when he moved there from Lisbon. He is married to María del Pilar, a Spanish journalist and his second wife. It may be that this marriage and his move to Spanish territory are indications of his Iberian, not just his Portuguese, loyalties. This is a theme that was already evident in *The Stone Raft.* At any rate, he is unquestionably one of the more important literary figures during the second half of the century in Europe, and with the Nobel Prize, he has achieved a well-deserved transatlantic fame as well.

References:

W. H. Auden, "Spain," in *Selected Poems,* edited by Edward Mendelson (New York: Vintage, 1979): 51–55;

Harold Bloom, *The Western Canon* (New York: Harcourt Brace, 1994);

Horácio Costa, *José Saramago: O Periodo Formativo* (Lisbon: Caminho, 1997);

Deirdre Donahue, "Writer, His Language are Nobel Winners," *USA Today,* 9 October 1998, p. 16;

Carlos Graieb, "O Nobel em Portugal," *Veja,* 14 October 1998, pp. 142–145;

Michael Hamburger, *The Truth of Poetry* (London: Weidenfeld & Nicolson, 1969);

Richard A. Preto-Rodas, "A View of Eighteenth-Century Portugal: José Saramago's *Memorial do covento,*" *World Literature Today,* 61 (1987): 27–31;

José Saramago, "Erratic Odyssey: The Novel's Return towards the Condition of Poetry," *Times Literary Supplement,* 20 November 1998, p. 14;

James Wood, "The Seeing I: Review of Saramago's *Blindness,*" *New Republic,* 219 (1998): 48–56;

Richard Zenith, "Letter from Lisbon," *Times Literary Supplement,* 23 October 1998, p. 18.

Nobel Lecture 1998

José Saramago

How Characters Became the Masters and the Author Their Apprentice

The wisest man I ever knew in my whole life could not read or write. At four o'clock in the morning, when the promise of a new day still lingered over French lands, he got up from his pallet and left for the fields, taking to pasture the half-dozen pigs whose fertility nourished him and his wife. My mother's parents lived on this scarcity, on the small breeding of pigs that after weaning were sold to the neighbors in our village of Azinhaga in the province of Ribatejo. Their names were Jerónimo Melrinho and Josefa Caixinha and they were both illiterate. In winter when the cold of the night grew to the point of freezing the water in the pots inside the house, they went to the sty and fetched the weaklings among the piglets, taking them to their bed. Under the coarse blankets, the warmth from the humans saved the little animals from freezing and rescued them from certain death. Although the two were kindly people, it was not a compassionate soul that prompted them to act in that way: what concerned them, without sentimentalism or rhetoric, was to protect their daily bread, as is natural for people who, to maintain their life, have not learnt to think more than is needful. Many times I helped my grandfather Jerónimo in his swineherd's labor, many times I dug the land in the vegetable garden adjoining the house, and I chopped wood for the fire, many times, turning and turning the big iron wheel which worked the water pump. I pumped water from the community well and carried it on my shoulders. Many times, in secret, dodging from the men guarding the cornfields, I went with my grandmother, also at dawn, armed with rakes, sacking and cord, to glean the stubble, the loose straw that would then serve as litter for the livestock. And sometimes, on hot summer nights, after supper, my grandfather would tell me: "José, tonight we're going to sleep, both of us, under the fig tree." There were two other fig trees, but that one, certainly because it was the biggest, because it was the oldest, and timeless, was, for everybody in the house, the fig tree. More or less by antonomasia, an erudite word that I met only many years after and learned the meaning of. . . . Amongst the peace of the night, amongst the tree's high branches a star appeared to me and then slowly hid behind a leaf while, turning my gaze in another direction I saw rising into view like a river flowing silent through the hollow sky, the opal clarity of the Milky Way, the road to Santiago as we still used to call it in the village. With sleep delayed, night was peopled with the stories and the cases my grandfather told and told: legends, apparitions, terrors, unique episodes, old deaths, scuffles with sticks and stones, the words of our forefathers, an untiring rumor of memories that would keep me awake while at the same time gently lulling me. I could never know if he was silent when he realized that I had fallen asleep or if he kept on talking so as not to leave half-unanswered the question I invariably asked into the most delayed pauses he placed on purpose within the account: "And what happened next?" Maybe he repeated the stories for himself, so as not to forget them, or else to enrich them with new detail. At that age and as we all do at some time, needless to say, I imagined my grandfather Jerónimo was master of all the knowledge in the world. When at first light the singing of birds woke me up, he was not there any longer, had gone to the field with his animals, letting me sleep on. Then I would get up, fold the coarse blanket and barefoot—in the village I always walked barefoot till I was fourteen—and with straws still tuck in my hair, I went from the cultivated part of the yard to the other part, where the sties were, by the house. My grandmother, already afoot before my grandfather, set in front of me a big bowl of coffee with pieces of bread in it and asked me if I had slept well. If I told her some

Dust jacket for the translation of Saramago's surrealistic novel about the inability of rational human beings to act rationally

bad dream, born of my grandfather's stories, she always reassured me: "Don't make much of it, in dreams there's nothing solid." At the time I thought, though my grandmother was also a very wise woman, she couldn't rise to the heights grandfather could, a man who, lying under a fig tree, having at his side José his grandson, could set the universe in motion just with a couple of words. It was only many years after, when my grandfather had departed from this world and I was a grown man, I finally came to realize that my grandmother, after all, also believed in dreams. There could have been no other reason why, sitting one evening at the door of her cottage where she now lived alone, staring at the biggest and smallest stars overhead, she said these words: "The world is so beautiful and it is such a pity that I have to die." She didn't say she was afraid of dying, but that it was a pity to die, as if her hard life of unrelenting work was, in that almost final moment, receiving the grace of a supreme and last farewell, the consolation of beauty revealed. She was sitting at the door of a house like none other I can imagine in all the world, because in it lived people who could sleep with piglets as if they were their own children, people who were sorry to leave life just because the world was beautiful; and this Jerónimo, my grandfather, swineherd and storyteller, feeling death about to arrive and take him, went and said goodbye to the trees in the yard, one by one, embracing them and crying because he knew he wouldn't see them again.

Many years later, writing for the first time about my grandfather Jerónimo and my grandmother Josefa (I haven't said so far that she was, according to many who knew her when young, a woman of uncommon beauty), I was finally aware I was transforming the ordinary people they were into literary characters: this was, probably, my way of not forgetting them, drawing and redrawing their faces with the pencil that ever changes memory, coloring and illuminating the monotony of a dull and horizonless daily routine as if creating, over the unstable map of memory, the supernatural unreality of the country where one has decided to spend one's life. The same attitude of mind that, after evoking the fascinating and enigmatic figure of a certain Berber grandfather, would lead me to describe more or less in these words an old photo (now almost eighty years old) showing my parents "both standing, beautiful and young, facing the photographer, showing in their faces an expression of solemn seriousness, maybe fright in front of the camera at the very instant when the lens is about to capture the image they will never have again, because the following day will be, implacably, another day. . . . My mother is leaning her right elbow against a tall pillar and holds, in her right hand drawn in to her body, a flower. My father has his arm round my mother's back, his calloused hand showing over her shoulder, like a wing. They are standing, shy, on a carpet patterned with branches. The canvas forming the fake background of the picture shows diffuse and incongruous neo-classic architecture." And I ended, "The day will come when I will tell these things. Nothing of this matters except to me. A Berber grandfather from North Africa, another grandfather a swineherd, a wonderfully beautiful grandmother; serious and handsome parents, a flower in a picture—what other genealogy would I care for? And what better tree would I lean against?"

I wrote these words almost thirty years ago, having no other purpose than to rebuild and register instants of the lives of those people who engendered and were closest to my being, thinking that nothing else would need explaining for people to know where I came from and what materials the person I am was made of, and what I have become little by little. But after all I was wrong, biology doesn't determine everything and as for genetics, very mysterious must have been its paths to make its voyages so long. . . . My gene-

alogical tree (you will forgive the presumption of naming it this way, being so diminished in the substance of its sap) lacked not only some of those branches that time and life's successive encounters cause to burst from the main stem but also someone to help its roots penetrate the deepest subterranean layers, someone who could verify the consistency and flavor of its fruit, someone to extend and strengthen its top to make of it a shelter for birds of passage and a support for nests. When painting my parents and grandparents with the paints of literature, transforming them from common people of flesh and blood into characters, newly and in different ways builders of my life, I was, without noticing, tracing the path by which the characters I would invent later on, the others, truly literary, would construct and bring to me the materials and the tools which, at last, for better or for worse, in the sufficient and in the insufficient, in profit and loss, in all that is scarce but also in what is too much, would make of me the person whom I nowadays recognize as myself: the creator of those characters but at the same time their own creation. In one sense it could even be said that, letter-by-letter, word-by-word, page-by-page, book after book, I have been successively implanting in the man I was the characters I created. I believe that without them I wouldn't be the person I am today; without them maybe my life wouldn't have succeeded in becoming more than an inexact sketch, a promise that like so many others remained only a promise, the existence of someone who maybe might have been but in the end could not manage to be.

Now I can clearly see those who were my life-masters, those who most intensively taught me the hard work of living, those dozens of characters from my novels and plays that right now I see marching past before my eyes, those men and women of paper and ink, those people I believed I was guiding as I the narrator chose according to my whim, obedient to my will as an author, like articulated puppets whose actions could have no more effect on me than the burden and the tension of the strings I moved them with. Of those masters, the first was, undoubtedly, a mediocre portrait-painter, whom I called simply H, the main character of a story that I feel may reasonably be called a double initiation (his own, but also in a manner of speaking the author's) entitled *Manual of Painting and Calligraphy,* who taught me the simple honesty of acknowledging and observing, without resentment or frustration, my own limitations: as I could not and did not aspire to venture beyond my little plot of cultivated land, all I had left was the possibility of digging down, underneath, towards the roots. My own but also the world's, if I can be allowed such an immoderate ambition. It's not up to me, of course, to evaluate the merits of the results of efforts made, but today I consider it obvious that all my work from then on has obeyed that purpose and that principle.

Then came the men and women of Altejo, that same brotherhood of the condemned of the earth where belonged my grandfather Jerónimo and my grandmother Josefa, primitive peasants obliged to hire out the strength of their arms for a wage and working conditions that deserved only to be called infamous, getting for less than nothing a life which the cultivated and civilised beings we are proud to be are pleased to call—depending on the occasion—precious, sacred, or sublime. Common people I knew, deceived by a Church both accomplice and beneficiary of the power of the State and of the landlords, people permanently watched by the police, people so many times innocent victims of the arbitrariness of a false justice. Three generations of a peasant family, the Badweathers, from the beginning of the century to the April Revolution of 1974 which toppled dictatorship, move through this novel, called *Risen from the Ground,* and it was with such men and women risen from the ground, real people first, figures of fiction later, that I learned how to be patient, to trust and to confide in time, that same time that simultaneously builds and destroys us in order to build and once more to destroy us. The only thing I am not sure of having assimilated satisfactorily is something that the hardship of those experiences turned into virtues in those women and men: a naturally austere attitude towards life. Having in mind, however, that the lesson learned still after more than twenty years remains intact in my memory, that every day I feel its presence in my spirit like a persistent summons: I haven't lost, not yet at least, the hope of meriting a little more the greatness of those examples of dignity proposed to me in the vast immensity of the plains of Alentejo. Time will tell.

What other lessons could I possibly receive from a Portuguese who lived in the sixteenth century, who composed the *Rimas* and the glories, the shipwrecks and the national disenchantments in the *Lusíadas,* who was an absolute poetical genius, the greatest in our Literature, no matter how much sorrow this causes to Fernando Pessoa, who proclaimed himself its Super Camões? No lesson would fit me, no lesson could I learn, except the simplest, which could have been offered to me by Luís Vaz de Camões in his pure humanity, for instance the proud humility of an author who goes knocking at every door looking for someone willing to publish the book he has written, thereby suffering the scorn of the ignoramuses of blood and race, the disdainful indifference of a king and of his powerful entourage, the mockery with which the world has always received the visits of poets, visionaries, and fools. At least once in life, every author has been, or will have to be, Luís de Camões, even if they haven't

Cover for Saramago's last novel before he won the Nobel Prize

written the poem *Sôbolos Rios.* . . . Among nobles, courtiers, and censors from the Holy Inquisition, among the loves of yesteryear and the disillusionments of premature old age, between the pain of writing and the joy of having written, it was this ill man, returning poor from India where so many sailed just to get rich, it was this soldier blind in one eye, slashed in his soul, it was this seducer of no fortune who will never again flutter the hearts of the ladies in the royal court, whom I put on stage in a play called *What Shall I Do with This Book?,* whose ending repeats another question, the only truly important one, the one we will never know if it will ever have a sufficient answer: "What will you do with this book?" It was also proud humility to carry under his arm a masterpiece and to be unfairly rejected by the world. Proud humility also, and obstinance too—wanting to know what the purpose will be, tomorrow, of the books we are writing today, and immediately doubting whether they will last a long time (how long?), the reassuring reasons we are given or that are given us by ourselves. No one is better deceived than when he allows others to deceive him.

Here comes a man whose left hand was taken in war and a woman who came to this world with the mysterious power of seeing what lies beyond people's skin. His name is Baltazar Mateus and his nickname Seven-Suns; she is known as Blimunda and also, later, as Seven-Moons because it is written that where there is a sun there will have to be a moon and that only the conjoined and harmonious presence of the one and the other will, through love, make earth habitable. There also approaches a Jesuit priest called Bartolomeu who invented a machine capable of going up to the sky and flying with no other fuel than the human will, the will which, people say, can do anything, the will that could not, or did not know how to, or until today did not want to, be the sun and the moon of simple kindness or of even simpler respect. These three Portuguese fools from the eighteenth century, in a time and country where superstition and the fires of the Inquisition flourished, where vanity and the megalomania of a king raised a convent, a palace, and a basilica which would amaze the outside world, if that world, in a very unlikely supposition, had eyes enough to see Portugal, eyes like Blimunda's, eyes to see what was hidden. . . Here also comes a crowd of thousands and thousands of men with dirty and calloused hands, exhausted bodies after having lifted year after year, stone-by-stone, the implacable convent walls, the huge palace rooms, the columns and pilasters, the airy belfries, the basilica dome suspended over empty space. The sounds we hear are from Domenico Scarlatti's harpsichord, and he doesn't quite know if he is supposed to be laughing or crying. . . . This is the story of *Baltazar and Blimunda,* a book where the apprentice author, thanks to what had long ago been taught to him in his grandparents' Jerónimo's and Josefa's time, managed to write some similar words not without poetry: "Besides women's talk, dreams are what hold the world in its orbit. But it is also dreams that crown it with moons, that's why the sky is the splendour in men's heads, unless men's heads are the one and only sky." So be it.

Of poetry the teenager already knew some lessons, learnt in his textbooks when, in a technical school in Lisbon, he was being prepared for the trade he would have at the beginning of his labor's life: mechanic. He also had good poetry masters during long evening hours in public libraries, reading at random, with finds, from catalogues, with no guidance, no one to advise him, with the creative amazement of the sailor who invents every place he discovers. But it was at the Industrial School Library that *The Year of the Death of Ricardo Reis* started to be written. . . . There, one day the young mechanic (he was about seventeen) found a

magazine entitled *Atena* containing poems signed with that name and, naturally, being very poorly acquainted with the literary cartography of his country, he thought that there really was a Portuguese poet called Ricardo Reis. Very soon, though, he found that this poet was really one Fernando Nogueira Pessoa, who signed his works with the names of nonexistent poets, born of his mind. He called them heteronyms, a word that did not exist in the dictionaries of the time, which is why it was so hard for the apprentice to letters to know what it meant. He learnt many of Ricardo Reis's poems by heart ("To be great, be one / Put yourself into the little things you do"); but in spite of being so young and ignorant, he could not accept that a superior mind could really have conceived, without remorse, the cruel line "Wise is he who is satisfied with the spectacle of the world." Later, much later, the apprentice, already with grey hairs and a little wiser in his own wisdom, dared to write a novel to show this poet of the *Odes* something about the spectacle of the world of 1936, where he had placed him to live out his last few days: the occupation of the Rhineland by the Nazi army, Franco's war against the Spanish Republic, the creation by Salazar of the Portuguese Fascist militias. It was his way of telling him: "Here is the spectacle of the world, my poet of serene bitterness and elegant skepticism. Enjoy, behold, since to be sitting is your wisdom. . . ."

The Year of the Death of Ricardo Reis ended with the melancholy words: "Here, where the sea has ended and land awaits." So there would be no more discoveries by Portugal, fated to one infinite wait for futures not even imaginable; only the usual fado, the same old saudade and little more. . . . Then the apprentice imagined that there still might be a way of sending the ships back to the water, for instance, by moving the land and setting that out to sea. An immediate fruit of collective Portuguese resentment of the historical disdain of Europe (more accurate to say fruit of my own resentment . . .), the novel I then wrote—*The Stone Raft*—separated from the Continent the whole Iberian Peninsula and transformed it into a big floating island, moving of its own accord with no oars, no sails, no propellers, in a southerly direction, "a mass of stone and land, covered with cities, villages, rivers, woods, factories and bushes, arable land, with its people and animals" on its way to a new Utopia: the cultural meeting of the Peninsular peoples with the peoples from the other side of the Atlantic, thereby defying—my strategy went that far—the suffocating rule exercised over that region by the United States of America. . . . A vision twice Utopian would see this political fiction as a much more generous and human metaphor: that Europe, all of it, should move south to help balance the world, as compensation for its former and its present colonial abuses. That is, Europe at last as an ethical reference. The characters in *The Stone Raft*–two women, three men and a dog–continually travel through the Peninsula as it furrows the ocean. The world is changing and they know they have to find in themselves the new persons they will become (not to mention the dog, he is not like other dogs . . .). This will suffice for them.

Then the apprentice recalled that at a remote time of his life he had worked as a proofreader and that if, so to say, in *The Stone Raft* he had revised the future, now it might not be a bad thing to revise the past, inventing a novel to be called *History of the Siege of Lisbon,* where a proofreader, checking a book with the same title but a real history book and tired of watching how "History" is less and less able to surprise, decides to substitute a "yes" for a "no," subverting the authority of "historical truth." Raimundo Silva, the proofreader, is a simple, common man, distinguished from the crowd only by believing that all things have their visible sides and their invisible ones and that we will know nothing about them until we manage to see both. He talks about this with the historian thus: "I must remind you that proofreaders are serious people, much experienced in literature and life, My book, don't forget, deals with history. However, since I have no intention of pointing out other contradictions, in my modest opinion, Sir, everything that is not literature is life, History as well, Especially history, without wishing to give offense, And painting and music, Music has resisted since birth, it comes and goes, tries to free itself from the word, I suppose out of envy, only to submit in the end, And painting, Well now, painting is nothing more than literature achieved with paintbrushes, I trust you haven't forgotten that mankind began to paint long before it knew how to write, Are you familiar with the proverb, If you don't have a dog, go hunting with a cat, in other words, the man who cannot write, paints or draws, as if he were a child, What you are trying to say, in other words, is that literature already existed before it was born, yes, Sir, just like man who, in a manner of speaking, existed before he came into being, It strikes me that you have missed your vocation, you should have become a philosopher, or historian, you have the flair and temperament needed for these disciplines, I lack the necessary training, Sir, and what can a simple man achieve without training, I was more than fortunate to come into the world with my genes in order, but in a raw state as it were, and then no education beyond primary school, You could have presented yourself as being self-taught, the product of your own worthy efforts, there's nothing to be ashamed of, society in the past took pride in its autodidacts, No longer, progress has come along and put an end to all of that, now the self-taught are frowned upon, only those who write

entertaining verses and stories are entitled to be and go on being autodidacts, lucky for them, but as for me, I must confess that I never had any talent for literary creation, Become a philosopher, man, You have a keen sense of humor, Sir, with a distinct flair for irony, and I ask myself how you ever came to devote yourself to history, serious and profound science as it is, I'm only ironic in real life, It has always struck me that history is not real life, literature, yes, and nothing else, But history was real life at the time when it could not yet be called history, So you believe, Sir, that history is real life, Of course, I do, I meant to say that history was real life, No doubt at all, What would become of us if the deleatur did not exist, sighed the proofreader." It is useless to add that the apprentice had learnt, with Raimundo Silva, the lesson of doubt. It was about time.

Well, probably it was this learning of doubt that made him go through the writing of *The Gospel According to Jesus Christ.* True, and he has said so, the title was the result of an optical illusion, but it is fair to ask whether it was the serene example of the proofreader who, all the time, had been preparing the ground from where the new novel would gush out. This time it was not a matter of looking behind the pages of the New Testament searching for antitheses, but of illuminating their surfaces, like that of a painting, with a low light to heighten their relief, the traces of crossings, the shadows of depressions. That's how the apprentice read, now surrounded by evangelical characters, as if for the first time, the description of the massacre of the innocents and, having read, he couldn't understand. He couldn't understand why there were already martyrs in a religion that would have to wait thirty years more to listen to its founder pronouncing the first word about it, he could not understand why the only person that could have done so dared not save the lives of the children of Bethlehem, he could not understand Joseph's lack of a minimum feeling of responsibility, of remorse, of guilt, or even of curiosity, after returning with his family from Egypt. It cannot even be argued in defense that it was necessary for the children of Bethlehem to die to save the life of Jesus: simple common sense, that should preside over all things human and divine, is there to remind us that God would not send His Son to Earth, particularly with the mission of redeeming the sins of mankind, to die beheaded by a soldier of Herod at the age of two. . . . In that Gospel, written by the apprentice with the great respect due to great drama, Joseph will be aware of his guilt, will accept remorse as a punishment for the sin he has committed and will be taken to die almost without resistance, as if this were the last remaining thing to do to clear his accounts with the world. The apprentice's Gospel is not, consequently, one more edifying legend of blessed beings and gods, but the story of a few human beings subjected to a power they fight but cannot defeat. Jesus, who will inherit the dusty sandals with which his father had walked so many country roads, will also inherit his tragic feeling of responsibility and guilt that will never abandon him, not even when he raises his voice from the top of the cross: "Men, forgive him because he knows not what he has done," referring certainly to the God who has sent him there, but perhaps also, if in that last agony he still remembers, his real father who has generated him humanly in flesh and blood. As you can see, the apprentice had already made a long voyage when in his heretical Gospel he wrote the last words of the temple dialogue between Jesus and the scribe: "Guilt is a wolf that eats it cub after having devoured its father, the wolf of which you speak has already devoured my father, Then it will be soon your turn, And what about you, have you ever been devoured, Not only devoured, but also spewed up."

Had Emperor Charlemagne not established a monastery in North Germany, had that monastery not been the origin of the city of Münster, had Münster not wished to celebrate its twelve-hundredth anniversary with an opera about the dreadful sixteenth-century war between Protestant Anabaptists and Catholics, the apprentice would not have written his play In Nomine Dei. Once more, with no other help than the tiny light of his reason, the apprentice had to penetrate the obscure labyrinth of religious beliefs, the beliefs that so easily make human beings kill and be killed. And what he saw was, once again, the hideous mask of intolerance, an intolerance that in Münster became an insane paroxysm, an intolerance that insulted the very cause that both parties claimed to defend. Because it was not a question of war in the name of two inimical gods, but of war in the name of a same god. Blinded by their own beliefs, the Anabaptists and the Catholics of Münster were incapable of understanding the most evident of all proofs: on Judgment Day, when both parties come forward to receive the reward or the punishment they deserve for their actions on earth, God—if His decisions are ruled by anything like human logic—will have to accept them all in paradise, for the simple reason that they all believe in it. The terrible slaughter in Münster taught the apprentice that religions, despite all they promised, have never been used to bring men together and that the most absurd of all wars is a holy war, considering that God cannot, even if he wanted to, declare war on himself. . . .

Blind. The apprentice thought, "we are blind," and he sat down and wrote Blindness to remind those who might read it that we pervert reason when we humiliate life, that human dignity is insulted every day by the powerful of our world, that the universal lie has replaced the plural truths, that man stopped respecting himself when he lost the respect due to his fellow creatures. Then the apprentice, as if trying to exorcize the monsters generated by the blindness of reason, started writing the simplest of all stories: one person is looking for another, because he has realized that life has nothing more important to demand from a human being. The book is called All the Names. Unwritten, all our names are there. The names of the living and the names of the dead.

I conclude. The voice that read these pages wished to be the echo of the conjoined voices of my characters. I don't have, as it were, more voice than the voices they had. Forgive me if what has seemed little to you, to me is all.

—Translated from the Portuguese by Tim Crosfield and Fernando Rodrigues

© The Nobel Foundation 1998

The Year in Fiction

George Garrett
The University of Virginia

"From *Don Quixote* to *The Great Gatsby* one of the great themes of western literature is the power of fiction to set up for a fall. As a girl Emma Bovary reads romantic novels and daydreams of elegant balls and sumptuous dinner parties, as a woman she finds her fantasies reduced to desperate adultery in one-night cheap hotels." – Michael Dirda, "Readings," *Washington Post Book World* (21 June).

"We read fiction because it makes us feel less lonely about being a human being. We read about what other human beings feel–what they're driven to do, how often they work for their own destruction, how they're in the grip of appetites that are beyond them and that they can't control or harness." – John Updike quoted in *The Washington Post* (16 December).

"Fiction is all about reliving things. It is our second chance." – Don DeLillo, quoted by Campbell Geeslin in *Authors Guild Bulletin* (Winter).

* * * * *

The problems facing all who deal with or are concerned by fiction–writers, publishers, booksellers, readers–as this century and the millennium stagger toward some kind of closure are enough to cause wonder why so many people read, write, publish, buy, and sell any fiction at all. There is the fact, far from unnoticed, that actual events, worldwide and close to home, are so drastically unusual that in the context of any forms of fiction, except perhaps pure fantasy, they would not be commonly credible. Who among all our crew of gifted fiction writers, for example, could have imagined and invented, with all of its implications and ramifications, the story of the president and the intern? The factual story has its literary implications. The president and the intern exchanged books as gifts, and when it became known that Nicholson Baker's satirical novel about phone sex, *Vox,* had been a gift from Monica Lewinsky

to the president, it was news in print and on television. Not to forget that one of the principals in this cast of characters was a literary agent (described in *The New Yorker,* 2 February, as "the conservative literary agent")– Lucianne Goldberg, who promptly became either a hero or the wicked witch of the west at the red-hot center of a vast right-wing conspiracy.

And even if the world of hard facts were not at once more outrageous and fascinating than at least most fiction, there are the simply practical problems of the age. In a year of great mergers–chiefly the takeover of Random House and all its parts by Bertelsmann, the already enormous communications conglomerate–what place, if any, is left for the serious literary writer and reader? Using final figures for 1997, *Publishers Weekly* informs us that of all the hundreds of titles of literary fiction (these among more than sixty thousand published titles overall) only twenty-one sold one hundred thousand copies or more. We learn also from a variety of sources that the average percentage of returns from bookseller to publisher for any given title is roughly forty percent. These are not good numbers for the mid-list author of literary fiction, of whom even the lucky twenty or so are in a relative sense mid-list writers. And one should not forget that even among some of the most celebrated and successful books, blockbusters in fact, some of them as literary as anyone could ask– Charles Frazier's *Cold Mountain* (Atlantic Monthly), Arthur Golden's *Memoirs of a Geisha* (Knopf) from 1997; Barbara Kingsolver's *The Poisonwood Bible* (Harper Flamingo), and, above all, Tom Wolfe's *A Man in Full* (Farrar, Straus) of 1998, in spite of these successes and surprises, there have also been significant failures among the packaged blockbusters. *Item:* Most obviously, among many examples, the millions of dollars squandered on books about the O. J. Simpson trial.

Meanwhile there has been much ado in the press about the various changes in the nature of the business of publishing, few of these changes being in any way advantageous to the art and craft of literature. Signs and portents–that there are one-third fewer editors working in publishing compared to a decade ago. See

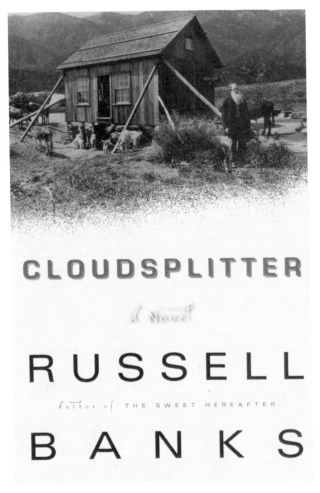

CLOUDSPLITTER

A Novel

RUSSELL

Author of THE SWEET HEREAFTER

BANKS

Dust jacket for the author's novel recounting the life of abolitionist John Brown

Doreen Carvajal, *The New York Times* (29 June). Carvajal writes: "With publishing cycles compressed, leaving less time for editing, and editors distracted by other corporate duties like acquiring new titles, writers are increasingly recruiting hired pens–independent editors who sharpen text or copy editors who correct grammar and spelling errors for fees ranging from $1,000 to $25,000." In another sign to be read as you please ("If you can't beat 'em, join 'em."), writers are fighting for survival in a celebrity-ridden world by trying to become public celebrities themselves. Witness (*The New Yorker,* 21 September, "Absolut Irving") author John Irving writing copy for an Absolut Vodka advertisement.

There is a wealth of anecdotal evidence, assumed by everyone involved, that times may never have been worse for the literary writer who has not created a bestseller or has not managed to earn one of the prestigious prizes. (And even the commercial value of these prizes, Pulitzer, National Book Critics Circle Award, PEN/ Faulkner Award, has diminished.) Grim prospects for

one and all, it would seem, and especially for the beginner. Hard numbers are not yet in and won't be for months; yet, as evidence, this year more than 120 titles were nominated for the PEN/Hemingway Award, given exclusively for first novels and collections of short stories. Many of these nominations came from the big commercial publishing houses, to be sure; but a significant number came from the growing number of small presses and, as well, from university presses which, in addition to extensive reprints and translations are now more and more engaged in trade publishing of original fiction. (See John F. Baker, "University Presses," *Publishers Weekly,* 1 June.)

Bad as the numbers have been and may continue to be for serious and talented writers of fiction, this year has been, nevertheless and taken as a whole, a remarkable and diverse year for fiction. This year *The New York Times Book Review* (6 October) lists 169 titles (mostly fiction) as "Notable Books of 1998: Fiction & Poetry," not counting the five works of fiction–*Birds of America* (Knopf) by Lorrie Moore, *Cloudsplitter* (Harper Flamingo) by Russell Banks, *The Love of a Good Woman* (Knopf) by Alice Munro, *The Poisonwood Bible* (Harper Flamingo) by Barbara Kingsolver, and *Preston Falls* (Knopf) by David Gates–selected by the staff of the *Review* as "Editors' Choice." Other lists, though parallel in many choices, proved different enough to indicate that reputable book editors and publications found other worthy titles, adding to the number of good books brought out in 1998. To be sure all lists are, to an extent, whimsical, inadequate, unfair, and almost always incomplete. Still there is some value and even some truth in the habit of listing. As R. H. W. Dillard wrote in *First Man on the Sun* (LSU Press): "It is a code, a hieroglyph, these lists that mean nothing apart from the context which they describe, and yet, to those who have eyes to see, lists that hold the flow and spin of the real, the reel and whirl of the things we think we know." And as critic Louis Menand wrote ("Novels We Love," *The New Yorker,* 3 August): "Having a favorite novel or movie when you are a grownup is like having a favorite color or a favorite Beatle when you were a kid: it's a way of explaining who you are to other people."

Herewith then, in alphabetical order by author, is my own list of Notable Books of Fiction in 1998.

*Beryl Bainbridge, *Master Georgie* (Carroll and Graff). A lean, quick-moving novel set in England and in the war in Crimea, chiefly dealing with four major characters–George Hardy, surgeon and photographer; Myrtle, a foundling; Pompey Jones, a street boy; and the scientist, Dr. Potter: "A dozen or more Russians were spilled round the cart. I opened the coat of one to see if there was anything of value inside, but Myrtle was watching me, so I tugged it off altogether and struggled into its folds. There was a leathery smell and the homely odor of sweat. For good measure I jerked free the metal cannister that hung at his belt and downed his vodka ration in one swallow. For the first time that day the blood ran warm in my veins. I would have worn his bearskin too if I hadn't feared I might be mistaken for the enemy."

*Russell Banks, *Cloudsplitter* (Harper Flamingo). The complex and often contradictory life (and death) story of the abolitionist martyr (or murderer), John Brown, as told many years later by a surviving son Owen: "But you must understand. The three-hundred-year-long War Between the Races, from before the Revolution up to and including Harpers Ferry, was being fought mainly as the War Against Slavery. Then, briefly, in '61, it became the War Between the States. And from then until now, there has been such a grieving, angry clamor that I knew I would not be heard, except as one of the sons of John Brown trying to justify his father's and his own bloody deeds–a puny, crippled man who fled the carnage he helped create and for the rest of his long life hid alone in the West."

*Andrea Barrett, *The Voyage of the Narwhal* (Norton). Winner of the 1996 National Book Award for her collection of stories, *Ship Fever,* Barrett here mixes fact and fiction as we follow the scholar and naturalist Erasmus Darwin Wells who leaves Philadelphia to join an exploration voyage to the far north (Ellesmere Island) on *Narwhal* 1855–1856: "A few nights later a great snowstorm descended, and with it a gale that shifted slowly from southwest to west to northwest. Erasmus and Ned heard the rush of feet on the deck above, excited chatter all night long as the ship shifted beneath them and their tilted world slowly leveled. Early the next morning Captain Sturrock rushed into their cabin, his hair sticking up and his eyes dark with excitement."

*Richard Bausch, *In the Night Season* (Harper Flamingo). Author of eight novels and four outstanding collections of stories, Bausch has here created a perfect match of the literary novel and the page-turning thriller in the story of Nora Michaelson and her son, Jason, following the accidental death of Jason's father, as their lives are invaded and endangered by ruthless strangers: "He was being carried, head down by the waist. He saw the ground moving below, only inches from his eyes. This was Bags carrying him, and he would die soon. It would be death. He would find out what it was, and he had the thought as if the dying were simply the next thing in his life. It raked through him that this was the thing itself, happening, and there wouldn't be any time, no person to look back on it and call it a name. His mind sped. Everything throbbed."

*Ann Beattie, *Park City: New and Selected Stories* (Knopf). This book is Ann Beattie's twelfth, a careful gathering of thirty-six short stories, eight appearing in book form for the first time. Since early in her career Beattie has been singled out as a kind of spokesperson of her generation and has been a significant influence on that generation and on younger story writers: "When the waitress does appear, Nell is sitting on the edge of her lounge, like the relative of someone in an operating room, frantic for news. The flavors are: Cherry Garcia (pink with cherries and chocolate) I explain: she'll like it; Swiss almond fudge; and nonfat banana yogurt. I order a Corona, which the man next to Lyric is drinking. Lyric decides on Swiss almond fudge. I cancel my beer and order banana yogurt. Nell, still squinting as she assimilates the information about Cherry Garcia, looks like the doctor has just explained the patient's condition in language too technical to understand." ("Park City")

*Louis Begley, *Mistler's Exit* (Knopf). Thomas Mistler spends the last six months of his life in Venice. Begley's fifth book is lean, poetic, funny, and sad: "On the vaporetto that crosses from the Zakere to the Giudecca a girl with hair that's naturally red and a man who hasn't shaved are embracing. He has her lean against the metal wall, next to the entrance to the passenger cabin, his tongue so deep he must be cleaning her tonsils. Mistler's view of the proceedings is excellent."

*Aimee Bender, *The Girl in the Flammable Skirt* (Doubleday). Sixteen stories comprise this first collection, mostly concerned with troubled women who (in the words of Lisa Zeidner in *The New York Times Book Review,* 23 August) share "devil-may-care attitudes and heavy hearts": "I want to jump the chair over and pounce on him, but I can't steer it very well, so instead I turn my head around and stare at him, first seductively and then like a pain in the ass."

*Carrie Brown, *Rose's Garden* (Algonquin). Set in a small New Hampshire town, this story follows the effects of an old man's vision of a visiting angel, and of a love that endures beyond the limits of a lifetime: "Sometimes, kneeling in the garden at Mt. Olive, near the double helix of rosebushes planted by the Pleiades in Rose's name, Conrad thought he saw Rose walking toward him through the flowers, a bouquet in her hands, her white dress fluttering around her."

*Frederick Buechner, *The Storm* (Harper San Francisco). This novel, Buechner's sixteenth (he is also author of fifteen books of nonfiction), is an up-to-date, shadow version of Shakespeare's *The Tempest.* Kenzie Maxwell (Prospero) is living on Plantation Island, an elegant, planned development off Florida. The characters and events, including a genuine tempest, reiterate and parallel the original result of this concept. It is stylish, witty, compassionate, and charitable: "Like Miss Sickert, the Bishop had started the cocktail hour early to steady his nerves, and he and his wife were having their second by candlelight when the phone rang. She could see by his face that something terrible had happened, but he didn't tell her what it was until he had drained off his glass in a couple of long swallows. Kennie Maxwell was a friend as well as a parishioner, he said, and he would of course have to go to him immediately even though it meant braving the storm on foot."

*Frederick Busch, *Girls* (Ballantine). This book, Busch's twenty-first, was inexcusably passed over last year, even though it was a *New York Times* Notable Book. I take the occasion of the 1998 publication of the trade paperback to remedy my error. *Girls* is a first-class literary thriller. Set in Upstate New York in bitter wintertime, it is at once a gripping mystery of missing children and the story of a complex and loving relationship that cannot endure. Asked, for the paperback edition's "Reader's Guide," why *Girls* is a dark book, Busch replied: "I live in a dark part of the country. My ancestors came from a dark part of the world, which is Russia, and I am a serious artist, which means that what I am looking to understand is the bad news, not the good news. . . . I think it is that side of life that the artist tries to explore. There are moments of joy, and he or she may bring explosions of joy to the page; but by and large I think our responsibility is to explore the more frightening moments on behalf of our readers. I think that's why they may value us, if they do."

*John Casey, *The Half-Life of Happiness* (Knopf). Casey's first novel since *Spartina,* winner of the 1989 National Book Award, is set in Charlottesville, Virginia, in 1978 and centers on the public life (politics) and private, complex family life of Mike Reardon, a lawyer: "Mike was in a rage. His hands shook when he lit his cigar. He hated his rage, he hated his rage, he hated every symptom of it. He would hate emerging from it into the hungover state with its after-cringes. He willed it all to end. He pressed it down. Then he tried to stop up the little leakages of puzzlement—Why was he so mad? What set him off? And then he tried to stop carrying on the argument—what argument?—in his head."

*Avery Chenoweth, *Wingtips* (Johns Hopkins). Nine interrelated stories, witty, satirical, sometimes funny, and never self-important, set across the country, from Martha's Vineyard to Tennessee, Oklahoma, Washington, D.C., and Jacksonville, Florida: "People calling to people, car doors slamming, and when this exodus of rubber over wet asphalt was over, Stuart found himself walking with people he had never seen before. They followed each other loosely through the woods and came onto the state road where Mac's neon

sign shone red and blue through the mist of silence." ("Going Back")

*Alan Cheuse, *Lost and Old Rivers: Stories* (S.M.U. Press). A rich variety of eleven new stories of various kinds (including, for example, "Hernando Alonso," the story of a sixteenth-century Spanish Jew in Mexico City) by this National Public Radio book reviewer who is also the author of three novels and two other short-story collections: "The time in which Hernando Alonso grew into manhood was filled with stories from other cities of funeral pyres piled with burning logs and Jews on fire. On Sundays, at Mass, he shivered in his bones at the stories about devilish Hebrews and the fiery rewards of sin that the priest howled down at them from the altar. Sometimes his mother would take him in her arms on a Sunday evening and hold him, rock him as though he were still a small child."

*Mark Childress, *Gone For Good* (Knopf). For his fifth novel Childress follows the life and adventures of Ben "Superman" Willis, a folk-rock star of the 1970s: "The El Paso Civic Auditorium sold out within ninety minutes of the first announcement on the *Today* show. Details were sketchy. The concert would go live nationwide on an exclusive NBC simulcast starting at seven central, eight eastern. 'Certainly one of the more interesting comeback stories in the history of pop music,' said Bryant Gumbel."

*Ethan Coen, *Gates of Eden* (Weisbach/Morrow). Not surprisingly, the author of these fourteen stories—who with his brother, has created the special genre of movies such as *Blood Simple, Raising Arizona, Barton Fink,* and *Fargo*—has invented his own version of the form, an off-the-wall, zany mixture of sex and violence, slapstick comedy cheek-by-jowl with the purely gothic grotesque, always hovering on the edge of the purely parodic: "They say that pictures don't lie. Well then, I guess I dreamed all of what happened between me and Miss O'Hara. These pictures didn't show a man and woman celebrating their oneness. They showed a sagging middle-aged guy screwing a Jap. Shame, shame—all I felt on looking at these pictures was dirty shame, shame that Miss O'Hara had seen me naked. And I was—well, if I just had a month or so to work out a little, get back in fighting trim. . . ." ("Gates of Eden")

*Martha Cooley, *The Archivist* (Little, Brown). The letters of T. S. Eliot are in fact sealed, not yet available to public scrutiny, but are here imagined and used as the occasion for this complex novel of love and memory: "Emily Hale followed the dictates of her conscience . . . I can picture the scene: a handsome, conservatively dressed woman in her seventies arrives at the library one warm spring afternoon. She asks to speak to the archivist about several cardboard boxes of letters piled in the trunk of her car: a lifetime's treasure. By training this woman is an actress. Her faith shows nothing of her pain, only her determination."

*Robert Coover, *Ghost Town* (Holt). For those with a taste for this kind of game, Coover's latest caper is a send-up of the western. As described in *The New Yorker* ("Briefly Noted," 5 October): "'Ghost Town' is both warped and scintillating, a cross between 'No Exit' and 'The Canterbury Tales.'"

*Michael Cunningham, *The Hours* (Farrar, Straus). Highly praised and awarded prizes for his previous two novels, *A Home at the End of the World* and *Flesh and Blood,* Cunningham here performs a virtuoso tour de force, more a reiteration of Virginia Woolf's *Mrs. Dalloway* than a single imitation of or homage to it, played out mostly in the present and in the haunted lives of two contemporary American women–Clarissa Vaughan (nicknamed Mrs. Dalloway by her lover, a poet) and Laura Brown–whose separate lives converge with the life and death of Virginia Woolf and some of the people around her–Leonard Woolf, Vanessa Bell, and Nelly Boxall: "She is borne quickly along by the current. She appears to be flying, a fantastic figure, arms outstretched, hair streaming, the tail of her fur coat billowing behind. She floats, heavily, through shafts of brown, granular light. She does not travel far. Her feet (the shoes are gone) strike the bottom occasionally, and when they do they summon up a sluggish cloud of muck, filled with the black silhouettes of leaf skeletons, that stands all but stationary in the water after she has passed along out of sight. . . ."

*Edwidge Danticat, *The Farming of Bones* (Soho). Born Haitian, Edwidge Danticat published her first novel at age twenty-five. This, her third book, concerns the Haitian orphan, Amabelle, who works as a maid for a Dominican family in 1937, the year of the massacre of Haitian workers in the Dominican Republic: "When I came to, I was in a large room with wooden walls and a tin roof like the face of a dirty mirror. The midday heat burned through the ceiling, as if trying to set us all on fire. People fanned themselves for relief and to frighten the flies and ants away from their wounds."

*Kiran Desai, *Hullabaloo in the Guava Orchard* (Atlantic Monthly). Called by Zia Jaffrey (*New York Times Book Review,* 19 July) "a parable, an allegory, a bittersweet reminder of the chaos of India," this first novel concerns a young Indian man, Sanpath, a former postman, who tries to escape reality in a guava tree, only to be taken for a prophet and guru: "Monkeys climbed up trees. Beatles lived in trees. Ants crawled up and down them. Birds sat in them. People used them for fruit and firewood, and underneath them they made each other's acquaintance in the few months between the time they got married and the babies arrived. But for someone to travel a long way just to sit in a tree was preposterous.

Dust jacket for the collection that includes the long, semi-autobiographical work, "On the Millstone River: A Story from Memory"

For that person to be sitting there a few days later was more preposterous still."

*Peter Dimock, *A Short Rhetoric for Leaving the Family* (Dalky Archive). In the form of an epistolary narrative divided into four rhetorical parts, this is a story, from an unusual angle, of the war in Vietnam. It is accurately described from the point of view of the political architects who created it: "Father signed the memorandum authorizing offensive action on the part of U.S. troops in the President's name, 6 April 1965. I am confident now of my trust in you especially because I am not aware of having omitted any of the rules of rhetoric from what I have written here."

*Susan Dodd, *The Mourner's Bench* (Morrow). Two sisters, Leandra in North Carolina and Pamela in New England, and one man, Pamela's husband, Wim, a professor, make up the triangle at the heart of this story, described by the publisher as an "affecting love story about memory, perspective, temptation and forgiveness." This is Susan Dodd's fifth book: "I'd grown restive by then, my fourth year of teaching at a small women's college. My students, drawn mostly from the mezzanine of privilege and accomplishment, were far too eager to please. It was 1974 and feminism was well on its feisty rise. I liked to think my own interests were feminist at heart. . . . It frustrated me to discover how many of them aspired to no more than my good opinion. And to grades reflecting that, of course."

*William H. Gass, *Cartesian Sonata and Other Novellas* (Knopf). Much praised and well-prized by an impressive number of prize-giving institutions, Gass has put together, for his tenth book, in the words of his publisher, "four interrelated novellas that explore Mind, Matter, and God." Depth and complexity coexist, in Gass's fictional world, with wit and a free-floating style: "Emma was afraid of Elizabeth Bishop. Emma imagined Elizabeth Bishop lying naked next to a naked Marianne Moore, the tips of their noses and their nipples touching; and Emma imagined that every feeling either poet ever had in their spare and spirited lives were present there in the two nips, just where the nips kissed. Emma, herself, was ethereally thin, and had been admired for the translucency of her skin. You could see her bones like shadows of trees, shadows without leaves."

*Denise Giardina, *Saints and Villains* (Norton). For her fourth novel Giardina, a former Episcopalian priest, has written, from the inside, the life story of the German theologian and martyr of the Nazi years–Dietrich Bonhoeffer: "Day 1. Late in the day the prisoner is moved to a regular cell, Number 92 on the third floor. Here his cot holds a thin mattress and thinner, but relatively clean, blanket. He has a wooden bench and a stool. The slop bucket stinks but is empty. Soon enough, he supposes, the odor will be his own and he will be able to stomach it, perhaps even be comforted by it, like a dog which has marked its territory."

*Samantha Gillison, *The Undiscovered Country* (Grove). Set in the remote, mountainous rain forest of Papua New Guinea, this first novel tells the story of what happens to biologist Peter Campbell, his wife June, and his daughter Taylor when they go to live in the village Abini. Needless to say, all does not go well. June dies and father and daughter are radically affected and changed by the experience of living in a strange world, among an alien people with an utterly different culture: "As we walked deeper and deeper into the forest, the most incredible symphony of bird calls, waterfalls, insects buzzing, and wind whistling through the trees surrounded us. The sound is all encompassing, and it is hard for me to believe that this music is not deliberate. I must say that now I am in an amazed, trance like state at nature, Darwin seems obscene. How could he have come up with such an unromantic and dyspeptic theory in a place as lovely as the Galapagos?"

The late John Hawkes praised this novel as being "as painful as Graham Greene's novels of Africa and as beautiful as any I've read."

*C. S. Godshalk, *Kalimantaan* (Holt). Described by Annette Koback (*The New York Times Book Review,* 26 April) as "a highly accomplished novel of the contradictions of empire" and "a brilliantly subtle panorama of life forces played out in the face of death," this is the imaginary story (closely parallel to historical facts) of Gideon Barr, an Englishman who, over four decades, made himself the ruler of a large part of Borneo during the nineteenth century: "There is a moment in those latitudes, a pause in the great revolution of winds, when they cease blowing from one quadrant and, for the first time in months, start from the reverse. With the southwest monsoon, everything lightens, a breeze flows through the innermost convolutions of the brain. Things slammed down in temper are picked up again. Jokes are cracked. Love is made in slow and imaginative ways. In November, the universe lurches again and the reverse occurs, wet winds shrieking from the sea."

*Lester Goran, *Bing Crosby's Last Song* (Picador). Goran, author of seven earlier novels and two collections of stories, here returns to the turf of those short stories, the Irish-American neighborhood of Oakland Park in Pittsburgh. Set in 1968, it tells the story of Daly Racklin who becomes a local leader while he slowly succumbs to change in a changing America: "Without language Daly felt himself in mourning connected to the other men, their histories as binding as the time now when they moved more or less forward in unison, but Daly felt the shuffle forward oppressive after a while. Their common pasts became lost. There was only the heat of the day, the death of Bobby Kennedy, all the people they had known together, dead, many deaths that united them, but irretrievable now in sunlit moments that became unreal."

*Nadine Gordimer, *The House Gun* (Farrar, Straus). The twenty-sixth book by the South African Nobel Prize winner tightly focuses on the crime and punishment of twenty-seven-year-old Duncan Lindgard and its impact upon his respectable parents, Harald, director of an insurance company, and Claudia, a physician. A complex and thoughtful picture of the new South Africa: "He seems now to abandon his text, to accuse the assembly and himself, the streets and suburbs and squatter camps outside the courts and the corridors, the mob of which he sees all as part, close up against the breached palace of justice.–But that is the tragedy of our present time, a tragedy repeated daily, nightly in this city, in our country. Part of the furnishings in homes, carried in packets along with car keys, even in the schoolbags of children, constantly ready to hand in situations which lead to tragedy, the guns *happen to be there.–"*

*Tom Graves, *Pullers* (Hastings House). Memphis journalist Tom Graves takes on the very real contemporary American sport of arm wrestling–the Professional Arm Wrestling Association, in the person of characters like Steve Strong, Carroll Thurston, Scud Matthews ("the great gay hope"), Snack Pack Harris, and Larry Lancaster: "One look at Larry Lancaster and the oddsmakers reacted as if they were caught in a flurry at the New York Stock Exchange. Lancaster was called on deck for the first match-up with a middleweight from Greece who had more balls than brains. The odds were ridiculously lopsided in Lancaster's favor. Lancaster easily stopped the puller in mid-move and audibly gritted his teeth as he applied a downward wrenching pressure. The puller's face twisted in agony as everyone heard a loud crack and a long slice of bone knifed through the side of his wrist. He fainted before he could scream."

*A. C. Greene, *They Are Ruining Ibiza* (North Texas). The story of Charles Martyn, author and academic, who returns to a changed Ibiza with his second wife, Susan: "Susan left him with the pile of baggage while she went out the front gate to see if Ledyard and his wife had arrived to pick them up. Charles watched the crowd, thinking to himself they looked very much the same as a bunch of people around a baggage carrousel at LaGuardia or O'Hare. 'There are no more natives,' he told himself. 'The world is populated with the same nomadic tribe, its members just speak local dialects.'"

*Ken Greenhall, *Lenoir* (Zoland). Greenhall's sixth novel is a picaresque adventure story set in seventeenth-century Antwerp and Italy, creating a life and history for its hero-narrator, the slave Lenoir who is here presumed to have posed for Ruben's *Four Heads of a Negro:* "I remove my costume and put on my robe . . . I wash my costume and then remove my robe and wash my body. A few people walk past and look at me with the surprise and admiring curiosity that I am used to. Without my makeup and costume, I still attract attention but no one smiles at me."

*James W. Hall, *Body Language* (St. Martin's Press). Since 1987, with *Under Cover of Daylight,* poet and story writer James W. Hall has been writing popular and successful thrillers. Here he takes a new turn with a new protagonist, Alexandra Rafferty, photographic specialist with the Miami Police Department, who keeps busy (and keeps the reader turning pages) with a breaking marriage, a father with Alzheimer's, and danger from a murderous rapist: "Rapists and killers in the movies were always flamboyant madmen . . . They were losers who wore polka dots and plaids together and their glasses were thick and greasy. The movie rapists slunk

around at night with whores and go-go dancers. But he was none of those things. He was well-informed, well-read, but without intellectual pretensions. He was handsome, but not strikingly so. He could be intense, but he could also laugh."

*Donald Harington, *When Angles Rest* (Counterpoint). This book is Harington's tenth novel, set in the Ozarks and featuring the wildly and variously imagined hamlet of Stay More, Arkansas, is accurately described in jacket copy by the publisher as "part American tall tale, part hillbilly *Paradiso.*" Here Harington gives us the story of twelve-year-old Dawny who tries to imitate his hero, Ernie Pyle, during World War II with his own newspaper, the weekly *Stay Morning Star:* "Among all the things that were hard to come by during the war–sugar, elastic, tin, chewing gum, coffee, and so on–one of the most precious was soap. Of course the womenfolks still rendered hog lard and ashes into a kind of crude lye soap that was okay, but not really suitable for sudsing and lathering and bathing. Latha Bourne could no longer stock the good-boughten soaps–Ivory, Lifebuoy, Lava, not to mention Cashmere Bouquet–which were scarce as hen's teeth. And even if she had, the Dinsmores couldn't have afforded to buy a bar."

*Jim Harrison, *The Road Home* (Atlantic Monthly). Widely reviewed, praised, and promoted (including a rare, full-page ad in *The New Yorker*), *The Road Home* is a capacious novel covering more than a century and telling the story of the Northridge family. It is, then, a continuation of the story begun in *Dalva,* Harrison's novel of ten years ago. Here the story of the family is told by several voices (including, finally, Dalva herself) speaking in and from the 1950s and 1986 and 1987, but ranging from the nineteenth century to the present: "I've often had the feeling that as I grow older the country is becoming more primitive, certainly more stupid and impolite. One certainly notes it with the airlines, the government, restaurants and hotels and among doctors. You are forever dodging the invisible shrapnel of free-floating contentiousness. You are frankly suspect if you don't act appropriately dead within the market-driven mono-ethic of pay and shut up. People yap about the bottom line as if it existed anywhere but in hell."

*William Harrison, *The Buddha in Malibu: New and Selected Stories* (Missouri). This gathering includes stories from Harrison's earlier collection, *Roller Ball Murder,* and consists of seventeen well-executed stories set in movieland, in Africa, and in the imaginary future. Forms are various and innovative. Novelist and screenwriter Harrison knows his places as well as his subjects and writes with deft sophistication: "The flames lick his breath away. The little hairs edging out from underneath his asbestos hairnet are singed off, he springs into the air, feet together, leaping, and pain is beauty, that is

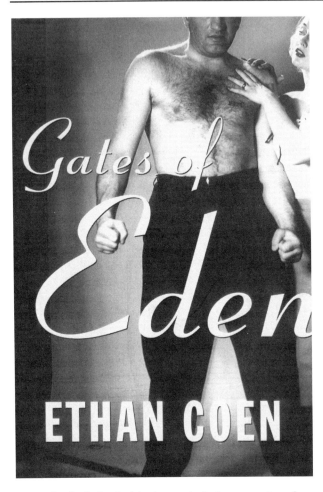

Dust jacket for the first book by the award-winning screenwriter, whose stories have been published in The New Yorker, Playboy, *and* Vanity Fair

all you need to know on earth, even the worst audiences know that much."

*Peter Hedges, *An Ocean in Iowa* (Hyperion). For his second novel, set in suburban Iowa in the late 1960s, Hedges centers on the lively consciousness and witness of a bright seven-year-old, Scotty Ocean, and his troubled, contemporary family: "Andrew pulled off Barbie's plastic go-go boots and then yanked off her leatherette skirt. He pointed to the space between her legs and said, 'Real girls have a hole here. Real girls have a patch of hair.'

"Scotty looked surprised."

*Robert Hellenga, *The Fall of a Sparrow* (Scribner). Classics professor Alan Woodhull goes to Italy to cover the trial of terrorists who killed his daughter. Somehow out of the suffering comes redemption and a form of joy for some of the characters involved: "During the long, hot days Woody sat in the rooftop amidst the bougainvillea and the fruit trees—palms, oranges, lemons, dates. He'd browse through a copy of the *Odyssey* that Allison

bought for him or pick up Babak's guitar, a National Steel, like his own, but with a large single-cone resonator instead of a tricone. Less sustain, but more punch."

*William Hoffman, *Tidewater Blood* (Algonquin). Hoffman's eleventh novel (he is also author of four story collections) is set in Virginia and centers on the first-person narrator Charles LeBlanc who is suspected of blowing up his family's ancestral home with his family in it: "I again had the sensation of being watched. Maybe this crazy land was doing it to me, the dismal hollers, the deserted camps, a people honed to insularity by the dark Appalachians. A dog barked. I looked behind me up the brightening mountainside. Nothing."

*Yoel Hoffman, *Bernard* (New Directions). A philosophy professor at the University of Haifa and author of five novels, Hoffman is widely regarded as Israel's leading avant-garde writer. This novel, set in the Palestine of the 1940s, follows the inner life of its distraught, widowed protagonist, Bernhard, while all the terrible events of the 1940s are played out, in fact and in flesh, elsewhere: "On the twenty-eighth of March, a great sea battle takes place. Two thousand four hundred Italians drown (five hundred others are fished out). Not a single English sailor is injured (but Virginia Woolf dies the same day). Bernhard tells himself to count from one to two thousand four hundred but gives up after a hundred and seventy. He wonders if anyone said (before drowning) 'Arrivederci.' Above the surface of the ocean the air was filled with cries, but within (the width of one little finger lower) silence prevailed. These sights do not gladden Bernhard's heart, nor do they sadden it."

*Pam Houston, *Waltzing the Cat* (Norton). Pam Houston made a literary name for herself with her first, widely praised collection of stories—*Cowboys Are My Weakness* (1993). *Waltzing the Cat* offers eleven new stories, all but one by a first-person narrator, and acknowledged by the author in interviews to be generally autobiographical in content. They are linked together as a narrative by sharing a central character (among a variety of other types)—Lucy O'Rourke, a photographer. Settings are various—the Rocky Mountains, the East Coast, the Amazon, the Gulf Stream; and, as in her earlier stories, Houston handles outdoor action scenes with grace, economy, and authenticity: "My hands are still on the oars and the water that has been so brown for days is suddenly white as lightning. It is white and it is alive and it is moving toward me from both sides, coming at me like two jagged white walls with only me in between them, and Thea is airborne, is sailing backwards, is flying over my head, like a prayer."

*John Irving, *A Widow for One Year* (Random House). Irving's tenth book chiefly concerns the life of writer Ruth Cole, as seen in three time frames: 1958, when she is a four-year-old; 1990; and 1995: "That

Very Important Person at Random House, Ruth's editor, was there. (The editor of Ruth's first two novels, a woman, had died recently, and now this man had succeeded her.) Eddie had met him three or four times, but could never recall his name. Whatever his name was, he never remembered that he'd met Eddie before. Not once had Eddie taken it personally, until now."

*Ruth Prawer Jhabvala, *East Into Upper East: Plain Tales from New York and New Delhi* (Counterpoint). Jhabvala, a MacArthur Fellow and author of many screenplays for Merchant-Ivory Productions, is also author of twelve novels and six story collections. This latest gathering has six stories firmly set in India and eight in the Upper Eastside of New York: "When the doctor told Sophie that her disease was incurable, she would have liked to share the information with her husband. But she knew that Dave had many troubles—like his business and his creditors and his young girl friend—to which she did not wish to add yet another." ("Fidelity")

*Charles Johnson, *Dreamer* (Scribner). Johnson, who received the National Book Award in 1990 for *Middle Passage* (Atheneum), offers what his publisher describes as "a magesterial homage" to the historical Martin Luther King Jr. through the story of the fictional Chaym Smith, a man who becomes King's stand-in: "With each box and shopping bag of Smith's things I found myself falling through his past and into passageways of a constantly mutating soul which, I'd wager, even his therapists at Elgin had not fully charted. Poking through a shopping bag, I pulled out expired passports stamped by half the countries left of Hawaii, a sketchbook filled with his poetry and drawings—penciled images of well-known locations in the Loop, and possible portraits of what his own father might look like (one was a derelict feeding himself from a Dumpster, another was Daddy King)—hypodermic needles I was afraid to handle, and eight scrapbooks in which he's posted news articles about, I thought, himself."

*Gayl Jones, *The Healing* (Beacon). African American writer Jones's first novel in more than twenty years, telling the story of a woman who changes from rock-star manager to faith healer. This book was a finalist for the National Book Award: "Me, I've worked hard. I worked my butt off. I hardly knew what fucking country I was in most of the fucking time. It was all for you, not me. Places you never would have got to go in a million fucking years, if it wasn't for me. Your husband took you over there to Africa, but you got to travel all over the world because of me."

*Ismail Kadare, *The File on H.* (Arcade). Two Irish scholars go to Albania during the reign of King Zog, before World War II, in an effort to explore Albanian oral folk poetry for possible connections with the Homeric tradition: "It must have been an unending struggle

of women and children moving forward to the muddled sounds of yelling and squalling, a cohort obeying no orders, leaving no milestones or monuments, more like a natural disaster than a military invasion. . . . All of a sudden they were in the midst of a Slavic sea: a gray, unending, anonymous Eurasian mass that could easily destroy all the treasures in a land where art had flourished more than anywhere else on earth."

*Wayne Karlin, *Prisoners* (Curbstone). Author of four earlier novels, a memoir, and editor of several books concerning the Vietnam War, Karlin is one of the most gifted, passionate, and powerful American writers of his generation. Set in the years 1990 to 1994 and with its episodes linked by the story of a runaway teenager named Kiet, *Prisoners* involves the lives of four men and two women whose lives were changed by the Vietnam War . . . and civil wars long before that: "Now a park ranger in a Smokey the Bear hat stands in front of us, megaphone in one hand, little cassette recorder in the other. Starts talking about how here on this ground under our feet blah-blah one of the largest prisoner of war camps from the Civil War, thirty thousand Confederate prisoners here, exposed to weather and abuse in Maryland. Talks about payback. While he's going on, this ragged ass white prisoner runs away and the sharp black guard I saw before raises his musket, shoots him down. Right. Just like real life."

*Terry Kay, *The Kidnapping of Aaron Greene* (Morrow). The latest by the author of *To Dance with the White Dog* and six other books follows all the implications and results of the kidnapping of a young mail boy, someone without wealth or connections: "Amos Temple's story on the kidnapping of Aaron Greene for the first edition of *The Atlanta Journal* was a repeat of the stories he had written for a week: nothing of substance to report from anyone. Law enforcement officials were turning over grains of sand and could find nothing. Tips flowed in like a high tide with thundering, whitecapped waves, but all evaporated under the heat of questioning. It was a thin story padded with the filler of terse comments. . . ."

*Nanci Kincaid, *Balls* (Algonquin). For her third book (following the novel *Crossing Blood* and a collection of stories, *Pretending the Bed is a Raft*), the author, twice-married to college football coaches, writes with earned, funny/sad knowledge about big-time college football from the point of view (and narrative voice) of the women whose lives are linked to the game and the coaches: "The death knell sounds at the end of our 3 and 7 season. It's like a clock striking midnight twenty-four hours a day. Mac has two more years on his contract, but the papers are full of talk of alumni buying him out—a lively crusade led by prosperous ex-players, some of whom had played with him in the sixties, who've gone on to become big-time car dealers and bar-

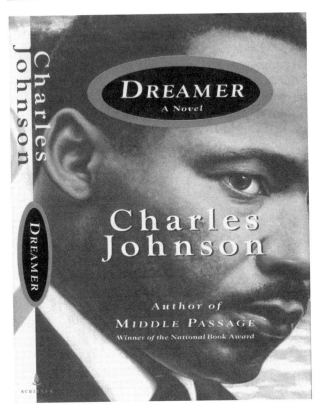

Dust jacket for the novel based on the life of Martin Luther King Jr.

becue-restaurant owners. The six o'clock news is unbearable. We all live life like there are nooses around our necks and any sudden move might leave us hanging."

*Barbara Kingsolver, *The Poisonwood Bible* (Harper). Drawing freely (as she acknowledges in her "Bibliography") on the best available firsthand studies and research, including Margaret Meyers's 1995 novel *Swimming in the Congo* (Milkweed), Kingsolver in her fourth book focuses on an American missionary family living in the Belgian Congo in 1959, during the beginning of postcolonial independence. Nathan Price, an evangelical Baptist, together with his wife Orleanna and their four daughters—Rachael, Leah, Adah, and Ruth May (each of whom serves as a narrator in the multiple narration)—set out to discover and to change the world (Africa). Not surprisingly, all are either destroyed or radically changed in and by the process. Firmly political in its ideology, the story is nonetheless elegantly written; and the topic helped the novel to find a place on the best-seller lists: "I can have a good laugh at my former self remembering how my sisters and I nervously made our list of prospects: oranges, flour, even eggs! At our low point as missionaries, we were still fabulously wealthy by the standards of Kilanga. No won-

der any household item we carelessly left on our porch quietly found a new home in the night. No wonder the neighbor women frowned in our doorway when we pulled out the linings of our pockets as evidence of our poverty. Not another soul in town even had pockets."

*Michael Knight, *Divining Rod* (Dutton) and *Dogfight and Other Stories* (Plume). Published simultaneously by the Penguin Group and both books freighted by a gathering of impressive blurbs, these two books mark the arrival on the scene of a gifted young writer who has already earned a string of prizes for his work. *Divining Rod,* set in the author's native Alabama, is a story of love, adultery, and murder, briskly told in a clear, energetic style. The ten stories of *Dogfight,* though various in form and subject, share the energy, clarity, and well-wrought structure of invention that marks *Divining Rod:* "Jay heads back out the door to get the beer we bought en route. The door has been open all day and there's a semicircle of moisture just inside. A cool, sloppy fall breeze moves through the house, pushing the new paint smell around the room. Oliver points at the screen and says to me, 'Do you think Drew Barrymore's too young for me? She's nineteen. Seventeen in this movie.'" ("Poker")

*Pavel Kohout, *The Widow Killer* (St. Martin's Press). Czech dramatist and novelist Kohout has here brilliantly joined together a page-turning thriller with a stylish literary novel. Two detectives, one a Czech and the other associated with the Nazi Gestapo, desperately try to find a serial killer in the early months of 1945 just as the Third Reich is falling apart and the Russians are approaching Prague: "What should have been a trifling problem for Buback, of all people, turned into a surreal scene with an even wilder script. Before he could speak, two SS men tackled him like butchers grabbing a meat calf and shoved him toward a handful of men they had evidently picked up before him. He could not find the courage to dig his Gestapo papers out from his socks and shoes in full view and decided to remain anonymous until a less awkward opportunity presented itself."

*Anne Linzer, *Ghost Dancing: Stories* (Picador). Eleven stories, in this debut collection, linked together through the characters of Jimmy One Rock and his wife Mary, set in Oklahoma and a reservation in the Pacific Northwest: "Once, back in Oklahoma, when Jimmy was younger and Grandma One Rock was still alive, Jimmy had watched as an earnest young man, a tourist, who had been hanging around a tribal gathering all weekend, talking and laughing too loudly, finally joined in a stomp dance at night, dancing with awkward, overly exaggerated gestures. Jimmy and Roy came alongside, making jokes and imitating him."

*Norman Mailer, *The Time of Our Time* (Random House). Fifty years following the publication (6 May 1948) of *The Naked and the Dead* and thirty books later, Mailer has assembled a huge (1,286 pages) representative gathering from all his work, early and late, more or less chronological according to the time *written about,* not the time of writing. And, more or less, as he reasonably argues, based on the ways and means of fiction as he perceives them: "There is little in this book, even when it comes under the formal category of non-fiction or argument, that has not derived, then, from my understanding of how one writes fiction. . . . Fiction, as I use the word, is a reality that does not cohere to received axes of fact but is breathed in through the swarm of our male and female movements about one another, a novelistic assumption, for we perceive the truth of a novel by way of the personality of the writer." ("Foreword")

*Hilary Mantel, *The Giant O'Brien* (Holt). Mantel's eighth novel is appropriately slender, poetic, and evocative. Set in 1782 in Ireland and London, it tells the tale of the storyteller and mythmaker, the Irish giant O'Brien, and of his antagonist, the Scots doctor, John Hunter, who aims to lay claim on the Giant's corpse for science. The Giant and the doctor are based on "real" historical figures. The story is fiction: "The mornings were icy now, and for the first time in his life the Giant began to feel the cold. Aching and snuffling, he brooded over the smoking fire, and when Claffey said to him, 'Coming to the Scotsman then?' he looked up, lethargic, and shook his head.

"'Hunter frightens me,' he said. 'When he laid his hand on me to feel my pulse, he felt right through to my bone.'"

*Kenny Marotta, *A House on the Piazza* (Guernica). A novella, "Asphodel," and seven short stories, linked by the stories of two families and by a common concern with the joys and sorrows of the immigrant experience: "A few weeks later, Enzo and his bride lay on a bed in a hotel near the docks of Palermo. It was still light, but they were tired from their journey, by cart, train, and street car. Above the stand with the ewer and basin hung tinted images of the king and queen, bidding a personal farewell. The hotel was full, and you could hear the sounds of many different families through the walls. All the same, it was more privacy than the couple had ever had. They might speak as loudly as they liked." ("Her Sister")

*Bobbie Ann Mason, *Midnight Magic: Selected Stories* (Ecco). Seventeen stories, nine of which appeared in *The New Yorker,* published between 1982 and the present have been chosen by this celebrated writer of Kentucky-based accountings of the clash between the values of a decaying rural and small town America and the invasive change of a new order: "Sitting behind the wheel,

he eats the chocolate-covered doughnuts he just bought and drinks from a carton of chocolate milk. They do something weird to chocolate milk now. His father used to drive a milk truck, before he got arrested for stealing a shipment of bowling shoes he found stacked up behind a shoe store. He had always told Steve to cover his tracks and accentuate the positive." ("Midnight Magic")

*Donald McCaig, *Jacob's Ladder* (Norton). Subtitled "A Story of Virginia During the War," this outstanding novel covers the whole of the Civil War, from John Brown's raid to Appomattox and after, following the lives of a wealth of diverse and memorable characters. Cited as "astonishingly immediate" by Mary Lee Settle, *Jacob's Ladder* earned extraordinary praise from Staige Blackford, editor of *The Virginia Quarterly Review* (Summer)–"*Jacob's Ladder* is in the judgement of this reviewer, the finest novel about the Civil War ever written . . . *Jacob's Ladder* is a better novel than *Cold Mountain.* It makes *Gone with the Wind* look like the soap opera it really is in the last analysis. And compared to it, Mary Johnston's *The Long Roll* and *Cease Firing* seem as much out of date as silent movies. McCaig has produced a masterpiece which deserves a wide readership."

*Cormac McCarthy, *Cities of the Plain* (Knopf). This final volume of McCarthy's much-praised *Border Trilogy* brings together John Grady Cole (from *All the Pretty Horses*) and Billy Parham (of *The Crossing*) and covers fifty years, beginning on a New Mexico ranch in 1952 and ending early in the coming century. It is a sad story of the end of one world, but is redeemed by passionate characters who are, in McCarthy's terms, "ardent hearted": "He was the best. We run off to Mexico together. When we was kids. When our folks died. We went down there to see about gettin back some horses they stole. We was just kids. He was awful good with horses. I always liked to watch him ride. Liked to watch him around horses. I'd give about anything to see him one more time."

*Jill McCorkle, *Final Vinyl Days* (Algonquin). The nine stories from this second collection of stories by Jill McCorkle, described by her publisher as "irrepressibly frank and funny," are marked by wonderfully rounded characters with memorable and inimitable voices: "The day my father died, the weatherman was on the news all afternoon, more or less apologizing for his error. His name was Joe Johnson and he was all right, curly blond hair and a nose a little off to one side, like a hockey player. Twyla decided she would write him and ask for his autograph. My mother said she certainly intended to write him a card and might even send a leftover floral arrangement." ("Last Request")

*Alice McDermott, *Charming Billy* (Farrar, Straus). This winner of the year's National Book Award,

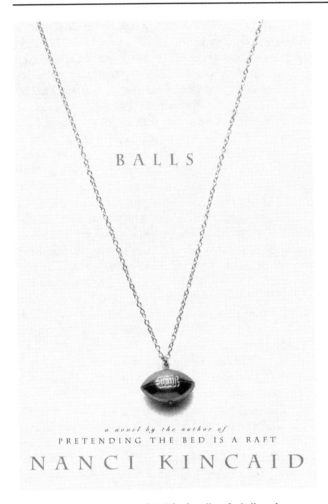

Dust jacket for the narrative of the life of a college football coach—as seen through the eyes of women on the sidelines

McDermott's fourth novel begins at the wake for Billy Lynch and follows, by stories and memories of kith and kin all around him, his life, the mysteries and ambiguities and contradictions of it, played out in Queens, East Hampton, and Ireland: "Telling the story, my father easily slipped from past to present: Billy was, Billy is, Billy drank, Billy drinks. Billy sets his heart on something. In the front seat of Mr. Holtzman's car, on Seventieth Street, just off Park Avenue, my father watched Mary, Eva's sister, worry a small handkerchief, Irish linen (naturally), embroidered in one corner with three small shamrocks."

*Ian McEwan, *Enduring Love* (Nan Talese/Doubleday) and *Amsterdam* (Nan Talese/Doubleday). McEwan is author of eight novels and two collections of stories. *Enduring Love* is a complex story of obsessive love which is triggered by a balloon accident: "What were we running toward? I don't think any of us would ever know fully. But superficially the answer was a balloon. Not the nominal space that encloses a cartoon character's

speech or thought, or, by analogy, the kind that's driven by mere hot air. It was an enormous balloon filled with helium, that elemental gas forged from hydrogen in the nuclear furnace of the stars, first step along the way in the generation of multiplicity and variety of matter in the universe, including ourselves and all our thoughts." Later in the year McEwan's *Amsterdam* won the prestigious and coveted Booker Prize for 1998 and was swiftly brought out in the United States. The triggering occasion is the funeral of Molly Lane, bringing together several of her former lovers: "The friends of Molly who made up the funeral gathering would have preferred not to be at a crematorium, but George had made it clear that there was to be no memorial service. He didn't want to hear three former lovers publicly comparing notes from the pulpits of St. Martin's or St. James's, or exchanging glances while he made his own speech. As Clive and Vernon they heard the familiar gabble of a cocktail party."

*Milena McGraw, *After Dunkirk* (Houghton Mifflin). A first novel that follows, in flashes and fragments of vivid language, the life of Flying Officer Wayne Luthie, age twenty, of the R.A.F. in the time of the Blitz: "Finally Luthie went to sleep. He was not watching over them, this time, as he had done the night after McGregor's death. He was not engineering their precise degree of drunkenness. Nothing like that! But he himself did not drink at all—my God he must be too exhausted even to get drunk!—and then he went to sleep."

*Jay McInerney, *Model Behavior: A Novel and 7 Stories* (Knopf). Once again, in his sixth novel, McInerney turns to New York City in this story involving Connor McKnight, journalist; his sister, Brooke; his friend, story writer Jeremy Green; Connor's girlfriend, Philomena, a model; and a stripper named Pallas. The stories, originally published in magazines such as *Playboy, Esquire,* and *The New Yorker,* are various and sundry takes on the same scene: "A refugee from the western suburbs, I used to skip school and take the bus into the city. I hung out on St. Mark's Place and the Bowery, copping the look and the attitude of punk, discovering Bukowski and the Beats in the bookshops. Returning to the subdivisions of New Jersey was an embarrassment. The soil was too thin for art." ("The Queen and I")

*Steven Millhauser, *The Knife Thrower and Other Stories* (Crown). The eighth book by this Pulitzer Prize–winning author has twelve stories and is marked by variety of form and subject even as he continues to explore the borders of the magical and the surreal, testing the limits and the possibilities of imagination: "By nature, then, our art is mimetic; and each advance has been a new encroachment on the preserves of life. Visitors who see our automatons for the first time are awed and even disturbed by their lifelike qualities. Truly our figures seem to think and breathe. But having acknowledged the mimetic or illusionistic tendency of our art, I hasten to point out that the realism of which I speak must not be misunderstood to mean the narrow and constricting sort that dominates and deadens our literature. It is a realism of means, which in no way excludes the fanciful." ("The New Automation Theater")

*Susan Minot, *Evening* (Knopf). For Susan Minot's third novel (also *Lust & Other Stories*) the author tells the story of Ann Lord who, dying, recalls and relives a three-day love affair that happened in her life some forty years earlier: "Her face seemed to Nurse Brown as if a light had been thrown from beneath it and she saw in Ann Lord the young face she'd seen in some of the photographs around the house. There was one of Ann Lord as a young woman with her hair blowing and her teeth white in profile. Nurse Brown picked up the tray and left the room."

*A. G. Mojtabai, *Soon: Tales From Hospice* (Zoland). The author's eighth book is a group of stories set in a hospice at Amarillo, Texas: "He was so restless, he couldn't wait to be gone from West Texas, he was ready to go. There were open fields on either side, a telephone cable stitching the air high overhead. The wire went humming with secrets it wasn't yet telling, bound for elsewhere, where he, too, was going."

*Lorrie Moore, *Birds of America: Stories* (Knopf). Author of two novels and three collections of stories, Moore was treated to significant, widespread critical attention and respect from the twelve stories collected and arranged as *Birds of America.* Jeff Giles's *Newsweek* (28 September) review was representative–"a marvelous, fiercely funny book about great and tiny jolts to the heart, about the push and pull of relationships, about the way loved ones, slowly or suddenly, become unrecognizable": "Because this is a research and teaching hospital, all the regular doctors are at home sleeping in their Mission-style beds. Tonight, as is apparently the case every weekend night, the attending physician is a medical student. He looks fifteen. The authority he attempts to convey, he cannot remotely inhabit. He is not even in the same building with it."

*Alice Munro, *The Love of a Good Woman* (Knopf). This gathering of eight stories, five of which appeared in *The New Yorker,* is Munro's tenth book. The stories, some of novella length, are gradual and cumulative in effect and depend upon the discovery and exploration of solidly dimensional characters, old and young, of several generations. As in her other works, the principal settings are rural or resort areas in Canada: "The beach was nearly empty–people had got used to its being a rainy day. The sand was too heavy for Caitlin to make a castle or dig an irrigation system–projects she would

only undertake with her father, anyway, because she sensed that his interest in them was wholehearted, and Pauline's was not. She wandered a bit forlornly at the edge of the water." ("The Children Stay")

*Kent Nelson, *Discoveries: Short Stories of the San Juans* (Western Reflections) and *Toward the Sun: The Collected Sports Stories of Kent Nelson* (Breakaway Books). Nelson is one of the most gifted and productive story writers in America and richly deserving of far more critical recognition than he has received so far. Perhaps these two impressive collections of twenty-four stories, many of which have appeared in the best quarterlies, will change his luck: "No one but a madman forgets who he is, but William Bryce Talbot had lived so long alone in the mountains he no longer thought of himself with a name. 'My name meant what my father wanted it to,' he said aloud to himself, as if to someone interviewing him. 'It might have been a name everyone knew, a famous name . . .' He stopped. Recently his voice sounded hollow. It broke in the back of his throat like an aspen leaning against another tree in the wind." ("A Way of Dying" from *Discoveries*)

*Patrick O'Brien, *The Hundred Days* (Norton). This latest in the hugely popular Aubrey-Maturin series, the nineteenth, follows the adventures of Commodore Aubrey and his surgeon friend in the Mediterranean and Adriatic seas during the breathless hundred days between Napoleon's escape from Elba and his defeat at Waterloo. Sea battles and close calls onshore in North Africa keep the pages turning. Authentic details of the life and times, as usual, enrich the narrative experience: "This, with the help of a clearing sky over the main ocean, the light of a splendid moon and a more regular sea, was soon done; and the squadron, well in hand, at the proper cable's length apart, ran down the Moroccan coast under courses and full topsails with our easier following sea and the wind on their larboard quarter; they were still in the order of their leaving, *Ringle* lying under *Surprise's* lee, as becomes a tender."

*Tim O'Brien, *Tomcat in Love* (Broadway). O'Brien's latest, his sixth book, tells all about the linguist Thomas H. Chippering, whose driving force is based on a deep appreciation, if not understanding, of women, even his former wife Lorna Sue: "After class, as a matter of good form, I was obligated to flag down my raven admirer. Lively chitchat ensued–invigorating, I thought–and naturally I inquired as to her name, which was Toni with an *i,* short for Antonia with a pair of firmly bracketing *a's.* To our mutual pleasure, the conversation ran on for a full twenty-two minutes. Toni's eyes appropriately aglow, each tick of the clock chiming with innuendo and possibility. The girl was smitten."

*Iain Pears, *An Instance of the Fingerpost* (Riverhead). Set in Oxford in 1663, early in the Restoration, this "intellectual thriller," with as many "real" characters as fictional, is partly a classic murder mystery, partly a spy story, and, finally, a religious book: "But how often now, late at night when I lie sleepless in my bed once more, or when I am deep in the frustration of prayers which no longer come, I fear my only hope of salvation is that His mercy will prove greater than was mine.

"I no longer believe it will."

*Leslie Pietrzyk, *Pears on a Willow Tree* (Avon). This first novel is the multigenerational story of a Polish American family. Five generations of the women of the Marchewka family deal with the clash of values and customs of the Old World and the ever-changing New: "My sisters especially liked stories about boys with blue eyes that moved like the sky and hands as big as loaves of bread and a voice steady enough to still rabbits. My mother frowned through these stories, so I did, too, even though I liked them and the way my sisters' faces turned soft as they talked."

*Chaim Potok, *Zebra and Other Stories* (Knopf). Six stories about various teenagers by the author of the best-selling novels—*The Chosen* and *My Name Is Asher Lev:* "In the third week of November, about an hour after the start of the day, Tim Boynton was called into the office of the headmaster and asked to open his locker. . . . By the start of the *Macbeth* rehearsal that day, everyone knew that the headmaster had found nearly half a pound of marijuana in Tim Boynton's locker. The police were notified, and he was taken from the school in handcuffs. His parents were called; he was suspended." ("Nava")

*Steven Pressfield, *Gates of Fire: An Epic Novel of the Battle of Thermophlae* (Doubleday). A sole survivor of the amazing battle at Thermopylae, where three hundred Spartans held off a huge Persian army for three days, recounts the event to Xerxes and to the other Persians: "There is a secret all warriors share, so private that none dare give it voice, save only to those mates drawn dearer than brothers by the shared ordeal of arms. This is the knowledge of the hundred acts of his own cowardice. The little things that no one sees. The comrade who fell and cried for aid. Did I pass him by? Choose my skin over his? That was my crime, of which I accuse myself in the tribunal of my heart and there condemn myself as guilty."

*Reynolds Price, *Roxanna Slade* (Scribner). Price's latest novel in a long and lucky career (twenty-eight books) is the fictional autobiography of a now ninety-four-year-old Southern woman: "Leela was the world's chief Jell-o provider. She claimed it was still made from baby calf's hooves, all of which kept her fingernails strong as any ox horn. She did have the longest nails in

the upper South, unbreakable as leather and painted Blushing Pink till the early 1960s when she switched to Jungle Drums, a lazy deep red."

*Richard Price, *Freedomland* (Broadway Books). The sixth novel of one of our most gifted and relevant novelists (he also has written a number of screenplays) is set in the same New Jersey urban wasteland as his highly praised *Clockers;* the story for *Freedomland* was inspired, he has said in several interviews, by the case of Susan Smith of Union, S.C. *Freedomland* takes place during a week in July and features as its protagonist a black detective—Lorenzo "Big Daddy" Council: "'Just keep your eyes down;' Lorenzo murmured to Brenda, hoping she would, hoping she wouldn't. . . . They beheld what seemed at first an inconceivable number of corpses in open storage, some fresh, some unclaimed, others back-logged for autopsy. More than half, Lorenzo knew, were guests from neighboring Essex County, where the Newark-based morgue had suffered a cooling-system blowout. . . . Their varying postures and conditions were like an inventory of final exits, the dead lying there on their backs, their bellies, curled and their sides as if cold or frightened, lying there in attitudes of agony, of repose, of resistance, of surrender."

*James Purdy, *Gertrude of Stony Island Avenue* (Morrow). In a version of the myth of Demeter and Persephone, Carrie Kinsella searches for the truth about her dead daughter, Gertrude, a gifted painter. Purdy, over the past forty years, has written twenty-seven books, sixteen of which are novels: "What was astonishing to everybody, including Cy, was not Gertrude's worship of this music but that her mother was as unconnected with the world of Sixty-third Street and bebop as a small child is unconversant with all the details of the fall of Pompeii and the biblical Sodom."

*Kit Reed, *Weird Women, Wired Women* (Wesleyan). Author of thirteen novels (and four under the pen name Kit Craig), Kit Reed has also published five collections of short stories, including this gathering of twenty "womanist" fantasies, written from 1958 to 1996. These stories are richly various in form and strategy, linked by the author's voice and irrepressible, ironic, often mordant wit: "The women had collected twigs and they were first about to set fire to Patsy and Andy when Sheena came out, closely followed by Dr. Ora Fesenden and a warlike Rap. Everybody started shouting at once and in the imbroglio that followed, Patsy and Andy escaped. They would surface years later in a small town in Minnesota, with an ecologically alarming number of children; they would both be able to pursue their chosen careers in law because they worked hand in hand to take care of all the children and the house, and they would love each other until they died." ("Songs of War")

*Mark Richard, *Charity: Stories* (Talese/Doubleday). Richard's earlier story collection, *The Ice at the Bottom of the World,* earned the PEN/Ernest Hemingway Foundation Award. Versions of the eleven stories in *Charity* appeared in *The New Yorker, Esquire, Harper's,* and many first-rate literary magazines. His stories are lean, generally brief, and tend to move to the near edges of surrealism: "The boy mistook death for one of the landlady's sons come to collect the rent. Death stood leaning against a tree scraping fresh manure off his shoe with a stick. The boy told death he would have to see his mother about the rent, and death said he was not there to collect the rent.

"My brother is real sick, you should come back later, the boy said. Death said he would wait." ("Memorial Day")

*David Robertson, *Booth* (Anchor). A first novel by an author who has published nonfiction and poetry, *Booth* is narrated by John Surratt, the only survivor among the conspirators who planned the assassination of President Lincoln: "In the darkness of the alleyway, I could make out a photographic print of my *carte de visite* posted on the cardboard. Below my image was hastily written in ink, as if in a dream: WANTED FOR APPREHENSION IN THE MURDER OF PRESIDENT LINCOLN. My heart stopped in my throat. What had happened? What had Booth done?"

*Philip Roth, *I Married a Communist* (Houghton Mifflin). This story of Ira Ringold, radio actor and political activist in the 1940s and 1950s, is remembered and retold by Nathan Zuckerman (who has starred in other books by Roth) and ninety-year-old Murray Ringold, once Zuckerman's English teacher in Newark. A complex, ambiguous story of the days of political witch-hunts and blacklisting in America: "All his ranting Ira now directed at himself. How could this farce have wrecked his life? Everything to the side of the main thing, all the peripheral stuff of existence that Comrade O'Day had warned him against. Home. Marriage. Family. Mistresses. Adultery. All the bourgeois shit! Why hadn't he lived like O'Day? *Real* prostitutes, trustworthy professionals who understand the rules, and not blabbermouth amateurs like his Estonian masseuse."

*Bart Schneider, *Blue Bossa* (Viking). Set in San Francisco in the 1970s, this is the story of a jazz trumpet player, Ronnie Reboulet: "Ronnie does his best to keep up, without trying any fancy Dizzy stuff, although the old hipster always hovers over his song. Ronnie wasn't able to make high notes like Diz, even in his prime. Still he flies through the changes, his teeth nearly coming unfixed from his gums, the damn drummer driving them all wrong, but still driving him."

*John Burnham Schwartz, *Reservation Road* (Knopf). Schwartz's second novel received wide and

Dust jacket for the novel about the self-discoveries the protagonist makes as she reminisces in the evening of her life

prompt review attention and praise. This is another of the year's crop of "literary" thrillers. A hit-and-run accident and the death of his ten-year-old son, Jason, turns Ethan Learner, college professor, into an obsessed hunter for the guilty driver. Multiple narrators tell the story from several angles: "I drove home that afternoon with the man's name in my mouth. Spitting out the vowels and consonants to myself, over and over, like a diver, alone in green watery light, murmuring to himself at the end of the high board."

*Jane Smiley, *The All-True Travels and Adventures of Liddie Newton* (Knopf). Smiley's tenth novel is the large, picaresque, first-person story of Liddie Harkness Newton, set in "Bloody Kansas" during the 1850s as the nation, torn apart by slavery, moved toward civil war: "It didn't take long for me to get out of Kansas City. I was eager and strong, and it was easy to walk in trousers, as I had noticed before. Giving away my petticoat had lightened my case some, and I contemplated tossing the whole thing aside, but in the end I couldn't quite do that. It represented too much who I'd been. I was afraid to lose that entirely."

*Robert Stone, *Damascus Gate* (Houghton Mifflin). In Stone's sixth novel Christopher Lucas, an American journalist looking for a subject to write about finds himself in Jerusalem, where he becomes deeply involved with a group of extraordinary characters and, among other things, a plot to blow up the *Temple Mount:* "At the entrance to the small camp was a pile of tires buttressed by gasoline cans, an instantly inflammable barricade. About a hundred feet beyond it, a group of youths were gathered about burning trash cans. In the light of the flames, he could see figures laid side by side under blue sheeting. The figures appeared to be corpses."

*Hunter S. Thompson, *The Rum Diary: The Long Lost Novel* (Simon & Schuster). In 1958 Paul Kemp (a shadow figure of the *Gonzo* author himself) leaves New York for Puerto Rico, where he finds work at the *San Juan Daily News.* Kemp describes his time in the sun accurately enough in his own words: "It was a greedy life and I was good at it. I made some interesting friends, had enough money to get around, and learned a lot about the world that I never could have learned in any other way." This novel, a product of his early twenties, shows some of the characteristics of his mature work, described by fellow reporter/novelist William Kennedy as "bizarre wit, supreme self-confidence, the narrative of the wounded meritorious ego, and the idiopathic anger of the righteous outlaw."

*Melanie Rae Thon, *Girls in the Grass* (Owl). Eleven stories, various in form, content, subject, place, and time, comprise this second collection of Thon's stories. Her first, *First, Body* won her the praise of critics and story writers and, as well, a Whiting Award in 1997. Here she shows a firm, imaginative mastery of complex characters of all ages and of diverse social backgrounds: "The boys said Henry Clay talked truth and nothing but. His ears were too big and stuck out straight from his head. His hair was shaved so close to the skin his skull gleamed. Ben heard his mama was white and never left the house. Then he heard she was only half white and ran away. Either way, Henry Clay got somebody's fine golden skin, and the girls at school giggled when they passed him, called him 'pretty boy' behind his back, and never seemed to notice those ears."

*Hector Tobar, *The Tattooed Soldier* (Delphinium). Set in contemporary Los Angeles, this is the story of Antonio Bernal, victim and refugee from Guatemala, and Guillermo Longoria, a former death-squad soldier. It soon becomes a manhunt. Tobar, a *Los Angeles Times* reporter, gives us an insider's view of the Third World city that is Los Angeles today: "There were so many Latinos in Los Angeles now, thousands upon thousands of Mexicanos, Guatemaltecos, and Salvadorenos, more than he ever imagined. He had come to the States expecting to be surrounded by blond, blue-eyed gringos, not a Spanish-talking sea of brown faces. Even the Mayan Indians of his country, people who had lived in the same little *Aldeas* in Guatemala since before the Spaniards came–even they were here."

*William Trevor, *Death in Summer* (Viking). This novel, the twenty-sixth published book by Trevor, concerns three deaths in a summer at Quincunx House and centers on Thaddeus Davenant, who owns it and lives there: "By the time Thaddeus was first conscious of his surroundings the days of the Davenants' enterprise and prosperity were over. Mismanagement in a single generation had initiated decline and the aftermath of war did not permit recovery. And Thaddeus witnessed in another way the effects of that same war: in his father's failure to recover from the distress of his experiences in battle."

*John Updike, *Bech at Bay: A Quasi-Novel* (Knopf). This is the third in the series of Bech books that Updike began with *Bech: A Book* (1970). *Bech at Bay* comprises five linked stories about Bech in his senior years, ending in "Bech and the Bounty of Sweden," with Bech being awarded, without warning, the Nobel Prize in Literature. Until then his adventures and misadventures take him to California, Czechoslovakia, and, of course, his home in New York and all over the map on a book tour: "This was on a radio swing down through Megalopolis, from Christopher Lydon in a dismal stretch beyond Boston University to Leonard Lopate in the dingy corridors of New York City Hall to Philadelphia's 'Fresh Air' in a canister-lined chamber of WHYY and on to Diane Rehm's WAMU aerie on Brandywine Street in the bosky midst of American University in Washington, D.C."

*Bailey White, *Quite a Year for Plums* (Knopf). This first novel is the third book of National Public Radio commentator Bailey White. Set in small-town Georgia, the story deals with a large and intricately interconnected cast of characters, many of whom are as eccentric as anyone you may ever meet in fact or in fiction: "It was a 1919 General Electric, three speeds, with copper blades that showed up as a golden glow at the root of the gale. One of the blades had a jagged chipped edge that threw the fan a little off-balance and set up a vibration that caused the whole store to rattle and shake. A pair of Mr. and Mrs. Santa salt and pepper shakers marched with wobbly steps to the edge of their shelf. Ethel caught Mrs. Santa (salt) just as she began to tip."

*Curtis White, *Memories of My Father Watching TV* (Dalkey Archive). Reviewing this lively, experimental novel ("Daddy was a Pontoon Bridge," *The New York Times Book Review,* 30 August), William Ferguson wrote: "White's wonderfully manic novel is built on the premise that the television industry manufactures dreams that wound and dehumanize even as they claim to entertain": "As Sarge walks back to meet his platoon, he feels no joy. He'd done his job, saved lives by the bucketful, frustrated *les boches,* and yet he felt gloomy. He couldn't understand, of course, but he had become my father. My father's essence could not be destroyed; it had to reside somewhere. It must have flowed back up the wires to the detonator at the moment of his death. Like me, Sergeant Saunders is now possessed by my father. The undead. They walk among us."

*John Edgar Wideman, *Two Cities* (Houghton Mifflin). Wideman's fifteenth book, set in the mean streets of Pittsburgh and Philadelphia, is told by the three central characters–Kassima, a widow; Robert Jones, who loves her; and Mr. Mallory, an eccentric artist (photographer) who is her tenant. Here is Mallory recalling his experience in World War II: "Yet all the war's ugliness could not hide the beauty of the landscape, the Italy that would return after war, just as it had thrived before war. How can I say it. So much death and danger, so much unhappiness surrounding me. Then a tiny flower, a breeze, dawn on the hills. . . ."

*Diane Williams, *Excitability: Selected Stories 1986–1996* (Dalkey Archive). Ninety stories and a novella ("The Stuperfaction") compose this gathering by an avant-garde story writer who has caught the attention and earned good words from such highly regarded story writers as Elizabeth Tallent, Amy Hempel, Lydia Davis, and Bob Shacochis. Most of the stories are very short, what Elizabeth Tallent called "Fictional Chips": "One point must be made and this concerns what we learn from the history of the world. It must be noted that usually men do not possess valuables or huge sums of money. Their sense of their being sorry about this grows and it grows and it grows. A woman may be their only irreplaceable object. That's why I think the meaning of life is so wonderful. It has helped millions of men and women to achieve vastly rich and productive lives." ("The Meaning of Life")

*Tom Wolfe, *A Man in Full* (Farrar, Straus). By year's end this expansive novel, set in Atlanta and lavishly plotted around the representative life and times of Charles Croaker, former football star and now a high-flying entrepreneur and developer, was already an extraordinary success by any standards and, as well, the subject of all kinds and forms of critical attention, pro and con. Whether the book is entertainment, pure and simple, or a powerful literary statement, it is a remarkable achievement, Wolfe at his vintage best, at once satirical and authentic: "Roger Too White–the old nickname was *really burning* up his brainstem tonight–sat in his Lexus, brooding. He could probably make it unscathed to the church, which was just over a block

away, but the bad boys would descend upon the Lexus like . . . like . . . like . . . He couldn't imagine what the bad boys here in this part of Southeast Atlanta would be like. He had a vision of a window bashed in until the remains looked like crushed ice and holes in the steering column and on top of the dashboard where there used to be air bags. . . ."

*Daniel Woodrell, *Tomato Red* (Holt). Ozark noir is perhaps the best description of the genre in Woodrell's five earlier novels and *Tomato Red*. This latest, with as odd a cast as Woodrell can imagine, takes place in the Venus Holler section of the town of West Table, Missouri: "The good world, regular happy life; I never had no hand in that, so it's interesting for me to watch it. They seem so sure of their road and what they'll pass along the way and what they'll find at the end."

*Kim Wozencraft, *The Catch* (Doubleday). Kim Wozencraft's third book presents a contemporary couple who are smuggling marijuana, but trying to break free and begin a new life in Upstate New York: "Kurt parked the rental in the garage and sat, psyched and freaked at once. Hadn't they given Kessler the real live slip but good? Divide and conquer. Catch me if you can, motherfucker. If you do, that makes me one, too."

Other Fiction

Here are other novels and collections of stories that received significant review attention (and promotion) during the year and in many cases were deemed worthy for other lists of the best and most notable books of the year: *The Antelope Wife* (Harper Flamingo), by Louise Erdrich; *Armadillo* (Knopf), by William Boyd; *Barney's Version* (Knopf), by Mordecai Richler; *Big Girls Don't Cry* (Atlantic Monthly), by Fay Weldon; *Blue Light* (Little, Brown), by Walter Mosley; *The Boy* (Houghton Mifflin), by Naeem Murr; *Bringing Out the Dead* (Knopf), a first novel about a paramedic, by Joe Connelly; *Cavedweller* (Dutton), by Dorothy Allison, who has published her first full-scale novel since *Bastard Out of Carolina*; *Dusk* (Modern Library), by Philippine writer F. Sionil Jose; *Gain* (Farrar, Straus), by Richard Powers, described by *The New York Times Book Review* (6 December) as "An erudite, penetrating novel that deals with the evolution of American industry and commercial practice over two countries. . . "; *The Healing* (Beacon), by Gayl Jones; *Icy Sparks* (Viking), by Gwyn Hyman Rubio, a first novel about a young woman's struggle with Tourette's syndrome; *Jack Maggs* (Knopf), by Peter Carey, a revised version of and homage to Charles Dickens's *Great Expectations*; *Kaaterskill Falls* (Dial), by Allegra Goodman, about life in an Orthodox Jewish community; *Karoo* (Harcourt Brace), a posthumous

Dust jacket for the author's novel that involves race relations and urban crime in the United States

Hollywood novel by the writer of *Breaking Away*; *The Last King of Scotland* (Knopf), by Giles Foden, in fact all about Idi Amin; *My Heart Laid Bare* (Dutton), by Joyce Carol Oates; *Nosferatu* (Knopf), by Jim Shepard; *On the Occasion of My Last Afternoon* (Putnam), a Southern historical novel by Kay Gibbons; *Paradise* (Knopf), by Toni Morrison, who has written this "complicated" novel that opened to mixed if well-meaning reviews; *A Patchwork Planet* (Knopf), the fourteenth novel by Anne Tyler; *Quarantine* (Farrar, Straus), by Jim Crace, a revised and reinterpreted version of Jesus' forty days in the wilderness; *The Rich Man's Table* (Knopf), by Scott Spencer; *Salt Water* (Chronicle), by Charles Simmons, a summer love story set in 1963; *The Smithsonian Institution* (Random House), by Gore Vidal, a quirky tour through American history; *T.C. Boyle Stories: The Collected Stories of T. Coraghessan Boyle* (Viking), sixty-eight stories and close to seven hundred pages; *The Treatment* (Knopf), by Daniel Menaker, editor at Random House and former fiction editor at *The New Yorker*. (Amazing how many of the books on these lists, and all the others, come from Knopf!) Not to ignore Alison Lurie's

Key West novel, *The Last Resort* (Holt); Marianne Wiggins's *Almost Heaven* (Crown), the story of a young journalist named Holden Garfield; Jack Butler's *The Dreamer* (Knopf); Ethan Canin's latest, *For Kings and Planets* (Random House); *The Ark of the Marindor* (MacMurray & Beck), by Barry Targan; Barry Gifford's *The Sinaloa Story* (Harcourt Brace); *Where the Sea Used to Be* (Houghton Mifflin), Rich Bass's revision and expansion of his 1987 novella with the same title; David Leavitt, *The Page Turner* (Houghton Mifflin); *Flights of Angels* (Little, Brown), by Ellen Gilchrist; or Nancy LeMann's *The Fiery Pantheon* (Scribner).

Among books published by African American writers, three not found on any lists did, in fact, earn considerable review attention—*The Edge of Heaven* (Doubleday), by Marita Golden; Gloria Naylor's *The Men of Brewster Place* (Hyperion); and *Up Jumped the Devil* (Avon), by Blair S. Walker. Several outstanding first books by African American writers appeared during the year. *Lady Moses* (HarperCollins), by poet Lucinda Roy, tells the troubled life story of Jacinta Moses, daughter of an African father and a white British mother. This novel received a great deal of review and press attention. Compared to Pynchon and Millhauser, Colson Whitehead follows the story of Lila Mae Watson, black female elevator inspector (and intuitionist) in the Department of Elevator Inspectors in *The Intuitionist* (Doubleday). In *The Moaner's Bench* (Harper Flamingo) polymath Mars Hill tells the coming-of-age story of an African American boy in a religious family during the Great Depression. A contemporary and complex blending of fact and fiction is found in David Dante Troutt's *The Monkey Suit,* ten short stories "on African Americans and Justice," each story a fictional version of famous cases in the law involving African Americans. In *Caucasia* (Riverhead) Danzy Senna presents the stories of the two daughters of a black father and a white mother in Boston in the 1970s. On the jacket Thomas Keneally, author of *Schindler's List* and other books, praises her as "a superb new writer" and "a fresh and robust American voice." Other first novels that received attention and earned the praise of reviewers include Tim Gautreaux's *The Next Step in the Dance* (Picador) and Peter Glassgold's *The Angel Max* (Harcourt Brace). *Glorie* (Zoland), by Caryn James, chief television critic for *The New York Times,* was included in "Notable Books" in *The New York Times*.

It was a good year for the publication of collections of short stories. Among debut story collections were the following: Mark Slouka's *Lost Lake* (Knopf), which includes twelve stories set in a Czech community on the shore of New York's Lost Lake. This collection is praised by Richard Bausch for its "powerful new lyric voice." Mark Brazaitis, whose collection *The*

River of Lost Voices (Iowa) won the Iowa Short Fiction Award, has ten stories set in Guatemala. Bill Oliver, who has earned many prizes for individual stories, in *Women & Children First* (Mid-List Press) gathers a dozen varied stories linked by theme and by the author's voice. The Midwest and the city of Manila are the settings for the dozen stories in Laura Stapleton's *The Lowest Blue Flame Before Nothing* (Aunt Lute Books). Joyce Hinnefeld won the Katherine Bakeless Nason Fiction Prize for the fifteen stories that comprise *Tell Me Everything* (Middlebury/Bread Loaf), stories mostly about the ordinary lives of women. The central characters are mostly women, also, in Southern writer June Spence's fifteen stories that make up *Missing Women and Others* (Riverhead). The title story was selected for *The Best American Short Stories 1997*. Michael Byers is Truman Capote Fellow at Stanford University, and the eight stories of his first collection, *The Coast of Good Intentions* (Houghton Mifflin), earned him a place as Best American Short Stories Discovery. A novella and four short stories make up Kathryn Trueblood's *The Sperm Donor's Daughter and Other Tales of Modern Family* (Permanent Press). A baker's dozen of stories dealing with "the lives of quirky characters of the Great Plains" form Nebraskan writer Ron Block's *The Dirty Shame Hotel* (New Rivers Press). The John Simmons Short Fiction Award was won by *Friendly Fire* (Iowa), by Kathryn Chetkovich. Writer Stuart Dybek praised the author for "the comic vision that gives these stories a memorable charm." Thom Jones called Joseph Clark—author of *Jungle Wedding: Stories* (Norton)—"An often hilarious, yet terrifying new voice in fiction." Some forty-three short stories are in Nancy Dillingham's *New Ground* (Worldcomm). Of the author, poet Fred Chappell writes in the foreword: "Things are as they are in her world and this very condition of their being is what caused her to write them. She could have fashioned them to a more contemporary taste; she could have falsified, though I have the impression this possibility never even occurred to her." All of the above books were nominated for the PEN/Hemingway Award.

Other noteworthy story collections include: Doug Lawson, *Patrimony of Fishes* (Red Hen); *Dirt Angel* (Ontario Review), by Jeanne Wilmut; Ehud Havazelet, *Like Never Before* (Farrar, Straus); *Hunger: A Novella and Stories* (Norton), by Lan Samantha Chang; Josip Novakovich, *Salvation and Other Disasters* (Graywolf)—a volume that was included in "Notable Books" in *The New York Times;* Dabney Stuart, *The Way to Cobb's Creek* (Missouri); *Where She Went* (Sarabande), by Kate Walbert; and Beth Lordan, *And Both Shall Row* (Picador). Richard Selzer's *The Doctor Stories* (Picador) is a selection from thirty years of his short fiction.

There was no shortage of anthologies of short fiction during 1998. *Prize Stories 1998: The O. Henry Awards* (Doubleday), edited by Larry Dark and a prize jury including Andrea Barrett, Mary Gaitskill, and Rick Moody, featured twenty stories selected from a variety of magazines and quarterlies—four from *The New Yorker,* two from *Atlantic Monthly,* and two from *Harper's.* First prize went to Lorrie Moore's "People Like That Are the Only People Here," celebrated by Rick Moody: "Moore's story is perfect because it unflinchingly takes on the most difficult of all dramas, the sickness of a child, without indulging once in sentimentality." Second prize went to Steven Millhauser for his title story "The Knife Thrower," and third place went to the distinguished Alice Munro for "The Children Stay." *The Best American Short Stories 1998* (Houghton Mifflin) was edited by Garrison Keillor and series editor Katrina Kenison, with a minimum overlapping of the two volumes: "People Like That Are the Only People Here" and "Flower Children," by Maxine Swann, appear in both. Each has a story by Annie Proulx. Although this volume has a couple of stories from *The New Yorker* and *Atlantic Monthly,* the stories have been selected from a variety of literary magazines, and there are more stories by first-rate young writers. Outstanding among them are Bliss Broyard ("Mr. Sweetly Indecent") and Tim Gautreaux ("Wedding with Children"). Close in spirit is *New Stories from the South: The Year's Best, 1998* (Algonquin), edited by Shannon Ravenel. This collection sports a satirical preface by Padgett Powell and more younger writers from a wider variety of magazines (Ravenel combs nintey-nine different magazines) than the others. The comments by the authors about the stories reprinted here are, at best, interesting and helpful . . . to other writers, at least. Houghton Mifflin is now publishing a separate anthology of short fiction, edited this year by Sue Grafton—*The Best American Mystery Stories 1998,* more or less following the familiar format of the traditional *Best American* anthology, except that other magazines and another crew of writers are involved. However, some straightforward literary writers who have written crime fiction are represented here—Joyce Carol Oates ("Faithless," from *The Kenyon Review*), Steve Yarbrough ("The Rest of Her Life," from *Missouri Review*), and Jay McInerney ("Con Doctor," from *Playboy*). A generally younger group of writers selected by editor Carol Shields, twenty-two from the 234 nominations, is found in *Scribner's Best of the Fiction Workshops 1998* (Scribner). It's a mixed bag and probably not representative of the best work in the creative writing workshops (some of the very best of those are not present here), but it is not without interest. An impressive anthology with a distinctly different cast of characters comes from Dalkey Archive Press—*Innova-*

tions: *An Anthology of Modern & Contemporary Fiction,* edited by Robert L. McLaughlin. Asserting simply that "fiction is and always has been an art form that allows writers the most freedom within which to play," McLauglin has gathered writers of several generations (Djuna Barnes and Gertrude Stein; John Barth, Robert Coover, and Donald Barthelme; Curtis White and David Foster Wallace) in compiling a book that demonstrates the power and pleasures of innovative fiction. Celebrating the ways and means of innovative fiction, the editor adds "A Highly Eccentric List of 101 Books for Further Reading," which includes fiction by writers from Kathy Acker to Marguerite Young.

More and more the case, literature from all over the world, in translation, has become important in American fiction. Sometimes it is in the form of new translations of work by foreign writers. In 1998, for example, Andrew Hurley published a new translation of *Collected Fictions* (Viking), by the enormously influential Jorge Luis Borges. Two new translations of Franz Kafka were brought out by Shocken–*The Trial,* translated by Breon Mitchell, and Mark Harman's translation of *The Castle.* Russian nineteenth-century writers influenced the literary scene in 1998. Richard Pevear and Larissa Volokhonsky produced a highly praised new translation of *Collected Tales* (Pantheon), by Nikolai Gogol, one that James Wood, writing in *The New Yorker* (17 August, "The Prankster and the Prophet"), labeled as "superb." Translator Peter Constantine brought forth *The Undiscovered Chekhov: Thirty-Eight New Stories* (Seven Stories Press), a collection of stories from the 1880s, all but two of which have never been rendered in English. Depending on the familiar translations of Constance Garnet, Ecco Press published *The Essential Tales of Chekhov,* edited and with an introduction, "Why We Like Chekhov," by Richard Ford. Ford writes: "More than anything else, though, it is Chekhov's great sufficiency that moves us and makes us admire; our reader's awareness that story to story, degree by degree around the sphere of observed human existence, Chekhov's measure is perfect." Another form of "translation" from nineteenth-century Russian to contemporary American is Charles Simmons's *Salt Water* (Chronicle), which turns out to be a revised version of Ivan Sergeevich Turgenev's "First Love." It was hailed by Katherine Webber (*The New York Times Book Review* 6 September) as "a small masterpiece."

The busy and fruitful year for translation from a variety of languages was made more extensive by the active translation programs of university presses. It is impossible in this space to do more than suggest the larger picture. For those readers with a special interest in translation of modern and contemporary literature *The Review of Contemporary Fiction* is a good source, a place to start. Not only are there a large number of reviews, but, from time to time, special issues feature the literature of other languages. For example, the Spring 1998 issue was chiefly devoted to "New Latvian Fiction." Not surprising, considering the significant and growing Hispanic population in the United States, there were many translations from Spanish. Among them were: *The Notebooks of Don Rigoberto* (Farrar, Straus), an erotic novel by the well-known Mario Vargas Llosa; *Loves That Bind* (Knopf), an epistolary novel by Julian Rios; and from Cuba *A Viewing from the Mangrove* (Massachusetts), by Antonio Benitez Rojo. Oxford University Press, as part of its ongoing Library of Latin America, brought out *Torn from the Nest* by Clorinda Matto de Turner, first published in 1889. From Portugal came the latest novel of Nobel Prize–winner Jose Saramago–*Blindness* (Harcourt Brace). Also from the Portuguese (Brazil) is *Quincas Borba* (Oxford) by Joaquim Maria Machado de Assis, originally published in 1891. There were many translations from French: Christopher Bataille, *Hourmaster* (New Directions), set in the seventeenth century in a French duchy near the North Sea; *Another November* (Nebraska), by Roger Grenier; Maryse Conde's *The Last of the African Kings* (Nebraska), set in Charleston, South Carolina; *Possessions* (Columbia), by Julia Kristeva; by the scientific journalist Bernard Webber–*Empire of the Ants* (Bantam); from Martinique writer (French Creole) Patrick Chamolseau came *Solibo Magnificent* (Pantheon); and from the University of Nebraska Press came Patrick Modiano's *Out of the Dark.* Widely and favorably reviewed was Andrei Makine's *Once upon the River of Love* (Arcade), of which the reviewer in *The New York Times Book Review* (7 September) asked and answered, "Can a whole novel be about adolescent boys watching Jean-Paul Belmondo movies through a Siberian winter? Resoundingly, yes." Sun and Moon Press published a translation of the final novel by Raymond Queneau, *The Children of Clay* (1938); Johns Hopkins Press published a translation of Michel Tournier's third novel, *Gemini.*

Among the Italian works translated this year were Dacia Maraini, *The Silent Duchess* (Feminist Press); Anna Maria Ortese's *A Music Behind the Wall: Selected Stories, Volume Two* (McPherson); *The Story of Tonle* (Northwestern), by Mario Rigoni Stern; and *Rules of the Wild* (Pantheon), by Francesca Marciano. Writers from other European countries and languages were well represented on the scene. Peter Hoeg of Denmark published *Tales of the Night* (Farrar, Straus). From Germany came *Once Again for Thucydides* (New Directions), by Peter Handke; Uwe Timm's *Midsummer Night,* also published by New Directions; another by Handke–*My Year in the No-Man's Bar* (Farrar, Straus); Ingo Schulze, *Thirty-Three Moments of Happiness: St. Petersburg Stories* (Knopf); and

Christa Wolf's *Medea: A Modern Retelling* (Talese/Doubleday). Among the middle European writers published in translation this year were Czech writers Josef Hirsal, with *A Bohemian Youth* (Northwestern), and Milan Kundera, with *Identity* (Harper Flamingo). A Polish first novel, *Miss Nobody,* by Tomek Tryzna was published by Doubleday. Polish Jewish writer Bogdan Wojdowski's *Bread for the Departed* came from Northwestern. Hungarian writer Peter Esterhazy was represented by two books, both published by Northwestern University Press—*She Loves Me* and *The Glance of the Countess Hahn-Hahn.* Another Russian book of more than passing interest is *How It All Began* (Columbia), by the early Soviet leader (and victim) Nikolai Bukharin.

From the Middle East: Israeli Aharon Applefeld had two books published by Shocken—*The Iron Tracks* and *The Conversion.* Other books from Israel include Dorit Rabinyan's *Persian Brides* (Braziller), a first novel; *The One Facing Us* (Holt), by Ronit Matalon; and Savyon Liebrecht's *Apples from the Desert* (Feminist Press). The University of Arkansas Press's Arabic series (the Arabic Translation Awards) produced *Dongola: A Novel of Nubia,* by Idris Ali, and Ghada Samman's *The Square Moon: Supernatural Tales.* Out of Egypt came Mohamed El-Bisatie's *A Glass of Tea and Other Stories* (Three Continents). Also translated from Arabic were the seventeen stories composing *I Sweep the Sun Off Rooftops* (Anchor), by Hanan al-Shaykh.

Several books from Japan received attention in the United States. The oldest known work of Japanese fiction, *The Tale of the Bamboo Cutter,* was published by Kodansha, also the publisher of Natsuki Ikezawa's *Still Lives.* Yukio Mishima's 1964 novel, *Silk and Insight,* was brought out by East Gate. First published in Japan in 1923, Taruho Inagaki's *One Thousand and One-Second Stories* finally appeared in English from Sun and Moon. The University of Michigan Press published Shohei Ooka's *The Shade of Blossoms.* From China came Ying Chen's third novel, *Ingratitude* (Farrar, Straus). Taiwanese writer Wang Chen-Ho's *Rose, Rose, I Love You* came from Columbia University Press. Curbstone published *Behind the Red Mist* by Ho Anh Thai of Vietnam. Two Indian novels, from among a goodly number of the same, were *Beach Boy* (Scribner) by Ardashir Vakil and *Cereus Blooms at Night* (Grove).

To come (almost) full circle, here are three good British novels not mentioned elsewhere in this article: *The Restraint of Beasts* (Arcade), by Magnus Mills, the story of a crew of Scots fence builders that was shortlisted for the Booker prize; Pauline Melville's *The Ventriloquist's Tale* (St. Martin's Press), which won last year's Whitbread First Novel Award in Britain and earned a place in "Notable Books" in *The New York Times;* and George MacDonald Fraser's *Black Ajax* (Carroll &

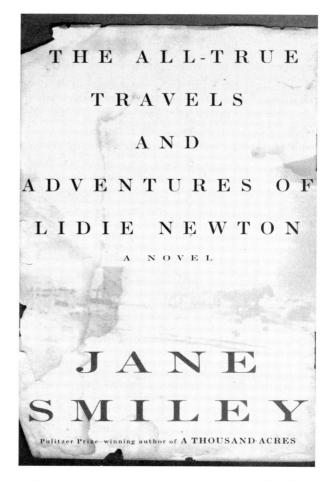

Dust jacket for the novel set in Kansas shortly before the Civil War

Graf), based on the life of great prizefighter Tom Molineaux.

University presses have influenced more things than translation. Many of them publish original fiction also. Here are only some of these books from 1998: Kathryn Chetkovich, *Friendly Fire* (Iowa); John J. Clayton, *Radiance* (Ohio State); Susan Neville, *In the House of Blue Lights* (Notre Dame); Toni Graham, *The Daiquiri Girls* (Massachusetts); Annabel Thomas, *Blood Feud* (Tennessee); Rick Bass, *Fiber* (Georgia); Joyce Hinnefeld, *Tell Me Everything and Other Stories* (New England); Charlotte Bacon, *A Private State* (Massachusetts); Debbie Lee Wesselman, *The Earth and the Sky* (SMU); and Ernest J. Finney, *California Time* (Nevada). Note that this brief list does not include titles from university presses that are already listed on the DLB's "Notable Books." Another area where university and small presses are becoming serious competitors of the mainstream commercial publishers is the matter of reprints and rediscoveries. For example, Iowa brought out a previously unpublished novel by the late Edmund

Wilson—*The Higher Jazz.* Russell Hoban's extraordinary novel of postapocalyptic England, *Ridley Walker,* returned to print in an "Expanded Edition," including an afterword, notes, and glossary, from Indiana University Press. Under the general title "The Virginia Bookshelf," the University Press of Virginia brought back into print several novels by Virginia writers—*The Shad Treatment,* by Garrett Epps; *A Blue Moon in Poor Water,* by Cathryn Hankla; and *The Blood of Paradise,* by Stephen Goodwin. Nebraska returned Harry Brown's World War II novel, *A Walk in the Sun,* to print. As part of their Library of Modern Jewish Literature, Syracuse University Press republished *The Continuing Silence of a Poet,* by A. B. Yehoshua, and Edward Lewis Wallant's *The Human Season.* Although no longer publishing original fiction, L.S.U. Press has produced almost fifty titles in its ongoing Voices of the South Series. The books reprinted in 1998 include: *Bobby Rex's Greatest Hit,* by Marianne Gingher; *Take Me Back,* by Richard Bausch; *The Inkling,* by Fred Chappell; *Augusta Played,* by Kelly Cherry; *The View from Pompey's Head,* by Hamilton Basso; *Easter Weekend,* by David Bottoms; *Slow Poison,* by Sheila Bosworth; and *Flight,* by Walter White. Smaller presses also entered (or continued) the reprint picture, bringing out new editions of all kinds of books, some obvious and some surprising. Turtle Point published *Bertram Cope's Year,* by Henry Blake Fuller, a book originally published eighty years ago; Edward Weismiller's *The Serpent Sleeping* (Fran Cass) is an espionage novel of World War II, first published in 1962. Dalkey Archive Press has an active program of reprints. Among its 1998 volumes are Flann O'Brien's *At Swim-Two-Birds* (with an introduction by William H. Gass); *Time Must Have a Stop* (preface by Douglas Dutton), by Aldous Huxley; *Cigarettes* and *Tlooth,* by Harry Mathews; *Take Five* (preface by John O'Brien), by D. Keith Mano; *The*

Age of Wire and String, by Ben Marcus; *The Dick Gibson Show,* by Stanley Elkin; and *Willie Masters' Lonesome Wife,* by William H. Gass. But there were reprints and discoveries by some of the mainstream publishers as well. Norton brought out a new edition, after years of neglect, of *Yesterday Will Make You Cry,* by Chester Himes. An abandoned Dorothy Sayers mystery was found among her papers after her death in 1957 and has just now been completed by novelist Jill Paton Walsh—*Thrones/Dominations* (St. Martin's Press). A genuine discovery among the papers of an aristocratic Italian family led ultimately to the publication of a little book, *Maurice, or the Fisher's Cot: A Tale* (Knopf), by Mary Shelley, edited by scholar Claire Tomalin. The Library of America devoted two volumes to the work of Gertrude Stein and also two volumes—one titled *Stories, Essays, and Memoirs* and the other titled *Complete Novels*—to the work of Eudora Welty. James Baldwin also earned two volumes in the same distinguished series—*Early Novels and Stories* and *Collected Essays.*

In the 6 December issue of *Washington Post Book World,* instead of a list of notables, editors were asked to come up with a list titled ". . . And overlooked, which includes"—good books that did not receive deserved attention. Among them were *Hell* (Ecco), by Kathryn Davis; *Waiting in Vain* (Ballantine), by Colin Channer; and *Thirst* (Milkweed), by Ken Kalfus. I should like to close with a little list of my own—good books I should have found a place for: Elmore Leonard, *Cuba Libre* (Delacorte/Seymour Lawrence); *Whistle* (HarperCollins), by Janice Daugharty; Carol Maso, *Defiance* (Dutton); and the inimitable Donald Antrim for his latest, *The Hundred Brothers* (Vintage), called, in praise, "a high test of literary absurdity" by critic Paul Maliszewski (*Review of Contemporary Fiction,* Summer).

Dictionary of Literary Biography Yearbook Award for Distinguished Novel Published in 1998

Donald McCaig, from the dust jacket of Jacob's Ladder
(photograph by Dan Deitch)

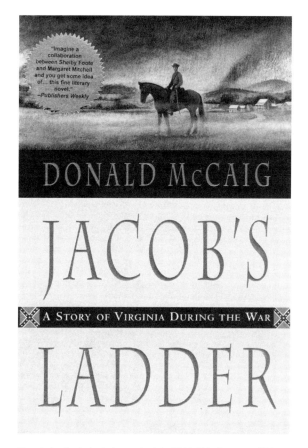

Dust jacket for the book that received the 1998 Dictionary of Literary
Biography Yearbook Award for a distinguished novel

Author of several novels and three "entertainments," Donald McCaig was best known for his two nonfiction books—*Eminent Dogs, Dangerous Men* and *An American Homeplace*—and for his role as an on-air essayist for National Public Radio. His new novel, *Jacob's Ladder: A Story of Virginia During the War* (Norton), received great and deserved praise when it was published in 1998. Calling it "a masterpiece," Staige Blackford, editor of *The Virginia Quarterly Review*, wrote: "*Jacob's Ladder* is a better novel than *Cold Mountain*. It makes *Gone With the Wind* look like the soap opera it really is in the last analysis." McCaig's years of experience raising sheep in Highland County, Virginia, enable him to give this tale of (mostly) rural Virginia in the Civil War a gritty authenticity. A large and wonderfully diverse cast of characters give life to this powerful, compassionate story.

–George Garrett

Dictionary of Literary Biography Yearbook Award for Distinguished First Novel Published in 1998

Dust jacket for the book that received the 1998 Dictionary of Literary Biography Yearbook *Award as a first novel*

Prizes are nothing new to young writer Michael Knight, who, as a student, won a Henfield Foundation Award and the *Playboy* 1996 college fiction contest and was selected for *Scribner's Best of the Fiction Workshops Anthology* for 1997. In 1998 he published two books simultaneously—*Dogfight and Other Stories* (Plume) and a novel, *Divining Rod* (Dutton). These books won him the New Writing Award given by the Fellowship of Southern Writers. *Divining Rod* tells a tale of adultery, love,

and murder, and is, in the words of Harry Crews, "the work of a man we will be reading for years to come." The ten stories of *Dogfight,* various in form and content, have already won the strong support of writers like Clyde Edgerton, Lewis Nordan, and Madison Smartt Bell. Taken together these two books put Michael Knight in the front ranks of the new fiction writers.

–George Garrett

Dictionary of Literary Biography Yearbook Award for a Distinguished Volume of Short Stories Published in 1998

Dust jacket for the book that received the 1998 Dictionary of Literary Biography Yearbook *award for a distinguished short-story collection*

Among the many good collections of stories that appeared during 1998, *Park City: New and Selected Stories* by Ann Beattie stands out as especially worthy of honor. There are thirty-six stories in this volume, twenty-eight carefully culled by the author from her earlier collections and eight new stories (enough for a collection in itself) published in book form for the first time. The combination of things that have made her work inimitable is strongly evident in this collection—a lyrical and witty voice, a sure sense of time and place, a deep awareness of the irony and sorrow at the center of our lives. She has been called "the chronicler of her generation," but she is more than that. She gives life and voice to all the living generations of Americans, and she gives joy to several generations of readers.

–George Garrett

The Year in Children's Books

Caroline Hunt
College of Charleston

The big news of 1998 was the resurgent popularity of British fantasy on both sides of the Atlantic. Two established authors had their centenaries; one modern fantasy author provoked a major controversy; and a debut fantasy novel took a fistful of prizes and became a best-seller. In all genres except nonfiction and young-adult fiction, many of the top titles had at least a touch of fantasy.

Dominating 1998 were the centenaries of Lewis Carroll (d. 1898) and C. S. Lewis (b. 1898). In an appropriately Carrollian reversal, the two centenaries provoked responses that were nearly opposite to the original reception of the two writers. The hundredth anniversary of the death of Charles Lutwig Dodgson, better known as Lewis Carroll, was celebrated worldwide with little hint of the subversive elements once seen in the Alice books. Radicals have become icons before; the metamorphosis of Lewis into a controversial figure, however, came as a surprise. Philip Pullman attacked the Narnia cycle in the *Guardian* (1 October) as "one of the most ugly and poisonous things I've ever read." Conceding that "[i]n a superficial and bustling way, Lewis could tell a story," Pullman excoriated Lewis's "vile moments," "nauseating drivel," "loathsome glee," "reactionary sneering," and, finally, "the sheer dishonesty of his narrative method." Readers around the world reeled, and E-mail discussion groups were kept busy. Because Lewis's conservative tendencies were already well known, Pullman's diatribe made news not for its content but for its tone—and because of its author's status as Britain's leading writer of fantasy. Nicci Gerrard's follow-up on the day of the centenary, 29 November, also in the *Guardian,* cautiously compromised: Narnia is flawed, but children love it so much that the series will remain popular: "doubtless, thousands more children, whether we like it or not, will step with Lucy through the wardrobe into the world of make-believe and magic."

Academic appraisals of Lewis were more ambivalent. *Oxford Today: The University Magazine* carried a generally laudatory piece with the subhead "Mary Rogers, who listened to C. S. Lewis's lectures in the 1930s,

C. S. Lewis, author of the seven Chronicles of Narnia books published between 1950 and 1956 (Wade Collection)

describes his uneasy relationship with the University." The article, despite the title "Rejected by Oxford," chronicles Lewis's life and conversion evenhandedly. *Oxford* magazine gives a more intimate picture of Lewis's life in Oxford, complete with an endearing elderly dog.

Meanwhile, the Royal Mail issued "Magical Worlds," a series of stamps commemorating British fantasy works for children—featuring Lewis and Carroll and also including works by E. Nesbit, Mary Norton, J. R. R. Tolkien, and Philip Pullman. Conspicuously absent was Roald Dahl, whose controversial books garnered seven of the top ten spots in a 1997 poll by the Waterstone's book chain and the BBC's Bookworm.

Centenaries made for good business; in *The New York Times Book Review* of 15 November, Bauman Rare Books advertised a first edition of *The Lion, the Witch and the Wardrobe* (1950) at $3,500, while first editions of *Alice in Wonderland* and *Through the Looking-Glass* carried a price high enough to warrant the notation "Please inquire." The general public, always keener on Lewis than most critics, snapped up Lewis items. Picture books adapted from the Narnia series sold nicely. Eerdmans brought out a centennial biography, Beatrice Gormley's *C. S. Lewis: Christian and Storyteller.* HarperCollins offered *The Narnia Cookbook,* with text by Mary Kate Morgan and drawings by Pauline Baynes.

MARKETING AND MEDIA

Like the old folktale about blind men describing an elephant, the story of 1998 in the children's book industry varied according to one's perspective. For publishers, an upswing begun in 1997 continued unabated. For independent booksellers, 1998 also marked a continuation—of threats from chains, of ever less well-informed publishers' representatives, and of shaving discounts to remain profitable. Parents and grandparents browsing in bookstores found reassuringly familiar authors and beloved titles from backlists; some, perhaps, noticed the relative scarcity of new items. Professional buyers found few "big" new books anywhere.

Some publishers showcased "new" titles by dead authors. *Beatrix Potter: The Complete Tales* (Frederick Warne) includes two previously unpublished tales and two sets of illustrations for unfinished stories. *Hooray for Diffendoofer Day!* (Knopf) expands a set of sketches left by Dr. Seuss (Theodore Geisel), with text by Jack Prelutsky and illustrations by Lane Smith. His editor of eleven years, Janet Schulman, explains "How This Book Came To Be" in an afterword. Meanwhile, Geisel's widow continued licensing his famous characters for tree ornaments, clothing, and a new theme park, despite his known dislike of such enterprises. Adaptations from Louisa May Alcott, Laura Ingalls Wilder, Frances Hodgson Burnett, and others raked in handsome profits.

Publishing executives were, generally, optimistic about the future of children's book publishing. At the annual meeting of the Children's Book Council (15 September), several singled out on-line marketing as an important area for future expansion. Dick Robinson of Scholastic, Michael Lynton of Penguin Group, and Jack Romanos of S&S Consumer Publishing, quoted in *Publishers Weekly* (5 October), also mentioned the "expanded retail environment" beyond bookstores, the

Philip Pullman (Random House)

need for more varied books for an increasingly diverse population, and the effect of recent mergers in the industry.

A few weeks later, the annual sales statistics for the industry confirmed this optimism: "Children's Publishers Rebound in 1997" (*Publishers Weekly,* 19 October) showed improvements ranging from Little, Brown's 77 percent sales increase to healthy sales figures for the recently merged Penguin/Putnam and Random House/Bantam Doubleday Dell. Of fifteen publishers, only Scholastic showed a decline (–15.5 percent), largely from dwindling sales of its Goosebumps series.

Independent booksellers were less sanguine. Some noted cynically the industry's focus on best-sellers and its highly selective promotion of small segments of backlists. Despite their misgivings about book selection, independents as a group did well. According to Caron Chapman of the Association of Booksellers for Children, new store openings compensated for store closings; Chapman, quoted in *Publishers Weekly* (6 April), believes that the threat from major chains has peaked as smaller stores have learned better strategies for positioning themselves in the market. A *PW* survey of independents opened within the past three years corroborated Chapman's ideas.

Anniversaries always provide good marketing opportunities. Two children's classics turned thirty-five: Maurice Sendak's *Where the Wild Things Are* (HarperCollins) and Madeleine L'Engle's *A Wrinkle in Time* (Bantam Doubleday Dell). Both publishers provided elaborate displays and posters. Bantam Doubleday Dell reissued the entire *A Wrinkle in Time* quartet, which sold well; HarperCollins threw a party in New York for Sendak. Marjorie Weinman Sharmat's Nate the Great, star of a twenty-book series, turned twenty-five, and appeared in a "Milk: Where's Your Mustache?" ad. In a Gruner and Jahr magazine group promotion, readers who bought a Nate the Great book and two gallons of milk could receive a poster and a Nate decal. David Macauley's *The Way Things Work* marked its tenth anniversary, and in the final quarter of the year, the author promoted a revised edition with an extensive tour in the northeast. Titled *The New Way Things Work* (Houghton/Lorraine), the volume adds a dozen new entries and a chapter on digital technology.

Motion-picture and television exposure also boosted backlist sales. *Madeline,* a movie based on Ludwig Bemelmans's classic, increased sales of Madeline books. Amazon.com promoted Madeline on its website, and sent its E-mail subscribers excerpts from Anna Quindlen's introduction to *Mad about Madeline: The Complete Tales.* A television series starring Marc Brown's Arthur sent the sales of individual Arthur books up three to five times their previous figures.

Meanwhile, the annual children's book fair in Bologna showed a relative scarcity of exciting new books. The changing marketplace, with mergers and buyouts occuring on the eve of the fair, attracted more attention than most of the titles on display. Several U. S. buyers returned without a "big book" for their lists and cited picture books as especially disappointing.

These trends—a dearth of new quality titles, combined with the aggressive marketing of a small, proven backlist—incited criticism. Laura Numeroff's *If You Give a Pig a Pancake* (HarperCollins) rode the best-seller lists for the second half of the year; then, as a result of a highly publicized author tour, sales of her earlier books, *If You Give a Mouse a Cookie* and *If You Give a Moose a Muffin,* rose spectacularly. By contrast, most backlist titles went unpromoted, and many went out of print. Small booksellers complained that they could not fill customers' requests and noted with distress the shrinking number of competent publishers' representatives. Several spoke strongly against the tendency toward telemarketing.

New launches often imitated previous successful ventures. American history through fictionalized diaries emerged as the most popular series format. (Here, too, it was noticeable that the American past was presented as a kind of fantasy.) Harcourt Brace/Silver Whistle continued its Young American Voices series with *Rachel's Journal: The Story of a Pioneer Girl* by Marissa Moss. Scholastic's lucrative "Dear America" series, consisting of fictional girls' diaries from different periods of American history, spawned a parallel series for boys called "My Name Is America." Other publishers followed suit. Hoping to cash in on the popularity of the American diary format, Doubleday brought out *A Cobtown Christmas,* by Julia (text) and Robert (illustrations) Van Nutt. The basis for the illustrations is a model in the authors' Greenwich Village apartment. Five further *Cobtown* books are planned. Another American history spin-off (though not in diary form) was Delacorte's "Orphan Train Children," by Joan Lowery Nixon, capitalizing on the successful "Orphan Train Adventures" by the same author. And, of course, the best-selling American Girls series continued to sell books, dolls, and other highly profitable merchandise. Meanwhile, Lothrop, Lee and Shepard launched a new African American series with *African Beginnings,* by James Haskins and Kathleen Benson. Six additional volumes are planned.

Several new imprints appeared. Growing Tree, from HarperCollins, specialized in age-coded preschool books. Random House launched Jellybean Books in July, featuring a low price ($1.99) and familiar Random House characters such as Thomas the Tank Engine, the Berenstein Bears, and Sesame Street figures. Dorling Kindersley inaugurated its 3D Eyewitness series and the historically based DK Discovery Guides series, as well as the paperback DK Eyewitness Readers. Avon/Camelot started a paperback series, Goners; Bantam countered with the Clearwater Crossing series and, under its Skylark imprint, the Soccer Stars. Simon and Schuster started a children's division in Great Britain. Two British companies, Element Children's Books and Bare-Foot Books, started marketing special U.S. editions of some of their titles. Owl's House Press, an offshoot of the internet children's store Owl's House Inc. (www.owlshouse.com), published two picture books, with plans for two new books per year. Marvel Comics began a book line, Marvel Kids, featuring Marvel's most durable superheroes such as Spiderman and the Incredible Hulk. *Riverbank Review,* a quarterly print journal, began publishing in May.

AWARDS

A pleasant start to each year in children's books is the announcement of the American Library Association's awards for books published in the United States during the preceding year. The John Newbery Medal, for best children's book by an American author,

Dust jacket for the book awarded the 1998 Caldecott Medal for its illustrations

went to *Out of the Dust,* a bleak account of the Depression by Karen Hesse. The Caldecott Medal, for best illustrations, went to Paul Zelinsky's ornate paintings for *Rapunzel.* Also at ALA's winter meeting, winners in specialty categories were announced. *Forged by Fire,* by Sharon M. Draper, received the Coretta Scott King Award. Javaka Steptoe won the Coretta Scott King Award for Illustrations for *In Daddy's Arms I Am Tall.* The Pura Belpré award went to Victor Martinez for *Parrot in the Oven,* a runaway favorite (and winner of a National Book Award), while Stephanie Garcia took the honors for illustration with *Snapshots from the Wedding.* The Mildred L. Batchelder award for an outstanding book in translation went to Josef Holub's *The Robber and Me,* a critically acclaimed story of World War II.

Also at ALA, the Young Adult Services Division (YALSA) announced the first winners of the "Alex," part of a five-year program to increase young-adult readership by promoting titles originally marketed for adults. YALSA's Margaret A. Edwards Award for Outstanding Literature for Young Adults, given for lifetime achievement, went to Madeleine L'Engle.

One ALA award is not given by a juvenile division and not announced until midsummer: the Gay,

Lesbian, and Bisexual Book Award, sponsored by the Gay, Lesbian, and Bisexual Task Force of the Social Responsibilities Round Table. The 1998 winner was *The Shared Heart: Portraits and Stories Celebrating Lesbian, Gay, and Bisexual Young People* (Morrow).

Other organizations gave equally prestigious awards. The International Board on Books for Young People announced its Andersen Award winners on Hans Christian Andersen's birthday, 2 April. Katherine Paterson (U.S.) received the author award, and Tomi Ungerer (France) the illustrator award. Both awards are for lifetime achievement. Laurence Pringle took the Orbis Pictus Award given by the National Council of Teachers of English for an outstanding work of nonfiction, with *An Extraordinary Life: The Story of a Monarch Butterfly,* illustrated by Bob Marstall (Orchard). A Christopher Award, for a "creative work that expresses the highest values of the human spirit," went to David Parker's *Stolen Dreams: Portraits of Working Children* (Lerner). The Mystery Writers of America gave the Edgar Award for best young-adult mystery to *Ghost Canoe,* by Will Hobbs (Morrow). Many state and regional awards were also announced throughout the year.

Dust jacket for the book that won both the 1998 John Newbery Medal and the Scott O'Dell Award for Historical Fiction

CENSORSHIP

Censorship cases throughout 1998 continued to revolve around the question of Internet access; a far smaller percentage of newspaper and journal articles concerned books than was the case a few years ago. Some observers felt that the furor over film and Internet censorship contributed to continued censorship of books. In Barron, Wisconsin, the school board removed from school library shelves four books about homosexuality, even though the district's review committee recommended keeping the books and was partially supported by the superintendent. After a series of problems between Family Friendly Libraries (a conservative group) and a coordinator of children's and youth services, the librarian, Kathy Herrin, was forced out by the Mexico-Audrain County library board. At issue was the presence of *It's Perfectly Normal: A Book about Changing Bodies, Growing Up, Sex, and Sexual Health* (Candlewick, 1994) in the juvenile collection.

In Brooklyn a censorship incident resulted in the teacher's leaving PS 75 abruptly. Ruth Sherman, who is white, selected Carolivia Herron's *Nappy Hair* (Knopf, 1997) to read with her elementary school class, thinking that this story of a child who accepts her unruly locks would boost the self-esteem of her young (mostly non-white) students. Parents, however, reacted with outrage to the book, which they found to be racist, and with little support from the school system, Sherman was forced out. (As a coincidence, the first children's book scheduled for early 1999 publication is by adult author Bell Hooks and will be called *Happy to Be Nappy*.) In "What Johnny Can't Read: Parental Protests Are Only the Latest Reason Teachers Shy Away from Books That Might Cause Controversy" (*Time*, 21 December), the *Nappy Hair* brouhaha introduces the thesis that few teachers know about children's literature (most states do not require children's literature courses for teacher certification); those who do have the necessary background may reject contemporary books as too risky. One author was quoted as saying that fully half the teacher-education students she encounters do not know E. B. White's classic *Charlotte's Web*.

NONFICTION

As usual, many nonfiction books concerned practical matters: college applications, self-help, smoking, tattooing, and so on. Nonfiction series continued to expand. Enslow added to its Holocaust Remembered series with *The Holocaust Ghettoes* by Linda Jacobs Altman and *The Holocaust Camps* by Ann Byers. From the same publisher, the Diseases and People series added volumes on AIDS, allergies, chicken pox and shingles, epilepsy, heart disease, Lyme disease, and other sexually transmitted diseases.

Biographies, most competent but unexciting, showcased stars of sports and entertainment: Monica Seles, Leonardo DiCaprio, Babe Ruth, and other predictable subjects. Two that critics anticipated were by veteran nonfiction writers Russell Freedman and Frederick and Patricia McKissack. Freedman's lucid and balanced *Martha Graham: A Dancer's Life* (Clarion) contains many previously unpublished photographs. Release of the McKissacks' *Young, Black, and Determined: A Biography of Lorraine Hansberry* (Holiday House), announced for fall publication and favorably reviewed in advance copies, was delayed until 1999. Picture-book biographies included Jeannette Winter's *My Name Is Georgia* (Harcourt Brace) and Josephine Poole's *Joan of Arc* (Knopf), illustrated by Angela Barrett. For somewhat older readers, Diane Stanley's *Joan of Arc* (Morrow) offered a more complicated Joan.

American history titles were, as in the past several years, of generally good quality. Dennis Fradin's *Samuel Adams: The Father of American Independence* (Clarion) portrays its subject's passion for liberty convincingly and with a candid look at some results of the man's single-mindedness–for instance, the impact on his family. *Mormons in America* (Oxford), by Claudia Lauper Bushman and Richard Lyman Bushman, gives a balanced overview of the growth of the church; the volume is part of Oxford's Religion in American Life series.

Once again, some of the best books dealt with African American history. Julius Lester's *From Slave Ship to Freedom Road* (Dial) is less a continuous text than a series of meditations (Lester's own term) on Ron Brown's paintings.

Walter Dean Myers's *Amistad: A Long Road to Freedom* (Dutton) gave a lucid portrayal of an often-sensationalized case. A parallel volume, Veronica Chambers's *Amistad Rising: A Story of Freedom,* illustrated by Paul Lee, told the story through the eyes of Joseph Cinque. From the prolific Jim Haskins came *Separate But Not Equal: The Dream and the Struggle* (Scholastic), a restrained account of education for African Americans from colonial times to the present. Another Haskins book, *Black, Blue, and Gray: African Americans in the Civil War* (Simon and Schuster) was less well received because it contained careless factual errors.

Two autobiographical books showed their authors to be far more complex than generations of admirers might have suspected. *Looking Back: A Book of Memories* (Houghton Mifflin/Walter Lorraine) began taking form when author Lois Lowry's son was killed in 1995 while on a military mission. Lowry combed family records to make a book for her infant daughter, who might otherwise have no memories of her father. Lowry connects personal experiences to incidents in her fiction in a fascinating way. More unexpectedly, Anita Lobel in *No Pretty Pictures: A Child of War* (Greenwillow) reveals a life starkly different from her cheerful illustrations. Beginning in Krakow during German occupation, the memoir documents a series of refuges for Lobel and her brother before they were discovered and shipped to a concentration camp.

Some nonfiction, mostly for young adults, defied categorization. Paul A. Winters edited a challenging collection of essays and interviews, *Cloning* (Greenhaven). Marc Aronson's *Art Attack: A Brief Cultural History of the Avant-Garde* (Clarion) was the veteran editor's first book for young adults. Fascinating glimpses of the juvenile book industry stud *Dear Genius: The Letters of Ursula Nordstrom,* edited by Leonard S. Marcus (HarperCollins). An all-ages book was *Throw Your Tooth on the Roof: Tooth Traditions from*

Dust jacket for the 1997 children's book that aroused controversy when officials in one American public school system questioned its ethnic subject matter

Around the World by Selby Beeler, with pictures by G. Brian Karas (Houghton Mifflin), paralleled by Marilyn Singer's *Bottoms Up! A Book about Rear Ends* (Holt).

COLLECTIONS

The most talked-about collection of 1998 was *Twentieth Century Children's Book Treasury* (Knopf), edited by Janet Schulman, which contains the full text of forty-four juvenile classics. Though received enthusiastically by many–*Newsweek* on 30 November called it "wonderful"–the *Treasury* attracted much criticism for its cavalier treatment of the illustrations and its omission of important texts such as *The Tale of Peter Rabbit*. Adele Geras retold some great old plots in *The Random House Book of Stories from the Opera,* illustrated by an astonishing array of artists. From Oxford came Dennis Peper's *The Young Oxford Book of Nasty Endings* and Michael Harrison and Christoper Stuart-Clark's *Oxford Treasury of Classic Poems*. Gary Paulsen's *My Life in Dog Years* (Delacorte) tells of the author's own dogs. A hard-to-classify volume was *Images of God,* by John and Katherine Paterson, with pictures by Alexander Koshkin, a biblical compendium of stories that connect to earthly images.

Cover for the book featuring British television characters who have become popular in a series for children in the United States

POETRY

Returning to the pervasive fantasy theme of 1998, *Imagine That! Poems of Never-Was* (Knopf), selected by Jack Prelutsky and illustrated by Kevin Henkes, introduced young readers to a slew of imaginary creatures (and yes, it does include "Jabberwocky"). One reviewer described Naomi Shihab Nye's collection, *The Space Between Our Footsteps: Poems and Paintings from the Middle East* (Simon and Schuster) as "mesmerizingly beautiful," as indeed it is. From Boyds Mills came two varieties of fantasy: *Lemonade Sun: And Other Summer Poems,* edited by Rebecca Kai Dotlich with illustrations by Jan Spivey Gilchrist, and Monica Gunning's Jamaican anthology *Under the Breadfruit Tree: Island Poems,* illustrated by Fabricio Vanden Broeck. From Harcourt Brace/Gulliver came *Antarctic Antics: A Book of Penguin Poems,* edited by Judy Sierra and illustrated by Jose Aruego and Ariane Dewey. Representing sports fantasy was *That Sweet Diamond* (Simon and Schuster/Atheneum), edited by Paul Janecsko and illustrated by Carole Katchen, which focused on baseball. On a more serious note, Neil Philip edited *War and the Pity of War,* with pictures by Michael McCurdy. Catherine Clinton and Stephen Alcorn edited *I, Too, Sing America: Three Centuries of African-American Poetry* (Houghton Mifflin).

PICTURE BOOKS

Fantasy triumphed as the much-loathed purple dinosaur, Barney, was conquered in the invasion of the British television series Teletubbies (creatures who talk infantile gibberish and have television screens on the front of their abdomens). Barney, at least, was based on something that once existed; also, he spoke something that was recognizably English, not baby talk. Teletubbies board books, stickers, and other paraphernalia sold briskly.

Some of the best-selling picture books of 1998 came from authors known chiefly for other careers. Two veteran cartoonists at the *New Yorker* brought out juvenile books. Both Jules Feiffer's *I Lost My Bear* (Morrow) and William Steig's *Pete's a Pizza* were favorites with reviewers; the former made the list of the ten best picture books of the year in *The New York Times Book Review,* an honor shared by Steig's other 1998 offering, *A Handful of Beans: Six Fairy Tales* (HarperCollins/ Michael di Capua), with text by Jeanne Steig. A third *New Yorker* cartoonist, Roz Chwast, illustrated Patricia Marx's *Meet My Staff* (HarperCollins), an ingenious tale in which young Walter organizes people to take on, for a fee of course, unwanted tasks such as swallowing medicine and doing homework. One from this group was more realistic: *Today I Feel Silly* (HarperCollins/Cotler), by Jamie Lee Curtis with illustrations by Laura Cornell, is the film star's third and best children's book. Reviewers liked it; Curtis made dozens of personal and television appearances; and consumers put it on the best-seller charts.

Chris Raschka's *Arlene, Sardine* generated strong comments pro and con—largely because, for about half the book, Arlene is dead. The cover picture, a sardine can, bears across one corner a strip saying "net wt. 12 oz." Arlene swims about in a fjord, then in the sea, then in a net. The inevitable happens: "Here, on the deck of the fishing boat, Arlene died." (At this point, Arlene's round eyes become stylized crescents.) "However, Arlene's story is not over, because she was put on ice, in a box, with her friends." At the sardine factory, she is graded, salted, and smoked, then packed, inspected ("I wonder if Arlene was a little nervous for the inspection"), covered with olive oil, cooked, and hermetically sealed in her can. "At last . . . Arlene was a sardine."

Based on original ideas were the riotously inventive *Insectlopedia,* by Douglas Florian, and *Beastly Feast* (Henry Holt), by Bruce Goldstone and Blair Lent. Audrey Wood and Mark Teague teamed up for *Sweet Dream Pie,* a fantasy that reveals new detail at each reading. Charlotte Huck invented a Halloween number book, *Creepy Countdown* (Greenwillow), with striking illustrations by Jos. A. Smith.

Patricia Polacco reveals her own secret—a childhood made miserable by dyslexia—in *Thank You, Mr. Falker* (Philomel), perhaps the only disability book to date that does not seem in the least didactic. At the other end of the spectrum for 1998's excellent fantasy offerings was a crowd of well-intentioned books. "I can report that many of them are frankly aimed at helping children calm the beast within," observed Joan Acocella in "The Big Bad Wolf: A Year When Picture Books Have Come of Age" in the *New Yorker* (30 November). "Some of these books we could live without," she adds. In addition to "calming the beast," juvenile self-help books battled intolerance, jealousy, and other undesirable traits. *Ian's Walk: A Story about Autism* (Albert and Whitman), by Laurie Lears, was typical, as was *Little Clam* (Greenwillow), by Lynn Reiser (who is a psychiatrist). *Pushkin Meets the Bundle* (Simon and Schuster/Atheneum), by Harriet Ziefert with pictures by Donald Saaf, deals with jealousy over a new baby (made more palatable because the jealous character is a small dog). The usual picture books urging conservation or extolling the natural world appeared at the usual rate. Gail Gibbons's *Soaring with the Wind* (Morrow), about bald eagles, was a typical example—nicely done but rather dull.

Monster and animal stories with an ironic twist were popular. Jon Scieszka and Lane Smith teamed up once more for *Squids Will Be Squids: Fresh Morals for Beastly Fables* (Viking). Mitra Modarressi's *Monster Stew* (DK Ink) turns three favorite stories inside out—starting with a hilarious sendup of the Princess and the Pea. Another popular monster book was Laura Numeroff's *Monster Munchies* (Random House), with illustrations by Nate Evans—a departure from her successful "If You Give" series.

Not all the good picture books were parodic; some veteran illustrators interpreted familiar themes freshly. Peter Sís wrote *Fire Truck* (Greenwillow), a tale for the very young, for his son Matej, "who loves fire trucks more than anything." Matt loves fire trucks so much that he becomes (in a stunning fold-out center page)—a fire truck! A more complex Sís title, *Tibet through the Red Box* (Farar, Straus and Giroux), attracted critical admiration but aimed at an older audience. In *Snow* (Farrar, Straus and Giroux) Uri Shulevitz creates a nearly perfect meld of text with pictures. Lois Ehlert's *Top Cat* (Harcourt Brace) and Brian Karas's *Windy Day* were much admired for their pictures, though some felt that the integration of text in Ehlert's book could have been better.

Some picture books used setting to great advantage. Eve Bunting's *So Far from the Sea,* with pictures by Chris Sontpiet (Clarion), and Sherry Rand's *My Father's Boat* (Scholastic/Polaris), illustrated by Chris Rand, portrayed Japanese American and Vietnamese American families in remembrance mode. Another family story was *Since Dad Left* (Millbrook), by Caroline Binch, concerning a family breakup. Two picture books with a New York flavor were Jacqueline Preiss Weitzman's *You Can't Take a Balloon into the Metropolitan Museum* (Dial), illustrated by Robin Preiss Glasser and Mark Karlin's *Music over Manhattan* (Doubleday), with pictures by Jack E. Davis.

Perception was the central idea in some outstanding picture books. Joan Steiner's *Look-Alikes* (Little, Brown) is a series of captivating puzzles—a chair back that is actually a tiny pretzel, for instance. A key at the end of the book identifies the objects. Richard Wilbur's *The Disappearing Alphabet* (Harcourt Brace) pairs witty poems with the concept of vanishing. Another Walter Wick extravaganza, *Walter Wick's Optical Tricks* (Cartwheel/Scholastic), succeeded with both reviewers and buyers. Two award-winning illustrator-authors turned to concept books: Kevin Henkes with *Circle Dogs* (about shapes), illustrated by Dan Yaccarino, and Tana Hoban with *More, Fewer, Less* (about quantity), both from Greenwillow.

Many authors successfully repeated formulas that had worked for them before. Sam McBratney's *Just You and Me* (Candlewick) continues the sentiments of *Guess How Much I Love You,* using geese. Martha the talking dog continued to delight her fans in Susan Meddaugh's *Martha Walks the Dog* (Houghton Mifflin). The team of Julius Lester and Jerry Pinkney produced another winner in *Black Cowboy, Wild Horses.* Ed Young's *Lost Horse* (Harcourt Brace/Silver Whistle) once again explored Chinese legend and visual tradition. Donald Crews wrought his magic of color and perspective in *Night at the Fair.* Tomie dePaola augmented the Strega Nona saga with *Big Anthony: His Story* (Putnam).

Caldecott Medal winner David Wisniewski produced a typically offbeat account of the psychology of adults, *The Secret Knowledge of Grown-Ups* (Lothrop, Lee and Shepard). *The Little Scarecrow Boy* (HarperCollins), by M. W. Brown, attracted attention for the striking pictures by another Caldecott winner, David Diaz. From the same publisher, Richard Egielski's *Jazper* and Thacher Hurd's *Zoom City* also garnered positive reviews, as did Peggy Rathmann's *10 Minutes till Bedtime* (Putnam). Two books by previous Caldecott winners had mixed receptions. Emily Arnold McCully's *Beautiful Warrior: The Legend of the Nun's Kung Fu* (Scholastic) was more popular with reviewers than with children. *To Every Thing There Is a Season: Verses from Ecclesiastes* (Scholastic), by Leo and Diane Dillon, was heavily advertised. While each illustration is splendid, the effect of a different period style for each double-page spread is disorienting.

No, David! (Scholastic), by David Shannon, portrays a small boy who finds many enticing things forbidden. Shannon based the book on a childhood production of the same title, written when his name and the word "no" were all he knew how to spell. His other 1998 title, *A Bad Case of Stripes* (Scholastic), shows a young girl plagued by a series of bodily changes: stripes, spots, and worse. The ingenious cure suggests that listening to one's own instincts is better than following peers. A more literal "sick" book was Vera Rosenberry's *When Vera Was Sick* (Holt), about chicken pox.

And finally, even in 1998 there were some promising first books. *Window Music* (Viking), by Anastasia Suen, with illustrations by Wade Zahares, won critics' praise both for its simple motif—scenery observed during a train trip—and for its vivid pictures. *Time* rated this book best in its "for little eyes" category on its seasonal best-of-'98 list (7 December)—an honor for a first-time illustrator.

RETELLINGS

Barbara McClintock's illustrations for *The Gingerbread Man*, retold by Jim Aylesworth (Scholastic) were widely admired, as were Gennady Spirin's characteristically elegant pictures for *The Crane Wife* (Harcourt Brace/Gulliver), retold by Odds Bodkin. Text and words merit equal praise in *Ouch!*, a tale by the Grimms retold with zest by Natalie Babbitt and illustrated by Fred Marcellino. Robert San Souci retold *Fa Mulan: The Story of a Woman Warrior* (Hyperion), illustrated by Jean and Mou-Sien Tseng.

As usual, Holiday House brought out a clutch of impressive retellings. Three stood out: Eric A. Kimmel retold the Grimms' *Seven at One Blow*, with illustrations by Megan Lloyd; Margaret Hodges interpreted the English tale *Up the Chimney*, illustrated by Amanda Harvey; and Lensey Namioka's *The Laziest Boy in the World* had pictures by Young Sheng Xuan (who also illustrated Eric Kimmel's version of *The Ten Suns: A Chinese Legend*). Nonny Hogrogian illustrated David Kherdian's *The Golden Bracelet,* an Armenian story.

In an ingenious version of *The Emperor's New Clothes* (Harcourt Brace), each chapter is told from a different perspective and written (and spoken, on the accompanying compact disk) by a celebrity: Madonna, Robin Williams, Stephen Spielberg, and so on. The project, organized by Spielberg, benefits a foundation for sick children. Retelling the same story, Jane Yolen's *King Long Shanks* substitutes a green frog for the emperor.

For older readers, ranging from the middle grades to adults, Katherine Paterson adapts Wolfram von Eschenbach's medieval epic as *Parzival: The Quest of the Grail Knight* (Lodestar). Though beautifully produced as a slender, small hardcover and though reviewed with great enthusiasm, the book seems destined for neglect by its intended readers.

MID-GRADES FICTION

The lead story in mid-grades fiction for 1998 was the runaway success of a British import, *Harry Potter and the Sorcerer's Stone* (Scholastic), by J. K. Rowling. Winner of a Children's Book Award and a Smarties prize and shortlisted for the Carnegie medal, the book was a best-seller with both juveniles and adults in Britain; Scholastic paid more than $100,000 for the U.S. rights, a record for a new children's author. A sequel, *Harry Potter and the Chamber of Secrets,* will be published in 1999.

World War II continued to provide material for mid-grades fiction. In *Greater than Angels* (Simon and Schuster), Carol Matas again explores the experiences of deported Jewish children during World War II. Set mostly in southern France, *Greater than Angels* shows a French side of the Holocaust that may be unfamiliar to most readers. *Foster's War* (Scholastic), by Carolyn Reeder, is a competent home front novel. Virginia Euwer Wolff's *Bat 6* (Scholastic), set in the immediate postwar years, combines a gripping account of softball and small-town life with such issues as anti-Japanese prejudice, illegitimacy, and emotional and academic disability. Told from the perspectives of twenty-one different characters, this is Wolff's best book to date.

By now, books set thirty years ago are period pieces, at least for young readers. Two of the best portrayed strong African American girls. Angela Johnson's *Songs of Faith* (Orchard) combines the themes of divorce, Vietnam War veterans, divided siblings, and lost friends. Pitched at a slightly younger audience than the author's earlier *Toning the Sweep* (1993), *Songs of Faith* will appeal to many readers in the earlier teenage years. Another retrospective aimed at the same audience was Nikki Grimes's *Jazmin's Notebook* (Dial), set in the 1960s.

Setting, often a casualty in recent fiction for this level, starred in a number of books. Jane Kurtz used her firsthand knowledge of Ethiopia in her latest novel, *The Storyteller's Beads* (Harcourt Brace/Gulliver), and Amy B. Zemser sets *Beyond the Mango Tree* (Greenwillow) in Liberia. In *The Islander* (DK Ink) Cynthia Rylant portrays the loneliness of an orphan boy on an island off British Columbia. *Return to Hawk's Hill* (Little, Brown), by Allen W. Eckert, picks up where *Incident at Hawk's Hill* (1971) left off—with a young boy tending a wounded badger in 1970s Manitoba. Though lacking the beautifully portrayed human-animal bond of its predecessor, *Return to Hawk's Hill* was favorably reviewed.

Lynne Reid Banks's new book, *Maura's Angel* (Avon), featured a convincing Northern Irish setting.

Many books focused on the here-and-now, especially in school settings. In their first collaboration, *Longer Letter Later* (Scholastic), Paula Danziger and Ann M. Martin use an epistolary form to tell of two friends who keep in touch after one moves away—a competent book, but not compelling. The latest Alice book from Phyllis Reynolds Naylor, *Achingly Alice* (Atheneum/ Simon and Schuster) continues the engaging heroine's story into the eighth grade. *Joey Pigza Swallowed the Key* (Farrar, Straus and Giroux) presents a believable story of attention-deficit disorder and its effects. Sharon Ciecchi's *Bloomability* (HarperCollins) follows a thirteen-year-old's experiences at an international school.

Some titles eschewed the world of school. *The Maze,* by Will Hobbs, follows an escapee from a juvenile detention center as he becomes involved in a project to save condors. *The Dog with the Golden Eyes* (Milkweed), by Frances Wilbur, mingles coming-of-age themes with ecology. At first, this tale of a thirteen-year-old attempting to save a homeless dog seems reminiscent of Peg Ehret's *Cages,* but when the "dog" turns out to be an Alaskan wolf, everything changes.

Some of the most impressive novels of 1998 made powerful statements about family relationships. In *Armageddon Summer* (Harcourt), by Jane Yolen and Bruce Coville, two teenagers struggle with their feelings about their parents' doomsday cult. Also pitting teen identity against parental beliefs was John H. Ritter's *Choosing Sides* (Philomel), in which a young man tries to reconcile his talent as a left-handed pitcher with his father's belief that both left-handedness and competitive sports are evil. Adele Griffen's much-discussed *The Other Shepards* (Hyperion) follows sisters Holland and Geneva as they try to overcome the legacy of siblings who died long ago. Set in 1957, *My Louisiana Sky* (Holt), by Kimberly Holt, concerns a normal girl with retarded parents. All four books avoid easy solutions and offer thought-provoking material for upper mid-grade readers on the edge of adolescence.

YOUNG ADULT

The hottest debate in the Young Adult (YA) community centered on whether YA books are "bleak." The American publication of *Smack* (Holt), by Henry Burgess, triggered this discussion; winner of the Carnegie Medal in Britain (where it was titled *Junk*), the book concerns young heroin addicts. In a *New York Times Sunday Magazine* article (2 August) Sara Mosle attacked recent realistic fiction such as this, also mentioning Virginia Walter's *Making Up Megaboy* (DK Ink), in which a teenager shoots a liquor-store owner. Print and E-mail

discussions followed, and many experts pointed out that Mosle did not even use the term "young adult" in its usual sense (age twelve and up), preferring to think it meant "suitable for children 14 and under." Beyond this point, however, the discussion reverted to the old question of whether there is a trend toward "abnormal, sick, and destructive subject matter," in the words of one letter writer. Most YA specialists took the view they have taken for many years, that adolescents are already living in a world frighteningly like that of the "bleak" novels.

Bleak or not, some 1998 titles were highly original. Mordicai Gerstein's *Victor: A Novel Based on the Life of the Savage of Aveyron* (Farrar, Straus and Giroux) examined a young man on the edge between human and beast. Equally acclaimed by reviewers was *Holes* (Farrar, Straus and Giroux) by Louis Sachar, winner of a National Book Award.

War continued to play a major part in youngadult novels. Ann Rinaldi continued her output of meticulously researched historical books with *Mine Eyes Have Seen* (Scholastic), covering John Brown's activities in the summer of 1859 and told by his daughter Annie. *Soldier's Heart* (Delacorte), by Gary Paulsen, follows fifteen-year-old Charley Goddard's fortunes as he enlists in the First Minnesota Volunteers and serves throughout the Civil War. Based on a true story, the book has all of Paulsen's usual deftness. Robert Cormier reexamined the nature of true courage in *Heroes* (Delacorte), the story of a Silver Star winner who returns home, maimed and disfigured, to confront his former idol, who is not only a war hero but also a rapist. An even grittier tale of the ravages of war was Patricia Anthony's *Flanders* (Ace), which takes place during World War I in the trenches.

Contemporary novels were many and, generally, of good quality. Francesca Lia Block's *I Was a Teenage Fairy* (HarperCollins/Joanna Cotler) is an identity story. Jacqueline Woodson's *If You Come Softly* (Putnam) deals with interracial romance. The difficult subject of obsessive-compulsive behavior received an uncommonly sympathetic telling in Tery Spencer Hesser's *Kissing Doorknobs* (Delacorte). Donna Jo Napoli's *In the Love of Venice* is a YA family story, and Gary Paulsen's *The Transall Saga,* also from Delacorte, verges on science fiction. In *Jungle Dogs* (Delacorte) Graham Salisbury returns to the Hawaiian setting he knows so well—this time in a contemporary story about Boy Regis, his paper route, his fears, and his family. Carolyn Coman's *Bee and Jacky* (Front Street), deceptively small in format and simple looking, dissects the lives of teenagers ravaged by incest.

Susan Fletcher, known for her humorous contemporary tales and for a fantasy trilogy, broke new ground with *Shadow Spinner* (Jean Karl/Atheneum), a retelling of the Scheherazade story with a Persian setting. Fletcher brings out the terrifying side of the tale convincingly. Another suspenseful novel, Joan Lowery Nixon's *The Haunting* (Delacorte), concerns an old plantation house with dark secrets. Lia, fifteen, eventually exorcises two ghosts and proves that she indeed does inherit the strength of the outstanding women in her family. A scarier tale was the British import *Clockwork* (Scholastic), by Philip Pullman.

A first novel, *The Tribes of Palos Verdes* (St. Martin's Press) by Joy Nicholson, covers familiar ground (such as a dysfunctional family, moving to California, surfers, and an overeating mother) in a fresh way. Fourteen-year-old Medina Mason is one of the most interesting first-person narrators in a long time, even though, or perhaps because, much of the time she is not particularly likeable. Also featuring a former beauty queen, Cherie Bennet's *Life in the Fat Lane* (Delacorte) centers on a teenager who suddenly gains one hundred pounds. Lara's attempts to cope with her new body and her peers' cruelty are complicated by the collapse of her parents' marriage. Though often a cliché in young-adult fiction, the issue of body image in this book really works.

Perry Nodelman's *Behaving Bradley* (Simon and Schuster) marks the author's first excursion into young-adult realism after a series of finely crafted fantasies for middle grades. Nodelman's mastery of teenage linguistic nuances makes his narrator, Bradley, a memorable character. Also centering around school, Daniel Pinkwater's *The Education of Robert Nifkin* (Farrar, Straus and Giroux) takes the form of a college application essay. This hilarious tale, set in the late 1950s, will delight Pinkwater's many fans.

A group of excellent novels concerned alcohol and highway accidents, connected in several different ways. In Joan Bauer's *Rules of the Road* (Putnam) a young woman chauffers an elderly business owner on a tour of her chain of shoe stores. Jenna's struggles with her father's alcoholism are tied in nicely with the journey theme. *Whirligig* (Holt), by Paul Fleischman, also centers on a journey and involves alcohol. Sixteen-year-old Brent's suicide attempt accidentally kills a recent high-school graduate whose infectious joy in life fills the entire book. As part of his community service sentence, Brent undertakes a mission for Lea's mother: to place whirligigs around the country in her memory. As the monuments are constructed, people living nearby become involved; their stories are told in interpolated chapters. Despite its derivative qualities—the stories from the author's own *Seedfolks* and the memorial whirligigs from Cynthia Rylant's *Missing May*—Fleischman's new book appeals. In *Cheat the Moon* (Little, Brown)

Patricia Hermes presents another alcohol victim: Gabby, mature beyond her not-quite-thirteen years, who mothers her six-year-old brother and her alcoholic father. In Sarah Dessen's *Someone Like You* (Viking) the aftermath of a fatal motorcycle accident stresses the friendship of two young women, one pregnant and the other struggling against a controlling mother.

Rearranging and Other Stories (Simon and Schuster), by David Gifaldi, shows teens coping with a variety of crises and relationships. The more explicitly titled *Trapped! Cages of Mind and Body* (Simon and Schuster), edited by Lois Duncan, contains stories by a number of name-brand authors: Joan Bauer, Lois Lowry, Francesca Lia Block, and many others. For female readers, a compilation by Marilyn Singer called *Stay True: Short Stories for Strong Girls* (Scholastic) earned strong reviews. Other short-story collections specialized more narrowly: there was a volume for Mormon teenagers and one on family secrets, for instance. Chaim Potok aimed at a wider audience with *Zebra and Other Stories* (Knopf), centering on important moments in the lives of young adults.

Nonfiction for the high-school audience continued to stress AIDS, drug education, illegitimacy, sports, and written-to-order lives of the famous, from Madeline Albright to Roseanne. A few titles, especially historical biographies, stood out—including two about Victoria Woodhull, an influential feminist who ran for president while in prison. VOYA reviewed them as a pair: Mary Gabriel's *Notorious Victoria: The Life of Victoria Woodhull, Uncensored* (Algonquin) and Barbara Goldsmith's *Other Powers: The Age of Suffrage, Spiritualism, and the Scandalous Victoria Woodhull* (Knopf). It recommended both but assigned a P value (for popularity) of only two on a possible five-point scale.

OBITUARIES

Rumer Godden, a prolific author of children's books for more than fifty years (and of adult titles for more than sixty), died on 8 November at her home in Scotland. Born Margaret Rumer Godden in 1907, she grew up in India and was taught at home until the age of twelve. Her experiences in remote areas of India contributed to many of her books, particularly the young-adult title *The Peacock Spring,* which was made into a television series in 1996. Many of her most successful juvenile books concerned dolls, beginning with her first title for children, *The Doll's House* (1947). Godden returned to Indian themes for her last book, *Premlata and the Festival of Lights* (Greenwillow, 1997).

New York lost several children's book authors. On 17 July, Lillian Hoban died of heart failure in New York City. Best known for her series of picture books about Frances the little badger, she had recently been successful with the Arthur series, about an engaging young chimpanzee. Kay Thompson, creator of *Eloise* (1955), died on 2 July after more than six decades in varied careers: singer, vocal arranger, entrepreneur, and film actress. She was believed to be between ninety-two and ninety-six.

Two trailblazers who promoted multiculturalism long before the term existed died in 1998. Like Hoban and Thompson, they had strong ties to New York City. The great storyteller August Baker died on 22 February at age 86. The first African American to appointed Coordinator of Children's Services at the New York Public Library (1961), she was influential in collection development, beginning with *Books about Negro Life for Children* (1948). Baker served as a mentor to generations of librarians and storytellers alike. Gyo Fujikawa, author and illustrator of the longtime best-seller *Babies,* died on Thanksgiving Day at age 90. In the early 1960s Grosset and Dunlap advised her that *Babies* and its companion *Baby Animals* should not include black babies—for fear of shrinking sales in the American South. Fujikawa refused; the black and Asian babies remained, and thirty-odd years later the two books have sold more than a million and a half copies and been translated into more than twenty languages.

The children's book world also mourned several influential editors and scholars. Mildred Batchelder, whose donation of her own international book collection and related materials made possible the American Library Assocation award that bears her name, died in Evanston, Illinois on 25 August. Dorothy Briley of Clarion Books died of a heart attack on 25 May. While at Clarion she had worked with authors such as Katherine Paterson, Karen Cushman, and Russel Freedman, and illustrators including John Steptoe, David Wisniewski, and David Wiesner. Fabio Coen died on 19 August at the age of eighty. As editor in chief of juvenile books at Pantheon and Knopf, he worked with Roald Dahl, Robert Cormier, and other leading authors. Earlier he had been responsible for Leo Lionni's turning to writing and illustrating books for children. Francelia Butler, founder of the journal *Children's Literature* and a major influence on the teaching of this subject in American universities, died on 17 September in Windham, Connecticut, at the age of 85.

Though Cleveland Amory as neither a children's author nor an editor, his death on 14 October affected the many young readers who enjoyed his books about his cat, Polar Bear. Amory was founder and president of the Fund for Animals, which lobbies for animal causes and also operates a sanctuary, Black Beauty Ranch, for abused and deserted animals. Fittingly, Amory's memorial service on 12 November was at the Cathedral of St. John the Divine in Manhattan, where a famous service including dozens of animals is held every September.

As 1999 approached, mainstream fantasy continued to sell. Readers looked forward to the third volume of Philip Pullman's Dark Materials trilogy and to *Harry Potter and the Chamber of Secrets,* and there seemed little chance that the preposterous Teletubbies would lose their popularity. Closer to home, publishers planned yet more volumes about a fantasy-like American past. Meanwhile, the growing number of new websites devoted to children's books, from Marvel comics to Amazon.com/kids, promised one area of dramatic change to be explored in next year's roundup.

Dictionary of Literary Biography Yearbook Award for a Distinguished Children's Book Published in 1998

Dust jacket for the author's first children's book, which won several prizes and recognition from readers in both England and the United States

The story of J. K. Rowling and her first book rivals the novel's plot in its fantasy elements: a penniless single mother, drafts written in a café, a last-ditch rescue through a Scottish Arts Council grant, and instant popularity for *Harry and the Philosopher's Stone* (Bloomsbury, 1997) with reviewers and young readers in Britain. Awards followed: the Smarties prize for its age group, the Children's Book of the Year award from the British Book Council, and a Commended status from the shortlist for the Carnegie Medal. *Harry* was also shortlisted for the Guardian Award. A tabloid tried to

buy the rights to Rowling's life story; she refused. In interviews and on tours, much of the story came out. Yes, it was true that after teaching English abroad (in Portugal), she had married, borne a child, divorced, and moved to Edinburgh with the beginning chapters of her book in hand. It was true that, without a job, she went on welfare and that, without child care, she wrote in cafés while her infant daughter slept in a stroller. The part about the grant was true, too. It also emerged that though the first agent whom she contacted from a list in a reference book immediately returned the manuscript, a second agent found in the same way succeeded in placing it on his fourth try—not bad for a first book, especially one of more than three hundred pages.

Harry and the Sorcerer's Stone (Scholastic), as it is known in the United States, continued its triumph after crossing the Atlantic, swiftly turning into a best-seller on the Amazon.com website and elsewhere. It defies tradition in winning the *Dictionary of Literary Biography Yearbook* award for 1998 in the Children's Book category; no previous winner has been either a first novel or a popular best-seller (although Philip Pullman's *The Golden Compass* later gained notable success in the U.S. marketplace). Further, because the award normally rotates from one category of juvenile book to another, the odds favored picture books this year.

In a year of mediocrity, *Harry* stands out—a page-turner with an event-filled plot, memorable characters (from Harry's porcine cousin Dudley to the gentle giant Hagrid), zippy dialogue, and humor on every page. The son of a witch and a wizard who were both killed by the evil Voldemort, Harry has survived, bearing only a lightning-shaped mark on his forehead. In the early part of the book, he lives with his ghastly aunt and uncle, relegated to a dark cupboard under the stairs. The petty meanness of the Dursley family reaches Roald Dahl-like heights of invention—a used coat hanger as a birthday present, for instance. After ten miserable years with Aunt Petunia, Uncle Vernon, and the unspeakable Dudley, Harry starts receiving letters, which for a time his uncle successfully intercepts. Finally, Harry learns that he has been admitted to Hogwarts School of Witchcraft and Wizardry, leaves the world of everyday ("Muggles"), and enters a fantasy world through platform nine and three-quarters at Kings Cross Station. The remainder of the book combines a generic, often hilarious school story (including an aerial soccer-like game called Quidditch, played on flying broomsticks) with the serious business of finding the Sorcerer's Stone, escaping Voldemort and his allies, and starting to take on his rightful identity.

No major part of the book is entirely original, as is often the case with fantasy of this type: everyone recognizes the hero with an important legacy from a parent he never knew, the distant but kindly mentor, the evil mage, and the helping animal. In his hobbit books, J. R. R. Tolkien treated, memorably, the quest for an object that may tip the balance between good and evil; C. S. Lewis defined for young readers, in the Narnia cycle, the idea of walking into a parallel world of fantasy; and Ursula Le Guin set the standards for stories of apprentice wizardry in *A Wizard of Earthsea* and its sequels. What distinguishes *Harry and the Sorcerer's Stone* is its lack of pretention. The elaborate philological trap-

pings of the hobbit world, the allegorical freight of Narnia, and the Jungian backdrop of Earthsea are nowhere to be seen, and young readers of the 1990s obviously do not miss them. Though lacking the lyrical prose style of the trio of major twentieth-century fantasy writers for children, Rowling has mastered a workmanlike, fast-paced prose with plenty of room for irony. The tongue-in-cheek narrator wickedly echoes whatever characters are being described, as in the innocuous opening:

> Mr. and Mrs. Dursley, of number four, Privet Drive, were proud to say that they were perfectly normal, thank you very much. They were the last people you'd expect to be involved in anything strange or mysterious, because they just didn't hold with such things.

Rowling's narrator handles terror equally well, and pathos adequately. Natural human speech is not always a strong point among fantasy writers, but Rowling's deftness of touch makes the dialogue sound natural yet not tied too closely to a single time or place; the school children, for example, speak colloquially but not in datable slang.

Rowling plans a total of seven volumes—one for each year that Harry will spend at Hogwarts. (She estimates that a wizard who begins training at eleven should finish at seventeen. Issues already present in the first book will unfold gradually; at least one major puzzle about Harry's past will not be solved until the fifth volume.) The second in the series, *Harry Potter and the Chamber of Secrets,* is already a favorite in Britain and will appear in the United States in 1999. The third and fourth reportedly have been completed. It's clear that Harry will keep young readers happy for years to come.

***Dictionary of Literary Biography Yearbook*
Award for a Distinguished Children's Book:
Honor Books for 1998**

Young Adult
Lois Sachar, *Holes* (Farrar, Straus & Giroux)

Picture Book
Uri Shulevitz, *Snow* (Farrar, Straus & Giroux)

—Caroline Hunt

The Year in Literary Biography

James R. Simmons Jr.
Louisiana Tech University

One might well call 1998 "The Year of the Edition of Letters." Although as in previous years many expansive volumes outlining the lives of literati were published, what was perhaps different in 1998 was the sheer volume of collections of letters that appeared, most of which are first-rate. Scholars interested in the correspondence of famous authors and poets were treated to collections of Ralph Waldo Emerson; Kate Chopin; Cleanth Brooks and Robert Penn Warren; Anaïs Nin and Felix Pollak; Dorothy L. Sayers; Robert Louis Stevenson; Anne, Emily, and Charlotte Brontë; and many others. Overall, these collections are well edited and informative, and many include correspondence seldom, if ever, read by the public. There were perhaps as many fine collections of letters as there have been in any previous year during this decade; as usual, though, there were also some good biographies.

Charles Dickens once wrote that Daniel Defoe's *Robinson Crusoe* (1719) was "the only instance of a universally popular book that could make no one laugh and could make no one cry," and the same might be said of Defoe's life as presented in Richard West's *Daniel Defoe: The Life and Strange and Surprising Adventures* (Carroll and Graf). West's work seems to cover every aspect of Defoe's life, and this is no small feat considering that Defoe was a religious and political chameleon and an author so versatile that he is generally considered to be the most prolific writer in the English language. Reading this biography however, creates the same emotional detachment that Dickens found in *Robinson Crusoe,* Defoe's most famous novel, and thus it is hard really to *care* about the Defoe that West presents. Defoe can be appreciated, but it is difficult to see him as anything more than an historical figure. Certainly he had enough misfortune in his life to warrant sympathy, but somehow West does not elicit these emotions in this biography.

This is not to say that the book is a bad biography, because it is not. West begins not only with a detailed background of Defoe's life but also with a careful analysis of the political climate of the late seventeenth and early eighteenth centuries. Though this

Dust jacket for the biography of the eighteenth-century author and political activist who published more than 560 pamphlets and books

background at times seems detached from the subject of the biography, it is important to understand these contexts, for without them the details of Defoe's life to come will be essentially meaningless. Thus, for roughly the first one hundred pages there is more about the Puritans and the Commonwealth government than about Defoe specifically.

Readers who want to know mainly about Defoe the novelist will also find the early part of the biography of interminable length; one should remember however, that Defoe did not write his first novel (and arguably the first novel in the English language), *Robinson Crusoe,* until he was fifty-nine. West is thus being a responsible biographer by taking his time getting to this stage of Defoe's life. Though the part of his life during which he was a novelist is the period for which he is best known, it was, in fact, preceded by nearly six eventful decades.

When the reader finally does reach that period of Defoe's career, the biography is a bit of a disappointment. A case in point is chapter 12, "*Moll Flanders* and *Roxana.*" Unlike *Crusoe,* these two novels are quite engaging; in fact, the subject matter is somewhat risque, especially parts of *Roxana.* Yet West offers no new insight into Defoe's composition process or any events in his life that may have influenced the writing of these novels. Overall there is nothing new in the latter half of this work, which is largely a collection of the plot summaries of Defoe's novels. While this may be good for the casual reader looking for a new read or for the student trying to avoid reading the whole novel while seeking a succinct account of the action, there is not much here for the scholar.

It is also interesting to note that while today Defoe is known primarily for being the author of *Robinson Crusoe, Roxana, Moll Flanders,* and *Journal of the Plague Year,* West feels that Defoe's most significant contribution as a writer was *Tour of the Whole Island of Great Britain,* which West calls "arguably the greatest of all his books." The operative word in West's claim is "arguably," and, indeed, most would argue with his contention about *Tour.* His statement belies his bias, as in the introduction he quickly informs the reader that it was not Defoe's novels that brought him to Defoe but *Tour.* "For as long as I can remember I have enjoyed exploring the English countryside," West says, and clearly he is allowing his personal likes to make the judgment that *Tour* is Defoe's greatest work. While this is a somewhat unexpected statement to find on the first page of the book, perhaps it is well to know about West's interests early on, for it explains a lot about the construction of the biography. One also has to remember, however, that West is a journalist and not a scholar, and this explains why he gives simple summaries rather than explications of the novels. Therefore, while this is a competent and solid work, there is nothing new here, nothing that is emotionally engaging. It may be safe to say that this is the biography Dickens would have expected to read about the man who wrote the "emotionless" *Robinson Crusoe.*

Another eighteenth-century novelist treated in a biography this year is Henry Fielding, and Harold Pagliaro's *Henry Fielding: A Literary Life* is one of two new volumes in St. Martin's Press's Literary Lives

series. In that tradition it is not simply a biography, and like other volumes in this series, Pagliaro's work not only examines Fielding's life but also provides a critical overview of his work as a playwright and as a novelist. As such, the work is a compilation of both biographical and critical sources, and while the research seems solid, this rather brief volume is most useful as a guide to other, more in-depth studies.

Pagliaro begins with a biographical sketch that amounts to a summary of other biographies, in particular Martin C. Battestin's *Henry Fielding: A Life* (1989). The sketch is useful if Fielding scholars, whom Pagliaro identifies as his intended audience, need one, although why any Fielding scholar who wanted biographical information would read Pagliaro's work instead of Battestin's is unclear. The sketch is, nonetheless, easy to follow. Some readers will take issue, however, with Pagliaro's tendency to apologize for or to excuse Fielding's worst behavior, particularly his alleged incestuous relationship with his sister. Furthermore, Pagliaro speculates on Fielding's ability to be a good husband and closes one passage with the remark that Fielding should have "moderated his behavior" for his wife's sake. Readers may also wonder what Pagliaro means when he states that Fielding's "morality easily survived" the "nominal betrayals" represented by his sudden reversal of political loyalty in *The Opposition: A Vision.* Pagliaro simply could have mentioned these matters without commenting on them; his speculations portray Fielding as an amoral opportunist, at least.

Pagliaro's sections on Fielding's drama and novels provide a useful, if limited, compilation of critical sources mixed with biographical detail. Here Pagliaro's approach works: readers receive a sense of the context in which each work was presented to the public, although this sense is filtered through other critical and biographical sources. But here also, his material becomes superfluous. Too often his critical comments are overshadowed by plot summaries of the plays; indeed, readers may question how much of the commentary is his own and how much he derives from others. Pagliaro seems most comfortable when writing about the novels: he supports details in his chapter on Fielding's novels with only 87 notes; his chapter on Fielding's drama includes 157 notes.

In short, Pagliaro's work offers a respectable review of what others have said about Fielding. But Fielding scholars, or those who wish to be, will find this book most useful as a guide to other important biographical and critical information about their subject.

Robert E. Schofield's *The Enlightenment of Joseph Priestley: A Study of His Life and Work from 1733 to 1773* (Penn State University Press) is an exhaustive biography of the first forty years of Priestley's life and examines the early influences on one of the most prolific intellectual figures of the eighteenth century. Beginning with Priestley's Yorkshire birthplace, Schofield explores Priestley's familial and religious roots as a dissenting Calvinist and identifies his repudiation of original sin as a first step toward his eventual position as a dissenter among dissenters. Recognizing Daventry Academy as the environment in which Priestley began to blossom intellectually, Schofield reveals the early signs of the vigor with which Priestley later approached controversies in science, religion, and philosophy. Schofield follows him through the difficult years at his first ministry in Needham Market to his happier days at Warrington Academy, where as a teacher-scholar he wrote on subjects as various as language and grammar, biography and history, and liberal education. At Warrington, the reader learns, Priestley also demonstrated his proclivity for synthesizing seemingly unrelated categories when he wrote his history of electricity, for which he was accepted into the Royal Academy. Finally, Schofield presents Priestley at his intellectual maturity in Leeds, an influential figure engaged in the controversies of his day.

Schofield's extensive research allows him to speculate about topics for which documentation is scarce or nonexistent. When lacking sufficient evidence to trace the origins of Priestley's developing interest in mathematics and science, for example, Schofield attempts to reconcile often competing influences from Priestley's religious beliefs, education, and readings. In doing so, Schofield considers not only what Priestley was reading but also how he was reading: when describing Priestley reading John Locke, for instance, Schofield reviews "the time, place, occasion, and circumstances of the reader as well as the author." In this way Schofield's intellectual energy certainly seems well suited to that of his subject.

The scope of Schofield's study encompasses the minutiae of Priestley's life, but in analyzing the personal and institutional influences on the young man Schofield also provides an expansive view of educational and scientific practices during the century. Indeed, if his work has a fault, it lies in allowing readers temporarily to forget the subject of his inquiry, often for several pages at a time, while he delves into the circumstances and practices of Locke, Isaac Watts, Sir Isaac Newton, and others. Furthermore, Schofield occasionally confuses readers by mixing his opinions with those of Priestley in such a manner that readers cannot, from Schofield's syntax, distinguish where Schofield ends and Priestley begins. Nonetheless, the biographer's passion for his subject is unmistakable: his biography gives readers a glimpse at the making of an eighteenth-century Renaissance man and thus provides a

Dust jacket for the biography of the Romantic poet whose letters T. S. Eliot praised as "the most notable and most important ever written by any English poet"

valuable service, to Priestley scholars particularly and to eighteenth-century scholars generally.

Though only a few new titles this year cover authors who wrote most of their works prior to the end of the eighteenth century, a plethora of new offerings in literary biography and collections of letters concerning writers from the advent of the British Romantic period through the end of the nineteenth century were published. One volume that appeared late in 1997 deserves at least a brief mention: Mark Storey's *Robert Southey: A Life* (Oxford University Press). Southey, who was an important literary figure in his own time—he was made poet laureate in 1813—has been neglected during this century. In his era Southey was as celebrated as his friends William Wordsworth, Samuel Taylor Coleridge, Robert Lamb, Percy Bysshe Shelley, and Sir Walter Scott—and was as well known as his detractors William Hazlitt and George Gordon, Lord Byron. While Southey's peers are still well known, Storey points out that audiences today do not even know how to pronounce his name correctly (Storey notes that it rhymes "with 'mouthey' as Byron joked"). Yet, Southey wrote in all genres of literature, was widely admired, and was considered a mentor for many aspiring authors and poets, including Ebenezer Elliott and Charlotte Brontë. Storey goes into much detail on Southey's being regarded as a mentor, which is surprising considering the obviously thick-headed advice he gave the aspiring young Brontë when she wrote to him in 1937. His now-infamous reply that "literature cannot be the business of a woman's life: & it ought not to be" is not included here, though it is difficult to blame Storey for that: he is trying to bring Southey back into the limelight, not relegate him permanently to the background. This biography brings to life a figure who deserves more recognition than he gets today, and like many Oxford books, it may well be the most comprehensive and important scholarly biography of its subject available.

Not every Romantic poet who is the subject of a biography this year is little known. One of the major Romantic poets, John Keats, was just as unknown while he was alive as Southey has become today. Shelley wrote his lines of tribute, "O weep for Adonais—he is dead!" in 1821, and the short life of Keats is seen today as embodying the Romantic archetype: Keats was the gifted yet tortured artist who lived briefly, wrote well, and died before realizing his full potential. In *Keats: A Biography* (Farrar, Straus and Giroux) Andrew Motion—who won the Whitbread Prize for Biography for his 1993 work on Philip Larkin—presents the most recent of many biographies of the poet. Motion does not take a typically maudlin approach by asking the reader to pity Keats and lament the poet's early death; instead, he evenhandedly examines what motivated the man. While it is impossible not to pity a genius who died at twenty-five with so much unrealized potential, the reader finishes this biography admiring the man who overcame much to produce the quality of work that he did and gaining a sense of respect for Keats and his works—and not simply because he is an idealized Romantic figure.

One of the strengths of this work, and what sets it apart from many other literary biographies, is that Motion adequately explores various literary, social, and political contexts of the period. Although these contexts are often acknowledged as important in academic discussions of Keats's work, they are often overlooked in biographies. Motion, however, balances his discussion of Keats's works and his life well, with his purpose being to present a Keats who is "more rounded" than in other biographies, and he does not deify the poet by ignoring facts that do not fit his idea of how he thinks we should regard Keats. For example, he rightly pre-

sents Keats as hovering precariously between the upper-working and lower-middle classes. Furthermore, Motion disabuses the reader of the notion that Keats was an apolitical poet: he was influenced by political events and liberal beliefs—as were his contemporaries, such as Wordsworth, Coleridge, Shelley, and Byron—and his work also incorporates these events and beliefs. Motion presents Keats a man whose life was a combination of "inspiration, accident, [and] genius," and the result is a biography that is one of the better works of the year.

Unlike Southey, who is not now well known, and Keats, who was not then well known, William Wordsworth was and still is quite well known, perhaps as much as any of the British Romantics. Although Wordsworth has been the subject of many studies, Kenneth R. Johnston's *The Hidden Wordsworth: Poet, Lover, Rebel, Spy* (Norton) promises to uncover a Wordsworth heretofore little seen. Johnston assumes (rightly, it seems) that the Wordsworth whom most people know is the somewhat dull, predictable patriarch of the Romantic poets, and as he notes, even Wordsworth's appearance was unexciting. Compared with "his great literary contemporaries," Johnston writes, "almost all of whom *look* Romantic . . . Wordsworth, from first portrait to last, looks calm and resigned at best, sleepy or weary at worst." The illustrations in Johnston's book substantiate this claim, and many scholars, while agreeing that Wordsworth was a poetic genius, find that—compared to the work of other well-known Romantic poets such as Shelley, Byron, Blake, Coleridge, and Keats—Wordsworth's has a dull predictability. Johnston seems to be trying to reshape this mundane Wordsworth and tries to lure readers with promises that he will provide new revelations that will uncover a "lover," a "rebel," and a "spy" in addition to the poet whom readers know. The results of this new exposé are mixed; far less is proven than is claimed on the dust jacket.

This book quickly becomes plodding, mired in details—every possible detail—of Wordsworth's life. It is doubtful that any more thorough study of the poet's life has been done, and certainly this may be a landmark work of Wordsworthian scholarship. After all, if a reader wants 960 pages of page-turning excitement, it is unlikely that a biography of Wordsworth is where he or she will be looking for it. Yet, excitement is what is supposed to separate this biography from previous studies of Wordsworth, for it is advertised as presenting a life of the poet that few have ever read before. While this biography is in some ways informative, it fails to live up to its promise of being a shocking exposé.

Certainly the "spy" appellation in the title seems intriguing, and advance notices of the book focused on the fact that Johnston had uncovered some startling new material indicating that Wordsworth may have been in the employ of the British Secret Service during the latter part of the eighteenth century. Readers expecting James Bond, however, will be disappointed. Though for a few pages Johnston almost begs the reader to accept the theory that Wordsworth may have been a British agent, the evidence is hardly conclusive.

If the reader is not convinced that Wordsworth was a spy, perhaps "lover" will work. Johnston carefully covers ground that relates to Wordsworth's French lover Annette Vallon and the illegitimate daughter she bore him. The dust jacket claims that "Wordsworth's complex relationship with his sister Dorothy changed disturbingly when she tried to initiate an overtly erotic involvement." Though almost anyone familiar with Wordsworth's life will acknowledge that his relationship with Dorothy was complex and that twentieth-century critics have often hinted about finding incestuous desire in his life and work, it is likely that any sexual urges the siblings may have felt were unconsummated. The reader is led to expect some evidence that Dorothy tried to seduce her brother, but Johnston never drops that bombshell. Nor is this information buried in the endless minutiae about Wordsworth's life; a rereading of index pages that even hint at any relationship between the two turns up nothing. In short, the information in this volume has been examined in countless other studies, and the only even slightly suggestive comments are the repeated references to Dorothy's "wild eyes." What the "overtly erotic involvement" claim refers to is unclear, and the blurb on the dust jacket was apparently designed to titillate.

Perhaps in the crowded wasteland of literary biographies produced every year publishers think that even books written primarily for academic audiences must promise to reveal lurid details and intrigue. When the dust jacket alludes to "sexually experienced" and "erotic" characters, "prostitutes," "eroticism," "clandestine" operations, and "most astonishingly of all, Wordsworth's likely spy missions, the reader expects a biography that will" that reveal a poet whose life is a cross between something recounted on a daytime talk show and a role played by Sean Connery. Perhaps there is no way to fulfill such a promise. Johnston's book emerges, however, as a fairly well-balanced study, and if it did not promise so much that it cannot deliver, reading it, though at times laborious, might at least end up being rewarding. As it is, the reader may feel cheated—or as if he or she missed something. Neither feeling is a good one to have upon finishing a book.

Some authors and editors, however, know the successful formula for literary biographies and collections of letters, especially when they have worked with

Dust jacket for the biography intended to revise conventional views of Wordsworth's political activities and personal life

a book-length study of their subject before. Therein perhaps lies a greater challenge: how does an author follow up a biography that has been generally considered one of the best ever written? When you are Juliet Barker, whose 1995 biography *The Brontës* was lauded as a landmark by reviewers in *Publishers Weekly, The New York Times Book Review, The Los Angeles Times,* and scores of other periodicals, you follow it with another first-rate work: *The Brontës: A Life in Letters* (Overlook). As a former curator of the Brontë Parsonage Museum, Barker has the background to claim authority for her work, yet she never slips into one mistake that befalls many critics and fans of the Brontës: suppressing information that may present the family in an unflattering light. Since Elizabeth Gaskell wrote *The Life of Charlotte Brontë* in 1857 and sanitized Charlotte's life by suppressing information that Charlotte had been in love with Constantin Heger, a married man, many biographies and collections of letters have attempted to present the Brontë sisters as perfect literary artists. Though the sisters were generally pious and reserved, they had failings. Barker does not sugarcoat the facts by withholding information, and thus her works always seem more credible than those of many other Brontë scholars.

Another problem in writing on the Brontës is that by now everything seems to have been done. Other than William Shakespeare and Dickens, few if any literary figures have received as much attention as Anne, Emily, and Charlotte Brontë. Editions of Brontë letters have appeared in the past, but Barker's new collection includes letters never before published. She debunks myths about Branwell Brontë (brother of the three famous sisters) in presenting letters indicating that Branwell's affair with an employer's wife was almost certainly sexual and that it is extremely doubtful that he ever attended the Royal Academy, as critics often have claimed. Furthermore, Barker's inclusion of letters and diary entries (both rare, indeed) by Anne and Emily keeps this from being another work that one might refer to as "Charlotte-centric." An added bonus is the inclusion of the most important letters sent *to* the Brontës—including Southey's letter of advice to Charlotte—as well as noteworthy epistolary comments about the Brontës, such as those Harriet Martineau published about Charlotte in her *Autobiography* (1877). (These are especially significant, since no edition of Martineau's autobiography is in print, and none will be until Linda Peterson's Broadview edition is published in late 1999 or early 2000.) In one passage from these letters in Barker's collection, Martineau notes that Charlotte was the "smallest creature I had seen except at a fair." Though Brontë scholars always seem to look for one weak spot in a work to reveal the fallibility of the author or editor, such a weak spot is not obvious here. All in all, this is a superb collection of letters and is largely without parallel for a single-volume work.

While the Brontës left only a few letters, other compilers must examine thousands, which certainly makes their decisions about what to include more difficult. In *The Selected Letters of Ralph Waldo Emerson* (Columbia) Joel Myerson has selected 350 letters from the more than 4,500 in existence; his stated purpose is to present a "'representative' Emerson." He does that quite well, as these letters provide a good overview of one of the most important American thinkers. The problem with selecting letters from such a voluminous number is that sometimes an issue is alluded to that is left unresolved in this volume: in a letter written in 1848, Emerson tells Lidian Emerson that he will be dining with John Forster, Dickens, and Thomas Carlyle the next week, and one feels a natural curiosity and wants to read a follow-up letter telling how these four famous men got along together that night. Such curios-

ity cannot be satisfied, however, because no subsequent correspondence about this matter is included in this collection. Nevertheless, this problem cannot be seen as a fault, as Myerson's work does not aim to present the complete letters of Emerson, just selected ones. Indeed, this well-edited and annotated collection merely makes one wish to read more.

Mary Moody Emerson seems to have had a formative influence on her nephew Ralph—that is, if we are to believe Phyllis Cole in *Mary Moody Emerson and the Origins of Transcendentalism* (Oxford University Press). As we see Mary Emerson's silhouette hovering above portraits of her nephew, Henry David Thoreau, and Bronson Alcott on the dust jacket, it is clear that Cole's purpose is firmly to place her at the forefront of the transcendentalist movement.

Cole's information is compelling, and she will almost single-handedly deserve the credit if a reevaluation of Mary Emerson's influence occurs. Having discovered Mary Emerson's diary in 1981, Cole has been able to add insight into the intellect of a woman known mainly as Ralph Waldo Emerson's "eccentric Calvinist aunt." Cole's biography is sure to establish an important place for Mary Moody Emerson in studies of transcendentalism, and thus this work succeeds as few biographies do. Enjoyable and imminently readable, this work and Myerson's (which has at least a dozen letters from the nephew to his aunt) give scholars of this period in American literature an impressive foundation of new works upon which to build as the next century approaches.

Like Myerson, Ernest Mehew must have found some difficulty in deciding what to include when compiling *Selected Letters of Robert Louis Stevenson* (Yale University Press). Mehew, who has been working on Stevenson's letters for more than twenty-five years, brought together all 2,800 known Stevenson letters in *The Letters of Robert Louis Stevenson* (1994–1995), an eight-volume collection that is the most comprehensive work ever done on Stevenson. In his current book Mehew has selected 317 letters by Stevenson, as well as one by his wife Fanny, and has presented them in a way that recounts Stevenson's life as well as any ordinary biography could.

The collection begins with letters written when Stevenson was eighteen and continues through one of the last letters he wrote, to Edmund Gosse, just days before Stevenson's death. They are arranged chronologically according to distinct periods in Stevenson's life, and each chapter has a full introduction that explains what is to come and why the letters are grouped as they are. In these letters Mehew presents the development of a sickly but inspired young man into a famous author wracked by the tuberculosis that

*Dust jacket for the edition of letters by the foremost figure
in the transcendentalist group*

eventually killed him. Yet, regardless of the state of his health, Stevenson was a prolific letter writer, and among his correspondence we find many letters not only to his friends and family but also to well-known literary figures such as Arthur Conan Doyle, William Butler Yeats, Mark Twain, Thomas Hardy, and Henry James. Because Mehew has carefully annotated the letters and has indicated every instance in which a letter has been abridged or extracted, this is a first-rate collection, valuable to anyone who wants to know more about a man who wrote some classic literary works.

Selected Letters is a proper title for Mehew's thorough and satisfying work, and readers who open Merlin Holland's *The Wilde Album* (Holt) should be advised that the title of this book is also not a misnomer, although *album* should not be construed as a positive term for a biography. Holland, who is Wilde's only grandson (Wilde's heirs adopted "Holland," a name from his wife's side of the family, after Wilde's trial), presents a fascinating array of photographs, and in them we almost literally see Wilde grow from childhood until his death in 1900. These photographs give us a sense of the man who, Holland claims, seemed to

relish publicity—any publicity, good or bad. Certainly anyone who was so often photographed valued his own image, and whether the photographs be of a two-year-old Oscar in a blue velvet dress or of the bloated ruin that he became later in life, the images are all here. Many of these photos previously had been unpublished, and Holland's kinship with Wilde has given him an opportunity to present a work with a true insider's perspective.

Perhaps the availability of the insider's perspective is what makes this such a disappointing work: Holland completely wastes the opportunity to give us anything really new other than the photographs. The biographical content is extremely superficial, and other than a few interesting factoids (for example, the reader learns that as a young man Wilde was six feet, three inches tall and powerfully built), most of the biographical material could have been written by a reasonably well-informed graduate student. Holland mentions that the Wilde family photo albums were sold at the time of Wilde's trial in 1895, but he does not indicate whether they have ever turned up or who bought them. Holland's father, Vyvyan, is mentioned only in passing.

Certainly one would think that Holland should be able to give us a unique perspective on Wilde's life, and through his father be able to share some knowledge to which perhaps no other living soul is privy. What were the feelings of Vyvyan, or of his brother Cyril, about their infamous father? The absence not only of anecdotes but also solid information in what Holland claims to be the result of twenty years of research on his grandfather makes this a biography that is far less than satisfactory. If a reader seeks a coffee-table book filled with images of Oscar Wilde, then Holland's work is perhaps unsurpassed; if a reader wants a good critical biography of the man who was perhaps the greatest British playwright of the nineteenth century, he or she needs to look elsewhere.

Jonathan Fryer's *André & Oscar* (St. Martin's Press) might qualify as that elsewhere. Though not a relative of Wilde, Fryer is an experienced biographer, having previously written lives of Dylan Thomas and Christopher Isherwood. Experience may make all the difference, for Fryer's is one of the year's most compelling reads. In a work that ironically begins with Fryer thanking Holland for giving him permission to quote from Wilde's correspondence, Fryer methodically writes a work that is substantially more than the advertised biographical examination of the lives of Wilde and André Gide, the Nobel Prize–winning French author. In addition, Fryer explores in some detail the lives of Constance Wilde and Madeleine Gide, the authors' wives, as well as the lives of many other major players in the fin de siècle decadence that characterized the literary circles in which they participated.

Fryer begins by introducing us to the French literary and artistic circles in which these two men moved, though at the time Wilde was just achieving popularity and Gide was still a few years away from literary recognition. Paul Verlaine, Stéphane Mallarmé, James McNeill Whistler, and Paul Valéry are just a few of the individuals encountered along the way, and it is easy to see how the young Gide would have been influenced by any of these great talents. Wilde may have influenced his life the most, as Gide noted that Wilde played Mephistopheles to his own Faustus. Though Fryer points out that the two men were never in constant contact and that Gide interacted with Wilde sporadically "in the ascendant, at the height of his powers and in final free fall" of Wilde's career, Wilde got Gide to admit for the first time his interest in pederasty.

Indeed, this biography draws us with the same appeal that makes us crane our necks to examine a horrible accident on the highway. There may be much more than we care to know about Wilde's sexual proclivities, his intercourse with Lord Alfred Douglas, and Gide's pedophilia involving boys of almost any age as

his sexual prey. Fryer notes that it is ironic that Wilde went to prison for being homosexual and Gide, although he was a confirmed pedophile, went free; today these consequences would surely be reversed. Though the history of the sexual conquests of these two men is often shocking, it makes for anything but mundane reading.

One thing that this work does conclusively is to indicate that Wilde was a fool. He completely overestimated his powers of persuasion and his popularity, and he firmly believed that he would emerge triumphant in his famous suit against the marquess of Queensberry. Perhaps he thought he would win because his lawyer agreed that he would, although Wilde had lied to his lawyer and denied that he was a homosexual, a matter that was easily proven. It is easy to feel sorry for Wilde, the prisoner who stood handcuffed in a train station as people jeered him and one man actually spat in his face; the memory of these details caused Wilde to cry whenever he recalled the experience.

Yet, any sympathy for Wilde dissipates as the biography progresses. Fryer relates instance after instance in which Wilde made decisions that proved to be disastrous, and they eventually cost him his wife, children, and fortune. As we see the near-toothless, shabbily dressed, semimendicant Wilde roaming France during the last days of his life, it is hard to feel sorry for him, though it does seem unfair that Wilde's lover—"Bosie," or Lord Alfred Douglas—did not share the shame. Douglas emerges as an almost satanic figure in this biography; he clearly tormented and tortured Wilde, as well as enthralled him. Our greatest sense of his evil comes when Douglas tells Gide that Cyril, the older of Wilde's sons, "will be for me." Douglas, unlike Wilde, never suffered for his deeds and escaped most of the misery that drove Wilde to an early grave. As these biographical details illustrate, Fryer's book does everything that Holland's does not, and thus Fryer's is an important work not only on Wilde but also for the insight it provides into the life of Gide. This is a volume that is essential reading for anyone interested in the lives and works of either writer.

Another literary figure whose life was a mixture of tragedy and triumph is Jack London, the subject of Alex Kershaw's *Jack London, A Life* (St. Martin's Press). Though the reader's first impression is that this work will be anything but enjoyable (it begins with a present-tense, "you-are-there" look at a time during London's last days), eventually Kershaw's approach becomes less experimental, and the biography becomes pleasurable to read.

Kershaw often depicts London in an unflattering light, and he acknowledges that throughout London's career the writer had a penchant for romanticizing his humble beginnings and his early, rough-and-tumble life, so much that at times London appears to be a twentieth-century Mr. Bounderby, the pontificating blowhard who conveniently embellishes his own childhood in Dickens's *Hard Times* (1854). Yet, while Kershaw rightly suggests that London mythologized his childhood, any reader recognizes that a boy who was a wharf rat, oyster pirate, and seal hunter–and who drank liquor and consorted with prostitutes before the age when most of us graduate from high school–has a right to embellish a bit. In his brief span of forty years London clearly did more living than most people could do in ten lifetimes, and his experiences served him well. His Klondike adventures shaped classics such as *Call of the Wild* (1903) and *White Fang* (1906); his seafaring adventures did so in *The Sea Wolf* (1904); and even his alcoholic excesses provided material for *John Barleycorn* (1913). As a surfer, war correspondent, hobo, gold prospector, prison inmate, socialist, and novelist, London's astonishing personal experiences and his literary canon of forty books that drew upon them probably have yet to be fully appreciated. This recognition seems to be part of Kershaw's mission, and he has chosen an interesting figure to champion. Yet, despite the wealth of material about London, Kershaw's book could have been more illuminating than it is about some events in London's life.

The most glaring deficiency is that Kershaw appears to be holding back information, either because of his own delicacy or because of his fear that such information may cast London in an unflattering light. For example, he hints that London may have been raped in prison by writing that "when Jack later wrote about his days on the road, he did not mention what really happened in prison," and he adds that "Jack had suffered all manner of 'unthinkable horrors' in prison." What exactly does that mean? It implies that he was raped, but it does not tell us anything. In 1998 it is safe to assume that most readers can handle such a revelation, but Kershaw never answers the question. If Kershaw does not know, that is fine, but the reader should be told that no one knows. There are several similar instances, and each is inexplicable.

Kershaw also relates incidents that have no logical conclusion and leave the reader wondering if he or she missed something. For example, Kershaw mentions a woman who was the only female contact London had for some months in Alaska. An attractive woman, she was married to an adventurer named Stevens, who regaled London with tales so enthralling that the latter was "blind to everything about him, even the woman." Later London visits the couple, and Stevens shows London how well he can shoot a rifle. Kershaw writes that

Dust jacket for the biography of Ralph Waldo Emerson's aunt

"it would be several months before Jack again braved the elements in search of female company."

Apparently the reader is to guess that London really went to see Mrs. Stevens, though that is never stated or even implied, especially since London knew that he was visiting the couple, not just her, when he went, and Kershaw has already written that Mr. Stevens's stories made London oblivious to all else. This is but one of many instances in which a few details, and then a conclusion that seems not to follow, are given. London's apparent death wish, as manifested in his insistence on living so hard and fast that he seemed hell-bent for an early grave, is puzzling enough for the reader, who does not need Kershaw's logical inconsistencies and veiled suggestions as a bonus. London seems to have been a man who was straight to the point, but Kershaw, unfortunately, is not.

Despite the problematic presentation, however, there is simply no way to completely ruin a biography about a man who lived as fully as Jack London. If read-

*Dust jacket for the selected letters by one of the more prolific
correspondents of the late nineteenth century*

ers can stand to maneuver through the literary mine-field that Kershaw has constructed, the material is sufficiently rewarding to make the experience worth-while.

Though Kate Chopin's life did not extend as far into this century as London's did, the author of *The Awakening* (1899) still seems a writer of the twentieth century rather than of the more staid nineteenth century. Emily Toth and Per Seyersted's *Kate Chopin's Private Papers* (Indiana University Press) is an important collection that brings together all the bits and fragments of Chopin's literary legacy that, if taken individually by type, would not make up a full volume. There are documents from her commonplace book, manuscript account books, letters, poems, newspaper pieces, and "rediscovered short stories," fragments of her work discovered in a Worcester, Massachusetts, warehouse in 1992. *Kate Chopin's Private Papers* is clearly not a work of interest to dilettantes, as a previous appreciation of Chopin's life and work may be necessary to realize the full importance of this collection. One does not have to be an expert on Chopin, however, to see that this is a

first-rate collection that will be a valuable supplement to Chopin scholarship.

In terms of her literary reputation Chopin has been lucky, as Seyersted did much to reestablish her importance as a literary figure when he began working with her oeuvre in the late 1950s. Usually seventy-five to one hundred years after an author has done his or her best work, the academy informally determines whether to make the writer one of the canonical names that will forever be revered and studied or to relegate him or her to the role of a minor figure receiving attention from those scholars dutiful enough to gamble basing a life's work on a writer who may or may not belatedly be appreciated. Three biographies published this year concern female literary figures of the early twentieth century who, unlike Chopin, are little known by the general public and perhaps known only by name to many scholars. In these books the biographers bid for recognition for their subjects, but whether they will be successful remains to be seen.

The first, Sally Cline's *Radclyffe Hall: A Woman Called John* (Overlook), is obviously targeted at capitalizing on the market for women's studies and gay studies in major universities, and it seems to be marketed as such. Though Hall published poetry as well as novels, today she is remembered almost solely for *The Well of Loneliness* (1928), a novel extremely risqué, for that time, about lesbian love. While this biography is a rather entertaining read, it is likely that it might not have been published if Hall had not been a lesbian—simply because her work was average. And if she were not a colorful personality in lesbian studies, where there are not many high-profile figures, there probably would not be much of a market for this biography. It is only the woman's life that sells this book, although readers may be interested in giving *The Well of Loneliness* a look after reading this biography. Perhaps Cline is happy with that result, and if so, the purpose of the biography is served.

The same cannot be said for Nathalie Blondel's *Mary Butts: Scenes from Life* (McPherson), which also tells of the life and times of an all-but-forgotten novelist, poet, and essayist of the early twentieth century. This biography follows reprintings of several of Butts's works during the past few years, and although Blondel does a good job of relating information about Butts's life, there is little insight into Butts's talent or into reasons for reading her today. Like Radclyffe Hall, Butts seems to have been an interesting personality but little more. Butts has never been a "name" in the United States, and despite the exacting detail with which this work was prepared, it is doubtful that this title alone will change her literary reputation. While Blondel's book probably will not convince readers to take a renewed interest in Butts's work, the biography is entertaining.

The third biography about a woman writer concerns one whose name we should know; but if asked to name fiction writers who won the Pulitzer Prize, many readers would be unlikely to volunteer Ellen Glasgow. This is perhaps part of why Susan Goodman has written *Ellen Glasgow: A Biography* (Johns Hopkins University Press). Glasgow, who won the Pulitzer Prize in 1942 for her novel *In This Our Life,* is not as familiar to us as are many of her contemporaries, such as John Steinbeck, who won the Pulitzer before her, and Upton Sinclair, who won it the year after her. Yet, Glasgow was a successful writer, and her 1902 novel *Battle-Ground* sold an amazing 1.5 million copies. Goodman informs us that Glasgow was a significant influence on Robert Penn Warren, Eudora Welty, and William Faulkner and that all were "indebted" to her. Thus, Goodman's mission seems to be to restore Glasgow to what she sees as Glasgow's place among twentieth-century literati.

Will it work? Goodman certainly does not present her material in a way that enables the reader to sympathize or empathize with Glasgow. The child of a wealthy Richmond family, Glasgow went through many trials throughout her life: the death of her mother in 1893, the suicide of her brother-in-law the next year, and, as Goodman informs us, "in the ensuing two decades, . . . more catastrophes; the end of her relationship with a married lover . . .; the suicide of her brother Frank; and the death of her favorite sister, Cary McCormack, after a prolonged battle with cancer." As Glasgow was born in 1873, these traumatic events seem to have occurred over a forty-year span. If the two suicides had been deaths by any other cause, how would this have been any more horrible than what the average person experiences in the course of a lifetime? This may be why this biography does not work: Goodman simply pushes too hard in trying to convince her reader that Glasgow, who was far more famous and fortunate than most mortals, has somehow been cheated by posterity.

Goodman says that Glasgow has been "ignored" and somewhat defensively tells the reader that, because Glasgow did not write about "The Astor Four Hundred," she is not as highly regarded as Edith Wharton—and now her literary reputation ranks a distant third to the reputations of both Wharton and Willa Cather. This seems to be an extremely generous assessment. Goodman also claims that though Glasgow anticipated much that we have come to regard as Faulknerian, she has little of the recognition that Faulkner receives. It is unclear whether Goodman thinks that Glasgow felt unappreciated or if Goodman simply believes that Glasgow truly was unappreciated. Every time we read that

Glasgow has a novel published, however, Goodman makes it seem as if Glasgow thinks that she will win the Pulitzer that year. Goodman writes that when Lewis won it for *Arrowsmith* in 1926, "Glasgow [thought] she had a real chance of receiving the Pulitzer Prize," and part of Goodman's justification for this assessment is that Wharton and Cather had already won prizes. Again, we are told that in 1932 Glasgow "once again expected to win the Pulitzer Prize" but failed. Since there are no quotations from Glasgow to confirm this claim, it is not clear how reliable it is. It is difficult to feel sorry for someone who is so successful and who constantly expects to win one of the highest literary awards, especially when the expectation resembles the give-and-take of childhood, in which one child expects a gift from the parents simply because another sibling got one.

What emerges from this biography is a portrait of a woman who seems not at all likable, and certainly this may largely result from Goodman's persistent efforts to force us to see that Glasgow was a wronged woman who should be as well known as any other American author of this century. Readers may well end up feeling as if they have just watched an especially irritating commercial, after which they vow not to buy the product just because of the way in which the commercial presented it. Readers of this biography also may not feel like buying any Glasgow afterward.

To American audiences at least, Enid Blyton's name may be just as unknown as Glasgow's, but in *Enid Blyton* (Sutton) George Greenfield assures us that such is not the case in England, where Blyton is known as the author of some six hundred books for children and adolescents. Blyton's biography is the latest in Sutton's Pocket Biographies series, and though most of the names in the series are familiar ones—the short but diverse list includes Dickens, Jane Austen, Alexander the Great, Abraham Lincoln, Sigmund Freud, Grigory Rasputin, Winston Churchill, and Ludwig van Beethoven—Blyton's name seems out of place among such luminaries. Anyone reading this work will, however, be treated to an account of the life of a fascinating character and will gain a greater appreciation for Blyton's work.

Greenfield, who was a friend and business associate of Blyton's, seems to be fairly straightforward in his representation of her, and unlike Goodman's treatment of Glasgow, Greenfield lets the details of Blyton's story unfold whether they are good or bad—and they are often both. Greenfield shows us a young girl whose parents divorced, and although Enid was bookish, her mother still believed that women should be raised as practitioners of domesticity. Thanks to her father, Blyton was allowed to pursue her academic and literary interests, and after a period as a teacher she became a

Dust jacket for the biographical study of the lives, times, and literary relations of two writers whose sexual behavior was received in different ways

full-time novelist and one of the most successful writers in England. Greenfield apprises us of her literary output, as well as of what she earned as a writer, and what emerges is his portrait of a woman whose work was loved by millions of readers through a long and productive career.

What also emerges is a portrait of a woman who could be quite different from the author who wrote didactically about treating others with fairness and compassion. The reader learns that Blyton was "brutal" toward domestics, whom she fired if they made even one mistake. When her first husband, Hugh Pollack, a British army officer during World War II, was injured when a mortar shell exploded and a piece of shrapnel lodged in his face, she chose not to visit him in the hospital. Claiming that she hated hospitals, she requested of the staff: "If he's going to be ill for some time, could you please let me know how he gets on? Perhaps you could ring me every day—keep me informed . . . the best time of day to ring me is in the evening."

When Blyton and her husband divorced, Pollack agreed to shoulder the blame (although Blyton had been having an affair) if she would agree not to limit his access to their children. As Greenfield notes, Pollack failed "to comprehend the character of his soon-to-be ex-wife," and after the divorce he never saw his children again. There are many such anecdotes, and Greenfield thus reveals a woman who was as complex and often abrasive as she was productive. The result is a brief but fascinating read that reinforces the point that a celebrity's true character may be far different from his or her public persona.

Different from what they appear to be is probably the best way to describe those works that appear each year with titles that indicate that at least a substantial part, if not all, of the text is biographical. The amount of biographical content can vary greatly, as three works this year reveal. Edgar J. Goldenthal's *Poet of the Ghetto: Morris Rosenfeld* (KTAV) has only a short biographical section of thirty-three pages in its more than four hundred pages, and thus the reader gets only a brief sense of the Jewish poet Rosenfeld's life and a much greater sampling of his poems, which are republished in the volume. This lovingly prepared book (Goldenthal is Rosenfeld's grandson) is written for the layperson and not the scholar, and, in fact, Goldenthal claims that he eschews any "boring attempts at pedantry." The book takes a decidedly nonscholarly approach by often directly addressing the reader, and many sentences end in exclamation marks. Overall, this work is suited for nonacademics, although anyone interested specifically in Rosenfeld's poetry probably could not find a better text as a departure point for studying his work.

Mary Lee Settle's *Addie: A Memoir* (University of South Carolina Press) is also an atypical autobiography, as Settle contextualizes her own life by writing a memoir of her grandmother, Addie. As an accomplished novelist, Settle weaves a tale of her life by telling us that "an autobiography that begins with one's birth begins too late," and, indeed, by meeting Settle's grandmother, the reader better knows the author. By learning how Addie survived turn-of-the-century life in the rough coal-mining country of West Virginia, a bad marriage, and social ostracism, the reader understands that Settle's toughness is congenital. Her memoir thus reveals how the diligence and perseverance mandatory for success may have much to do with where we come from and how we are raised—no matter how smugly we may congratulate ourselves on our educations and personal accomplishments. Settle is willing to acknowledge that she owes much to both her grandmother and her mother—not talent, but simply a certain something that they passed along that makes Settle who she is. This work is a convincing testament to Settle's belief that beginning an autobiography with one's own birth is, indeed, too late.

James A. Davies's well-annotated *A Reference Companion to Dylan Thomas* (Greenwood Press) does not tell us about anybody's grandmother, but Dylan Thomas's life was eventful enough that we do not need to know about his ancestors. Davies's work is similar to Rosenfeld's in that only the first section of the book is a biography (the second section discusses Thomas's works, and the third is a critical history of his literature), and those first one hundred pages are compelling reading. Davies has the power to make us both loathe and pity Dylan Thomas, and although Thomas's reputation as a hard-drinking, disruptive bohemian is fairly well known, this biography reveals an individual who was a reprobate, coward, liar, and thief, as well as a brilliant and admired poet. As Davies notes, had Thomas died in his twenties, already productive yet with his reputation untarnished, we might now see him as "a younger Keats . . . attractively heroic, with infinite potential, struck down in youth's full flower." Some might also wish that, like Arthur Rimbaud, Thomas had written brilliantly early and then disappeared for the rest of his life—to be rediscovered only on his deathbed, so that the public would have no chance to witness any diminution of his abilities or embarrassing personal revelations. Thomas did not, however, die or disappear; he left a trail of shattered lives, broken hearts, and alcoholic anecdotes for us to follow with wonder.

Davies begins with a careful look at Thomas's origins and parents, especially his father's frustrated academic ambitions and his pretty but nonintellectual mother. Throughout Thomas's childhood his every whim was indulged, as he was coddled by his mother. Although he cared little for academic pursuits other than literature, his father, a teacher at the boys' school, seems never to have taken him in hand. The makings of the later, tragic Dylan Thomas are in the boy we see: he was an intellectually lazy child, prone to stealing money from his family and friends. As an adult he generally subsisted entirely on literary genius and cared little about anyone or anything else.

During those early years it is easy to feel for the struggling young artist, even when he seems to waste almost all of his income on alcohol. Especially during the 1940s this pity turns to disgust, and Davies presents a mind-shattering narrative detailing Thomas's use and abuse of almost all who came near him. We learn that Thomas was a habitual beggar of sorts, constantly putting the pinch on everyone he knew for loans, which, of course, he invariably failed to pay back. Also, as his wife Caitlin has written, she and Thomas were "apt to be rather too 'at home' in other people's houses," and this often provided opportunities for their stealing and pawning their hosts' belongings to pay for drink. Thomas often took advances for books that he never wrote, and although in his later years he had an income that should have made his family wealthy, they lived almost always in abject poverty as he squandered his earnings on drinking and socializing.

Certainly many famous people have money problems, but Davies informs us of personal qualities even more repugnant—among them that Thomas was quite likely a coward. During World War II, as patriotic fervor ran high in England, Thomas looked for a way—any way—to get out of going into the service. He may have convinced a doctor friend to declare him unfit for service (his wife thought this may have been how Thomas managed to avoid serving, but it was never proved), and his civilian wartime experiences are no more endearing. His wife recalls him hiding, "whimpering, under the bedsheets" as German bombers flew overhead and on several occasions Thomas and his wife went out to get drunk and apparently left their baby alone at home under a glass roof while the bombers flew over. Thomas emerges as a horrible, neglectful parent, and his wife only slightly less so.

As these details show, whatever Thomas did always seemed to come back to drinking, and Thomas was not a "good" drinker. If he were angry at others and had been drinking, he might urinate on their walls or possessions or, worse, defecate on their floors. He seems at some time or another, to have alienated almost everyone with whom he came into contact while he was drunk: Davies writes that Thomas may have been "offensively suggestive about Shelley Winters's breasts; his drunken behavior certainly offended Charlie Chaplin." Thomas was often violent while drunk, prone to play the "pub fool" by crawling on the floor and barking like a dog, and he once failed to appear at a wedding at which he was to be the best man. He did not write the bride and groom with a lame excuse until almost a month later.

Certainly Thomas seems not only a tragic figure, a genius ruined by alcohol, but also a man with just enough mean-spiritedness to revolt us. Davies's biographical section details all of this and more, and it is certainly an engrossing and informative read. The latter sections of the work seem to be as good as the opening biographical one, and this is a book that anyone interested in Thomas and his work would do well to have.

While reading a biography about someone such as Thomas may be enjoyable even if the reader does not know much about the subject, reading a collection of letters is generally something that should be done only after the reader has a fairly comprehensive knowledge of the letter writer's life and work; otherwise, trying to understand the subject matter can be frustrating.

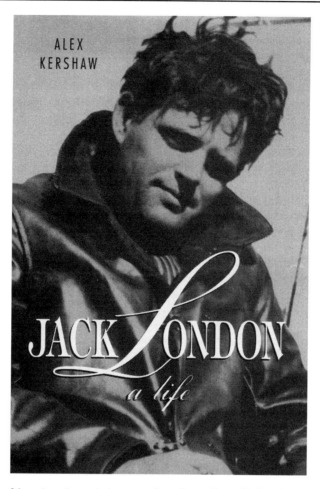

Dust jacket for the biography of the writer whose experiences were bases for autobiographical works such as Martin Eden *(1909) and* John Barleycorn *(1913)*

To that end, three of the following four collections of letters may be for scholars only. The collection with the widest range is Don Reneau's translation of Hans Wysling's *Letters of Heinrich and Thomas Mann, 1900–1949* (University of California Press). Here are collected all known letters between the two brothers, and many are appearing here in English for the first time. The correspondence of the two novelists is interesting, and their letters shed considerable insight on their personal and quite different feelings about the political direction of Germany during these years, especially the most fractious years of their relationship throughout World War I. While this well-annotated edition is a superb achievement, readers who are not familiar with the brothers' work, or who have no concern for German culture and politics, may find little of interest here.

It may come as a shock to fans of the work of Dorothy L. Sayers that they may find little to interest them in the collection that Barbara Reynolds has

edited, *The Letters of Dorothy L. Sayers: 1937–1943, from Novelist to Playwright* (St. Martin's Press). It is not that Reynolds has done a poor job–quite the contrary. The problem is that this was a period in Sayers's life when she had forgone her detective fiction and begun to concentrate on Christian writings. Since Sayers's reputation was made primarily as a writer of mysteries, and most of the literary references in these letters are about her plays, articles, and lectures on Christianity, admirers of her fictional hero Lord Peter Wimsey will probably not enjoy this second volume of her collected letters.

James A. Grimshaw's *Cleanth Brooks and Robert Penn Warren: A Literary Correspondence* (University of Missouri Press) will also appeal to a somewhat narrow audience, no doubt an intellectual one. Brooks and Warren were friends for almost a lifetime, and their paths crossed and in many ways merged from the time they were young adults to the later periods when they taught at Louisiana State University and Yale. In more than three hundred letters the reader can follow the correspondence of these two stellar scholars who were among the fathers of New Criticism, a formalist literary criticism that received its name from John Crowe Ransom's *The New Criticism* (1941). The problem is that if you do not know that Brooks and Warren were influential New Critics, you probably will not be interested in the material in this collection, although it concerns more than New Criticism. It is a valuable work, for in their letters Brooks and Warren discuss much about the literary world that will fascinate scholars of several types of literature.

The fourth collection of letters is a bit different. Despite a disturbing first impression (the first thing the reader encounters when picking up the book is a typo inside the front flap of the dust jacket: *Madison,* Wisconsin, is spelled *Madision*), Gregory Mason's collection *Arrows of Longing: The Correspondence between Anaïs Nin and Felix Pollak, 1952–1976* is a superb collection that even readers unfamiliar with the novelist and diarist Nin, the poet Pollak, or both can understand and enjoy.

Mason provides a clear introduction sufficient for understanding the letters to follow. He explains that he has included approximately 170 of the 201 known letters and cards that Nin and Pollak wrote to each other between 1952 and 1976. When they began corresponding, Nin was going through a low point in her career and was having trouble finding a publisher for her novel *A Spy in the House of Love* (1954). Pollak, the rare-books librarian at Northwestern University and an admirer of Nin's work, wrote her a letter of appreciation, and a long friendship ensued. Pollak had his first volume of poetry published in 1963, and with five subsequent volumes of poetry he also became well known. The importance of their correspondence should not be trivialized, as Nin wrote in her diary: "These are the letters which have kept my writing alive." Since it was late in her career that Nin's work at last gained the recognition it deserved, on her own authority one would have to regard these letters as significant.

In addition to novels and diaries, Nin wrote several volumes of erotica, kept a household with a husband on one coast and a household with a lover on the other, and had several affairs, and readers may expect that the relationship between Nin and Pollak was a sexual one and that this collection of letters will be an exposé of it. Given the title (taken from Pollak's suggestion to Nin that Nietzsche's phrase "'Pfeile der Sehnsucht' [Arrows of Longing] would make a good title for a collection of poems"), such an expectation would be reasonable; but it will be disappointed.

Despite their long correspondence Pollak and Nin met face to face only once, in 1955, and clearly it was not a tryst. Perhaps one of the saddest aspects of their relationship is that briefly after that meeting Pollak was somewhat infatuated with Nin, and the content of his letters thereafter justifies the rather suggestive title of the collection. Although Pollak was married, he writes like a love-stricken teenager after the meeting: passages such as "Miss you, miss you terribly, and I wish we could have had more time together, more time together" and "There would be so much to say, so much that it is best to say nothing more" reveal both the poet-to-be and a man who felt more than mere friendship for Nin. She did not encourage him, if her letters are any indication, and soon their relationship soured, ostensibly because of artistic differences. After ten years she contacted Pollak again, and the two older, wiser, and more mellowed authors remained friends until her death from cancer in early 1977.

In terms of the content and the systematic way in which Mason has arranged the letters into chapters, prefacing each section with an overview of what is to come, this collection is easy to understand and reads as well as any collection could. Mason's endnotes and appendices added to this work make it a collection that scholars interested in either Pollak or Nin would do well to read. This fairly engrossing collection can be appreciated by anyone with a basic interest in why and how people do what they do.

"A study of why people do what they do" might describe Ellis Amburn's biography *Subterranean Kerouac: The Hidden Life of Jack Kerouac* (St. Martin's Press), but more in regard to Amburn's work than Kerouac's. What is Amburn's purpose here? His background as Kerouac's last editor puts him in a league with only a handful of Kerouac biographers, as few others actually knew their subject. Furthermore, Amburn has written other biographies—of Janis Joplin and Buddy Holly—and his research seems sound. As Amburn had unlimited access to Kerouac's papers, there should be no way that this biography could go wrong. So what is it here that does not seem quite right?

The preface is a tip-off. Amburn writes that Kerouac's concerns about "his sexuality, and the paradoxical world in which he existed, a world not unlike our own, where increasingly twisted values and ingrained prejudices still warp human nature" are part of what is new to this biography, and on the first page Amburn notes that Kerouac "moved restlessly from homoerotic to bisexual and heterosexual liaisons." This book is not so much about Kerouac's life as it is about his sex life. Of course, it is not that Kerouac's sex life was unimportant, but sex and his struggles with his sexuality appear to be almost all that were important and motivating to him, as Amburn presents Kerouac's life. For example, Amburn blatantly proclaims that although many people

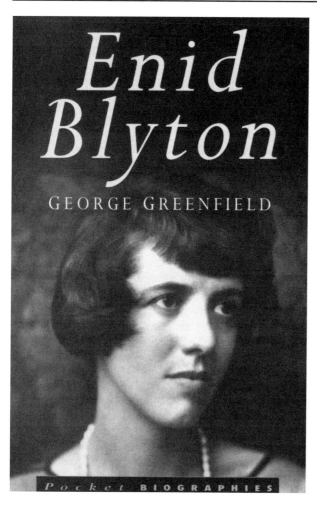

Dust jacket for the biography of the prolific British writer of children's books

assume alcohol killed Kerouac, it did so only because "he could not accept his sexuality."

This is not a bad biography, however. It is well written and informative, and anyone who has any interest in Kerouac should read it. What is problematic is that Amburn's main goal appears to be to titillate, as if a biography without the references to Kerouac's sexuality simply would not suffice. Amburn seems to try to lay out as much dirt as he possibly can, and it is easy to attribute this proclivity to his background as a biographer of rock stars. Albert Goldman's biographies of Elvis Presley and John Lennon proved long ago that dirt sells better than adulation, and perhaps Amburn's previous experiences as a biographer of pop culture icons taught him that. While this biography is not overtly mean-spirited—Amburn does not feel any hostility toward Kerouac—it is what might be called a "businessman's" biography, one written with the biographer's bank account in view. While this book undoubtedly has sold and will continue to sell well, it is

regrettable that Amburn could not have taken the edge off its blatant sensationalism by using some moderation.

If Amburn is determined to tell every possible detail of Kerouac's sex life, Ian MacNiven is just as resolutely determined not to tell us enough in *Lawrence Durrell: A Biography* (Faber and Faber), even if we think he should. MacNiven's lengthy biography of Durrell is masterfully presented, chronicling one of the central figures of twentieth-century prose fiction. Though Durrell's *The Alexandria Quartet* (1957–1960) was read by the flower children of the 1960s, who saw in it a testament to their own call for sexual freedom, Durrell's work is today not as well known as it should be. Perhaps MacNiven's biography will contribute to a greater knowledge of and appreciation for Durrell's work. At the least, the richness of detail and the ample documentation of MacNiven's book ensures that it will supersede Gordon Bowker's *Through the Dark Labyrinth,* which appeared just a year ago.

Bowker's failing is MacNiven's strength. Where Bowker has been unable to obtain permission to quote from Durrell's works, MacNiven's biography is full of quotation from Durrell's letters, novels, and poems. MacNiven, a keen critic of Durrell, is well aware of his subject's violent, turbulent side, but he is also, perhaps, too respectful and forgiving toward Durrell, especially toward Durrell's relationships with women. Leaving his first wife in Alexandria to care for their daughter, Durrell took up with Eve Cohen, the reputed model for Justine in the novel of that name. The marriage ended in disaster, brought on in part by Durrell's brutality and monomania, though Durrell saw the cause as Cohen's "Jewish hysteria and religious mania." Where Durrell's novels often show the male as a victim of a manipulating female, in Durrell's personal life it was probably the other way around.

MacNiven is also circumspect and vague about whether Durrell cuckolded Henry Miller, though there is some evidence that Durrell slept with Miller's Japanese wife, Hoki. MacNiven is tight-lipped about the affair. He relates that Hoki wrote Durrell an angry letter over his silence about the affair, that Durrell visited the Millers while on a book tour, and that Hoki accompanied Durrell to Walt Disney World. He gives no concrete answers, but an abundance of inference. MacNiven dismisses (perhaps rightly) any attempt to blame Durrell for his daughter's suicide. Sappho accused Durrell of incest after the death of Durrell's third wife, Claude, but MacNiven finds the only evidence to be based on recovered memories and a few hints or clues during her psychoanalysis. Though incest is pervasive in Durrell's fiction, MacNiven reminds us, it is almost never between father and daughter, but rather between brother and sister.

This biography will certainly increase interest in Durrell's career and work, and the mere fact that Durrell's life is much like a travelogue—India, England, Egypt, Rhodes, Argentina, Yugoslavia, Cyprus, and France were his residences at one time or another—only makes reading about his life more compelling. Durrell witnessed or participated in many of the major events that shaped our century, from his official duties during World War II and his diplomatic role in Yugoslavia under Marshal Tito to his direct involvement in Cypriot independence, as recorded in his travel book, *Bitter Lemons* (1957), and his friends and acquaintances (Miller, Nin, T. S. Eliot, Richard Aldington, and George Seferis) read like a Who's Who of twentieth-century literati. So there is something here to interest every reader. While a more balanced biography may eventually replace MacNiven's work, it probably will not be for many years.

Like Durrell, who died in 1990, several other recently deceased authors were subjects of biographical works this year. In *The Quest for Graham Greene* (St. Martin's Press) W. J. West explores the novelist's life in a way that underscores how many of our favorite authors were far from tweed-coated eggheads who sit around and think about literature all day. Through diligent research, West has uncovered letters and papers that shed additional light on the life of the enigmatic Greene, who was a British agent for MI6 and was also involved in some rather shady tax evasion schemes in the 1960s. Whether it be Greene's dealings with espionage or communism, there is much to interest the reader in this well-researched work.

Communism also lurks in the background of Eric Jacobs's *Kingsley Amis: A Biography* (St. Martin's Press), as Amis, who died in 1995, was a communist as a young adult. Despite Amis's wit, intelligence, and literary genius, the novelist had his share of skeletons in his closet, and his exploits as a boozer and womanizer are carefully referenced here. This is an entertaining read, especially as it is easy to sense that Jacobs, who began this project before Amis died in 1995, got much of his information and anecdotes straight from Amis, and the biographer's closeness to his source is evident in his presentation. Readers of Amis's literary works who are interested in his life will no doubt be pleased with this project, as it exposes a man who was as caustic and at times self-destructive as he was intelligent.

It is doubtful, however, that any work published this year depicts a man who was more intelligent and self-destructive than James Dickey, and in Christopher Dickey's *Summer of Deliverance* (Simon and Schuster) these qualities are explored fully. Christopher must

have questioned his father's behavior and their relationship many times through the years, and his presentation of that relationship makes *Summer of Deliverance* succeed where so many other biographies or memoirs fail. Many biographers plead for our sympathy but Christopher Dickey never does: he does not have to, because his story wrings it from us. In exploring the author's relationship with his father, which vacillated between love and hate for many years, the work resembles the relationship itself: up and down, back and forth, but not all hero-worship—the style that befalls, and befouls, so many biographies. This is no dry academic biography, as Christopher Dickey, the bureau chief for *Newsweek* in Paris and an accomplished author of several nonfiction works and a novel, knows how to write with style and emotion.

"My father was a great poet, a famous novelist, a powerful intellect, and a son of a bitch I hated," Dickey writes on the first page, and this sentence may well sum up their complicated relationship. When we read of the athlete, flyer, and creative genius that the elder Dickey was, it is hard not to admire many things about the man. At times, too, especially in the first half of the work, which covers the years before the biographer entered college, the reader never knows whether to pity or envy Christopher Dickey. Certainly as James Dickey's fame and alcoholism increased, the Dickey household at times must have been a hellish place. On the other hand, how can we read that Christopher Dickey as a child was sketched by Pablo Picasso; lived in Paris and then in Positano, Italy, where neighbors were John Steinbeck and Mary Norton, author of *The Borrowers* (1953); had his own Jaguar XKE in high school; and "rubbed elbows" with literary greats such as Norman Mailer and William F. Buckley—and not wish ourselves in his place? Still, these amenities came at a high price, and Christopher Dickey's candor is refreshing. He does not sugarcoat, and he tells us about his father's affairs, his parents' fights, and long bouts of drinking. Perhaps this candor shows the journalist in Christopher Dickey, but there is also much of the ability to manipulate language that his father possessed. It may be that Christopher Dickey, who has worked hard to succeed on his own and not through his father's influence, would take this as a compliment: he writes much like his father at times. And no matter what James Dickey may have done that was ill advised or reprehensible, no one has ever argued that he was not a superb writer.

It is perhaps ironic that among nonacademics Dickey is known better as a novelist than as a poet, primarily because of the success of *Deliverance* (1970). There is ample discussion of this work and of its impact on the Dickey household, as well as some interesting behind-the-scenes information about the filming of the movie. We also see James Dickey's downward spiral that came with the success of *Deliverance,* including his increasing problems with alcohol, Maxine Dickey's alcohol-induced death, his quick marriage a few months later to a troubled young woman, and subsequently his almost total estrangement from his sons. It is amazing that Christopher Dickey can still love his father after the many trials he went through, and it is amazing that the reader can, also. Christopher Dickey did, and we do: when James Dickey tells his son, "I do love you so much," 260 pages into this memoir, we feel the emotion that his son must have felt that day. Christopher Dickey recounts the good and the bad for us, and at the end we, like the biographer, still care about James Dickey because the author can write with power and emotion, can make us feel as he does.

Just as Christopher Dickey's ability to tell us the good with the bad makes his work an excellent memoir, withholding information can severely harm a biography. Does the fact that the subject is living influence the biographer to overdo the platitudes? Ezenwa-Ohaeto's *Chinua Achebe* (Indiana University Press) is a work with much insight that a reader will find nowhere else, but the hero worship of Ezenwa-Ohaeto, Achebe's former student, makes the work too sugary. As a look at the life of one of the more important African writers, it is informative, though biased. Yet, by comparison, Millicent Dillon's *You Are Not I: A Portrait of Paul Bowles* (University of California Press) makes Ezenwa-Ohaeto's work look less slanted than it is. Dillon's biography—which is as much about her as it is about Bowles (and this may be the biggest problem with her book)—is all about hero worship, and it becomes difficult to read. If you love both Bowles and Dillon you may like this biography; otherwise, it is a doubtful read.

Some biographers, of course, know how to treat a living subject effectively, and D. M. Thomas's *Alexander Solzhenitsyn: A Century in His Life* (St. Martin's Press) does so. Perhaps Thomas's skill as a novelist makes this work so readable, and though it is clear that Thomas must admire Solzhenitsyn, this biographer never purely glorifies his subject. Thomas treats the Nobel Prize winner as honestly as he can—and in a way that brought Solzhenitsyn's wrath on him.

The book caused a furor even before it was released, and St. Martin's Press, one of the leaders in the field of literary biography (it has more titles reviewed in this essay than any other publisher), wrung every ounce of publicity out of Solzhenitsyn's ire. His displeasure was primarily aroused because, like any good biographer, Thomas knew that the way to get the whole story was to get not only the subject's version of events but also opposing viewpoints. Thomas therefore

interviewed Natalya Reshetovskaya, Solzhenitsyn's first wife, and this angered Solzhenitsyn. While Reshetovskaya's versions differ from Solzhenitsyn's on many points, Thomas appears to be trying to do no more than to tell a story as accurately as he can. In any event, the publicity generated by the bad feelings between Solzhenitsyn and his biographer worked to Thomas's advantage. Readers should not let the public furor obscure the fact that this is a good biography: Thomas's years of research provide a balanced look at an important man and important author.

"Balanced" is not a term one would use to describe Auberon Waugh's autobiography; "insufferable" is more apt. Perhaps self-worship was the motivation for writing *Will This Do?: The First Fifty Years of Auberon Waugh; An Autobiography* (Carroll and Graf), because the reader has to wonder: why did Waugh write this book? Was it to write about his father, Evelyn Waugh (who, as presented here, is interesting)—or to write about himself (who, as presented here, is not)? The writer of this autobiography is ostensibly its subject, but we get much insight into his father, especially when we read Evelyn Waugh's comments on his oldest son, such as one declaring that "Bron is clumsy and disheveled, sly, without intellectual, aesthetic or spiritual interest." Indeed, this autobiography seems most appealing as we read Evelyn Waugh's thoughts about his children, thoughts that he recorded for posterity. Peppered throughout the father's diaries are comments such as "My children were much in evidence and boring," and "My children weary me. I can only see them as defective adults: feckless, destructive, frivolous, sensual, humorless."

While we may read these as representative comments of a creative man who was unable to bring himself down to his children's level, his other comments strike us otherwise. When we read that during World War II, when Auberon was four, his father had his books sent away from London to ensure that they would not be destroyed during an air raid and yet took Auberon to London at the same time, we feel that this is odd. When his father writes, "It would seem that I prefer my books to my son . . . but the truth is that a child can be easily replaced, while a book destroyed is utterly lost," it makes us feel something more than merely uncomfortable.

Perhaps many American readers wonder who Auberon Waugh is, besides Evelyn Waugh's son. He has written several novels, but he seems to be more journalist than artist. When he recalls his first meeting with James Dickey and Dickey's first wife, Maxine, he insultingly refers to her as Dickey's "speechless, catatonic wife." In condescendingly recounting details of his visit to Dickey's home in South Carolina, Waugh notes

Dust jacket for the autobiography of the American literary and social critic and man of letters

that "I had never heard of Dickey or his poetry" and that bookshop owners from whom he sought to acquire some of the poet's works in Virginia told him that they "had never heard of him." (This seems odd, since Waugh's visit was just three years after Dickey had won the National Book Award for Poetry and the Melville Cain Award of the Poetry Society of America). In any event most readers will find little interest in this autobiography other than in Waugh's reminiscences about his father because most readers simply have never heard of Auberon Waugh. Much of what is in this autobiography is one long inside joke, a narrative that we can neither fully enjoy nor fully understand. Certainly Auberon Waugh, as someone unfamiliar with a prominent American literary figure of the latter half of this century, should understand that.

Just as Auberon Waugh attracts an audience primarily through what he offers about his more famous and interesting father, one of the main selling points of Joyce Maynard's autobiography, *At Home in the World* (Picador), is that she had an intimate relationship with

J. D. Salinger: not a tawdry, sex-only, one-night stand but an extended live-in relationship that lasted about a year, when she was nineteen and he was fifty-three. What makes this an effective work is that it does not seem mean-spirited, and her purpose does not seem to be to ruin that sacred privacy that Salinger is so determined to permit no one ever to invade. It seems as if Maynard fell truly and deeply in love with Salinger, and when the crash came, it nearly wrecked her life.

In 1998 the young-woman/famous-older-man situation may suggest the Monica Lewinsky/Bill Clinton fiasco. Salinger instigated the relationship and urged Maynard to move in with him. Even as a freshman at Yale University, she was a young writer of promise, and after Salinger had read about her in *The New York Times Magazine* he began to correspond with her. Naturally flattered by such attention from a man who was not only a famous writer but also extremely guarded, she entered into a relationship that blossomed. While their days together sound hardly perfect, it is easy to see how this impressionable young girl filled with doubts about her own worth and sexuality would have leaped at an opportunity to become Salinger's lover.

Eventually Salinger sent her packing, but these revelations convey more disappointment and hurt than malice. Frankly, it is surprising that Maynard is not more bitter and vindictive than she is. Certainly legions of Salinger followers may see the work as a way for Maynard to get even by doing what Salinger hates the most–invading his privacy–but they are not reading closely enough. While a few critics have complained that Salinger is the centerpiece and that readers would not buy the book if he were not, anyone who reads it will realize that–while this may have some truth–Maynard has her own story to tell. Unlike Auberon Waugh, though, she is not smug and does not seem to be making claims of her own greatness. She simply wants to tell us about her fascinating, often painful and pathetic life. Readers seem either to love or hate this book, but either way, it is one of those books that a person well informed in literary biography will consider a must-read.

George Steiner's *Errata* (Yale University Press) will have to sell on its own merit, because there are no Salingers or Evelyn Waughs here. There do not have to be. Steiner is an important figure in twentieth-century literature, and readers will enjoy this memoir for what it tells about the author. It would be unfair, however, to say that this is simply an autobiography; it reads more like a novel than a recounting of the author's life. His life is and has been interesting, and the graceful, flowing, intelligent style of this book makes it a joy to read.

Perhaps it is a measure of Steiner's skill that we often forget we are reading about his life when we peruse these pages. The book is so beautifully written that, even as he writes of the Nazis murdering millions of Jews, we forget how terribly such events must have affected this bookish young Jewish boy living in Paris and then, by 1940, in the United States. In the first chapters, and only there, Steiner's talents as a writer work against him, because certainly he does not intend that we forget or minimize the horrific events occurring in Europe when he was a boy. Yet, in reading a book crafted with the elegance of a watercolor, we tend to forget that we are reading about someone's life at a horrible time in our history.

The novelistic tendencies never disappear, and when Steiner recounts his first days in college, his adventures with his roommate–a former paratrooper named Alfie who arranged for Steiner to lose his virginity to a prostitute whom "Alfie had briefed"–seem both beautiful and poignant, despite the subject matter. Each chapter seems to start with a retelling of Steiner's life, but each just as systematically evolves into often-philosophical essays on diverse subjects.

This is not an autobiography for literary dilettantes. Steiner–who began learning Greek before the age of six and who holds a B.A. from the University of Chicago, an M.A. from Harvard, and a Ph.D. from Oxford–writes in a way that uses his deep, varied knowledge. He offers his reflections on Shakespeare, Voltaire, Leo Tolstoy, Samuel Johnson, Alexander Pope, Virgil, and other famous writers, and he incorporates references to theoretical approaches ranging from New Criticism to deconstruction as casually (and, one suspects, as effortlessly) as another autobiographer might refer to a spouse. (It is odd, but Steiner's wife is one person in his life about whom we never read much in this book; she is mentioned only twice, and only once by name.) There is simply no getting away from the fact that this memoir is written by a superbly talented, intelligent man. As a result, *Errata* provides a nice finish to a year in which many autobiographies promised much but delivered little.

Dictionary of Literary Biography Yearbook Award for a Distinguished Literary Biography Published in 1998

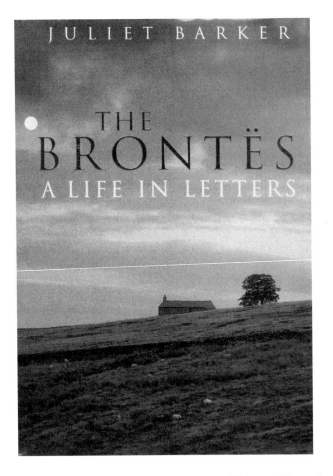

Dust jacket for the book that received the 1998 Dictionary of Literary Biography *Award for a distinguished biographical work*

Juliet Barker's *The Brontës: A Life in Letters* is, as the title suggests, a collection of letters and not a biography. Yet, it reads like a biography, as every important letter both by and about the Brontës is in this collection, including many published for the first time. Preferring to have the reader get to know the Brontës from their correspondence, Barker has suppressed nothing that might paint them in an unflattering light. This collection will be indispensable to Brontë scholars for years to come.

–James R. Simmons Jr.

The Year in Drama

Amy S. Green
John Jay College of Criminal Justice

The year 1998 was an active one in American drama, some of it dealing with issues of private versus public morality, much of it written by and about gay people, and the best of it produced off Broadway. Big-budget musicals, European imports, and productions built around featured celebrities continue to provide the chief interest on Broadway. By year's end there were only a few new American plays on the Great White Way–three of which were musicals. The bulk of the box office for musicals in one of Broadway's biggest revenue seasons came from long-running stalwarts such as *Cats, Les Miserables,* and *Miss Saigon* alongside more-recent megahits such as *Chicago, Rent,* and *The Lion King.* In 1998 they were joined by remountings of established musicals, including *On the Town, High Society, As Thousands Cheer,* and *Little Me.* The most noteworthy of these was a dark British revisioning of John Kander and Fred Ebb's *Cabaret,* directed by Sam Mendes and starring Natasha Richardson as Sally Bowles and Alan Cumming as a libidinally-unleashed Emcee. On 21 July the production's Times Square nightclub-turned-Kit Kat Club fell victim to the collapse of a construction elevator on a nearby building. After closing for the summer, the show reopened in a converted Studio 54, where Jennifer Jason Leigh took over the lead.

Broadway also enjoyed two successful classical revivals in 1998, both with London origins. Geraldine McEwan and Richard Briars played the elderly couple in Eugène Ionesco's *The Chairs* under the crisp, funny, and poignant direction of Simon McBurney. Zoe Wanamaker took the city by storm in the title role of *Electra* in a boldly revisionist staging of a new translation by Frank McGuiness, whose version of Henrik Ibsen's *A Doll's House* enjoyed similar success a couple seasons ago. The stunning new production, directed by David Leveaux, originated in London and switched to its current American cast for a limited run at the McCarter Theatre in Princeton, New Jersey, earlier in the year. Claire Bloom co-starred in the role of Clytemnestra.

Otherwise, the year on Broadway consisted of several new American musicals, including two adaptations– *Ragtime,* from the E. L. Doctorow novel, and *Footloose,* a

screen-to-stage extravaganza of youthful energy, acrobatic dance numbers, and mindless sentiment. *The Capeman* (book by West Indian playwright Derek Walcott), Paul Simon's salsa-spiked story of a Puerto Rican American youth who spent twenty years in prison for the schoolyard murder of two rival gang members in the summer of 1959, and *Parade,* the true story of Leo Frank, a Northern Jew tried and convicted for killing a girl in Atlanta in 1913, with book by Alfred Uhry and lyrics and music by Broadway first-timer Jason Robert Brown, were the two other American musicals. There were also nonmusical imports from Europe (*Art, The Beauty Queen of Leenane, The Judas Kiss,* and *The Blue Room*), from Australia (*Honour*), and, from the off-Broadway and regional circuits, a meager three new American plays: *Golden Child* by David Henry Hwang, *Side Man* by Warren Leight, and *Getting and Spending* by Michael Chipega.

In smaller New York venues and the lively circuit of regional theaters several dozen new American plays hit the boards, a steady stream of new works by established writers such as Arthur Miller, Sam Shepard, A. R. Gurney, and Lanford Wilson, none of whose plays were produced on Broadway. Off-Broadway theaters presented a far livelier and more innovative array of new American plays and musicals, and among these new works Terrence McNally's *Corpus Christi* and Paul Rudnick's *The Most Fabulous Story Ever Told* rubbed our noses in the hypocritical coexistence of Christian tolerance and homophobia, while Craig Lucas vented a gay artist's outrage in *The Dying Gaul,* a searing, Hollywood-bashing thriller. Hollywood skulduggery was also the subject of *Mizlansky/Zilinsky or "schmucks,"* Jon Robin Baitz's biting satire about a sleazy former horror-film producer who becomes an illegal tax-shelter salesman. This production ran at the Manhattan Theatre Club, with Nathan Lane as the oddly appealing main character.

Miller (*Mr. Peters' Connections*), Michael Christofer (*Amazing Grace*), and newcomer Margaret Edson (*Wit*) pondered the fear and mystery of impending death, while William Finn turned a near-fatal medical episode into *A New Brain,* a new musical that premiered at Lincoln Center's Mitzi Newhouse Theatre. Gurney added

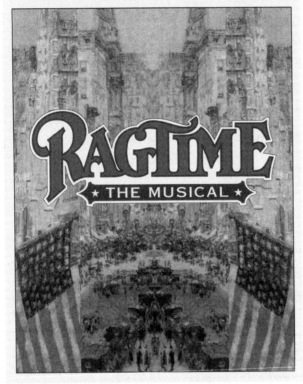

Program for the production based on E. L. Doctorow's portrait of changes in New York City life at the turn of the twentieth century (Playbill® used by permission)

Shange, Marsha Norman, and William Finn, each of whom contributed a short play in response to a particular Shakespearean sonnet.

Several off-Broadway plays concerned African American history. These included *Dinah Was,* Oliver Goldstick's musical that starred Yvette Freeman in a rousing portrait of jazz vocalist Dinah Washington; John Henry Redwood's *The Old Settler,* a tale of lonely-hearts romance in Harlem during the 1940s; and Doug Grissom's *Deep Down,* in which a black convict, just released in 1963 and hired by a poor white Florida farmer to dig for treasure on his land, finds artifacts from nineteenth-century slaves. Set in the same turbulent decade, *The American Jesus Christ* by Don Wilson Grissom portrayed five black women working in a Southern coffee shop.

As usual, the regional theaters produced a mix of classical revivals, New York hits from last season, and a healthy share of new work by established and brand-new playwrights. Highlights of those new works produced in the regionals range from off-beat, postmodern experiments to Broadway-bound music spectacles. In addition to the Wanamaker *Electra,* the McCarter Theatre in Princeton produced a searing revival of Garcia Lorca's *The House of Bernarda Alba,* directed by Artistic Director Emily Mann; *Meshugah,* Mann's adaptation of a novel by Isaac Bashevis Singer; and Richard Greenberg's *Safe as Houses,* also directed by Mann. Greenberg's play is a cautionary tale about a middle-aged man's infatuation with his son's teenage babysitter. The plot covers the fifteen years after the crush begins; the humor of the first act gets stuck in the throat as one watches the marriage of Ken and his wife Irene unravel. David Margulies and Michael Learned brought depth and enormous emotional truth to the roles of unhappy husband and wife. Greenberg also had a second regional-theater premiere in 1998 with *Hurrah at Last,* a biting comedy at the South Coast Repertory.

Further yet from New York City, Steppenwolf Theatre in Chicago presented *The Berlin Circle,* a retelling of the ancient Chinese fable that provides the story for Bertolt Brecht's *The Caucasian Chalk Circle.* Playwright/historian Charles L. Mee updates the setting of this tale to Berlin, 1989, when the wall that has divided the city tumbles. A baby boy is abandoned in a melee at Brecht's own Berliner Ensemble, and a wealthy American woman and a ragged but good-hearted East German babysitter appropriately named Dulle are forced to take charge of him. The future is promising and precarious.

To underscore the raison d'être of this adaptation—an examination of the underlying cultural and economic forces that compete for the soul of the city just as the women finally tussle for custody of the baby—Mee's imaginative postmodern text introduces historical charac-

three new chapters to his chronicle of WASP America with *Labor Day* at the Manhattan Theatre Club, *Far East* at the Mitzi Newhouse, and *Darlene and The Guest Lecturer* at the George Street Playhouse in New Brunswick, New Jersey. In addition, Beth Henley teamed with actress Holly Hunter for *Impossible Marriage,* their sixth consecutive collaboration and another gothic Southern fable. Alan Arkin and Elaine May joined forces as writer/performers for *Power Plays,* three comic one-acts; Frances McDormand took the role of Jocasta in Dare Clubb's modern twist on *Oedipus;* and Sam Shepard's *Eyes for Consuela* retold the grim morality tale of Octavio Paz's short story "The Blue Bouquet," in which a lonely American on the run is confronted and transformed by an ominous Mexican whose wife collects blue eyeballs. Perhaps the most eclectic evening of theater this year was in *Love's Fire,* an anthology of one-acts by Eric Bogosian, Wendy Wasserstein, Tony Kushner, John Guare, Ntozake ters such as Warren Buffet, Andy Warhol, and Heiner Muller. Under Tina Landau's imaginative direction, the cast celebrates the new era with a brisk rendition of "Y.M.C.A.," and the surrogate mothers and the baby, a trio on the lam, cross a rope bridge suspended over the auditorium. Following the contours of the classic tale, the mothers are eventually captured by a pair of clownish cops in this production. The mothers are tried for kidnapping the boy, but in Mee's fillip of an ending, the child's rightful mother is determined by compromise—the morally murky stuff by which contemporary social and political upheavals are so often resolved.

In Atlanta the Alliance Theatre joined with Disney, Incorporated, to host the first staging of *Elaborate Lives: The Legend of Aida,* the latest musical collaboration by Elton John and Tim Rice. The big-budget production, from the book by Linda Woolverton, starred Heather Headley as the legendary Nubian princess and Hank Stratton as her star-crossed Egyptian lover. Critics found the pre-Broadway tryout to be numbingly overproduced, so it is a good bet that the show will be substantially renovated by the time it makes its way to New York.

On the West Coast, The Mark Taper Forum in Los Angeles invested heavily in an epic dramatization of novelist John Irving's *The Cider House Rules.* Countering the trend toward leaner budgets and briefer playing times for nonmusicals, Peter Parnell wrote the six-hour, sixty-character script, which covers four generations in a small Maine town where Dr. Wilbur Larch devotedly performs abortions. Like other marathon theatrical productions that followed the Royal Shakespeare Company's *Nicolas Nickelby* (Peter Brook's *Mahabarata,* Ariane Mnouchkine's *Les Atrides,* and Tony Kushner's *Angels in America* come to mind), the play was presented in two parts that could be seen consecutively on a single day/evening schedule or separately on different nights. Parnell's script retains large chunks of Irving's verbally acrobatic inner monologues that give the characters a lot of depth and the cast members a lot to wrap their mouths around.

Taking an overview of the social and political affairs of new American plays produced in 1998 gives one a dim optimism about the theater. Despite strides for women, African Americans, Latinos, and Asian Americans as performers and subjects of American plays, American playwriting—at least the kind that gets produced—is still largely the province of white males. One significant change behind that iron curtain must be noted, however, in that plays by gay men seem to have attained prominence on the American stage. Alongside many highly acclaimed regional—and far more explicit—revivals of lesser-known plays by Tennessee Williams were new works about openly gay issues by Terrence McNally, Craig Lucas, Paul Rudnick, and others.

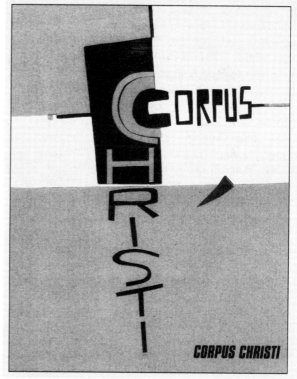

Program for Terrence McNally's controversial play presenting a contemporary gay Christ figure (Playbill® used by permission)

Indeed, McNally's depiction of a modern-day, gay Christ figure in *Corpus Christi* became the cause célèbre of the theatrical year. The Manhattan Theatre Club scheduled the production but then removed it from the list because of threats from right-wing Christian groups. When the arts community protested this acquiescence of the theater, MTC reinstated the play—and installed metal detectors at the entrance to the lobby. A continuing vigil by protesters for and against the production formed outside the theater at every performance, and the media engaged in yet another debate about censorship versus free artistic expression.

As 1998 continued the trend toward bigger musicals and smaller dramas (with fewer characters, smaller budgets, shorter playing times—most of the new plays were ninety minutes long and without intermissions), the ultimate minimalist theater form also continued to flourish. On and off Broadway one-person shows proliferated, ranging from John Leguizamo's hilarious, dead-on impersonations of his Latino friends and family in *Freak,* comedian Jerry Seinfeld's one-week summer solo stint, *I'm Telling You for the Last Time,* and Sandra Bernhard's irreverent celebrity sendup/rock-and-roll concert, *I'm Still Here . . . Damn It!* to Mandy Patinkin's all-Yiddish evening of songs, *Mamaloshen.* Solo acts off Broadway included those such as Karen Findlay in *The Return of the Chocolate-Smeared Woman* at the Flea Theater in Tribeca; Tom Driscoll's *Creative Fluid,* in which he devoted the entire hour of stage time to "America's preoccupation with the dick"; Danny Hoch's exploration of the young urban male in *Jails, Hospitals, and Hip Hop* at P.S. 122; and more traditional monodramas such as *All Under Heaven,* featuring Valerie Harper as Pearl S. Buck, and *Mystery School* by Paul Selig, which cast Broadway and televison veteran Tyne Daly as five women, each grappling in her own way with millennial anguish and visions. One wonders whether virtual reality might displace live actors altogether in the new millennium.

If the death knell of the American theater echoed less thunderously than usual in 1998, it was because the doomsayers have finally learned to look beyond Broadway for the dramatic vitality of the nation. Dramatic production off Broadway was just as it should be—adventurous, uneven, controversial, and outspoken. What follows are more-detailed assessments of some of the year's dramatic highlights.

BROADWAY IN 1998

The first new American musical to open on Broadway in 1998 was *The Capeman,* an ambitious but flawed attempt by pop performer/composer Paul Simon and Nobel Prize–winning playwright Derek Walcott to chronicle the jailhouse redemption of Salvador Agron, the young Puerto Rican American who spent twenty years in prison for stabbing to death two members of a rival youth gang in a schoolyard brawl on the West Side of Manhattan in 1959. With its controversial subject matter, Simon and Walcott heading the creative team, and two major Latino pop stars (Marc Antony as the teen and Ruben Blades as the adult incarnation of Agron), *Capeman* attracted considerable pre-opening attention. Friends of the late Agron clashed with relatives of his victims over how willing the show was to honor the murderer's memory. Puerto Rican community leaders resented Simon's appropriation of Latino musical forms and feared that the show would reinforce negative stereotypes of savage Hispanic teens.

Walcott admitted to having taken a while to come around to Simon's sympathy for the main character, who earned his titular sobriquet by the garment he wore on the night of the killings. Defending himself as a victim of anti–Puerto Rican prejudice and oppression, Agron ini-

tially refused to repent his violent crime. The first act traces his troubled childhood, when his father left him and his forsaken mother in Puerto Rico. After she remarried a fervently religious man who tyrannized the young Sal, the family arrived in Hell's Kitchen, where Agron sought acceptance and solace in the gangs and drugs and fights that led him to commit the double murder. Walcott's second act focuses on the spiritual and intellectual transformation of the imprisoned adult through poetry and Communism. Simon's salsa-spiced songs inspire the same nasty accusations of co-opting and exploiting native forms aroused by his previous forays into South African and South American genres. Critics liked the score, however, and *The Capeman* is expected to survive beyond Broadway.

The most awaited new musical of the year was *Ragtime,* adapted from E. L. Doctorow's 1975 novel, with book by Terrence McNally and music and lyrics by Stephen Flaherty and Lynn Ahrens. *Ragtime* finally made its way to Broadway after three years of development outside New York City. Doctorow's sprawling story of New York as microcosm of American society at the turn of the twentieth century chronicles the simultaneous fortunes of three representative families. Members of the first are well-to-do New Rochelle WASPs; the second, struggling urban blacks; and the third, Russian-immigrant Jews on the rise.

McNally's stage version faithfully retains the period details from the novel and neatly points and counterpoints the triptych of sagas to their devastating climax. In the spectacular twelve-minute opening number of the show all three groups present themselves to the audience in meticulously metered lyrics set to Flaherty's intricate thematic rag. From there the three stories unfold and intersect. McNally's script retains appearances by historical figures such as Henry Ford, Booker T. Washington, Evelyn Nesbit, Emma Goldmann, and Harry Houdini, whose presence underscores the theme of dizzying technological progress and the social upheavals it causes. Frank Galati directed the opulent production, which takes its aesthetic cues from these two preoccupations.

Headlining the cast were Audra McDonald and Brian Stokes Mitchell as Sarah and Coalhouse Walker, the hapless black couple who begin the play looking forward to their son's better future in a tender duet, "On the Wings of a Dream," and end with Walker's tragic death. Peter Friedman played Tateh, who goes from Ellis Island to finding success as a silent-film director.

Despite its generous funding, production pedigree, and box-office draw, *Ragtime* received mixed reviews. The most frequent criticisms cited a stilted, almost mathematical quality to its dramaturgy and pacing, a result of its perhaps too-reverent fidelity to its source. In *The New York Times* on 19 January, Ben Brantley wrote that he was reminded of "an instructional diorama in a pavilion at a world's fair" rather than the penetrating, dynamic tale of confusion, frustration, and thwarted optimism in the novel. Other critics noted that characterization was sacrificed to spectacle, and this lack of characterization left them intellectually stimulated but not emotionally involved.

The new musical season limped along with *Footloose*, yet another screen-to-stage adaptation. Youthful, energetic, and beside the point, the Broadway version whitewashed the last trace of the smoldering sensuality that the movie has and replaced it with good-natured acrobatics. When a Chicago bad-boy (Kevin Bacon in the movie) moves to the small, high-minded Midwestern town and threatens to teach his high school mates to dance, there is something seductive and dangerous enough to upset the town elders' equilibrium. The sanitized version of the main character in the musical is so good-natured that it is impossible to understand the fuss. It is equally hard to imagine why Dean Pitchford, who wrote both the screenplay and the stage adaptation (with director/co-author Walter Bobbie), participated in neutering his playful original.

The musical year ended with *Parade*, Uhry and composer/lyricist Jason Robert Brown's dramatization of the life of Leo Frank. In one of the first "trials of the century" in 1913 Frank was accused and convicted of murdering a thirteen-year-old girl who worked in an Atlanta pencil factory where he was a supervisor. Professing his innocence as a wrongfully prosecuted Jewish Yankee in a deeply anti-Semitic South, he spent two years in prison. After his death sentence was commuted in a stunning move by the governor of Georgia in 1915, outraged protesters marched through the streets, abducted Frank from prison, and lynched him. The story assumes the proportions of a genuine American conflagration of race, class, sex, and religion because a black delinquent, who may in fact have done the killing, had been the prosecution's star witness, and there were other accusations that Frank had been having sex with female employees.

The late-year Lincoln Center premiere of the complex musical drama based on this story was directed by Harold Prince. The script documents the trial and its aftermath, especially Frank's arranged marriage to a rather superficial woman who develops into his most ardent supporter. Musical numbers that reveal the thoughts and feelings of the various characters include a hoedown, in which white Atlantans celebrate Frank's conviction; "A Rumblin' and a Rollin'," in which black citizens vent their resentment of Northern whites who come to protest Frank's conviction; and the fanciful solo in the middle of the trial, when the prim-and-proper Frank (Brent Carver), forced to sit through the excruciating testimony of office girls who accuse him of having

Program for Alfred Uhry and Jason Robert Brown's drama of racial, sexual, and religious turmoil aroused by an Atlanta murder in 1913 (Playbill® used by permission)

demanded sexual favors, bursts out with "Come Up to My Office"—in which he becomes the predator whom the women describe. Vincent Canby, writing for *The New York Times* (27 December), found the material to be compelling but the script and all but the two central characters to be flat and stereotypical.

European imports dominated the nonmusical year on Broadway. From France via London came the American premiere of *Art*, Yazimina Reza's 1994 comic meditation on taste and friendship, in its English translation by Christopher Hampton. As a trio of old pals who clash and spar over the purchase of a white-on-white painting, Alan Alda, Victor Garbor, and Alfred Molina starred in the New York production. The painting itself, hardly avant-garde in the 1990s, is really a pretext for Reza's exploration of the triad's shifting tensions and allegiances. As their arguments progress swiftly from the aesthetic to the personal, the three men peck away at the trendy values that they had thought bound them together, only to recoil from the brink of breaching their unmasked friendships. As the action of the play shifts to each man's apartment and reveals each character's favorite work of art, Yvan suffers most from his companions' squabbles. Reza's most accomplished writing is in Yvan's long manic monologue about the trials of arranging his coming–and uninspiring–wedding. In the happy ending the trio preserves the status quo by settling for tolerance of both their varying artistic tastes and their personal foibles.

Honour, by Australian Joanna Murray-Smith, was notable for bringing Jane Alexander back to the stage after her stint as chair of the National Endowment for the Arts. It is unfortunate that the script barely deserves the attentions of such a major talent. The formulaic plot concerns the marital dissolution of Honor (Alexander) and Gus (Robert Foxworth), whose thirty-two-year liaison is rent asunder by the wiles of twenty-nine-year-old Claudia (Laura Linney), a go-getter journalist in a miniskirt who jolts Gus out of his midlife crisis and the familiar embrace of his family. Years ago Honor had given up her creative pursuits (she used to write poetry) to raise the couple's daughter Sophie (Enid Graham), now twenty-four years old. Gus's desertion forces Honor to reassess her choices and commitments. In an early scene of ironic foreshadowing Gus has wondered aloud, "What is it about facing death that makes a man turn to a tanning salon?" The all-too-clever dialogue in this ninety-minute series of two-character scenes remains frustratingly glib.

The straight play most likely to go down in Broadway history from 1998 would have to be twenty-seven-year-old Martin McDonagh's *The Beauty Queen of Leenane,* which in April was transferred, in its native production by the Druid Theatre Company of Galway, from its limited run at the off-Broadway Atlantic Theatre Company. McDonagh's queen is Maureen Folan, forty-something, unmarried, unemployed, and living with her overbearing, slovenly mother (she empties her chamber pot into the kitchen sink) in a run-down cottage in western Ireland after having suffered a nervous breakdown in England fifteen years earlier when she had tried to branch out on her own. McDonagh's finely crafted, emotionally charged four-character drama presents Maureen's last grasp at love, which comes, much to the dismay of her mother, Mag, in the person of Pato Dooley, the none-too-successful older brother of Mag's neighbor, Ray. Pato has been working in England and is ready to try his fortune in America. Mag does her best to intervene when Pato asks Maureen to go with him. A conflict of gothic proportions follows, unearthing the intense loneliness, boredom, and longing that are familiar parts of life in the economically and culturally depressed rural areas of Ireland.

McDonagh's now-wrenching, now-hilarious script is beautifully served by its Irish cast, including Marie Mullen (Maureen), Anna Manahan (Mag), Brian F. O'Byrne (Pato), and Tom Murphy (Ray), who eked every last morsel of humanity from these four pitiful souls. Directed by Garry Hines, *The Beauty Queen* is the first in a trilogy that received full production in London last year. New York has something to look forward to.

The noteworthiness of *The Beauty Queen* seemed almost predictable in a year in which the Nobel Prize was awarded to the brokers of the Good Friday peace accord in Northern Ireland. Nearly a dozen Irish and Irish American plays enjoyed productions in New York and the regions. The steady stream of Irish-related plays and performances included everything from another sensational new play by McDonagh, *The Cripple of Inishmann* (directed by Jerry Zaks at the Joseph Papp Public Theatre), about a misshapen young man from an Irish backwater, to *Binlids,* a verbatim-drama about the women of Northern Ireland who warn their sons and husbands of the arrival of British police by beating the tops of garbage cans. There were also revivals of at least half a dozen plays by Eugene O'Neill, and *Colin Quinn: An Irish Wake,* a comic one-man show by the anchorman of "Saturday Night Live's Weekend Report."

Another Irish playwright was the subject of yet another Broadway import in 1998. *The Judas Kiss,* by David Hare, starred Liam Neeson as Oscar Wilde, the subject of multiple plays and films in recent seasons. Hare focuses this play on two particular moments in Wilde's notorious life. The first, in 1895, is the day when Wilde decides to stay in England and face his accusers. The second, in 1897, depicts Wilde in Naples with Lord Alfred Douglas, for whose love he had just spent two grim years in an English prison. Wilde died three years later, at the age of forty-six, financially broke and physically, psychically broken. An intimate portrait, this picture of Wilde is without his customary extravagance of wit and defiance. Hare's figure suffers quietly if intensely, observing rather more than he dares to say about the man he loves and yet continuing his inevitably self-destructive course. Neeson's performance, suitably restrained and delicately etched, helps strip the dandified veneer of legend and peer behind the mask at the man.

The year in Broadway imports ended with a second work by David Hare, *The Blue Room.* The West End production of Hare's adaptation of Arthur Schnitzler's *La Ronde* garnered much press for the nude scene by its female lead, Hollywood star Nicole Kidman, in one scene of an encounter between its five male and five female characters, all of whom are looking for love in all the wrong boudoirs. The play casts two actors in the ten parts, serially coupling and uncoupling in a futile quest for carnal and spiritual satisfaction. Kidman's quick-change marathon included portrayals of a teenage Cockney prostitute, a French au pair, the wife of a politician, a bored American model, and a grande dame of the theater. Each role demanded a different accent and affect. Her costar, Iian Glen, plays an equally daunting range, as their various characters meet, mate, and move on to what they hope will be more satisfying pairings.

In spite of the explicit love scenes and hot pre-publicity (an oft-quoted quip from the London *Daily Telegraph* calls the original production "pure theatrical Viagra."), New York critics found the one-hundred-minute, intermissionless play a tepid affair focused more on the characters' loss, disappointment, and disaffection than on their lusty entanglements. On 14 December, Ben Brantley of *The New York Times* summed up the play's message: "erotic satisfaction is a chimera, the elusive quarry on an eternal and fruitless hunt." All told, he wrote, in *The Blue Room* "the expectation of sex is as good as it gets."

Of the few nonmusical plays by American playwrights that opened in Broadway theaters, *Getting and Spending* by Michael J. Chepiga could hardly be considered a major work. The trite comic drama by a first-time playwright who is perhaps better suited to his day job as an attorney in California premiered at the Old Globe Theater in San Diego in August and somehow found its way to New York by October. The script recycles, in sitcom/soap opera plotting and dialogue, the theme of material versus spiritual fulfillment in the greedy world of investment banking in the 1990s. Victoria is under indictment for insider trading and wants Richard to represent her, but Richard is fed up with his exorbitant lawyer's income and has just entered a monastery. Victoria goes to the abbey to lure him out, where, in order to prove how far she will go to get Richard to comply, she ends up running through the sacred halls in her underwear, much to the amusement of Brothers Alfred and Thaddeus. Enough said.

More worthy of its high-profile placement is David Henry Hwang's *Golden Child,* a memoir of his maternal grandparents' journey from pre-Revolutionary China to the United States and the impact of their choices on the family that put down roots in American soil. Hwang's grandfather, Eng Tieng-Bin (Randall Duk Kim) decided to convert to Christianity and Westernize his polygamous household. The play frames the historical action in the present, as Chinese American Kim appears in his mother's ancestral dream. Hwang tackles a host of East-West, old world–new world issues such as the binding of girls' feet, traditional versus modern marriages, and class and gender role conflicts in a changing society.

The play was three years in the making, from a 1995 first draft commissioned by the South Coast Repertory in California through workshops at Trinity Rep and productions at New York's Joseph Papp Public Theater,

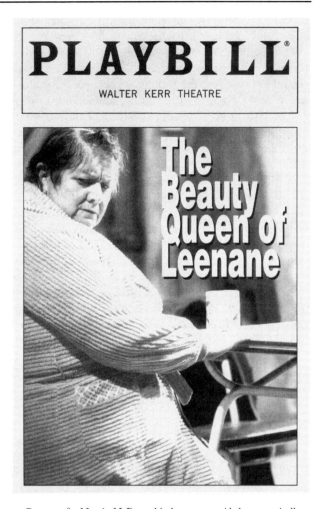

Program for Martin McDonagh's drama set amid the economically and culturally deprived provinces of Ireland (Playbill® used by permission)

the Kennedy Center in Washington, D.C., the American Conservatory Theater in San Francisco, and a run at the Singapore Repertory Theater in December 1997. According to interviews with the playwright, his collaborators, including director James Lapine, had enormous impact on the script along the way. From all accounts the final text shed the static, predictable dramatic structure with which Hwang had begun. Gone are long autobiographical monologues that alternated with scenes from his grandparents' life in China. The family patriarch grew older in subsequent drafts, and this makes more poignant his eventual transition to the New World. Exposition has been whittled away so that more of the story is dramatized, and the play balances domestic comedy and serious undertones. The version that played Broadway was clearly an improved play, yet it still carried the weight of didacticism and chunks of clunky, pseudo-Chinese English dialogue. This "final" draft raises questions about the development process now typical for works by playwrights with enough clout to win so much time, effort, and backing. Just what constitutes a new American play, and who is—or are—its author(s)? Does the wonderfully collaborative nature of theatrical production extend its benefits to the crafting of play texts, or can too many cooks spoil the dramatic broth? In the case of *Golden Child,* group effort seems to have helped the script along. The unanswered question is, how many other new plays lay dormant in literary managers' in-boxes while this one absorbed so many developmental resources?

Warren Leight's *Side Man* also found its way from off- to on-Broadway this year. The tender, often-humorous memory play about a jazz-crazed, itinerant musician premiered at the cozy Classic Stage Company before moving to the Roundabout in June. True to its jazz story line, the play zigs and zags through time and space as Clifford (Robert Sella), the narrator, insinuates himself into scenes from his family's past, from 1953, when Clifford's father, Gene (Frank Wood), fell for foul-mouthed Terry (Wendy Makkena), married her, and got her pregnant, to 1985, when the baby is twenty-nine years old. Gene's single-hearted devotion to his music creates a sorry childhood for Clifford. Incapable of a firm connection to his new family, Gene hovers on the emotional sidelines at home, as he does on stage with the bands he backs up for one-night gigs. Terry drinks herself into a stupor and threatens suicide. Clifford time-travels through their disintegrated relationship as if he were flipping through a scrapbook and wishing he could rearrange the pictures, rewrite the end, and make peace with his past.

Layered into Leight's detailed domestic melodrama are snippets of the music that Gene lives for. Using music by the likes of Hoagy Carmichael and Billy Strayhorn, director Michael Mayer (whose 1997 Roundabout Theater revival of Arthur Miller's *A View From the Bridge* moved to Broadway and enjoyed a successful run throughout 1998) infuses Leight's play with a moody period flavor. The Broadway venue opened up the claustrophobic, seedy nightclub setting from which each of the family members seeks figurative relief: Gene through his music, Terry in alcohol and finally suicide, and Clifford by reconciling himself with his memories. In the process, the domestic scenes of the play lost some intensity and the nightclub segments their late-night, smoky haze.

OFF BROADWAY

The furor that the Catholic League voiced over the gay Christ figure at the center of Terrence McNally's *Corpus Christi* attracted extraordinary publicity to what critics felt was an essentially flawed script. Joshua/Jesus (Anson Mount) and his thirteen friends/apostles form the cast of this modern passion play. Act 1 presents Joshua as he grows up gay in conservative Corpus Christi, Texas. In just a few of McNally's strained parallels between the lives of Jesus and Joshua, Josh's mother, Mary (Sean Dugan), gives birth to him in a cheesy roadside motel, and his friends have names such as Matthew (Drew McVety), John (Michael Irby), Judas (Josh Lucas), and Philip (Matthew Mabe), who gives up street hustling under Joshua's influence. Joshua's purpose on earth is, of course, to cure AIDS and rid the world of homophobia, especially the kind that comes cloaked in religious rhetoric. Equally predictable, though not inconsequential, is McNally's deeper purpose.

This deeper purpose may have led the usually clever writer of playful dialogue and complex if recognizable characters to go astray. Absent are McNally's humor and wordplay. Too often the characters spout pseudo-biblical phrases such as "Thank you, Lord. I can see," the kind of stilted lines that even Charleton Heston barely pulls off in epic technicolor movies. Religious persecution of sexual minorities is indeed serious, even dangerous, as violence against gays is increasing, but McNally appears to have taken his dramatic task too seriously and so flattened his characterizations. As Alexis Greene writes of the final scene in her 23 October review for *InTheater* magazine, "In McNally's version, there is no resurrection. At the end, Joshua is just nailed to the cross. But by the time the script fumbles to this disturbing close, you are past caring about his unidimensional and uncharismatic hero."

If McNally's work on the status of gays and the Bible errs on the side of solemnity, Paul Rudnick's madcap Old Testament farce takes off in the opposite direction. In *The Most Fabulous Story Ever Told,* which was produced by the New York Theater Workshop, Adam (Alan Tudyk) and Steve (Juan Carlos Hernandez) are the denizens of Rudnick's Eden—the first humans, they believe, until they leave paradise and meet Jane (Becky Ann Baker) and Mabel (Kathryn Meisle), a lesbian couple who are equally convinced that they were created first. The four central characters, comic stereotypes of butch and femme in both genders, spend act 1 traveling through the trials of the Old Testament, including flood, famine (when they're not munching on such blatantly homoerotic produce as carrots and bananas), and Egyptian slavery (when they join in a number from *A Chorus Line* while layering stones on a pyramid). Of course, they also discover geography, anatomy, and physiology, at which point the actors' loincloths give way to full-frontal nudity. When God asks Adam what he thinks of Creation, the reply is perfect: "Fabulous. I mean I would have put the lake over there. . . ."

Act 2 reincarnates the two couples as contemporary characters at a stylish Christmas party in New York

City. Jane is pregnant by artificial insemination. Steve is HIV positive. But the play does not become maudlin. It keeps up the satirical high jinks and moves into gentler emotional territory. Life for these latter-day gays is bittersweet, tinged with fear and confusion, friendship and hope. Rudnick is not bitter, however. He relishes the fundamental Judeo-Christian mythology and our need to believe it, just as his humor relishes the homosexuals who prance, preen, and plod around his stage. The open question is not of Rudnick's willingness to embrace Christian religious heritage but the willingness of its most extreme adherents to return the hug.

McNally and Rudnick are compassionate toward AIDS victims and opposed to heterosexual contempt and religious persecution in 1998; at the Vineyard Theater, Craig Lucas produced *The Dying Gaul,* an angry thriller about a Hollywood screenwriter who gets caught in a devastating triangle involving a bisexual movie producer and his Internet-surfing wife. Robert (Tim Hopper) is still in mourning for the lover he recently lost to AIDS when he is approached—sexually as well as professionally—by Jeffrey (Tony Goldwyn, a member of the studio-mogul family and thus no stranger to real-life Hollywood producers). When Jeffrey's wife, Elaine (Linda Emond), learns of their liaison, she cruelly engages Robert in an on-line romance by posing as the cyber-ghost of Robert's dead lover. Like other plays that rely on the contents of their characters' correspondence, Lucas's 1990s treatment of the genre frequently sets its characters in chairs facing the audience and reading aloud. The difference in this production is the absence of the ubiquitous writing desks. Balanced on their knees are the laptops on which Robert and Elaine compose and receive their e-mails. Few reviewers admired the play; most found its melodramatic plot to be clumsy, its characters mean, and its overall bitterness unpalatable. The whimsical fantasy in earlier Lucas plays such as *Prelude to a Kiss* and *Reckless* takes a decidedly demonic turn in *The Dying Gaul,* as Elaine practically tortures grief-stricken Robert with her cruel deception.

The sleeper triumph of the year off-Broadway was *Wit,* a strikingly well-written character study by first-time playwright Margaret Edson, a kindergarten teacher from Atlanta. Kathleen Chalfant earned unanimously glowing reviews as Vivian Bearing, a John Donne scholar who is waging a war of words and will with ovarian cancer. The play is set in Vivian's hospital room, where she wears a red baseball cap to cover her chemotherapy-shorn scalp and pushes her IV pole around the stage. Vivian intermittently breaks out of the action to address the audience directly, providing ample evidence of the cleverness that gives the play its title. Over the course of the play, however, this brave woman comes to see that the same intellectual bite that carries her through her medical ordeal has in fact kept her feelings and her loved ones at arm's length throughout her life.

Medical travails with a happier ending comprise the plot of William Finn's *A New Brain,* the most noteworthy off-Broadway musical of 1998. Finn wrote the music and lyrics and co-authored the book with his long-time collaborator, James Lapine. The gay Jewish central character of this show faces potentially fatal illness harkening back to *Falsettos,* Finn's musical contribution to the genre of AIDS-related drama in which the main character deals with his lover's demise. *A New Brain* also shares its predecessor's fully scored format, exuberant musical line, and jump-cut plotting, but there are significant differences in the mood and tone, if not the subject and style, of the new play.

In Finn's most autobiographical play to date, the protagonist's life-threatening illness sets the action, and the play has a happy ending. Finn's stand-in, protagonist Gordon Michael Schwinn (Malcolm Gets, in the Lincoln Center Theater production), is an aspiring composer who collapses suddenly. His extended family of friends, relatives, and caretakers fears the worst. Schwinn worries over the songs he'll never get to compose. The members of his support network ponder his fate and buck him up with songs such as "Brain Dead," "Heart and Music," and "Don't Give Up." When his diagnosis turns out to be less dire than was feared and the condition is operable, Schwinn recovers to finish with "I Feel So Much Spring."

There's something guilt-inducing about faulting a true story for its happy ending, and it's never a good idea to compare siblings. But as clever, bracing, and tuneful as it is, Graciela Daniele's well-cast and well-directed staging of *A New Brain* never quite achieves the emotional punch of the *Falsetto* plays. Still, it is a charming, witty, and thoroughly enjoyable piece of theater, a welcome addition to Finn's body of work.

The Year in Poetry

John E. Lane
Wofford College

In newspapers, on television, and over the World Wide Web the words of politicians, paramours, lackeys, and lawyers followed us through every turn and twist of 1998: conversations were secretly recorded, then revealed; questions were asked on videotape and in person; answers were recorded and pondered; transcripts were transformed into melodrama by a novelist-consultant. All year words were placed under the pressure of cross-examination. "It depends on what the definition of 'is' is," our president answered to one inquiry from the grand jury. As the year unfolded, words at times showed the tensile strength of steel—but often, at other times, the brittleness of straw.

In this year when the president's statement fixed public attention on a single word amid a storm of accusations, the lives of poets went on. There were submissions. There continued the usual publications, the usual prizes. In considering collections of poetry published this year, one wonders how much it's all really mattered, a year of poets publishing their work with large and small presses, in hardbound and in soft cover, in editions ranging in size from a thousand to many thousand books.

There are so many ways to judge the value of a book; critical reception and sales figures are two familiar measures. For poetry, reviews are often slow to come, and sales have never been a very accurate barometer. In sales of poetry this year a phenomenon worth noting has developed. It used to be that poets had to imagine volumes selling in bookstores in far-flung parts of this country. Now, however, with the high-speed connection of the Internet, readers can access their money, their friends, and, yes, even sales figures of books in which they may be interested. Amazon.com, the on-line bookstore, has begun to post sales figures to rank all of the million-plus books it lists in its virtual bookstore.

On one typical morning a new poetry collection, *A Night Without Armor* by country singer Jewel Kilcher, was ranked 710th in sales; Donald Hall's new book of poems, *Without,* is ranked 27,653rd. Which is the better collection? No doubt it is Hall's, but sales figures tell us

(and can tell Hall, if he logs on) that a book by a country singer is outselling his five to one.

This is not to suggest that Donald Hall should watch Amazon.com to see whether his sales are rising and falling like stock on a given day, but some writers may find it hard to resist the urge to check in on their own collections of poems from time to time. The presence of poetry in our culture is always more mysterious than sales and reputation. So often books arrive as gifts, as surprises. So often they are old, out-of-print. So often they are what we are drawn to at the moment.

Birthday Letters, Ted Hughes's last book of poems, was published early in the year and may be one collection that draws readers. Published in Britain by Faber and Faber and in the United States by Farrar, Straus and Giroux, this book-length poetic sequence addresses in image, metaphor, and loose narrative the ill-fated relationship of Hughes and Sylvia Plath. The book was something the poet had been writing for twenty-five years, but most of the poems he kept unpublished. When it was published, the book became a best-seller in both England and America, and there is even talk of a movie deal, probably something like *Tom and Viv* (1994), for it. Hughes's death from cancer in October punctuated its publication, a last word to the living crafted as letter poems to his famous dead wife.

Why did the infamous relationship between Hughes and Plath go so bad? Why was this young, talented couple so unlucky in love? Why do we still care thirty years later? Maybe it's because Hughes destroyed his wife's last journal. Maybe because he stayed quiet about the relationship, even as feminists accused him of everything short of murder. Now, decades later, Hughes writes of his budding love for Plath as an "obsession" in the odd poem "Fidelity," in which the twenty-five-year-old poet courts Sylvia but sleeps naked in the arms of a soup kitchen attendant "a month of nights" and never "once made love." The speaker explains, "I was focused, / So locked into you, so brilliantly, / Everything that was not you was blind spot."

Hughes uses *Birthday Letters* to craft his final (and solitary) response to Plath's much-debated life and

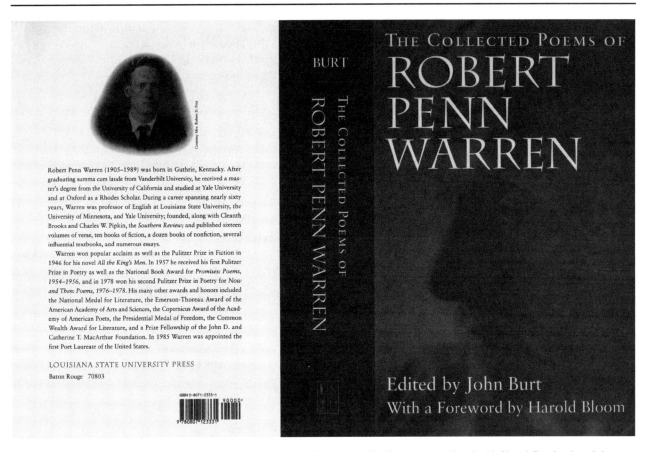

Robert Penn Warren (1905–1989) was born in Guthrie, Kentucky. After graduating summa cum laude from Vanderbilt University, he received a master's degree from the University of California and studied at Yale University and at Oxford as a Rhodes Scholar. During a career spanning nearly sixty years, Warren was professor of English at Louisiana State University, the University of Minnesota, and Yale University; founded, along with Cleanth Brooks and Charles W. Pipkin, the *Southern Review*; and published sixteen volumes of verse, ten books of fiction, a dozen books of nonfiction, several influential textbooks, and numerous essays.

Warren won popular acclaim as well as the Pulitzer Prize in Fiction in 1946 for his novel *All the King's Men*. In 1957 he received his first Pulitzer Prize in Poetry as well as the National Book Award for *Promises: Poems, 1954–1956*, and in 1978 won his second Pulitzer Prize in Poetry for *Now and Then: Poems, 1976–1978*. His many other awards and honors included the National Medal for Literature, the Emerson-Thoreau Award of the American Academy of Arts and Sciences, the Copernicus Award of the Academy of American Poets, the Presidential Medal of Freedom, the Common Wealth Award for Literature, and a Prize Fellowship of the John D. and Catherine T. MacArthur Foundation. In 1985 Warren was appointed the first Poet Laureate of the United States.

LOUISIANA STATE UNIVERSITY PRESS
Baton Rouge 70803

ISBN 0-8071-2333-1

THE COLLECTED POEMS OF
BURT
ROBERT
PENN
WARREN

THE COLLECTED POEMS OF ROBERT PENN WARREN

Edited by John Burt
With a Foreword by Harold Bloom

Dust jacket for the poetry of the Southern writer whose 1938 college text, Understanding Poetry, *co-authored with Cleanth Brooks, shaped the ways that generations of college students read poetry*

death. The book is personal, even private at times; however, it never feels confessional. "Sylvia," the dead poet, is addressed directly as "you," and the poems have the feel of a whole. Hence the interest of Hollywood.

Hughes gets the last word. Instead of describing his wife as having fallen victim to the brutal march of patriarchy, Hughes imagines Plath caught in the huge machinery of the artist's fate. Plath's life was lived and lost "to announce to the world / What Life had made of you, / Your whole body borrowed / By immortality and its promise, / Your arms filled / With what had never died, never known Death."

Hughes, the concrete, atavistic poet of *Crow* (1970), often places daily events in the lives of Plath and himself in mythological time and space. He uses the zodiac early on as a metaphor for the epic collision of their stars: "Our Chaucer would have stayed at home with his Dante, / Locating the planets more precisely . . . And Chaucer / Would have pointed to that day's Sun in the Fish / Conjunct with your Ascendant exactly . . . That day the solar system married us / Whether we knew it or not" ("St. Botolph's"). "Always bad news from the Ouija board," begins another poem. After

Plath's famous suicide, Hughes speaks of his fate in terms of the Tarot: "By night I lay awake in my body / The Hanged Man / My neck-nerve uprooted . . ." ("Life after Death"). In these poems death is not a conclusion but instead a theme, a poet's trope.

In the end, *Birthday Letters* is darkly compelling and worth the wait. Though somewhat mannered and maybe too mythological, as if some muse of History and Tradition were listening to the poet laureate over Queen Elizabeth II's shoulder, many of the poems in *Birthday Letters* call for a closer reading. The book lives up to its hype.

There were other deaths this year besides Hughes's. A short list of the dead includes Kathy Acker, Brendan Gill, John Malcolm Brinnin, Beat poet Jack Micheline, Vassar Miller, and David Ignatow. Micheline styled himself a "vagabond poet" in the tradition of Vachel Lindsay; Brinnin will always be remembered as the man who invited Dylan Thomas to America; Miller, for his Southern formalism, and Ignatow, for dark urban dreams and the strong will of his working-class origins. Ignatow, like the late William Stafford, believed in daily writing, and his production was often brilliant. "As I tread the dark, / led by the light of my pulsating mind, / I am faithful to myself," he writes in *Tread the Dark* (1978). He remained faithful to the end. An edition of selected poems is still available.

Though *Birthday Letters* overshadows most of the year's imports, several other overseas collections deserve serious notice. Nobel laureate Seamus Heaney released a fat new selected poems in 1998, *Opened Ground: Selected Poems 1966–1996* (Farrar, Straus and Giroux). His poems offer readers a full harvest of his thirty-year career, and, since *Opened Ground* has been chosen as the *Dictionary of Literary Biography Yearbook* Distinguished Poetry Book of the Year, it is discussed in detail in that citation. Also of special note is *Wooroloo* (HarperCollins), a collection of poems by English painter and children's book author Frieda Hughes, the daughter of Ted Hughes and Sylvia Plath.

With strengths borrowed from both parents, Frieda Hughes in *Wooroloo* presents a dark, sharply drawn (and charged) poetic universe. Like her father, Hughes creates a place where foxes and birds move in the shadows; and, much as her mother might observe, the speaker of one poem says, "I am a monster of pieces. / My spirit watches from the corner and follows at a distance, / Doesn't recognize its home." It is fascinating how impossible it is to read these poems without looking for clues to the great mystery of the poet's famous mother. In the poem "Thief" Hughes writes:

It was years before I dug her out
From where her shadow lay, like a bloodstain
Beneath the black stones I had
Weighted her down with.

How can one not help but read into these lines—and many more in this fine, grainy collection—hints of the continuing influence that Sylvia Plath and Ted Hughes have on their daughter. There are ghosts in every poem.

This year the Kentucky poet, essayist, and novelist Wendell Berry has published two new books, *The Selected Poems of Wendell Berry* (Counterpoint) and *A Timbered Choir: The Sabbath Poems 1979–1997* (Counterpoint). Berry, who has lived and worked on a hillside farm in Henry County, Kentucky, has published more than thirty books, always conscious of community, land, and commitment to craft. Heaney, in his Nobel address, describes how he spent years "bowed to the desk like some monk . . . in an attempt to bear his portion of the weight of the world." Berry is of a similar character.

A Timbered Choir is one of the best books of the year. It is the type of achievement only Berry would contemplate and then continue with a monk's steadiness. For more than twenty years he has practiced a

kind of "walking meditation" on his farm and written poems "in silence, in solitude, mainly out of doors." Here, from a Sunday in 1982, is a brief example of one of his "Sabbath poems":

The pasture, bleached and cold two weeks ago,
Begins to grow in the spring light and rain;
The new grass trembles under the wind's flow.
The flock, barn-weary, comes to it again,
New to the lambs, a place their mothers know,
Welcoming, bright, and savory in its green,
So fully does the time recover it.
Nibbles of pleasure go all over it.

Berry's *Selected Poems* feels slim at 170 pages, and avid readers of the poet will have to return to early collections for some of their favorites. Berry notes in a short preface, "I like the idea of a 'selected poems' because I like the idea of culling and condensation and compactness." He might have included more of his Mad Farmer poems. "Go with your love to the fields," the Mad Farmer tells us in his "Manifesto: The Mad Farmer Liberation Front" (included in the collection). One would hope that Berry gets shortlisted for the Nobel Prize someday.

The Collected Poems of Robert Penn Warren (Louisiana State University Press), edited by John Burt with a foreword by Harold Bloom, was also published in 1998. Warren, who died in 1989, was, like Berry, a Kentuckian by birth and in love with his native land, though Warren often wrote of other places—Vermont, Louisiana, the West. He also shares with Berry the ability to publish with distinction in different genres (he's still the only writer to win the Pulitzer Prize for both prose and poetry). This collection gathers all of Warren's published poems with the exception of the verse drama *Brother to Dragons* (1953). It is a particular pleasure to revisit the long narrative *Audubon: A Vision* (1969; "We never know what we have lost, or what we have found. / We are only ourselves, and that promise. / Continue to walk in the world. Yes, love it!"), the shorter "Pondy Woods" ("The buzzards over Pondy Woods / Achieve the blue tense altitudes"), and "Weather Report" ("Rain taps on the roof of my air-swing workhouse, / On one side in pine-tops above the gorge. / This is the code now tapped: *Today is today*"). Robert Penn Warren's "today," though now decades in the past, still glimmers through his images and metaphors. He is a powerful poet.

With the publication of Donald Hall's *Without* (Houghton Mifflin) we open a window into his deep grief over the death of his wife, the poet Jane Kenyon. The book is similar to Hughes's *Birthday Letters* in that it attempts to communicate beyond the grave, though Hall chooses to contact Jane not directly but through shifting points of view including letters.

Dust jacket for the collection in which the poet responds to the death of his wife

Kenyon, who died of leukemia in 1995, is always a strong presence, and she fights her coming death with spirit: "Today, / she looked at her bald head and at / her face swollen / with prednisone: 'I am Telly Savalas.'" Though the poems at times have a feel of a bedside journal, they often leap beyond the particular: "Remembered happiness is agony; / so is remembered agony." This is a difficult book to ignore, full of articulated sadness and love.

A durable selected poems has finally appeared for William Stafford, *The Way It Is: New & Selected Poems* (Graywolf Press). This collection includes one of the most striking cover layouts of the year, a closeup of crisscrossed fall leaves, beautifully balanced in burgundy, blue, and yellow by designer Tree Swenson. The flap copy praises Stafford's "rugged domesticity" and notes the "political edge of his irony." These insights are true enough, but Stafford's daily commitment to the life of poetry always impresses one most. Included in *The Way It Is* is a good selection of the daily poems Stafford was writing right up to his death in 1993 at the age of seventy-nine. Here are a few lines from "Are you Mr. William Stafford?," the poem he wrote on 28 August, the morning he died:

Well, it was yesterday.
Sunlight used to follow my hand.
And that's when the strange siren-like sound flooded
over the horizon and rushed through the streets of our
town.
That's when sunlight came from behind
a rock and began to follow my hand.

Robert Creeley has a new collection, *Life & Death* (New Directions). It is the poet's fourteenth, and it offers the familiar compacted Creeley utterance of one of our greatest living poets. The long poetic collage "Histoire de Florida" offers history, insight, literary echo (The last part of the poem is a gloss on Wallace Stevens's "The Anecdote of the Jar"), and sharp wit driven by line break ("You've left a lot out / Being in doubt / you left / it out"). One is always drawn deeply into Creeley's poems by the care he takes and the way he makes language primary in the life of the poem.

Two collected and one selected poems by poets known mostly as prose writers: Raymond Carver's *All of Us: The Collected Poems* (Knopf), George Garrett's *Days of Our Lives Lie in Fragments: New and Old Poems 1957–1997* (Louisiana State University Press), and Jim Harrison's *The Shape of the Journey: New & Collected Poems* (Copper Canyon Press) were also published in 1998. Carver says on the flap copy, "I began as a poet, my first publication was a poem. So I suppose on my tombstone I'd be very pleased if they put 'Poet and short-story writer—and occasional essayist' in that order." There are three hundred poems collected, and many read like tiny imagistic drafts of Carver's minimalist stories. They are poems full of lively dialogue, and they have the clarity of Anton Chekhov's journals, but in the end the stories are still the center of Raymond Carver's creative wheel.

Though maybe best known for his many novels, George Garrett is a fine poet and has practiced his craft for almost half a century. *Days of Our Lives Lie in Fragments* draws poems from seven previous collections, and most of these poems are well-known to readers of contemporary poetry. Here is "Crows," one of the new poems with which Garrett leads off this collection:

Lord, but I do dearly love
these, your large, slow reedy messengers,
your spies clad in shiny feathers,
sentinels of high places squawking
and cawing arrivals and departures,
raggedy fliers rising in a black caucus
or, grounded, the shifty epitome
of pure swagger and bravado.
Old crows, nosy flock,
we came through bad weather together
when all the trees were a cruel glitter
of ice and earth was a hard-hearted stranger
who wished only catastrophe upon us,
you and I, shabby and insufferably proud,
perched here to witness the robin's return.

Jim Harrison, on the other hand, is a highly underrated poet, and *The Shape of the Journey* shows once and for all how his poetry needs to be considered as seriously as his fiction. Harrison may be a *better* poet than fiction writer, though this could be hard to believe for someone familiar only with the epic and successful *Legends of the Fall* (1979), *Dalva* (1988), and just this year, *The Road Home*. Harrison's "The Theory and Practice of Rivers" is a fine poetic sequence that explores the nature of our connection to landscape, and in his shorter poems Harrison celebrates the self, dark water, and northern light. Here is the second section from "Three Night Songs":

Moving in liquid dark,
night's water,
a flat stone sinking,
wobbling toward bottom;
and not to wait there for morning,
to see the sun up through the water,
but to freeze until another glacier comes.

Harrison's early poetry collections—*Plain Song* (1965), *Locations* (1968), *Outlyer and Ghazals* (1971), and *Letters to Yesenin* (1973)—are hard to find. It is good to see them finally together.

Each year brings its new flood of selected and collected poems, and the stream this year included Stephen Sandy's *The Thread* (Louisiana State University Press), which draws on poems from five previous distinctive collections. Sandy's poems always prove attentive to the natural world. In "From the Fastest Train," Sandy enters the landscape from a Kyoto/Tokyo train window: "Each field is gone again / freak snow erasing boundaries / and still the same as yesterday / save a few edges softened here and there. . . ." In "The Tack," a poem from his 1992 collection *Thanksgiving Over the Water,* Sandy observes the metamorphosis of a tack that he contemplates in his own study. One moment the tack is a "steely convex eye," and the next, the "beveled head of tack / No longer beamed a guttering eye; it was / Only a tack, flush with the wood." These are the moments that are Stephen Sandy's territory.

Relations: New & Selected Poems (Graywolf Press) by Vassar College professor Eamon Grennan offers poems that rage over thirty years and two countries. Grennan, an Irish citizen who has lived in the United States for three decades, has produced lyrics of medieval monastic Ireland and meditative narrative poems exploring his adopted countryside. In "Outing" he writes to a sick friend: "Here among woods and hills of New Hampshire / it's you I think of when I watch the mountains / appear and disappear in mist, the shape of things / changing by the minute."

Like Grennan's collection, Ben Belitt's complete poems *This Scribe, My Hand* (Louisiana State University Press) gathers together poems from a distinguished career as professor and poet. Lately Belitt's poems use famous men—Henry David Thoreau and Charles Darwin, to name two—as the backdrop for a lyric intensity some have compared to Hart Crane's. His poems remain difficult and elegant. Many are long and resist excerpting, but here are six lines from "Sumac," a poem in six sections from Belitt's latest collection, *Possessions* (1986):

The incunabula of the malign
that bloodies a summer with no obvious intent
to harm, raising the sumac's fist

on a gargoyle of waxes and berries,
a coxcomb with its brickdust wattles
bared, like maggots swarming . . .

Alicia Suskin Ostriker's *The Little Space: Poems Selected and New, 1968–1998* (University of Pittsburgh Press) selects poems from eight previous collections.

Dust jacket for the 1998 collection of poetry by a writer known for his aesthetic precept that "form is never more than an extension of content"

Her poems have remained accessible and celebratory, though their simple repetitions and lack of punctuation early on now seems dated. Here's "Wrinkly Lady Dancer," from her first book:

Going to be an old wrinkly lady
Going to be one of those frail rag people
Going to have withered hands and be
Puzzled to tears crossing the street

Hobble cautiously onto buses
Like a withery fruit
And quite silently sitting in this lurching bus
The avenues coming by

Some other passengers gaze at me
Clutching my cane and my newspaper
Seemingly protectively, but I will really be thinking about
The afternoon I danced naked with you
The afternoon I danced naked with you
The afternoon! I danced! Naked with you!

Gerald Barrax's *From a Person Sitting in Darkness: New and Selected Poems* (Louisiana State University Press) is a collection full of social consciousness and formal experimentation. His poems range all over the page, split punctuation off from lines, and isolate words for

emphasis. In "I Called Them Trees" he doesn't miss "the old darkie ringing / the banjo" at the feet of a statue of Steven Collins Foster or, in "Uniforms," the "hooded men" who "shame their faith as Christian Knights / of burning crosses, / enhance with sheets the color of the faces / that we often would die not to see, for just one day."

Louisiana State University Press has also published a unique "selected" poems this year: *A New Pleiade: Selected Poems,* featuring poetry by Fred Chappell, Kelly Cherry, R. H. W. Dillard, Brendan Galvin, George Garrett, David R. Slavitt, and Henry Taylor. There should be no need to introduce any of these poets to readers of contemporary verse. What most would not know is that these poets have been friends for years. All have long careers, prizes, and positions of honor. What makes this book unique is the manner in which the poems were selected. Each poet selected about thirty pages of work by the next poet in alphabetical order. What the collection displays is, according to the cover copy, the "affection, fun, and mutual respect of this happy association of poets." The selection is masterful and offers many surprises when the work of one poet rubs up against the work of another.

David R. Slavitt has also published a separate collection of poems, *PS3569.L3* (Louisiana State University Press). This collection, his sixtieth book, gathers translations (Slavitt is a highly respected translator of Latin poetry and prose), imitations, parodies, and poems. Here is "Bucolic Lines Composed en Route to Lyon's U-Pik'Em Strawberry Fields, Creedmore, N.C.," a light poem that appears in the final section of the collection:

> Let's all live somewhere in Creedmore,
> where life is simpler. We need more
> solitude. We'll prune and weed more,
> go to nightclubs less. We'll read more,
> drink Wild Turkey, go to seed more,
> fool around a lot of breed more,
> maybe slash our wrists and bleed more,
> where good old boys have R.I.P.ed more
> tranquilly out here in Creedmore
> than anywhere I know.
> It's calling us. Let's go!

John Ashbery has a new collection, *Wakefulness* (Farrar, Straus and Giroux), in which the poet presents fifty new poems. In the title poem he writes: "Little by little the idea of the true way returned to me." It's always enjoyable to watch Ashbery's mind move from decade to decade. He is one of our masters of consciousness, always aware, always tracking his fear and joy. *The Mooring of Starting Out,* a compilation of Ashbery's first five collections of poems, is also available this year from Ecco Press.

Mark Strand also has a striking new collection, *Blizzard of One* (Knopf). These new poems by the former poet laureate of the United States carry on Strand's long career of the chilly illumination of the normal. They are witty (as Strand's poems often are) and hint at loss more strongly than past collections do. The titles are particularly strong as well. Among them may be found "The Great Poet Returns," "Our Masterpiece Is the Private Life," "Some Last Words," and "The Delirium Waltz." Strand's poems nod toward our time and its blizzard of sensation. He mentions the next century in one poem and seems to be meditating on our larger social reality (Kenneth Starr, President Clinton, and the death of privacy) in another. "There is something down by the water keeping itself from us," begins "Our Masterpiece Is the Private Life." "Why should we care?" the poem's speaker asks. Strand's answer is that we should care, because this inner world he opens to us is one of heavy weather and needs watching.

W. W. Norton has an impressive list this year. There are new collections from Adrienne Rich, *Midnight Salvage Poems 1995–1998;* Sherod Santos, *The Pilot Star Elegies;* Thomas Lynch, *Still Life in Milford;* and Maxine Kumin, *Selected Poems, 1960–1990.* Other new collec-

tions include those from the Irish poet Eavan Boland, who splits her time between Stanford University and Dublin, and Ai, an African American–Native American–Asian American poet. Boland's *The Lost Land* (Norton) continues her exploration of Irish life from the end of the telescope opposite that of Seamus Heaney's recent poems. Boland, like Rich and Kumin, creates her own mythic history, both private and personal. In these new poems she reads the land as the absent daughter and imagines herself "on the underworld side of that water, the darkness coming in fast. . . ."

Vice New and Selected Poems (Norton) is generously drawn from Ai's four previous collections, with the addition of some new poems. The titles of Ai's early collections speak to their darkness and the testimony of violence toward women and people of color: *Cruelty* (1973), *Killing Floor* (1979), and *Sin* (1986). With her fourth collection–*Fate* (1991)–Ai's tone shifted a little. Obviously she has returned with *Vice* to the darker vision of her earlier work.

Two collections of poems about mills and millwork have been published this year: *The Weave Room,* (University of Chicago), by Michael Chitwood, and *Eureka Mill* (Bench Press), by Ron Rash. Rash's *Eureka Mill* is his first poetry collection, but it has been anticipated for years. *Eureka Mill* is a sequence of forty-two poems, a red-clay version of Edgar Lee Masters's *Spoon River Anthology* (1915), and one after another the lyrics carry the reader deep into the emotional and concrete world of a Carolina cotton mill. The "real" Eureka Mill is just east of Chester, South Carolina, but Rash has created a whole new world. He writes beautifully of lost farms, long shifts, drought, fever, fights, religion, and family. Here's "Mill Village," an example of the powerful poems found in the collection:

> Mill houses lined both sides of every road
> like boxcars on a track. They were so close
> a man could piss off of his own front porch,
> hit four houses if he had the wind.
>
> Everytime your neighbor had a fight,
> then made up in bed as couples do,
> came home drunk, played the radio,
> you knew, whether or not you wanted to.

If you had to re-create the emotional DNA of a South Carolina mill working existence, this would be the book to clone. Rash's book is one of the best of the year.

Michael Chitwood has published two other collections, *Salt Works* (1992) and *Whet* (1995). In these collections Chitwood demonstrates a quirky genius for metaphor and country image. *The Weave Room* (University of Chicago Press), published this year, is just as good as the earlier collections but in different ways. More than in the earlier volumes, Chitwood works with narrative and creates recollections similar to Andrew Hudgins's poems in *The Glass Hammer* (1994). Chitwood's poems, set in southwestern Virginia and recalling a college summer job at a plant his father managed, are all Michael Chitwood, both in tone and subject. In "Threads, End of Another Day," he writes,

> Country tunes trailed them out the gate
> while I waited for my ride, my evening.
> The chainlink trolled those still moments
> with its shadow net, and sparrows
> gathered the string they let go.
>
> That's it, all that happened, then, there,
> and again, here, now, clinging to another day
> where I'm working them in.
> What you notice becomes your life.

Ecco Press has published new collections from Louise Gluck, *Vita Nova,* and from James Tate, *Shroud of the Gnome,* and has also republished two early collections of Jorie Graham, *The End of Beauty* and *Materialism.* There seems to be a growing market for republishing "classic" contemporary collections, and more may be coming.

Tate seems every year to offer a new collection, and *Shroud of the Gnome* is his twelfth. There are good, playful poems here; he remains a master of titles. Who would have thought he could top the 1994 National Book Award winner, *Worshipful Company of Fletchers*? Tate's work will have quite a heft when a volume of his collected poems appears.

Four very strong collections this year are by poets in mid career: *Four Testimonies* (Louisiana State University Press) by Kate Daniels; *Deepstep Come Shining* (Copper Canyon Press) by C. D. Wright; *Thieves of Paradise* (Wesleyan/New England) by Yusef Komunyakaa; and *Babylon in a Jar* (Houghton Mifflin) by Andrew Hudgins. All four of these poets write with a seriousness of purpose, and these collections should receive close attention.

Daniels has published two previous collections, *The White Wave* (1984) and *The Niobe Poems* (1988). She now teaches at Vanderbilt University and has edited *Out of Silence: Muriel Rukeyser's Selected Poems* (1992). Her new collection is made up of one powerful dramatic monologue ("The Testimony of Simone Weil") and three long sequences of poems ("In the Marvelous Dimension," "The Smash-Up," and "Portrait of the Artist as Mother"). The seriousness of this poetry is underscored by the brief introductory note to the Simone Weil poem, in which Daniels introduces the importance of biographical details about Weil, the radical French

philosopher and political thinker (who is also, it seems, the guiding ghost of the entire collection), and Engene Atget, the French photographer who in the late nineteenth century set out to photograph "the visual remains of Old Paris." Daniels's work is rooted in the history of ideas and places, and she alerts us—with epigraphs, introductions, notes, even a bibliography—to the importance of human joy and suffering seen in relief against the backdrop of longer histories.

Her poems are not dry and intellectual, though. Reading the collection is like sliding along a knife blade of sharp emotion. "In the Marvelous Dimension" is a series of monologues by survivors of the collapse of the Nimitz Freeway in Oakland during the San Francisco earthquake in 1989. One of the "voices," Mary, tells how she "picked the kids up / at 4:45, as usual." And then, "I was just about / to yell, *Goddamnit, shut up for once,* / when the whole thing went. I mean / the whole thing, the whole world, / I thought. . . ." The woman loses all three of her children in the earthquake (which actually killed forty-two people), and her "testimony" is powerful and exact. How to go on living after the loss of children? This question rhymes with Weil's life: "She never married, but remained close to her mother, father, and only brother," Daniels tells us in her introduction.

"In my book, poetry is a necessity of life," C. D. Wright says on the back cover of *Deepstep Come Shining.* "It is a function of poetry to locate those zones inside us that would be free, and declare them so." So it seems Wright attempts a project similar to that of Daniels. She wants to ground us in history, yet introduce us to the here-and-now of life. Her book is formally challenging (long lines, lyrical prose paragraphs at times, and sections prefaced with a photograph by Deborah Luster showing strange, ghostly banners of type) and registers a voice deeply confident. The book begins in motion and rain:

> Meanwhile the cars continued in a persistent flow down
> Closeburn Road.
>
> The refrain to the rain would be a movement up and
>   down the
> clefs of light.
>
> Chlorophyll world. July. Great goblets of magnolialight.
>
> Her head cooling against the car glass. The mind apprehends
> the white piano, her mother. Who played only what she
>   chose,
> who chose only to play "Smoke Gets in Your Eyes."

From beginning to end, Wright spins and digresses into memory ("white splotches in a clearing, a fat, diapered baby in a field of timothy chasing another"), graffiti ("God is Louise. Is that what it says."), surrealism ("In the living room of a saint . . . With an icecream head-ache.") and word play ("Come my sultry refulgence"). The language of *Deepstep Come Shining* is both colloquial and sharply poetic.

Komunyakaa's new collection, *Thieves of Paradise,* is his tenth, and it mixes "multiple traditions," classic forms (odes, eclogues, and quatrains), contemporary prose poem meditations ("*Did you kill anyone over there?* Angelica shifts her gaze from the Janis Joplin / poster to Jimi Hendrix . . ."), and monologues (one involving two paleontologists working at the La Brea Tar Pits). One section of the book is called "testimony" and deals with Charlie Parker, poverty, jazz, and cheap chicken shacks: "Like a black cockatoo / clinging to a stormy branch / with its shiny head rocking / between paradise and hell, / that's how Yardbird listened."

Through five books of poems Andrew Hudgins has proven to be one of the most watched of American poets. Each book is anticipated and praised. He has viv-idly imagined the Civil War in *After the Lost War: A Nar-rative* (1988) and has explored his Southern childhood in *The Glass Hammer*. In *Babylon in a Jar* (Houghton Miff-lin) Hudgins writes of dogs, ashes (there are two poems about cremation), backyards, order, disorder, and trees. Often, of trees.

In "The Chinaberry," the first poem of the collec-tion, Hudgins describes grackles covering, then leaving, a chinaberry tree. This moment in childhood is indeli-ble and survives. Hudgins is aware that he has chosen to elevate to poetry that most common and unvalued of birds, the grackle, and that most lowly of Southern landscaping trees: "Oh, it / was just a chinaberry tree, / the birds were simply grackles. / A miracle / made from this world and where I stood in it." When reading a Hudgins poem, one often feels this way—that the poet has recovered the "miracle" under the commonplace.

This collection also creates a huge sense of things passing, though. After the book opens with the "miracle" of the grackles leaving the chinaberry tree, it ends with another miracle. In "Stump," a poem about sacrifice, mys-tery, and loss, the poet imagines himself as a poet chop-ping at a stump and as an imaginary chicken whose head is loosed from his body on an old oak stump:

> I flapped my elbows, crowed.
> I knelt and pressed my hot face on the stump,
> then stood and cut my head off. I raced down the yard
> in crazy circles, blood spurting from my neck,
> and when I, flailing, dropped dead at my own feet, I stood,
> ran back to my imaginary head, and kicked it
> to the foot of the unstumped oak . . .

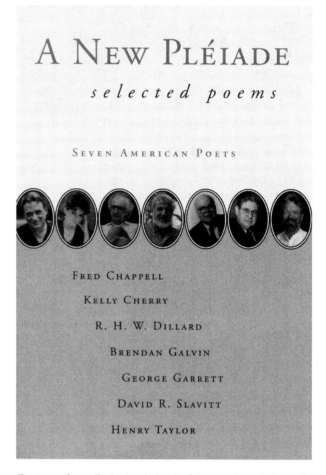

A NEW PLÉIADE

selected poems

SEVEN AMERICAN POETS

FRED CHAPPELL

KELLY CHERRY

R. H. W. DILLARD

BRENDAN GALVIN

GEORGE GARRETT

DAVID R. SLAVITT

HENRY TAYLOR

Front cover for a collection in which each of the poets chose selections to be included from the work of one of the other poets

This is a move typical of Hudgins—the humor, the imagination, and yet the ability to see so much in so common an act. Hudgins's voice is at times as common as a grackle and as quick as a hummingbird.

Of the many award winners in 1998 two notable ones were Barbara Ras, whose *Bite Every Sorrow* (Louisi-ana State University Press) won the Walt Whitman Award (judged by C. K. Williams), and Sandra Alcosser, whose *except by nature* (Graywolf Press) was selected by Eamon Grennan for the National Poetry Series. The four sections of Ras's *Bite Every Sorrow* offer one- and two-page poems with long lines and much travel. The ever-shifting rhythm, the humor (the cover of the book shows four pastel dogs ready to bite the sorrows), and the love of place, any place, are what draw one to these poems.

Occasionally a Spanish word will creep into the poet's consciousness, and the very sound of the word will turn into a meditation, as in "Abundancia":

On the train as it rolls in and out of stations, abundancia
    underground,
abundancia above, the sequence constant,
dark dark light, dark dark light,
then the longest dark, abundancia under the bay, and
    abundancia
in the mother combing her son's hair, pulling the
    ten-cent-comb
again and again through the already yielding strands,
and in the bending of the boy's head abundancia as he
    holds still for the part,
his hair obeying the invisible line she makes on his head.

Ras uses the rhythm of the train, of her meditation, to give the moment intensity and range. One is reminded of another Bay Area poet, Robert Hass, so often in this collection: Hass is able to make every moment luminous. Ras, now living in Athens, Georgia, has the same genius.

Though all the poems in Sandra Alcosser's *except by nature,* which won the 1998 James Laughlin Award for best second book of poems, do not grapple with the natural world and our place in it, many of the strongest do. The issue of place is never far from the surface of Alcosser's concerns. She writes about things and relationships with what judge Eamon Grennan calls "buoyant verbal manners." He points out how Alcosser describes a mallard she is holding in her hand as a "hoodlum heart whooping like a blood balloon" and the Louisiana bayou as "mushed together and sticky as gumbo." The reader wants to be there when she is watching grizzlies dance, when she asks, "Have you never wanted / to spin like that / on hairy, leathered feet, / amid the swelling berries / as you tasted a language of early summer?"

A few more eye-catching collections of poems published this year include Lola Haskins's *Extranjera* (Story Line), a collection in which the speaker is a foreigner on a trip through Mexico; Greg Miller's *Iron Wheel* (University of Chicago Press); Stephanie Brown's *Allegory of the Supermarket* (University of Georgia Press); Kathryn Stripling Byer's *Black Shawl* (Louisiana State University Press); and Frederick Pollack's *happiness* (Story Line).

Three anthologies are worthy of mention this year: *Wild Song Poems of the Natural World* (University of Georgia Press), cdited by John Daniel; *Verse & Universe Poems About Science and Mathematics* (Milkweed), edited by Kurt Brown; and the second volume of *Poems for the Millennium* (University of California Press), edited by Jerome Rothenberg and Pierre Joris.

Wild Song Poems is a helpful collection of poems to introduce many poets who "decry ecological injuries, celebrate nature's beauties, point to its many mysteries." It includes selections by many poets one would expect—Wendell Berry, Robert Bly, William Stafford, Pattiann Rogers, Mary Oliver, and Maxine Kumin—and the collection adds to this list poets less well-known, such as C. L. Rawlins,

Alison Hawthorne Deming, Jane Hirshfield, and Reg Saner. *Verse & Universe* includes work by many of the same poets, but it ranges much further. Many of its poems are really about science or mathematics and actually use these fields as metaphors. The poetry also opposes the concerns of science. Hence, Bill Knot's "The Consolations of Sociobiology" presents a spurned teenager understanding his rebuff in terms of E. O. Wilson's sociobiology, in which human mating is driven by Darwinian survival: "I sat at a drive-in and watched the stars / Through a straw while the coke in my lap went / Waterier and waterier . . . / –Then you explained your DNA calls for / Meaner genes than mine. . . ."

Volume one (published in 1995) and this year's second volume of *Poems for the Millennium* together constitute, as the subtitle indicates, *The University of California Book of Modern & Postmodern Poetry*. These books, which include at more than 1,600 pages, place (and "reconceptualize," according to Marjorie Perloff) poetry in a global context. Yes, there *are* poets here from all over the globe and from 1,000 years ago, from literate and nonliterate cultures–poets well-known and unknown in this country until this anthology. The context for this book is not understandable, however, and the introductions are not very helpful.

The most fascinating feature of the index is in noting whom the editors have left out. Among American poets since 1945, Theodore Roethke, Robert Lowell, and Elizabeth Bishop do not make the millennium cut; John Ashbery, Frank O'Hara, and Anne Waldman do. Ted Hughes does not; Langston Hughes does. Sylvia Plath is out; Anne Sexton is in. The poetry that matters, for Rothenberg and Joris, is poetry that is "an instrument of change."

"Poems are made of words," Donald Hall writes in *To Read Literature* (1981). Maybe 1998 made words matter to the public in a way they had not mattered a year earlier. W. H. Auden comes to mind often as one combs through the year's poetry collections, as one listens to our Chief Executive and his accusers: "For poetry makes nothing happen: it survives / In the valley of its saying where executives / Would never want to tamper."

This quotation comes from the great poem "In Memory of W. B. Yeats" (1939), a poem of note for the century. What does Auden mean in saying that poetry "makes nothing happen?" Does it mean (as today's freshman survey students repeat often enough) anything one wants it to mean? If Auden's *Collected Poems* is ranked 4,002 by Amazon.com, this means that he's charting better than Hall but worse than Jewel Kilcher. Does it matter? I think not. Auden, the most public of poets, drew our attention to the work at hand, the public and private business of reading and writing poetry. That's what matters, for this year or any year.

Dictionary of Literary Biography Yearbook Award for Distinguished Volume of Poetry Published in 1998

With thirty years of publishing and twelve volumes of poetry, the Irish poet Seamus Heaney has proven to be one of the most challenging and satisfying twentieth-century poets. Through a long career teaching at Harvard University, Heaney seems almost American in his presence. His picture—face broad as a moor, hair tossled, tie askew, and dark eyes slightly squinting into the camera—fills the back cover of his new collection and announces his singular presence.

Opened Ground: Selected Poems 1966–1996 finally expands on *Poems 1965–1975,* the twenty-years-out-of-date volume that until now came closest to being a selected or collected edition of Heaney's poetry. *Opened Ground* offers the best of the poet's work to date to new readers that Heaney has acquired since his 1995 Nobel Prize. (For those who do not have a copy of his 1995 Nobel lecture, "Crediting Poetry," it is reprinted at the conclusion of the collection.)

In his first book, *Death of a Naturalist* (1966), Heaney offers the taut, acoustic "Digging," with its well-known beginning:

> Between my finger and my thumb
> The squat pen rests; snug as a gun.
>
> Under my window, a clean rasping sound
> When the spade sinks into gravelly ground:
> My father digging. I look down
>
> Till his straining rump among the flowerbeds
> Bends low, comes up twenty years away
> Stooping in rhythm through potato drills
> Where he was digging.

A music similar to that of "Digging" can be enjoyed almost thirty years (and in this volume, 400 pages) later in "Two Stick Drawings" ("Claire O'Reilly used her granny's stick– / A crook-necked one–to snare the highest briars"), from *The Spirit Level* (1995).

Opened Ground offers old comforts and new surprises. In a section of *The Cure at Troy* not selected for this volume Heaney writes:

Seamus Heaney, from the dust jacket of Selected Poems 1966–1996 *(Farrar, Straus and Giroux)*

> Human beings suffer,
> They torture one another,
> They get hurt and get hard.
> No poem or play or song
> Can fully right a wrong
> Inflicted and endured.

In this year, when it is still in question whether peace may finally come to the troubled territory of Northern Ireland, Heaney's poems—passionate, accurate, gravelly, historical—come as close as any to righting the wrongs of the world. This volume of selected poems pulls to- gether, under one cover, his best work.

–John E. Lane

The Year in Book Reviewing and the Literary Situation

George Garrett
The University of Virginia

"Increasingly, what matters to writers, as to everyone in a celebrity culture, is getting noticed." –Scott Donaldson, "The Literary Situation Today," *The Sewanee Review* (Fall 1998).

"More publishers exist to perpetuate myths—about celebrity, self-help, money-making, politics, history—than to dispel them." –Celia McGee, *The New York Observer*, 30 March 1998.

SOURCES

It would probably be better for all concerned if all of us living outside of what *Esquire* (Rust Hills) once called "the red hot center" of the literary world made no effort at all to find out what's happening there and didn't try to keep up with events and people, the news from New York. We might be a lot happier. But, for reasons beyond fathoming, and often beyond good common sense, we writers and readers are urgently curious. More or less outsiders in a multicultural, corporate, and celebrity-driven (if not ruled) society, we try to find out. We try to keep some kind of score.

How? If you are not at the moment directly involved, how do you keep up? Answer: The best you can from a wide variety of sources. Here are mine for 1998. To begin—the newspapers. Three papers seem to be essential to coverage of book reviewing and the literary scene: *The New York Times* and *The New York Times Book Review*, *The Washington Post* and *Washington Post Book World*, and *The New York Observer*. In 1998 I read these faithfully and with interest. Irregularly I read the book pages of *The Boston Globe* and *The Washington Times*, both of which are excellent though neither focuses much attention on the publishing business or on the literary scene except insofar as they are revealed by the books reviewed. In the past, for this piece, I read most of the major papers with book pages in the country. Reading these offered a variety of views, sometimes interesting in their contradictions, of much the same books as those reviewed in *The New York Times* and *The Washington Post*.

Magazines, especially the literary magazines and quarterlies and other magazines devoted mainly to the

Cover for the journal that began its second year of publication in Raleigh, North Carolina, with this issue

books, were (for a lot of reasons) somewhat more independent than the newspapers and, all in all, a good deal more diverse in the books they chose to review. It is true that most of these "serious" magazines (as distinct from slick, popular magazines that dealt with publishing as yet another arena of celebrity and gossip) do not concern themselves much with looking at publishing and the literary scene. Still, in 1998 several of the best pieces about those subjects appeared in magazines. Two that were outstanding are *Chronicles*, the May issue of which was headlined "Who Killed the Book?" and included first-rate articles by Thomas Fleming ("Dial M for Murdoch"), Tony Outhwaite ("A Hothouse of Goofiness: *The American Book Industry*"), Clay Reynolds ("Maxwell Perkins Is Dead: The Decline of Commercial Publishing"), Gregory McNamee ("The Unscholarly World of

Scholarly Publishing"), and others. Likewise *The Sewanee Review* (Fall) published an important essay by Scott Donaldson, "The Literary Situation Today," a piece for which another piece, a follow-up, is promised. Of course, from the point of view of those involved in the publishing business, and for other interested parties as well, the best source of all remains *Publishers Weekly*, which has improved even as it has expanded to spend more time and space on children's books, audio books, and other pertinent topics. The best ongoing report card, one that includes a careful look at *Publishers Weekly*, too, is Campbell Geeslin's column, "Along Publisher Row," which appears in each issue of *Authors Guild Bulletin*. Not much that happens escapes Geeslin's notice.

The New York Times, in addition to its daily book reviewers, has the services of journalists such as Doreen Carvajal; Martin Arnold with his column "Making Books"; and Sarah Lyle, covering the business and the buzz of publishing. *The Washington Post* and *Washington Post Book World* have three veteran regulars who handle the news of publishing and general literary journalism as well as occasional book reviews–Jonathan Yardley, Michael Dirda, and David Streitfeld. As is the case in other forms of journalism these writers have, over time, assumed certain roles. Yardley serves as curmudgeon-in-chief, geezer-in-residence with the long view of things. Streitfeld is, in his excellent interviews, profiles, and features, the literary stockbroker of *The Washington Post*, alert to the least nuance of celebrity and notoriety, precise in his measure of who's out and who's in. Dirda is the book lover. His column, "Readings," is humane and concerned. In keeping with its image as sassy and irreverent, *The New York Observer* has Elizabeth Manus writing "Publishing" and Philip Weiss and regular reviewer Adam Begley handling various literary chores. Typical is Weiss's review and commentary of *Sir Vidia's Shadow: A Friendship Across Five Continents* (Houghton Mifflin), by Paul Theroux–"Theroux Slams Naipaul, Weiss Slams Theroux," 28 September: "All the same, I must admit that I had great pleasure reading this book. This is because in his urgency to burn H.M.S. *Naipaul* to the deck, Mr. Theroux traces the lineaments of his former friend's genius. He affords us a great view of a fierce and afraid Naipaul, dependent on strong women, crabby and needy and successful and self-protective, but always sensitive, always loving literature." In a year in which full-fledged "tomahawk chops" were, for whatever reasons, few and far between, one could always count on the *The New York Observer* to fight against the trend.

How about the magazines? What magazines, other than the quarterlies and literary magazines, are especially helpful in the struggle to keep up with book reviewing and the literary scene? From the point of view of writers and would-be writers there are the basic

"trade" magazines ranging from specifically limited publications such as *The PEN Newsletter, The American Poet*, and the recently spiffed up *Journal of the Academy of American Poets: Poets & Writers*, which has revised and refurbished its format and appearance this year and expanded its coverage to include more critical and personal pieces in addition to professional how-to and self-help articles. The *AWP Chronicle* had a facelift and appeared (six times a year) as *The Writer's Chronicle*–"Providing news, information, and inspiration for writers," aiming at a somewhat larger audience than the member institutions and individual membership of the Associated Writing Programs. Even the spartan *National Book Critics Circle Journal*, though unconcerned with aesthetics, has added features of interest for this special professional readership, as, for example, Bill Eichenberger's defense of "gratuitously nasty" book reviews in "Nasty Reviews" (August). *The Hungry Mind Review: The National Book Magazine*, published in St. Paul, Minnesota, which showed up in large and small bookstores all over the country (often given away free by booksellers), helped with splashes of color and offered reviews and articles on "literary" books, especially on the international scene and translations. So was *The Boston Book Review* ubiquitous nationwide. *Brightleaf: A Southern Review of Books* survived its first year, ably edited by former journalist David S. Perkins. Reviews are supported by columns (writers such as John Shelton Reed and Janet Lembke), profiles, interviews ("Atlanta in Wolfe's Clothing" by John Bentley Mays in the Winter issue), and special sections ("Unraveling Race," Fall issue).

Other southern magazines, more general than strictly literary, shine with all the signs of money behind them. Jump-started by a huge grant from the Lindhurst Foundation and by the actively engaged stewardship of Robert Coles, *DoubleTake* is certainly one of the most handsome and elegant magazines to appear in a long time, a kind of *Flair* for intellectuals–for those with a memory of that elaborate and expensive magazine. Coming from the Center for Documentary Studies at Duke University, it has an impressive layout of visual arts, chiefly photography, and publishes poetry, fiction, and book reviews. Like many other assertively "arty" publications, particularly those coming from the South, who are fearful of presenting an image too regional, *DoubleTake* has become a trendy supporter and defender of the literary establishment. You would be wasting your time if you looked there for any real news or any kind of discovery. Still, it has plenty of good work and is a pleasure to hold and to look at. *The Oxford American: The Southern Magazine of Good Writing*, supported by the kindness and beneficence of its publisher, John Grisham, is equally and expensively good looking, though it tends to be a little more desperately trendy than *DoubleTake*.

Even newer on the scene, and as flashy or more so than either *DoubleTake* or *The Oxford American* is *Book: The Magazine for the Reading Life,* which tries to do a little of everything concerned with the literary life and publishing trends and troubles. It is more than a little like a *People* magazine or a *Vanity Fair* of the literary scene, but, so far, it remains lively and interesting.

The space allotted for "Book World" in *The World & I,* the book-length monthly magazine of *The Washington Times,* has shrunk a little, but this magazine remains, all in all, one of the best places in the country for book reviewing. The quality of the essay-length reviews, edited and maintained by Susan B. Reno and Clark Munsell, has not diminished. And, in fact, there has been some improvement in the timing of their reviews. In the past their reviews often came onto the scene too late to be influential in any practical sense. In 1998 they were able to feature essay reviews of significant books during the actual, all-too-brief shelf life of the works. Some of the novels given thorough coverage and subjected to serious scrutiny included: Reynolds Price's *Roxanna Slade* (Scribner), Anne Tyler's *A Patchwork Planet* (Knopf), Jim Crace's *Quarantine* (Farrar, Straus and Giroux), Cormac McCarthy's *Cities of the Plain* (Knopf), Steven Millhauser's *The Knife Thrower* (Crown), Robert Stone's *Damascus Gate* (Houghton Mifflin), and Andrea Barrett's *The Voyage of the Narwhal* (Norton). Extra columns—"Books from Abroad" and "Writers and Writing"—offered more information. If there is a flaw or fault in "Book World," it is that the pool of reviewers seems to be smaller than it used to be. At times some issues have seemed to be dominated by reviewers all coming from the Raleigh–Durham–Chapel Hill triangle, as if "Book World" and *Brightleaf* and *DoubleTake* were coordinating their efforts. And it might as well be added that, like some of the others, "Book World" has little time and space for discovery and rediscovery. But in 1998 these aims were ignored by almost all the book-reviewing publications—except, maybe, for the extraordinary and firmly independent *Review of Contemporary Fiction.* Dedicated to discovery and rediscovery, championing the offbeat, the avant-garde, and the small press, the review edited by John O'Brien of Normal, Illinois, appears to have appropriately concluded that most literary novels and novelists are species as much endangered as any other. In "Book Reviews" there is plenty of space for unusual talents, foreign and domestic, and for discovery also—*item: The Collected Stories of Calvert Casey* (Duke), called "a visionary stylist" by reviewer David Ian Paddy (Fall). That same issue contained thoughtful reviews of mainstream mid-list writers such as William H. Gass, Mario Vargas Llosa, Milan Kundera, John Edgar Wideman, Jerome Charyn, Cormac McCarthy, and John Fowles. A relatively new addition to the package of the

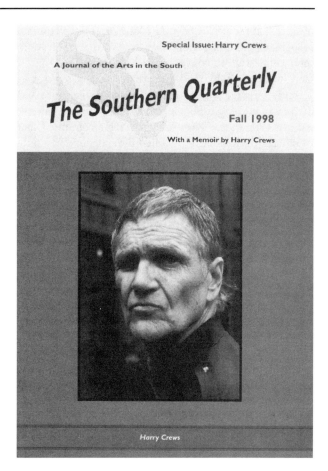

Special Issue: Harry Crews

A Journal of the Arts in the South

The Southern Quarterly

Fall 1998

With a Memoir by Harry Crews

Harry Crews

Cover for a special issue of one of the major Southern reviews

review is editor O'Brien's "School of Stupidity," which allows him to take a poke (or a tomahawk) at some of the literary sacred cows—as, for example, when he welcomed Michiko Kakutani of *The New York Times* into his "school" and honored her in the Spring issue with a "Lifetime Achievement Award": "In conclusion, we would like to congratulate Ms. Kakutani. We would also like to ask how she ever got her job."

Among the major mainstream magazines, *The New Yorker,* which had given over space to consideration of the publishing world, made news on 9 July when both *The New York Times* ("Editor of the New Yorker Leaving for New Venture") and *The Washington Post* ("Tina Brown quits The New Yorker") had prominent stories about Tina Brown's departure from *The New Yorker* after serving as its editor for six years. S. I. Newhouse had owned the magazine for thirteen years, including the years of Brown's tenure, during which he lost an estimated $100 million. Brown went to work for Miramax and was almost immediately replaced by staff writer David Remnick. On 27 July, Brown wrote "Something Old, Something New," her farewell accounting of the six years of her editorship: "Members of a vast cosmopolitan community, extending far beyond Manhattan have come to recognize in the pages of *The New Yorker* a civilization, their civilization in conversation with itself." In point of fact, after a shaky and uncertain start, Brown had recently devoted a good deal of space to literature and literary matters. Both book reviews and literary journalism thrived. Editor Remnick has so far continued that trend. On 5 October he "pushed the envelope" by publishing a group of writers–Toni Morrison, Janet Malcolm, James Salter, Lorrie Moore, Louis Begley, Jane Smiley, and Ethan Coen–venting their opinions on the subject of President Clinton and his problems. Other than a demonstration of verbal facility and some high and low forms of irony, and other than Toni Morrison's assertion that the president's behavior makes him, "white skin notwithstanding, our first black President," all this expensive brainpower and creativity added up to nothing much. Nevertheless, *The New Yorker* of 1998 remained one of the principal sources for cutting-edge book reviewing and for news of the literary scene.

For book reviewing, the chief quarterlies and some of the literary magazines assumed increasing importance. In the past the major quarterlies (*The Sewanee Review, The Hudson Review, The Virginia Quarterly Review, The Southern Review,* and *The Georgia Review*) had seen their influence diminish because of timing. By the time their reviews of literary books appeared, the effective shelf life of these books (four to six weeks) was over and done with. Some new developments have changed this. For one thing, until recently the publishers sent only finished books, not bound galleys or advance readers' copies, to the quarterlies. Now more and more publishers send out galleys to the quarterlies just as they do to the press and to the mainstream magazines. (These latter, with noted exceptions, do very little serious reviewing anyway.) Reviews from the literary quarterlies are more timely. In addition, the triumph of the computer has changed things considerably. With contemporary marketing, books can be ordered and delivered from distributors easily, swiftly, and at any time, which means that the brief shelf life of a literary book, as distinguished from the life of a blockbuster, is less relevant. The big chain bookstores have to fill their extensive shelves, anyway. Moreover, on-line direct marketing through big companies such as Amazon.com and Barnes & Noble.com gives a book a much longer lifetime, and it aids the marketing of books published by small presses. Thus book reviews in the literary quarterlies are now as important and influential as they have ever been. It is true that the direction of large conglomerate publishing is altogether different. A two-track system of publishing and marketing is evolving. For the conglomerate direction see Robert S. Boynton's "Annals of Publishing: The Hollywood Way" in *The New Yorker* (30 March), a profile

of Michael Lynton, chairman of Penguin Books: "In big publishing, books are increasingly being regarded less as discrete properties than as one vital link in a media food chain that begins with an idea, takes early shape as a magazine article, gets fleshed out between book covers, gains bigger life in a movie or TV screen, and enters the hereafter as a videocassette or the inspiration for a toy." Of course, in "bigger publishing" the majority of "ideas" stumble and fail long before arriving at the hereafter.

If the quarterlies and literary magazines are more important than they used to be, especially in the life and fate of literary, mid-list books, most of them have not risen to the challenge. Serious reviewing and criticism have become rare and whimsical in most of the literary magazines and in once-vital quarterlies such as *The Southern Review* and *The Kenyon Review*. To be sure, there are other magazines that are exclusively devoted to reviewing and criticism and are more and more concerned with the contemporary rather than the literary-historical scene. For example, *The Southern Quarterly: A Journal of the Arts in the South* has done adventurous work for a basically academic quarterly, including a special issue (Fall) celebrating the life and work of Southern "outlaw" writer Harry Crews. But their venue is all the arts, and the arts of poetry and fiction must compete with the visual arts for space and attention. Only three of the major quarterlies have remained true to their identities as reviews: *The Hudson Review, The Sewanee Review,* and *The Virginia Quarterly Review*. These three, though they publish poetry, fiction, and essays as do the other literary magazines, devote much space to book reviews and to literary essays. *The Hudson Review* on the average devotes fifty pages to book reviews; both *The Sewanee Review* and *The Virginia Quarterly Review* average roughly eighty pages of book reviews. All three magazines allot ample space for reviews of current fiction. In this point they are against the trend in the newspapers and the mainstream magazines that, following the example of *The New York Times Book Review,* routinely use two-thirds of their reviewing space for nonfiction. One of the results of all this is that literary fiction depends more than ever on the attention of the quarterlies or on other forms of attention–National Public Radio reviews and interviews, for example, and the variety of television programs on C-Span.

Taken altogether, the situation of book reviewing tends to favor the already known, the "literary establishment," at the expense of discovery and rediscovery and reappraisal. Still, it was an active, lively, and interesting year in book reviewing, and here is my list of outstanding book reviews from 1998:

*Bruce Allen, "A Writer's Harvest," *Brightleaf* (Winter). Review of *Stories, Essays and Memoirs* (Library of America) and *Complete Novels* (Library of America), by

Eudora Welty: "The more ambitious tales gathered in the *Wide Net* (1943) are more varied explorations of the paradox that engaging the world, daring and living are both departures from the self's security and, in the largest possible sense, the whole reason for living. The brilliantly comic title story (Welty's version of the Orpheus-Eurydice legend), the provocative 'At the Landing' . . . and the lushly mythic 'Asphodel' are all neglected stories that very nearly equal her acknowledged masterpieces."

*Sven Birkerts, "Don DeLillo's Brave New World," *DoubleTake* (Fall): "There is something urgent in the movement of the second hand, the ticking of the cursor. Our image- and data-saturated culture is pushing us toward some sort of critical mass. We are in the moment of the paradigm shift, when the old has clearly given way but the new has not yet announced itself. A Don DeLillo world. . . ."

*Greg Bottoms, "Strange Frame," *Gadfly* (January 1999). Review of *Glamorama* (Knopf), by Bret Easton Ellis: "If we're charitable enough, we might convince ourselves, based on publicity alone, that Ellis is a real maverick, a Poe or a Beckett or a Joyce, not just ahead of his time but beyond the constraints of cultural time, a writer to be truly and finally appreciated by a future generation. But it's also easy, given he knows what he's doing, to wonder if *carte blanche* from editors because of big sales and a big name is such a good thing when the talent is, at times, suspect."

*Hal Crowther, "The End of the Trail," *The Oxford American* (23). Review of *Cities of the Plain* (Knopf), by Cormac McCarthy: "A century from now, if the habit of literature survives the current cultural holocaust, *Suttree* will be a benchmark . . . like *Huckleberry Finn* or *The Sound and the Fury*. It pains me to see *Suttree*'s author chided by some light-weight New York reviewer for 'portentous rhetoric' and 'pop existentialism': But McCarthy has been asking for it. He should pay a visit home to Tennessee, where stoic cowboys and desert oracles don't much signify, where even the best readers resent untranslated Spanish dialogue."

*Michael Dirda, "The Final Deduction," *Washington Post Book World* (8 March). Review of *An Instance of the Fingerpost* (Riverhead), by Iain Pears: "As haunting as *The Name of the Rose* and as gripping as *Tinker, Tailor, Soldier, Spy,* it is a novel about deception and self-deception, about the scientific method and Jesuitical chicanery, above all about political expedience and religious transcendence. Every sentence is as solid as brick and as treacherous as quicksand."

*Thomas M. Disch, "Being One Being a Genius Sometimes," *The Hudson Review* (Autumn). Review of *Gertrude Stein: Writings 1903–1932* and *Writings 1932–1946* (Library of America): "What mainly accounts for

the occluding elements in Stein's style was the fact that she had something to hide. Not her reservations about the greatness of Matisse, though a veil can be handy in those circumstances, too. Her guilty secret, like most everyone's, was sex. After the cautionary example set by Oscar Wilde, writers in the early 1900s were not about to advertise themselves as sodomites."

*Thomas R. Edwards, "The Gang's All Here," *New York Review of Books* (13 August). Review of *The Half-Life of Happiness* (Knopf), by John Casey: "In splitting the book between the demise of the gang and Mike's congressional campaign, Casey seems to be asking what useful relation may now be imaginable between sensitive, educated, intelligent people and the proper running of the nation. 'None at all,' appears to be the book's answer, which seems true enough for our time and place. . . ."

*Jeff Giles, "The Human Comedy," *Newsweek* (28 September). Profile of Lorrie Moore and review of her book *Birds of America* (Knopf): "There are times when 'Birds' seems almost *too* cynical about the distance between people, and the collection feels long by a story or two. Still, most everything is so smart and so full of absurdist pathos that you can't look away."

*Todd Gitlin, "Crazy in Jerusalem," *The Nation* (11 May). Review of *Damascus Gate* (Houghton Mifflin), by Robert Stone: "This is Stone's longest novel, and it is overlong and overstuffed, the action often badly slack. Shake the likes of his whole sick crew and bake them in the Middle East oven, send them on criminal missions into the Gaza Strip, expose them to angry Palestinians and millenarian settlers, and *Damascus Gate* ought to be superb. It has Stone's characteristic lizard eye for human tension and pretension. It has the morally pained view, that which nothing could be more apposite for Israel and Palestine. But the intricacy comes at a steep price. Stone's largest population of characters is too dense, too much a cobbler of bad apples."

*Paul Gray, "Better Red than Dead?," *Time* (12 October). Review of *I Married a Communist* (Houghton Mifflin), by Philip Roth: "What Zuckerman/Roth does with this imagined material is constantly mesmerizing. Library shelves groan under the Truman and Eisenhower presidencies, but it would be hard to find one among them that presents as nuanced, as humanly complex an account of those years as *I Married a Communist*."

*Pat C. Hoy, II, "Virginia Woolf and the Art of Recovery," *The Sewanee Review* (Fall). Chronicle review of several recent books about Virginia Woolf: "Civilization seemed on the brink of collapse. Woolf's audience was disappearing into the collective hysteria that war evokes, and there was no one to write to. There seemed little left but the darkness. Yet here in this particular version of Virginia Woolf's story, [Hermione Lee's *Virginia*

Cover for the quarterly review published by the Center for Documentary Studies at Duke University

Woolf, 1997], we can feel the ebb and flow of her life, just as we feel the rhythms of her work. Life and work overlap, reinforcing one another, illuminating death and forever and making a mockery of those who judge too harshly her final surrender."

*Alfred Kazin, "God's Own Terrorist," *New York Review of Books* (9 April). Review of *Cloudsplitter* (Harper Flamingo), by Russell Banks: "The book brilliantly comes alive only in the violent scenes that are the central part of Brown's story—his Kansas killings and the attack on Harpers Ferry. Russell Banks is a talented and agile novelist who moves easily from one American subject to another; he is strong in short descriptive effects but weak in creating characters equal to his larger design for the book."

*Peter LaSalle, "Tempest-Tossed," *Book* (December/January). Review of *The Storm* (HarperCollins), by Frederick Buechner: "Of course, any retelling of Shakespeare (the jacket copy calls this a 'shadow version') has to survive on its own and make for moving, solidly crafted fiction, the connection to the original offering an extra, yet important, dimension. And Buechner succeeds here."

*M. G. Lord, "Image on the Living Room Screen," *Washington Post Book World* (20 December).

Review of *Breaking News* (Doubleday), by Robert MacNeil: "Yet I didn't learn anything from *Breaking News* that I hadn't already seen on 'Murphy Brown.' It did, however, offer an insider's view of what was, for me, exotic territory—the brain of a mature man. Except when placed by John Updike into the head of Rabbit Angstrom, I have never been as conscious of the extent to which testosterone influences a storyteller's perceptions."

*Norman Mailer, "A Man Half Full," *New York Review of Books* (17 December). Review of *A Man in Full* (Farrar, Straus and Giroux), by Tom Wolfe: "Writing a best-seller with conscious intent to do so is, after all, a state of mind that is not without comparison to the act of marrying for money, only to discover that the absence of love is more onerous than anticipated. When a putative and modest writer of best-sellers finally becomes professional enough to write a winner, he or she thinks that a great feat has been brought off, even as a man void of love (and money) will see a wealthy marriage as a helpful union."

*Scott L. Malcomson, "The Color Line," *The New Yorker* (6 April). Review of *Cloudsplitter* (Harper Flamingo) by Russell Banks and *The All-True Travels and Adventures of Liddie Newton* (Knopf) by Jane Smiley: "One can't help wondering whether Russell Banks ran into Jane Smiley out on the Kansas prairie, dowsing for abolitionist spirits. It's certainly curious that two prominent white American writers have just published historical novels about abolition. It may be odder still that the two writers' books have so little in common."

*Thomas McGonigle, "The Best Fiction of 1998," *Los Angeles Times Book Review* (13 December). Review of several European novels published in 1998: "Sadly now in America only three publishing companies can be said to reliably, season after season, produce significant translations: Farrar, Straus and Giroux, the University of Nebraska Press, and, most extravagantly, Northwestern University Press, which almost single-handedly are keeping alive the idea that many countries in Eastern Europe are replete with marvelous writers worthy of our attention."

*Daphne Merkin, "Glass House," *The New Yorker* (24–31 August). Review of *At Home in the World* (Picador), by Joyce Maynard: "But if there is something unsavory about a fifty-three-year-old man's fascination with an unformed girl, there's something equally creepy about an unformed girl's deliberately shaping herself to fit a role, a recurring motif in Salinger's imagination."

*William Mills, "Beyond the Crossing," *Chronicles* (October). Review of *Cities of the Plain,* by Cormac McCarthy: "Buy the book and enjoy it now as a virgin experience before Disney makes a movie of it, or the literary theorists tell you what they think it means."

*Jack O'Brien, untitled review in *The Review of Contemporary Fiction* (Fall). Review of *Keeping Literary Company* (State University of New York), by Jerome Klinkowitz, and *Namedropping* (State University of New York), by Richard Elman: "While many of the writers that Klinkowitz covers still remain unrecognized in contemporary American literature, and since yet another university is willing to give him space in its catalog, the book could have been an opportunity for much-needed discussion; instead it becomes an occasion for the author's self-imposed illusion that he made them well-known."

*David R. Slavitt, "Revenge Fantasy," *The New York Times Book Review* (14 June). Review of *Medea* (Talese/Doubleday), by Christa Wolf: "Wolf reportedly wrote much of his novel on a grant from the Getty Center for the History of Art and the Humanities (socialists have to be realists sometimes) in an apartment hotel in Santa Monica, California. In that spirit of accommodation, the SS, who cowed her father into submission, and their Stasi successors, for whom Wolf worked, could seem very far away, almost as remote as Medea's fabulous homeland, into which she is clearly projecting herself."

*Lisa Russ Spaar, "Wild Imperatives in Character and Prose," *The Virginia Quarterly Review* (Spring 1998). Review of *Kneeling on Rice* (Missouri), by Elizabeth Denton, and *Nightwork* (Knopf) by Christine Schutt: "Except for a few startling sketchy props, Schutt's characters experience themselves and each other in a kind of spatial and material wasteland. Not so with Elizabeth Denton. Like other 'Yankee sensualists'–Elizabeth Bishop, Alice Munro, Edna O'Brien, Elizabeth Bowen, Virginia Woolf–she shapes her characters in *Kneeling on Rice* out of an acute attention of external phenomena that is so aptly restrained and quirky that it at times borders on the erotic."

*Walter Sullivan, "An Uncertain Jesus," *The World & I* (August). Review of *Quarantine* (Farrar, Straus and Giroux), by Jim Crace: "*Quarantine* is well constructed and efficiently written. The prose is clear and subservient to the story; that at-times almost surreal ambiance is skillfully maintained. The book has many literary virtues, and it is a sort of parable of our faithless times."

*Deborah Sussman Susser, "Women on the Brink of Enlightenment, or Breakdown," *The Washington Post* (3 December). Review of *In the House of Blue Lights* (Notre Dame), by Susan Neville: "There is stunning language in these stories, many of which have the hearts of poems. . . . If Neville has a weakness, it's one that arises from her strength; in places she offers the reader so many striking turns of phrase that they threaten to cancel each other out."

*John Updike, "Awriiiiighhhhhhhht!: Tom Wolfe Looks Hard at America," *The New Yorker* (9 November). Review of *A Man in Full* (Farrar, Straus and Giroux), by Tom Wolfe: "For Faulkner, Southern life was life; for Wolfe it is a provincial curiosity, though one he cherishes. The lush landscape moves him to nature lyricism; the suburban luxury of Atlanta's Buckhead neighborhood sets off idyllic catalogues of sun-splashed antiques and shrubs. He is, disarmingly, dazzled, and something of this dazzlement rubs off."

A long view of American book reviewing is to be found in a large anthology from Times Books: *Books of the Century: A Hundred Years of Authors, Ideas and Literature From the New York Times,* edited by Charles McGrath (who edits *The New York Times Book Review*). Chronologically arranged from 1896 through 1997, the gathering of reviews is, as McGrath points out in his "Introduction," essentially an expansion of the centennial issue of *The New York Times Book Review,* which appeared in October 1996, on the occasion of the one-hundredth anniversary of the review. "We've included a number of reviews that we didn't have room for back then, and also some non-review material (the annual Editor's Choice selections for the twenty-five years from 1972 to 1997, letters, essays and commentary) intended to suggest a fuller sense not only of what *The New York Times Book Review* was actually like from week to week but also of some of the larger cultural issues that helped shape the literary climate at various points." More or less aware, at least admitting that the present editors are limited in their choices and selections and that those who come along in the next century "will no doubt find many of our choices quaint, not to say incomprehensible," the collection opens with a 20 February 1897 review of *The Spoils of Poynton,* by Henry James, and closes (not counting the final section, "Editor's Choice 1972–1997," which may be best described as the editors' brief celebrations of what they took to be the best books of each year) with a review by Martin Amis of *Underworld,* by Don DeLillo, on 5 October 1997. The text is generally enlivened by editorial marginalia that serve to set the reviews in the context of the literary scene. Here, for example, is the note for the year 1980: "Lillian Hellman sues Mary McCarthy for $2.25 million after McCarthy says of Hellman, 'Every word she writes is a lie, including "and" and "the".'" *Books of the Century* is at once interesting and worthwhile, though it is, perhaps inevitably, as much a picture of the tastes and notions of the library establishment of the 1990s as it may be a record of the views of past decades. In an odd sense all past time, including its judgments and failures, is simultaneous when viewed from the shifty observation point of the present. So, in a sense, *Books of the Century* demonstrates the state of book reviewing in America in 1998.

What sort of a year was it? What happened, large and small, to shape the literary scene?

Close readers of *Publishers Weekly* and of Campbell Geeslin's "Along Publishers Row" (*Authors Guild Bulletin*) found plenty of evidence of the by-now-usual comings and goings at publishing houses (more going than coming) and minor mergers. But everyone was taken by surprise by two almost unimaginably huge events. Jocelyn McClurg of the *Hartford Courant,* who wrote on 3 January 1999 that "1998 was a year to remember in books and publishing," was not exaggerating when she commented: "The biggest story inside New York publishing was the acquisition of Random House by German publishing giant Bertelsmann AG. Bertelsmann already owned Bantam Doubleday Dell when it decided to buy Random House and all of its imprints." Some in the business hoped that the Federal Trade Commission (FTC) might block this huge merger, and indeed Authors Guild and the Association of Authors' representatives joined in protest to try to convince the FTC's federal antitrust regulators to block the purchase. The original announcement of the merger came in late March.

By the end of April the FTC had already acted, and the *Authors Guild Bulletin* (Spring) covered the story in "Bertelsmann Bid For Random House Passes FTC Scrutiny: Guild Protest Leads to Closer Look, but Fails to Block Purchase": "Bertelsmann's purchase of Random House creates a publishing giant controlling more than 36 percent of the U.S. adult trade book market, the Guild reported to the FTC. The top four publishers would control 73 percent of the market should the merger be completed." A thorough article about the acquisition appeared in *The New Yorker* (27 April and 4 May)—"Springtime For Bertelsmann: The Publishing World," by Daniel Johnson. Johnson pointed out that with the acquisition of the Random House conglomerate from Advance Publications, Bertelsmann would become one of the world's three great media conglomerates, together with Disney and Time Warner. Johnson also wrote that the aim of these companies to attain 15 percent profit on total assets was a goal that, even if achieved, could radically change the publishing business, being in no known way advantageous to independent publishers and bookstores and mid-list, literary authors.

In the fall came another surprise for the literary world. In November, Len Riggio of Barnes and Noble announced the intention to buy the chief distributor in the nation, Ingram Book Company, for $600 million, a prospect that seemed likely to be a trump card in the competition between Barnes and Noble and Amazon.com. (See Yahlin Chang, "Books Caught in the Web," *Newsweek,* 28 November: "The certain victims of this deal will be, as always, the struggling independent booksellers.")

On a smaller scale, money talked in 1998. Tom Clancy's new multibook contract with Putnam was reported to be for $100 million. Meanwhile, Stephen King signed on at Simon and Schuster with a new deal giving him $2 million per book plus 50 percent of the profits. And in another deal, authors Dominick Dunne and John Irving were paid $25,000 for five hundred words in narrative form about the pleasures of Absolut vodka. Pat Conroy was reported (in many places) to be negotiating to write the next sequel to *Gone with the Wind* for a very large advance. Reliable sources also indicate that, under contract, Alexandra Ripley will automatically earn a comfortable percentage of royalties from any sequel of *Gone with the Wind,* including one by Pat Conroy.

Hype played an increasingly larger part in the publishing marketplace. In the spring there was much advance publicity about Helen Fielding's novel, *Bridget Jones's Diary* (Viking), which had been a blockbuster in Great Britain. Blockbuster it was not on this side of the Atlantic, though it found a niche on the lower echelons of the national best-seller lists. Reviews were mixed and, as is often the case with manufactured best-sellers, irrelevant.

Nothing in recent literary history can equal the end-of-the-year attention accorded to Tom Wolfe and his new novel, *A Man in Full* (Farrar, Straus and Giroux), the first since the hugely successful *Bonfire of the Vanities.* Drumbeats for the book, scheduled for fall publication, began early in the year. *The New York Observer* ran a front-page story, "Tom Wolfe's Magnum Opus Is Ready! Farrar Hopes to Make Serial Killing," in the 27 April issue. (At that time the still unpublished work had another title—*Red Dogs.*) A little later according to *Publishers Weekly,* 22 June, at Book Expo America 98 came the public announcement from Farrar, Straus and Giroux that the first printing would be 1.2 million copies. Judy Quinn of *Publishers Weekly* ("A Full Fall") reported that other publishers were "astounded." In September *Vanity Fair* ran a long profile/interview, "The White Stuff," by David Kamp about Wolfe and the book, replete with more than one full-page photograph of Wolfe in his trademark three-piece white suit. By October, even before *A Man in Full* was published, it was already nominated and shortlisted for the National Book Award. (It did not win, of course, but it was the subject of news stories all across the country, anyway.)

The official publication date was 10 November, but many important reviewers jumped the gun. In *The New York Times* Michiko Kakutani weighed in on 28 October with "Wolfe Turns 'The Bonfire' Upside Down," a mixed review, but no harm done. Many reviews were mixed at best, but harmless, indeed serving as an excuse for more coverage of the book and the author.

Both Norman Mailer and John Updike labeled the book more entertainment than literature, and that became the occasion for more hype: see, for example, Martin Arnold, "A Snubbed Tom Wolfe Parries With 2 Men of Letters," *The New York Times,* 10 December. There Arnold quotes Wolfe's classic response: "I think you have to take Mailer and Updike as a matched set, and ask why those old bones are rising up to try and shoot down this book." Earlier (15 October), *Rolling Stone* had run an excerpt from the forthcoming novel, headlined on the cover–"Exclusive Sneak Preview: Tom Wolfe's New Novel." On 2 November, Wolfe, a man in a white suit with a white hat and matching gloves, smiled from the cover of *Time,* followed by a highly favorable cover story–"A Man in Full: Tom Wolfe's Bodacious New Novel, His First in 11 Years, Proves He Still Has the Right Stuff." On 9 November *The New York Observer* ran a lengthy review by literary pundit Harold Bloom, a mixed review to be sure, but helpful–"Mr. Wolfe's Atlanta is bad news, but then what part of the United States is anything else, in the age of Gingrich, Trent Lott and all of our other splendors!" Bloom also thanked Wolfe for resurrecting the stoic philosophers in his story: "An immense dose of Epictetus would do all of us a great deal of good, and I am grateful (beyond irony) to Tom Wolfe for reviving Epictetus and making him available to the hundreds of thousands whom Mr. Wolfe will reach." *A Man in Full* arrived instantly atop the best-sellers list of *The New York Times* and all the others.

On Monday, 16 November *The Washington Post* ran a full-scale interview (with a large white-suit picture) by David Streitfeld–"Still Master of His Universe." Three days later Wolfe was again the lead story of the "Style" section with Sue Anne Pressley's "Atlanta, Proud to be Picked On":

> "We don't care if he calls us 'boys with breasts,'" says Jeanne Sauban, owner of Jeanne's Body Tech, the supposed prototype of a Buckhead fitness gym featured in the novel. "We interpret that to mean the women are really fit–we're pumped up about it."

Jonathan Bing in *Publishers Weekly* gave extra pages to his interview with Tom Wolfe–"Tom Wolfe On Top" (7 December): "Making an appearance at the National Press Club in Washington, which was televised on C-Span, Wolfe declared that the 'money fever' of the 1980s has been replaced by the 'moral fever' of the 1990s." There were a multitude of interviews in the final weeks of 1998 (you could make a bibliography of the inter-

Cover for a monthly review of literature and the arts, with emphases on cultural studies and the history of ideas

views alone), even in the literary magazines, as shown in *Brightleaf* (Winter), where, in "Atlanta in Wolfe's clothing," John Bentley Mays wrote: "The book is well-stuffed with neat facts about contemporary American follies and fancies, and funny-sad portrayals of scores of heterosexuals in crisis." *The New York Times* even found a way, in its "Think Tank" column by Joyce Jensen (2 January 1999), to celebrate the Stoics and Tom Wolfe at the same time.

Meanwhile, other writers well known and little known received brief spotlights of public attention. Salman Rushdie was back in the papers. A piece in *The New Yorker* (26 October) by James Atlas, "Ink: Salman Rushdie has a brief glimpse of freedom," covers the basics. The 1989 *fatwa* was "formally repudiated" in 1998 by the Iranian government. Rushdie was free, walked the streets of London, and talked to reporters about his new novel, *The Ground Beneath Her Feet,* a version of the Orpheus story in the person of Vina Aspara, an Indian rock singer. All was well until Iranian Muslim clerics, allowing that the government of Iran had no right to repudiate the *fatwa,* renewed it, and Rushdie once again dropped out of sight. *Newsweek* (16 November) broke the news that Binjamin Wilkomirski's much praised and prizewinning memoir of the Holocaust, *Fragments,* turns out to be, in fact, a work of fiction. Novelist Barbara Chase-Ribaud lost her case (*Chase-Ribaud* v. *Dreamworks*) for copyright infringement of her novel *Echo of Lions* by the makers of the movie *Amistadt. The City of Light,* by David Selbourne, supposedly an authentic account of an early (before Marco Polo) medieval voyage to China, turned out to be a work of fiction. Bangladeshi poet Taslima Nasrin, charged with blasphemy, (like Rushdie) surrendered to authorities to stand trial. On a book tour Paul Auster discovered a set of page proofs of a lost book he had translated from the French twenty years earlier—*The Chronicle of the Guayaki Indians,* by Pierre Clastres. The original publisher for whom Auster did the translation is now defunct. Zone Books of New York announced its intention to publish the book. Critic D. T. Max published the results of a preliminary scholarly examination of the papers of Gordon Lish (now held by Indiana University) and concluded that Lish had great influence, as the editor, on the celebrated work of Raymond Carver ("The Carver Chronicles," *New York Times Magazine,* 9 August). Writing in Max's former home place, *The New York Observer* (24 August), columnist Todd Gitlin was critical of Max's opinions: "The issue D. T. Max does not raise in 'The Carver Chronicles' is why Mr. Lish archived his own edits in the first place. If not to burnish his own reputation, why save them at all? Certifying one's contributions sounds like itemizing expenditures during a marriage to start building a case for a post-divorce settlement" ("Editing: An Act of Generosity, Not a Stab at Co-Authorship").

One item of news caught the public fancy (as well as the interest of reporters) and was widely reported and commented on. (The reaction to this event is discussed in more detail elsewhere in the *DLB Yearbook 1998.*) On Monday, 20 July, *The New York Times* published as the leading story in its "The Living Arts" section Paul Lewis's "Ulysses at Top As Panel Picks 100 Best Novels." The editorial board of *Modern Library,* consisting of Christopher Cerf, Gore Vidal, Daniel J. Boorstin, Shelby Foote, Vartan Gregorian, A. S. Byatt, Edmund Morris, John Richardson, Arthur M. Schlesinger Jr., and William Styron, produced a list of the one hundred best works of fiction published during the past one hundred years. The list was "officially" released at the Radcliffe Publishing Course on Friday, 24 July, by which time most of the newspapers and magazines in the country had picked up the story and reprinted the list and the first reactions to it.

Newsweek ("The Dated and the Dead," by David Gates and Ray Sawhill, 3 August), in addition to covering the story, reported on the reaction to it:

By the end of the week, reporters were trying to track down board members. . . . And two counterlists had appeared. Students at Radcliffe College's summer publishing course picked *The Great Gatsby* first, *The Catcher in the Rye* second, *Ulysses* sixth–just after *The Color Purple*–and sneaked in *Charlotte's Web, Winnie-the-Pooh, The Wonderful Wizard of Oz* and *The Wind in the Willows* as well as three novels by Morrison. . . .

Almost immediately everybody, from English professors to stand-up comics, joined in and had a list. Letters poured in to *The New York Times* (Sunday, 26 July).

Nobody seemed happy with the original list or anybody else's list except, perhaps, Ann Godoff, president and editor in chief at Random House, who was quoted in Lewis's original story: "It's a way to bring the Modern Library to public attention. We want to grow the Modern Library and its stable of classics." Lewis pointed out in the same piece that all but one member of the editorial board are writers published either by Random House or its new owner, the Bertelsmann group. It was also noticed at the outset that only one woman, A. S. Byatt, was on the board and that the list contained works by only eight women.

Other reactions–William Styron's in "The Talk of the Town" in *The New Yorker;* Edmund Morris's "Bookend" in *The New York Times Book Review;* David Streitfeld's "Lowdown on the Literary List" in *The Washington Post* (5 August); and Frank Rich's op-ed column, "Who Chose 'The Magus'," in *The New York Times,* 8 August– are dealt with elsewhere in the *DLB Yearbook.*

In *The Boston Globe* (Saturday, 25 July) Beth Carney and Maureen Dezell wrote in "Boomers' Bests Borrowed from Other Lists" that at the first announcement of the Modern Library list, they had "asked readers born between 1946 and 1964 to tell us the names of their own favorites." At once they received three hundred letters in reply, and a new title, *To Kill a Mockingbird* by Harper Lee, was number one. *Style OnLine,* the online magazine published at Richmond, Virginia, tried another approach (4 August): "Not wishing to be silly, but looking for a little fun, *Style* has asked its writers to share their three favorite books. . . . In order to avoid the millennium hysteria, we have not limited our titles to the twentieth century, and they are not all novels." Their highly personal lists were diverse from *Great Expectations* and *The Count of Monte Cristo* to Daniel Pinkwater's *The Snarkout Boys and the Avocado of Death* (Farrar, Straus and Giroux). Two of the five staff writers (for reasons beyond all comprehension) picked John Irving's *A Prayer For Owen Meany.*

My own favorite list, among all the lists and counterlists, is the one prepared by Steve Martin, "The Hundred Greatest Books I've Ever Read," in *The New Yorker* (21 September). "Ulysses (first sentence only)" is number 85, followed immediately by the September issue of *Vanity Fair. Cliff's Notes* stands proudly at number 18 but is overtopped by *Owner's Manual, 1966 Mustang,* at number 12.

Finally, a word or two about trends in 1998. I would call attention to two in particular. Many literary books took on the coloration of the thriller. Novels, for instance, by Richard Bausch, Frederick Busch, William Hoffman, John Burnham Schwartz, Richard Price, and Michael Knight are characterized by strong, suspenseful plots joined with demonstrably literary writing. Year by year some of our finest genre writers–Elmore Leonard, Tony Hillerman, James W. Hall, and James Lee Burke, for example–are being reviewed and treated as mainstream novelists rather than strictly genre writers. There is some kind of meeting of the minds that is taking place. (See Elizabeth Manus, "Age of the Literary Thriller: Serious Writers Smell Blood," *New York Observer,* 21 September.)

The memoir is now finally in place. (See "Betrayal Between the Covers," by David Streitfeld, *Washington Post,* 27 October: "When all else fails, just be vicious.") Creative writing programs around the nation are now offering courses in writing the memoir as if it were a genre, equipped with a set of rules and conventions and a basic formula to be followed or ignored. But the nature of the memoir, especially the literary memoir, appears to be changing, also. In a society where privacy is allowed, but nonetheless more and more unobtainable, where public figures, living or dead, have no private lives, it is no surprise that a new kind of memoir, close kin to "confessional poetry" and to the trends in biography, should emerge. Composed in narrative much like autobiographical fiction, the form insists on hard facts, factual truth at its core. There were a number of outstanding examples of this kind of memoir during the year, books that were widely reviewed and discussed. Ted Hughes's *Birthday Letters* (Farrar, Straus and Giroux) was, remarkably for a book of poems, a best-seller because it dealt with his life with Sylvia Plath. Two appeared in serial version in *The New Yorker*–Paul Theroux's *Sir Vidia's Shadow: A Friendship Across Five Continents* (Houghton Mifflin), concerned with Theroux's long and complicated relationship with his former friend and mentor, V. S. Naipaul, and *Summer of Deliverance: A Memoir of Father and Son* (Simon and Schuster) by Christopher Dickey, a kind of biography of the poet, James Dickey, told from the complex point of view of his eldest son. This latter book earned strongly favorable notice.

Rosemary Mahoney, author of a pair of highly regarded and award-winning nonfiction books, turns back to the summer of her seventeenth year in *A Likely Story: One Summer with Lillian Hellman* (Doubleday). Here she recapitulates a very unpleasant story of working one summer for Lillian Hellman on Martha's Vineyard. Hellman was seventy-three years old and, evidently, a difficult person at any age. The portrait of the old lady is brutally unflattering, though, in fairness and probably not accidentally, the seventeen-year-old Mahoney seems to be a pain as well. Something of the same angle, a teenager's view of an older and prominent literary person, is the main (and most interesting) part of the story of Joyce Maynard's life so far–*At Home in the World: A Memoir* (Picador). For the first time Maynard writes, and in some detail, of her affair with the eccentric and reclusive J. D. Salinger. This memoir received mixed review at best, but was widely and promptly reviewed in all the media. Maynard might have done well to listen carefully to him in one of their serious conversations about writing: "Does anybody actually need to open up *Esquire* magazine and take in one more hysterically amusing little excuse in assassination by typewriter? Sooner or later you need to soberly consider whether what you write is serving any purpose but to serve your own ego."

Other literary memoirs that made a mark during the year included two books about William Shawn, longtime editor of *The New Yorker*: *Remembering Mr. Shawn's New Yorker* (Outlook) by Ved Mehta, and Lillian Ross's *Here and Not Here: A Love Story* (Random House), which tells of a long love affair between *The New Yorker* writer and her editor. *A Transatlantic Love Affair* (New Press) offered the public a selection of the love letters exchanged between Nelson Algren and Simone de Beauvoir. Novelist James Alan McPherson's *Crabcakes* (Simon and Schuster) is primarily autobiographical, but, as Jonathan Yardley put it (*Washington Post Book World,* 11 January), the book "contains a good deal of impenetrable self-indulgence."

Near year's end there were two other literary memoirs that received considerable attention. Susan Cheever's story of her three marriages and of her battle with alcoholism is recapitulated in *Note Found in a Bottle: My Life as a Drinker* (Simon and Schuster), and it gains added interest for its views of family life with her famous father, John Cheever. At the end of December there was *Elegy for Iris* (St. Martin's Press), John Bayley's account of his life with Iris Murdoch, who suffered from Alzheimer's disease.

At the far edge of the new trends and directions in narrative nonfiction writing stands Ellen Douglas's *Truth: Four Stories I Am Finally Old Enough To Tell* (Algonquin), described and defined by her publisher, in jacket copy: "A novelist revered for her story telling, here she crosses into the mirror world of historical fact to tell four stories in which she seeks the truth. . . ." A more frivolous and amusing example of the fusion and confusion of fact and fiction was a book by novelist William Boyd, *Nate Tate: An American Artist* (21 Publishing), in which the fictional artist Tate was passed off as "real" and became the subject of media attention and of a large publication party for New York literati. (See Sarah Lyall, "Raising Obscurity to an Art, A Book Gives A Painter Undue Fame," *The New York Times,* 9 April.)

LITERARY JOURNALISM

Finally, a word or two about literary journalism. With all that was happening in 1998 it is no wonder that literary journalists kept busy on all fronts. More and more it is the profiles, articles, and interviews that reach readers rather than the conventional book reviews. Here, from among many of their kind, is my selection of the outstanding literary journalism of 1998:

*Fouad Ajami, "The Traveler's Luck," *The New Republic* (13 July). Profile/review of V. S. Naipaul and his book of "Islamic Excursions"–*Beyond Belief* (Random House): "Naipaul's old unease with Islam persists, alas, into his new inquiry. True, the tone is slightly different. There is that opening disclaimer that it is a book about 'people' and not 'opinion.' This time the work is informed by the traveler's desire to be fascinated but neutral, to be a 'manager of narrative,' to stay in the background."

*Martin Arnold, "A Snubbed Tom Wolfe Parries with 2 Men of Letters," *The New York Times* (10 December). Account of the public (and modest) quarrel between Tom Wolfe and two reviewers, John Updike and Norman Mailer, of Wolfe's new novel–*A Man In Full* (Farrar, Straus and Giroux): "What perhaps can only be truly said now about 'A Man in Full' is that it's one novel that people are clamoring to read. What will be considered literature or entertainment 100 years from now no one can know."

*James Atlas, "The Uses of Misery," *The New Yorker* (24–31 August). Profile of Saul Bellow: "Bellow got to a point in every book, he confided to one of his girlfriends, where he had to 'tear up his life.' It wasn't a conscious policy–more a matter of encouraging conditions in which the chaos could flourish."

*Douglas Brinkley, "In the Kerouac Archive," *Atlantic Monthly* (November). Profile of Jack Kerouac based on "unpublished materials, including letters, notebooks and a voluminous diary that he started at the age of fourteen" : "As the 1960s progressed, Kerouac could not understand how Ginsberg could flash the peace sign and pronounce the imminent 'fall of America' while ignoring, as Kerouac saw it, mass murders by China's Mao Zedong, a brute worse than Stalin. 'Genet and Burroughs do not offend half as much, because they are metaphysically hopeless,' Kerouac continued in his letter to [Nanda] Pivano, 'but Ginsberg and [the poet Gregory] Corso are ignorant enough to be metaphysically

healthy and want to use art as a racket.' (See a selection from the Kerouac journals, "On the Road Again," in *The New Yorker,* 22 and 29 June.)

*David Denby, "The Contender," *The New Yorker* (20 April). Profile of Norman Mailer: "As James Baldwin and others pointed out, Mailer was no hipster himself; he was far too earnest ever to lose himself in spontaneous hedonism. In Mailer's writing, for instance, sex is rarely a flight into sweet or stormy clouds of pleasure; it is more likely to be a turbulent existential undertaking, caught in the dialectic of past and present, in which lovers draw forces and expectations from themselves and each other and either ascend into greater daring or sink back into timidity."

*Sebastian Faulks, "Forever a Mistress," *The New Yorker* (27 April and 4 May). Profile of French novelist Françoise Sagan: "But when a reputation has been down for so long there is only one way it can go. During the last decade of the century, various critics, tired of the excesses of French literary theory and its novelistic offspring, have tried to reinvent Sagan as an artist. The names of Nancy Mitford and Evelyn Waugh have been invoked. The writer François Nourissier has also compared her with F. Scott Fitzgerald, and speaks of her 'gaiety, disenchantment, a certain sadness against a background of naughtiness.'"

*Richard Ford, "Good Raymond," *The New Yorker* (5 October). Personal essay about the author's friendship with the late Raymond Carver: "What he liked when he got to Princeton was our whole setup. I had made some movie money the year before, and we had a good house on a pretty street. We made our mortgage payments. We owned our French car. Kristina was Kristina–she looked like a million bucks, loved to laugh, and had a professor's job at Rutgers. I wrote. There were no dependents. We didn't get drunk and take swings at each other late at night. We didn't frequent lawyers. The credit companies didn't threaten us. We were solid little citizens, and we were not even thirty-five."

*Paul Gray, "The Birth of a Poet," *Time* (19 October). Profile of poet Frieda Hughes, daughter of Sylvia Plath and Ted Hughes: "*Wooroloo* would be an impressive debut coming from any new poet, but the book will be read by many out of plain curiosity: In what manner does a child of those parents write? And although Hughes denies being consciously influenced by the work of her mother and father, traces from both are easy to see."

*Michael Kenney, "Briny Bestsellers Prepare to Do Battle," *Boston Globe* (28 July). Discussion of reissued nautical classics designed to profit from the huge recent success of Patrick O'Brian: "In the publishing wardrooms where the grand strategies are mapped out, the success of the O'Brians is credited with heightening interest in the genre—even by editors and publishers of O'Brian rivals like Murray, who is steering the Hornblower relaunch at Little, Brown, and Alexander Skutt, who is publishing yet another series."

*Peter Manso, "Chronicle of a Tragedy Foretold," *The New York Times Magazine* (19 July). Profile of African American writer Gayl Jones and her complex relationship with her husband, Bob Higgins: "Relentlessly playing on the race theme, he not only received basic help for Lucille [Gayl Jones's mother], but also apologies, even groveling mea culpas from city officials. One letter—an excoriation of Porter Peebles, the head of Lexington's Urban League, as a traditional Southern black—almost got Higgins into trouble when Peebles notified authorities, but no alarms went off with the cops. Nor, apparently, were the letters red flags to Jones; even his invocations of Hitler and his rampant anti-Semitism did not shake her belief in Higgins."

*Elizabeth Manus, "Dale Peck: Now It's Time to Say Goodbye to Farrar," *New York Observer* (13 July). Details of wheeling and dealing and hanky-panky involved in moving a writer from one publisher to another: "On May 29, Farrar's vice president and executive editor John Glusman was stroking his strong jaw and wondering why he still hadn't heard from agent Andrew Wylie about his offer on Mr. Peck's next book. It had been over a week. He gave Mr. Wylie until the next day. When he didn't hear back, he conserved his flinty voice and promptly fired off a fax withdrawing his offer."

*D. T. Max, "The Carver Chronicles," *The New York Times Magazine* (9 August). Examination of the Carver archives at the Lilly Library at Indiana University to determine the extent of the influence of Gordon Lish (and others) on the work of Raymond Carver: "What I found there, when I began looking at the manuscripts of stories like 'Fat' and 'Tell the Women We're Going,' were pages full of editorial marks—strikeouts, additions and marginal comments in Lish's sprawling handwriting. It looked as if a temperamental 7-year-old had somehow got hold of the stories."

*Michael Nelson, "Ward Just's Washington," *The Virginia Quarterly Review* (Spring). Critical profile and appreciation of Ward Just's novels: "In general, what fiction is, especially for writers of Just's generation, is the summit of the writing profession. Journalists have the

manuscripts of unpublished novels in their desk drawers; novelists don't have nonfiction manuscripts in theirs. The writers Just singles out for special admiration are Flaubert, Fitzgerald, Hemingway and James, not Mencken, Liebling and Steffens."

*Henry Taylor, "A Form of Patience: The Poems of John Haines," *The Hollins Critic* (December): "We have for several decades been aware of Haines as a poet of wilderness solitude; it takes a little effort, now, to recall how unusual his subject matter seemed when it began to appear in the 1960s. In his first book, *Winter News* (1966), he presented, among other things, a kind of short poem whose style appears simple and straightforward, but whose effect is to arouse a strong sense of mystery."

*George Watson, "Iris Murdoch and the Net of Theory," *The Hudson Review* (Autumn). "In any case there is a better answer than empiricism to explain the enormous and ever-recurring power of realism in England since Defoe, and it was Iris Murdoch who found it. It is the unique presence of Shakespeare. This is a highly original intuition about literary history, and from someone who has never been a literary historian, so I do not conceal my envy."

*William Weaver, "Roman Candle," *The New York Review of Books* (25 June). Memoir of the author's friendship with Alberto Moravia: "Since he had no teachers and saw his parents seldom, Moravia was a man without received ideas—there had been no one to receive them from—and, both in his writing and in his daily life, he maintained a free, skeptical mind, immune to political creeds of intellectual fashions. While some other Italian writers and thinkers, including many future left-wing eminences, had a youthful moment of Fascist flirtation, Moravia was not attracted by the regime's superficial allure."

*Philip Weiss, "Hey! Grandpaw Was Right—Doctorow Stole *Ragtime*," *New York Observer* (23 March). Discussion of E. L. Doctorow's debt to *Michael Kohlhaas* by Heinrich von Kleist: "Mr. Doctorow's comments on the matter in interviews back in 1975 also strike me as sly. He brought up Kleist himself, but the reporters then characterized Coalhouse as a 'tribute' or a reflection of Mr. Doctorow's 'admiration' for Kleist. When Mr. Doctorow used the word 'adaptation' in our conversation, that was more to the point."

The Publishing Industry in 1998: *Sturm-und-drang.com*

Michael L. Lazare

Four events helped define book publishing and bookselling in 1998. **23 March:** German publishing and entertainment giant Bertelsmann AG announced it would purchase Random House, one of the most prestigious imprints in American book publishing, from Advance Publications Inc. Advance retained newspapers such as the *Cleveland Plain Dealer, Portland Oregonian, New Orleans Times-Picayune,* and *Newark Star-Ledger,* as well as cable television companies and the Condé Nast family of magazines, which includes *The New Yorker, Glamour, Allure, Vogue, Vanity Fair,* and *GQ.* The Bertelsmann purchase of Random House was consummated on July 1, after approval by the Federal Trade Commission. Bertelsmann and Advance are privately held and do not disclose financial data, but the consensus of industry analysts was that the sales price was between $1.2 billion and $1.4 billion. **17 May:** The equally well-known Simon and Schuster was dismembered alive and divided between two companies. Allyn and Bacon, Macmillan, and part of Prentice Hall were sold to Britain's Pearson PLC, owners of the *Financial Times* and half of *The Economist,* Mindscape software, and book publishers Penguin, Viking, and Putnam. The professional and reference operations of Prentice Hall were sold to Hicks, Muse, Tate & Furst of Dallas, which owns radio and television stations, movie theaters, and consumer goods ranging from Stetson hats to Chef Boyardee canned pasta. Simon & Schuster kept Pocket Books and Scribners. **6 October:** Bertelsmann bought 50 percent of Barnes & Noble's on-line bookselling operations, barnesandnoble.com. **31 December:** Trading on the stock market ended for the year with shares of Amazon.com at $3213, $291 higher than at the end of 1997. The stock subsequently split and gained 50 percent in the first week of trading in 1999. Amazon.com, which does business only on the Internet, is the largest on-line bookseller and barnesandnoble.com's fierce competitor. Anyone with the foresight to buy $10,000 worth of Amazon.com stock at the low price in 1998 would have made a profit of $96,639 by the end of the year. Perhaps other investments have done as spectacularly well, but what made Amazon.com doubly astounding was that as its stock was increasing 966.4 percent, its losses more than quadrupled, from a 22-cents-a-share loss in the last quarter of 1997 to a 90-cents-a-share loss in the third quarter of 1998. barnesandnoble.com is nowhere near making a profit, either. But neither deals in Dutch tulip bulb futures. Both are legitimate businesses that are expected to make healthy profits in the future. Bertelsmann predicted that on-line book sales would account for 20 percent of its business by the year 2010.

In sum, two main trends marked the year. On the one hand, control of book publishing was concentrated in fewer and fewer hands, and American ownership of venerable American corporations was rapidly dwindling. On the other hand, the growth of books being funneled through modems was increasing logarithmically. Looked at from any point of view, 1998 was truly the year of sturm-und-drang.com.

The hue and cry that followed Bertelsmann's announcements in 1998 focused on three main points: One, the sale to foreigners of a prestigious American marque (Random House owns Knopf, Crown, Ballantine, Fawcett, Times Books, Villard, and Pantheon). Two, the effect on writers and the book-buying public of yet further concentration of publishing power. Three, the effect on writers and the book-buying public of mushrooming on-line sales of books.

There was little outright xenophobia, but the German factor certainly was mentioned prominently in commentaries about the sale of Random House. Almost forgotten was the fact that there already existed a formidable foreign presence in American publishing. Australian-born Rupert Murdoch's News Corporation owns HarperCollins, and Germany's Verlagsgruppe Georg von Holtzbrinck GmbH owns St. Martin's Press, Henry Holt, and Farrar, Straus and Giroux. But with the stroke of a pen, Bertlesmann became the world's largest English-language publisher, controlling an estimated 10 percent of the American market. It now owns literary rights to John Grisham, Michael Crichton, Anne Rice, Toni Morrison, Norman Mailer, John

Updike, James Joyce, Eudora Welty, Truman Capote, Dr. Seuss, and James Michener, among many others.

Bertelsmann already owned Bantam Doubleday Dell (BDD), itself the union of three paperback publishers. More than 30 percent of Bertelsmann's sales, estimated at $12 billion annually, are now in America; the company's new CEO, Thomas Middlehoff, has said he intends to increase the percentage to 40. (He is 45 years old and is expected to run Bertelsmann until the company's mandatory retirement age of 60.) Until 23 March, most American book buyers probably had never heard of Bertelsmann. Yet the firm has been publishing books longer than most American companies. Carl Bertelsmann published his first book, a collection of Christian songs, in 1835, predating the first publications by Charles Scribner, Frederick Stokes, George Ticknor, J. B. Lippincott, Alfred A. Knopf, and dozens of other American publishers—including Bennett Cerf and Donald Klopfer, who launched a new imprint in 1927 to publish a few good books "at random." Bertelsmann's first famous authors were the Brothers Grimm. From these beginnings, Bertelsmann grew into the world's third-largest media empire, outstripped only by Walt Disney and Warner Brothers. It owns books, magazines, broadcasting companies, and digital pay television operations and is a partner with America Online in European on-line services. No stranger to America, Bertelsmann already owned the RCA and Arista record labels and a group of American magazines that includes *McCall's* and *Family Circle,* as well as BDD. Bertelsmann is run by German businessmen who are not under the pressure of their American counterparts to show quarter-to-quarter increases in profit. It is not publicly held and therefore does not have stockholders who demand a steady growth in share prices. It can afford to keep its focus on the long term, and in the long term it sees America and the on-line selling of books as profitable. Bertelsmann wanted to buy into Amazon.com. But long, intense negotiations foundered on price because of the steadily rising price of Amazon.com's shares. Bertelsmann then announced it would start its own bookselling venture but chose instead to buy part of the existing barnesandnoble.com operation.

Writers and agents were understandably concerned when the Bertelsmann–Random House marriage was announced. Equally understandably, the debate about who wins and who loses will be settled only by time, not by letters to the *Times.* In one such letter, Authors Guild President Letty Cottin Pogrebin wrote, ". . . Random House books have taken more than 50 percent of the Pulitzer Prize awards for fiction and nonfiction in the past four years. That record reflects the work of talented editors working for autonomous imprints. Bertelsmann reportedly plans to rein in

that autonomy, coordinating the imprints' bids on new works as a first step. Books continue to drive much of our cultural and political discourse, but the quality of that discourse is fragile. Permitting a single publisher to control one-third of the market is discomforting to writers and readers alike" (2 April 1998). In an article the day after the merger became official, the *Times* quoted Kay Murray, assistant director of the Authors Guild: ". . . we've maintained all along that the merger isn't good for writers. We are afraid of a decrease of diversity in the books published, with one publisher having a third of the market share" (2 July 1998). (The *Times* noted that Bertelsmann in fact would control only one-tenth of American publishing.) Many agents also said they feared the growing international consolidation would mean less freedom to negotiate in different countries.

Less lofty but more practical were fears about advances to authors. A few days after the Random House announcement, the *Times* ran a long article by Doreen Carvajal and Geraldine Fabrikant in which it noted, ". . . interviews with publishing figures over the past few days suggest that the consolidation of the major publishing houses into the world's largest English-language trade publisher could accelerate a relatively new trend. And that is a reduction in advances to midlist authors who sell fewer books than brand-name authors with bestseller status. That result could make it much more difficult for the nonstars to earn a literary living. 'You'll see a reduction for advances in the middle of the lists through the next level, where authors will have to earn their way—I think we've all been a little bit more cautious about how much we want to gamble on writers with less potential," said Jack Romans, president of consumer publishing for Simon and Schuster. He added, though, that superstar authors would continue to command "top dollars" (25 March 1998).

It should be noted that Random House had been setting new standards for huge advances—$5 million for Marlon Brando's autobiography, more than $6 million for Gen. Colin Powell's autobiography, and $2.5 million to Dick Morris, former adviser to President Clinton who also was involved in an adultery scandal. English literary agent George Greenfield, who represented John Le Carré among others, noted, "The worst thing to my mind about over-large advances is their effect on the publisher, not on the author. One publisher produced a deficit of around $10 million on one of their author's last three-book contracts. They will make profits from other books and authors, but that $10 million will never come back. It could have been better spent in so many other ways—on publicity for deserving newcomers, for backing gifted but not highly commercial writers—and so on."

Speaking with the voice of experience was Thomas McCormack, former chairman of St. Martin's Press, a casualty of the Holtzbrinck purchase. Shortly after the Bertelsmann announcement McCormack commented, "The *Times* quotes a Writers Guild spokesman on the consolidation: 'Our fear is that with his sort of situation they're going to look for efficiencies and some ways to cut costs.' They will, and they should—as Random House did when it acquired Knopf: instead of two accounts-payable departments, it will have one, and one accounts-receivable department, and one CEO. They'll combine shipping to cut stores' freight expenses. And more. They shouldn't do this? Study an old Literary Market Place and see how many publishers aren't around any more, killed by costs. Why do you think Newhouse sold Random? The Guild fears 'restricted bidding,' but Doubleday-Dell had it long before Bertelsmann arrived. And don't think there hasn't been imprint control at Random House. To this day there is resentment at Vintage Books about *The Joy Luck Club*. Vintage had the floor in the paperback auction—and they were forced to transfer it to Ballantine. Contrary to prejudice, you'll find the Germans even less controlling than Americans. The policy at Holtzbrinck . . . allows unlimited competitive bidding among those imprints. . . . Over the decades, every conglomeration has been bewailed as a sign of doomsday—when Macmillan bought Scribner and Atheneum, Simon and Schuster bought Macmillan, Pearson bought NAL and then Putnam. No doomsday has arrived. And Bertelsmann, huge though they are, won't make it arrive, either."

Finally, there remains the matter of physical versus on-line bookstores. Industry analysts point out that 60 percent of books are now sold through nontraditional bookstore channels ranging from book clubs to supermarkets—and those statistics predate the Amazon.com explosion. McCormack again: "On-line book buying and therefore bookselling will continue to increase sharply. Ours is an industry of doom-speak.

The closest analogy I can think of to the rise of on-line buying is the rise of book clubs before World War II. The apocalyptic prediction then was that the clubs would kidnap the bookstores' customers, the stores would fail, the publishers would be sorry for having shot themselves in the foot. Of course it didn't happen. . . . Doomspeak about the book business has always been false. Movies, TV, videos, mass-market paperbacks—none of these have done anything except parallel the steady, strong increase in hardcover book sales over the decades. On-line selling should have one particularly salubrious effect—and that's on small publishers. Small houses can't afford the selling teams needed to get their titles into independent bookstores across the country. On-line reduces that need immensely. They still need some publicity . . . but their titles will be on equal footing with the biggest guys."

For a final comment, turn to the English publication *The Economist*—now Macmillan's and Allyn and Bacon's stablemate: "Other publishers are surprisingly enthusiastic about this deal [Bertelsmann-Random House]. That is because they fear their suppliers and their customers—the agents and the retailers—more than they do the competition, and they hope that this deal will shift the balance back in their favour. It may, for example, mean lower advances: unlike Random House, BDD forbids its units from competing against each other for books. Bertelsmann will presumably implement this policy throughout the group, which will cut the number of potential bidders for a big title from eight to five. . . . It [Bertelsmann] seems to be planning to be the first huge vertically integrated publisher, in order to capture the value that currently slips away into the booksellers' hands. Suddenly the bookselling business loses its charm, and publishing looks much more attractive" (28 March 1998).

Of one thing there could be no doubt: it will take months or even years for the events of 1998 to play out in full.

E-Books Turn the Corner

Richard Curtis

Media historians will look back at 1998 as a pivotal moment in the evolution of authorship and publishing. This was the year that the full implications of the marriage of text to computer dawned upon denizens of the book business. For many of them, the dawn came up like thunder, leaving a host of shell-shocked authors, agents, editors, and industry executives staggering like so many gassed soldiers after a battle in The Great War.

Indeed, The Great War may not be hyperbole, for a couple of technological developments exposed–or simply intensified–the underlying hostility between those who create intellectual property and those who exploit it commercially. Most combatants were so deeply involved in hand-to-hand combat over language for such contractual terms as revenue splits and territorial rights that it was hard for anyone to step back to view the larger issues. What, then, was it really about?

What it really seemed to be about is that we are tumbling on the crest of a paradigm shift of almost unimaginable proportions. Those who grasp it understand one truth clearly: the traditional structure of our publishing industry has been permanently altered. But– has it been fatally altered as well? Even the most fanatical of digitalists believes that books will always be with us. But very few publishing people know any longer what constitutes a book. Though the old-fashioned Gutenberg model is still the device of choice for delivering information, ideas, and entertainment, its enhancement by computer technology offers options and improvements for which readers have longed for centuries, such as a way to look up unfamiliar words without having to get up and take the dictionary off the bookshelf.

Three events that occurred within a month or two of each other stunningly dramatized the magnitude of the revolution.

The first was a demonstration at Chicago's Book Expo America of a computerized "print on demand" press capable of economically printing single copies of any book upon request by a customer. Publishers witnessing Lightning Print realized in a flash that the tide of returns, which had been devastating their industry

Richard Curtis (photograph by Leslie Curtis)

for decades, might at last be turned. For now they could issue small, even tiny, printings cheaply and print only as many copies as they could reasonably expect to sell. Any book worth publishing could now be kept in print indefinitely at a contained cost.

The second phenomenon was the rollout of handheld electronic reading devices, quickly dubbed "e-books" by the pundits. Companies such as NuvoMedia and Softbooks Inc. demonstrated production models of these gadgets, which had long been predicted by science-fiction writers and media futurists. Publishers invited to attend the introduction of NuvoMedia's Rocket E-book at Barnes & Noble's Union Square store saw that in addition to storing the texts of many books in their memories, e-books had dictionary lookup, note-taking, highlighting, font and large-print options, and other computerized word-processing capabilities. This brief demo was all they needed to realize that such a product could reach populations of readers undreamed of only a year or two before. And think of it: for senior citizens, every book could now be a large print book. For students, no more spine-straining book bags—all their text and notebooks could be carried in the memory of a single portable e-reader. For travelers, a small library in one compact container, plus travel guides, plus whatever work they needed to take on their trip.

The third event went all but unnoticed by most publishers, authors, and agents, because it occurred at the same time as the more widely celebrated annual Frankfurt Book Fair. But the first conference on e-books sponsored by a government agency (the National Institute of Standards and Technology), held outside Washington, D.C., in October, may end up having the greatest impact of all, for it celebrated the maturation of e-book technology and promoted the creation of standards that would accelerate mass acceptance. With federal encouragement, the advent of a viable electronic-book industry seemed assured and only a few technological generations away—and in modern life, such generations are measured in months.

It didn't matter that these technologies had technical or other problems (the price of a Rocket Book or Soft Book was a pricey $500, for instance); their impact was immediate and profound. And not everybody embraced it wholeheartedly. What spelled salvation for publishers filled authors with anxiety, for the new technologies seemed to provide publishers with an excuse for cutting royalties and seizing perpetual control over copyrights. Battle lines were drawn and the first skirmishes reported.

No matter which side of the fence one stood on, it was clear that publishing would never be the same again. Only yesterday our lives, our careers, our businesses, were predicated on a centuries-old publishing model based on physical objects, actual places, and hard currency. Typewritten manuscripts of books were acquired by publishing companies, edited and prepared in an editorial office, printed in factories, stored in warehouses, transported on trains, planes, and trucks to distribution depots and stores, and sold for cash. But now? In a stroke, we were looking at a model with no manuscripts, no publishing company offices, no editorial functions, no printing plants, no vehicles, no warehouses, no stores, no distributors, no hard copies of books, and no cash. Is it any wonder that most of us felt the way that people on horseback at the turn of the last century must have felt after seeing their first automobile?

Even Amazon.com, the online store that transformed book distribution overnight and led Internet stocks on a rocket ride into the stratosphere, seemed anomalous in light of systems for delivering books in digital form. After all, Amazon's stock-in-trade is still the good old book, and the expense of handling good old books may explain the huge abyss between the company's stock price and its net income. What Amazon did show us above all was the simplicity of moving *anything*—hard merchandise or invisible electrons—by means of a website.

As we pondered the instant transformation of all that we had taken for granted, some corollary realizations quickly followed.

The first is described in a two-dollar word: *disintermediation,* which might be defined as the elimination of unnecessary connecting links—popularly referred to as middlemen—between seller and buyer. (As I type "disintermediation" on my laptop, my Word for Windows spell-check underscores it in red to warn me that there is no such word, an amusing irony considering Microsoft's role in bringing the phenomenon about!)

The old publishing model is rife with intermediaries. Publishers are middlemen between authors and readers; trucking companies are middlemen between printing plants and distribution outlets; bookstores are middlemen between publishers and consumers. Indeed, to place the matter on my own doorstep, are not literary agents middlemen between authors and publishing companies? And all those in the middle of these processes have suddenly been confronted by a potentially shattering question: if authors can offer their work directly to readers, are middlemen such as we still relevant?

Plenty of arguments have been advanced to support the contention that we are. The most cogent is that publishers are the gatekeepers, the taste-makers that help readers to distinguish between good and bad. An immense infrastructure has developed over the centuries to filter out junk from gems: editors and agents, book reviewers and critics, best-seller lists and publicity campaigns. If these are "disintermediated," readers will be exposed to a direct assault by countless untried or untalented writers and quickly find themselves overwhelmed.

Like the transition from horse-and-buggy to auto, the transition from traditional to e-publishing will be gradual, and there is little immediate danger of extinction for agents, editors, critics, and others vital to the taste-making process. But with each innovation of the 1990s, such as spell- and grammar-checking software, desktop publishing programs, and, above all, an Internet on which every author can build a personal promotional site, publishing people began to see pieces of their exclusive franchise chipping off the infrastructure. By some mysterious and spontaneous process, website surfers seem able to discover interesting and entertaining authors without anyone's assistance. Best-seller lists began to yield ground to lists of most-visited sites.

A second recognition is that *digital is forever*. In the good old (pre-1998) days, books could be defined as hard merchandise, manufactured items with a measurable shelf life, like shoes or lamps. Though the contents of some books may be characterized as immortal, looking at them unsentimentally as hard goods it can be said that they are born, they live for a while, and then they die.

But a book stored in digital format, in the memory of a computer hard drive or on a floppy disk, has an infinite life. At the stroke of a key it can be materialized: displayed on the screen of a computer or e-book, teleported over phone lines or via satellite, or printed on demand. There is no time limit: today, tomorrow, twenty years from now, or seventy years after the author's death (the current statutory term of copyright under American law), this capability will exist.

Another realization is that *e-books do not respect international boundaries*. Under the old rules, authors and agents negotiating with American publishers could reserve the right to license English language editions of their books outside of the United States, such as Canada, the United Kingdom, or Australia. The American publisher restricted distribution of those books so as not to infringe on the territory controlled by publishers in those nations. Fugitive copies occasionally made their way across borders, but the scale of such transgressions was modest.

Not so with e-books. A Rocket e-book owner living in England can instantly download an American edition of a book—and instantly violate the territorial exclusivity of that book's British publisher.

Yet another product of the paradigm shift was the *realignment of allies, competitors, and bedfellows*. Traditional rivals became partners and vice versa, and sometimes they were both at the same time. For example, Bertelsmann, a publisher, invested in the on-line division of Barnes & Noble, a bookstore chain. Barnes & Noble in turn acquired Ingram, a book distributor that owned Lightning Print, a competitor of Bertelsmann's own printing division. Other book-industry mergers, acquisitions, and alliances suggested that conflict of interest seemed to be the order of the day.

Finally, we realize that *publishing is no longer a place*—there is no *there* there. In the virtual world of electronic publishing, all the familiar landmarks simply vanish. And with them vanish all the comfortable touchstones of that world—manuscripts and blue pencils and galley proofs, printing plants and binderies, cardboard cartons and UPS trucks, checkout counters and cash registers, the sound and aroma of a freshly opened book . . . gone. Gone, too—gone, above all—are people. Lots and lots of them: editors and art directors, sales reps, designers, publicity and marketing folks, independent distributors—all those warm bodies that make traditional publishing the cozy, nurturing environment that all but the youngest of us grew up with.

These homes, however, have been growing ever more expensive. All costs connected with traditional book publishing, acquisition and advertising, paper and printing, production and promotion, marketing and management, have risen steadily for decades, and so has the cost of the real estate on which the whole enterprise rests. These costs have not only eaten into profits but also forced publishers to become more and more conservative, paying outlandish advances for guaranteed front-runners and celebrities while sacrificing new talent to the familiar and formulaic.

Enter the electronic book.

The cost of carrying electronic versions of books in the memory of a computer and selling them on-line is preposterously cheap. Once acquisition, production, publication, and overhead have been amortized, digital exploitation of electronic rights is pure profit. Because there is no inventory and next to no overhead, even a book that sells no more than a dozen copies a year can make a positive contribution to a publisher's bottom line. If you multiply that dozen sales by the thousands of books on that house's backlist, and that number in turn by the decades that publishers now expect to keep books in print, it is easy to appreciate why the industry has embraced the new technology. Remember, these books are not to be found in a *place*—they exist in the memory of a server compact enough to function in somebody's closet. Imagine all of Simon and Schuster, or Random House, or Warner contained in the memory of a server in a closet—indeed, imagine all of Simon and Schuster *plus* Random House *plus* Warner contained in that server's memory! Even the most visionary of futurists quakes at the implications of what we have wrought.

For an ailing publishing industry, the potential for exploiting the rights to books in perpetuity offers the perfect answer to those soaring overheads and diminished profit margins. And publishers hesitated no more than thirty seconds to act on this epiphany. Between the end of the summer, when print-on-demand and e-books were announced, and the end of autumn, publisher after publisher had revised its acquisition strategy, and most were feverishly revising their contract boilerplate as well. The Great Electronic Land Grab was on.

The battle was waged on three fronts.

Out-of-print provisions. Before the electronic revolution, authors could recover rights to their books when hard copies were no longer available for sale and/or when reprint licenses, such as book club or reprint editions, had expired. Upon ascertaining that their books were out of print, authors could request reversions of rights to them and sell them to other publishers.

Such reversions had never been granted with alacrity, as they occupied a low place on publishers' priority lists, and besides, by stalling on reversion requests, publishers could hold onto books and gamble that they would one day become valuable again—if, say, the author became a best-seller.

Now, however, reversion was out of the question, even if there wasn't a hard copy to be found and all reprint licenses had expired. With on-demand reprint available at the touch of a computer key, and the term "in print" suddenly becoming synonymous with "accessible for display," the definition of in-print was extended to a period as long as copyright law permitted—and that, as we have seen, is seventy years after the author's body lies a'moulderin' in the grave.

Royalty. With no precedent to guide them, publishers resorted to the familiar in defining electronic rights and setting an appropriate royalty structure. Though a sale to an e-book publisher could arguably be defined as a reprint license entitling authors to 50 percent of the original publisher's net receipts, publishers elected to define it instead as a form of distribution. As such, existing contractual boilerplate entitled them to pay authors a much smaller royalty, as little as 5 percent of net receipts, making the term "peanuts" sound like a windfall.

Territory. The fact that e-books are blind to international borders did not seem to prevent some American publishers from exercising their electronic rights whether they controlled worldwide English-language rights or not. Though the immediate effect on British publishers was negligible because the e-book business is still negligible, the long-term effects on the British book business could be devastating, dependent as it is on American authors. What is more, in order to legitimize their distribution outside the United States, it is being predicted that American publishers will step up their efforts to acquire worldwide English-language rights to all books they acquire, threatening to reduce author choices and revenue.

It did not take authors and agents long to respond to the publishers' co-option of electronic rights. But they were at a serious disadvantage, because publishers held the high ground. Authors eager to sell their books were put in a take-it-or-leave-it position over those deal points. Faced with losing a sale, what choice did authors have but to go along with contracts that in effect mortgaged their rights in perpetuity, offered meager elec-

tronic book royalties, and deprived them of the option of licensing British rights?

Some publishers, perhaps hoping to gain an edge over the most intractable of their colleagues, did offer some concessions or flexibility in the e-rights area, and a variety of formulas was proposed that offered hope for the future, such as a minimum annual royalty to keep a given book in print. But the first round was unquestionably won by the publishers.

As all military people know, however, winning a battle is not the same as winning a war. As the big publishers, reinforced by the aggressive expansionist activities of Barnes & Noble and Amazon.com, locked their contractual grip on authors, an alternative publishing industry was being wheeled out of the delivery room. Small e-book presses offered authors comparatively favorable terms such as nonexclusivity, reversion options, and relatively respectable royalties. To authors horrified by the prospects of losing their rights forever by selling their books to the big publishers, publication by e-book presses offered a tempting path.

Though authors approached such companies cautiously (one important reason is that their unencrypted texts were not protected from unauthorized reproduction), they knew that eventually the path would be cleared, and some of those wildcatters would find a way to publish safely and profitably. The fact that this alternative publishing paradigm is author-driven is a very appealing feature. Authors using the World Wide Web can leverage promotion of their work cheaply but effectively from their home page. No longer do they have to beg their publishers for a crumb of the publicity budget reserved for megastars.

And perhaps it is their subliminal grasp of this potential revolution that caused publishing people to break into a sweat in 1998. Although many elements must fall into place for such an "author-centric" paradigm to replace the old "publisher-centric" one, the prospects of fame, fortune, and fun for authors in an immature e-book industry compare favorably to those of fear and frustration in the mature—and some say ossifying—world of conventional publishing. Authors live for exposure, and the Internet offers nothing if not exposure. The dream of communicating their stories effectively to an audience of millions is as potent to writers as any drug, and if they can't fulfill it one way, they will try to fill it another.

Indeed, 1998 was a year of significant seismic rumbling. And, if you listened intently, you could detect the flutter of the author tail wagging the publisher dog. It can only get louder.

It should be an interesting millennium.

The Great Modern Library Scam

The list of the "100 Best [English-language] Novels of the 20th Century" ostensibly selected and ranked by the Modern Library Editorial Board in 1998 is now old news; but it is worth examining here because the extent of its misrepresentation has not been fully documented. To be sure, it is impossible to identify the 100 best novels of a century in any language: 100 is too few or too many. What does *best* mean? It is feasible to nominate the 100 most influential novels or the 100 novels that a well-read person should have read. Beyond that, literary rankings are games. Nearly all the commentators on the list have taken the easy position that any booklist that attracts attention and possibly new readers is good. But the pernicious consequences of this list have not been examined: it has no literary authority; the basis for selection was not promulgated; members of the so-called jury have disclaimed responsibility for the 100 titles and their rankings; there are highly dubious omissions. Any list that claims to be a reader's guide to the 100 best novels of this century but omits *Look Homeward, Angel* and *Guard of Honor* is silly. General readers who consult booklists are presumably seeking guidance; to conceal masterpieces from them is to cheat these trusting seekers.

Background. The origins of the project and the selection process have not been made clear by Modern Library; but this is what has been disclosed. The idea originated with Harry Evans, the now-deposed head of Random House, publisher of the Modern Library. The list was drawn up by the "editorial board" of the Modern Library, which appears to be the same body referred to as the jury: Daniel J. Boorstin (historian and former Librarian of Congress), A. S. Byatt (British novelist), Shelby Foote (novelist and historian), Vartan Gregorian (former director of the New York Public Library and academic administrator), Edmund Morris (historian), John Richardson (art historian), Arthur Schleisinger Jr. (historian), William Styron (novelist), and Gore Vidal (novelist). One Brit, four historians, three novelists, and one novelist/historian. The chairman was Christopher Cerf, the son of Bennett Cerf, who co-founded Random House. Chairman Cerf has characterized the project as "to some degree a scam" but "a good scam." The rationale for the scam has not been revealed. Some observers have concluded that the purpose of the scam was to sell Modern Library titles: 21 of the 100 are in the Modern Library; 59 of the 100 are on the Random House backlist.

Two of the jurors, Edmund Morris and William Styron, have published articles on the process. Morris reported that the selections were "debated over many ruminative lunches" and that the final 100 were chosen from the jury's combined list of 404 (*The New York Times Book Review,* 23 August 1998). Styron has described the final list as "weird," noting that the voting was done by mail without a selection meeting: "A luncheon meeting with a good wine that allowed for lively disputation would have soon eliminated such toothless pretenders as *The Magnificent Ambersons* and *Zuleika Dobran*" (*The New Yorker,* 17 August 1998). Apparently he was not invited to the luncheons Morris attended. An instructive *Washington Post* article by David Streitfeld disclosed that the jurors were not permitted to approve the final 100 after it was compiled by Random House. Modern Library Managing Director Ian Jackman declined to be specific about how the voting was done, but he says more than one vote was needed to make the final list.

"I didn't set up the system as Price Waterhouse might have set it up," he concludes. "I personally didn't feel that I could go back to the board and say 'Rank them all.' I knew that was a lot to ask" (5 August 1998).

Why was that "a lot to ask?" Their names were used to legitimize the list; they should have demanded final approval. What method did Jackman use to cull and rank without jury participation? Moreover, there was no basis of selection; the jury had no ground rules. Schlesinger has stated that "I was going for artistic vitality—which of the books would still be alive a century from now." Foote chose "not the best-written books, not even the best books, but the 100 novels that would have to be included in literary history of the 20th century." Cerf admitted that he voted for books he hadn't read. Did others?

The ML 100 is actually the ML 121: it included all the volumes in certain series—which was not a good idea. The *U.S.A.* trilogy certainly belongs there, but one *Studs Lonigan* is more than enough. *Parade's End* is probably obligatory, but is *The Alexandria Quartet?*

Including the 12 volumes of *Dance to the Music of Time* means that 10 percent of the best novels in the English language were written by Anthony Powell.

The idea of ranking the 100 greatest novels is absurd. There is no such thing as the best or the greatest novel in English. There is no such thing as the 47th best novel. The project might have been useful if it had generated two lists—one for American fiction and one for British fiction—without rankings.

Inevitably the interest generated by the Modern Library 100 inspired counter-lists. At the invitation of Modern Library, the students in the Radcliffe publishing course used the 404-title list to come up with 100 titles headed by *Gatsby, Catcher, Grapes of Wrath, Mockingbird,* and *Color Purple. Library Journal* invited its readers to nominate one or more books, with each nomination to count one vote, no matter how many titles were on each respondent's list. The result was 150 books—including fourteen translations—of which fifty-three were also on the Modern Library list. Since most *LJ* readers are librarians, their votes presumably represent books they cherish and books sought by library patrons.

The *DLB Yearbook* invited well-read people (writers, publishers, scholars) to recommend deserving titles that failed to make the Modern Library 100, not to delete titles from that list. These authorities provided 215 different titles—with *Look Homeward, Angel; Guard of Honor;* and *Rabbit, Run* receiving more than four nominations.

In January 1999 Modern Library announced that a list of 100 twentieth-century nonfiction works would be prepared. The selection board has been augmented by Caleb Carr, Ron Chernow, Stephen Jay Gould, Charles Johnson, Jon Krokauer, Elaine Pagels, and Carolyn See. "The board has gone so far as to contract the services of a statistician, who will numerically weigh the subtleties of each member's expertise in compiling the nonfiction rankings" (*Publishers Weekly,* 11 January 1999).

                                                                                            –M.J.B.

The Modern Library List of the 100 Best English-Language Novels of the Twentieth Century

1. *Ulysses* (1922), James Joyce
2. *The Great Gatsby* (1925), F. Scott Fitzgerald
3. *A Portrait of the Artist as a Young Man* (1916), James Joyce
4. *Lolita* (1955), Vladimir Nabokov
5. *Brave New World* (1932), Aldous Huxley
6. *The Sound and the Fury* (1929), William Faulkner
7. *Catch-22* (1961), Joseph Heller
8. *Darkness at Noon* (1940), Arthur Koestler
9. *Sons and Lovers* (1913), D. H. Lawrence
10. *The Grapes of Wrath* (1939), John Steinbeck
11. *Under the Volcano* (1947), Malcolm Lowry
12. *The Way of All Flesh* (1903), Samuel Butler
13. *Nineteen Eighty-four* (1949), George Orwell
14. *I, Claudius* (1934), Robert Graves
15. *To the Lighthouse* (1927), Virginia Woolf
16. *An American Tragedy* (1925), Theodore Dreiser
17. *The Heart Is a Lonely Hunter* (1940), Carson McCullers
18. *Slaughterhouse-Five* (1969), Kurt Vonnegut
19. *The Invisible Man* (1952), Ralph Ellison
20. *Native Son* (1940), Richard Wright
21. *Henderson the Rain King* (1959), Saul Bellow
22. *Appointment in Samarra* (1934), John O'Hara
23. *U.S.A.* (trilogy, collected 1938), John Dos Passos
24. *Winesburg, Ohio* (1919), Sherwood Anderson
25. *A Passage to India* (1924), E. M. Forster
26. *The Wings of the Dove* (1902), Henry James
27. *The Ambassadors* (1903), Henry James
28. *Tender Is the Night* (1934), F. Scott Fitzgerald
29. *The Studs Lonigan Trilogy* (1932, 1934, 1935), James T. Farrell
30. *The Good Soldier* (1915), Ford Madox Ford
31. *Animal Farm* (1945), George Orwell
32. *The Golden Bowl* (1904), Henry James
33. *Sister Carrie* (1900), Theodore Dreiser
34. *A Handful of Dust* (1934), Evelyn Waugh
35. *As I Lay Dying* (1930), William Faulkner
36. *All the King's Men* (1946), Robert Penn Warren
37. *The Bridge of San Luis Rey* (1927), Thornton Wilder
38. *Howards End* (1910), E. M. Forster
39. *Go Tell It on the Mountain* (1953), James Baldwin
40. *The Heart of the Matter* (1948), Graham Greene
41. *Lord of the Flies* (1954), William Golding
42. *Deliverance* (1970), James Dickey
43. *A Dance to the Music of Time* (series; 1955, 1962, 1968, 1976), Anthony Powell
44. *Point Counter Point* (1928), Aldous Huxley
45. *The Sun Also Rises* (1926), Ernest Hemingway
46. *The Secret Agent* (1907), Joseph Conrad

47. *Nostromo* (1904), Joseph Conrad
48. *The Rainbow* (1915), D. H. Lawrence
49. *Women in Love* (1921), D. H. Lawrence
50. *Tropic of Cancer* (1934), Henry Miller
51. *The Naked and the Dead* (1948), Norman Mailer
52. *Portnoy's Complaint* (1969), Philip Roth
53. *Pale Fire* (1962), Vladimir Nabokov
54. *Light in August* (1932), William Faulkner
55. *On the Road* (1957), Jack Kerouac
56. *The Maltese Falcon* (1930), Dashiell Hammett
57. *Parade's End* (1950), Ford Madox Ford
58. *The Age of Innocence* (1920), Edith Wharton
59. *Zuleika Dobson* (1911), Max Beerbohm
60. *The Moviegoer* (1961), Walker Percy
61. *Death Comes for the Archbishop* (1927), Willa Cather
62. *From Here to Eternity* (1951), James Jones
63. *The Wapshot Chronicle* (1957), John Cheever
64. *The Catcher in the Rye* (1951), J. D. Salinger
65. *A Clockwork Orange* (1962), Anthony Burgess
66. *Of Human Bondage* (1915), W. Somerset Maugham
67. *Heart of Darkness* (1902), Joseph Conrad
68. *Main Street* (1920), Sinclair Lewis
69. *The House of Mirth* (1905), Edith Wharton
70. *The Alexandria Quartet* (1962), Lawrence Durrell
71. *A High Wind in Jamaica* (1929), Richard Hughes
72. *A House for Mr. Biswas* (1961), V. S. Naipaul
73. *The Day of the Locust* (1939), Nathanael West
74. *A Farewell to Arms* (1929), Ernest Hemingway
75. *Scoop* (1938), Evelyn Waugh
76. *The Prime of Miss Jean Brodie* (1961), Muriel Spark
77. *Finnegans Wake* (1939), James Joyce
78. *Kim* (1901), Rudyard Kipling
79. *A Room with a View* (1908), E. M. Forster
80. *Brideshead Revisited* (1945), Evelyn Waugh
81. *The Adventures of Augie March* (1953), Saul Bellow
82. *Angle of Repose* (1971), Wallace Stegner
83. *A Bend in the River* (1979), V. S. Naipaul
84. *The Death of the Heart* (1938), Elizabeth Bowen
85. *Lord Jim* (1900), Joseph Conrad
86. *Ragtime* (1975), E. L. Doctorow
87. *The Old Wives' Tale* (1908), Arnold Bennett
88. *The Call of the Wild* (1903), Jack London
89. *Loving* (1945), Henry Green

ULYSSES

by

JAMES JOYCE

SHAKESPEARE AND COMPANY
12, Rue de l'Odéon, 12
PARIS
1922

Title page for the first edition of the book at the top of the Modern Library List of 100

90. *Midnight's Children* (1981), Salman Rushdie
91. *Tobacco Road* (1932), Erskine Caldwell
92. *Ironweed* (1983), William Kennedy
93. *The Magus* (1966), John Fowles
94. *Wide Sargasso Sea* (1966), Jean Rhys
95. *Under the Net* (1954), Iris Murdoch
96. *Sophie's Choice* (1979), William Styron
97. *The Sheltering Sky* (1949), Paul Bowles
98. *The Postman Always Rings Twice* (1934), James M. Cain
99. *The Ginger Man* (1955), J. P. Donleavy
100. *The Magnificent Ambersons* (1918), Booth Tarkington

Letters of Response to the Modern Library 100

Madison Smartt Bell

. . . the truth is that I have had a hard time working up any reaction to the 100 novels list, other than a dull feeling that it is probably a pretty dumb idea (except, perhaps as a publicity stunt to direct fresh attention to some forgotten classics). I did not pay enough attention to know the method of selection but the result seems scattershot–I can't really detect any organizing principle (except that nice round number of 100). On the other hand I think their selections of novels by dead people are pretty well legitimate. There are few I'd quarrel with. Among contemporary novelists I don't agree with the choices half so well, but that's to be expected.

Anyway here's a few I think would merit inclusion.

The Violent Bear It Away, Flannery O'Connor
The Velvet Horn, Andrew Lytle
Death of the Fox, George Garrett
The Chaneysville Incident, David Bradley
Continental Drift, Russell Banks
Merry Men, Carolyn Chute
Fifth Business, Robertson Davies
A Flag For Sunrise, Robert Stone
Mr. Bridge and *Mrs. Bridge,* Evan S. Connell
The Optimist's Daughter, Eudora Welty
The Fathers, Alan Tate

And that's without thinking about it much. Like I said, I ain't much good at lists.

André Bernard

. . . I was appalled by the exclusion first of all of John Updike's Rabbit books, which represent to me the finest achievement in fiction writing in this century by an American. *Rabbit, Run* is in itself a masterwork, but when combined with the other three books of Rabbit's life the tetralogy is a towering mountain.

Then there is Robert Stone, whose *A Flag for Sunrise* and *Dog Soldiers* should have been included.

And Don DeLillo–he, Stone, and Updike are our greatest living writers, I feel–whose *Libra* or my own personal favorite, *Mao II,* or *Underworld,* for that matter, should have been there.

And where is *Last Exit to Brooklyn? The Color Purple? Lucky Jim? The Man with the Golden Arm?* Mailer's *The Executioner's Song?* Paul Scott's *Raj* books?

Kick off the 100 List numbers 12, 44, 68, 78, 87, 91 and 100 to include the above, and we'll be part way there.

And what about *Lord of the Flies?*

Matthew J. Bruccoli

Restricted to dead writers:
By Love Possessed, James Gould Cozzens

Guard of Honor, James Gould Cozzens
The Galton Case, Ross Macdonald
The Long Goodbye, Raymond Chandler
Look Homeward, Angel, Thomas Wolfe
The Love of the Last Tycoon, F. Scott Fitzgerald
The Octopus, Frank Norris
For Whom the Bell Tolls, Ernest Hemingway
Ten North Frederick, John O'Hara
A Walk on the Wild Side, Nelson Algren
You Know Me Al, Ring Lardner

Frederick Busch

Publishing is, more and more, about free advertising–which is also called publicity or marketing. The profession is about turning over units of product–which are also called books. The list of the 100 "best" novels is a triumphant marketing maneuver, and we are working on behalf of Random House, Inc., publishers of the Modern Library, when we discuss that list. The point of the list was not the list; it was the attention to Random House, Inc.'s backlist–which includes so many of the titles among the hundred "best." We talk, now, as if the list were serious and literary, while it is only business–and we ought, really, to know the difference, or to desire a difference–and, conducting business on behalf of Random House, Inc., we serve not literature but the sales department.

I know that it seems unsophisticated to remind oneself of the realities of this phenomenon. But if such notables as were on the committee to write the list decided to curtsy and bow in spite of what *their* intellect and sophistication told them was going on, it would seem to me that scolding just a little, and feeling annoyed, and a wee bit soiled by the conversation, is a good corrective to the cynical and complacent ease of our literary elders and betters.

William Cagle

Who could resist playing this game! The following are 60 British novels not included in the Modern Library's list, along with a few American novels listed at the end.

Arthur Conan Doyle, *The Hound of the Baskervilles* (1902)
Erskine Childers, *The Riddle of the Sands* (1903)
W. H. Hudson, *Green Mansions* (1904)
Frederic W. Rolfe, "Baron Corvo," *Hadrian the Seventh* (1904)
H. G. Wells, *The History of Mr. Polly* (1910)
Joseph Conrad, *Under Western Eyes* (1911)

John Galsworthy, *The Forsyte Saga* (1922)
Liam O'Flaherty, *The Informer* (1925)
Virginia Woolf, *Mrs. Dalloway* (1925)
Agatha Christie, *The Murder of Roger Ackroyd* (1926)
Henry Williamson, *Tarka the Otter* (1927)
Dorothy Sayers, *The Five Red Herrings* (1931)
Stella Gibbons, *Cold Comfort Farm* (1932)
James Hilton, *Good-bye, Mr. Chips* (1934)
Dorothy Sayers, *The Nine Taylors* (1934)
J. R. R. Tolkien, *The Hobbit* (1937)
Richard Llewellyn, *How Green Was My Valley* (1939)
C. P. Snow, *Strangers and Brothers* (1940)
W. Somerset Maugham, *The Razor's Edge* (1944)
Kingsley Amis, *Lucky Jim* (1953)
John Wain, *Hurry on Down* (1953)
J. R. R. Tolkien, *The Lord of the Rings* (1954–1956, 3 vols.)
Samuel Beckett, *Molloy* (1955)
Angus Wilson, *Anglo-Saxon Attitudes* (1956)
Alan Sillitoe, *The Loneliness of the Long-distance Runner* (1959)
Doris Lessing, *The Golden Notebook* (1962)
John le Carré, *The Spy Who Came In From the Cold* (1963)
William Trevor, *The Old Boys* (1964)
Paul Scott, *The Raj Quartet,* (1966–4 vols.)
John Fowles, *The French Lieutenant's Woman* (1969)
Elizabeth Taylor, *Mrs. Palfrey at the Claremont* (1971)
John Berger, *G* (1972)
Margaret Drabble, *The Needle's Eye* (1972)
J. G. Farrell, *The Siege of Krishnapur* (1973)
Nadine Gordimer, *The Conservationist* (1974)
David Lodge, *Changing Places* (1975)
John Fowler, *Daniel Martin* (1977)
Iris Murdoch, *The Sea, the Sea* (1978)
Nadine Gordimer, *Berger's Daughter* (1979)
Isabel Colegate, *The Shooting Party* (1980)
Ian McEwan, *The Comfort of Strangers* (1981)
Thomas Keneally, *Schindler's Ark* (1982)
J. M. Coetzee, *The Life and Times of Michael K* (1983)
Graham Swift, *Waterland* (1983)
Vikram Seth, *A Suitable Boy* (1983)
Julian Barnes, *Flaubert's Parrot* (1984)
Martin Amis, *Money: A Suicide Note* (1984)
Anita Brookner, *Hotel du Lac* (1984)
Margaret Atwood, *The Handmaid's Tale* (1985)
Peter Carey, *Oscar and Lucinda* (1988)
Bruce Chatwin, *Utz* (1988)
Kazuo Ishiguro, *The Remains of the Day* (1989)
A. S. Byatt, *Possession* (1990)
Michael Ondaatje, *The English Patient* (1992)
Barry Unsworth, *Sacred Hunger* (1992)
Pat Barker, *The Ghost Road* (1995)
John Banville, *The Untouchable* (1997)

Peter Carey, *Jack Maggs* (1997)

And now for the Americans:

John Barth, *The Floating Opera*
John Barth, *The Sot-Weed Factor*
Ray Bradbury, *Fahrenheit 451*
Ray Bradbury, *The Martian Chronicles*
John Cheever, *The Wapshot Scandal*
Robert Coover, *The Origin of the Brunists*
James Gould Cozzens, *By Love Possessed*
John Irving, *The World According to Garp*
Carson McCullers, *The Heart is a Lonely Hunter*
Carson McCullers, *The Member of the Wedding*
Larry McMurtry, *Lonesome Dove*
John Updike, *Rabbit, Run*
Alice Walker, *The Color Purple*
Tom Wolfe, *The Bonfire of the Vanities*
Thomas Wolfe, *Look Homeward, Angel*

Two of the Conrads listed by the ML editorial board don't belong on the list: *Lord Jim* was published in 1900, the last year of the 19th century, not the first year of the 20th; *Heart of Darkness* is something between a long short story and a novella, not a novel. Quibble, quibble, quibble.

The ML editorial board list is weak in the second half of the century, especially the last two decades. They chose Iris Murdoch's *Under the Net,* her first book but certainly not her best. They include Hammett and Cain but not Christie and Sayers. Is *Winesburg, Ohio,* which they list, a novel? How about Raymond Chandler, or Ian Fleming? But this could go on endlessly, so enough.

Robert Coover

As for your 100+ query, I don't have my own bookshelves in front of me, but some books I'd add would include John Hawkes's *The Lime Twig, Second Skin,* and *The Passion Artist* (add *The Cannibal* and call it *The Providence Quartet*); Samuel Beckett's trilogy of *Malloy, Malone Dies,* and *The Unnamable;* William Gaddis's *Recognitions* and *J. R.;* Thomas Pynchon's *V* and *Gravity's Rainbow* and maybe (still reading it, loving it) *Mason and Dixon;* Cormac McCarthy's *Blood Meridian;* Angela Carter's *Infernal Desire Machines of Doctor Hoffman;* Djuna Barnes's *Nightwood;* Nicholas Mosley's *Impossible Object;* Stanley Elkin's *The Living End;* Donald Barthelme's *The Dead Father;* Wilfrido Nolledo's *But for the Lovers;* William Burroughs's *Naked Lunch;* Jim Crace's *Gift of Stones;* Felipe Alfau's *Locos;* John Barth's *Sot-Weed Factor.* Also I don't see Don DeLillo, Flann O'Brien, or Toni Morrison here. Was Sadegh Hedayat's *The Blind Owl* written in English? Must be many more. Hate such lists. This one is peculiarly rubbishy.

Robert Cowley

Actually, I think the Modern Library list is pretty good, though there are several books that I feel are overrated or that don't belong: *Slaughterhouse-Five*, *A High Wind in Jamaica* (I prefer *The Fox in the Attic*), and *Finnegans Wake* (the most unreadable book in the English language). I could also quarrel with the ranking. Why is *Catch-22* seven and *All the King's Men* (which comes close to being my favorite novel) thirty-six? Or *Slaughterhouse-Five* eighteen and *Lord Jim* eighty-five? But I'm glad to see books from the early part of the century recognized—like *Kim*, *Zuleika Dobson*, and *The Way of All Flesh*.

What books would I have nominated? Certainly more Nabokov. *Pnin* (absolutely!) and *Invitation to a Beheading* (which I believe was written in English and so qualifies). I would include not just the wonderful *Ironweed* but the whole *Albany Trilogy*. There are Conrad novels better than the ponderous *Secret Agent*, which is chiefly famous for one image (the anarchist who goes everywhere carrying a live bomb) but is hung with more chains than Marley's ghost: *Typhoon*, *Victory*, or his rarely-mentioned and hard-to-obtain last novel, *The Rover*. Better, though, to save the space for another deserving book—and there are many that really belong here: *For Whom the Bell Tolls* (even with the silly love-talk, it's Hemingway's best), *Guard of Honor*, *Brighton Rock*, *The Recognitions*, *Look Homeward, Angel*, and Rolvaag's *Giants in the Earth* (yes, I know he wrote the book in Norwegian, but it's an American book through and through, one of the great American novels, in a class with *U.S.A.* and *All the King's Men*). I'd also include some recent books: *All the Pretty Horses* (but not the rest of the trilogy), *The Shipping News*, and Don DeLillo's brilliant *The Names*. Where is *Lucky Jim* (the funniest book of the century), *Blood Meridian* (the most unpleasant), or *The Spy Who Came In From the Cold* (the best novel of the Cold War)? And why not add that little gem of realism, *The Friends of Eddie Coyle*—George V. Higgins is our most underrated good novelist—or a whodunnit, such as *Farewell, My Lovely*.

R. H. W. Dillard

The choosing of the best one hundred anything of the closing century is at best a game, often an entertaining one and even a meaningful one, but a game nonetheless. Since the rules of games are arbitrary, I set myself some quite arbitrary limits before I place my counters on the board:

–I would only choose novels by authors who do not appear either on the Modern Library list or on the widely disseminated Radcliffe Publishing Course list, making the point that there are many worthy books whose authors were completely overlooked and also saving myself the task of adding yet another Faulkner (*Absalom, Absalom!*) Or Green (*Back*) or Lawrence (*The Plumed Serpent*) or Nabokov (*Ada*) or whoever;

–I would only choose novels by dead authors, not that they are better than the living, but that I would avoid thereby the Styron Syndrome (the appearance that the fix was in) or the cold, steady stares of my friends whose books happen not to appear on my list;

–I would limit myself to only one title per author;

–I would follow the lead of the Modern Library list by including as single novels multivolume works composed of separate but interlinked books;

–I would only choose books that I believe, for one reason or another (simple merit as I see it, or literary and cultural significance beyond simple merit), honestly belong on a list of the century's best novels in English.

Here, then, without further comment, are a dozen books that meet all of my criteria for inclusion, arranged in alphabetical order by author:

Biography of the Life of Manuel (1904–1930), James Branch Cabell (series)
　The Horse's Mouth (1944), Joyce Cary
　The Flower Beneath the Foot (1923), Ronald Firbank
　The Sheltered Life (1932), Ellen Glasgow
　A Voyage to Arcturus (1920), David Lindsay
　Under the Volcano (1947), Malcolm Lowry
　At Swim-Two-Birds (1939), Flann O'Brien
　Ship of Fools (1962), Katherine Anne Porter
　A Glastonbury Romance (1933), John Cowper Powys
　Pilgrimage (1915–1967), Dorothy Richardson (series)
　The Code of the Woosters (1938), P. G. Wodehouse
　And, for good measure, to make it a baker's dozen,
　Tarzan of the Apes (1914), Edgar Rice Burroughs

Irvin Faust

The list needs Pynchon. My vote goes to *V*.

It also needs chronicles of the immigrant experience. The BEST are *Call it Sleep*, by Henry Roth, who wrote grandly and beautifully about Jews in New York, and *Christ in Concrete* (the most resonant title of the 100+) by Pietro di Donato, who was toughly tender

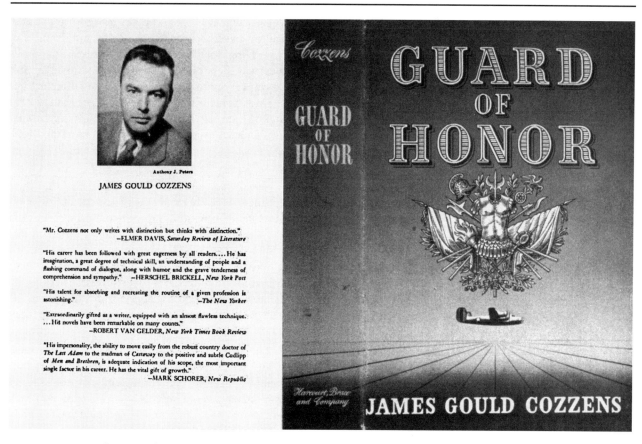

Dust jacket for the 1948 Pulitzer Prize-winning novel overlooked by compilers of the Modern Library List

with Italians in the city, a group that has received very little serious attention.

The best (and most neglected) novel about THE war is *The Gallery,* by John Horne Burns. It is set in Fifth Army country, a theater that is as little noted in good WW II literature as its author. But take it from an old GI; this book is the real thing, plus which Burns can write.

When Alan Sillitoe is digging into his hardscrabble, boozy roots, he's great. Give me *Saturday Night and Sunday Morning.*

I want an American Historical Novel that delivers history through the straight-crazy prism that is history. I'll take any of these: *The Sot-Weed Factor,* by John Barth; *Little Big Man,* by Thomas Berger; or *Willy Remembers,* by Faust.

I like Styron and think he belongs, but please make it one of his best: *The Long March, Lie Down in Darkness,* or *Set This House on Fire.*

Finally, I wish William Dean Howells could have made the 1900 cut-off, but his two GREAT ones missed by a couple of years. But because he was an upper-class American Zola who needs rediscovery and a champion, I'll include *The Rise of Silas Lapham* and *A*

Hazard of New Fortunes. (One could ask why I don't then anoint *The Red Badge of Courage,* which also missed by a few years. My answer is that Crane had such a sensational flaming-up and out that his book, and reputation, will always ride high on the shooting star; correct conclusion, wrong reason. The solid and outwardly stolid Howells didn't have that literary luck. Ergo my push for restoration; he rates it.)

George Greenfield

. . . on the whole, I go along with the Modern Library 100. There are five different candidates I would include, as follows:

The Jungle, Upton Sinclair. One of the first realistic novels.

Her Privates We, Frederic Manning. A great WW I novel.

Babbitt (or *Main Street*), Sinclair Lewis. Small-town America—marvelous.

Goshawk Squadron, Derek Robinson. A fighter squadron in WW I. A real tour de force—by an author who wasn't even born at the time of the events described.

The Spy Who Came In From the Cold, John le Carré. *The* Cold War novel.

And which five would I eliminate? First, out goes Anthony Powell. Unreadable prose and ultra-snobbish attitudes. One of the Hemingways would have to go. Salman Rushdie has cost the British taxpayer too much in protection–out. Henry Green was brilliant but a minor talent, so he goes. Finally, it would be a toss-up between losing J. P. Donleavy or Lawrence Durrell.

Joseph Heller

I would certainly include on a list of 100 Great Novels written in English, in preference to a number already there, John Barth's *Sot-Weed Factor* and *The Floating Opera,* Toni Morrison's *Beloved,* William Faulkner's *Absalom Absalom!,* Nelson Algren's *The Man with the Golden Arm,* and my own *Something Happened.*

George V. Higgins

I surmise most of the exclusions of novels I admire are attributable in the most instances to the winnowing policy obeyed by orthodox self-consciously intellectual readers of the late twentieth century. It requires–or enables–them to screen out all fiction preliminarily appearing to them either as:

–potentially entertaining and challenging in a manner unlikely to reinforce and advance the prevailing agenda, attitudes and conventions enforced by their group(s) (in order to expedite the process of perfecting man), or

–appearing to be the work of a person who has not to their knowledge been vetted and accredited as Good, Sensitive, Very Evolved, and Valid and is therefore likely if not certain to be heedlessly if not deliberately subversive of the prevailing agenda, attitudes and conventions enforced by their group(s) (in order to expedite the sundry processes of perfecting man, With or Without His Consent).

To illustrate: none of Charles McCarry's novels appears on the list. His espionage trilogy: *The Miernick Dossier, The Tears of Autumn,* and *The Secret Lovers,* and his more recent *Shelley's Heart,* are works of truly remarkable intellect and understanding. But he is an autodidact, an achievement and condition that late-twentieth-century American intellectuals usually find threatening, tolerable only among victims of autism and members of what their predecessors denominated lesser breeds without the law–then, of course, they find it admirable. And McCarry is *known* not only to have served his country but to have done so as a member of the Central

Intelligence Agency (a.k.a. the Great Satan), *and* in that capacity to have performed with valor and distinction. Your well-bred intellectual, once informed of these disabilities, was therefore on notice that any novel he produced was certain to be unwholesome and therefore not to be read. Something similar I'd bet accounts for no citation of John le Carré; *The Spy Who Came In From the Cold* crystallized an era of international mortal danger; *Smiley's People* is but one work of his genius. He is missing.

Novels that one has not read in belief that their provenance or content render them insalubrious of course do not spring to mind when the person who has not read them is invited to enumerate the Best of this very mixed Breed. The contributors to the ML list most likely felt no need to read James Gould Cozzens published in the forties and fifties precisely because he told stories suggesting that life is as much the art of the possible as are the politics of the compromise that they found so repellent–I would have listed *Guard of Honor.*

The same sort of dismissal, differently reasoned, may very well account for the omission of all of J. P. Marquand's masterly tales of Boston. On the rough-justice-to-as-many-as-possible theory of limiting each author to one citation, I believe I would have named *The Late George Apley,* but a very good case could be made for *H. M. Pulham, Esq.* Marquand's problem, I think, was his habit of paying off his marital misadventures by writing high-quality junk. Even in his heyday–and the halcyon pre-TV days of American fiction–more books were published than the diligent and discriminating reader could hope to buy and savor as they appeared; the author who proffered an excuse to overlook his work–and "cheap writer" was a *far* better excuse then than it is now–had principally himself to blame when they did.

But why no A. B. Guthrie? *The Way West* was my introduction, and I recall *Arfive* and *The Big Sky* with the same enthusiasm. Was his work omitted because he wrote "westerns"? Those were good, solid books, at least as meritorious as Wallace Stegner's *Angle of Repose*–but Stegner had the Sierra Club mantle of the conservationist; so he didn't write mere "westerns."

Larry McMurtry's sin is probably that he's made too much money, but he's good, and one of his novels would've been on my list–*Lonesome Dove,* most likely. John Irving's *The World According to Garp* was a splendid piece of work. I'm not sure Glen Ross ever published another novel after his brilliant tale of the Korean Conflict, *The Last Campaign;* that could explain his absence, along with Harper Lee, who seems to have stopped after *To Kill a Mockingbird.* But then how on earth did the nominating folks manage to leave out John Updike?

The man's a pure writing machine: any if not all of the four *Rabbit* novels would have graced the list.

Of course all lists are compendiums of subjective judgments, as are these I have made. And anyway, why ask me? I'm said to write crime novels and we all know where they rank.

John Jakes

I believe Larry McMurtry's *Lonesome Dove* is a serious omission. Certainly it could replace #90 on the list. I don't believe there are any real human beings who read Salman Rushdie; among my widely read friends I have never met one yet.

With a slightly higher degree of uncertainty about its literary value I would cite Tom Wolfe's *Bonfire of the Vanities.*

A third WWII novel to join the Mailer and the Jones might be Irwin Shaw's *The Young Lions,* though I suppose Shaw is slightly too "light" and/or "popular" for such a list.

William Jovanovich

As for the 100 Best, it's like all lists, fun to make and always suspect. My choices, listed below, are meant to redress the lack of Southern and Western writers, and, secondly, to add novels which cannot be ignored in a literary history.

As to the first,
Ellen Glasgow   *The Deliverance*
William March   *The Looking Glass*
Nelson Algren   *The Man with the Golden Arm*
Frank Norris   *The Octopus*
K. A. Porter   *Pale Horse, Pale Rider*
Hamlin Garland   *Son of the Middle Border*
Thomas Wolfe   *Look Homeward, Angel*

As for the second,
Arnold Bennet   *Clayhanger*
Booth Tarkington   *Alice Adams*
J. G. Cozzens   *Guard of Honor*
Mary McCarthy   *The Group*
Djuna Barnes   *Nightwood*
John Marquand   *Point of No Return*

Some of the books on the present list are indeed dubious for several differing reasons.

I, Claudius is good cinema but not a great novel. It would not go on a list compiled in 2050.

Zubeka Dobson was on reader's lists for undergraduates in the 1930s, 40s, and 50s. It's gone.

The Moviegoer is not in the league of Wolfe or Algren.

The Wapshot Chronicles is on the list because of *The New Yorker* cabal.

The Clockwork Orange is a clever show but there's little behind the curtain.

The Alexandria Quartet is precious, vaporous stuff, like forgotten fragrances, lost evenings. It's on the list in 2050 with *Arabian Nights.*

A High Wind in Jamaica is like the short story "The Lottery," startling, relevant, but is a concerto with a single chord.

A House for Mr. Biswas—if it has appeal, it's partly owing to our current move to cultural remove.

The Golden Bowl is very fine but three Henry James are too many on a list of 100.

The Bridge of San Luis Rey shows its age—it belongs to the age when authors were God and the world was made of sad irony.

Point Counter Point is too much Huxley—you already have *Brave New World.*

The Secret Agent is fine but *three* Conrads?

The Rainbow is one too many D. H. Lawrence.

Scoop is plainly not good enough. It's Waugh to a fault.

Finnegans Wake is a phenomenon, not a readable book. The words are balloons, a send-up.

Angle of Repose is good but not memorable. I could recommend it to my three grandchildren in college now, but not sonorously.

Ragtime is a fluke, an organ grinder made transparent so you can see the gears in motion.

The Sheltering Sky is one of those things: a hundred writers have gone to see the author in his hot and depraved setting and many think they owe him a notice.

Midnight's Children and *The Ginger Man* are minor works: make a list 25 years from now and they'll not appear.

If I were to attack my own suggestions, I'd say Marquand is on the edge, but like James Gould Cozzens, he speaks to America in the first half of the 20th century. *Nightwood* is not worth *Finnegans Wake* but it's a lot more readable. Is March a great writer? No. But *The Looking Glass* is a major book. (P.S. I met March in Mobile.)

Well, compiling lists is like compiling virtues in applying for a visa to heaven. Will it pass? Do I look smart? Does God read fiction?

Thomas McCormack

As for explicit omissions from the Modern Library 100, the most egregious in my opinion is *By Love Possessed,* which reduces some of those other titles to vaudeville. It's been decades since I read *The Cruel Sea,* but I remember being awed by it at the time. I suppose somebody would disqualify *The Last Tycoon* on the grounds of its being incomplete, but I'd certainly rather reread it than many of the other 100.

And as for general reaction to the whole notion of the top 100 list, I expressed it in the following letter to *The New York Times,* which they printed in slightly shortened form:

Modern Library's list of the 100 Great Novels is a good thing for several reasons, but the happiest one is: it will result in more books being read. AFI's list of the 100 Greatest Movies sent countless viewers to their video store to rent old films. The same will happen with books–not despite, but because of the lively disputes. Wrangling, for once, becomes salubrious.

But, to promote reading, an even more salubrious list can be imagined. This would be the 100 best "fun-reads." It would include many titles from the "Great" list, but would also celebrate various supernal jobs of sheer storytelling–books we'd be shy about mentioning alongside such "profound" efforts as *Ulysses.* If some young nonreaders could be persuaded to try the like of *The Caine Mutiny, Red Dragon,* and *Eye of the Needle,* the chances of their getting hooked on books are greater than if the bait is *The Golden Bowl* or *Finnegans Wake.* I've read James and Joyce, but, possibly, only because Mark Twain hooked me in the first place.

And now a somber anecdote with a possible happy ending. Compton Mackenzie, whose novel *Sinister Street* was such an influence on Fitzgerald and others, was prolific and greatly admired by the likes of Edmund Wilson, who said he'd rather read Mackenzie than the much more disciplined Somerset Maugham. The major work of his life was called *The Four Winds of Love.* For various dismaying reasons its frequently-interrupted writing was sprawled over nine years, from 1935 to 1944. This had two effects. It was released in many short volumes, scattering the impact of its reception (which was further vitiated by the tumult of World War II). And, as the years passed, Mackenzie's original plan wandered astray. So he wrote too much: in all, it is perhaps a million words or more. As a publisher, I hoped one day to find an inspired editor who could pull out of those million words the one-volume masterpiece buried within. If that were ever done, I'm certain it would deserve a place among the 100 Best.

Mackenzie is not the only great writer who could use editing. Booth Tarkington at his peak was among the best we've had, but his adult novels cry out for pruning. And finally there's the tragic story of William Brinkley. His farewell novel was *The Last Ship.* It is a masterpiece, scuttled by incessant superfluous, ruminative paragraphs. When published in 1988, it failed. Within weeks, Brinkley committed suicide. Artfully edited, it too would be among our 100.

Patrick O'Connor

It was mean-spirited of them not to include *Gone with the Wind* and *To Kill a Mockingbird.* William Styron some years ago in *Esquire* said *Gone with the Wind* was either the great American novel or the best piece of kitsch ever written (not an exact quote and I would never be able to find it). One way or another it deserved to be on there.

An outrage not to include *Look Homeward, Angel.* For many of my generation the great American novel. Though almost none of us have read it since we were teenagers.

Shocking not to include *The Fountainhead.* I was Ms. Rand's editor during her waning years (believe me, she didn't wane much), and though *The Fountainhead* is execrably written and full of her Loony Tune economic theories (theories that we are still living with), nevertheless *The Fountainhead* is one of the most important books of the century.

Any list that does not include P. G. Wodehouse is not worth the paper it's written on. I'm sure if he were alive, Waugh, mean as he was, would have stepped aside for Wodehouse.

Other major omissions: *Guard Of Honor; Rabbit, Run;* and for me the most outrageous omission, *Nightwood* by Djuna Barnes.

The only unexpected surprises which please me: *A High Wind In Jamaica* and *The Wapshot Chronicle.*

And one timid vote each for *The Lonely Passion Of Judith Hearne* and *Precious Bane.*

Outraged, shocked and disappointed.

Marjorie Perloff

The big omission is Samuel Beckett, as in
Molloy
Malone Dies
The Unnamable

Another is Gertrude Stein:
The Making of Americans
The Autobiography of Alice B. Toklas
Lucy Church Amiably

Dust jacket for the author's autobiographical first novel, which the Modern Library List failed to include

And for Faulkner:

I believe almost every novel of his should be on here: *Absalom, Absalom!,* of course. And finally,

Eudora Welty: *The Ponder Heart*

These would be the main omissions, as I see it.

Peter S. Prescott

Anyone familiar with 20th-century literature, or with how lists are generated, knows that this list is misnamed. It should be called "20 Great Novels We've Actually Read This Century Plus 80 More We've Heard Of and Suspect We Should Have Read." I'm on friendly terms with two of the jurors, Arthur Schlesinger Jr. and Vartan Gregorian, and I'm sure that neither of these distinguished men has spent much of his adult life reading novels. When I mentioned *Under the Volcano* (#11), which is, with *The Golden Bowl* (#32) and *Finnegans Wake* (#77), one of the novels that every intellectual has heard of but few have actually read, to Dr. Gregorian he freely admitted he hadn't read it.

The "I've heard of it" aspect of the list prompts one genuine howler: Anthony Powell never wrote a series of novels called *A Dance to the Music of Time* (#43).

He wrote a series called *The Music of Time,* which was republished in four volumes, each with the phrase "*A Dance to*" added to the title to indicate its incomplete state. Everyone has heard of *Portnoy's Complaint* (#52), and has probably read it, but no one who knows Philip Roth's work would call it his best novel: either *American Pastoral* or *The Ghost Writer* is. *Ragtime* is E. L. Doctorow's most famous novel, but he's written better: *The Book of Daniel* and *Lives of the Poets.* Again, everyone knows Kurt Vonnegut's *Slaughterhouse-Five* (#18), in my view a brave failure–but there it squats above Ralph Ellison's *Invisible Man* (#19), an incontestable masterpiece that I'm beginning to fear has entered the "I really should have read it" arena.

It's easy, but useless, to continue. Incredibly, Random House didn't allow collections of short stories to be considered. Thus we have so-so novels by Somerset Maugham and John Cheever, because the jurors thought that these writers we've all heard of couldn't be ignored, but informed readers know that these writers' real achievement was in the short-story form. As was John O'Hara's. V. S. Pritchett's *Collected Stories* and Rudyard Kipling's late stories, when he virtually reinvented the short story for the 20th century, would make my top ten list. Few readers know them at all. Probably William Trevor's *Collected Stories*–he is the best living writer of short fiction–would be there too. And

Donald Barthelme's stories, collected in two volumes, should be somewhere in the 100: he reinvented the short story for our postmodern times.

Who else is missing? Toni Morrison's *Beloved* is a seminal novel for our time–not an easy read, but then the jurors who gave us *The Wings of the Dove* (#26) probably haven't read it either. John Updike, arguably the best American writer of fiction in our day, should be here somewhere. I would vote for his *Collected Stories,* but it doesn't exist; he has said that he distrusts such enterprises. I think he's wrong, and hope that we will have it someday. For the moment, let's put *Rabbit, Run* on our 100-best list. Larry McMurtry tells stories so well that critics recoil, yet *Lonesome Dove* is a great novel. Hilary Mantel's *A Change of Climate* is that rare thing: a novel that provokes a metaphysical shudder. John le Carré's *The Little Drummer Girl* should be here: the best novel about a terrorist's mind since Conrad's *The Secret Agent.* Finally, from recent times, William Gaddis's *J. R.* and J. M. Coetzee's *Waiting for the Barbarians.*

As for the past. . . . The problem with the "I've heard of it" approach to a list assembled by people who read little fiction is that many of the best books are now forgotten. L. H. Myers's tetralogy, sometimes called *The Root and the Flower,* sometimes *The Near and the Far,* may be the century's greatest historical novel, but no one knows it today. Joyce Cary's *The Horse's Mouth,* a supremely comic novel, should be here–and, yes, P. G. Wodehouse's masterpiece, *The Code of the Woosters.*

Charles Scribner III

Graham Greene, *The End of the Affair*
Alan Paton, *Cry, The Beloved Country*
Louis Auchincloss, *The Rector of Justin*
John Knowles, *A Separate Peace*
Morris West, *The Devil's Advocate*
Graham Greene, *The Power and the Glory*
Marjorie Kinnan Rawlings, *The Yearling*

John F. Thornton

Thanks for the chance to vote in books additional to the ML 100 list. I have two candidates: Flann O'Brien's (Brian O'Nolan's) wonderful novel-in-a-novel, *At Swim-Two-Birds* (1939), recently revived by Dalkey Archive Press, and Aldous Huxley's Hollywood satire, *After Many a Summer Dies the Swan* (1939), which anticipated many a later work, chiefly Waugh's *The Loved One,* to which I think it is superior.

Library Journal Readers' List of 150 Most Influential Works of Twentieth-Century Fiction

1. *To Kill a Mockingbird* (1960), Harper Lee
2. *The Catcher in the Rye* (1945), J. D. Salinger
3. *Lord of the Rings* (1956), J. R. R. Tolkien
4. *Gone with the Wind* (1936), Margaret Mitchell
5. *Beloved* (1987), Toni Morrison
6. *The Color Purple* (1982), Alice Walker
7. *Nineteen Eighty-four* (1949), George Orwell
8. *Animal Farm* (1954), George Orwell
9. *Lord of the Flies* (1954), William Golding
10. *Catch-22* (1961), Joseph Heller
11. *The Good Earth* (1931), Pearl Buck
12. *Charlotte's Web* (1952), E. B. White
13. *The Great Gatsby* (1925), F. Scott Fitzgerald
14. *Slaughterhouse-Five* (1969), Kurt Vonnegut
15. *One Hundred Years of Solitude* (1970), Gabriel García Márquez
16. *Lonesome Dove* (1986), Larry McMurtry
17. *Lolita* (1955), Vladimir Nabokov
18. *Fahrenheit 451* (1952), Ray Bradbury
19. *Rebecca* (1938), Daphne Du Maurier
20. *The Grapes of Wrath* (1939), John Steinbeck
21. *A Tree Grows in Brooklyn* (1947), Betty Smith
22. *The Hobbit* (1937), J. R. R. Tolkien
23. *One Flew Over the Cuckoo's Nest* (1962), Ken Kesey
24. *The Prime of Miss Jean Brodie* (1962), Muriel Spark
25. *My Ántonia* (1918), Willa Cather
26. *The Old Man and the Sea* (1952), Ernest Hemingway
27. *Lady Chatterley's Lover* (1928), D. H. Lawrence
28. *The Invisible Man* (1952), Ralph Ellison
29. *Exodus* (1957), Leon Uris
30. *Sophie's Choice* (1979), William Styron
31. *Native Son* (1940), Richard Wright
32. *Little House on the Prairie* (1935), Laura Ingalls Wilder
33. *A Farewell to Arms* (1929), Ernest Hemingway
34. *Winnie the Pooh* (1926), A. A. Milne
35. *The Jungle* (1906), Upton Sinclair
36. *The Handmaid's Tale* (1986), Margaret Atwood
37. *The Age of Innocence* (1920), Edith Wharton
38. *Rabbit, Run* (1960), John Updike
39. *On the Road* (1957), Jack Kerouac

40. *Stranger in a Strange Land* (1961), Robert A. Heinlein

41. *Brave New World* (1932), Aldous Huxley

42. *Angle of Repose* (1971), Wallace Stegner

43. *All Quiet on the Western Front* (1929), Erich Maria Remarque

44. *Ulysses* (1922), James Joyce

45. *The Sun Also Rises* (1926), Ernest Hemingway

46. *The Stranger* (1942), Albert Camus

47. *The Sound and the Fury* (1929), William Faulkner

48. *Possession* (1990), A. S. Byatt

49. *Stone Diaries* (1994), Carol Shields

50. *Song of Solomon* (1977), Toni Morrison

51. *The Joy Luck Club* (1989), Amy Tan

52. *Roots* (1976), Alex Haley

53. *A Portrait of the Artist as a Young Man* (1916), James Joyce

54. *Look Homeward, Angel* (1929), Thomas Wolfe

55. *Pale Horse, Pale Rider* (1939), Katherine Anne Porter

56. *Ethan Frome* (1911), Edith Wharton

57. *The Lover* (1972), Marguerite Duras

58. *A Clockwork Orange* (1962), Anthony Burgess

59. *Winesburg, Ohio* (1919), Sherwood Anderson

60. *To the Lighthouse* (1927), Virginia Woolf

61. *The World According to Garp* (1978), John Irving

62. *The Wonderful Wizard of Oz* (1900), Frank Baum

63. *The Lion, the Witch, and the Wardrobe* (1950), C. S. Lewis

64. *The Hound of the Baskervilles* (1902), Sir Arthur Conan Doyle

65. *The Fountainhead* (1943), Ayn Rand

66. *The Burger's Daughter* (1979), Nadine Gordimer

67. *The Call of the Wild* (1903), Jack London

68. *One Day in the Life of Ivan Denisovich* (1963), Alexander Solzhenitsyn

69. *The Mists of Avalon* (1983), Marion Zimmer Bradley

70. *I, Claudius* (1934), Robert Graves

71. *From Here to Eternity* (1951), James Jones

72. *East of Eden* (1952), John Steinbeck

73. *Cry, The Beloved Country* (1948), Alan Paton

74. *Advise and Consent* (1959), Allen Drury

75. *A Passage to India* (1924), E. M. Forster

76. *2001: A Space Odyssey* (1968), Arthur C. Clarke

77. *The Good Soldier* (1927), Ford Madox Ford

78. *Their Eyes Were Watching God* (1937), Zora Neale Hurston

79. *The Wind in the Willows* (1908), Kenneth Graham

80. *Portnoy's Complaint* (1969), Philip Roth

81. *The Plague* (1947), Albert Camus

82. *The Little Prince* (1943), Antoine de Saint-Exupéry

83. *The Bluest Eye* (1969), Toni Morrison

84. *The Bean Trees* (1988), Barbara Kingsolver

85. *Tarzan of the Apes* (1914), Edgar Rice Burroughs

86. *Sister Carrie* (1900), Theodore Dreiser

87. *A Good Man Is Hard to Find* (1955), Flannery O'Connor

88. *Remembrance of Things Past* (1960), Marcel Proust

89. *Ragtime* (1975), E. L. Doctorow

90. *Ordinary People* (1976), Judith Guest

91. *Of Human Bondage* (1915), W. Somerset Maugham

92. *Heart of Darkness* (1902), Joseph Conrad

93. *Babbit* (1922), Sinclair Lewis

94. *All the King's Men* (1946), Robert Penn Warren

95. *Women in Love* (1920), D. H. Lawrence

96. *Waiting for Godot* (1953), Samuel Beckett

97. *U. S. A.* (trilogy, 1938), John Dos Passos

98. *The Unbearable Lightness of Being* (1984), Milan Kundera

99. *A Death in the Family* (1957), James Agee

100. *The Once and Future King* (1958), T. H. White

101. *The Maltese Falcon* (1930), Dashiell Hammett

102. *The Golden Bowl* (1904), Henry James

103. *The Golden Notebook* (1962), Doris Lessing

104. *The Forsyte Saga* (1922), John Galsworthy

105. *The Big Sleep* (1939), Raymond Chandler

106. *The Bell Jar* (1963), Sylvia Plath

107. *The Ambassadors* (1903), Henry James

108. *The House of the Spirits* (1985), Isabel Allende

109. *Of Mice and Men* (1937), John Steinbeck

110. *The Naked and the Dead* (1948), Norman Mailer

111. *Magic Mountain* (1924), Thomas Mann

112. *Johnny Got His Gun* (1959), Dalton Trumbo

113. *Ironweed* (1983), William Kennedy

114. *A Farewell to Arms* (1929), Ernest Hemingway

115. *Dune* (1965), Frank Herbert

116. *Doctor Zhivago* (1958), Boris Pasternak

117. *Death Comes for the Archbishop* (1927), Willa Cather

118. *Cat's Cradle* (1963), Kurt Vonnegut

119. *Brideshead Revisited* (1945), Evelyn Waugh

120. *Breathing Lessons* (1988), Anne Tyler

121. *Are You There, God? It's Me, Margaret* (1970), Judy Blume
122. *The Accidental Tourist* (1985), Anne Tyler
123. *A Thousand Acres* (1991), Jane Smiley
124. *A Room with a View* (1908), E. M. Forster
125. *Wise Blood* (1952), Flannery O'Connor
126. *The Tin Drum* (1959), Günter Grass
127. *Wide Sargasso Sea* (1966), Jean Rhys
128. *White Noise* (1985), Don DeLillo
129. *Where the Wild Things Are* (1963), Maurice Sendak
130. *The Wapshot Chronicle* (1979), John Cheever
131. *Under the Volcano* (1947), Malcolm Lowry
132. *Tropic of Cancer* (1934), Henry Miller
133. *Things Fall Apart* (1959), Chinua Achebe
134. *The Yearling* (1948), Marjorie Kinnan Rawlings
135. *The Winds of War* (1971), Herman Wouk

136. *The Moviegoer* (1961), Walker Percy
137. *The Razor's Edge* (1944), W. Somerset Maugham
138. *The Rebel* (1954), Albert Camus
139. *The Pearl* (1947), John Steinbeck
140. *The Outsider* (1956), Colin Wilson
141. *Call It Sleep* (1934), Henry Roth
142. *The Heart Is a Lonely Hunter* (1940), Carson McCullers
143. *The Godfather* (1969), Mario Puzo
144. *A Curtain of Green* (1941), Eudora Welty
145. *The End of the Affair* (1951), Graham Greene
146. *The Color of Water* (1996), James McBride
147. *The Caine Mutiny* (1951), Herman Wouk
148. *The Bridge of San Luis Rey* (1927), Thornton Wilder
149. *The Agony and the Ecstasy* (1961), Irving Stone
150. *Studs Lonigan: A Trilogy* (1935), James T. Farrell

A Celebration of Literary Biography

Tracy Simmons Bitonti

and

Mori Thomas

On 13–14 November 1998 the University of South Carolina hosted "A Celebration of Literary Biography," sponsored by the University Office of the Provost, The Gale Group, Bruccoli Clark Layman, the Thomas Cooper Library, the Thomas Cooper Society, and the Department of English at the university. The purposes of the celebration were to commemorate the publication of the two hundredth volume of the *Dictionary of Literary Biography* (*DLB*) and to launch the Literary Biography Depository at the Thomas Cooper Library.

The Literary Biography Depository was conceived to fill a gap in existing scholarship. As Patrick Scott, professor of English and associate librarian for Special Collections, pointed out, most libraries neglect to adequately preserve literary biographies; the books "will not be there for the long run," because they are consulted so often and for so many reasons, that they "not only get used, but they get used up." The intent of the depository is to ensure that these books, an essential element of cultural heritage, will be "available for the future and adequately recognized." The plan is to acquire a copy of every biography of every American author that is written in the English language, and "biography" is intended in its fullest sense to encompass resources both published and unpublished: memoirs, autobiographies, letters, diaries, journals, notebooks, and other documentary and archival materials. The depository will thus provide a survey of the accomplishments in this field since William Dunlap's *Memoirs of Charles Brockden Brown, The American Novelist* (1815). Publishers have been asked to donate copies of new biographies as they appear, and contributions have already been received from Harcourt Brace and Scribners.

There is currently no bibliography or checklist of American literary biographies; thus, the working list compiled as the basis for collection assessment and inventory will be an important resource that will be maintained on-line as part of the planned World Wide Web site for the depository. At least three thousand items from existing collections will form the initial basis of the depository, with some biographies remaining in general circulation and scarce or valuable volumes being moved to Special Collections. A want list will be circulated to book dealers in the United States and abroad as part of an ongoing acquisitions program, a massive search project also involving scholars from several departments. The web page will provide periodic updates on activities associated with the depository.

With this unprecedented project the University of South Carolina is creating an international resource—a central location where authors, editors, publishers, and subjects of literary biography can place their papers for the use of students and researchers, and where scholars will be able to find more of this material than anywhere else. Courses on literary biography are being developed at the university, and lectures and conferences in the field will be sponsored.

The uses of literary biography were explored in the keynote address given by John Updike. Following remarks by Dr. George Terry, Vice Provost and Dean of Libraries and Information Systems at the University of South Carolina, Dr. John Palms, president of the university, introduced Updike to the crowd that filled the Law School Auditorium to hear his reflections on how reading literary biography can be a valuable endeavor.

Updike opened with two epigraphs conveying familiar reservations that many writers have expressed about literary biography: as F. Scott Fitzgerald wrote in his notebooks, "There never was a good biography of a good novelist. There couldn't be. He is too many people if he is any good," and, as Octavio Paz remarked about Portuguese poet Fernando Pessoa, "Poets don't have biographies. Their work is their biography." If such views are true, Updike asked, why do we need literary biography at all? What, of any significance, can a biographer add to the literary record that authors—in drawing on their personal experiences, feelings, and memories—have left in their works, which surely ought to be the main interests of readers?

John Palms, President of the University of South Carolina, and John Updike (courtesy of Thomas Cooper Library, University of South Carolina)

Readers are drawn to literary biography for various reasons, Updike acknowledged. Perhaps George D. Painter's two-volume biography of Marcel Proust illustrates what readers find to be the most worthy reason, as the biographer makes his work a way for readers to reexperience Proust's *Remembrance of Things Past* by allowing them to delight in seeing memories, places, settings, and events often treated evasively in Proust's fiction transformed back into real ones in Painter's biography. By masterfully prolonging and extending the experience of that intimacy which readers of Proust's novel enjoyed in reading it, Painter renews (from his different perspective as biographer) the delight that readers felt while they were communing with Proust, the novelist whose voice or mind provided them with such joy.

By contrast, Updike continued, other biographies such as Richard Ellmann's of James Joyce may give readers not a reflection or an extension of their initial delight in reading Joyce's works so much as a kind of comprehensive anthology that deepens their understanding of his creative process. For example, in its detailed record of quotations Ellmann's biography

helps readers to comprehend how Joyce created his works, how those works manage to re-create for Joyce's readers the Dublin that he transformed from the drab facts of Irish poverty, politics, and priest-laden life into the vivid art of *Dubliners* (1914), *A Portrait of the Artist as a Young Man* (1916), *Ulysses* (1922), or *Finnegans Wake* (1939).

Updike admitted that biography cannot explain the literary accomplishments of some writers for whom recorded details of their lives are lacking or incomplete. For instance, the lack of verifiable details on which biographies depend necessarily ensures that no record can adequately explain why a William Shakespeare or a Jane Austen achieved the literary renown that their works have brought them. Yet, he contended, it is understandable how a work such as Dennis Kay's 1922 biography of Shakespeare appeals to reader curiosity about what the biographer might offer as evidence to illuminate the life of the greatest writer in the English language—even though much about artistic genius or creativity remains inexplicable by recourse to the purely historical facts on which biography depends.

Reader curiosity is also a basis for the appeal of biographies written as diagnoses of how some deprivation or presumed sickness that an author suffered drove him to write literature as a compensation for what the biographer finds the artist's life must have lacked. Edmund Wilson's *The Wound and the Bow* (1941) and similar studies of writers such as Franz Kafka, Nathaniel Hawthorne, or Herman Melville present their subjects' lives in this way, but, as Updike reminded his audience, the lives of such "invalids" merit interest chiefly because of the truths incorporated in their literary works. Their "wounds" may have existed, but so did the admirable "bows" that such wounded creators used masterfully to strike their targets, he concluded—and the biographical exposition of such wounds thus enhances readers' appreciation of significant obstacles that these writers successfully transcended or transformed into their art.

Another use of literary biography is one that Updike found to be a basis for the objections that authors (including Updike) express toward the genre. Biographies such as those by Lytton Strachey seem written primarily to gratify readers by making them feel superior to the authors whose lives are presented, lives that are exposed and belittled in these literary biographies that appear to be growing in popularity. As an example of such studies, Updike cited Michael Sheldon's 1995 biography of Graham Greene, whom the biographer portrays as a bad Catholic, a bad husband, a sadistic joker, a burnt-out writer, the actual murderer in an unsolved homicide case, and (as was his friend, Kim Philby) a British traitor.

Updike identified an even more reprehensible subset of this class of biography: the "Judas biography," in which the biographer (a former spouse, friend, or coworker of a writer) presents a most unflattering portrait that the reader does not expect to find. Claire Bloom's portrait of the insensitivity, selfishness, adultery, and financial vengeance of her former husband, Philip Roth; Paul Theroux's reports of vain, cruel, racist, and misogynistic remarks made by V. S. Naipaul (in what Naipaul apparently felt were private confidences); and Joyce Maynard's exposé of J. D. Salinger's personal eccentricities and private character during the years she lived with the author all illustrate this subclass of unflattering literary biography. Updike acknowledged that readers could be fascinated to discover such private details of the life of a writer whose works they have enjoyed, but he found that such biographies offer strong evidence that the obligations of the biographer and the fiction writer toward their readers differ, and must do so in important ways.

Biographers must be sure not only that their facts are accurate, he insisted, but also that their selection and presentation of these do not misinterpret their significance or assign to them an importance that the subject of the biography knows to be inaccurate. From the fiction

writer's ignorance, the speculations about what he or she knows, the fiction writer designs his or her art. From the many facts that the biographical investigator examines, the biographer (if thorough) knows many things that may merit being included in his or her biography. "Truth" in fiction denotes what the reader *feels* to be true; "truth" in biography must be referred to the verifiable facts, the evidence that a study of the life of the author bears out. Given these differences in what these genres demand of each writer, Updike cautioned, the biographer must not appropriate the artist's license to *make* truth: his or her aim must remain that of leading readers of literary works—who should expect to find greater enjoyment and a sharpened understanding of them—back to those works that the author has written.

Henry James's literary achievements, even without biographer Leon Edel's extensively detailed tracing of connections between James's psyche and his growing canon, remain as highly regarded as they have ever been, Updike concluded. What makes Edel's biography so admirable, he noted, is that it enables a reader familiar with the novelist's works to watch the "different people" that James was at different times throughout his life thereby to coalesce in some way. By so extending and deepening the reader's enjoyment of the writer's works through presenting the reader with thought-provoking, tangible renderings of the various "people" whom Fitzgerald saw comprising the personality of the writer, literary biography continues to serve useful and worthy ends.

Updike's presentation was followed by the Thomas Cooper Society dinner. After remarks by President Palms and Dean Terry, Updike was presented the Thomas Cooper Medal, awarded by the society for distinguished literary achievement. Previous recipients include Pat Conroy, Joseph Heller, and James Dickey. Updike remarked that the medal is "a nice little piece of Southern hospitality to take back to New England and make all my friends envious." Then two speakers addressed the main reasons for the celebration: Dedria Bryfonski, president of the Library Education Division of the Gale Group, summarized the achievement and importance of the *DLB*, while John Cole, executive director of the Center for the Book at the Library of Congress, saluted the establishment of the Literary Biography Depository.

As the foreword to *DLB 200* indicates, that volume "is actually the 252nd *Dictionary of Literary Biography* volume: 216 in the main series, including the early multi-volume titles; 18 in the *Documentary Series;* and 18 *Yearbooks.*" These books "include 8,500 entries by 8,000 editors and contributors worldwide: more than 62,000,000 words." Bryfonski called the *DLB* "scholarship unbound," and she recalled that when the idea of the *DLB* was first formulated in a shipboard meeting convened by publisher Frederick Ruffner in 1975, the plan was to create three volumes

George Terry, Dean of Libraries and Information Systems, University of South Carolina; Helen Ann Rawlinson, President, Thomas Cooper Society; and John Updike, at the presentation of the Thomas Cooper Medal (courtesy of the Thomas Cooper Library, University of South Carolina)

and see if the market could support ten. The *DLB* was founded on the same principle as other Gale projects such as *Contemporary Authors* and *Contemporary Literary Criticism:* "that ordinary people, high school students, college students, patrons of public libraries, want good and accurate information about books and authors." Bryfonski emphasized the commitment to accuracy that is part of Gale's contribution to literary biography.

Bryfonski also read a statement from C. E. Frazer Clark Jr., one of the founding partners of Bruccoli Clark Layman, who could not attend the celebration. Reading *DLB 200*, Clark said, he was "struck by how faithful to the original plan is the 200th volume." The *DLB* was initially designed to fill gaps in history and publishing left by the *Dictionary of American Biography*, but now, Bryfonski said, "the child has outgrown the parent." The success of the project has led to its expansion beyond American authors to encompass world literatures, and "each new volume that we create continues a story that has no foreseeable end."

The future of the *DLB* also encompasses electronic media. In a world that is increasingly "plugged in" there is a premium on high-quality information, expertise, access, and the kinds of connections between authors, places, themes, and contexts that electronic media can facilitate. While it is important to have the *DLB* in its entirety housed in the reading room at the Bodleian Library, Oxford University, Bryfonski continued, it is even more important to know that its information is "just a mouse click away" for students and others with questions about literature. She concluded her remarks by saying that the last twenty years have been "just a prelude to the future that we're looking for," one in which *DLB* information will be available to "all the people who are connected electronically to literature that moves through the world."

In his remarks on the Literary Biography Depository, Cole congratulated Thomas Cooper Library and the university for having "the imagination and, indeed, the nerve" to begin this project. He called the depository "a most ambitious bibliographic and archival task" that will provide "a substantial contribution to our nation's cultural and literary heritage." Noting that the University of South Carolina is the first American institution to develop such a collection, Cole linked the university to the Library of Congress, which also celebrates literature and the printed word. The Literary Biography Depository "will greatly benefit scholarly research and appreciation of literature and of the community of the book itself." Cole cited two quotations that are etched on the walls of the Jefferson Building and that confirm the value of the depository: Petrarch's statement that "Glory is acquired by virtue but preserved by letters" and Samuel Johnson's assertion that "The chief glory of every people arises from its authors."

Two exhibits were mounted at Thomas Cooper Library in conjunction with the celebration. The first was an exhibition of John Updike materials from the extensive collection of Donald J. Greiner, professor of English and associate provost. As Patrick Scott pointed out, "the best introduction to an author is his books, and unless someone has the books, nobody knows the author." At the opening of the exhibit on 14 November, Greiner recalled how his collection got started. He had admired Updike's work ever since he read a copy of *Pigeon Feathers and Other Stories* (1962) in graduate school. By 1980 he had decided that he wanted to write about Updike, and his first challenge became "to figure out what he had written"–identifying not only Updike's books but also all of the other writings, including articles, reviews, prefaces, forewords, broadsides, and galley proofs. The second challenge was to "go buy every one of them, because it was clear that one library was not going to have them all." The twenty-four-page catalogue of the exhibit, available at no charge but in limited supply from the Special Collections Department at Thomas Cooper Library, includes Greiner's descriptions of the approximately 150 items exhibited.

Commenting that "Every loved child has the correct sensation that everything he or she does is precious," Updike compared Greiner's collection of his work to the baby book kept by his mother, "in which she wrote down each tiny advance I made in the journey of life." He spoke of being both grateful for the interest of collectors and a bit embarrassed by the sheer bulk of the exhibit. Of the items on display, he said "they're all old friends, and various details of jacket design and struggle over typography and all kinds of intimate working details came back to me–and would come back only to me–as I saw these things." He recalled a few of those details for the audience, pointing out, for example, graphic artist Harry Ford's striped dust jacket design for the novel *The Poorhouse Fair* (1959), a design that Updike kept for other books.

While the Updike exhibit documented the milestones of one author's professional biography, a second exhibit, "The Biographical Part of Literature," charted the development of literary biography and featured some of the materials that comprise the beginning of the new Literary Biography Depository. William R. Cagle, director emeritus of The Lilly Library at Indiana University, spoke about the history of the genre and

Dedria Bryfonski, President of the Library Education Group of the Gale Group, at the Thomas Cooper Society dinner (courtesy of Thomas Cooper Library, University of South Carolina)

about the possibilities for collections such as that begun by the University of South Carolina. The full text of his remarks is published in this *Yearbook* volume.

In addition to featuring many of the noteworthy items mentioned by Cagle, the exhibit incorporated many key concepts of biography, including its process (identifying greatness, augmenting and correcting the record, tracing the writings, collecting the primary documents, and sifting the myths); the potential of biography to restore or revive an author's professional career; the problems for a biographer when his subject's life was less than exemplary or when family members got involved; and issues of biographical practice such as compassion, distortion, friendship, and detachment. A case of items from the Matthew J. and Arlyn Bruccoli Collection of F. Scott Fitzgerald provided examples of the primary materials of biography, including records such as the author's 1925 tax return, royalty statements, correspondence with his editor, and his own self-assessments in his *Ledger*. A case of modern literary biographies selected from the

John Y. Cole, Director of the Center for the Book, Library of Congress
(photograph by Michael Rogers)

18,000-volume library of James Dickey (which the Thomas Cooper Library recently acquired) demonstrated not only the breadth of Dickey's reading but also the range of biographies available, from standard works to new examinations of traditional subjects.

A sixty-one-page illustrated catalogue for "The Biographical Part of Literature" prepared by Scott is also available at no charge but in limited supply from the Special Collections Department of the Thomas Cooper Library. It describes the importance of the various items displayed and their places in the development of the genre of literary biography. For example, Dunlap's treatment of Charles Brockden Brown is "the first full-length biography of the first professional author of the United States," while Pierre Munro Irving's *Life and Letters of Washington Irving* (1862–1864) "gave for the first time to an American author the multi-volume life-and- letters treatment that had long been standard in Britain." British items included a 1787 second edition of Sir John Hawkins's *Life of Samuel Johnson, LL.D.*, the first biography of Johnson, later "completely overshadowed by Boswell's" (which was also displayed). The exhibit emphasized the

value of preserving this genre and showed the possibilities for study that the depository project will offer.

The presence of Dickey's books in the exhibit was also a reminder of the poet's importance to the university, a point reinforced by the dedication of the James Dickey Poetry Seminar Room at the library and by the premiere of *James Dickey on Film,* produced by Ed Breland of Instructional Development Services at the university. The videotaped tribute to Dickey was produced from excerpts of movies in which the poet reads his works and discusses experiences that he transformed into poetry. Illustrated with photographs and visual materials, the tribute opens with Dickey reading "For the Last Wolverine." Another Southern poet appears on an outing with Dickey in the section from *Two Poets, Two Friends: James Dickey and Robert Penn Warren,* produced in 1982 by CBS Cable. The tribute closes with Dickey, introduced by Bette Davis, at inauguration ceremonies for President Jimmy Carter in 1977, as the poet reads "The Strength of Fields," which he wrote for that occasion.

Dean Terry then introduced Henry Hart, professor of humanities at the College of William and Mary, who is writing the authorized biography of Dickey. Hart recalled his first meeting with the poet in August 1996 at Dickey's home in Columbia, where, despite being ill, Dickey was sitting up in a chair, surrounded by his books and other possessions that seemed to present contradictory images: mementos of his days as a track and football athlete, his flight jacket, and other possessions seemed to reinforce the typically "non-bookish" character of the writer.

Yet Dickey's sister, Maibelle, insisted to Hart that her brother had been "born with a book in his hand." At age five Dickey wrote "You and Yourself," a book only a few pages long, its binding made of string and its cover illustration (of a child) clipped from a magazine. His second book, a narrative of his boyhood ambition to become a fighter pilot, was written at age six, titled "The Life of James Dickey," and illustrated with crayon-drawn airplanes.

Through grammar school Dickey was a dedicated reader of boys' books: the Tarzan stories and science fiction of Edgar Rice Burroughs, the Bomba the Jungle Boy tales by Roy Rockwood, the Baseball Joe books by Lester Chadwick, the Hardy Boys series, and the Westerns of Zane Grey. In high school his reading interests broadened to include the poetry of Robert Frost and Edgar Allan Poe as well as the fiction of Thomas Wolfe, Erskine Caldwell, and W. Somerset Maugham, although Dickey maintained, as Hart indicated, "a voracious appetite" for the fiction of pulp magazines such as *Popular Detective, Amazing Stories, The Shadow, Terror Tales, The Phantom Detective,*

Main entrance to the Thomas Cooper Library, the site of the new Literary Biography Depository (courtesy of Thomas Cooper Library, University of South Carolina)

Horror Stories, Doc Savage, War Birds, and *Flying Aces.* Hart remarked that Dickey's youthful enjoyment of adventure stories foreshadowed the interest in quest literature that he displayed as an adult.

After Dickey enlisted in the Army Air Corps in World War II, his love of books continued to grow—and to broaden. Hart stated that in 1944 Dickey wrote home to his mother to ask that she sell some of his war bonds and buy copies of Joyce's *Ulysses* and Ernest Hemingway's *A Farewell to Arms* to send him. In a 30 June 1945 letter Dickey asked her to buy and mail him copies of fifty books on a wide range of subjects, books such as Sigmund Freud's *General Introduction to Psychoanalysis,* Will Durant's *The Story of Philosophy,* Thomas Bulfinch's *Mythology,* Eugene O'Neill's *The Complete Greek Drama,* Bernard Guerney's *A Treasury of Russian Literature,* Barney Ross's *Fundamentals of Boxing,* Philip Goepp's *Great Works of Music,* and Charles Darwin's *The Origin of Species* and *The Descent of Man.* He also enjoyed reading poetry by W. H. Auden, C. Day Lewis, Kenneth Patchen, Trumbull Stickney, Richard Aldington, Dylan Thomas, Robert Penn Warren, R. P. Blackmur, Stephen Spender, and Randall Jarrell.

While Dickey was attending Vanderbilt University after the war, Zibart's Bookstore in Nashville, Tennessee, became one of his favorite hangouts. Surprised and impressed that a football player could have so much interest in books and could talk so knowledgeably about them, Carl Zibart, the owner, gave Dickey his first job working in the bookstore. His great memory of what he read, Hart added, enabled Dickey accurately to quote long passages of poems (such as Frost's "After Apple-Picking") and even prose (such as André Gide's *Journals*) by writers whose works interested him. Throughout his life the poet "enjoyed living in the sensual world," Hart acknowledged,

> but he also enjoyed treating that world as if it were a book—full of sound of fury and consequence. The world wasn't entirely real until he made it so in his imagination. To borrow a phrase Ward Briggs [a friend and colleague at the University of South Carolina] used in a final conversation with Jim, Jim's most cherished world "was real in the dream"—in the dream that was the book.

Dickey's library and the Dickey Poetry Seminar Room, Hart concluded, are therefore fitting memorials to the

John Updike and other participants at the Celebration of Literary Biography, in the James Dickey Poetry Seminar Room (courtesy of Thomas Cooper Library, University of South Carolina)

poet at the Thomas Cooper Library, where "his spirit is palpable, . . . is in it–and part of it–from now on."

In celebrating the poetry seminar room, Provost Gerald Odom closed the morning session with an additional tribute to Dickey, whose teaching and publishing after his arrival at the university in 1969 brought him many distinctions. Odom praised Dickey for having been not only a superb teacher but also "an intellectual presence," a mentor and a friend to young writers and colleagues. Throughout his career at the University of South Carolina his colleagues honored Dickey–for example, by making him its first Carolina Distinguished Professor and awarding him an honorary doctorate of letters. He also received the Thomas Cooper Medal. It is therefore appropriate, Odom remarked, that the Dickey Poetry Seminar Room will be more than a shrine or a museum: it is a teaching room "for the kind of small-group teaching Jim did so well." The provost concluded, "We believe that James Dickey's library will be a resource and an inspiration–both for future scholars of Jim's work and for students following in his intellectual path."

The celebration also featured four panel discussions on related topics. A pre-conference panel, "Libraries and Literary Biography," was moderated by Linda Lucas-Walling, professor in the College of Library and Information Sciences at the University of South Carolina. Participants included Sharon Verba, reference librarian at Thomas Cooper Library; Clo Camarota, information services librarian at Richland County Public Library; and Lynn S. Barron, librarian at Hammond Academy. These panelists discussed the needs of various users of biographical resources, including students of all ages working on school projects, teachers seeking to plan lessons or refresh their memories, and librarians seeking to answer questions for book-club members who need information about books they are reading or authors who will be speaking at their events. Other topics included the need for more information about international and world authors and the importance of illustrations–such as photographs of the author at various stages in his or her career, dust jackets, and manuscript pages–not just to interest younger readers but to provide better understanding for all users.

The panelists also discussed advantages and disadvantages to using electronic forms of information as well as traditional print forms. Electronic resources offer multimedia and hyperlink possibilities, indexing and search features not available with print, the ability

Dennis Poupard, Gale Research Group; James Rettig, University of Richmond; James L. Harner, Texas A&M University; and Richard Layman, Bruccoli Clark Layman (photograph by Michael Rogers)

to keep material updated more easily, and wider access to one source of information—a particular advantage for larger libraries with several branches. As an audience member pointed out, however, a library can buy a print resource such as a set of the *Encyclopedia Britannica,* and patrons will still have access to the information if the library decides not to buy another set the next year; but if a library discontinues a subscription to an Internet resource, patrons lose access to the material since the library does not physically own it. On-line resources also bring further expenses for equipment such as additional computer terminals, and all of the librarians agreed that cost determines which biographical resources they can make available.

The first panel on 14 November continued discussion of on-line issues. "The Delivery of Reference Material in Electronic Form" was moderated by Richard Layman of Bruccoli Clark Layman, and participants were Dennis Poupard, vice president for product development at the Gale Group and a reference publisher for twenty years; James Rettig, university librarian at the University of Richmond and the author of hundreds of reviews of reference books in the Wilson Library Bulletin as well as the creator of *Rettig on Reference,* a review service on the World Wide Web; and James L. Harner, professor of English at Texas A&M

University, the author of sixteen books including *A Guide to Reference Sources for the Study of Literatures in English and Related Topics* (published by the Modern Language Association), and the editor of *The World Shakespeare Bibliography,* an ongoing series published by Cambridge University Press. Poupard began by saying that in the warnings of those who fear a computer culture he hears echoes of other warnings such as "television is going to kill film," or "rock and roll will destroy culture." New technology will kill some things we love, he said, but it will also create new possibilities. Some of these possibilities include unprecedented abilities to constantly update reference materials and to provide what Harner said users want most: "splash," speed, and links. Rettig also mentioned the demands of users who want the ability to link information and to have nonlinear experiences interacting with images on a screen, as today's generation is accustomed to doing. The downside, he said, is the potential reduction of information to what can fit on one screen.

The growth of on-line resources raises problems of authority, and there is an increasing need for students to learn how to discriminate between good and bad sources of information. Another result of the growth of electronic media will be an increasing demand for people who can understand, or learn to

George Garrett, University of Virginia; Darlene Unrue, University of Nevada, Las Vegas; Henry Hart, College of William and Mary; and Joel Myerson, University of South Carolina (photograph by Michael Rogers)

integrate, the needs of both the humanities-trained editor, who thinks in terms of what students and teachers want, and the scientifically trained software engineer, who thinks in terms of what the technology can do. In discussing problems of copyright, the panelists differed in their opinions of whether the concept of "fair use" is endangered by Internet technology.

The second panel, "Writing Literary Biography," was moderated by Joel Myerson, professor of English at the University of South Carolina. The participants were George Garrett, Henry Hoyns Professor of Creative Writing at the University of Virginia and author of poetry, fiction, drama, and a biography of James Jones; Darlene Harbor Unrue, professor of English at the University of Nevada, Las Vegas, currently at work on a comprehensive biography of Katherine Anne Porter; and Henry Hart. Illustrating the importance of careful research, Garrett shared the story of how he located an important archive of Jones's papers from a footnote in a reference work. He also spoke about the ways in which his work on the Jones biography increased his understanding of the choices and problems involved in that type of writing.

Unrue described the surprises (such as the discovery of an additional marriage) she has encountered in her research into Porter's life. In answer to a question about potential difficulties in working on contemporary authors and considering the feelings of survivors, she pointed out that a biographer must weigh the necessity

of a revelation and decide how important a piece of information is to the overall picture.

Hart identified the biggest difficulty he has encountered with the Dickey biography as the necessity of sifting fact from invention and legend; he added that a biographer can never know the whole person. In answer to a question about the utility of writings about the theory and practice of writing biography, Hart said he found some of them, such as *Writing Lives: Principia Biographica* (1984) by Leon Edel, to be sources of consolation by showing him that other biographers have faced the same issues he is tackling.

Some of these points were discussed further in the third panel, "Publishing Literary Biography," moderated by Catherine Fry, director of the University of South Carolina Press. Panelists were Barry Blose, acquisitions editor of the University of South Carolina Press; Virginia Spencer Carr, professor of English at Georgia State University and biographer of John Dos Passos and Carson McCullers; and Patrick O'Connor, who has had a long and influential publishing career at several mass-market paperback houses. Blose pointed out that literary biography is "a niche product" with a relatively small market, and that the literary biography that sells usually has some special attraction such as debunking or exposing its subject, illustrating a social or cultural trend, or simply being interesting and well written.

Barry Blose, Acquisitions Editor, University of South Carolina Press; Pat O'Connor, paperback book editor; Virginia Spencer Carr, Georgia State University; and Catherine Fry, Director, University of South Carolina Press (photograph by Michael Rogers)

Carr spoke about the process of working with an editor in deciding what to cut from a lengthy manuscript and how to handle the threat of lawsuits. She mentioned potential lawsuits that developed during her writing of the McCullers biography and that she avoided by a slight change of wording or by her being less specific. She also discussed the growing trends of biographers who put too much of themselves into a biography or who become jealous and possessive of their subjects; she described a better attitude of friendly rivalry such as the one she had with Townsend Ludington, who was working on Dos Passos at the same time she was. She stated that the more biographers there are for a subject, the better, because each one will bring a different approach.

O'Connor told several stories about the publishing business. He described how Ayn Rand once invited to dinner the top executives of New American Library, the house that had been making steady income for years from publishing her works. She asked them which of her books they liked best and why; but "not one of them had read one word." O'Connor later became her editor because he had read her books, and she admonished him to be a good editor "and do everything I say."

In answer to a question about how to handle authors who demand that their work be published exactly as written, O'Connor recalled an occasion when Morrow had a

contract to publish a book by Johannes Mario Simmel, who had a great international reputation but had not been published successfully in the United States. When Morrow wanted to trim his 1,000-page manuscript, Simmel insisted that "not a golden word" be cut. So O'Connor "bought the manuscript for $2,000 . . . and I cut every other word." He knew that Simmel would never read it. O'Connor also recommended several books, including *Laurette* (1968), a biography of actress Laurette Taylor by Marguerite Courtney, and *Lovely Me: The Life of Jacqueline Susann* (1987) by Barbara Seaman. The latter, he said, includes everything one would want to know about the book business.

Other concerns of publishers were also discussed, such as the importance of fact-checking, which in some cases can be done by outside readers or specialist copy editors. Fry pointed out that university presses, because they do not have to be as concerned as trade publishers with big sales figures, can publish more specialized materials. She also advised writers to be their own best editors and be willing to cut their manuscripts so that they can reach a broader audience.

The range of topics addressed by these panels reveals the enduring appeal and importance of literary biography as something worth celebrating and preserving, as the University of South Carolina has begun to do.

Remarks at the Opening of "The Biographical Part of Literature" Exhibition

William R. Cagle
Director Emeritus, The Lilly Library

For all its recognized position in the world of letters today, biography—and especially literary biography—was slow to develop as a literary form. Plutarch, born in the first century A.D., is traditionally regarded as the pioneer of biographical writing. His *Vitae Romanorum et Graecorum,* published in Florence in 1517 and translated into French by Jacques Amyot in 1559 and from French into English by Sir Thomas North in 1579, remains in print today as *Parallel Lives.* Plutarch established the concept of biography as moral example, a notion that continued to intrude itself on biographical writing through the end of the nineteenth century. The medieval lives of the saints followed the same pattern, their subjects portrayed as exemplary rather than lifelike figures.

Biographical writing in English, the focus of this exhibition, got its start in the sixteenth century with John Bale's biographical collection, the *Illustrium Maioris Britanniae Scriptorum Summarium,* published in 1548. Bale's interest, as his title indicates, was more in providing bibliographical catalogues of English writers than in recording the events of their lives. Nevertheless, this work stands as the first rudimentary history of English literature and provides at least some basic facts about Tudor authors.

The two most notable biographies of the sixteenth century were political rather than literary— George Cavendish's *Life of Cardinal Wolsey,* and William Roper's biography of his father-in-law, Sir Thomas More. Both are encomiums of great men, more like eulogies one would expect at a funeral than a balanced study of their subjects. Such literary biographies as existed in the sixteenth century consisted of essays prefaced to an author's works, as in the case of Thomas Speght's life of Chaucer in the 1598 edition of Chaucer's works shown in the exhibition.

Lives of authors written in the seventeenth century continued to appear as introductory matter rather than as separate books, but many were more thoroughly researched and better written than their predecessors of a century before. Isaac Walton's "Life of John Donne," which was published in the 1640 edition of Donne's *LXXX Sermons,* was based both on interviews Walton had with men who had known Donne and information provided in Donne's letters. Thomas Sprat also used letters as source material in his "An Account of the Life and Writings of Mr. Abraham Cowley," prefaced to the 1668 edition of Cowley's *Works*—arguably the first true English literary biography in that it presents both Cowley's personality and an analysis of his writings. It is regrettable, however, that once Sprat had completed his work, he burned Cowley's letters, judging them to be too intimate and "scarce ever fit to see the light," a censorial practice still the bane of biographers.

The seventeenth century also saw the publication of an increasing number of biographical dictionaries. Following the example of John Bale were Thomas Fuller's *The History of the Worthies of England* (1662); Edward Phillips's *Theatrum Poetarum Anglicanorum* (1675); Anthony à Wood's *Athenae Oxoniensis* (1691–1692); Pierre Bayle's *Dictionnaire historique et critique* (1695–1697), translated into English in 1710; and, from the other side of the Atlantic and just into the next century, Cotton Mather's *Magnalia Christi Americana* (1702).

Bayle's dictionary in particular inspired similar biographical collections in eighteenth-century England, the outstanding example of which, as shown in the exhibition, is the *Biographia Britannica* (1747–1760). Other notable eighteenth-century literary biographical collections include Giles Jacob's *The Poetical Register* (1710–1720), Theophilas Cibber's *Lives of the Poets of Great Britain and Ireland* (1753), Horace Walpole's *Catalogue of the Royal and Noble Authors of England, Scotland and Ireland* (1758), Samuel Johnson's magnificent *Lives of the English Poets* (1779–1781), and David Rivers's *Literary Memoirs of Living Authors of Great Britain* (1798). While these collections offer only sketchy portraits, more résumés than biographies, Johnson's *Lives of the English Poets* stands out

William R. Cagle speaking on the history of literary biography, 14 November 1998 (courtesy of Thomas Cooper Library, University of South Carolina)

for its critical judgments and sympathetic portrayal of its subjects.

Biographical dictionaries published in the United States, in addition to Mather's work, include Jeremy Belknap's *American Biography* (1794), Jared Sparks's twenty-five-volume *Library of American Biography* (1834–1848), and, almost a hundred years later, the twenty-volume *Dictionary of American Biography* (1928–1937), a less ambitious undertaking than its British counterpart, the *DNB*. The *Dictionary of Literary Biography* commenced publication in 1978.

Johnson and Boswell stand out as giants in the world of literary biography, not only for their century but for all time. Boswell's *Life of Samuel Johnson,* published in 1791, is regarded as the supreme achievement in biographical writing. Not only did Boswell make extensive use of both correspondence and interviews, but he took detailed notes which allowed him to reproduce Johnson's conversations with great vitality. Their separate accounts of the journey they made to the Hebrides–Johnson's *Journey to the Western Islands of Scotland* (1775) and Boswell's *Journal of a Tour of the Hebrides*

with *Samuel Johnson, LL.D.* (1785)–are the two finest examples of travel memoirs (a form of autobiography) written during their century. As the exhibition demonstrates, interest in Johnson called forth several works about the great man following his death in 1784. Hester Lynch Piozzi was first into the field with her *Anecdotes of the Late Samuel Johnson,* published in 1786. She was followed by Sir John Hawkins's *Life* in 1787, which she, in turn, followed with her 1788 edition of *Letters to and from the Late Samuel Johnson.* Arthur Murphy published his 187-page *Essay on the Life and Genius of Samuel Johnson* in 1792. All of these remain curiosities for the scholar or the collector while Boswell's masterpiece has not been out of print in more than two hundred years.

The nineteenth century produced ambitious and expansive biographies, many of which drew on and included extracts from the letters and journals of their subjects, frequently resulting in works of several volumes and sometimes, notably with political figures, written as the life-and-times, not merely the life, of an individual. Thomas Carlyle's *Frederick the Great* (1857–1865), for example, ran to six volumes and is as much a

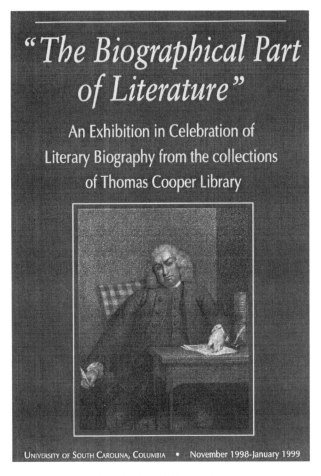

"The Biographical Part of Literature"

An Exhibition in Celebration of
Literary Biography from the collections
of Thomas Cooper Library

UNIVERSITY OF SOUTH CAROLINA, COLUMBIA • November 1998-January 1999

Cover for the exhibition catalogue

between 1885 and 1900. Underwritten by London publisher George Smith and edited by Leslie Stephen until 1891 and then by Sidney Lee until its completion in 1900, the *DNB* includes about 30,000 lives written by many contributors. As a work of cooperative scholarship it is rivaled, in the English-speaking world, only by the *Oxford English Dictionary,* published between 1884 and 1928, and the *Dictionary of Literary Biography,* the publication of the two hundredth volume of which we celebrate with this exhibition.

American literary biographies of the nineteenth century tend to be less notable. Among them are R. W. Griswold's biographical essay on Edgar Allan Poe in *The Literati* (1850) in which Griswold blackened Poe's character; Henry James's extended essay on Hawthorne published in 1879 in the "English Men of Letters" series; Julian Hawthorne's *Nathaniel Hawthorne and His Wife* (1884); and, just into the twentieth century, William Dean Howells's *My Mark Twain* (1910). But it was in the twentieth century, rather than in the nineteenth, that the art of biography was to achieve greatness in the United States.

In the years following World War I, three changes occurred which affected the writing of biographies: there was a revolt against the restrictive moral attitudes of the Victorian era; the trauma of the war with its great loss of life upset the old social order; and the writings of Sigmund Freud, Carl Jung, and others offered new insights into human behavior and personality. Biographers began to place a new emphasis on the inner life of their subject—the revelation of aspects of character—and showed a new ruthlessness to "tell it as it is." Examples of the "new biography" include Van Wyck Brooks's *The Ordeal of Mark Twain* (1920) and *The Pilgrimage of Henry James* (1925) as well as Katherine Anthony's *Margaret Fuller* (1920). But perhaps the most influential book in revolutionizing the writing of biography at this time was Lytton Strachey's *Eminent Victorians* (1918). Strachey reacted against the Victorian laudatory life-and-letters biographies with their reverential attitude toward their subjects. He took the past off its pedestal and didn't hesitate to show that even the most eminent Victorians could have feet of clay. As John Updike stated last night, he was widely imitated.

While the emphasis in this exhibition is on English-language biographies, it has not overlooked the Frenchman who is perhaps the most popular twentieth-century writer of writers' lives. André Maurois's *Ariel, ou la vie de Shelley,* published in 1923, began a series of biographies which, combining fullness of information with the readability of a good novel, tell the life stories of Benjamin Disraeli, Lord Byron, George Sand, the elder Dumas, Balzac, Victor Hugo, and Marcel Proust. His

history as it is a biography. And yet, while the Victorian biographies were voluminous, they also left much unsaid. The socially conservative climate of the era, one in which ideas of decorum and propriety imposed a self-censorship, colored such biographies as John Forster's *Life of Charles Dickens* (1872–1874) and John Cross's *George Eliot* (1885), in which the texts of letters were silently altered. It was a time in which a biography told all of a life that was fit to tell, and anything likely to offend family values was swept under the carpet.

Yet, for all their faults, there were some truly notable British literary biographies published across the nineteenth century, works such as John Gibson Lockhart's *Memoirs of the Life of Sir Walter Scott* (1837–1838), Thomas Carlyle's *Life of John Sterling* (1851), Elizabeth Gaskell's still popular *Life of Charlotte Brontë* (1857), and James Anthony Froude's *Thomas Carlyle* (1882–1884).

But the greatest achievement in biographical writing and publishing during the nineteenth century rests not with individual lives but with the massive *Dictionary of National Biography,* published in sixty-three volumes biographies continue to enjoy a wide readership both in French and in English translation.

Toward the end of the exhibition there is a selection of recent biographies from the library of James Dickey. If we had any doubt, these clearly demonstrate that the biographical art is not only alive and well but that it is flourishing as never before. Improbable as it may seem, this state of affairs was at least in part prompted by an event that happened in the Soviet Union just over forty-one years ago. In October 1957 the then-Soviets launched into space a rocket carrying the first sputnik, beginning the space race and sending shock waves through the United States. Our science was lagging behind and in the determination to catch up, the U.S. government poured great sums of money into American universities. While this was largely aimed at scientific research, it generated an era of general prosperity for the academic world in which libraries as well as laboratories benefited. In university libraries that had never dreamed of possessing rare books and manuscripts, departments of special collections were opened. As it was probably too late, and certainly too expensive, to build a rare-book collection along traditional lines—medieval manuscripts, incunabula, Elizabethan drama—many of the libraries beginning special collections focused on contemporary culture. Modern first editions and the archives of contemporary figures, predominantly writers but occasionally a scientist or politician, were sought in what quickly became a highly competitive environment. Literary archives increasingly found their way into American libraries so that biographers from the 1960s onward had at their disposal substantial bodies of research materials organized by trained professionals.

It is clear that the large-scale institutional collecting of the materials on which biographies are based has influenced the way biographies are now being written. The aggressive accumulation and systematic preservation of great quantities of biographical data make possible more thorough research into the lives of subjects. During the time this collecting activity has flourished we also saw a growing academic interest in writing the lives of writers. Indeed, in spite of John Updike's reservations—a case of the great man looking over his shoulder—the past four decades have proved a golden age of literary biography.

These years have seen publication of the last four volumes of Leon Edel's life of Henry James (1962–

1972), Michael Holroyd's life of Lytton Strachey (1967–1968), as well as books by Joseph Blotner on William Faulkner (1974), Matthew J. Bruccoli on F. Scott Fitzgerald (1981), the revised edition of Richard Ellmann's life of James Joyce (1982), Victoria Glendinning on both Vita Sackville-West (1983) and Rebecca West (1987), Scott Donaldson on John Cheever (1988), Richard Ellmann on Oscar Wilde (1988), Holroyd on George Bernard Shaw (1988), Anne Stevenson on Sylvia Plath (1989), Michael Reynolds on Ernest Hemingway (1986–1997), and Hermione Lee on Virginia Woolf (1996).

But why, if there have been so many interesting literary biographies written between the reigns of the two Elizabeths, has this area of writing held so little appeal for the collector of books? In a paper delivered at the University of Texas last month, Lewis Carroll's biographer, Morton Cohen, noted that Disraeli urged us to read no history, only biography; that Thomas Carlyle believed that history was the essence of biographies; and that Ralph Waldo Emerson wrote that there is no history, only biography. Yet with all of this praise of biography, in my now nearly forty years of involvement with book collecting I have known only one serious private collector who built a collection with biography as a theme. The late James Hart, author of the *Oxford Companion to American Literature* and for many years director of the Bancroft Library, collected American presidential campaign biographies. There are collectors of entertainment biographies—film, television, music. Yet I know of no collector of literary biography.

I would like to suggest in closing that the volumes of the *DLB,* with their groupings of writers in a variety of categories, map out some interesting new paths for aspiring book collectors. Take two examples: one from early in the *DLB* series—*DLB 4: American Writers in Paris 1920-1939,* and one of more recent date, *DLB 186: Nineteenth-Century American Western Writers.* Broaden the definition of biography to include autobiography, collections of letters, memoirs, travel accounts, interviews, and biography in fiction and picture the fascinating collections of books that could be built around the authors in either of these two *DLB* volumes. There are now two hundred volumes of the *DLB* to inspire such collections. They should provide valuable guides for collectors for years to come.

Interview with Thomas McCormack

Before retiring in 1997, Thomas McCormack was that rare entity in publishing—an editor who rose to top editorial responsibility. He started editing at Anchor Books of Doubleday in 1959, founded the paperback line of Dolphin Books there, and moved to Harper and Row, where he founded Perennial Books. After running Mentor Books for New American Library, he joined St. Martin's Press in 1969 as Director of the Trade, becoming president in 1970. An author of books on fiction and editing, he has also written a Publishers Weekly *op-ed column, "The Cheerful Skeptic," for two years.*

This interview with McCormack was conducted in New York City on 27 June 1998.

DLB: The name of the course is "The Profession of Authorship in America." I've been going around with my tape recorder talking to people in New York publishing about various aspects of how, in the twentieth century, an American author makes a living and how an author's relationships with his editor and publisher may shape his career.

McC: I'm not always going to be encouraging here. When we're talking about what the writer can expect from his publisher I'm going to be very straight. I'm not going to try to paint a picture one way or another. You get the right publisher, the right editor and one hell of a lot can be done for you, the writer. But the awful truth is they are many fewer in number than we all wish they were—good publishers and good editors. Look at a *Literary Market Place* from eight years ago, five years ago and see who was running things and notice how many aren't there anymore. And yet at the time that they had those jobs they looked like they knew something. You know, they had the command presence; they had the buzz words at tongue tip. They were terrific talking percentages, and, in point of fact, what they had was all of the trappings and very little of the substance required for the job. Which, incidentally, is an inducement to go into book publishing because it is a talent-poor industry, and if you've got the intelligence, the sensibility, and the application, you're going to go up very fast in this business. There's lots of room at the top because it's just not an industry that manages to attract and keep very many gifted people.

Thomas McCormack

I think at the outset it's because the starting salaries for young people in publishing are so very, very low. I think currently if you're getting out of college this year you probably come in at nineteen, twenty, or maybe some places twenty-one thousand. But think of twenty thousand dollars as the starting salary. In New York City? You're going to move here from South Carolina or from Missouri and live in this city on twenty thousand dollars a year? It may sound like a lot out there, but you come here, you find it's not. So a lot of smart people tend not to look to publishing. They love books. They love to work with books and with authors, but they also have this despicable appetite to eat three times a day, and publishers are always poor-mouthing the industry. And they do start out at a very low salary, so we tend to have difficulty attracting people who are both smart and have something of an eye on the dollar. When I first came into publishing, I used to be astonished at the young people around me at Doubleday many, many years ago. They dressed so well. The young ladies came in and they had the designer A-lined dresses and the nice accessories, and I said, "I just don't know how they do. Man, they must know how to manage money." And of course how they did it was they had a rich daddy. Again and again as you walked down the hallway back then in those days, these young people were only able to make it because they had subsidies from home. And that obtains still today to a certain degree. I don't know, if one turned to another industry, what the frequency of very talented young personnel would be either. In other words, I can look from publishing house to publishing house and say, "Good God, the caliber of the people at almost every level isn't what it ought to be." If I knew anything about the record business or about the movie business or about the motorcar business, I might be saying the same thing. For example, *The New York Times* or *The Wall Street Journal* or sophisticated newspapers like that do stories about book publishing, especially the business side of book publishing, and they consistently get it, sometimes not one tick wrong but one-hundred-eighty degrees wrong. Again and again they just don't begin to understand the book business that they're writing about. This has to say to me: if they don't understand book publishing, why believe that they know about any of these other businesses that they're writing about? You can write about a business fluently and articulately, know the old buzz words, and yet know next to nothing. Two lessons: there's incompetence in every industry, and don't believe the media too quickly—especially about publishing.

DLB: The profession of authorship. What should a writer expect from his publisher?

McC: Now my grad work was in philosophy, linguistic analysis and mathematical logic and this sort of thing. So I'm constantly going to make distinctions in the questions. Let's look at the word *expect*. There are two ways in which. . . .

DLB: Has a right to expect.

McC: Has a right to expect. Good. That's distinguished from "probably will get." You certainly have a right to expect honesty. Why should you have to mention it? The next column in *PW* [*Publishers Weekly*] is going to be "An Occupation for Gentlemen," which is a catalogue of the crimes in publishing. You want honesty. You would like all the things you want to encounter in your lawyer and your doctor. You want competence. You want intelligence. You want application. But how does that manifest itself in the particular pursuit of book publishing? In the ideal instance you have an editor who is up to the job. Now, did you get

that book I sent you [McCormack, *The Fiction Editor, the Novel, and the Novelist* (New York: St. Martin's Press, 1988)]? Well, that's a whole book about what you should expect from an editor if you're a novel writer. What you want in your editor in fiction is spelled out in that book. He's got to have sensibility; he's got to have craft; and he's got to have application. The nonfiction editor, among other things, the first thing he's got to be able to perceive is when something is not clear if he is going to edit your text. Editors do four things. They acquire books; they help to publish the books—working on the jackets and the publicity; they support, comfort, and retain authors; and they edit. That fourth thing. Editors make great reputations and have long careers doing really just the first three. The editor who can really edit is a very rare bird, as you and I have touched on in our discussions about Max Perkins, who I do think one would be very lucky to have as an editor but who was in truth imperfect as hell himself in certain ways. You're just never going to find the perfect editor.

Let's go through what happens to your manuscript in a publishing house. First hint: send it to a particular editor, rather than just to "Editorial Department, Doubleday Inc." When your manuscript arrives, you want it read at as high a level as possible. Still, sometimes an editor, noticing the script is unsolicited by him, will send it to the first-operation. Here it's usually read by an editorial assistant. This isn't necessarily so bad—believe it or not, though your impression may be they don't want to be bothered by you, they're eagerly hunting all the time for publishable books. It helps their career. Let's assume the assistant likes it enough to get an editor to read it, and the editor wants to publish it. He goes to the editor in chief or publisher—and the forum for doing this is usually the "editorial meeting." At St. Martin's we held—and they still hold—these meetings once a week. I used to have lots of people at that meeting—thirty or thirty-five of them—because I wanted the young people to see how decisions are made, to understand what factors are key to publishability, to grasp the physiology of the business. This requires not just being able to analyze a book editorially. Editors have to understand the numbers and the planning entailed by publishing anything.

At these meetings we would usually talk about the quality of the book, its market, and how much we should—in terms of author-advance—offer for the book. (This can be done based on just a proposal rather than a full manuscript. Novels are almost never signed up on a proposal alone unless it's a well-known author, but nonfiction books frequently are. Professional writers are often reluctant to commit a huge amount of time to writing, say, a biography, unless they're sure a publisher will want to do the thing when they're finished.)

Assuming the editor gets the okay to put the book under contract: while the editor works on the script with the author, other departments in the house start to boot up. Marketing, production, and sales start their planning. The publication of a book is a multiplicitous event. It gets edited; it gets catalogued; it gets written about—in the catalogue, on the book jacket, in publicity releases. Pray God your editor can write and can oversee the writing of those other people. Then there's the sales conference. The editor often goes to the sales conference to tell the sales reps—who've come in from all around the country—what the book's about, who's the market, and why it should sell well. The reps, after the sales conference, go back out to their territories, from Portland [Maine] to Portland [Oregon], and carry a bag from store to store and try to talk the booksellers into ordering copies of the book. The sales conference for the books that are going to be published say from September through December are usually held April/May. So that about June they're out there selling the book in June, July, and August. There isn't any book yet. It's being typeset and put into proofs maybe, but they've got to sell it this far ahead of time so that they've got orders in the can for when the book finally comes out of the bindery in September. And it does that thing and gets shipped all around the country at that time if—one of the things you hope for from your publisher—they have done a good job of selling it in. How you do a good job of selling it in is an extremely multiplicitous event.

"Selling it in" is the phrase that covers the effort to get sufficient orders from bookstores, chains, jobbers, so that on the day of release from the bindery you have enough books out there so that you and your family can go find it in a reasonably close bookstore. The range of selling-in is extremely vast. You can have books with advances of two thousand copies, and there have been books with advances of two million copies. That's literally how much they can vary. You can be under two thousand. If you're writing a novel, you sure like to think that there will be books sold-in, in the sense that there will be books standing in a bookstore on publication so that when reviews occur and the people say "That sounds interesting to me," they can go and find the book in the bookstore. There's nothing more frustrating to an author than getting good reviews or good publicity and nobody can find the book anyplace because the publisher did not succeed, let's put it that way, in selling the book in. Now the elements that go into selling the book in are numerous. A book gets sold-in, in a sense, about five times.

DLB: What I really want you to get to talk about is how writers live. How they live from book to book. What a writer can expect to earn from a book. What a publisher

should do as a matter of commitment to an author to keep the author alive from book to book. It's about money. Everything is about money. When you grow up you understand that. Unless you're an English professor, in which case you deny it. How does a writer in America in the twentieth century make a living? Especially writers who could be supplementing their incomes by writing magazine articles, only the magazines are gone.

McC: I once saw a statistic from the Writers Guild or someplace like that saying, "Do you know what the average writing income last year in America was? Four thousand one hundred dollars." I said to myself, "Wait a minute. Who the hell are they including in this collection?"

My daughter is a young girl in her twenties. Wants to be an actress, and she just had her off-Broadway debut in a play. It's called *Boom. The Lost Generation.* Fitzgerald, Hemingway. She played Dorothy Parker. Well, there were thirteen young people in there, and none of them got paid. If you asked any of them in an interview on the street, "What do you do?" they would probably say, "Well, I'm an actor." Well, what's your income this year? "Thirty-seven dollars. I was an extra in a Pacino movie." If you do that with actors you can do the same thing with writers. There's lots of people who will say to you "I am a writer." In point of fact they're driving a taxi cab or they are teaching school, and it is difficult to make sense of including everyone who wants to write and everyone who does scribble in the compilation of any statistics about writers. Again, as I said earlier, you can get from two thousand to two million in the number of copies of a book sold. The amount of money you can make as an author ranges so massively it is like other professions if you get to know them. In entertainment, how much money did you make this year? Thirty-nine dollars. How much money did you make this year? Thirty-nine million dollars. That's the range of things. For writers, if you're a good writer and to some extent we're talking about book writers as distinguished from journalists. . . .

DLB: What's a good writer?

McC: A good writer can be defined in about three or four different ways and different planes of consideration.

DLB: One is he gets published.

McC: One, he gets published? All right. If you want to make that part of the defining element—he gets published. There will be writers out there who say, "I'm good, but I can't get published." If he does get published, we go to your question number 4: What makes a book sell? There is a difference if you're nonfiction and if you're fiction. If you're a fiction writer you don't have very often at hand the great elements that make for huge sales. Publicity, news, front-page stuff–that's nonfiction. Anne Tyler, very good writer; she had to go seven books before she made the best-seller list. If you're a fiction writer, as a general rule, you've got to build a reputation. Things like *Cold Mountain* and *Bridges of Madison County* are very, very much the exception–first novels that have become huge sellers. Most of them don't. So if you're a fiction writer, you've got to look forward to putting in a kind of apprenticeship, as you produce your works. Ideally you are published and published frequently enough so that your market continues to grow as you feed the readership. One of the things that gives a publisher a pang is when he's got a hugely selling author who produces a book every ten years or so because he knows if he had three books every ten years from the guy, the guy would be even bigger. Stephen King sells these millions and millions. He didn't always sell the millions and millions of copies. I published *The Silence of the Lambs,* by Tom Harris, and when his next book came up for auction, I went to the auction, but I dropped out because one of the competitors was offering him a million dollars on signing. I knew he'd taken six years to write his second book and seven years to write his third. That was I believe, 1988. Ten years ago. There's no book. There's no sign of a book. That million dollars has already cost over a million dollars in interest costs to the publisher. I was not about to do that. I can't charge that to the author's royalty account, but it's an expense. What the writer can expect and should expect from the publisher is intelligent effort, strong enough effort in selling the book in, and promoting the book and getting it out there, and then moving it out of the stores. But publishers also have things they can legitimately ask from authors. In nonfiction you've certainly got to expect responsibility, honesty, intelligence, and clarity so that you can understand what they're talking about. But, among other things, you've got to count on them to say what they will do. "Here: I'm going to take an advance from you. Now: You're going to give me cash now, publisher, and I'm going to deliver my book in one year's time."

It's an interest-free loan. I can argue each side of the table on this, but that is in fact what it is. It's an interest-free loan, and I'm going to deliver you a manuscript in one year. And at the end of the year if there's no manuscript you almost never see the author give the money back. But when he does give the money back, usually what he does is he gives the money back, and all that interest has been his. These are the kinds of gripes that publishers can have.

DLB: Isn't it rare for the author to give the money back?

McC: It occurs, though. Every once in a while a publisher will just get pissed off and he will actually come after the guy. But sometimes you don't have to. There are some authors who say, "Look. I can't do it. I'm wrong. I thought I could do this book, and here's the money back." You know writers are almost like people, which is to say, they're honest–they're dishonest. But the publishers and the writers can expect responsible, honest, and capable behavior from one another. As a writer the key thing for you to find if you possibly can, and it's very hard–I can't give you a formula for this–is finding a good editor. Because, as I say, editors do four things. All four. They sign your book up. They help to publish it. In other words, they'll push the publicity; they'll devise the marketing campaign to the extent that they can. They'll write copy. They'll go to the sales conference, and they'll sell it. The third thing–they support, comfort, and retain authors. They take your calls. They answer your mail. They see that your queries are responded to and that your checks go out on time.

DLB: I had a conversation once with a man who made fishing reels. He expressed interest in how authors earn a living, and he couldn't believe what I was telling him. He felt that the division of the income, the cutting of the pie, was completely wrong. He couldn't see why the bookstore gets 40 to 45 percent of the ticket price, and the author gets 10 percent of the ticket price. This successful executive who knew nothing about books or publishing felt that the author was being victimized by the publishing industry. That the author deserved more of the pie. What's wrong with that system that once prevailed in England of half-profits?

McC: What's wrong with it is writers won't stand for it. What do you mean they won't stand for it? Again and again I would have been more than happy to give an author half the profits. Now, how you define profits is a tricky thing, but it can be done in a way that is satisfactory to both sides. But the author wants an advance, and suppose you said, "But wait a minute. I can't pay you an advance because if I pay you an advance and there isn't any profit what happens? You going to give me the money back?" No. They want an advance. From time to time I've offered editors, very good editors, the following deal. I say, "Look. I'm going to arrange so that you get a percentage of the contribution of your books, but of course it does mean that we're going to drop your guaranteed portion of your salary way down because this will allow you, if you have a blockbuster, to get rich."

DLB: Anybody go for it?

McC: No, thanks. "I'd like a percentage of the profit but I also want a guaranteed income." "Ah? And can you guarantee the publisher a profit?"

DLB: The personal imprint does that, doesn't it?

McC: No. Why do you believe that? Often enough the editor gets his name on the books just 'cause he wants them that way. There is no formula that obtains from house to house and indeed within the house. At St. Martin's I had a number of editors with imprints. Joan Kahn was the great mystery editor through the years. Joan had her own imprint and was always just on salary. Joan had zero interest in money. I guess her father, her family had money. Never wanted participation. You want participation, OK, but you know you can't get a quarter of a million dollars a year and participation. It's got to be one or the other. You want this? Fine. And again and again you find that what they want is the guarantee, which is very understandable. The numbers that comprise the pie are probably fairly opaque to your friend. You know the one who said, "Gee, I think the authors are getting screwed here." I can give you a printout, a lot of numbers, and when you're old, you can look at them. Perhaps you should have them just to get a sense of where the money comes from and where the money goes in publishing. Royalty starts out usually–this is a standard royalty rate–10 percent of the list price, the price on the flap of the book for the first five thousand copies sold. Twelve-and-a-half for the next five thousand copies and fifteen percent thereafter. Since publishers' discounts to bookstores average about 47–48 percent by the time an author is at the 15 percent–let's say it's a $10 book just to make the arithmetic obvious–on a $10 book the publisher is receiving only $5.20. 48 percent discount. If you're at a 15 percent royalty, you're receiving $1.50 of the $5.20 that the publisher received. The $4.80 stays with the bookstore. So you're already at 28 percent of receipts. The publisher has to pay for typesetting, artwork, paper, printing and binding, and for the shipping, and if there's any advertising and promo. Meantime he's also got to have something left over to pay the rent, the heat, and the light and the salaries. And a successful publisher does that, but a lot of publishers don't. There are publishers who come up with red ink, and certainly individual books are very uneven in the percentages of contribution that they produce. But if your $10 book that we just talked about had a million dollars in total sales, it does say that you, the author, are going to get about $150,000. How much the publisher gets is hard to discern because the questions are: How much was the paper, printing, and binding? How much was the plant cost? How many books did he print that he didn't

sell but nevertheless had to pay for? The arithmetic is not Einsteinian, but it's complex because there are many, many different elements. It is not the case–I believe this–that the publisher is running off with great tons of money when the author is not. As a general rule. It certainly has occurred. The following interesting data was in one of my *PW* columns. On a given book the entity that makes the most money is the bookstore. Now they don't make the most money in some sense because all we're saying is they sell the $10 book and they pay only $5.20 for it. They've got $4.80. Don't call it profit. They've got to pay the rent that day, the salaries of the clerks that day, the heat, the light, the insurance, and everything. What they've got to do is they've got to collect enough of those $4.80s in a year's time so that they cover all those what are called "fixed overheads." And if they do to the extent that at the end of year they've got $4.80s coming after they've paid the year's rent, then they've got some profit for that year. But of the dollar that the customer hands over, the one that keeps the most and applies the most to their fixed overheads is the bookstore. It's not the publisher because remember the bookstore has $4.80. The publisher has $5.20. Nope. Got to give $1.50 to the author so I've got $3.70. I've got to give $1.70 of that to the printer so now I'm down to $2.00. But now I've got to pay plant cost. The one-time-only cost of typesetting and the art for the jacket and stuff like this. Oh, I've got a little ad campaign here for $3,000. I've got to pay that. All of these disbursements that I've just referred to on the publisher's part are genuinely disbursements. Money sent to the outside. They pay the newspaper for the ad space. They pay a printer down the street to print the books. A typesetter across town to typeset the book. Money is going out. The author keeps $1.50, let's say, of the $10 list price; but there're the bookstores who are always talking about the publishers, those terrible publishers, yet on any given single book published the ones who keep the most are the bookstores. Not the author. Not the publisher. Things that people just don't analyze. They'll sit back and they'll have feelings. They'll opine about the gouging publisher or these terrible authors who take these huge advances because when they get this huge advance, the publisher doesn't have any money left to do my book. If I didn't publish James Herriot and Tom Harris and people like that and make huge amounts of money on them, then I certainly wouldn't have had any money to sign up the tiny literary novels. A lot of people get accused one way or another in publishing of things that they shouldn't be, that they're not guilty of, but in many other ways publishers have failed their authors and other people.

DLB: You think the 10, 12½, 15 escalator is right and proper, and there's nothing that can be done about it?

McC: I mean there are many other possible ways. Suppose we did that and suppose we did this: Look, author, here's what I'm going to offer you. We're going to receive 52 percent of the list price of the book. Now out of the 52 percent, what I want to do is I want to take out the paper, printing, and binding. And all the rest that is left, first we'll apply it toward paying for the plant (the typesetting and the art) and we'll apply it towards the promo campaign here, this $4,000 or $8,000 whatever, we'll do that. I will have to do the following. I will have to take a certain percentage, 7½ percent, 12½ percent whatever the wrangle comes to, that is to cover the what we will call direct variable overheads. Every time I ship a book I've got to bill someone. I've got to pick, pack, ship. There's all kinds of things here. So we'll take that out of everything that remains and what's left after all of that we'll divide. Well, wait a minute. Let's review what we just said. Ten dollars. I receive five-twenty. I deduct from it immediately the paper, printing, and binding, and I'm going to deduct 10 percent ($.52) for picking, packing, shipping, billing, processing returns, and this sort of thing. Then all the rest of that remaining margin, after the paper, printing, and binding and the 10 percent for fulfillment are taken from the $5.20, we're going to collect until we pay off the plant and the promotion. Everything after that we will, by definition, call profit, we're going to split it with you. You get half and I get half. Now since I don't spell out for you all the percentages, you the author really don't know, am I getting screwed or not. Wait a minute. If I just take a 15 percent royalty, I know I'm going to receive 28 percent of the receipts. If I am going to get half of the profits, are the profits really going to be 56 percent of the receipts? I don't know because I don't know what paper, printing, and binding . . . it's not obvious at all, again and again, that that's what the author should do. And you do notice that big authors turn it down constantly. The ones that could have it any way they want, they say, "No, thanks. I'll take my five-million-dollar advance, and I'll let you worry about whether or not the book is profitable." The offer is out there. I made it to James Clavell. I've made it to people. They don't take it. I don't blame them. Among other things, then you got to worry about, in all truth, the conniving dishonesty of the publisher. You know, what are they going to say is a cost? It's like a movie. Do you really want to live on the profits of a movie? Buchwald had to sue the producers and the studio. Wait a minute! Three hundred million dollars in dollar volume on this goddamned movie, and there's no profit? I used to really spell out in contracts; I used to take pride in spelling out contracts that had no shadows. That had no tricks. No bear traps. Because I've seen so many people screwed by them.

By contracts that had all kinds of trapdoors that they had no idea of. There's no guaranteeing that you would come out. That half the profits are going to be better than 28 percent of the receipts. It's not the case.

DLB: You've made a convincing case. How does an author who is not a blockbuster writer but who is a hardworking, productive writer put together a thirty-year career or a forty-year career of writing, being published, and making enough to support his family above the level of minimum wage? How does an author construct a career, and how can, does, should a publisher collaborate with the writer in constructing a career?

McC: Whether or not there can be that kind of cooperation is a function of the productivity of the writer. As I say, writers are uneven in their productivity. Some write a book every ten years. There are people who do produce a book every three months. And people like that can constantly produce these books and they will make money. They will never make a hell of a lot except in accumulation. There are certain kinds of books, fiction, where that will probably never happen: if someone is doing a book every three months—unless your name is Barbara Cartland or something along those lines—because you can't make a work of fiction good enough in three months, and so it's always going to be a nice four-thousand-copy mystery sale, and a writer can produce four mysteries like that a year. And you'll work your way along. In the ideal instance, you do have the likes of an Anne Tyler or Joyce Carol Oates—producing books frequently, of high quality. In the ideal instance, you have a system not unlike what *The New Yorker* magazine used to have when they would actually keep writers on retainer, which is in effect to say, on salary. And you the writer would, up in Westchester County, produce your stuff and send it in when it was ready. They knew that what you wanted to do with your life was to write and therefore you weren't off doing some other thing on their money, and they took their chances that you were going to produce enough to earn your retainer, so to speak. I used to publish authors year after year after year, and some of their books were uneven, and some weren't as good as the ones before, but I said, "OK, it's a bad day, but I'll do it." I used to do that. Over the course of time you saw less and less of that as you saw the rise of the role of the agent. Because one of the things that happens, especially to small publishers like Louisiana State University Press and Naval Institute Press, you publish a guy and by God he's got a great big goddamned book, and you are sure that someone from New York is going to come and try to kidnap him from your list. It's going to happen. Why? Because he's got an agent and the agent says, "I'm only trying to do the best thing for my client." So the publisher gets shafted. Small agents get shafted. You know, they work with an author for three, four, five, six, seven years trying to break him through. He finally breaks through. Bam! Good, I'll now go to William Morris. It's no longer an industry where you see a hell of a lot of that loyalty over the course of decades. You do see some. It has occurred.

DLB: Can you give a case history of a writer whose career you took an interest in and attempted to nurture?

McC: Well, early on from Britain in large part is where this would occur. I took authors of whom you would not probably have heard because they'd write very good adventure novels. Anthony Trew, Duncan Kyle, people like that, and they would produce a book a year, and I would do their books every year. And I would do a book a year from them for fifteen years; then Anthony Trew had *HMS Ulysses,* and it was a big book and he had himself a best-seller. Finally, Duncan Kyle had a couple of movies made of his books. But neither of them got what you would call very, very rich. One of the authors that did get very, very rich was a guy named James Herriot when we took on *All Creatures Great and Small.* There's another speech in there about everything that we did on that one because that turned out to be something of a phenomenon. We were a small publisher and he was a total unknown. We did do something of value on that book: we constructed the book for him, with him. But the quality of the writing was the key, and that was all his. All we did was the carpentry to create *All Creatures Great and Small.* He did not write a book called *All Creatures Great and Small.* He wrote two other books. We bought them together, got him to add three chapters and marry the girl at the end. That was the creation of *All Creatures,* and we stayed with James throughout his career. We were his publisher the day he died twenty-five years later. So those relationships did obtain. With Tom Harris we didn't do his first two books. He did *Black Sunday,* and then he did *Red Dragon.* We did *The Silence of the Lambs.* With *The Silence of the Lambs* we sold twice as many hardcovers as he had ever sold before, and eventually with the movie we sold five times as many paperbacks as he'd ever sold before. His next book was auctioned. I was allowed to go to the auction. I had no special entree at all. It happens. And we lost the author, but as I say he's never written another book. We didn't lose anything in that instance, but around the house there was great sagging pain for my colleagues when I had to tell them it's gone. We were in the auction, and we dropped out. Oh, how could you? He took six years between book one and book two, and seven years between book two and book three, and there's no evidence he's got anything in mind for book four. I don't know when it's going to come. So I lost him. If

he were more regular perhaps we would have been in a position to stay in, but we only did one book from Tom, and we were just a stopover for him. We were a pit stop. You know his next publisher is whoever it's going to be, and that's the way lots of authors work because the agent would like, almost every single time, to go to auction. You know, let's test the market every single time. But we also hear complaints about publishers who don't have any loyalty towards authors. You know, they'll do three books, and then they'll reject their fourth. Loyalty in the book world was largely slain by agents.

You will never find an agent trying to talk an author into a profit-sharing arrangement in lieu of the big advance. No. No. I'll take money right here and now. That's what I'll take. The agent would say, "Look, you know you don't owe the publisher anything. You made him a lot of money off the last book. He's a much richer man because of you." So then the question is, why should the publisher believe he owes the author anything? I often did. If, after a successful book, an author's next book was a bummer, I tried to do it anyway—especially if his mode was to produce, say, one modest-selling book a year. If I said no to the book and no one else would take it, it meant a year of his life was wasted—and so was his small bank account. So I'd do it and hope the next one was better. In truth, most of the time the next was not better, but you still tried to hang in there as long as you could, out of respect for the days when you were small, and they were a dependable part of your list. I worked with authors, as I said, one of them for twenty-five years, but a lot of them for ten or fifteen years, but you don't see it much anymore. Except in invisible ways. Where you see it is on the level of mysteries. St. Martin's does more mysteries than anyone else probably in the world, and there are many recurring authors on there. But even there, when an author gets big, breaks through, then she goes to auction. We were Ann Perry's first publisher in the United States. We don't do Ann Perry anymore. Collin Dexter. We did his first half-dozen novels. Then he got the TV thing and went to auction. Good-bye. But when he was small and needed the money, we were there. It's all right. We weren't being saintly. We were making money on his books, and that was the relationship.

DLB: We've covered all the important points except maybe the case history of the editing, revising, rewriting of a promising bad book into a successful book. Can you name titles and authors who received that treatment at St. Martin's—whose books were made successful because of what St. Martin's did?

McC: Yeah. But we never made a big success of anything that didn't have a hell of a lot already brought to it by the author. *All Creatures Great and Small* is a four-hundred-page book, and you know the story of that. The big book called *The Far Pavilions,* by M. M. Kaye. It was a huge manuscript, 1,529 manuscript pages. I remember it vividly. The last three hundred and something pages of that book were the siege in Kabul where all the Brits were wiped out a hundred and fifty years ago, and our hero was trapped in a prison cell looking out and seeing the action. I said to the author, "Molly, you can't. He's been our hero for 1,150 pages, and now he's just going to watch the action. I don't care what you do." I went off into the hills of Pennsylvania with that manuscript for three weeks and worked on editing the thing. She did the rewrite and got him down there into the battle, and it was wonderful. We were helpful on James Herriot's *All Creatures Great and Small,* and he was always generous about saying so (authors, understandably, frequently don't want to say publicly what the editor did—nor should an editor expect them to). He wrote a 192-page book titled *If Only They Could Talk.* I read it and made a speech to the agent: "There are two kinds of books—caper books and milieu books." A caper book, like a mystery, you want to read it tonight, finish it tonight. A milieu book, in which the author creates a rich new world for you, you don't want to finish tonight. You want to be able to look forward to getting back to it tomorrow night. "Herriot," I said, "has written a milieu book at caper length. It should be much longer." "How nice you should say that." She pulled down a brand-new book just published—as the first one was—in England. It too was 192 pages, titled *It's a Vet's Life.* I read it—and it was as marvelous as the first book—but, like the first book, it was a year in the life of a veterinarian. It didn't have an ending—it just stopped, though the vet had obviously met a wonderful young woman. I called Herriot and told him my thought was to combine the two books—which gave me milieu length—but, I said, we need an ending. This is clearly the girl—can he marry her? Here I was, the American publisher talking from New York City, speaking to a veterinarian in a small town in northern England. What would he make of me and my suggestion? Would he think it Hollywood-crass? No, he didn't, he wrote three more chapters, married the girl, and gave us an ending that clanged like *The Sound of Music.* James Herriot was a species of storytelling genius. He did more with the suggestion than I ever could have dreamed up, and so did Molly Kaye. What we did was come up with general suggestions on how to make the book better. When we did *All Creatures Great and Small,* I printed up six thousand copies of chapter one. Gave away three thousand at the ALA. Gave away 3,000 at the ABA meeting—because the book is such if you just get a nibble, a taste

of *All Creatures Great and Small,* you want more. I made up little animals and I sent them to reviewers. I wrote to the *Farm Journal* and *Veterinary Quarterly* and all the rest of them. I wrote to anyone, and I said you can have any chapter that you want in this book for nothing. Free. And all of these things were attempts to get the book going. No magazine took me up on it until after it was a big best-seller and then they did. Well, OK—you learn some things.

When you get a publisher who is fanatically committed to a book and has muscle and a certain amount of mental alertness, then you're a lucky author. You want a guy who really believes this is great stuff. I did. I mean I had such religion about James Herriot and about *The Far Pavilions* and in all truth about *The Silence of the Lambs.* I thought this ought to be a big seller. And there are other things. Not all authors are guys you'd want your sister to marry—for example, Gordon Liddy. I published Gordon, and I enjoyed publishing Gordon. We did his autobiography. We actually went from manuscript to finished books in eight days in total secrecy. The manuscript was edited at this table. We blind-shipped eighty-two thousand copies to bookstores. They came in on Monday morning and there's a box of books.

John Sirica we felt might have had the grounds actually to stop the book from being published. And you hated to see that happen. Then we put on a promo campaign with this man. He's the first guy ever to be on both *Good Morning America* and the *Today Show* on the same day. And on *Good Morning America* he looked at Jack Anderson, the columnist who revealed the CIA man's name and address in Greece—that man was immediately kidnapped, tortured, and killed—and Liddy looked at Jack Anderson on television and he said, "Yeah. I would have killed you. I only wished they had asked me to." Number-one bestseller because he's such a showman. Such an actor, but we gave him the platform to do it. You never, publishers never, make best-sellers from nothing. The author and the book is constantly the key. Sometimes it's just the author's promotability; sometimes it's just the sheer quality of the book. The publisher sits back and tries to take credit, and they didn't write a line of the book, and that's what made the book. A publisher can't do it, but he can allow it to get done. Put it that way. It's like teaching how to write. You cannot teach someone how to write a terrific novel. What you can do is teach them how to allow it to get done if it is within them. You can teach them craft and various other things, and if it's in there, now you've cleared the debris away for the runway; but if it's not in there, it's never going to get airborne because of what you did. All you can do is allow it to get done, and there are lots of things a good publisher and a good editor can do and should do with a potentially good writer.

DLB: In my twenty, twenty-five years of working with publishing houses I've noticed year by year the collapse of literary standards, literary knowledge, literary education in the people I deal with. I have been asked by editors who were not trainees, full editors, who Ring Lardner is. A dumbbell at Scribners recently asked, "How do you know about these books you're always talking about?" I said, "Because I've read them." And she said, "Ohh—you read books?" Where the hell are these dopes and dumbbells who hold important editorial positions in major houses coming from and why are they hired and why are they kept?

McC: Well. I don't want to sound like an antediluvian here, but you're actually asking, I think, a question about the direction of university-level education in America. When I went to college, we had to take certain requirements. I went to Brown University, and I had to take four humanities, four social studies, four sciences, and this sort of thing. I had to have languages, and I had to have English competence and math. We get kids now, out of Brown. . . . My own children went to Brown. I'm a contributor to Brown. There are no requirements of that kind anymore. They can get out of there without ever taking a language course. They can get out of there with a minimal liberal-arts education of the kind that you and I are used to. You see what I'm doing here? Elementary classical Greek. I've got five of those textbooks in the house at the moment. Different places. I'm starting classical Greek now. Why? Because the amount of pleasure I've gotten over the course of my life out of the Latin that I took has been immense, and I remember five years ago studying Chaucer and for the first time reading him in the Middle English that he wrote. I don't see that impulse very much in the young people that are coming to us from the colleges. I wonder what the hell has gone wrong. It may be that thing over there called the television set. But the wonderful luxuriating in language and the literary heritage of the past seems to me rarer and rarer. What am I reading over there? I'm reading *The Wings of the Dove* now—admittedly, from looking at the movie—and as I'm reading, incidentally, I said to myself, "James Gould Cozzens obviously read this book."

DLB: He didn't read James. He thought Henry James was unreadable.

McC: Aha! But how did he find out?

DLB: Well, he tasted it.

McC: You read the opening pages of *The Wings of the Dove* and compare it to the opening pages of *By Love Pos-*

sessed and that ushering-in of things. Cozzens does it wonderfully, does it better than James because he's more of a disciplined artist in a strange way than James. In any case, it is such a lovely thing to be able to hear the echoes from one to another. To read *Sinister Street* and know why it had the influence on Fitzgerald that it did and then to read Fitzgerald and then to see—not clones, they're not clones of Fitzgerald—but Fitzgerald's children. It's unendingly interesting to see how many people were influenced by him, and to see all of writing as a growing thing through the generations. You've got the same thing in music. You wouldn't have had the Beethoven we know if you didn't have Mozart, no matter what the hell he says.

I look at one book after another and say where was the goddamned editor. Where was the editor? I'm a notorious growler on the subject. You saw the first line of my book. Something to the effect of "The greatest secret influence on American writing in the last century has been the fiction editor. And in large part it has been a history of opportunity either lost or actively destroyed by the editor." Finding an editor who can do the job is, among other things, you touched on it four minutes ago—it's someone with an education. You can't just do it with sensibility. You have to be educated. You can have terrific sensibility, and if it isn't educated, if you don't know something about the heritage of the language and the literature, you can be doing things all goddamned day and not know what you're doing. Don't you see this is a take-off on the whiteness of the whale? What's the whiteness of the whale? It's a shame because you love the idea of being able to sit down with someone who knows books and can tell you things about books that you recognize and they know more than you do, but at least you can appreciate what they're saying.

DLB: I'll leave you with a sardonic joke—only it's not a joke. The erstwhile head of trade at Scribners once asked me to edit a book for her, and I responded "Barkis is willin'." And she said, "If Barkis is going to do it, why are we paying you?" My fault for talking like an English professor.

McC: If you can't do that, it's like being in prison. You know, I'm writing now. I'm writing plays, and indeed even in these columns I'm slipping things in there that I'm getting a giggle out of, and I know all kinds of people are not getting it. And it's too bad because I love to write things with second meanings and third meanings and echoes of what other people have said. I think T. S. Eliot was an awful snob and very many things, but he was absolutely right that there is, let's say, a certain kind of writing that can only be enjoyed if you know, so to speak, all the writing that went before it. I mean *The Waste Land* itself.

Book Publishing Accounting: Some Basic Concepts

Thomas McCormack
New York, New York

The business side of publishing is often discussed in my column "The Cheerful Skeptic" in *Publishers Weekly*. Columns on topics such as returns and overheads prompt an immense amount of e-mail that conveys an avid craving—and need—for information about some of the most basic concepts and procedures in book publishing. No textbook or business school teaches these things, because they are so specific to the book world. For example, in what other industry can we find companies that regularly launch a thousand "new products" every year?

In this essay I will address some of the most frequent queries and concerns that readers have expressed. In giving answers, I find it necessary to explain and clarify certain fundamental notions and practices that shape the book business as we know it. This is far from a complete textbook; I won't even touch on large areas of the business, and I don't know all the answers, anyway. I'll be content if I can give some of the answers and stimulate a healthy skepticism in anyone seeking more of them.

Be warned, however: I will struggle to be clear, but I'm aware that *clear* and *simple* are not always the same thing, and if all these numbers are new to you, you may go into oxygen debt halfway through this piece. But, as with any complex discipline, concepts that seem bewilderingly complicated in the first week will seem elementary after you're six weeks into the semester—if you do your homework. If you're looking at this essay on a screen, you may want to print it out. Publishing is not subatomic physics, but it does have its complexities. But then, I know few things that are interesting and valuable—as book publishing is—that are utterly simple, too.

We can start to understand and critique the thinking of some execs and accountants in book publishing with this query from a chief financial officer (CFO). The query was prompted by one of my "Cheerful Skeptic" columns, in which I wrote that accountants are wrong to charge individual titles with a "cost" for fixed overhead:

You took to task those of us who are bean counters and make up formulas for applying costs to projects/books in order for a business to project a balance in its expenses and revenues . . . most of us do something like taking the budgeted overhead expenses for the year and dividing them by the number of books and using that figure or ratio to guide pricing and list planning. I believe you think there is something wrong about assigning to books/projects the fixed part of overhead—that is, the rent, the executive salaries, the insurance, etc. How would you have these costs covered? Would you not assign them to each book in some proportionate way? How would you know when the benefits of a project might be outweighed by the costs?

Assigning overheads is a delicate problem for execs during at least three important tasks. All three have an impact on everyone from editors to owners:

(a) Projecting the forthcoming year's company results and doing the "planning" that those results indicate is needed.

(b) Deciding whether or not to okay proposed new titles.

(c) Pricing those titles.

That CFO's query stems from a failure to realize that applying fixed overhead must be done differently for each of the three tasks. The "Cheerful Skeptic" column on overheads to which the CFO is responding criticized execs for only one thing: their failure at assignment (b) above. They fail because—when they construct a "projected p&l" (profit and loss) statement on a proposed new title—they insist on deducting from the title's "profit" a fixed percentage of sales, which they attribute to "corporate overhead" costs. By conveying that if they publish this new book there will be a mythical, title-specific "cost," execs do three things: they obliterate the actual dollar value of the new title; they commit themselves to an unjustified formula that will repeatedly make them reject books they should accept; and they muddle the thinking of the very people they

155

most need to be perspicacious—those who go hunting for new books, and those who judge the potential financial worthiness of those books. In what follows I'll be saying, among other things, this to execs in publishing: *You* should *demand a certain percentage-contribution to fixed overhead when pricing books; but when deciding to buy a book, you should* not *use a percentage—you should look at absolute dollars; if fixed overheads are truly* fixed, *they are utterly irrelevant in judging whether a project's benefits outweigh its costs.*

Discussion in our industry is often confused because different people have different things in mind when they're using the same words. I'll try to make clear what I mean by each of the special terms I use, and I'll spell out important distinctions between those meanings. I'll begin with *overhead* (OH). There are three kinds of OH (I will, more often than not, use the plural—*overheads*—as part of my effort to keep distinct those things that are distinct):

Fixed overheads (FOH). Everything that recurs on a steady basis, whether you shop no books or a million books—i.e., the salaries, rent, insurance, etc.

Direct variable overheads. The portion comprising those costs that rise almost linearly with sales—e.g., shipping, commissions, and more.

Indirect variable overheads. The quintessential indirect variable is promo—i.e., it *tends* to rise with sales, but it isn't locked in linearly; you elect to spend it or not, but you tend to spend it if you think you see sales resulting from the expenditure.

Of course, in real life "fixed" isn't fixed (you can hire or fire in midyear); "direct" is only roughly linear (often, the more books you ship, the lower the cost per unit shipped); and "indirect variable" can vary mightily (Jane Fonda's famous workout book became the number one best-seller without a cent having been spent on advertising). Still, the trichotomy is useful. Two of those three types of overhead are title-specific costs (TSC).

TSC includes all and only those costs that occur solely because you're publishing a particular title. These costs specifically exclude any expenses such as rent and salaries that would be paid whether or not you publish this book. They include:

Production. This does not mean salaries of people in the production department; it means disbursements for plant and for paper printing and binding (pp&b) of each title. "Plant" refers to the one-time-only costs of a title—typesetting, artwork, freelance costs that wouldn't have occurred except for this particular title. Pp&b isn't one-time-only, because it recurs every time you print a title. Plant and pp&b are clearly title-specific costs—you incur them only because you publish given titles.

Royalty. Obviously the same here—you have royalty costs only because you have specific titles. In a given month if you sell no books at all, you will still have rent and salary costs—but not royalty expense. (Note: On company financial statements you "expense" the pp&b and royalty only on books *sold*. But when preparing the p&l of an individual title, you charge the cost of all the books *printed* and either the earned royalty or the author-advance, whichever is higher. See the appendix for further explanation of this point.)

Occasionally, as in reference-book publishing, a huge project requires hiring new people to work solely on this project. This is a case in which salary *is* a TSC. For tax purposes the exec may try to expense this as a fixed overhead, but the Internal Revenue Service may step in and say, "No, this is a plant cost and can't be expensed until the work is published."

Direct variables. The title-specific costs here are those that rise only as you sell books. You pay a shipping cost on a copy-by-copy basis—but the salaries of the personnel in fulfillment are fixed, and in doing a title p&l you shouldn't include salaries as a charge, because the shipping of this particular copy doesn't increase anyone's salary. The selling cost that should be charged to an individual title should be restricted solely to commissions or bonuses that rise as sales rise. Sales reps' salaries are fixed, as are the salaries of sales managers in the home office. In practice—for both company and title projections—almost everyone uses a percentage for direct variables—e.g., 4 or 5 percent of sales for fulfillment—because the variations from linear tend to be so negligible and numerous. There are exceptions; for example, when you're doing a title projection on a book with an advance sale so large that you arrange, say, a bindery shipment that eliminates costs such as freight-to-warehouse and certain warehouse handling costs. Then, often, a cents-per-book cost is projected instead of 4 or 5 percent of sales.

Indirect variables. Again the truth is that in practice most execs take an assumed percentage of sales rather than a dollar amount. That is, they do this in projections, not in actuals. They'll say, "We will spend 7 percent of sales on promotion." In calculating the postmortem actual profit and losses on individual titles, they must use the actual dollar amount spent on promo. For these postmortem purposes every bill coming into the house for plant, pp&b, and variable overheads such as ads and tours should be title-coded—so that the computer can in the end produce the TSC on each title. A trade house that knows well ahead of time that it'll be doing a huge promo campaign of, say, $500,000 for a particular title will enter that dollar amount when doing the projection.

One other stipulative definition: within TSC, I'll distinguish between "sunk" and "non-sunk" costs by saying that "direct TSC" includes only pp&b, royalty, and direct variables. This distinction will be useful when considering the theoretically best way to price a book.

Thus, here's what execs usually do with TSC when they make annual company forecasts (as distinguished from actuals, which they can't do until year end). They take the total sales projected and say, "50 percent of these revenues will have to be used to pay for 'cost of sales'"—the production and royalty costs. The remaining 50 percent—what's left after deducting cost-of-sales from revenues—is usually called "gross profit" or "gross margin." Execs will often break down gross profit this way: they assume 10 percent will go to pay the two kinds of variable overheads, and the remaining 40 percent will be available as a "contribution to FOH." To the extent that FOH is less than 40 percent (in this example), the remainder will be a contribution to "profit"—that is, to "operating profit." Such things as interest and amortization are then deducted to reach "pre-tax profit," the company bottom line. Execs will break down gross profit this way whether they're forecasting annual company results or a single title's p&l. (Note: I use these percentages—50, 40, and 10 percent—because they approximate norms in trade publishing, but in practice they vary from house to house. University presses, for example, often have an FOH percentage that's much higher than 40 percent.)

Execs break down gross profit this way in their first-pass annual projected operating statements for new books. (Backlist, returns, remainders, and special sales are another calculation to be done differently.) I say "first pass" because at this early budget/forecast stage execs have actually been estimating, in one room, the dollars of sales and cost-of-sales while estimating in another room the anticipated dollars of FOH. They usually get the FOH number by looking at the past year's FOH and adjusting for changes such as raises, rent increases, and new hires and departures. They don't get it by looking at sales. They know that FOH is an absolute amount determined by adding up specific costs such as rent and salaries. Those costs can't be projected by taking a percentage of sales. Planning often begins when they compare the projected "contribution"—for example, the 40 percent of revenues they hope are left, in effect, after deducting TSC—with the projected FOH

during a second pass—their official projected company-wide financial results for the year.

There is in all of this a vexing chicken-and-egg question. For example, where has that sales projection come from? From estimated unit sales times list prices minus discount-to-customers. But where do the list prices come from? Usually from management fiat. Management has told the editor that when he proposes a new title he must project his list price this way: calculate the "unit cost of sales"—that is, take all the projected production costs (including plant cost and that of all the books printed) plus all royalty/advance costs and divide this sum by the projected number of copies to be sold. If cost of sales is to be no more than 50 percent of what is received, then what is received on each book sold must be at least double that unit cost of sales. So double the unit cost, and that's what the firm has to receive after discount. Price the book accordingly.

There are several ways of doing this, and I lay out this method only for its clarity (although this clarity may not be altogether simple to understand). Let's say the royalty rate is a straight 10 percent of list, and received-after-discount is 53 percent of list. So the firm will be paying 19 percent of what it receives—ten fifty-thirds—to the author. If the royalty rate reaches 15 percent, the firm pays the author 27½ percent of what it receives. Let's say a given title has a plant cost of $12,000 and a pp&b cost of $20,000 to print 10,000 copies. The firm expects to sell 8,000 copies at the projected list price. That yields a unit production cost of $4 (that is, $32,000 divided by the 8,000 sold). This implies that, if the firm is going to spend no more, $4 must be no more than 31 percent of the price received, because the author is being paid 19 percent of what is received. Four dollars is 31 percent of what? Answer: $12.90. If $12.90 is thus 53 percent of list, list is $24.34. (Round up to, say, $25.)

Test the example as if you had priced the book at $24.34. Assume that 8,000 copies are sold, and you're receiving 8,000 times $12.90 = $103,200. Your production costs were $32,000. Your royalty at 10 percent of list is $24.34 per book times 8,000 copies = $19,472. Total cost of sales: $51,472. That's 50 percent of your revenues of $103,200—leaving 50 percent of revenues for all overheads (fixed and variable) and for profit.

The management fiat that in setting the price of the book you should aim for a 50 percent gross profit comes largely from little more than looking at company history. In fact, a house will sometimes ignore unit cost and "price the book to market." Although you may grumble about the percent demanded, every house, when it prices a book, needs *some* gross profit. If the publishing house prices all its books so that what it receives equals only production-and-royalty (and variables), then it'll have nothing left from revenues to pay rent and salaries. We're getting closer to the questions of when and when not to use an "allocated" FOH and how much that FOH should be.

Later I'll explain why *in setting the price of a book, you should use an allocation*. For now, however, I'll merely urge that it not be called an allocation. Call it a contribution—for two reasons. First, the danger of using a term such as *allocated cost* is that if we say it enough, we come to be mesmerized by the words—to the point that we believe that a new title actually does cost new fixed overhead, when it emphatically does not. This belief may not hurt us when we're pricing a book, but it can kill us when we're deciding whether or not to publish a book. The second reason for using the term *contribution* rather than *allocation*: I guarantee your editors will understand and accept the word *contribution* better.

I said that the notion of FOH comes into play in performing three important tasks. Notice this difference among the three: you feel an urge to "apply" FOH when you're pricing a book and when you're deciding whether or not to publish it. This insidiously suggests that FOH somehow varies with sales, that a book with much bigger sales costs lots more in FOH. But when you do your projected annual operating statement, there's no such temptation to think of FOHs as being in any way contingent on sales. Your lump-sum FOH is what it is—you calculate it in "another room" from the one in which sales and TSC are being projected. (Reminder: *FOH* means "fixed overhead"; *TSC* means "title-specific-costs"; *contribution* means what's left after you deduct all TSC from sales revenues.)

I'll dwell a bit longer on the exec's assignment in making his company-wide projections and planning before getting back to the jobs of approving and pricing new titles. Having completed his first-pass projections, the exec compares the projected total annual contribution with the total annual FOH—and if the FOH is larger, he says, "Oh-oh, I'm going to have a red-ink year unless I do something."

If you're the exec, you might consider many things in your planning, but I want to focus on only one: you should look to see if you're using your FOH to capacity. Obviously, you don't apply FOH when you make the company projections; you simply add up rent, payroll, etc. The only times that you're tempted to apply FOH are in pricing and acquiring titles. Examining the capacity of your fixed apparatus such as staff or space may prompt you to ask a fruit-

ful planning question such as this: could you, with the same fixed apparatus you have, publish more books this year?

Publishing additional books usually entails no increase in FOH. In the house where I worked, the number of books published in the trade division went from 42 per year to 151 before we had to hire a single extra employee. Eventually the company was publishing three hundred times as many titles with only eighteen times as many employees. Often during the year we would sign up for titles and then publish them within a matter of months—with no increase in payroll, rent, or any other fixed cost. In a "Cheerful Skeptic" column in which I talked about allocated overhead I cited a big book that eventually contributed $1.5 million to FOH; if the house had not published that book, it would have had the same FOH—and $1.5 million less to pay for it. Granted, eventually a publishing house will be publishing up to capacity, and to take on any more books it will indeed have to hire more people—but chances are that most firms are far from that stage yet. And when they get there, their FOH does not *slope* up; it *steps* up—and stays there on a plateau, unmoved by an extra title here and there. Then, twenty or thirty titles later, another step up may be required.

"Displacement" of sales of one book by another seldom occurs. Though it can happen, it's a rare occasion when the late appearance of book A on a list reduces the sales of book B on that list. Even rarer is it that by publishing A we make it impossible to publish B. In the old days of mass marketing when each imprint was allotted a fixed number of pockets by the wholesalers, displacement was a constant preoccupation, because if you shipped one title that meant you couldn't ship another. But in trade publishing the elasticity in size-of-list is far greater than most people think. At the house where I worked we expanded the number of titles, in every genre, year after year; contrary to conventional expectation, the number of copies sold per title actually went up.

I'm also aware that in talking about the elastic market, I have to be wary about large lead titles. Again, paperback publishers saw this clearly. For each month they could have only one lead title. If title B was to be your lead and you moved title A onto the list ahead of it, B's potential sales would be reduced, and this is one reason why mass-market houses started creating additional lines with entirely different imprint names. Each imprint could have a lead title. But this displacement occurs much less often in hardcover publishing. The $1.5 million windfall-title was, despite its lead-title size, essentially an add-on to the publisher's list that year. And—by adding it on–the firm dropped an additional $1.5 million to the bottom line.

At the house where I worked, late-appearing titles often came to our door after the coming season's list was closed. One time a controversial book was surreptitiously offered to me on 10 August. Six weeks later we had published it, and it was number one on the nonfiction hardcover best-seller list in *The New York Times*. We saw no diminution in the anticipated sales of any other book on that season's list. (Again, I concede there's a limit to this flexibility. If you're asking for a fifty-thousand-copy advance on ten titles, you're more likely to meet your target than if you're pushing for fifty-thousand on twenty-five titles. But we're seldom considering a 150 percent increase in the number of titles.)

I'm assuming for this discussion that availability of cash is not a problem. I'm talking about what to do *this year*–meaning that the time gap between cash-out and cash-in is small. (This implies that what I've said applies most usefully, say, to fiction and hot-topic nonfiction. For scholarly and reference books, cash tied up in long-gestation projects can certainly mount up to the point where the house simply has no more money to invest.)

I also assume that "cost-of-money" for so short a time is not an issue. I know of no publisher who ever tries to recognize the positive-interest-in-perpetuity that profitable titles produce. An even more arcane point: a division in a large company is often charged with interest for "funds employed"–money tied up in inventory, author advances, and even accounts receivable–but when do you ever see that division credited with positive interest on last year's after-taxes profit?

When you are confronted with a potential red-ink year in making first-pass calculations, your first step in "planning" should not be to run through the list canceling all the titles with low contribution percentages. *A low contribution percentage to FOH should not be the reigning factor in deciding whether or not to publish a book.* Absolute dollars of contribution should. In deciding whether or not to publish a book, if you reject books automatically when they fail to meet the percentage of "allocated overhead" you demand, you will consistently burn money.

Thus, if a new book that can be quickly published can contribute an interesting amount in absolute dollars is proposed–even though the percentage of how much it can contribute to what you receive is below the pricing formula standard–you should publish the book. Any exec who declines such a title because its contribution percentage is less than "formula"–or who cancels a similar title that is already

scheduled–has almost certainly reduced the potential pretax profit for the year, because there is almost no way that he can simultaneously reduce FOH by an amount greater than the aggregate contributions of the canceled titles. If he cancels ten small books with an aggregate contribution of $80,000 and somehow manages to cut FOH by $30,000, he's a $50,000 loser. And his move is even sillier if the plant cost is already spent and the advance paid to the author is unrecoverable.

Suppose an editor says that he has been offered two books and he can accept only one of them. He wants you to choose which one to publish. You believe that the first book would have $50,000 in sales, and, after TSC, would contribute $17,500. That's 35 percent of sales. The second book would have $300,000 in sales, but its high TSC would leave only $60,000 as its contribution–20 percent of sales. Which book do you choose? It's pretty easy to think that no one would be so terminally stupid as to choose the first, but I guarantee that there are publishing execs who would. It happens often because, under the crush of a thousand decisions every month, execs have laid down formula-dictated fiats based on percentages rather than on absolute dollars: "Don't come to me with any proposals that show a contribution of less than thirty-five percent!"

Seven months into the year an editor rushes in with a book based on a late-breaking hot topic. He says, "It's from a packager. It's ready to go; I know I can make catalogue. It's costly, and the contribution will be only 25 percent of sales–but that's still one hundred thousand dollars, and we can have it in ninety days!" The exec who briskly produces his book-proposal form and says, "Can't you see it says here that a book is a loser if it doesn't have a contribution of thirty-five percent?" should be asked in return: "Can't *you* see you just said no to one hundred thousand dollars in extra profit this year?"

Every title the execs can squeeze out of their apparatus this year–provided each title makes at least *some* contribution–will increase the annual pretax profit. This is because the annual FOH is a large, fixed amount of absolute dollars–twelve months of rent, salaries, and the like. Thus, the more absolute dollars of contribution you can accumulate, the faster the year's FOH bill will be covered–and any additional accumulation of contribution before year-end will go toward the year's "profit." The publisher who accepts the $1.5 million book is fully aware that the book's contribution *as a percentage* is below the company formula, and this means that when he prices the book, his task is to price it not to formula but to market. The size of the book's absolute-dollar contribution is persuasive, and it should be.

Every reasonable publisher occasionally allows a highly profitable editor to smuggle onto the list a personal favorite that has a low contribution. The publisher does this even though he suspects, rightly, that every title has direct costs that escape detection because nobody can track every cent of expense back to the title that generates it. A tiny title with a projected sale of two thousand copies will occasion letters, messengers, in-house and catalogue postings, and the like—all of which will erode the gross profit. He also suspects that, with a finite number of employee working hours available, each new title reduces the amount of attention each of the titles can receive, causing an adverse effect that he can't quantify. If he could assign values to and sum up all these concerns, he knows the sum would be small—but, still, it's some amount of money and some percentage of the revenues from the book.

This is to say that you should prepare a projected p&l on every proposed new title, and it's useful to have that p&l statement specify the percentage of what that book can contribute as well as the dollars it can contribute. (*Percentage* here means the dollars-of-contribution as a percent of dollars-of-book-sales.) If every title that an editor proposes has a small contribution percentage, then he should have many of those titles, and the amount of in-house time required for each title had better be small. In sum, even the most flexible publisher should draw an absolute-dollar line: the contribution a book makes must be at least such-and-such in absolute dollars, unless there is some ulterior reason for publishing this no-contribution title.

The absolute-dollar threshold will vary from house to house. In a small house a $7,000 contribution might be prized. Very large houses are alleged to have told editors to bring forth nothing but books that would sell fifty thousand copies or more. If that takes your breath away, it should: it's a policy based on a toxic combination of stupidity and laziness. The peril of the analysis I've given here is that editors may use it to justify approving one small-contribution title after another, to the detriment of acquiring and publishing more profitable books: "They're all contributing absolute dollars, aren't they?"

If you have an editor who year after year wants to do only ten books, all of which are projected to have small dollar-contributions, chances are you should ask him to find another job. Other editors who can do better than that are available. (There are also editors who can produce a lump-contribution that is literally negative for you, if you're not care-

ful.) You can try to educate such an editor this way: add up this year's aggregate contribution from all his new titles. Take his annual salary and that of his assistant, multiply the sum of their salaries by 125 percent to take into account such out-of-pocket costs as fringes, and add his t&e (travel and entertainment expenses). Subtract all that from the contribution of his new titles, and call this result his "net contribution." Then you can show him what he has really contributed this year to the rent and to the salaries of all the support people in production, sales, and so forth. If you want, you can sum all FOH except editorial. If, say, the editor in question is one of ten editors in the company, you could multiply his total contribution by ten and say, "If all the editors do as you've done, this is what the total contribution would be toward all these other FOH for the year: we'd go bust."

In the long run it's not a distortion to say that if that ten-editor house publishes one hundred titles a year, each title has a lifetime contribution of only ten thousand dollars, and the FOH is $2 million, the house will suffer an annual loss of $1 million. However, if each editor manages to produce twenty-five books a year (each with the same $10,000 contribution) and the FOH can remain fixed, the "profit" will be $500,000. The point is, as long as the FOH stays fixed, you want as many dollars of contribution as you can get. All other things being equal, I would rather have an editor who regularly produces twenty-five titles with a total contribution of $500,000—even if his contribution percentage is a low 20 percent of sales volume—than an editor who regularly produces ten books a year with a contribution percentage of 35 percent and a total contribution of only $250,000.

One implication of all this: the larger the title, the less relevant the percentage of contribution. Embrace $1.5 million in contribution, even if that's a mere 20 percent of sales. The smaller the title, the more important it is to be aware of the contribution percentage. To use cartoon numbers to make the point: if some "undetectable" TSC amount to 3 percent of sales, then a title with an ostensible 10 percent contribution is actually contributing only 7 percent. (Still, if the 7 percent amounts to $1 million and it's a guaranteed instant profit—as certain special sales are—think three times before walking away.)

Exam question: a respectable packager comes in with an idea for a series he calls, "The Year in Sports." It includes five titles—"The Year in Sports: Football," "The Year in Sports: Baseball," and so on. He'll deliver finished books year after year. The books are solid; you check the market, which convinces you that the series will bring $4 million a year but with a price-ceiling that means the contribution of FOH and profit will be *only twenty-five percent of sales.* The added in-house burden will be minimal with no increase in FOH, and the sales department says it won't cut into the success of other titles. What do you say?

In a roundabout way this gets us back to why you *should* use a required contribution—when *pricing* books—and why, except for the biggest books and the editor's small personal favorite, using a percentage-of-sales number is okay. Few things bother responsible financial officers more than foolish editors who always want to price their books real low so they'll sell a lot of copies. "Hey," the editor says, "I know what my title-specific costs are, and I know my book's revenues are covering them—so I know I'm not losing money." If such editors were allowed to have their way, the house would soon be out of business. So, *we usually* should *use a contribution-percentage requirement in pricing, for the glum reason that no one has figured out a better way to do it.*

What's the best price to put on a book? Here is the entirely correct, semi-useless answer: *the optimal list price for a book is the one that maximizes the contribution in absolute dollars.* This is what "pricing to market" should mean, but too often it's used to mean something vaguely like: "Price it so low that making it any lower wouldn't sell any more copies."

Calculating this dollar contribution involves using the "direct TSC" that I introduced earlier. You estimate the contribution of a title at a given price by taking the estimated number of copies you will sell at that price and multiplying it by what we might call the "direct margin"—which is what's left from the amount received per copy minus the per-copy pp&b and the expenses of the royalty and the direct variables such as shipping and commission. It ignores plant and promo. The calculation can look like this: "At $15 list, I receive $7.50; pp&b is $2.50; shipping, etc., is $.50; and royalty is $1.50. This leaves a margin of $3. I think I'll sell ten thousand copies at $15, so the amount in absolute dollars of contribution—to plant, indirect variables, FOH, and profit—is $30,000.

Notice that the previous examples in which editors have asked you to decide what book to publish or whether a book contributing $100,000 (but only 25 rather than 35 percent of sales, as ordained by management fiat) should be published both assume that you can't always solve a contribution-percentage problem merely by raising the price—because at some point raising the list price will so reduce the number of copies sold that the move will be counterproductive. Reducing the price so that you can sell more copies also carries the peril of reducing and thus damaging the direct margin per book. Suppose you price a book so low that it sells fifty thousand copies—but with a contribution of only $1 copy. Or suppose you price it so high that it has a contribution of $10 per copy but sells only five thousand copies. Then suppose you price it so that it has a contribution of $4 per copy—and it sells twenty-five thousand copies. It's obvious that the best price is not the one that sells the most copies or the one that has the highest contribution per copy. The first two prices each produce contributions of $50,000. The last produces $100,000.

This is all correct, but what makes this semi-useless is that the optimal price is the one at which, when you multiply the number of copies sold by the direct margin, you get the highest product, the highest total contribution to sunk costs and FOH—and no one, absolutely no one, has a sure way of knowing what that price is. There is no question more important to the profitability of a company than this: what will be the impact on the consumer of *this* price for *this* book? Realize that we're talking about hundreds of annual pricing decisions on products with total expected revenues as low as $35,000. You can't do consumer research on products such as that.

If you don't impose a required contribution percentage when pricing, you have to rely on your fallible gut feeling. You ask, "Suppose we price this book at twenty-five dollars. What percent fewer units would it sell at twenty-six dollars? At twenty-seven dollars? What percent more at twenty-four dollars? At twenty-three dollars?" And so on up and down. Make sure all your guesses are right. And how do you do that? Once I told the sales department that I wanted to price a book at $25 and sell fifteen thousand copies. No one protested. It sold two hundred thousand. There's no doubt that if two hundred thousand had been the announced target, the sales department would have pleaded for a $20 list. Their gut would have told them to do so.

If gut guesses about relative unit-sales at different prices are correct, you obviously can calculate what the total dollar-contribution of a title would be at those various possible prices. You'd then pick the price that has the highest contribution in total dollars—again, not the one with the highest dollar-contribution *per copy,* and not the one with the highest *percentage* contribution, either per copy or as a percent of the total sales.

If there are times when you feel you must rely on gut, the reason to ask what percent fewer copies rather than how many fewer copies, as in this example, is twofold. If you're taking a percentage, it's easier to do the math; consider the confusion if the calculations all start with a different unit-sales number at the $25 price. More important, experience has shown that there is less capricious irrationality if the guessers work with percents: I owe this insight to the most perceptive, creative thinker American publishing has ever seen–Leonard Shatzkin.

The guts of many salesmen and editors (not all) tend to be influenced by passion to sell lots of copies. So their first impulse is to go for a low price, but they can be trained to focus on total contribution instead of total copies. I've watched it happen. The best training tool for editors is the one I've sketched out: produce each editor's annual p&l that sums up the results of all his books that year–and the big, bold-faced bottom line is total annual contribution. I've seen editors so changed that *they* are the ones pushing for a higher list price.

Now you know why I say no one has figured out a better way to enhance chances for a useful contribution per title than to impose a required contribution expressed as a percentage of sales. Although everyone knows there's a counterproductively high and a counterproductively low price, no one knows for sure what these are. So, in our ignorance of how to price to market, if we should price to a formula with a required contribution percentage, the question remains: What should that percentage be? I've cited a common decision-procedure: demand 50 percent gross margin, or 40 percent after TSC. But is that the right way?

You can't get your answer from history. One of the great vexations about book publishing is your inability to verify what effect a price has had. Titles regularly sell more or fewer copies than expected. Neither those who favor lower prices nor those who favor higher ones can be refuted by the results. Let's say "formula" dictates a $25 price for a particular book, but the Low Guys prevail and it's priced at $24. If it sells more copies than projected, they'll say, "See!" If it sells fewer, they'll say, "It would have sold a ton fewer yet at twenty-five dollars." The High Guys meantime will be saying, "It would have sold the same at twenty-five dollars, and we would have made a lot more money!" Whose gut is right?

In the end, the boss has to impose some rules, and they're bound to be somewhat arbitrary. Suppose the boss has been hoping for a profit of 10 percent of sales. He got it last year and the year before, and both years his actual FOH was 30 percent of sales. Let's say he knows that he's doing better than other publishers, and, not wanting to fix something that ain't broke, he requires from the "pricing formula" he uses this year the same 40 percent contribution that he has used for the last few years.

Let's say further that suddenly, when the budgeting process is almost over, it becomes evident that a certain title expected to be relatively modest will obviously be a blockbuster. Its sales not only will be much larger than projected in first-pass projected financials but also will raise the total company sales by 50 percent. Quick arithmetic reveals that FOH this year will be only 20 percent of sales, not 30 percent. What should he do? Should the boss revise his formula?

The answer is yes, if he wants to ensure that he never makes more than 10 percent profit. In other words, the answer is no. By using his formula in the past, he seems to have done well enough–that is, he seems to have escaped pricing his books too high for the market or too low to produce an acceptable contribution. He should retain his formula and, if the projections are right, break his company profit record. (The guy who prices the books has a cruel assignment if he's interested in his public image. If he prices a title high and it sells far more copies than expected, no one will give him the credit. But if it sells far fewer, lots of people will give him the blame.)

By sticking to his formula, he *seems* to have escaped. He doesn't know if he could have been doing even better all along, however, and he never will know for sure. But here's a rule of thumb: if you're going to change the contribution percentage required by your pricing formula, chances are that it will be better to increase it rather than to decrease it.

The prices of books throughout the years have gone up–not because the required contribution percentage has been raised but because–with rising paper costs, etc.–unit costs have risen. In hardcover books the first publisher to price a novel above $19.95 was considered foolhardy and foresighted, depending on whether the name-calling was before or after the success of the book. In the mass paperback trade, $3.95 was once considered the highest acceptable price no matter how long or what the unit-cost of the book was. Then $4.95, then $5.95. . . . One barrier after another was broken, and I can't think of single case in which the higher price is thought to have killed the book.

Thus the generalization: tolerance for higher prices is greater than, say, our sales execs and certain customers will tell us it is. Don't try to break price barriers with ho-hum books, however, or everybody who doesn't *need* the book will seize the occasion to "teach you a lesson." Most people outside the highest exec offices, including bookstores and libraries, like lower prices.

When we think we're "pricing to market," often enough we're simply "pricing to competition."

This misconception is not so feckless as it may sound, because again and again what customers will tolerate paying depends not on what they can actually afford but on what they've been conditioned to feel is a reasonable price. All of us have passed up purchases that we can easily afford, but the notion of being "gouged" or "ripped off" stops us.

The most powerful source of conditioning here is the range of prices that customers regularly encounter in the marketplace. Thus, somewhat willy-nilly, by using the same general pricing formula as all your fellow publishers, you are pricing to competition—but pricing to competition, it turns out, usually *is* pricing to market.

But suppose your FOH year after year runs at 70 or 80—or even 90—percent of sales, a number put to me by a university press exec. In pricing books, can you possibly use a required contribution-percent equal to that? Probably not. And you can't simply say, "Well, why don't we just publish books that sell more?" You can do standard things such as checking for extravagances in FOH and production costs or author advances, and you can undertake the difficult task of reevaluating the abilities of your editors and sales operation. There are two other things you can do: first, you can test the upper limits of price-tolerance in the marketplace. As I've said, it's often higher than we think. And second, you can publish more books—provided that they all have revenues higher than their TSC. It's extraordinary how often execs choose the wrong action: given a couple years of red ink while publishing two hundred forty titles, their solution is to cut back to one hundred eighty—with nothing like a 25 percent reduction in FOH. Their strategy is to "publish fewer books but better books"—as though they've known all along which titles would lose money. They consistently find that their percentage of losers remains constant—but now they lack the aggregate contribution of the sixty titles they've canceled for the year. Within two years they're out of a job.

Certainly if every title on the list is a sure-thing, red-ink loser, then you cut your company's annual loss by cutting the number of titles. But if they all make some small contribution and if when you cancel titles you do not make a cut in FOH equal to the aggregate loss in contribution, you have increased the company red ink for the year.

Much of what I seem to advise about university presses will not apply to them, because the first objective of university presses is often not profit but the spreading of information. What I can say is not intended to tell them what to do; it's meant only to help them understand what they are doing.

I also can offer a strategic tip for the small publisher who asked me what percentage to use to satisfy his investors. They wanted to see the projected p&l statements on all proposed new titles—and to see how these p&ls would show a contribution percentage. Here's what to do. First, sum projected annual sales. Next, sum your annual FOH and a little bit for profit. Then take the second number as a percent of the first. Use that percent as the required contribution percent on the p&l for each title, and adjust projected unit-sales and prices accordingly. Finally, pray. Pray that they're not canny enough to match up each print-and-price sheet with each projection sheet; pray that happy lightning strikes early in the year and stuns them into inattention thereafter; and pray that you have, in fact, picked good titles and that the projected units and prices are reasonable. Failing those prayers, pray that you remember how to prepare a résumé.

Recent buzz-notions among financial planners have names such as "activity-based costing" and "uniform capitalization." These forms of accounting—which basically aim to make all costs TSC—are diametrically wrong for the kind of book publishing we're discussing. Such accounting methods are prompted by several motives. The first is a sincere, well-intended but misplaced effort in book publishing to tie essentially all costs in a company to the product that the company produces. This way, these financial planners believe, when they look at the sales that the product generates, they can better judge whether the product was worth it. But, as I have been arguing, there is in book publishing a disjuncture between FOH and actual product cost—TSC. It's thus a delusive fiction—with potential damaging consequences—to say that all FOH can be traced to the individual titles causing it.

These accounting methods may work just right for a services company or for a company such as General Motors that creates a few new products a year. If General Motors decides to launch a new model, chances are that it *will* have to increase its payroll and rent new space. If you embark on a new ten-volume reference work with an eight-year period of gestation, that's not a new book: it's a start-up subsidiary that requires its own special accounting. But the book publisher who decides to produce an extra novel or biography won't have to raise the president's salary or hire another body and other office staff to produce the book. By making all costs TSC, you ignore totally the indisputable fact of how infrequently new products and higher sales create any new FOH. When my company sold five million copies of the paperback edition of *The Silence of the Lambs*,

I guarantee our rent stayed the same. The only way to compare project A to project B is to compare their dollar contributions—which, by the definitions I have given, requires charging the book solely with the disbursements it caused and not with any FOH that, since it would have occurred anyway, could not have been caused by the title in question.

The second motive behind such methods is often suspect. For example, a company may capitalize a large percentage of its editorial costs in its financial statements by categorizing that cost as part of its plant. It then expenses the total plant cost for this year over, say, the next five years. Its argument is that the editorial work went into a product that was expected to sell for five years—so this is just matching costs to revenues. But the effect of such an accounting method is to make this year look good at the expense of later years. As long as the company's sales continue to slope up, the next day of reckoning will be delayed. But once the sales plateau, the "plant" that has to be expensed will require a larger and larger percent of sales—with greater consequences on the profit line. Livent, the theater producers who created the musical *Ragtime,* even capitalized the huge initial promotion on each production by expensing it over five years. Consider what a boon that could be to a publisher desperate to look good this fiscal year. He puts $1 million into launching a new title for this Christmas, picks up all those initial sales with their alleged contribution, and, by capitalizing the promo cost and spreading it over five years, has to expense only $200,000 in promo. Of course, four or five years from now, when the title is as dead as Gorboduc, the publisher will still be expensing $200,000 a year for the deceased.

It's a method that start-up organizations who want to look good from day one might be eager to adopt. Or it could be used by a company that anticipates selling itself three years from now. The method makes the next few years look nifty—with the new owner unwittingly picking up costs that were incurred years ago to produce sales years ago. The auditors that a buyer chooses to examine a company's books diligently before an acquisition should be very familiar with the accounting twists and loopholes that are special to publishing.

Much more, of course, could be said about "pricing to market," about "planning the list," about what markets for which product are elastic or inelastic, and much, much more—but I'd better stop here, or the core points I've been trying to make will be obscured even more by the surfeit of detail. To summarize the answers to the questions of the CFO whom I quoted at the outset:

1. *When pricing books, use a pricing formula, and see that the formula demands a contribution-percentage.*

2. *When deciding whether or not to do a book at all—i.e., when you're making a* publishing *decision rather than a* pricing *decision—focus not on the* percentage *of the contribution but on the amount of* absolute dollars.

3. At the beginning of the year, when you're doing the annual forecasts, if you see that your FOH is projected to eat up an astronomical percentage of your revenues, do not think you are remedying the problem by cutting titles with low contributions. This is an effective treatment only if you can replace a deleted title with another title that has a greater contribution. If the first title provides any contribution at all and you delete that book without a replacing it, you have just increased your loss for the year. Here's a sweeping generalization. Any mature company that has FOH of 70 or 80 percent needs to do one of two things: find better editors—i.e., editors who can bring in books that will have higher contributions—or increase the number of titles being published, because—I say categorically—any mature company with a FOH so robust is not using it to capacity.

I'm aware that I haven't supplied a checklist of hard numeric dicta—"Here's what your contribution-percentage must be, your profit percentage, your number of books per editor." I haven't done it because I would be wrong—not just for your house, but wrong in principle. I understand those who admire mathematical adroitness, logic, and consistency and completeness of systems. Departures from any of these practices make such people uneasy. So when they have power, they tend to impose forms, formulas, and formats on their troops. Most of the time who wants to have to reinvent the wheel? And many of the forms make sense, by and large.

But it's a fundamental truth—and not just in business—that the very best of thinkers and leaders have to rise above their passion for formulas. The world is infinitely complex, often indeterminate, and as changeable as a river. We can't devise formulas complex enough to embrace this indeterminacy, and even if we could it would be infinitely hard to apply these formulas. Thus the ultimately most effective minds learn to live occasionally with loose ends, with ad hoc decisions, with lack of mathematical certainty—with gut. If they're good enough, they don't go to pieces when confronted with the small daily chaos of life, and they don't become mad totalitarians commanding the patternless seas to conform. They'll live with the fact that sometimes departing from formula is the right thing; sometimes this means making a guess and sometimes taking a chance. They may prefer a world of calculation, of deduction, but they know that much of it can be mapped only by induction, by experiment, by feel. History has shown them that permanent concrete bunkers do not serve either to defend or to advance, and they know that they must advance. If they're good enough, their imperfect gut will still be adequate when their calculator goes blank—and it will.

ANNEX

Re: One difference between a *company* p&l and a *title* p&l:

You expense pp&b and royalty in different ways, depending on whether you're doing the company's annual projections and actuals or doing individual title p&ls. We can say this as a generalization: accepted accounting practice and the IRS allow a company to list as a cost only the royalty and pp&b on books *sold*. But when you're trying to evaluate a given title's worth to you, you should charge it with the cost of all the books *printed* and with the royalty earned or the author-advance, *whichever is higher*.

In the company statements, the unsold books and unearned author-advances are carried on the balance sheet as assets—until they are written off. If you're never going to sell those books or earn out those unearned portions of advance, your auditors will require you to expense them as write-offs, because their job is to see that your statement—which includes your balance sheet—gives an honest picture of the health of your company. The auditors' responsibility is not so much to management as to owners and potential buyers of the company. Meantime, the IRS doesn't want you to write off these "assets" as expenses prematurely—because you may just be trying to reduce this year's taxable-income line by expensing everything in sight.

The more heinous sort of quasi-cheating goes the other way, however: management (and owners looking to sell) will delay making write-offs as long as they can. This makes their profit line look better, and

their balance sheet will seem to show valuable assets that in fact are worthless. That's why the inspection of the company by a potential purchaser requires digging deeply into the entries on the balance sheet. The *Inventory* entry on a book publisher's balance sheet will often be a huge number—tens of millions of dollars. It's supposed to express the sum of the value of all the books in the warehouse. A good auditor will go look for those books—sometimes they don't exist at all—and, when he finds them, will look at the sales history title by title. He's apt to find, say, ten thousand copies of a title for which sales have totaled only one hundred copies in the last three years. This, he will say, is an "inflated asset," and it should be recorded as such in order to arrive at a true picture of the value of this company.

It's even more important to examine on hands and knees the items that constitute the *Royalty Advances* entry on the balance sheet. For example, here are three categories to look for: (1) Books already published. These advances can be justified as assets only if there is evidence for believing that future royalty earnings or rights income will exceed the currently unearned portion of the advance. (2) Advances outstanding on very old contracts. Is it probable that these manuscripts will never be delivered? (3) Large advances for books with values that have clearly dropped since these books were signed up. Your imagination can probably supply ten examples of such books in the time it takes to wince thrice.

Still another asset to be inspected closely is the alleged *Accounts Receivable*. We've been led to believe that a clerk at Penguin granted important customers a large discount on what they owed if they would pay the lower amount early. She retained the kick-back amount in the accounts receivable balance, and she did this, we've been told, for years. But surely the auditors year after year went through the standard year-end practice of asking each large debtor, "Here's what our ledgers say you owe us. Is this an accurate figure?" As I said at the beginning, a knowledge of how the business of publishing really works can be interesting and valuable.

George V. Higgins Interview

This telephone interview with George V. Higgins was taped on 19 June 1998.

DLB: How did you break into print?

Higgins: Mostly by sheer stupidity. I didn't know enough to be discouraged. I had fourteen books rejected numerous times by the best and most reputable publishing houses on both sides of the Atlantic.

DLB: No agent? You were just sending them over the transom?

Higgins: That's right. Then I got an agent after I got a few stories published in the small literary quarterlies. She was the next-door thing to useless. When I sent her a copy of *The Friends of Eddie Coyle,* she told me she couldn't place it and wished me luck in finding a publisher. Thereafter it was turned down by a publisher in Boston. I sent it out again, dogged fellow that I was, and it stayed at Alfred A. Knopf in New York. It was luck and determination, or stupidity. I don't know which.

DLB: It was accepted by an editor named Ashbel Green.

Higgins: Correct.

DLB: Did he fish it out of the slush pile himself?

Higgins: Yes. Ash was one of the few people of his eminence in those days who actually did read the slush pile. It was usually assigned to somebody who had sat on a top officer's hat in the corporation, an effort to discourage the poor young person determined to get a career in publishing. It was just an awful job. Most of the stuff that came in, of course, was terrible in those days, and it's probably even worse today.

DLB: What did you expect then; what do you expect now—if the situation has changed—from an editor?

Higgins: What I expected then was that the editor would publish what I wrote. It didn't really occur to me

that the editor would actually remove parts of what I had written or ask me to remove them. Or suggest additions or emendations or rewrites or anything of the sort. And Ash Green really didn't. He suggested that I cut about 175 words from *Eddie Coyle,* which I did, and with that one small exception what was published was the first draft. Thereafter I have occasionally taken suggestions from editors, primarily having to do with pace, which means that my characters—since I allow them to tell the stories—occasionally get too long-winded even for my long-suffering editors, and the story has to be cut. My *Change of Gravity,* which came out in 1997, went as high as 275,000 words in one draft; what was published was about 225,000. *Eddie Coyle,* for reference, was somewhere in the neighborhood of 100,000 words. So there's a great range in the amount of material in a novel. It all depends on the complexity of the story. It takes a fairly wise editor to know when he's dealing with one that's got to be long and when he's dealing with one that can be fairly short. Not all editors enjoy that kind of sagacity, and therefore I have not always enjoyed that kind of understanding. But I've been uncommonly lucky. I can think of only one editor who really gave me problems, and I guess I gave him problems too, with the happy result that he handed me off to a colleague who was able to deal with me in a much more agreeable fashion. I will not name them.

DLB: You've never been line-edited? That is to say, one of these editors who does it word by word, line by line.

Higgins: I have on nonfiction. Generally with fiction, my editors have deferred to what is considered to be my expertise on dialogue—as they'd damned right well better.

DLB: Do you ever give your editor a preview? Such as, "I'm thinking of writing a novel about. . ." to get a response from them as to whether they think the idea, the premise, is good.

Higgins: I have given editors a preview of what I'm working on. The general subject, and when I expect

George V. Higgins at the Locke-Ober Cafe (photograph by Boston College Magazine)

it to be finished, but that's all. And it's been not a matter of seeking approval, at least from my point of view; it's been a matter of keeping the editor informed. I think it is the useful view that he know what I'm doing, if I'm under contract to his company. But no editor has any effect or influence whatsoever upon my work until the draft is finished. And that includes nonfiction. I don't let anybody mess around with what's going on in my head until after I put it on paper—because of course I don't know what I think until I see what I've written.

DLB: Of course. How much rewriting do you do in proof? Or do you feel that all you do in proof is proofread?

Higgins: Well, I wish I could do a better job of proofreading. By the time I get galley proofs of anything I've written I have a form of snow blindness on the subject. If the word is spelled correctly it must be OK, and I let it go through. One illustration of that is in *Eddie Coyle*. I was doing a reading from a chapter some years after the book had come out. And by some years I

mean fifteen or twenty. The passage had been requested by the person who had scheduled the reading, and I honored the request. In the middle of performing as requested, I came upon a sentence that read, "The black teller," mentioned in the course of a bank robbery episode. There was absolutely no relevance whatever—and as far as I could recall no prior or subsequent reference whatsoever—to the race of any of the characters. It should have been *bank* teller. I suppose my brain had taken a small rest while my fingers kept moving on the keyboard. I left it alone when I saw it in copy because it was spelled correctly. But it made no sense at all.

In my 1999 book, *The Agent,* I probably read that story, oh, fifteen times before I saw galley proofs. Then I realized for the first time that the victim of the murder—which in part 2 occurs in February of the book—is vigorously alive, carrying on business, and being a general-purpose son-of-a-bitch in part 1—which occurs in March. The explanation for that is fairly easy. I set the times, the season of the year in my novels, during the seasons when I write them. I wrote part 2 in February, before I decided I needed part 1. So when I wrote part 1, it was March. Therefore the time was out of joint.

What impresses and frightens me is that not only I, but my editor, his deputy, and the copyeditor, had let the whole thing go through, several times: Victim fully alive and vigorous in part 1 in March, quite dead in part two in February. And none of us noticed. So it's a near thing when those mistakes are caught.

I think if it's spelled correctly, it's laid out correctly, we get lulled. I recently did an article for *The American Lawyer:* there were four people seated in the jury box at a hearing, one of them a major subject. An editor compressing a sentence changed it so that it read that *in addition* to the major subject there were four other guys. So who was the ghost? Hamlet's father?

These things can be extremely embarrassing. It's like putting the Pacific Ocean on the East Coast. You destroy the credibility of the entire enterprise.

DLB: But these still come under the heading of—if not proofreading—proof-checking. Catching errors. Catching blunders, if you don't mind the term. You don't rewrite or heavily revise?

Higgins: Oh, not in proof I don't. For one thing it's very expensive.

DLB: You pay for it. And the publisher gets mad anyhow, even when you do pay for it.

Higgins: Because the publisher figures he has to postpone all his plans because you weren't swift enough to get it right in the first place. And he's right.

DLB: It doesn't look different to you in print?

Higgins: No. It looks old.

DLB: It does to me.

Higgins: It looks to me like what it is: something I did awhile ago. By then usually—in fact almost always—I'm far more concerned with, and absorbed by, what I've started since then.

DLB: By the time the book is in proof, you're into another book?

Higgins: Yeah. Almost always.
DLB: That's a form of protection, isn't it?

Higgins: Sure it is. Fitzgerald said, "There were no second acts in American lives." I read that long before I

got anything published, and I'd made up my mind that if I ever did get anything published, my life was going to have a second act.

DLB: George, can we talk about your writing habits?

Higgins: When I originally started, I always wrote fiction on a typewriter.

DLB: Like most guys who came out of the newspaper newsroom.

Higgins: Yeah. But I started writing it on a typewriter when I was fifteen, long before I ever got into a newsroom. I taught myself to type—which was why I was not allowed to take typing in high school. The typing teachers refused to give the course to college-bound students until they were juniors. I learned to type when I was a sophomore, so that took care of that. And she also said it would take longer for me to unlearn my butcher method than it would to learn the right way of doing it in the first place, but the damage was done. So, to this day, I still don't really know how to type. I look at the keyboard all the time and I do ninety words a minute. When I wrote on the typewriter, I would type multiple drafts if I felt the story wasn't right when I read the final draft. I believe that a professional writer ought to turn in clean copy, not all marked up with marginalia and inserts and elisions and excisions and all the rest of it.

DLB: You're costing yourself a fortune when your manuscripts come up for sale.

Higgins: Tough. I do it my way. I've done it my way ever since the beginning. I can't tell you how many typos I can stand to have corrected by pen on a given page, but it's probably around four. That means one letter omitted or one definite article inserted or something like that. Anything more and I've always retyped the page.

I did *Choice of Enemies* on the typewriter. It was a long manuscript, about 750 pages. I had to get a certain weapon of destruction into the story near the beginning. I was delighted to find that that chapter had room enough at the end of it so that I could work it in without repaginating the whole manuscript. Unfortunately, when I started retyping to get the tire iron onto Roger Knox's desk at the gas station, I found a lot of other things that needed changing. Improving. By the time I'd finished that insert I'd added about three or four pages to the chapter, so then I had to rewrite the whole damn book. I probably rewrote, and therefore retyped, front to back, first word to last period, *Choice of Enemies* five times. Four times at least. And then I figured it was ready to send to Ash Green.

DLB: When you retype, are you just retyping for cleanliness?

Higgins: I start to, but I can't do it. When I start retyping, I rewrite. I can't leave it alone. I'm obsessive-compulsive in that respect. When I went to the computer back in 1982, I had a terribly difficult time making the transition, as I did when I went to a better computer in 1992. But after I found my ease with each of them, I became even more obsessive.

DLB: Why did you do it?

Higgins: I was working on a nonfiction book that required me to amass and order a large amount of factual data, and I thought it would be easier to do on the computer. You can move blocks of material around on a computer. You can probably do it even easier if you really know how to use one. My son who works for Microsoft tells me that I use about 12 percent of the capacity of the machine. Which is OK with me because it's the 12 percent I want. If I needed 30 percent, I'd learn how to use eighteen more, I guess.

But at any rate I soon found I had changed my procedure. Now I write by accretion. I start writing chapter one, say, on Monday, and that evening let's say I'm at page five. I do anywhere from one to three thousand words a day when I'm cooking. So I've got about five pages when I start on Tuesday morning. I begin again at page one, and I rewrite everything up to page five, as needed, and continue on that day until the close of business. By the time I finish Tuesday night I've got perhaps ten pages. On Wednesday morning I start again at page one and proceed through the day in the same fashion until Wednesday night. Maybe now I've only got thirteen pages. Maybe I've sixteen pages or maybe seventeen. By now it's hard to say because I've been rewriting all day getting to the point of starting something new. And so on through Friday, and if necessary to Saturday, and if necessary Sunday, and so on into Monday, until I finally finish chapter one, which is now probably anywhere from sixteen to thirty-five or forty pages.

I have had chapters in some of my books run forty, fifty thousand words. Many others have come close to that before I finally decided, this isn't working, it's too long, and started breaking them down. This too is a lot easier to do with a computer. It can mean that by the time I get through with those forty thousand words

they're sixty thousand—in chapters one through five, or seven or eight. Each of them somewhere between four thousand and ten thousand words.

That means the first draft that my editor sees is the first draft that satisfies me, usually about draft 3.4, draft 4.1, or 4.3, if you figure all the times that I've rewritten it as I've gone along. It's tiring, but it leads to neater copy. It also leads to prolixity. It's much easier to get wordy when you use a computer.

DLB: You have any tricks to discipline yourself from getting wordy?

Higgins: Unfortunately I don't. The reason I don't is because my characters do the talking—I always feel as though I'm taking dictation. My inclination is to follow the old rule of the Associated Press when we had a hot story: Let it run till it's cold. I figure if I put it in, and I don't see that it ought to be cut, and if my editor doesn't think that it should be cut, then it was necessary, and it should be in there. But if it was necessary, and I left it out, it will be missing forever. I figure it's better to err on the side of generosity and then edit on the side of severity. Well, that's what I try to do anyway—it's hard.

DLB: John O'Hara said that what he got out of journalism was pre-paper discipline, that when he sat down every night along about eleven o'clock or midnight to start writing, he wrote as though he was writing against a deadline, and he didn't have time to waste with frilly writing. Do you feel that your years as a newspaperman gave you this sense of pre-paper discipline of writing against a self-imposed deadline?

Higgins: I have a self-imposed deadline, but it's one of urgency: I want to see how the story comes out, and I really don't know that when I start writing.

DLB: O'Hara said he did.

Higgins: Oh, I don't.

DLB: You write to discover.

Higgins: I write to find out what the ending is, what these characters did to themselves and to each other. Furthermore, O'Hara for an old newspaperman had a fairly strange weakness, and it was a real weakness, too: he refused to rewrite. When he finished his story, it was finished. I don't think he was ever dissatisfied with anything he ever wrote. As much as I revere his memory and honor his production, I think he wrote a lot of stuff that really needed rewrite. His rewrite—not some editor's chisel or knife or scissors.

DLB: But great work.

Higgins: He still needed to rewrite it. He didn't have it right.

DLB: Some of the late work. Some of the late novels. *Lovey Childs* for example.

Higgins: Which is a stinker, unfortunately, but it is. I got into a deep pit some years ago with Lew Lapham at *Harper's.* I called him up one sort of dawdling day in the summer doldrums and told him I was convinced that *From the Terrace* was America's most unjustly neglected novel.

DLB: You're right.

Higgins: I was wrong. Have you read it lately?

DLB: Yes.

Higgins: It's slovenly. It's unkempt. It's poorly organized, and in many respects the characters do uncharacteristic things—things such persons would never do. It really should have been rewritten. It could have been a wonderful novel, but it wasn't. I now think the neglect of it is fortunate. I think John O'Hara's only fully successful novel is *Samarra.*

DLB: Ten North Frederick?

Higgins: Good, but, once again, self-indulgent. O'Hara was the man who needed to enforce discipline, and he just didn't do it. He had a very high opinion of his own effectiveness the first time out, and so do I.

DLB: We can agree, though, that O'Hara was . . .

Higgins: A master.

DLB: Our greatest short-story writer.

Higgins: In my mind. No question about it.
DLB: We've talked about what you expect from an editor, and in effect you said, "Nothing!" To accept the book and publish it.

Higgins: That's a lot. It's a lot to ask an editor to leave a writer alone. We are not a breed renowned for the uniformity of our obedience to contractual terms and so

forth. My editors have shown a great deal of circumspection and forbearance in dealing with me. And I think I've shown them I reward that. I meet deadlines or I beat them, and I don't raise a lot of contractual uproar after I've signed the paper. I think I'm fairly easy to deal with—except when somebody starts telling me how to write dialogue, and then I'm extremely difficult to deal with. But that's deliberate. I figure if I'm as difficult as possible when I'm trifled with, then I won't be trifled with as often.

DLB: What do you expect from the publisher as against what you expect from the author? Do you draw a line between the editor as editor and the publisher as publisher?

Higgins: Yeah, I have to because I have to deal with the editor, and I don't want to be on terms of hostility with him. I therefore transfer and tally all offenses, real and imagined, to the publisher's ledger. Of course, like every other scribbler, I sometimes think I don't know of a single publisher in America today who knows how to sell books. The one I knew in England is out of the publishing business.

DLB: Tom Rosenthal, formerly of Deutsch?

Higgins: Yeah. Economic circumstances drove him out of the business. But he sure did know how to promote a book. I've got this magnificent reputation in England, a country of fifty-five million people, and not much reputation at all in America, a country of two hundred sixty-five million people, and I think the explanation is that Tom published me there, but not here. Too bad.

DLB: Talk about that please. You have two reputations, as did for example, Raymond Chandler.

Higgins: Well, Chandler was half English. One of theirs, raised and educated in England.

DLB: And the Brits recognized him somehow as that.

Higgins: Whereas, I'm an import. Furthermore I'm an Irish American. That should have caused a lot of problems. At least I kind of half expected that it would, the first time I went to England. But it didn't. I was greeted with open arms. Tom arranged that. Thanks to him, in England I was treated from the beginning as a general-purpose fiction writer. But in America I've been treated as a crime novelist ever since Christopher Lehmann Haupt reviewed *The Friends of Eddie Coyle* in *The New York Times* and called it a crime novel. I don't know what a publisher could have

Dust jacket for the author's 1999 novel about the murder of a sports agent

done to counteract that, but none of them really has done very much. In retrospect, I might have been wiser if I had just sighed, laid back, and enjoyed it.

DLB: What was the English review, or who was the English reviewer, initially responsible for your serious reputation in England?

Higgins: There were two of them. There was Julian Symons, the late Julian Symons, quite a wonderful writer of detective fiction himself, but far better known as a critic and man of letters. He was enthusiastic about my work from the very beginning. The other was Lord Greystiel Gowry, very much of an aficionado of American literature. But it was Tom Rosenthal who thumped the tub and called their attention to my work, first at Secker and Warburg and later at André Deutsch.

DLB: Which one of your books was, to your way of thinking, published in the best way? I'm referring now to promotion, review copies, good dust jacket, everything. The package.

Higgins: Gee, I don't know. I've never really taken much of an interest in the mechanics of it, how many review copies were sent out, or to whom they were sent—plans for distribution or any of the other nuts and bolts of the publishing side. Perhaps that accounts for some of my disappointments.

DLB: Your attitude is that you write the books, let them publish them?

Higgins: I don't know much about publication, about what to do to get the books out into the field and get them displayed properly in the stores. I doubt I'd really want to read a novel by somebody who did know a lot about that side of things. Recently a Massachusetts politician published what he called a novel; his editor invited me to plug it. I declined with thanks. I said, "I'll plug his novel when he agrees to finance and endorse my next gubernatorial campaign."

I don't like people who screw around with writing novels, on the evident assumption that it's something that you can do on weekends with your left hand. It insults me, personally.

I don't like people who claim to have written nonfiction either, such as Hillary Clinton, who did no such thing. She gave a writer a title and the bare outline of some thoughts she had about child raising. The writer wrote the book and ol' Hillary didn't even give her the courtesy of a co-author designation. Hillary instead claimed to have written the book. Okay, then I'm First Lady of the United States, but my voice has changed and I have whiskers on my face.

DLB: Why don't you put on the record what you told the automobile dealer who said that he was number one on the library waiting list for your books.

Higgins: When my daughter turned sixteen and got her Massachusetts driver's license, I decided to preserve peace in the family. Since she was not going to drive my BMW or my wife's BMW, I thought it might be best to get her a beater to drive around town. Preferably one that wouldn't go too fast. So I went over to the local Chevrolet dealer, and out on the lot I found an old Mercury Cougar that didn't look as though it had too hard a life up 'til then. I went into the showroom and found a salesman who wasn't occupied and told him what I had in mind. He asked for my name and I told him and he said, "You're the writer." I pleaded guilty. He said, "I love your books!" Of course I beamed. He said, "My name is always first on the reserve list at the library when you have a new one out. What can I do for you?" I said, "Loan me that Cougar. If I don't bring it back in two weeks, I'll pay you a nickel a day until I do."

My butcher once said to me, "Where is my book?" And I said, "Same place as my roast. It's in the display case waiting for someone to come up with the money to buy it."

DLB: You can never convince civilians that an author gets ten copies.

Higgins: Twenty.

DLB: I get ten.

Higgins: Well, you don't fight hard enough on that clause. You have to fight them on every single clause. Editors are nice people. Publishers deserve to go to the trenches.

DLB: Civilians are sure, they are convinced, that you get all the free books you want.

Higgins: Not that you get ten or twenty. All you have to do is call the publisher up and say, "Send a gross. At once!" And they'll be on your doorstep immediately.

DLB: And when you politely try to explain to them you get ten, in my case, or twenty in yours, they tell you you're lying.

Higgins: And furthermore, they know better. The truth is, they think, that you just don't like them very well. And quite often they're usually the people to whom you have given not one book but several— who have never thanked you for one. And then after you stop, they take you to task the next time they see you and say, "I see you've got a new book out. Where's my copy?" I have been known to say, somewhat grouchily, I suppose, "Where're my thank-you notes?"

DLB: Has any of your books been hurt, damaged by bad publishing? A book that should have done much better?

Higgins: At least one. *The Judgment of Deke Hunter.* I think Atlantic/Little, Brown were concerned that it would fall into wrong hands, and so they did nothing to promote it. They did have some excellent Boston subway car posters. I still have one. It could be the best because it's the only one ever done, but still, it's a very good piece of work. But it didn't sell the book, and nothing much else was done.

The Friends of Richard Nixon wasn't published at all. The people publishing the book disagreed with the conclusions I expressed—that the judge, Sirica, was not a hero but in fact a mountebank; that a couple of the lawyers for the Senate Select Committee on Campaign Practices were pretty close to being bumbling idiots; *and,* that the Senate Chairman, the lovable Sam Ervin, was something of a buffoon. These were not popular views in fashionable East Coast salons, and consequently the book was shunned. And therefore scuttled.

Generally speaking I think the publishers have done about as much as they felt they could do. Except for television, word of mouth is the only way to sell books and no more than anyone else do I know how to inspire that.

DLB: I would have said that reviews sell books.

Higgins: They used to.

DLB: No more? Why? Why the change?

Higgins: I don't know. Certainly the reviews that *Eddie Coyle* got sold the book. That and the fact that Norman Mailer—and I had no idea then how important this was or how fortunate I had been—read the galleys and plugged the book. Norman Mailer's word on the jacket of a book in those days. . . . well, it could make one. And I'm convinced it made *Eddie Coyle*. It got *Coyle* readers that it never would have had, without that endorsement.

DLB: Something about, "I'm amazed that the fuzz can write this well." Isn't that it?

Higgins: Yeah. "What I can't get over is that so good a first novel was written by the fuzz." I was a federal prosecutor at the time, so I could understand his consternation. He was not in good aroma with the feds in those days.

DLB: What changed it? You say that it is no longer true that good reviews sell books.

Higgins: The Friends of Eddie Coyle in hardcover didn't sell twenty-five thousand copies in its first year. If it has since then, it's over the course of years, and we're talking now since 1972. *Eddie Coyle* got to number five, I think it was, and stayed on *The New York Times* best-seller list for ten or eleven weeks. Today to get on the best-seller list—not ten slots but fifteen—you've got to sell forty thousand copies in the first month. People no longer buy books because they've read reviews. Most of the books that are sold today are bought in superstores, book supermarkets or discount stores, and warehouse chains—where they're offered at cut-rate prices. I think they're bought because the woman in the next aisle bought one and she looks like she might enjoy it, so maybe you will.

So it's advertising and celebrity, and Oprah: she sells books and Don Imus sells books, and I hope Gordon Liddy sells books, because I got him out of jail and he remains a friend of mine. I don't think we agree on much, but he has a radio show and he remains a friend of mine. And I hope that Tom Snyder sells books. I know television, celebrity, notoriety sell books. And, of course, infamy sells books. If Monica Lewinsky can be somehow persuaded to pretend to write a book, that book may sell. I don't know how many it will sell, and I don't think it will earn back a twelve-million-dollar advance—which probably some publisher in America's foolish enough to give her. But it will make a lot of money, because it will sell to people who are basically not readers but who scarf up the gossip and notoriety purveyed to them in the supermarket tabloids. And so now we print them as books. Big thick supermarket tabloids, in hardcovers.

DLB: You're not one of the authors who's outraged because his publisher doesn't take big ads?

Higgins: I don't know if ads sell books. I've never known.

DLB: Publishers say they don't.

Higgins: Well, they could be right.

DLB: Publishers agree with you. They say books sell word of mouth. Somebody reads the book and tells his friends. That's what publishers say.

Higgins: Yeah, but you've got to get somebody to read the book. I tried to do what I can for Donald McCaig. His new book is *Jacob's Ladder,* about the Civil War. It's a big, heavy, meaty, novel, very well done. Donald is an excellent writer and a man of many parts. A long time ago he wrote an excellent book called *Nop's Trials*—it completely violates the rule against anthropomorphism; it's about a talking, thinking dog. It's a wonderful book. *Charlotte's Web* violates the rule too, and it's a wonderful book. But *Jacob's Ladder* is a sort of. . . . This is the book that Margaret Mitchell would have written about the Civil War if Margaret Mitchell had been able to write really well. And McCaig does write well, and it's good. Now is that book going to sell because I've been talking about it? Probably not. I don't have a television show. I don't have a radio show. But then again maybe it will sell a few more copies than it would have if I hadn't liked it.

A former editor of mine is of the opinion that there are a million readers in the United States—out of 265 million people. The problem is how to find them. You could sell a million books if you just knew how to get these people notified that you've got a good book out. That would be pretty impressive. But nobody knows how to target them. That's the difficulty. My wife is convinced that you do it on the Internet in the chat rooms. When you have a new book coming out, your publisher makes you available on the World Wide Web, and you answer questions and diddle people, sort of, the way we used to do at the library readings that nobody goes to very much anymore because they're all surfing the net, I guess. I don't know what the answer is. I really don't. I wish I did. I'd patent it and make several million bucks just selling books, never mind writing them.

DLB: The profession of authorship really means making a living from this book so that you can feed yourself while you're writing your next book. George, how the hell does a writer make a living?

Higgins: The writer who can get a success his first or second time out would be best advised to invest it and try to get some good advice so he doesn't get swindled as I did, and then get in trouble with the Internal Revenue Service. I didn't do that. I've been living off the advance on the next book since about the end of the Seventies. By the time this book comes out I will have spent the advance I got for it. And then it won't sell enough in most cases to pay the advance back, much less pay royalties.

So I've been betting on the come, as they say in the gambling circles. This has become more and more problematical because as my sales have declined, my advances have declined. Arbitrarily: say that in the mid eighties I was getting hundred-thousand-dollar advances. That's fifty thousand dollars on signing the contract and fifty thousand dollars on delivery. Since signing a three-book contract with Knopf about fifteen years ago drove me crazy, I have never signed a contract for a book that didn't exist. The first book was done, but that left me with two to write, and those books were *work*—writing books never had been for me until then. I'd never felt as though I was toiling at it. I currently have a two-book contract with Harcourt. I'm on the second book, but I had more than the vague idea for it when I signed the contract in '97.

Anyway, my advances have steadily declined as my sales have declined. In '97 I was downsized by Holt. The publisher had determined to take this initiative in '96, but he lacked the decency or gentlemanly qualities to tell me he was going to do it. So it caught me by surprise, a very nasty surprise. I had to deduce the fact that I was going to be high, dry, and friendless, and then find another home. When I was in the process of looking, I sent the draft of the new, complete book to seven editors who had expressed personally to me over the years the hope that if I ever did leave Holt I would have the kindness to come to them, and they would embrace me with open arms and give me large bags of money. This turned out to be in all but one case utter bullshit. It was sort of like having a rattlesnake bite your arse and having to ask somebody to suck the wound: That's when you find out who your friends are. Anyway, the consequence of it was that having gone from a hundred thousand dollars—fifty now and fifty later—in the eighties, I am now at twenty now and twenty later in the nineties. And damn lucky to have that, if you go by my recent experience.

I've found this extremely disconcerting, not to say depressing. I was lucky to be able to recover from it. I

did have the book in hand after all, and it did find a publisher, and now things are going swimmingly again.

But were it not for the fact that I am employed by Boston University, I would have been in serious financial trouble. There are such things as medical insurance and the necessity for pensions and that sort of thing, that you don't think about a lot when you're in your twenties, and your thirties, and even in your forties. It's a good thing for me that when I was in my late forties that somebody else thought of it and got me into this line of work, which I love to do, because it does provide an anchor to windward. Being a freelance writer today doesn't.

DLB: Like many writers, in America, the basis of your income comes from a university.

Higgins: The reliable part. It is awfully nice to know that when the mortgage comes due each month, you will have the money to pay it and your health insurance too, or most of it. And there will be something set aside for your old age, when you become completely toothless and your imagination runs out. Otherwise, it's very hard to work solely as a writer in the United States today, if you want to enjoy a nice life.

When you're in your twenties and your thirties, well, maybe not in your thirties, but when you're young, you don't think of that. You can say, "I will give all for art. And when I'm in my fifties I won't have a nice house. So what. Unless I strike it rich, which most writers don't, I won't have a nice car and I won't have a beach house and I won't have vacations in Europe, nice dinners in restaurants, all the fine things that your average stockbroker who's fourteen years old takes as a matter of course."

Those renunciations are all very noble, and in your twenties, very easy. But when you're in your fifties and you look around you, if you have in fact made that sacrifice for art, and your friends haven't, and they have the beach houses and they have the nice homes and they have the nice cars. . . .

DLB: You left out the boat.

Higgins: And the boat. I forgot that, didn't I? I managed to get most of those things, but it was because I was practicing law, and I did have some good fortune now and again with book sales, *and I have worked like a horse.*

Not that it's been an act of the will on my part, working like a horse. I love to work. Jack McCrae said I'm the only writer he ever had in his stable of writers who loved to write. And I do. To my way of thinking the worst thing you can do to me—or pretty nearly the worst thing anyway—is interfere with my writing. My idea of a vacation is to write in the mornings and sail in the afternoons. And if it rains in the afternoon, then write in the afternoon too—that's an excellent vacation. When I can't work, I go nuts. That's why I have always been so hostile to people who have said I should write less because I'm asking too much of the readers too often. Tough for them.

DLB: I'm sure somebody gave that great advice to Charles Dickens.

Higgins: Probably, and I know they gave it to O'Hara because he had the same reaction I did.

DLB: Let's talk about teaching writing. What can you do for the kids?

Higgins: You teach them how to learn to write. Nobody can teach anybody how to write. Nobody could teach me.

DLB: Define "teaching them how to learn to write."

Higgins: I am of the old, old school. Dead white males, I suppose, only I'm not dead yet. I believe that a story should have a beginning and a middle and an end. So I tell my students that I want them to start at Point A and escort me through Point B to Point C. By "escort" I mean write down the stuff so that I will know what the characters are doing and what they're saying and maybe what they're thinking if you're using omniscient narrator. But *not* what *you* think of what they're doing, saying or planning to do. That will bring me happily to Point C, where I see the results of their behavior.

If you leave out the beginning and the end, you will have a *New Yorker* story and you may get published there, as I have not been able to do. And you will make a lot of money, but you will not have a story that I will want to read, and I don't think it will be one that you'll be proud of. What you'll have is a long vignette. I teach the Aristote-

lian triad: unity, emphasis, and coherence. I enforce that in my classes. They are self-selecting. Students get in by applying. Each submits a piece of fiction. If I think you have the stuff to weather the kind of criticism you're going to get, I'll let you in. And if I don't, I won't.

The "stuff" is first, you have to *want* to write. I can tell instantly if you really want to write or you think you've found a gut course here. Secondly, you have to know *how* to write, by which I mean, understand the English language, know what the words mean, how to form short declarative sentences, and, if you wish, long declarative sentences, compound sentences, and all those other things. When you start breaking the rules of grammar, you'd better know how to do it, and not do it so often that you annoy me.

All this stuff is kind of tedious, so usually fewer than thirty-five kids a semester take my two seminars. I think that's about the right number. They have a good time and I'm content. That's probably the most that should be subjected annually to that amount of abuse.

DLB: Does teaching writing make you self-conscious when you're writing?

Higgins: No. It invigorates me. Writing is a solitary sport like masturbation. You need some refreshment from it. I used to be a trial lawyer, and I enjoyed showing off in court—although I was often somewhat hindered by the judges and always interfered with by opposing counsel who didn't want me to do some of the things that I wanted to do to their clients. In the classroom I get to show off once more, but now I'm not interfered with by judges and opposing counsel. So it's enjoyable from that point of view. It gets me away from the machines too, for one afternoon a week, and that doesn't do any harm either. I enjoy it greatly, and when I get graded by the students, as required by the administration, I get high marks—so I guess they enjoy it too.

DLB: That's a good way to end.

Higgins: Yeah.

The Anthony Burgess Archive at the Harry Ransom Humanities Research Center

Stacey Peebles
Harry Ransom Humanities Research Center

In the spring of 1998 the Harry Ransom Humanities Research Center announced the acquisition of an extensive collection of author and composer Anthony Burgess, virtually complete except for several early manuscripts held elsewhere. The archive consists of manuscripts and corrected typescripts, reviews, correspondence, musical compositions, and Burgess's nearly complete collection of all of his own editions, including translations in various languages. The wide range of Burgess's interests reflects the broad interests of the HRC as well; the principal rare-books and manuscripts library of the University of Texas at Austin and one of the great libraries of the world, the HRC houses a collection of approximately one million books, thirty million manuscripts, more than five million photographs, and more than one hundred thousand works of art.

Liliana Burgess, the author's widow, felt that the HRC was the appropriate place for such a collection because of Burgess's place in world literature and his ties with writers whose works are also available for study there, such as strong holdings in James Joyce, Evelyn Waugh, T. S. Eliot, E. M. Forster, and hundreds of other modern British and Irish writers. The HRC's director, Thomas F. Staley, echoes her sentiments: "It was important for us to acquire Anthony Burgess's archive because he is such an important figure in the continuum of this century's literature. His work is an extension, on the one hand, of Joyce's experimentation while on the other it reflects a substantial broadening in theme and subject matter of British fiction as a whole. This is evident from his early *Malayan Trilogy,* which exposes brilliantly the absurdities of the last days of British imperialism, to *A Clockwork Orange,* with its anticipation of the turmoil of the 1960s, through his later darkly comic works of the 1980s."

The archive now at the HRC was previously housed in five different locations where Burgess had lived: Rome, two apartments in Monaco, London, and Lugano, where most of the musical material was held.

Anthony Burgess (photograph by Jerry Bauer)

A brief inspection reveals that the material is as diverse as the locations, as the collection includes everything from screenplays to a concerto grosso for guitar quartet and orchestra. The abundance and variety of material from such a prolific writer make the collection a fascinating one to examine.

Anthony Burgess, whose full name was John Anthony Burgess Wilson, was born in 1917 and

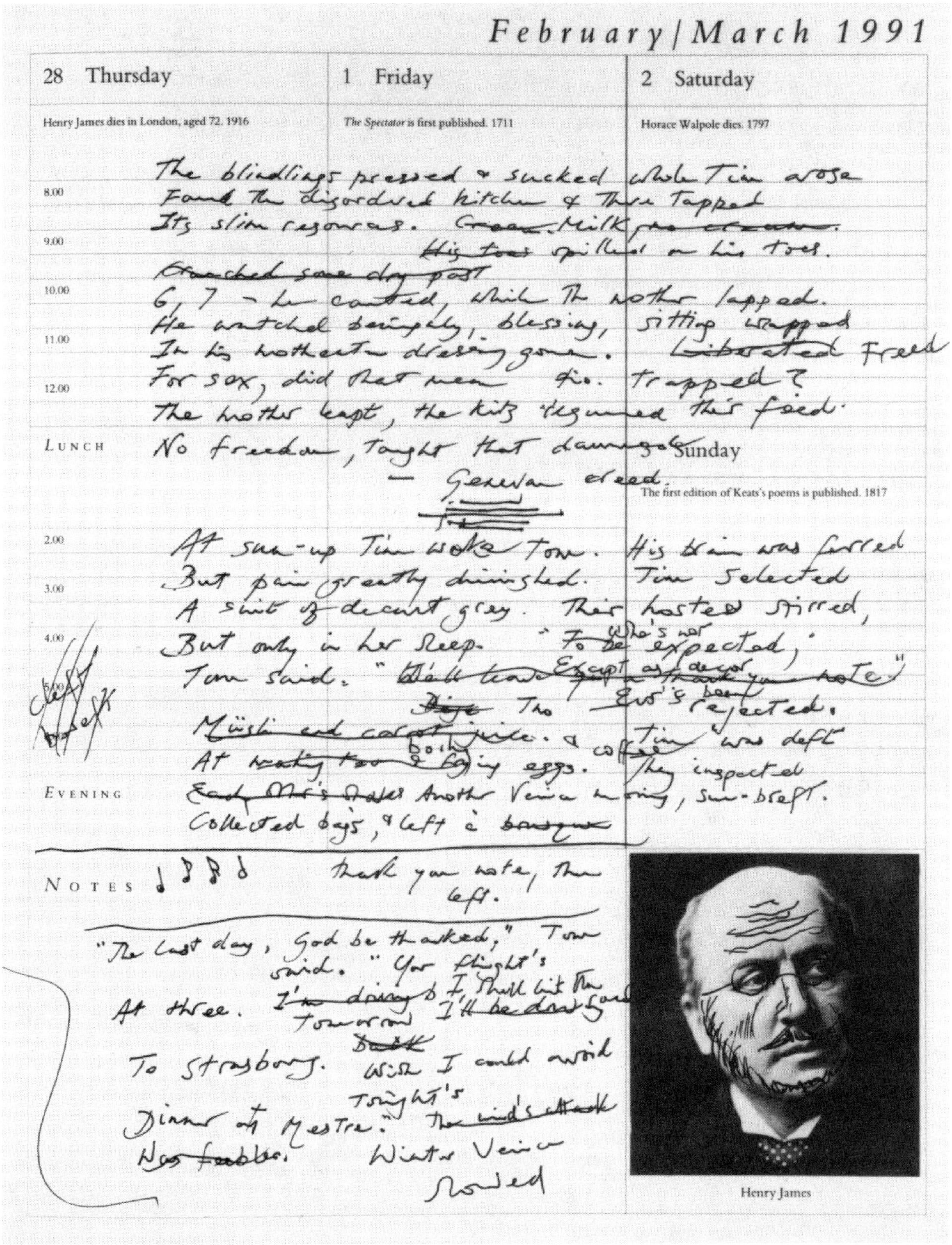

February / March 1991

28 Thursday	1 Friday	2 Saturday
Henry James dies in London, aged 72. 1916	*The Spectator* is first published. 1711	Horace Walpole dies. 1797

(handwritten draft verse, largely illegible)

The blindlings pressed & sucked while Tim arose
Found the disordered kitchen & there tapped
Its slim resources. Milk ...
His toes spilled on his toes.
...
6, 7 — he counted, while the mother lapped.
He watched boringly, blessing, sitting wrapped
In his mother's dressing gown. Freed
For sex, did that mean ... trapped?
The mother leapt, the kits resumed their feed.
No freedom, taught that damned — General creed.

At sun-up Tim woke Tom. His brain was furred
But pain greatly diminished. Tim selected
A suit of decent grey. Their hostess stirred,
But only in her sleep. "To be expected,"
Tom said. ... Evo's rejected.
... was deft
At ... eggs. They inspected
Another Venice morning, sun-bright.
Collected bags, & left a ...

NOTES ♪♪♪ thank you note, then left.

"The last day, God be thanked," Tom said. "Your flight's
At three. I'll ... I'll be dead ...
To Strasbourg. Wish I could avoid
Dinner at Mestre." Tonight's ...
No ... Winter Venice snowed.

Henry James

Page from Burgess's draft of Byrne, *his last novel (The Anthony Burgess Archive, Harry Ransom Humanities Research Center, The University of Texas at Austin)*

Page 1 from Burgess's musical adaptation of "The Wreck of the Deutschland," Gerard Manley Hopkins's poem (The Anthony Burgess Archive, Harry Ransom Humanities Research Center, The University of Texas at Austin)

became one of the most prolific and innovative writers of fiction in English of this century. His early interest in music and composition expanded into a love for literature when he began writing during a trip to Malaya in the 1950s. By the 1960s he was writing almost constantly, and in the early part of that decade he wrote five novels as well as a flood of reviews, scripts, and plays. Because of the large amount of material he had produced, his publisher convinced him to release two novels under the pseudonym Joseph Kell, and as a result one magazine unknowingly assigned Burgess to review his own book. It was a perfect opportunity for the sharp-witted author, and he did not hesitate to do so–presenting, of course, a favorable review. He traveled much during his life, and many of his novels are based on experiences in Gibraltar, Malaya, and Borneo, to name a few countries he visited. Burgess also taught at many universities in the United States and abroad; among other appointments, he was a visiting professor at Princeton University, a Distinguished Professor at the City College of New York, and a writer in residence at the University of New York at Buffalo during his career. He continued to work on a variety of projects, both in literature and music, until his death in 1993.

Rich Oram, head librarian at the HRC, sees the Burgess collection as an interesting one precisely because of this diversity: "Burgess was one of the major novelists of the post-war period, and he was especially engaging because of his interest in so many different areas of the humanities–from his traditional work in literary history to his imaginative view of the future. He is interesting not only because of his work, but also because of the shape of his unusual literary career."

The majority of the materials in the archive are from Burgess's work after 1970, and several of his earlier papers are held at the Mills Memorial Library of McMaster University in Ontario. Among many items of interest in the literary portion of the HRC's collection are the corrected typescripts of two of Burgess's Enderby novels, *Enderby Outside* (1968) and *Enderby's Dark Lady, or, No End to Enderby* (1984), the latter of which is accompanied by corrected proof copies and reviews of the book. The archive also includes several drafts of *Earthly Powers,* his 1980 novel that many critics regard as his masterpiece. The book, which took the author almost a decade to finish, was successively titled "The Affairs of Men," "The Prince of the Powers of the Air," and finally *Earthly Powers.* Burgess wrote a second draft in 1987 to adapt the novel to television, and this is supplemented by correspondence regarding the screen agreement. Both the Enderby novels and *Earthly Powers* are excellent representations of Burgess's work, because in them he explores two of his favorite themes: the condition of the poet and poetry in the Enderby books, and

the Pelagian/Augustinian cycle of history he foresees in *Earthly Powers.*

Burgess's most widely read novel is *A Clockwork Orange* (1962), the popularity of which increased with the release of Stanley Kubrick's motion-picture version in 1971. Written in a hybrid version of Russian and English, the book presents the life of the young teenager Alex, whose appetites are for brutal violence and Beethoven. Multiple editions of the book were published, which are included in the archive along with translations into Spanish, French, German, Russian, and several other languages. In 1987 Burgess adapted the novel into a one-act play with music. Burgess was disappointed with Kubrick's screen version of the story, which leaves out the crucial final chapter in which Alex decides to pursue marriage and family instead of anarchy. He once stated that he wrote the play in part to "stem the flow of amateur adaptations." The typescript of the play is accompanied by various reviews, correspondence, and catalogues.

In the 1970s Burgess wrote what he called his "TV tetrology" of specials on Moses, Shakespeare, Michelangelo, and Jesus of Nazareth, the last of which is represented in the collection by both the corrected typescript for the movie and the corrected typescript for his novel, *Man of Nazareth* (1979). Other biographical projects of interest are film scripts of his television portrait of Ernest Hemingway, *Grace Under Pressure* (1978), the unpublished typescript for a television project, *Marco Polo* (1978), the typescript for the television program *Attila* (1982), and the typescript of a television tribute to Benny Hill (1992). In 1993 Burgess published *A Dead Man in Deptford,* a study of the life and death of Christopher Marlowe, and the original typescript accompanies correspondence and reviews of the novel.

Burgess also did many translations, and perhaps his most famous is *ABBA ABBA,* a collection of sonnets by the nineteenth-century poet Giuseppe Giocchino Belli. Burgess translated the poems while maintaining the Petrarchan rhyme scheme, ABBA ABBA CDC CDC, a challenge that he thought of as a literary exercise. Belli wrote approximately three thousand poems, and in *ABBA ABBA* Burgess translates seventy-two of them. The original corrected typescript of the book is accompanied by notes for Burgess's novella about John Keats's death in Rome and his possible meeting with Belli. He also published a translation of Edmond Rostand's *Cyrano de Bergerac* (1971), and the manuscript is available for study with several drafts of theater adaptations. Also reflecting the author's fascination with translation of a sort is his corrected typescript of *Joysprick* (1973), an introduction to the language of James Joyce. This followed his controversial success in 1966 with *A*

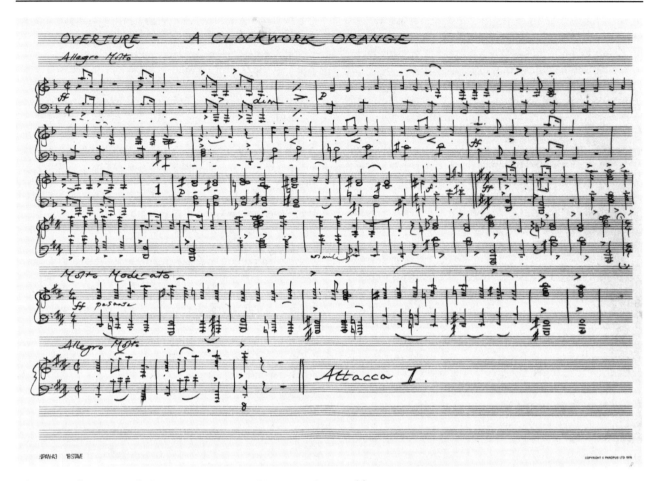

Sheet music from the score for Burgess's one-act play, A Clockwork Orange *(The Anthony Burgess Archive, Harry Ransom Humanities Research Center, The University of Texas at Austin)*

Shorter "Finnegans Wake," which reached a broad academic audience.

Burgess published a two-volume autobiography in 1986 and 1990: *Little Wilson and Big God: Being the First Part of the Confessions of Anthony Burgess* and *You've Had Your Time: The Second Part of the Confessions.* The first volume covers the years from 1917 to 1959 and ends with the diagnosis of an inoperable brain tumor that impelled him to start writing seriously. In it he openly describes his sexual escapades, a practice that led many critics to frown on the book. The more discreet second volume continues the story from 1959 until 1982. The HRC holds a copy of the corrected draft of the first volume, and a copy of the corrected typescript of the second.

Although most of his drafts are typewritten, the manuscript of his final novel, *Byrne,* published in 1995, is a notable exception. It was written in Monaco, by hand, across the pages of a Waterstone's Literary Diary of 1991. Each page of the daybook has a small picture of an author in the bottom corner, usually corresponding to the page with the date of their birth, death, or other noteworthy event. Burgess scrawled his novel across the space provided for appointments and notes and occasionally defaced or enhanced the writers' portraits. The result is a unique manuscript that reveals Burgess's signature sense of satire and inventiveness even in his final literary effort.

Burgess's collection of his own editions is extensive and will be available in tandem with the manuscript materials. It is comprised of Burgess's copies of many editions of his books in several languages, including first editions of *ABBA ABBA, Beard's Roman Women* (1976), and *Nothing Like the Sun: A Story of Shakespeare's Love Life* (1964).

Burgess's musical compositions comprise much of the archive, and though less well known than his literary work, they are nevertheless astonishing in their sophistication and variety. He wrote in practically every form, and the diversity probably results from his tendency to write for people and specific purposes rather than from simple inspiration. For example, for the 50th anniversary of the death of the Italian writer Gabriele

D'Annunzio, he set the rather long poem "La pioggia nel Pineto" to music, a piece for piano and countertenor that was performed in Amsterdam and Spotorno. Burgess published the autobiographical *This Man and His Music* in 1982, and in it he tells of listening to Claude Debussy's *L'Apres-midi d'un Faune* on a homemade crystal radio when he was twelve, which was the experience that inspired him to begin studying music fervently. He was mostly self-taught, and he failed to enter the Music Department at Manchester University only because he could not pass the required exam in physics. He decided then to enter the English Department instead. Dell Hollingsworth, music specialist at the Harry Ransom Center, notes that "composing was his first love, and had circumstances not, in his words, 'forced' him into a literary career, that is the vocation he would have chosen."

The musical portion of the archive includes manuscripts for approximately 130 works such as songs, piano works, concertos, scores for plays and motion pictures, string quartets, guitar quartets, sonatas and other chamber works, choral pieces, overtures, and even symphonies. There are also vocal pieces that set music to texts by James Joyce and Gerard Manley Hopkins, as well as songs based on texts by D. H. Lawrence for voice, flute, oboe, cello, and piano. Highlights of this part of the collection include the autograph score for the play *A Clockwork Orange,* which combines arrangements of Beethoven with some of Burgess's own music, and the autograph score for his radio play *Blooms of Dublin* (1986). The play is a musical version of *Ulysses,* and the score accompanies the original corrected typescript.

The Anthony Burgess archive is an impressive addition to the already formidable collection of contemporary British and American authors at the Harry Ransom Center. It also appropriately shares space with the first four folio editions of Shakespeare and the personal libraries of Wyndham Lewis, Ezra Pound, and Evelyn Waugh. Of special interest to Burgess scholars is the James Joyce archive, which includes the corrected first-edition page proofs of *Ulysses* and his library from his years in Trieste.

Director Staley is optimistic about the collection's potential value for scholars: "Anthony Burgess's archive is certainly one that reflects very well the life of a prolific and productive writer. I can think of very few writers in the twentieth century whose talent was as diverse as Burgess's; he was a major novelist, a screenwriter of note, a first-class composer of music, an incisive critic and also a frequent and engaging reviewer in the popular press. I would guess that although there will be immediate attention to the literary portion of the archive that music colleges and students of music will also benefit greatly from study of the materials."

Since the time of the original acquisition more of Burgess's material has become available, and the Harry Ransom Humanities Research Center has since added to the collection and will continue to pursue additional materials. Because the archive arrived at the same time as several other collections did, at press time only the musical material has been fully catalogued and made available for public use. A preliminary find list will be prepared in the future for the remaining portion of the archive.

University Press of Kansas

Fred M. Woodward
University Press of Kansas

The progress of scholarly publishing in Kansas corroborates the state's motto, *ad astra per aspera,* which is usually glossed as "to the stars through difficulties." Kansans pride themselves on their doughty survival through cyclones, droughts, blizzards, and grasshoppers. In contrast, the University Press of Kansas for almost four decades suffered an unnatural inclemency—section 4 of article 15 of the state constitution, which prescribed that all public printing must be performed by state printing facilities. At every crucial turn, that legislation played a major role in thwarting the ascent of the press to publishing prominence.

Like the history of any press, that of the University Press of Kansas has been shaped by the main currents of higher education and scholarly publishing and by the tributaries of local influences. For its first thirty-six years local forces arrested the development of the press. From 1946 until 1982 Printing, Money, and Bureaucracy rode together as the Three Horsemen of the Apocalypse. Of this unholy trinity, Printing proved to be the most baneful.

The prehistory of the University Press of Kansas, like that of other university publishers, hinted at the difficulties with which it would grapple. As early as 1911, University of Kansas (KU) Chancellor Frank Strong, who regarded published research as an effective way to publicize the school, reported that "important work done by members of our Faculty . . . had of necessity been sent for publication to other Universities and to Commercial publishers." He explicitly complained that laws governing state printing hampered university printing and binding. Joining Strong's brief, Professors Merle Thorpe and William Carruth also deplored the excessive printing and binding costs that constrained the university's fledgling efforts in publishing.

Twenty American university presses were founded in the 1920s and 1930s, a fact that doubtless contributed to growing faculty interest in the University of Kansas having its own publishing house. On 9 January 1940 the KU Committee on Publications

and Printing recommended to the Faculty Senate "that the Administration be invited to consider establishing a University of Kansas Press." The senate adopted the recommendation, but World War II intervened before the university administration could act on the faculty's invitation.

War or no war, other universities joined the publishing fray: Tennessee and Vanderbilt in 1940, Nebraska and Wayne State in 1941, Kentucky and Syracuse in 1943, South Carolina in 1944, and Alabama and Florida in 1945. At KU the machinations chiefly involved an American serviceman in Australia, a graduate school administrator, and a former executive of the Dole Hawaiian Pineapple Company. Dr. Clyde K. Hyder (1902–1992), a wartime cryptographer in the United States Army Air Force and a peacetime English professor at the University of Kansas, received an unexpected invitation from John H. Nelson, assistant dean and secretary of the Graduate Research Council, to serve as the first editor of the yet-to-be established publishing operation at KU. The former pineapple executive was Chancellor Deane W. Malott, who had most recently forsaken the Harvard faculty for Kansas. While Malott's approval was necessary for the plan to succeed, Nelson was the moving force behind the organizing of the University of Kansas Press.

Malott seemed poised to endorse Nelson's initiative. In August 1941 he had changed the name of the Bureau of Printing to the University of Kansas Press, a change that prefigured a more organized approach to publishing but blurred the distinction between printing and publishing. In November 1943 his executive secretary, Raymond M. Nichols, had answered an inquiry from the University of Alabama about setting up a press: "Just before the war broke out we were studying the possibility of establishing a press for publication of research work of the faculty but that plan has, of necessity, been pigeon-holed for the duration. . . . After the war we hope that we will find it possible to complete our plans. . . ."

Fred M. Woodward, director of the press since 1981 (photograph by Doug Koch)

I. 1946–1967

The postwar influx of students most likely diverted Malott from thoughts of publishing. But Nelson persevered, and the Publishing Division of the University of Kansas Press was formally established with Hyder as its part-time editor. Nelson, who chaired the Press Publications Committee until 1963, called the inaugural meeting to order on 9 January 1946. The committee promptly approved *A Malariologist in Many Lands,* by Marshall A. Barber, as the first book to be published by the new operation.

For those familiar with the founding of university presses, it is superfluous to observe that the University of Kansas Press in its infancy was understaffed and undercapitalized. In fact, Hyder *was* the staff; the Printing Division had to fill the book orders; and the graduate office handled the bills. Other presses managed to outgrow similar humble origins, but local conditions constrained the University of Kansas Press. Its godfather and overseer from 1946 until 1963, Dean Nelson "had thought of the Press as necessarily remaining a small one, financial resources being limited, but always publishing good books." Small at birth and malnourished, the press hardly grew. Handicapped by the state's printing regulations and forced to rely on the limited capabilities of the on-campus printshop, the press published only seven titles in its first five years. Although admitted to the Association of American University Presses in the year it was founded, the press was briefly placed on probation for not meeting minimum standards of staffing and publishing output. Even in the early 1950s Thomas Ryther, head of KU's Printing Division, professed an inability to print more than four books a year.

During these early years and afterward Clyde Hyder subscribed to the principles in the policy statement that he had drafted in 1946 for the committee and the chancellor to approve. "We believe," he had written, "that the chief purpose of a university press, like that of a university, is to contribute to society by the enlargement and propagation of knowledge. The Press should publish some books which interest only particular bodies of scholars and which can hardly have a wide circulation. . . . University presses have long stressed the principle of intrinsic value, rather than the immediate appeal, of what is put into print."

What the University of Kansas Press put into print upheld these principles, but its growth was stunted. In the 1950s the press published seventy-one books; in the 1960s it managed only seventy-five. Lack of money cramped the press at a time when the university was short on everything but students. Printing problems continued. The formulaic lament dwelled on the binding bottleneck at the state printing plant in Topeka. Understaffing was a chronic condition for the first twenty years. Not until fall 1953 did Hyder become the full-time director (and editor), and his entire staff consisted of no more than 1¼ clerk-typists until July 1965.

Despite these constraints the press published meritorious works, including the monumental 18-volume *Treatise on Invertebrate Paleontology* (1953–1966) and Lawrence S. Kubie's *Neurotic Distortion of the Creative Process* (1958), which was translated into German, Spanish, and Japanese. Perhaps its most distinguished titles concerned eighteenth- and nineteenth-century English literature: for example, Ralph Wardle's *Mary Wollstonecraft: A Critical Biography* (1951), Kathleen Williams's *Jonathan Swift and the Age of Compromise* (1958), W. P. Albrecht's *Hazlitt and the Creative Imagination* (1965), and Alan Dugald McKillop's *James Thomson* (1967). Like other presses at the time, the University of Kansas Press had an eclectic list. Through 1966 its output could be categorized roughly as one-third in literature and the humanities; one-third in history, biography, and the social sciences; and one-third in medicine and the sciences. Indicative of the eclecticism were L. E. Richdale's *Sexual Behavior in Penguins* (1951), James Seaver's *The Persecution of the Jews in the Roman Empire (300–438)* (1952), Thomas Bonner's *The Kansas Doctor: A Century of Pioneering* (1959), and Robert Riegel's *American Feminists* (1963).

In November 1963 the Press Publications Committee, with the encouragement of Dean W. P. Albrecht, concluded that the press had accumulated financial reserves sufficient to contemplate an expansion. Academic presses in Oklahoma to the south and Nebraska to the north had helped to raise awareness that other presses were prospering in comparison with the University of Kansas Press. Inhibiting its growth, the committee concluded, was the ever-present printing problem.

With faculty sentiment favoring the growth of the press, interest flared about how it might be achieved, and the administration commissioned a wide-ranging report by the press committee to examine "the present state of the University of Kansas Press and [to make] recommendations for its expansion and improvement." In addition to inadequate staffing and space and the restrictive legal handicaps, the June 1964 report faulted the "lack of sufficiently positive directives from the University Administration concerning the role and eventual stature desired of the Press."

Among the early results of the report was the edict from Raymond Nichols that henceforth the name *University of Kansas Press* belonged solely to the publisher. The press also moved into better quarters in Watson Library and began to add to its staff in 1965. Casting a pall on this progress, however, was a failed attempt that same year to pass a law exempting the press from the printing statute. The bill died in committee, and its death augured ill for the expansion plans.

In January 1966 the administrations of the University of Kansas and Kansas State University (KSU) began talking seriously about cosponsoring the press. Doubtless KU's desire for a larger, better-funded operation dovetailed with the urge of KSU's faculty, led by Robin Higham, a military historian from a British publishing family, to get involved in scholarly publishing. Earlier inquiries into the possibility of starting up a separate press in Manhattan, Kansas, had been found to be economically unfeasible. Hyder recalled that the Oklahoma press director, Savoie Lottinville, had advised the KSU contingent to cooperate rather than compete with the University of Kansas Press.

In short order Wichita State University (WSU) joined the talks. A Tri-University Press Committee, under the guidance of KU administrator Francis Heller and with KU geographer T. R. Smith as chair, was appointed to study the proposal. The committee issued its report in April 1966. Recommending staff and space increases, the report called for the annual production of titles to increase from a range of eight to ten to a range of twenty-five to thirty, with the objective of increasing the backlist from seventy to two hundred fifty "within 5 to 10 years." With Hyder's retirement looming in 1967, the report advocated "the appointment of a full-time professional Director." In October 1966 the Board of Regents authorized the "joint operation in the publication of scholarly books," and on 1 July 1967 the cooperative enterprise began operations as the University Press of Kansas.

In the words of the *Kansas City Star,* the press harbored "lusty intentions of becoming a major university press" (9 July 1967). Provost James R. Surface of KU sounded the keynote: "By combining the resources of the three state universities of Kansas, we hope to make possible the creation of an expanded and more significant scholarly press than any of us could provide singly." At the 16 November 1967 official founding of the reorganized operation, the poet Bruce Cutler, Distinguished Professor of English at WSU, hailed the cooperative effort as "a powerful leaven in our state's academic loaf."

II. 1967-1969

To meet these rising expectations, the Board of Trustees hired as director John P. Dessauer (1924-) from Indiana University Press, where he had served as associate director. Dessauer, who arrived in Kansas just as the golden era of university publishing started to wane, fought three familiar battles–printing, money, and bureaucracy–with mixed results. The tangled thicket of the state's bureaucracy especially complicated matters. For example, publishing contracts were held up for a time until February 1968, when the state attorney general issued an opinion that the press was indeed authorized to enter into such agreements. The impervious state printing statute resisted every legal maneuver, including one that sought to persuade the attorney general to rule that manufacturing scholarly books did not constitute "public printing"–a distinction that naturally comes to the minds of academic publishers when they contemplate piddling sales figures or visit their overstocked warehouses.

Dessauer, whose frequent faculty visits to the member campuses helped to solidify the consortium arrangement, resigned in summer 1969 and headed off to the Grolier Press in New York City. His departure took the steam out of the heralded expansion plans. Dessauer went on to write *Book Publishing: The Basic Introduction* and to become a well-known statistician for the publishing industry. His greatest legacy is the American Presidency Series, which to this day remains one of the chief adornments of the University Press of Kansas publishing program. The idea for the series originated in early 1968 with James O. Maloney, a member of the Editorial Committee and a KU professor of engineering who had looked futilely for concise biographies of presidents. The idea was refined by KU historian Donald R. McCoy, who was inspired by Richard Neustadt's landmark book, *Presidential Power,* and astutely reasoned that what was really needed were not biographies but histories of presidential administrations. Currently thirty-two volumes of the highly regarded series are in print.

Although his directorship was too brief to have lasting impact on the list, except for the presidency series, Dessauer oversaw the publication of some noteworthy books, including artist Thomas Hart Benton's autobiography, *An American in Art* (1969), and a biography of a Kansas newspaperman, *Ed Howe: Country Town Philosopher* (1969), by Calder Pickett.

In looking for Dessauer's successor, the search committee discovered at least one potential candidate who found the restrictive printing statute intolerable. "The printing problem," he observed upon withdrawing his name, "is analogous to forcing a race horse to run on three legs, and a University Press that cannot take a given job to the best-qualified printer in the country . . . is forever condemned to either unsatisfactory or heavily overpriced work."

III. 1970-1981

From Dessauer's departure in 1969 to spring 1970, Assistant Director and Editor in Chief Yvonne Willingham served as acting director. In May 1970 John H. Langley (1914-1988) became the third director of the press. A publishing veteran, Langley came from Duke University Press, where he was assistant director and business manager. The 1970s was a period of cautious readjustment for scholarly publishers, and the word *crisis* appeared with alarming frequency in their shop talk, speeches, and writings. But under Langley the University Press of Kansas enjoyed something of a boomlet during the decade. Production of titles increased 67 percent over the level of the 1960s, and sales during the fiscal year 1980 were 162 percent higher than in 1970-1971. The size of the staff increased from six in 1970 to seven in 1981. In constant dollars the deficit that Langley had inherited did not worsen, even though financial support for the press languished during a period of high inflation. In 1978 the annual production of titles rose to eighteen, but budgetary stringencies–exacerbated, of course, by overpriced state printing–dropped this production total below ten by 1981, when Langley retired in June.

During Langley's tenure, another milestone in the history of the press occurred when the Board of Regents reorganized it in February 1976. Effective 1 July 1976, the universities of Emporia State, Pittsburg, and Fort Hays joined in sponsoring the state's publishing enterprise, which was renamed the Regents Press of Kansas. As before, its Board of Trustees was composed of the chief academic officers of the sponsoring institutions. A lively raconteur, Langley demonstrated a deft public relations touch in

Covers for award-winning books published by the University Press of Kansas (photograph by James Busse)

his vigorous and continuing efforts to make the consortium work.

In acquisitions he had a straightforward philosophy: publish the best available books. That he succeeded can be seen in books such as the two-volume autobiography of Chang Kuo-t'ao, *The Rise of the Chinese Communist Party* (1971–1972)–which the *American Historical Review* hailed as "an important event"–and the eight-volume *Opera Omnia di Sidney Sonnino* (1973–1976, 1982), which received the Howard R. Marraro Prize in Italian Historical Studies. Other notable works include John T. Alexander's translation of S. F. Platonov's *Time of Troubles: A Historical Study of the Internal Crisis and Social Struggles in Sixteenth- and Seventeenth-Century Muscovy* (1970) and Hal Sears's *Sex Radicals: Free Love in High Victorian America* (1977).

Some of the titles published during the Langley era prefigured the list-building initiatives of the 1980s and 1990s. Of course, the American Presidency Series was begun, with the inaugural volumes being Paolo Coletta's *The Presidency of William Howard Taft*

(1973) and Forrest McDonald's *The Presidency of George Washington* (1974). As exemplars of regional publishing, *Kansas Impressions: Photographs and Words* (1972) by Wes Lyle and James Fisher, *The Land of the Post Rock: Its Origins, History, and People* (1975) by Grace Muilenburg and Ada Swineford, and *Wildflowers and Weeds of Kansas* (1979) by Janét Bare showed the possibilities of publishing books on Kansas that would reach a wide audience. The roots of the American West list can be traced to books such as John Clark's edited volume, *The Frontier Challenge: Responses to the Trans-Mississippi West* (1971); Jimmy Skagg's *The Cattle-Trailing Industry: Between Supply and Demand, 1866–1890* (1973); Craig Miner and William Unrau's *The End of Indian Kansas: A Study in Cultural Revolution* (1977); and Robert Athearn's *In Search of Canaan. Black Migration to Kansas, 1879–80* (1978). Even the faint outlines of the future commitment to military studies can be glimpsed in the Eisenhower Foundation's *D-Day: The Normandy Invasion in Retrospect* (1971), Norman Saul's *Sailors in Revolt: The Russian*

Baltic Fleet in 1917 (1978), and Coletta's *Admiral Bradley A. Fiske and the American Navy* (1978).

Although they ultimately proved to be a cul-de-sac in developing the list, books in the humanities published by Langley maintained high standards. Among the most noteworthy belonged to American and English literary criticism. W. P. Albrecht's *The Sublime Pleasures of Tragedy: A Study of Critical Theory from Dennis to Keats* (1975), Robert Hipkiss's *Jack Kerouac: Prophet of the New Romanticism* (1976), and Daniel Schneider's *The Crystal Cage: Adventures of the Imagination in the Fiction of Henry James* (1977) all came to be regarded as standard references on their subjects. In recognizing the quality of what the press contributed to humanistic scholarship, the American Council of Learned Societies awarded it a $7,500 grant in May 1976.

IV. 1981–1998

When Langley retired in 1981, the Regents Press of Kansas was a good but small press in some financial difficulty. Its very existence was called into question. To help provide an answer, the trustees invited David H. Gilbert, then director of the University of Nebraska Press, to review the operation in February 1981 and make recommendations. His sensible report carried the day, and the trustees once again set the press on a course toward expansion. If the trustees' plans were to succeed, the state printer's grip on the press had to loosen.

It did. Fred Woodward (1943–), formerly marketing director at the University of South Carolina Press, arrived in November 1981 as the fourth director, and he was given a mandate to build the publishing program and put the press on a sound financial footing. In February 1982 the state printer, at the urging of the KU administration, at last granted the press permission to purchase book printing and binding (but not typesetting) in the commercial marketplace. From this beneficence, all else flowed. Heartened by this action, the trustees agreed to pay off the $162,000 deficit the press had and to increase the annual operating subsidy. With access to commercial printers, the press realized immediate improvements in pricing and scheduling. The change also permitted it to begin publishing for the popular market color-illustrated regional books such as *Kansas in Color,* a perennial best-seller since the fall of 1982. The long-sought expansion began to occur.

Another obstacle to success was surmounted when the imprint changed. In the opinion of many, *Regents Press of Kansas* proved to be an unsatisfactory name on two counts: (1) outside the state it was not

immediately recognized as the name of a scholarly publisher; and (2) the operation was then regularly confused with the now defunct Regents Publishing Company of New York City. Without ruffling too many feathers, the Board of Regents in June of 1982 restored the name *University Press of Kansas* to the press.

In April 1986 the printing problems were resolved when Kansas Governor John Carlin signed into law Senate Bill 643 exempting the press altogether from the state printing requirement. This action freed the press to work with commercial typesetters and printers for all of its printing.

Annual title output has grown incrementally during the past sixteen years: from 9 titles in fiscal year 1983 to 31 in 1989 to 50 in 1997. As of mid 1998, the press had published 827 books since its founding. Of that total, 525, or 63.5 percent, have appeared since mid 1982. Annual sales have increased 918 percent during this period.

Adequately capitalized and liberated, the press managed to solve many of its long-standing problems. Needing room to grow, it moved its book inventory into a newly built warehouse with a storage capacity of 535,000 books in 1989. In 1991 on land donated by the Kansas University Endowment Association it constructed an office facility just north of the Yankee Tank Creek that runs through the West Campus. The costs of both the warehouse and offices were paid from funds generated by book sales. In early 1986 the press converted from a manual to an electronic order fulfillment system. By the end of 1998 the permanent staff had grown to thirteen, but these physical and staffing improvements, however crucial, were only means to a greater end. Former University of Chicago Press director Roger Shugg said almost thirty years ago on the KU campus that "a press exists only to publish and what it publishes tells the world who and what it is."

The mission of the press is "to extend the reach and reputation"–to borrow University of California Press Director James Clark's pithy phrase–of the six Kansas Regents universities. It fulfills that mission by publishing scholarly books that advance knowledge and regional books that contribute to an understanding of Kansas, the Great Plains, and the Midwest. In contrast to his predecessors, who embraced a catholic acquisitions program in order to represent the diverse interests of the home faculties, Woodward set out to focus list-building efforts in specific areas as a means to attract the best possible manuscripts and thereby to build a national reputation for excellence. In choosing this path the University Press of Kansas was emulating some but not all academic presses.

Since 1982 the editorial program has evolved–in often linear but sometimes convoluted ways–into one that focuses most broadly on history, political science, and philosophy, excluding the regional list. It concentrates specifically on military studies, American history (especially political and western), presidential studies, U.S. government and public policy, legal studies, and social and political philosophy. Active series include: Modern War Studies, American Presidency Series, Development of Western Resources, Studies in Government and Public Policy, American Political Thought, and Landmark Law Cases and American Society. Still evolving, the University Press of Kansas has recently announced two new series: Feminist Ethics and CultureAmerica, the latter being a new venture in American studies.

By most impartial accounts the strategy of specialization or niche list-building has succeeded. The lists in presidential and military studies are regarded by the cognoscenti as nonpareil. Lists in constitutional and legal studies, the American West, urban studies, and American political thought rank among the very best. While the University Press of Kansas is not a major press if judged solely in terms of title production and sales volume, it has steadily ascended toward the stars. Its ascent is confirmed not only by such objective criteria as a disproportionate number of book prizes and commendations, major media reviews, and book club adoptions but also by commentators who say as much in print. In a cover feature that appeared in its 3 July 1998 issue *The Chronicle of Higher Education* (*CHE*) profiled the press as "a distinctive model of success in turbulent times." Kathleen McDermott, the editorial director of the History Book Club, concurrently observed that Kansas "has really started to climb up to that top tier of university presses."

Accounting for this growth in eminence are, of course, the actual books and authors. Some of the award-winning books published since 1982 include: *Novus Ordo Seclorum: The Intellectual Origins of the Constitution* (1985) by Forrest McDonald, the 1987 Jefferson Lecturer in the Humanities; two Lincoln Prize winners, *The Presidency of Abraham Lincoln* (1994) by Phillip Shaw Paludan and *Decision in the West: The Atlanta Campaign of 1864* (1992) by Albert Castel; two Fletcher Pratt Award winners by Steven Woodworth, *Jefferson Davis and His Generals: The Failure of Confederate Command in the West* (1990) and *Davis and Lee at War*

(1995); the monumental *Flora of the Great Plains* (1986); *Regime Politics: Governing Atlanta, 1946–1988* (1989) by Clarence Stone; *The Mythic West in Twentieth-Century America* (1986) by Robert Athearn; and *The Middle West: Its Meaning in American Culture* (1989) by James Shortridge.

Among other prizewinning titles are Richard DeLeon's *Left Coast City: Progressive Politics in San Francisco, 1975–1991* (1991); Donald Baucom's *The Origins of SDI, 1944–1983* (1992); William Skelton's *An American Profession of Arms: The Army Officer Corps, 1784–1861* (1993); David Adams's *Education for Extinction: American Indians and the Boarding School Experience, 1828–1928* (1995); Charles Walcott and Karen Hult's *Governing the White House: From Hoover Through LBJ* (1995); Gareth Davies's *From Opportunity to Entitlement: The Transformation and Decline of Great Society Liberalism* (1996); Norman Saul's *Concord and Conflict: The United States and Russia, 1867–1914* (1996); William Davis's *The Cause Lost: Myths and Realities of the Confederacy* (1996); Charles Shindo's *Dust Bowl Migrants in the American Imagination* (1996); and Michael Durey's *Transatlantic Radicals and the Early American Republic* (1997). Almost certainly the most prestigious award bestowed upon a University Press of Kansas book is the 1997 Bancroft Prize, which David Kyvig's *Explicit and Authentic Acts: Amending the U.S. Constitution, 1776–1995* (1996) received.

The history of the University Press of Kansas testifies to the resilience of scholarly publishing as well as to the value of persistence. Handicapped, stunted, and beleaguered for more than half of its life, the press has persevered for more than a half century of enlarging and propagating knowledge. As the twentieth century closes, like other scholarly publishers it faces new challenges occasioned by declining markets for serious nonfiction, the rapid pace of technological change, and the diminishing prestige of humanities and social science research in academe. To thrive in this shifting environment, the University Press of Kansas must find better ways of disseminating knowledge to a larger public. To cope with this uncertain future, Woodward acknowledges his guiding principles in the *CHE* article: "I say to myself: thrift, selectivity, creativity. Don't exceed your reach. Keep an eye on content, content, content." Circumstances may change, but the commitment stays the same: *ad astra per aspera*.

James Jones Papers in the Handy Writers' Colony Collection at the University of Illinois at Springfield

Thomas J. Wood

University of Illinois at Springfield

To some extent the fiction of James Jones is always autobiographical. His novel *Some Came Running* (1957) and many of his short stories are based on his childhood and early adult years in the Wabash Valley of southeastern Illinois. Drawing on his army experiences in Hawaii, on Guadalcanal, and in the United States before, during, and after World War II, Jones created his great war trilogy—*From Here to Eternity* (1951), *The Thin Red Line* (1962), and *Whistle* (1978)—and from his experiences in Paris and Europe during the 1960s he wrote his novels *Go to the Widow-Maker* (1967), *The Merry Month of May* (1971), and *A Touch of Danger* (1973).

Jones published seven novels and two nonfiction books, and he wrote short stories, screenplays, and letters. His papers, like the settings of his fiction and of his life, are geographically dispersed: collections of materials related to him are at Boston University, Harvard University, New York University, Princeton University, the University of Illinois at Urbana-Champaign, and the University of Oregon. However, the largest collections of Jones's papers are divided among three major depositories: the Beinecke Library at Yale University, the Harry Ransom Humanities Research Center at the University of Texas at Austin, and the Brookens Library at the University of Illinois at Springfield.

Of these three major collections, the James Jones papers at the University of Illinois at Springfield is the smallest. However, it has special significance because it includes materials from Jones's formative period in his development as a successful writer. The manuscripts, correspondence, photographs, and other items at Springfield illuminate his life from his awakening desire to write while in the peacetime regular army in Hawaii and through his intense experiences during combat at Pearl Harbor and on Guadalcanal, his return to his hometown and first serious attempts at writing, his

remarkable success with *From Here to Eternity,* and his marriage and final departure from Illinois in 1957.

The Jones papers at the University of Illinois at Springfield are part of a larger collection that reveals his association with Harry and Lowney Handy of Robinson, Illinois. With the encouragement and financial assistance of the Handys, Jones wrote his first unpublished novel, "They Shall Inherit the Laughter," his first published short stories, and *From Here to Eternity.* In 1950 Jones and the Handys began a writers' colony that operated in the nearby town of Marshall until the death of Lowney Handy in 1964.

In 1983–1984 J. Michael Lennon and Jeffrey Van Davis of Sangamon State University (now the University of Illinois at Springfield) produced *James Jones: Reveille to Taps,* a PBS television documentary on the life of Jones that was first broadcast in 1984. Lennon and Van Davis interviewed many of Jones's friends and acquaintances in Robinson and Marshall, and the two producers discovered a large collection of material in the possession of Margaret Turner, Lowney Handy's sister-in-law. Turner generously donated the material to the university, which currently maintains it as the Handy Writers' Colony Collection in the archives at Brookens Library.

The material was in disorder when the university archives received it, and only after five years was the collection—which occupies thirty-four cubic feet of space and fills seventy-seven boxes on 42.5 linear feet of shelving—finally organized in a logical, useful way. The scope and depth of this collection are impressive. Lowney Handy had collected an array of documents about the Handy Colony and her association with Jones, and among these are photographs; newspaper clippings; bank, insurance, and other business records; more than two thousand letters; personal papers of the Handys; and manuscripts and galleys of many of the writers associated with the colony. Even notes that the

James Jones in Illinois

A Guide to the Handy Writers' Colony Collection

in the Sangamon State University
Library Archives

by Thomas J. Wood and Meredith Keating

Cover for the catalogue of Jones material from his early years as a writer

colony writers left in Lowney Handy's screen door were preserved.

The most valuable components of the collection are the hundreds of letters between Jones and the Handys; copies of correspondence between Jones and his Scribners editors, Maxwell Perkins and Burroughs Mitchell; a small collection of Jones's personal papers; and the notes, drafts, manuscripts, and galleys of his early novels and short stories. Many magazine and newspaper clippings in the Handy Writers' Colony Collection are also pertinent to Jones's early life and writing career.

Several illuminating items are from Jones's years in the regular army on Oahu, Hawaii (1939–1942). Jones had enlisted soon after graduating from high school in 1939 because the ruin of his family's fortunes in the Great Depression had made it virtually impossible for him to attend college. Although he had rather vague aspirations to write, his authorial ambition was inspired by his reading of Thomas Wolfe's *Look Homeward, Angel* (1929) in the library at Hickam Field in

Hawaii. After the attack on Pearl Harbor, Jones realized that he was fated for combat duty, and he brooded on the possibility that he might be killed before he could realize his dream of becoming a writer.

While most of his surviving correspondence from this period is in the Yale collection, one particularly moving letter to Mary Ann Jones, his younger sister, is in the Handy Writers' Colony Collection. Jones's mother had died in 1941, and his mood had been darkened by his father's suicide two months before he wrote this bitter and despairing letter, dated 20 May 1942. In it Jones expresses his disgust at the calculated dehumanization of military life, which he calls a "corrupt, ignorant, monotonous rut." He also rankles at the "favoritism . . . graft and red tape" imposed by the officers, and these became important themes in *From Here to Eternity* and his other writings. He concludes this letter with a postscript: "I wish I was a dog. Dogs just eat and sleep and bark."

Jones's only bright spot in this gloomy letter is in the prospect of attending writing classes at the University of Hawaii one day a week. The University of Illinois at Springfield collection includes some examples of his assigned writing–which already demonstrates a characteristic sincerity and realistic power of expression–that he completed for his classes at Hawaii. Most notable is his eight-page typed essay on Stephen Crane's *The Red Badge of Courage* (1895). In this piece–which has been published in *The James Jones Reader* (1991), edited by James R. Giles and J. Michael Lennon–Jones dismisses Crane's fictional depiction of courage in combat for being unrealistic when he compares it to his own experiences during the attack on Pearl Harbor. But the primary interest of the essay lies in its vivid, detailed, eyewitness account of the morning of 7 December 1941. Jones proved to be the only major writer who witnessed the event, and he wrote about it in autobiographical and fictional accounts at least four more times in his career.

Other items dating from Jones's time in Hawaii include snapshots that he took in and around Schofield Barracks and two small notebooks in which he recorded his impressions of incidents and personalities that he used as bases for shaping both some stories and some later characters and episodes in *From Here to Eternity*. One notebook records an incident involving a comrade named Maggio being sent to the stockade, and when Jones incorporated this incident into *From Here to Eternity* without even changing the name of his character, the writer was sued–although unsuccessfully–by the real Maggio.

The centerpiece of the Jones papers in the Handy Writers' Colony Collection is the material dating from years when Jones was associated with the Handys. After he was wounded in combat on Guadalcanal early in 1943, he was sent back to the United States to recover. That fall Jones was on furlough and visited Robinson, Illinois, where he met the Handys, a prosperous but childless couple. Lowney Handy had a deep interest in creative writing and was immediately impressed by Jones's desire to write. In 1944 she obtained a psychological discharge for Jones, and he came to live with the couple in their home on Mulberry Street in Robinson. Quickly convinced of Jones's potential as a writer, she wrote in a letter to one of his commanding officers, "how can you or I say that the war today, or the things that Jones may write tomorrow, are the greater in importance. Only a hundred years and the voice of many can answer that."

Harry Handy was also friendly with Jones and accepted him into the household almost as a son. There, with Lowney Handy's advice, Jones labored on "They Shall Inherit the Laughter," his first novel, about a bitter young veteran returning home from the war. The Handy Writers' Colony Collection includes Jones's preliminary notes, sketches, and three complete

drafts (the last of which is 788 pages long) of this unpublished novel. Of special interest is a list of characters in the novel and their real-life counterparts. "They Shall Inherit the Laughter" was indeed a roman à clef based on Jones's friends and family in Robinson.

In 1945 Jones took this manuscript to New York, to the editorial offices of Charles Scribner's Sons, and boldly insisted on showing it to Maxwell Perkins, the renowned editor of Thomas Wolfe's fiction. Although Perkins saw some merit in "They Shall Inherit the Laughter," he did not feel the novel could be published. He recognized Jones's talent for writing realistic prose, however, and encouraged him to pursue his idea for a novel based on his experiences in the peacetime army in Hawaii and culminating with Pearl Harbor. Encouraged by a $500 advance from Scribner's, Jones eagerly set to work on the new novel and eventually fashioned these extensive notes, sketches, and time lines for the themes, characters, and action of the novel into *From Here to Eternity*. Much of this preliminary material is preserved in the collection of the University of Illinois at Springfield.

From 1946 until 1950 Jones worked hard on this novel, and, since much of his writing was being done in Robinson, the Handys added a room to their home to accommodate his work. Every winter during this time he and Lowney Handy traveled through the Southwest to California, and Jones worked there as well. In 1949 the Handys purchased a jeep and trailer for him, and these made the trips convenient and productive for Jones. Because Harry Handy often stayed home in Illinois to work, dozens of letters written between him, Lowney Handy, and Jones document these travels and the writing of *From Here to Eternity* in great detail. When Jones and Lowney Handy were apart during that period, they exchanged many letters that chronicle in searing detail their complex, often troubled relationship. George Hendrick published a revealing sample of these in *To Reach Eternity: The Letters of James Jones* (1989).

Jones's papers in the Handy Writers' Colony Collection reveal the diligence and care he spent in writing his first novel to be published. The collection includes the untitled, 200-page, fourteen-chapter draft that Jones in 1946 sent to Maxwell Perkins, who apparently was impressed with it and dispatched a second $500 advance, although he suggested extensive revisions. Lowney Handy, who had a fondness for diet fads, recorded Jones's reaction to Perkins's encouragement in red ink on the first page of this draft: "Jim *was dazed!* It threw him for *six months.* . . . I had him on a fast." The collection also includes a partial draft that Jones prepared in response to Perkins's comments and that Lowney Handy labeled "second trial rewrite . . . (*strug-*

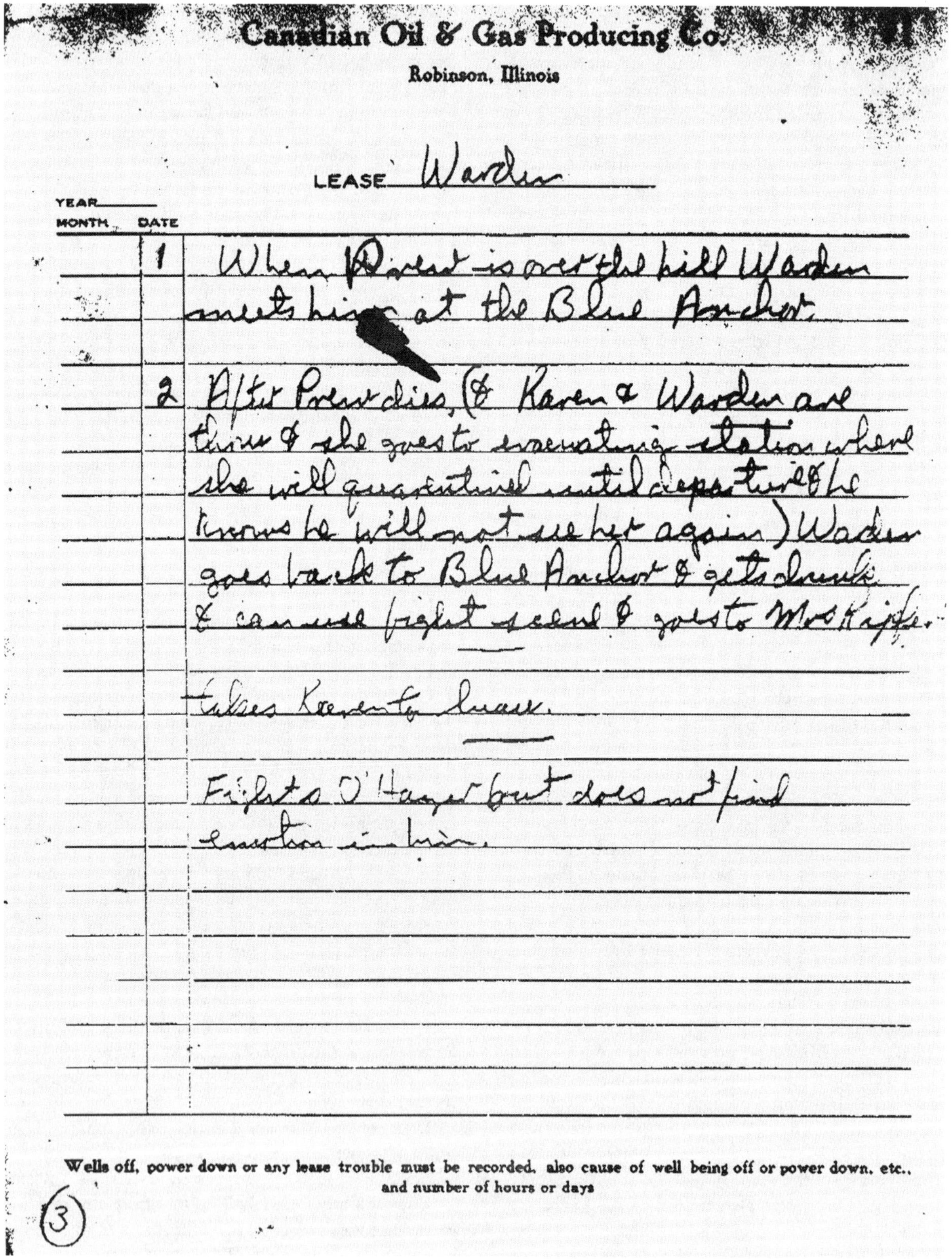

Canadian Oil & Gas Producing Co.

Robinson, Illinois

LEASE Warden

YEAR		
MONTH	DATE	

1 When Prewit is over the hill Warden meets him at the Blue Anchor.

2 After Prew dies, (& Karen & Warden are thru & she goes to evacuating station where she will quarantined until departure & he knows he will not see her again) Warden goes back to Blue Anchor & gets drunk & can use fight scene & goes to McKiff.

Takes Karen to leave.

Fights O'Hayer but does not find emotion in him.

Wells off, power down or any lease trouble must be recorded, also cause of well being off or power down, etc., and number of hours or days

③

Jones's 1945–1946 notes on the character Sgt. Warden of From Here to Eternity *(Handy Colony Writers' Collection, University of Illinois at Springfield)*

gling)." Also preserved are rejected pages and chapters as well as a complete, annotated, and corrected carbon copy of the final draft.

During his early work on *From Here to Eternity,* Jones corresponded extensively with Perkins. After Perkins died suddenly in 1947, Jones worked with Burroughs Mitchell and John Hall Wheelock as his editors, and their correspondence is preserved in the Charles Scribner's Sons Archives at Princeton University. Jones maintained photostatic copies of much of his correspondence with all three of these editors, and his copies are included in the Handy Writers' Colony Collection.

When Jones felt drained by his labors on *From Here to Eternity* he took breaks and worked on short stories. He was particularly pleased with one of these, "The Way It Is," and he remarked about this story: "Whenever I get blue and low and cannot write I sit down and read it over again and I am high again because I know I wrote it." The Jones papers at Springfield include several typed drafts of this story and others he wrote at such times–"Greater Love," "None Sing So Wildly," and "Just Like the Girl"–and the galley proof of "The Temper of Steel," his first published work: it appeared in the *Atlantic* in March 1948. All of these stories were collected in *The Ice-Cream Headache and Other Stories* (1968).

Jones completed the final revision of *From Here to Eternity* in a trailer camp in North Hollywood, California, on 27 February 1950, and the collection includes his telegram addressed to Harry Handy:

FINIS. CONGRATULATIONS TO YOU BOTH AND HEALTH AND EVERY HAPPINESS TO THE NEW ARRIVAL. YOUR LOVING SON,
MACK

To this Handy replied:

GRADUALLY RECOVERING FROM SHOCK STATE WITH GENTLE MINISTRATIONS OF SCORCH [*sic*]. CONGRATULATIONS, LOVE AND KISSES.
DOC

Jones spent much of 1950 editing the manuscript. Scribner's attorneys feared that publishing the book would bring obscenity charges, for Jones had faithfully recorded the language of soldiers in it. The attorneys advised him to reduce his use of one particular obscenity from 259 instances to about 25, but Jones insisted on retaining 106 because Scribner's had promised to print the word "in unprecedented scale." The collection at the University of Illinois at Springfield includes two complete sets of galley proofs of this novel, and these document the struggle over language that Jones had

with attorneys as well as the usual deletions, additions, and last-minute changes that were made.

Following Scribner's publication of *From Here to Eternity* in February 1951, Jones enjoyed a success that most writers only dream about. He appeared on the cover of *Saturday Review of Literature,* which hailed the book as "a work of genius." *The New York Times Book Review* declared that "in James Jones an original and utterly honest talent has restored American realism to a pre-eminent place in world literature." The Book-of-the-Month Club made the novel a special alternate selection because of its potentially shocking language and content. Columbia Pictures purchased the film rights for more than $80,000. Jones and the Handys were featured in *Life* magazine; and in 1952 the novel won the National Book Award. Jones and Lowney Handy gathered and annotated many of the reviews and articles that document the success of the novel, and these are conveniently assembled in the collection at the University of Illinois at Springfield.

Jones's success with this first novel was so great that he increasingly spent more time in New York and Hollywood than in Illinois with the Handys. The amount of material related to Jones in the Handy Writers' Colony Collection decreases after the publication date of *From Here to Eternity,* a decrease reflecting his growing independence from the Handys. In 1952 Jones began building his own home near the Handy Writers' Colony in Marshall, and he maintained his own files there. The collection at the University of Illinois at Springfield, however, contains photographs of him taken for magazines and newspaper articles in addition to informal photographs taken by the Handys or Jones before and during this time of his first success. For example, it includes copies of the photographs taken for the 7 May 1951 article in *Life* that did much to establish his celebrity as a novelist. Also included are 8- by 10-inch Kodachrome color prints of Jones and the Handys that were taken at the Handy Colony in Marshall, in Florida, and in the Southwest during their working vacations. The connections Jones established in Hollywood during the making of the movie *From Here to Eternity* (released in 1953) are evidenced by a series of photographs of Jones and Montgomery Clift, who played Robert E. Lee Prewitt, the central character.

The Handy Colony, which had opened in Marshall in the summer of 1950, was incorporated in 1951, and the publicity attending the success of *From Here to Eternity* attracted writing students from all over the country. By 1952 as many as twenty students were living in the tents and barracks of the colony, where they worked under the eccentric direction of Lowney Handy. Although Jones was not directly involved in operating the colony, he donated some of his profits

Dust jacket for the author's best-selling first book

from the book and the movie to support it, and he lived there much of the year. Most of the Handy Writers' Colony Collection consists of correspondence, financial records, manuscripts, and photographs documenting the operation of the colony from 1950 to 1964. These materials are primarily related to Lowney Handy, but items by writers such as Tom Chamales, Edwin Daly, Jere Peacock, Jon Shirota, Gerald Tesch, and Charles Wright—all of whom were associated with the colony—are included, as are manuscripts written by Mary Ann Jones, James Jones's younger sister and a promising writer who died at the colony in 1952 at the age of twenty-seven.

Soon after publishing *From Here to Eternity,* Jones began working on an epic novel about a young man returning from the war to his Illinois hometown and confronting the decadent, materialistic values of post-war America. In 1957 Scribner's published this novel as *Some Came Running,* a 1,266-page work that, despite being disliked by critics, sold well and was produced as a successful movie by M-G-M. Although the collection at the University of Illinois at Springfield includes little material relevant to the composition of this novel, there are two unannotated carbon copies of its typescript in addition to some rejected pages and early drafts of two chapters of it.

In February 1957 Jones married Gloria Mosolino, an actress and an unpublished writer from New York

whom he brought home to Marshall that summer. When relations between the Joneses and Lowney Handy became intolerable, the Joneses left Illinois for New York and later Paris. The material that they left behind in the possession of Lowney Handy is what remains in the collection at the University of Illinois at Springfield. She continued to operate the colony after Jones's departure, although on a reduced scale. Harry Handy died in 1963, and she died at the colony in 1964.

James Jones in Illinois: A Guide to the Handy Writers' Colony Collection (1989), a published inventory and index to the collection at the University of Illinois at Springfield, has been compiled by Thomas J. Wood and Meredith Keating. In the preface written for this volume by John Bowers, who was at the colony between 1952 and 1954, Bowers observes that Jones "came to [Lowney Handy] a disturbed out-of-control veteran in 1943 and left in 1957 one of the most celebrated novelists in America. The major thing Lowney gave Jim—and at a most pivotal time in his life—was improbable understanding." The Handy Writers' Colony Collection does not document the entire life and career of James Jones, but it is the primary source of information on the "most pivotal" time of his life, when he realized his youthful desire to be a writer and produced *From Here to Eternity,* the work that maintains his place in the ranks of great American realists.

The Life of James Dickey: A Lecture to the Friends of the Emory Libraries

Henry Hart
The College of William and Mary

I'd like to thank Steve Ennis and his colleagues in the Emory Special Collections Department for being so helpful with my research over the past four years and for inviting me to talk about writing the biography of James Dickey. I once told a journalist at the University of South Carolina that working on the biography has been a little like paddling down the Chattooga, the river where *Deliverance* was filmed and where I took an adventure-filled canoe trip with some Citadel friends about a decade ago. There have been rapids, waterfalls, and calm pools along the way. The Special Collections room has definitely been one of the calm pools. I remember immediately feeling at home here the first time I got off the elevator and walked down the hall with the glass exhibition cases. I looked to my left and saw the picture of Richard Ellmann, who had been the Robert W. Woodruff Professor at Emory before he died in 1987. Dick, as he insisted on being called, was my D.Phil. supervisor at Oxford and later turned from being a kind of benevolent taskmaster to a friend who always encouraged me to write a biography. While I was his student, he kept trying to persuade me to change my doctoral dissertation from a critical thesis into a biographical one. He often talked to me about his renowned biographies of James Joyce and Oscar Wilde, and if there is one man responsible, or, maybe I should say, to blame, for my decision to write a biography of James Dickey, Dick's the man.

Usually when I begin an interview to gather information about Dickey, I get asked one question: "Why are you writing a biography of James Dickey?" Sometimes the stress is on different words. Some will ask: "*Why* are you writing a biography of James Dickey?" Or others might ask: "Why are *you* writing a biography of James Dickey?" Sometimes the Deity is invoked, so the question becomes: "Why in *God's name* are you writing a biography of James Dickey?" For those of you who attended Dickey's memorial service at the University of South Carolina, you probably remember Pat Conroy saying: "Pity the biographer of James Dickey. If this biographer . . . gets all of the

far-flung, outrageous stories on paper, then the life of James Dickey will make Ernest Hemingway look like a florist from the Midwest. This is a promise, not a premise, a certainty, not a guess" (*Carolinian,* p. 25). When I phoned Pat Conroy not long ago, I reminded him of his remark and told him that, although I don't yet feel pitiful, I certainly do feel the many responsibilities and burdens of writing the life of James Dickey. I told him I sometimes felt like Ahab chasing a white whale. I also said I had every intention of ending up like Ishmael, telling the story rather than, like Ahab, going down with the ship.

The biographer inevitably begins his perilous adventure in relative innocence. The point of his research is to know as much as possible about his subject. If he is like Ishmael trying to learn about whales, he is also like Adam in Eden. He wants to be omniscient. He wants to pluck the apple of knowledge and devour it—stem, skin, flesh, seeds, and all. And yet he quickly realizes that there are those—not to mention God Himself—who would rather he left the apple alone. He realizes that at least some of the knowledge he has worked hard to get is private knowledge, forbidden knowledge, harmful knowledge. Of course there are some biographers, the Kitty Kellys or Andrew Mortons of the world, who write about public figures with reckless abandon, who thrive on publishing private facts or rumors of private facts, and who don't seem to care too much about the moral issues involved.

Writing a biography is a complex business, especially when your subject or your subject's family and friends are still alive. It was Oscar Wilde who noted that the biographer added one more fear to the prospect of death. Wilde also said that the great writer has many apostles, and usually it's Judas who writes the biography. John Updike admitted that when a biographer approached him, he was struck by such angst that he decided to preempt him by writing his autobiographical *Self-Consciousness.* Shortly after I began doing research on Dickey's life, I read a long article in *The New Yorker* by Janet Malcolm on the many biographies of Sylvia Plath.

James Dickey in 1989 (photograph by David Murray Jr.)

About the genre, Malcolm said: "Biography is the medium through which the remaining secrets of the famous dead are taken from them and dumped out in full view of the world. The biographer at work, indeed, is like the professional burglar, breaking into a house, rifling through certain drawers that he has good reason to think contain the jewelry and money, and triumphantly bearing his loot away" (23 and 30 August 1993, p. 86). Stern stuff for somebody just starting out on what he feels is a journey toward valuable knowledge! And Malcolm doesn't even mention ransacking the private property of the famous living, which of course goes on all the time.

For those of you who might be suspicious, I can assure you that I don't have a police record; I'm not a burglar who rifles through drawers and bears away jewelry or money that belongs to the living or the dead, even if I did want one of those gaudy medallions that Dickey used to wear around his neck. So why did I decide to write a biography of James Dickey? The answer, in some ways, is quite simple. As an undergraduate who had no idea of a college major or postgraduate career, I was lucky to take freshman English with a fine poet named Robert Siegel. Siegel adored James Dickey's poetry. He had invited him to campus for a

reading several months before I arrived. In one of the poetry courses I took from Siegel, he assigned Dickey's magnificent *Poems 1957–1967*. Like many others stumbling upon Dickey's poetry for the first time, I was electrified. Dickey liked to quote Rainer Maria Rilke on how poetry should change your life. I can say in all honesty that Dickey's poetry was instrumental in changing mine. To my parents' consternation, I began consuming great quantities of poetry and writing my own poetry. For better or worse, Dickey's poems continue to influence my own.

In some high-powered academic circles, biographers are often considered lightweights. The New Critics, who dominated academic discussions of poetry in the 1940s and 1950s, felt biographical information was extraneous to an understanding of the text. The Structuralists and post-Structuralists held similar views. The critic should concentrate on the play of language in the text; biographies were simply other texts, other fictions. Literary biographies, in my view, are more than that. Simply put, they help us better understand a writer's work. When I first started studying literature in high school, my teachers said almost nothing about writers' lives. It was as if the poem or short story or novel being scrutinized had arrived by some immaculate conception or had been produced by a printing press rather than a person. I always felt something was missing. The text seemed abstract, a satellite orbiting the earth rather than vitally connected to it. Biographies can provide that vital connection. They can show us that living, breathing, feeling, thinking human beings who walked the earth during a certain time in history actually created the artifice we admire.

James Dickey, as Pat Conroy suggested, presents daunting problems for the biographer. Dickey once wrote: "No one will ever be able to reconstruct my life. It is more complicated and more unknowable than that of Lawrence of Arabia" (*Sorties,* p. 89). Other biographers approached Dickey during the 1970s and 1980s, and he made it clear that he didn't want a biography written. Around 1992, when I first wrote him about the possibility of doing a biography, I didn't hear back, but I heard from mutual friends that he was leery of the idea. He must have realized, however, that a biography was inevitable. In a way he was already cooperating. During the 1960s he had sold many of his early papers to Washington University in St. Louis, and in 1993 he sold to Emory University the monumental collection of his letters, manuscripts, notebooks, military records, teaching materials, subject files, appointment books, sound recordings, photographs, financial records, and even—as I discovered yesterday—his key to all the Playboy clubs in the world. The 233 boxes containing all the material cover almost 100 feet of shelf space. It's a treasure trove for a biographer as well as any other Dickey scholar.

About a year before he died, Dickey and I began to talk on the phone and correspond. I remember very distinctly my trepidation when I first called him. I had been working hard on the book for a couple of years, and, even though I had heard through the grapevine that he had warmed to the project, I was still afraid he might try somehow to restrict it. There are many well-known cases of biographies being obstructed by the subject or the subject's family. J. D. Salinger managed to prevent Ian Hamilton from writing his biography. Ted Hughes and his sister have tried hard to prevent or at least curtail certain biographies of Sylvia Plath. Valerie Eliot has made it difficult for biographers of her famous husband. Henry James burned many of his letters in England and instructed his nephew and executor to keep the biographical hounds at bay. Matthew Arnold instructed his heirs to do the same. When I called Dickey, I didn't know what to expect. As I quickly learned, Dickey's way of answering the telephone, like so much about him, was unique. I nervously told him my name and where I was calling from. There was a pause. "Henry Hart!" he nearly shrieked. "That's not your name." And then he made up some

menacing Italian name that sounded like something from *The Godfather.* "You're not Henry Hart. You're Henrico Corleone! You're a hit-man for the mafia!" (25 April 1996)

What do you say to that? As quickly as I could, I tried to think of the most menacing organization I had ever belonged to, and I remembered the militia I had been forced to join at The Citadel when I taught there from 1984 to 1986. Around the time of my phone call, there had been a lot in the news about the horrors of militias. I hoped Dickey would be suitably surprised and/or impressed by this outfit to drop the subject and move on to more civilized topics. So I told him about the South Carolina Unorganized Militia– S.C.U.M., or "SCUM," as the cadets liked to call us. I told Dickey that we never killed anybody; we were officially "unorganized," but if some national crisis transpired, South Carolina might organize us. Dickey wasn't quite sure what to make of this information. In any case he laughed, and then we started talking about the biography.

To my great relief, Dickey showed no animosity toward the project. But he obviously had worries. His main worry was about the gap between his actual life and the romanticized versions of his life he frequently dished up for public consumption. He told me very candidly that he felt a poet had the right to make up stories about his life. He said he liked to give one account of an experience, and later give another, and later still another. I knew he had defined a poem as a "creative lie" that pointed toward the truth. And of course I knew that many of the stories he had told about his life, and that people believed were true, were "creative lies." Many of his poems and novels, in fact, are about creating these fictions and getting people to believe them. In his interviews, especially the ones conducted in the 1980s and 1990s, he often discussed the business of fabricating selves, playing roles, wearing masks, inventing myths, and telling tales.

Although Dickey sometimes ridiculed T. S. Eliot's self-conscious aesthete J. Alfred Prufrock, he shared Prufrock's need to "prepare a face to meet the faces that you meet." In an anecdote about his first poetry reading, which he approached with diffidence and fear, he said of himself:

> The public image, whatever that may be, notwithstanding, I'm really a rather shy person. It made me very nervous to get up in front of even as few as ten or fifteen people. My wife noticed how nervous it was making me. We were on a relatively modest salary at the time at a small West Coast experimental school [Reed College, where he taught in 1963], and even though I got a couple of hundred dollars that we very much needed for a week's work, I just didn't know if it

was worth what I was going through to get it. (*Voiced Connections,* p. 121)

Dickey finally told his wife, Maxine, he would decline the offer to read at Oregon State. His wife advised him to relax and just be himself on stage. He responded: "But what self, which one?" To mask his insecurities, he admitted, "I had to invent a self" (Suarez, p. 131). His model, he said, was the "big, strong, hard drinking, hard fighting" Ernest Hemingway, and, he added, "Nothing could be less characteristic of the true James Dickey, who is a timid, cowardly person" (Suarez, p. 132).

Right after telling this story to the interviewer, Ernest Suarez (and it *was* a story; Dickey had given many poetry readings long before teaching at Reed), he named Hemingway and T. E. Lawrence as the twentieth century's "two great invented selves, people who wished to become other than they really were and who wrote and acted out of the assumed personality" (Suarez, p. 131). He could have included William Butler Yeats as well, who wrote: "All happiness depends on the energy to assume the mask of some other life, on a rebirth as something not one's self, something created in a moment and perpetually renewed." Yeats went on to explain that "The poet finds and makes his mask in disappointment, the hero in defeat" (*Mythologies,* pp. 334, 337). Like his self-conscious and self-inventing forebears, Dickey sometimes chose to overcome disappointment and defeat by creating and then wearing heroic masks. When he wrote that no biographer could do justice to his life because he was more complicated than Lawrence of Arabia, what he meant was that he wore more masks and played more roles than Lawrence. Dickey once told Hubert Shuptrine, the painter who collaborated with him on *Jericho: The South Beheld,* that he had six different personalities. After Shuptrine finished his month-long book tour with Dickey, he was convinced that Dickey had fifty.

During my second phone conversation with Dickey, he again brought up the matter of lying. He asked me what I planned to call my biography. I said I might call it *James Dickey: A Rage to Live.* I knew he greatly admired a couplet from Alexander Pope's "Epistle to a Lady": "You purchase Pain with all that Joy can give, / And die of nothing but a Rage to live." He thought for a moment and then said: "No. Henry, we've got to shake them up out there. We've got to call it: *James Dickey: The World as a Lie*" (15 July 1996). The title reminded me of a line from Arthur Schopenhauer quoted by one of Dickey's favorite writers, Joseph Campbell, in *The Mythic Image.* The world of time and space, Schopenhauer proposed, was "a vast dream, dreamed by a single being, in such a way that all the

dream characters dream too" (p. 490). What Dickey meant, I think, was what Schopenhauer meant: that the world could be viewed as a dream or lie or invention—something created mysteriously out of the void—in which all the characters dreamed or lied, too. In other words, we fabricate the world we live in, and the world I live in is different from the world you live in. The Greek word behind poetry is *poesis,* a making, and Dickey was suggesting that we all are poets or artist-gods making up the world.

Again, if you went to the memorial service for Dickey you will remember the story told by Ward Briggs, a classics professor at the University of South Carolina. Dickey, Briggs said, once recounted a dream in which he had starred in a high school football game and then gone out with the most beautiful girl in Georgia for a moonlit tryst in his car. The girl proceeded to fall in love with him. Dickey said to his dream girl: "This is the greatest day of my life, but I can't be happy." "Why not?" she asked. He responded: "This is just a dream; it's not real." She responded: "Sure it's real. It's all real within the dream." Dickey asked Briggs to repeat the end of that story whenever the end came to him. In the hospital shortly before Dickey died, Briggs took his hand and said: "Just remember, Jim, it's all real in the dream." Dickey replied, "I know it is," and squeezed his hand (*Carolinian,* p. 25).

There was something of the eternal boy and eternal dreamer about Dickey. With every advancing year, he liked to boast that he was the oldest adolescent alive. Like most boys, he was curious about everything; he was mischievous, and he was wildly imaginative. He liked to play with interviewers, just the way he played with me. He liked to create himself anew just the way he created me anew as Henrico Corleone. After I asked him what he liked to read as an adolescent and he told me Edgar Rice Burroughs's *Tarzan* books, he began signing his letters to me as "Bolgani, the Gorilla." I would sign my letters to him as "Lord Greystoke II," which was Tarzan's original name before he became Tarzan. The fact that Greystoke in his incarnation as "king of the jungle" killed Bolgani didn't seem to deter Dickey from playing the game. In fact, he probably took secret delight in framing me as the murderous biographer and himself as the formidable victim.

When interviewers probed Dickey for biographical facts, his dreaming, boyish side leaped into action. Journalists often failed to realize that Dickey was testing them to see how much he could get away with. I can give you an example—a profile of Dickey written for Vanderbilt's alumni magazine in the late 1960s which I first found in the Emory collection. The journalist began her article with a statement by Dickey that she should have taken as a warning: "Everyone is several

Henry Hart, speaking at the opening of the James Dickey Poetry Seminar Room at the Thomas Cooper Library (photograph by Michael Rogers)

Walter Mittys. . . . Everyone has in him something saintly and something unspeakably vile" (Lawlor, p. 15). Dickey was referring to the daydreamer in James Thurber's "The Secret Life of Walter Mitty," a character who believes that he is a heroic navy pilot, a world-famous surgeon, an infamous criminal, and a daring army captain all while driving his wife to the hairdresser in Waterbury, Connecticut—a rather humdrum industrial city where my father used to work when I was a boy. For Thurber's Mitty, reality was an enemy. At the end of the story Thurber compares reality to a firing squad that shoots down Mitty's heroic fantasies with grim facts. Before the fusillade Mitty stands like a martyr, "erect and motionless, proud and disdainful . . ., undefeated, inscrutable to the last." For the undaunted and sometimes inscrutable Dickey, Walter Mitty was a role model.

Ignoring Dickey's clue, the journalist for the alumni magazine conducted her interview and then proceeded to render the facts of Dickey's life as follows:

Born [in] 1924 in a suburb of Atlanta, Dickey grew up with the nickname "Crabapple Cannonball," prowling the dusty roads of north Georgia on a Harleymotor-

cycle, trysting with farm girls in auto graveyards, and bootlegging liquor in a '34 Ford. At Clemson University, he was a prize football back but left after freshman year for the War, flying almost a hundred Pacific combat missions in a Black Widow night fighter. After the War, he transferred to Vanderbilt. When he was barred from football by a Conference rule designed to prevent coaches from stealing each other's returning service athletes, he turned to track and became Tennessee state champion in the 120-yard high hurdles. He graduated *magna cum laude* in 1949 and got his master's degree the next year. (Lawlor, 16)

Much, although by no means all, of Dickey's Mittyish life is contained in this paragraph, and nearly all of it is untrue. He was not born in 1924. His nickname was not the "Crabapple Cannonball." He did not drive around north Georgia on a Harley-Davidson trysting with farm girls in junked cars. He was not a pilot who flew a hundred combat missions in the Pacific. He never bootlegged liquor. He was not one of the top football players at Clemson. He was not prevented from playing football at Vanderbilt because of eligibility rules. He was not a Tennessee state champion hurdler. Only two sentences are true. He did transfer to Vanderbilt, graduate *magna cum laude* in 1949, and earn his master's degree the next year.

Dickey continued his cat-and-mouse teasing of this Vanderbilt journalist. He decided to pontificate about the morality of lying, and the journalist dutifully recorded Dickey's comments—comments that must have intensified the laughter of those few readers who knew the facts of his life. "People," he said, "are sick of being lied to and manipulated by politicians and public relations men. Poets are the only ones with veracity" (p. 17). In Dickey's capacious imagination, the politician, the public relations man, and the poet often shared the same stage, and they comprised only a few of his dramatis personae. A Renaissance man, Dickey early on adopted a Shakespearean approach to life. The world was his theater. With great zest he bestowed upon his multitudinous selves the costumes and actions of high and often hilarious drama.

As his writing amply demonstrates, Dickey was obsessed with disguise and camouflage. His desire to hide behind masks was fed in high school by dozens of pulp magazines that documented the "undercover" adventures of shape-shifting crime-fighters such as The Shadow and The Spider. He devoured these melodramatic tales, just as he later devoured more sophisticated books—such as those by Henri Bergson—about the unknowable flux of the self. Before the age of post-Modernism, Dickey was postmodernist in casting doubt on an identifiable self. He practiced what he preached, confounding audiences with a motley troupe of personae and impersonations from Marlon Brando to Burt Reynolds and Shirley Temple. Who was the real James Dickey? Few knew the answer. After World War II the French writer who vowed to treat his life as a work of art, André Gide, became one of his principal guides, as did Gide's mentor, Oscar Wilde. Wilde had once told Gide: "I have put my genius into my life; I have put only my talent into my works" (Painter, p. 45). To improve upon Wilde, Dickey tried to put his genius into both his life and his art.

In his controversial endorsement of lying, Dickey found his most sympathetic ally in Wilde, who once bemoaned what he called the "decay of lying" with his usual wit:

One of the chief causes that can be assigned for the curiously commonplace character of most of the literature of our age is undoubtedly the decay of Lying as an art, a science, a social pleasure. . . . Lying and poetry are arts—arts, as Plato saw, not unconnected with each other—and they require the most careful study, the most disinterested devotion. . . . The fashion of lying has almost fallen into disrepute. Many a young man starts in life with a natural gift for exaggeration which, if nurtured in congenial and sympathetic surroundings,

or by the imitation of the best models might grow into something really great and wonderful. But as a rule he comes to nothing. He either falls into careless habits of accuracy . . . or takes to frequenting the society of the aged and the well-informed. Both things are equally fatal to his imagination, as indeed they would be fatal to the imagination of anybody, and in a short time he develops a morbid and unhealthy faculty of truth-telling, begins to verify all statements made in his presence [this sounds like the biographer!], has no hesitation in contradicting people who are much younger than himself, and often ends by writing novels which are so life-like that no one can possibly believe in their probability. . . . If something cannot be done to check, or at least to modify, our monstrous worship of facts, Art will become sterile and beauty will pass away from the land. (Ellmann and Feidelson, pp. 17–18)

Unleashing the imagination without concern for truth and morality was a goal of fin-de-siècle aesthetes. It should come as little surprise that when Dickey was a young man one of his favorite poets was Wilde's friend Ernest Dowson, an Englishman who became famous in the South for coining the phrase "gone with the wind." During World War II, Dickey compiled a pamphlet of his poems that began with "Dedication," a poem paying homage to Dowson.

Dickey considered his long novel *Alnilam* to be his most significant work partly because it was his most extensive exploration of the imagination's ability to transform facts into captivating lies. The two main characters, Frank and Joel Cahill, reinvent the world in ways Dickey espoused. In a lengthy abstract for the novel and its projected sequel "Crux Australis," which I found in the Emory University archive, Dickey wrote of his alter-ego Joel:

He evidently has some notion of a society which he calls "circulatory," or "cyclic." The society would depend very heavily on *role-playing* and *lying*. Joel believes that lying exercises the creative and imaginative faculties, and, when indulged in on either an individual or a group basis, raises the consciousness of the party or parties concerned. The process is what Joel calls "continuous invention," and he believes, apparently, that such systematic practice of fabrication will create a new human world and the transfigured world of the human ability to fabricate. There is a kind of sketchy notion to the effect that there will be "truth areas," where empirical fact is rigorously adhered to and communicated truthfully. This is the area that will enable the state to function. All the citizens are indoctrinated both to truth and invention, so that they can be circulated in and out of both areas, as the state desires. It might even be a kind of law that one must spend equal time in both, or perhaps more time in the "invention area" than in the "truth area," but surely, some time in both. The real basis for the *mind* or imagination of the state will be in the invention area, where people are constantly exercising their creative abilities by making up stories about themselves, about their neighbors, about anything and everything there is. People would soon learn to live with this, Joel says, exploit it, and rejoice in it. It is a kind of freedom human beings have never before had on a large-scale, systematic basis. There might be a kind of hierarchy of lying here where one class of "inventors" would be compelled to enter the truth area or indicate by some sign or other, in case vital or necessary information was required, that this was indeed truth. The rest could be lies, but the highest group of all, the group that corresponds to the philosopher-kings or sages are those that need make no sign as to whether what they say is true or whether it is fantasy. These are the master inventors, and the state reveres them. (Emory, Box 128, n.p.)

Joel's conception of utopia turns Plato's Republic on its head. According to Plato, the philosopher-kings committed themselves to the eternal truths; the poets were the inventors or liars who sought divine frenzy rather than calm reason. For this reason Plato expelled poets from his ideal Republic. Joel sketches the sort of imaginary state Dickey aspired to and often lived in, the state where everything was real in the dream.

James Dickey entered popular awareness most memorably when he played the role of sheriff at the end of the motion picture based on his novel *Deliverance*. When I talk to friends or acquaintances about my biography, most of them don't know that Dickey wrote other novels, about a dozen volumes of poetry, children's books, essay collections, screenplays, journals, and coffee-table books. They know of James Dickey as the tall, beefy, drawling Sheriff Bullard in the film. For his detractors—and there were many by the time the movie appeared in 1972—his role confirmed a perception of Dickey as a sort of hulking Southern redneck who prized the savage ways of the Georgia hinterland over the more progressive ideals of the city.

From the early 1970s on, Dickey became the prisoner of an image, a stereotype, a role he sometimes played that was really a parody of the friendly, book-loving, multifaceted man who was James Dickey. In his moving eulogy in *The New York Times Book Review*, Reynolds Price wrote of the damaging effects of this image of "The Viking berserker stoked with mead":

Only a few weeks before his death, I tried to nominate Jim for an important poetry prize only to discover that my colleagues on the committee—all eminent writers and critics—were still in various states of rejection; and it seemed to me likely that their aversion was occasioned more by the memory or rumor of Dickey Berserk than by extensive knowledge of the imposing quantity of unassailable work he produced till the end. (23 March 1997, p. 31)

When Dickey's *Whole Motion: Collected Poems, 1945–1992* was published, it won no significant prizes—no Pulitzer, no National Book Award, no National Book Critics Circle Award, no Bollingen—even though it represented Dickey's lifework as a poet. It created hardly a ripple among reviewers and readers. It should have created a tidal wave.

I've experienced what Price spoke of in many ways. When I first started contacting agents in New York to try to sell my biography proposal to a publisher, I heard the same thing again and again. "Nobody reads James Dickey anymore. James Dickey is a has-been. Very few people would buy such a biography. I'm sorry I can't represent you." Finally I did get an agent, someone who had known Dickey personally, and she sent my proposal to about half a dozen editors in New York. I got the same response from editors: "If you were writing this book in the 1970s, we might be interested. Now we could only sell a few thousand copies. Sorry." At first I was mystified by the cold-blooded rejection of Dickey and his writing, and of my projected biography, too. There were many factors at work, among them the old divisions between North and South. The quality of Dickey's work had been inconsistent during his last two decades, but the stereotype of Dickey the Viking Berserker had done the most damage to his reputation.

Because of all the research travel and telephone interviews, writing a biography is an expensive proposition. Early on I hoped to get an advance from a New York publisher to defray some of the bills I had been paying out of my regular salary. I also hoped to get grants for my work, but none were forthcoming. Finally I decided to give up on agents, editors, and major grants until I had completed most of the manuscript. Luckily, two years ago I interviewed Jacques de Spoelberch, the most influential of the several editors assigned to *Deliverance* at Houghton Mifflin. Spoelberch had left Houghton Mifflin to become an agent, and after our interview he asked if anyone were representing my book. I said no, and he told me to send him the proposal. In about a month he had an interested editor, George Witte, at Picador/St. Martin's Press.

Dickey told me several times he hoped to read my biography, but he feared that death would intervene. An enthusiastic biography reader, he once wrote in a review of Lawrance Thompson's biography of Robert Frost: "I'm very high on literary biographies" (*Voiced Connections*, p. 135). He was especially interested in the way Frost created a persona that facilitated his career as well as his writing. Like Frost and most other writers worth reading, Dickey was all too aware of his flaws—tragic and otherwise—and in his best writing he explored and expressed them to dramatic effect. He also had many virtues. He could be the most sensitive, understanding, and hilarious companion. He was a charismatic and encouraging teacher, as almost all his students attest. He could make the shyest admirer feel at ease, just as his curiosity and empathy could make the same person feel that whatever he or she said was eminently important. He could be extremely generous to beginning writers. Barnstorming around the country to read to even the humblest community college or high school audience, he was a successful ambassador for poetry. His vast knowledge of literature, which his memory kept at the tip of his tongue, had few rivals among writers of any age.

What the Emory collection surely proves, and what I hope my biography will also prove, is that the popular image and the academic image of James Dickey are severely limited. He was much more complex than these stereotypes allow. On my ten weeklong trips to Emory, I've read through much of Dickey's correspondence and many of his manuscripts. My eyes grow dim thinking of the thousands of letters I've perused. I consider the letters as the bones that make up the skeleton of the biography. I've conducted many face-to-face interviews, probably fifty in all, including a weeklong series of interviews with Dickey six months before he died, and I have done hundreds of interviews on the phone. But the stories people tell, because of the deficiencies of memory, are often vague. It's difficult enough to recall *what* happened; it's often impossible to recall *when* it happened, especially when an event occurred fifty or sixty years ago.

So perhaps I should end by thanking Emory and the Special Collections Department for providing the bones of my book—I realize these are expensive bones (like those Tyrannosaurus Rex bones recently sold at auction). I'd also like to thank those of you who have talked to me about Dickey. Biographies, one quickly learns, are collaborative efforts. They cannot be written without the help of others. I'm hoping that my archival research and interviews—the bones and flesh—will make a whale of a book, and, yes, that I don't go down with the ship.

References:

Joseph Campbell, *The Mythic Image* (Princeton: Princeton University Press, 1974);

James Dickey, *Sorties* (Garden City, N.Y.: Doubleday, 1971);

Dickey, *The Voiced Connections of James Dickey,* edited by Ronald Baughman (Columbia: University of South Carolina Press, 1989);

Richard Ellmann and Charles Feidelson, *The Modern Tradition: Backgrounds of Modern Literature* (New York: Oxford University Press, 1965);

"It's All Real Within the Dream," *Carolinian,* 23 (1997): 24–25;

Jean Lawlor, "The Poetry," *Vanderbilt Alumnus,* 53 (1967): 15–19;

Janet Malcolm, "The Silent Woman," *The New Yorker,* 27 (1993): 84–159;

George D. Painter, *André Gide: A Critical Biography* (New York: Atheneum, 1968);

Ernest Suarez, "An Interview with James Dickey" *Contemporary Literature,* 2 (1990): 117–132;

William Butler Yeats, *Mythologies* (New York: Macmillan, 1959).

Fire at the Old Kentucky Home

Ted Mitchell
Thomas Wolfe Memorial

. . . Dixieland.

It was situated five minutes from the public square, on a pleasant sloping middle-class street of small homes and boarding-houses.

. . . a big cheaply constructed frame house of eighteen or twenty drafty high-ceilinged rooms: it had a rambling, unplanned, gabular appearance. . . .

Look Homeward, Angel

Flames ravaged the Thomas Wolfe Memorial on 24 July 1998, seriously damaging nearly all of the rooms of Thomas Wolfe's boyhood home in Asheville, North Carolina. From 3 to 5 A.M. firefighters fought the blaze that shot flames thirty feet toward the night sky. Fire officials later announced that the three-alarm blaze was the act of an arsonist.

Besides damaging the bedrooms of the former boardinghouse once owned by Wolfe's mother, Julia E. Wolfe, flames destroyed the slate roof, the attic, and the dining room of the 116-year-old structure. Hardly an inch of the white, wood-frame house renowned as "Dixieland" in Wolfe's first novel, *Look Homeward, Angel* (1929), escaped the effect of soot, water, or smoke. Although the quick response of the Asheville Fire Department rescued the building from total loss, one-quarter of the rooms sustained major damage. The ceilings throughout the second floor collapsed, causing timber and plaster to fall upon the furniture. Artifact damage was extensive, but a large percentage of the items can be conserved.

More than forty firefighters were called to the Wolfe Memorial at 3:07 A.M., after an alarm had been called in from the Radisson Hotel nearby. The fire was not brought under control until two hours later. "If we'd been ten to fifteen minutes later, it would have burned to the ground," Asheville Fire Chief John Rukavina said. Rukavina told reporters that ordinarily it would be impractical to rebuild a house that has sustained as much damage as the Wolfe house had. "Were this a house in Montford [historic district in Asheville]," he added, "we'd tear it down." But since the house at 48 Spruce Street is no ordinary house and has become a

pilgrimage for Wolfe's readers from all over the world, extra efforts were made to rescue the structure.

Only hours after firefighters finished spraying water on the smoldering roof, Wolfe Memorial staff and dozens of volunteers began sorting, cleaning, and cataloguing hundreds of surviving artifacts from Thomas Wolfe's life. An estimated 15 percent of the collection was lost, and 25 percent of the house was destroyed. Wolfe's diplomas from the University of North Carolina and Harvard University were lost, as well as the famous photograph of Wolfe that had hung in the hallway: the child with Lord Fauntleroy curls.

Three days after the devastating fire the Asheville-Buncombe Arson Task Force told Wolfe Memorial staff and reporters that the fire had been intentionally set. The fire was started in the dining room and spread to the upper levels. Asheville residents and visitors reacted with sadness and disbelief when learning of the attack on the historic structure. Although the arson investigation continues, no one has been charged with the crime. Three separate reward funds totaling $22,000 were established for information leading to the arrest and conviction of the arsonist.

The house, built in 1883, became a memorial to Wolfe in 1949 and was made a state historical site in 1976. It was furnished with the Wolfe family's personal possessions, including the piano with which Wolfe's sister Mabel entertained boarders and the bed where Wolfe's brother Ben died. The Queen Anne–influenced house is one of the few Victorian-era homes left standing in Asheville.

Central to Wolfe's work, the house was the setting for *Look Homeward, Angel,* a fictionalized account of Wolfe's youth in Asheville. Nearly every room in the house was remembered by the writer in the pages of his best-known novel. Wolfe moved into the house at the age of six in 1906 with his mother, and the boarders provided the models for many of the vivid characters in *Look Homeward, Angel.*

State officials guaranteed that damaged sections of the house, which is owned and operated by the North Carolina Department of Cultural Resources,

The Old Kentucky Home, where a July 1998 fire gutted the second floor (photograph by Ted Mitchell)

would be rebuilt. The architectural firm of Philipps and Opperman, P. A., have been contracted for the restoration. The Winston-Salem, North Carolina–based firm specializes in conserving and restoring historic properties that have sustained fire and water damage. Renovating the house and thousands of artifacts will be a long-term project. The house will not reopen for approximately two years.

The Thomas Wolfe Memorial visitor center adjacent to the Wolfe house still operates on a daily basis (it is closed on Mondays during the winter). The center houses an exhibit hall with many displays, including Wolfe's personal possessions, such as his typewriters, writing table, clothes, and furniture from his New York apartment at the Hotel Chelsea.

The cost of rebuilding the Wolfe house will be $ 3.3 million; less than half is covered by insurance. Monetary donations to assist with the rebuilding and preservation of the house and its artifacts can be sent to:

Thomas Wolfe Memorial Advisory Committee
52 N. Market Street
Asheville NC 28801

The Thomas Wolfe Memorial after the fire destroyed the roof and walls on the north side of the house (photograph by Ted Mitchell)

Special Collections at the University of Colorado at Boulder

Charles L. Egleston
Pierpont Morgan Library

and

Susan Thach Dean
University of Colorado at Boulder

Special Collections at the University of Colorado at Boulder is a significant repository of books and manuscripts in the West. Its notable strengths are first editions of English and American authors, fine-art photography books, children's books, mountaineering books, Romantic poetry by women, nineteenth- and early-twentieth-century publishers' bindings, beat materials, and fine- and small-press publications. Its fine-art photography book holdings are among the finest in the world.

As a separate space at the University of Colorado at Boulder Libraries, Special Collections began with the move in 1939 into the Norlin Library building designed by Charles Klauder. In the Buckingham Library a cage had been used to protect the treasures that had been acquired through the years, but in the new library the administration established the Treasure Room. No inventory of what was held in the Treasure Room survives, but one item may have been a 1938 donation of a signed letter from King Ferdinand and Queen Isabella of Spain relating to the conquest of Navarre and dated 27 July 1492, a few months before Columbus began his exploration. This letter remains in Special Collections, which also holds a copy of a deed signed by Abraham Lincoln in October 1849 and transferring title to Illinois property that he and his wife, Mary Todd Lincoln, owned.

Beginning in 1950 Professors Henry Pettit of the Department of English and Jacques Barchilon of the Department of French helped staff the Treasure Room with volunteers so that it could be open a few hours each week. Pettit, who was named honorary curator of rare books in the early 1950s, managed the collections, searched the library stacks for materials that deserved to be protected, and worked with the library to process donated material. He encouraged acquisition of materials, especially eighteenth-century English literature and examples of early and fine printing. In 1952 the Treasure Room was furnished, and policies were created for users of the collection; that same year Sam Tour, an alumnus of the university, donated a remarkable collection of books on metallurgy that includes William Gilbert's *De magnete, magneticique corporibus* (1600), Galileo's *Discorsi e dimostrezioni matematiche* (1638), and Robert Hooke's *Micrographia* (1665). In November 1955 Pettit began to publicize Special Collections in "Notes from the Rare Books Room," a flyer distributed to Associates of the Rare Books Room and to others interested in Special Collections.

Two items that Pettit found in the stacks are the core of the university's fine-art photography book collections. In 1905 the university had paid $13.69 for Lionel Tennyson's copy of Julia Margaret Cameron's *Illustrations to Tennyson's Idylls of the King, and Other Poems* (London: H. S. King, 1875), which includes photographs taken by and printed by Cameron. The volume is inscribed by Cameron to Tennyson: "Lionel Tennyson. A birthday gift from his life-long friend Julia Margaret Cameron 16 March 1875." Another significant work that Pettit found in the stacks is a twenty-volume text and twenty-volume portfolio, limited edition of Edward S. Curtis's *The North American Indian* (Seattle: Edward Curtis, 1907–1930).

In 1955 an additional room in the library was allocated to rare books; some items in the collection were added to the card catalogue; and a shelflist was created. In 1957 the Associates of the Rare Books Room for Friends of the Library began as a formal organization, and it assumed direction of an annual lecture in rare books that had been inaugurated in 1955 with Carl Jefferson Weber speaking on fore-edge painting. Lecturers in this series included James Gilmer McManaway, Don Cameron Allen, western historian Nolie Mumey, James Lowry Clifford, Richard Blackwell, Germaine Brée, John C. Gerber, David Lavender, d'Alté A. Welch, Charles Seymour Jr., Donald C. Baker, Jean Stafford, Lillian de la Torre, and Richard Shoeck. Following 1975 the annual lecture was replaced by lectures given throughout the year and sponsored by the Rare Book Associates.

Another notable collection acquired before 1963 is the Leavens Collection of more than one thousand items on the monetary aspects of silver and gold, a collection that had been acquired by Dickson H. Leavens and bequeathed to the university on his death in 1955. Three other collections also acquired before 1963 include the papers and books of American poet Marjorie Allen Seiffert, a set of early printings of Tobias Smollett's novels, and the Willard Tracts—more than two thousand pamphlets published in Great Britain between 1660 and 1832 and acquired by James Willard, a professor of history at the University of Colorado until his death in 1935.

Lack of cataloguing to make the Leavens Collection available to scholars heightened the need for professional administration of Special Collections. In 1963 the administration appointed Henry Waltemade, a professional librarian who had been with the University Libraries since 1938, to direct Special Collections. At the same time an annual fund for purchases was established. Ellsworth Mason, head of Special Collections from 1976 until 1982, writes in *The University of Colorado Library and Its Makers, 1876–1972* (1994) that under Waltemade "the Rare Books Room was established for the first time on a respectable level of presentation to the public through cleaning, anointing bindings, inventorying, adequate storage of manuscripts, and catalog records put into respectable condition."

In 1962 Agnes Fowler—widow of biographer, novelist, and newspaperman Gene Fowler—donated many of his typescripts, filmscripts, source materials, and papers to the University of Colorado, of which he was an alumnus. Among the Fowler materials held by Special Collections are his source materials for *A Solo in Tom Toms* (New York: Viking, 1946), his first autobiography, and the typescript for *Trumpet in the Dust* (New York: Horace Liveright, 1930), his first novel.

In December 1964, Special Collections moved into a large and elegant space in the library. In the records of the department are many complaints about lack of funding during the 1960s, but despite this lack Waltemade collected early imprints and first printings of nineteenth-century American authors such as James Fenimore Cooper, Ralph Waldo Emerson, Bret Harte, Nathaniel Hawthorne, Henry Wadsworth Longfellow, Herman Melville, Harriet Beecher Stowe, Mark Twain, James Greenleaf Whittier, and Walt Whitman and twentieth-century American authors such as Sherwood

Anderson, Willa Cather, E. E. Cummings, Theodore Dreiser, William Faulkner, Ernest Hemingway, Kenneth Patchen, Gertrude Stein, John Steinbeck, and Eudora Welty. Among the nineteenth-century treasures he acquired was the first edition of Whittier's *The Panorama* (1856), an association copy presented to Samuel E. Pierce by his friend William Winter, later the drama critic of the *New York Tribune*. Twentieth-century treasures include limited, signed editions of Dreiser, Cummings, Frost, and Anderson.

Pettit and Waltemade continued to publicize Special Collections by making "Notes from the Rare Book Room" a regular column in *Occasional Notes*, the newsletter of the University Libraries published from January 1963 until 1976. This newsletter was distributed to the Friends of the Library and to other interested parties; as the Friends of the Library group was the chief support of Special Collections at this time, *Occasional Notes* was instrumental in bringing in donations. In July 1965, for example, "Notes from the Rare Books Room" records that a Mrs. Caroline Taylor of Boulder has given fifteen letters, mostly from literary figures. In one of these, a 11 July 1898 letter in English from Count Leo Tolstoy to Ernest Crosby, Tolstoy discusses his efforts on behalf of the Doukhobors, a Russian religious sect who wished to emigrate to North America.

In June 1972, Pettit gave the libraries his Edward Young Collection, which he describes in his offering letter as "the greatest [Young] collection, or at least one that is not to be exceeded in the world including those of the Yale and the British Museum, especially as it includes many items probably unique." The capstone of this collection of 184 volumes is the edition of Young's *Night Thoughts* illustrated by William Blake in 1797 and acquired by Special Collections in 1987. In 1989 Pettit donated his personal library of more than four hundred books, mostly printed from the seventeenth to the nineteenth centuries, to Special Collections.

During the 1930s the university was given nearly three thousand children's books by Emily Wood Epsteen. Waltemade moved these books into Special Collections in 1965, and he was instrumental in acquiring other children's book collections. In the early 1960s he acquired for the university the books, manuscripts, and papers of children's authors Franklin Folsom, Mary Elting, and Aylesa Forsee. The Franklin Folsom/Mary Elting Collection consists of 183 volumes of the works of these two authors—including translations into languages other than English—and manuscripts. The Forsee Collection consists of sixty titles and manuscripts. In 1990 the university purchased the Donald Beaty Bloch Children's Literature Collection, approximately 2,400 nineteenth- and twentieth-century children's books and periodicals with an emphasis on illustration.

Interested in early and fine printing, Waltemade in 1966 acquired from Alex Warner many books printed in the northeastern states before 1850. This collection includes German books printed in the Philadelphia area, among the most notable of which is Christopher Dock's *Eine Einfaeltige und Gründlich Abgefasste Schul-ordnung* (Germantown: Christoph Saur, 1770). In 1970 Special Collections acquired Cotton Mather's *The Servicable Man* (Boston: J. Browning, 1690), Abel Morgan's *Anti-Pædo-Rantism* (Philadelphia: Benjamin Franklin, 1747), and books from the Kelmscott Press, Doves Press, and Ashendene Press. Special Collections now has all of the imprints of the Kelmscott Press, and in the 1970s Waltemade purchased other works, including two Aldines and Andreas Divius's edition of *Comoediae Undecim* (1568) by Aristophanes. In 1970 the library acquired Saur's 1776 Germantown Bible, a very rare edition, and in 1976 Professor Gayle Waldrop gave Special Collections a first edition of *The Book of Mormon*, printed in Palmyra, New York, in 1830.

Jean Stafford, Pulitzer Prize–winning author and an alumna of the university, began donating her papers and manuscripts in 1971. She designated the university as her beneficiary, and on her death in 1979 Special Collections received her personal library, her typewriter, her correspondence, published and unpublished short stories, and unfinished novels.

In the "Notes from the Rare Books Room" column in March 1972, Waltemade laments that

> nearly all the books added to the rare books research collection during the past year have been acquired as gifts, or have been purchased with funds provided by benefactors. There has been and there is little or no money in the library book budget available for the purchase of books and manuscripts for the Rare Books Room. It appears this lamentable situation will continue for several years. Any progress in the immediate years ahead will be largely the result of contributions of books or money from those interested in supporting the Rare Books Room.

Consistent development of particular strengths in the holdings of Special Collections began in the late 1970s with a larger commitment of funds from the administration.

Waltemade retired in June 1974, and William Webb, university bibliographer, was curator of Special Collections from 1974 until September 1975. He was followed by Gladys Weibel, who served as curator on a part-time basis until the appointment of Mason, who as one of his first steps devised a long-range acquisitions policy.

Mason was interested in James Joyce and Robert Graves, and he added significant materials of these authors during his tenure. Special Collections holds more than 125 copies of books by Graves, seven of which are signed, and among its most significant Joyce holdings is a 1922 Paris printing of *Ulysses*. In the 1970s Mason began correspondence with Elliot Paul, one of Joyce's friends and advisors in Paris during the 1920s, and this correspondence provided a basis for Special Collections to acquire the books and papers of Camille Cummings, who married Paul in 1928. One of the books she donated is a copy of Donald Friede's unauthorized printing of the first part of the book that became Joyce's *Finnegans Wake*. In Slocum and Cahoon's bibliography of Joyce, Friede writes that "in connection with my edition of *Work in Progress*, 15 copies only were printed for copyright purposes, all of them identically bound. The publication date was in early January 1928. The reason that the title-page reads 1927 was that the book was set up in 1927 and we neglected to change the title-page before printing." Elsewhere Friede reports that no more than twenty copies were printed. Cummings's papers also contain thirty-three letters from Gertrude Stein.

A memo dated August 1982 in the Special Collections administrative files records that "about 80% of our gifts came directly from or through contacts established by the Rare Book Associates, our support group with a membership of about 115 people." Significant holdings added through these contacts include the Michael John Bowen Faulkner Collection, 443 books by, or including selections from, William Faulkner; the George L. Creamer Library; the Goldman Collection of fine printing; the John L. J. Hart Mountaineering Collection of approximately 450 volumes; and the Josiah Holland Collection of manuscripts.

The Goldman Collection, given by Sam Goldman in 1977, includes 668, mostly small- and fine-press books. It builds upon the core of early- and fine-imprints assembled by Waltemade. In 1984 Nora Quinlan, head of Special Collections from 1983 to 1991, helped acquire the Walter W. Smith Vale Press Collection, which includes, in addition to manuscripts and ephemera, thirty-nine of the forty-five books published from 1896 to 1903 by Charles Rickett's Vale Press—one of the finest private presses active during the revival of fine printing at the turn of the century. She also began preliminary negotiations to acquire the James Hayes Collection (purchased in 1994 and 1995)–1,800 books, serials, and manuscripts dealing with calligraphy and the history of printing and letterforms—collected by calligrapher James Hayes. With its previous holdings in manuscript Bibles, prayer books, and two collections of disbound leaves comprising the Otto Ege Collection and the S. Harrison Thomson Collection, the Special Collections holdings in the Hayes Collection support teaching in paleography and illumination as well as in printing history.

With nearly eight thousand books on mountains, mountaineering, and related topics to which material continues to be added, the John L. J. Hart Collection has become the core of the Mountaineering Collection. The Josiah Holland Collection consists of ninety letters to Holland, who was editor of *Scribner's Monthly*, by correspondents such as Mark Twain, Richard Henry Dana, Emily Dickinson, Edward Everett Hale, Thomas Hardy, John Hay, Bret Harte, Oliver Wendell Holmes, Helen Hunt Jackson, Henry James, Sidney Lanier, Henry Wadsworth Longfellow, Henry M. Stanley, Harriet Beecher Stowe, Walt Whitman, and John Greenleaf Whittier.

In May 1992, Special Collections began to acquire the David H. Tippit Photobook Collection, which originally included seven thousand books. It is unique among photobook collections in that the books are preservation copies, most with dust jackets. Among the rarities of the collection is a complete run of Alfred Stieglitz's influential journal *Camera Work* (1903–1917). Tippit writes that

> the collection concentrates on first-edition books and catalogues by important European and American photographers. Books by lesser-known photographers are included if the book was published as a fine-art photography book. The collection also has photobooks by unknown photographers if the subject matter of the photographs is historically important and interesting.

With the help of Tippit in 1992 and 1993 Special Collections acquired 4,084 photo-illustrated books from collector Alan Scuba, and it also holds many photographic portfolios by photographers such as Ansel Adams, Imogen Cunningham, Lee Friedlander, John Pfahl, and Eliot Porter.

Appointed in September 1992 as head of Special Collections, Susan Thach Dean has particular interests in the history of the book and in Victorian literature. In 1996 the department acquired the nucleus of an expanding collection of poetry by women writers of the Romantic period. The scholarly rediscovery of these prolific and influential poets is profoundly influencing how the entire Romantic period is viewed. The Boulder collection, called Women Poets of the Romantic Period, 1770–1839, provides more than two hundred volumes of primary sources that are contributing to this ongoing reevaluation.

Women Poets of the Romantic Period includes both writers who are famous and those who are virtually unknown, and many of the volumes are rare. The prolific Felicia Hemans, for example, is represented by the relatively scarce *Forest Sanctuary* (1825) and *The Sceptic* (1820). Mary E. Cockle's *An Elegiac Tribute to the Memory of Lieut. Gen. Sir John Moore* (1809) is not recorded as being held by any other library. Many volumes include subscriber lists that illuminate literary friendships of the period. The subscriber list for Isabella Lickbarrow's *Poetical Effusions* (1814), for example, contains the names of Thomas DeQuincy, Robert Southey, and William Wordsworth.

This collection also supports studies in the history of the book: the places where these works were published include not only London but also Bristol, Hull, Edinburgh, Kendal, and Maidstone, and the collection demonstrates that writing by women transcends social classes. It includes works by aristocrats such as Lady Catherine Rebecca Manners and Lady Sophia Burrell as well as domestic servant Frances Greensted, who wrote to support her elderly mother, and Mary Robinson ("Perdita"), an actress and mistress of the Prince of Wales who began writing while sharing her husband's confinement in debtor's prison.

Another collection begun under Dean's tenure is the Publishers' Bindings Collection, which consists of some 1,700 late-nineteenth- and early-twentieth-century books having decorated covers. The nucleus of the collection was acquired from Charles S. Kamen, a private collector, in 1996, and the collection was augmented in 1997 by more than eight hundred volumes collected by David Anderson. It also has been supplemented through books found in the general collections of the library and transferred into Special Collections.

From its modest beginnings when it depended heavily on book lovers and the Friends of the Libraries, Special Collections at the University of Colorado at Boulder now contains seventy thousand volumes and is staffed by five persons. In the 1997–1998 academic year it served 3,013 readers and gave eighty-five presentations to university classes, local schools, and community groups.

British Literary Prizes

Merritt Moseley
University of North Carolina at Asheville

The British have a prize-giving culture. The long tradition of school prizes, prize poems, even yearly ranking of universities according to whose graduates received the highest percentage of first-class degrees (another prize) finds a counterpart in the panorama of literary prizes and awards. More than just a love of ranking seems to explain the popularity of literary prizes; there is also a love of ceremony and a desire by people with money to associate themselves with literature. And, as Simon Brett declared while announcing the 1997 Society of Authors awards, "As Robin Hood found out—apart from Maid Marian, there are few more enjoyable human activities than handing out someone else's money." The typical prize is sponsored by a company which may or may not have anything to do with literature; it is chosen by a well-publicized panel of judges; and it is awarded at a gala banquet by a celebrity who is as likely to be an actor or politician as an author, though there is more overlap in these categories in Britain than in the United States.

The Society of Authors, a membership organization founded by Sir Walter Besant in 1884, administers many prizes and awards in addition to grants and loans that are noncompetitive. For instance, each year the society announces the Cholmondeley Awards for poets (endowed by the late Dowager Marchioness of Cholmondeley in 1966); the Encore Award (sponsored by Miss Lucy Astor) for second novels; the Eric Gregory Awards to encourage promising poets under thirty years old; the Richard Imison Memorial Award for the best dramatic work broadcast by a writer new to radio (created in 1994 and sponsored by the Peggy Ramsay Foundation—Peggy Ramsay is a recently deceased literary agent); the McKitterick Prize for first novels written by authors over forty years old; the Royal Society of Medicine Awards for medical writing and illustration in electronic form; and the Sagitarius Prize for a published first novel by an author over sixty years old. There is a biennial Tom-Gallon award to fiction writers of limited means on the basis of a short story.

These are the less-acclaimed awards the society has to offer. Its two most highly sought prizes are the

Betty Trask Prize and Awards, for first novels by writers under the age of thirty-five, and the Somerset Maugham Awards for British authors under the age of thirty-five, given on the strength of a book and designed to enable the winning author to travel abroad.

The value of these prizes is widely variable. The Tom-Gallon Award is £500; the six winners of the Eric Gregory Awards for poetry get either £4,000 or £3,500 each; and the four winners of the Somerset Maugham Awards receive £3,500. The winner of the Betty Trask Prize receives £12,000 and there are awards of £5,000 for two runners up and an additional £1,500 for two others. The annual Society of Authors awards total £85,000.

The *Literary Review,* whose editor Auberon Waugh argues that "literary competitions are a good idea and we should have more of them," awards two prizes each year. The richest is the Annual Grand Poetry Prize of £5,000 that the *Literary Review* awards. It is limited to poetry that (according to Waugh's definition of "real poetry") rhymes, scans, and makes sense. The money for the prize is provided by the *Mail on Sunday* and, in the most recent year, the winner was announced by celebrity presenter and actor Richard E. Grant.

Worth considerably less money (£250) but much more sensational is the *Literary Review* Bad Sex Prize, a sort of booby prize for incompetently written or tasteless sex scenes in novels. The prize money provided by Rowbotham Films goes to the person who submits the winning passage, not its author—though many authors turn up for the award, which takes place at a lavish ceremony sponsored by Hamlet cigars—and the winning passage and the other finalists are printed in the *Literary Review.* Several novelists including Jonathan Coe, Cristina Odone, and James Blinn have, according to Waugh, sworn off all attempts to write sexual passages in their fiction, for fear of winning the Bad Sex Prize.

There have been further new prizes in the past two decades, which must certainly be the heyday of British literary prizes. In 1988 the *Sunday Express* announced an award for a best novel; it was stipulated

Dust jacket for the American edition of the book that won the 1998 Commonwealth Award

that this would be a "readable," or "accessible" novel–that is, less highbrow than the Booker Prize winner–and its value of £20,000 made it the richest literary prize of its time. Auberon Waugh and Kingsley Amis were associated with its launch, and Brian Moore's *The Colour of Blood* won the first award. This prize is now nonexistent, however, as it never established a niche: authors may have been wary of winning an award that seemed to be for novels not clever or complex enough to win the Booker Prize. Moreover, according to the literary editor of the *Sunday Express,* a prize sponsored by a newspaper has trouble getting any publicity (unless it is negative) in other newspapers. Another newspaper-based prize, the *Irish Times* International Fiction Prize, started as the *Irish Times*–Aer Lingus International Fiction Prize but, after losing its airline sponsor, lowered the value of its prize. It is given every two years, for an international English-language novelist; E. Annie Proulx won it for *The Shipping News* in 1993. The *Irish Times* also awards Irish literature prizes, which are restricted to Irish-born authors of fiction and poetry.

The Arts Council of England, a government funding agency, gives a series of Writers Awards worth £7,000 each, but, since they are designed to enable their winners to complete a work in progress, they do not fall into the same category as those which reward finished work of excellence. An award that does this is the David Cohen British Literature Prize in the English language. It began in 1993 with an award to V. S. Naipaul and is given every other year. The Cohen Prize is also administered by the Arts Council. It is unusual in that nominations are encouraged from the general public; its total value–£40,000–makes it the most lucrative of all British literary awards, and, of that sum, £30,000 is for the winner to keep and £10,000 to permit the winner (most recently, Muriel Spark) to use in encouraging younger writers and readers. Spark gave the £10,000 to James Gillespie's High School, Edinburgh, on which she had based her novel *The Prime of Miss Jean Brodie,* to stimulate pupils to develop their creative abilities. Since 1965 the *Guardian* newspaper has awarded the *Guardian* Fiction Prize, chosen by a panel of five judges and limited to a work of fiction by a British or Commonwealth author and published in the United Kingdom, and the Yorkshire *Post* makes an annual Book Award.

There are many other British literary awards large and small in addition to these, but the major awards, either in terms of the amounts of money

Whitbread Novel of the Year

Quarantine

JIM CRACE

'A marvellous book' *Guardian*

Cover for the novel about the spiritual crises of four travelers in the Judean desert

involved, or the public interest, are these: the Betty Trask Award, the Orange Prize, the Commonwealth Writers Prize, the Whitbread Prize, and the Booker Prize. All of them of course limit eligibility in some way, usually by nationality; aside from the Whitbread, all are fiction awards only; the Orange is the only prize open only to one sex.

As Richard Todd explains in his invaluable *Consuming Fictions: The Booker Prize and Fiction in Britain Today* (London: Bloomsbury, 1996), the Society of Authors astonished the world of books with the news in 1983 that a reclusive author of romantic novels named Betty Trask had died and bequeathed £400,000 to the Society to endow an annual prize to a young author less than thirty-five years old, "on the strength of a romantic novel or other novel of a traditional rather than experimental nature." The authors must be citizens of the British Commonwealth, and the prize is given for a first novel. How romantic, or how traditional, the novel must be has been subject to debate, and no doubt Betty Trask might have disagreed with some of the winners—

for instance, Tim Parks's *Tongues of Flame* (1986) and John Lanchester's *The Debt to Pleasure* (1996). The 1997 winner, Alex Garland's *The Beach,* is about hippies on an Asian beach and features drug taking, suicide, and multiple murders. There is only one winner of the Betty Trask Prize (although in 1987 and 1988 two novels tied) and a handful of Betty Trask Awards. One odd feature, surely, is that unpublished novels are eligible, and as often as not at least one unpublished novel wins an award. In 1998, when Kiran Desai won the Betty Trask Prize for *Hullabaloo in the Guava Orchard,* Tobias Hill received a £1,000 award for an unpublished book called "Underground."

Despite the founder's sex and what one may presume to be a healthy presence in romantic fiction by women authors, most of the Betty Trask Awards have gone to men, and the perception that women could not be treated fairly by the existing literary awards lay behind the announcement in 1994 that there would be a new fiction prize limited to women authors. This prize was to be called the Uni Prize, sponsored by Mitsubishi, and funded at a level that would make it the most lucrative fiction prize. The motive for awarding this prize was said to be "the dissatisfaction of senior women in the book world—publishers, agents, literary editors, booksellers, journalists and writers—with the neglect of women writers shown by the major fiction prizes." Mitsubishi withdrew its sponsorship, but in time Orange PLC, a mobile telephone company, stepped in and the Orange Prize was launched in January 1996. Both the nominees for the award and the judges are, of course, necessarily and exclusively women; and the exclusivity of the prize, with perhaps a suggestion that women fear an open competition, has been controversial from the beginning. Several well-established women novelists including Doris Lessing and Anita Brookner have refused to be considered for the Orange Prize. Though only women are eligible, they can be women of any nationality so long as the novel is in English and has been published in the United Kingdom.

This permissiveness has worked against British novelists, or so it would seem. Most of the nominees have been North American; the 1997 winner, Anne Michaels, is Canadian, and the 1998 winner, Carol Shields (for *Larry's Party*), is an American-born novelist living in Canada. Only one British novelist, Pauline Melville, made the 1998 shortlist, which also included Ann Patchett of Nashville, Deirdre Purcell of Dublin, and Kirsten Bakis and Anita Shreve of New York. Aside from its tendency to suggest a shortage of good novels by English women writers—or even a shortage of good novels by women writers, since some of the judges of the 1996 award deplored the quality of the work they were having to read–the Orange Prize seems well established. It attracts an eminent panel of judges, including a prominent broadcaster, a celebrated novelist, American professor Elaine Showalter, and the literary editor of *The Times*. The value of the prize, £30,000, keeps it one of the most desirable awards for fiction.

Carol Shields, the most recent Orange winner, is an interesting case, having been shortlisted for the Booker Prize–for which U.S. writers are *not* eligible–in 1993 for *The Stone Diaries,* which also won the Pulitzer Prize. One must presume that living in Winnipeg initiates her into the Commonwealth. Since 1987 the Commonwealth Writers Prize has been awarded by the Commonwealth Foundation to "reward and encourage the upsurge of new Commonwealth fiction, and to ensure that works of merit reach a wider audience outside their own country." Determinedly cosmopolitan, it holds each final judging and award ceremony in a different one of the fifty-three Commonwealth countries. Its shortlisting procedure is designed to ensure this cosmopolitanism. For the purposes of the award the Commonwealth is divided into four regions, Africa, the Caribbean and Canada, Eurasia (which includes the United Kingdom), and Southeast Asia and the South Pacific. In each region a best book and a best first book are chosen: these comprise the overall shortlist. The regional winners each receive a prize of £1,000; the winner of the book of the year receives £10,000; and the winner of the best first book receives £3,000. In addition the best book winner is invited to London to have a private audience with the queen. Over its eleven-year history Commonwealth prizewinners have included famous names such as David Lodge, V. S. Naipaul, Michael Ondaatje, A. S. Byatt, and Jeanette Winterson, and less famous writers Fotini Epanomitis, Syl Cheney-Coker, and Tsitsi Dangarembga. In 1998 the regional winners for best books were Canadian Mordecai Richler, Indian Vikram Chandra, South African Pamela Jooste and, the eventual winner, Australian Peter Carey (for *Jack Maggs*). Canadian Tim Wynveen won the Best First Book prize for *Angel Falls.*

The two remaining prizes are in many ways the most important awards in British literary life: the Whitbread Prize and the Booker Prize. The Whitbread, which was established in 1971, is slightly more valuable (the overall winner receives £23,000 compared to the £21,000 Booker award) but is perceived to be less prestigious. The Whitbread award, sponsored by a brewery, names prizewinners in five categories–biography or autobiography, fiction, poetry, first novel, and children's fiction. These "regional" or "generic" winners, announced in November, each win £1,000 and in effect constitute the shortlist for the Whitbread book of the year, announced in January. The overall winner, then,

need not be a novel. Comparisons are required between, say, a fine first novel and a collection of poetry: how the judges make these comparisons is not revealed. In January of 1998 Ted Hughes won the Book of the Year prize for his poetry volume *Tales from Ovid* (and the chairman of the judging panel announced that the decision had been unanimous). Thus he won over novel of the year, *Quarantine* by Jim Crace; first novel of the year, *The Ventriloquist's Tale* by Pauline Melville; children's book of the year, *Aquila* by Andrew Norris; and biography of the year, *Victor Hugo* by Graham Robb. The 1999 Novel of the Year was Justin Cartwright's *Leading the Cheers;* the first novel winner was Giles Foden's *The Last King of Scotland.* The Whitbread is one of the more liberal awards in terms of nationality; the winner is required only to be an author who has lived in Great Britain or Ireland for over three years–though an examination of the winning novelists shows that they are almost always British or from the Commonwealth or South Africa or the Republic of Ireland– exactly the geographical boundaries governing the Booker Prize. Expatriate American Paul Theroux did win the Whitbread best novel prize in 1978.

The Booker, or Booker-McConnell Prize, is the most eminent literary prize available to a British novelist. Sponsored by Booker-McConnell PLC, a food wholesaling company, it has been offered since 1969, though it seems to have begun to fascinate the public only about 1980. In that year William Golding's *Rites of Passage* and Anthony Burgess's *Earthly Powers* were seen as being in a two-horse race (an apposite term considering that large sums of money are wagered on the Booker each year). Golding won; Burgess went on to win the Yorkshire *Post* Book Award. The 1981 shortlist included novels by Doris Lessing, Muriel Spark, Ian McEwan, and D. M. Thomas, and the winner was Salman Rushdie's *Midnight's Children*–which, in 1993, was named the "Booker of Bookers," the outstanding Booker winner of the first twenty-five years. In the early 1980s the Booker Prize stood alone as the most prestigious and most lucrative award of its kind. The increased visibility of the Whitbread, with a boost in the cash award and the development of the Orange Prize, has made for a more crowded field.

Presumably the sponsors underwrite the Booker Prize because of its beneficial publicity for their company, though they cannot have been happy in 1996 when judge A. N. Wilson, unhappy about the result, denounced the whole prize process, adding for good measure that its sponsor was "a somewhat sleazy food chain." From the point of view of the Book Council and the individual who administers it for the Council, Martyn Goff, the purpose is to sell books, or more broadly to generate and sustain conversation about books, leading to sales. For this reason the shortlist is announced about five weeks before the final selection, for no particular reason except to permit discussion and wagering, since the judges choose the winner on the night of the announcement. Moreover, a canny system of leaks and hints—some of them emanating from Goff, others from careless judges, and still others invented by journalists—keeps the Booker being discussed for much of the year. In 1998 it was disclosed that Patricia le Roy's *The Angels of Russia* and Les Murray's *Fredy Neptune* were under serious consideration; le Roy's book was downloaded from the Internet and Murray's was in verse. Neither appeared on the official shortlist. Traditionally there is some acrimony surrounding the decision procedure. Some judges have resigned in a huff; others have denounced the results; and others have leaked accounts of their deliberations that fellow judges have contradicted. Two of the winners have taken an opportunity during their speeches to affront the sponsors—for instance, when John Berger in 1972 announced that he would be giving the prize money he received for *G* to the Black Panthers. None of the other British book awards seems to generate the same kind of dissent or occasional confusion.

From the beginning the Booker Prize has been aimed at the public, not just the literary intellectuals. The award ceremony is televised live. The judging panel always includes some representatives of the wider public; in 1998 the chair was Douglas Hurd, a novelist and a former Conservative minister, over the years Mrs. Harold Wilson, actress Joanna Lumley, and Rabbi Julia Neuberger have served as judges. Rabbi Neuberger resigned in protest against the 1994 winner, James Kelman's *How Late It Was, How Late.*

The dominance of the Booker puts the other prizes in the position of needing either to go their own way or to compete head to head. Sometimes an outcry over what is perceived as an injustice in the Booker selections may be rectified by Whitbread, the Orange, or the *Guardian* Fiction Prize. The Booker shortlist is announced in September, the winner in late October or early November. The Whitbread category winners are announced in November, the winner in January. The Orange Prize is announced in May, and any novel published in the year ending on March 31 is eligible. Thus, for instance, Beryl Bainbridge's *Master Georgie,* which was shortlisted for the 1998 Booker and made the betting favorite but lost to Ian McEwan's *Amsterdam,* may well be eligible for the 1999 Whitbread Book of the Year and the 1999 Orange Prize.

Presumably none of the organizations sponsoring the other prizes wish to be perceived as living on the scraps of the Booker; nor do they wish too sedulously to duplicate it. It is quite surprising how seldom the *Booker* winner wins another of the major awards, though it is not uncommon for the same book to win two awards—so long as neither is the Booker. In 1988, 1996, and 1997 the Whitbread Best Novel awards went to books that had made the Booker shortlist but failed to win. The *Guardian* Fiction Prizes for 1983 and 1996 went to novels on the Booker shortlist. Similarly, the Commonwealth Writers Prize for best book in 1998 was awarded to Carey's *Jack Maggs,* almost as a compensation for its missing the Booker shortlist against expectations. In a similar fashion Beryl Bainbridge's *Every Man For Himself,* a Booker finalist, won the Commonwealth Writers Prize for the Eurasia region in 1997. Pauline Melville's *The Ventriloquist's Tale,* on the Orange shortlist in 1998, won the 1997 Whitbread prize for best first novel, and *The Debt to Pleasure,* which won the same award in 1996, also won the *Guardian* Fiction Prize in 1997. Rhidian Brook's *The Testimony of Taliesen Jones* won both a 1996 Betty Trask Award and a 1997 Somerset Maugham Award. Even *The God of Small Things,* which won the 1997 Booker Prize, was on the shortlist for the *Literary Review* Bad Sex Prize.

The 1998 Booker winner, Ian McEwan, once said that it must be hell to win it. V. S. Naipaul, a former Booker winner (for *In a Free State,* 1971), has denounced it: "The Booker is murder. . . . It is useless. I have no regard for it at all. . . . Absolutely nothing would be lost if it withered away and died." A. N. Wilson, a novelist as well as a disgruntled judge, insisted in 1996 that "It would be good idea if we could announce that there would be no more Booker Prizes from now on." Like many observers, he believes that too many mediocre books have won it, too many good ones have not, and the very act of prize giving misleads the public into believing that the best book somehow has been—or *can* be—identified and rewarded. Awards like the Whitbread and the Orange never seem to attract so much animus—another demonstration of the supremacy of the Booker—but some writers object to the whole idea of choosing winners and giving prizes for art. Their objection is worthy of respect. Nevertheless, so long as prizes stimulate discussion and augment sales, so long as food or beer or cellphone companies wish to associate their brand names with literary fiction, and so long as the British continue to enjoy the giving and receiving of prizes, the prospects are for more literary prizes rather than fewer.

The 1998 Booker Prize

Merritt Moseley
University of North Carolina at Asheville

The 1998 Booker-McConnell Prize for fiction, awarded in a ceremony at London's Guildhall on 27 October, was the thirtieth Booker award and, suitably, the event was something of a reunion. All the previous winners were invited, and many of them attended, including the thrice-nominated Salman Rushdie, who won the prize in 1981, and Penelope Fitzgerald, one of the five-person judging panel. The shortlist of six nominated books included three by authors who had been nominated before–Julian Barnes (once), Ian McEwan (twice), and Beryl Bainbridge (a remarkable four previous nominations, most recently in 1996). McEwan's *Amsterdam* and Bainbridge's *Master Georgie* had been recognized as the two favorites, in part for extraliterary reasons since the list was announced on 24 September. Bainbridge, after all, had been a bridesmaid four times but never a bride, and many critics believed that McEwan's *Enduring Love,* published in 1997, was a masterpiece unjustly neglected by that year's Booker panel.

Bookmakers (who, having read none of the entries, make their calculations entirely on extraliterary considerations when they announce a betting line on the day the shortlist is announced) had initially made McEwan the favorite, but as the announcement approached and sentiment clearly favored Bainbridge, they lowered her odds. Before awarding the prize to McEwan for *Amsterdam,* the chairman of the judges, Douglas Hurd, Margaret Thatcher's foreign secretary and the author of political thrillers, acknowledged in his speech that McEwan and Bainbridge had been the only two novelists with a chance.

Response to the announcement was muted compared to the kind of outrage that the Booker has generated in many years, with judges resigning in protest, other judges leaking the supposedly secret deliberations to the press, and journalists ridiculing the decision. Some commentators had confidently predicted that McEwan could not win with Hurd chairing the jury–since his novel features the sensational exposure of a Conservative foreign secretary who happens to be an enthusiastic transvestite. And

Dust jacket for the novel that won the 1998 Booker Prize

there was considerable sympathy for Bainbridge for coming so close and losing again.

The whole Booker process was muted this year. It began in early spring, with advance touting for books likely to be considered; it gathered speed over the summer, with more detailed discussion of which books had been submitted by their publishers and which had been "called in" by the jury; in late summer there was much speculation, more or less well informed, about the "long shortlist"—about twenty novels that were, in effect, semifinalists; then the real shortlist of six novels was made public, setting off a month or so of vigorous second-guessing and odds-making. The man who administers the prize on behalf of the Book Trust (the prize money comes from Booker-McConnell plc, a food wholesaler) is Martyn Goff, and, faithful to his terms of employment, he fed the press a steady trickle of surprising predictions and sometimes misleading tidbits, in effect marketing the Booker. Two of the tidbits in 1998 were the suggestion that the Booker jury might consider a book downloaded from the Internet (but nothing came of this, perhaps because no one knows how to market such a book), and the idea that the jury would "call in" David Caute's novel *Fatima's Scarf*, self-published under the imprint of Totterdown Books. Caute has written an ambitious, panoramic, tragicomic novel based loosely on Salman Rushdie's experiences in 1988 after publishing *The Satanic Verses*, which richly deserved the panel's consideration though it was rejected by twenty-five publishers on the grounds, as Caute believes, of cowardice. Just before the shortlist appeared, Chris Smith, the Secretary of State for Culture, Media and Sport, attacked the forthcoming list for being too elitist and called for another, "lower-brow" prize for books ordinary people like to read.

Something always goes awry with the Booker, and in September 1998 someone accidentally downloaded the secret "long shortlist" to journalists. This showed that the semifinalists did include Caute and other highly praised authors such as William Boyd, Nadine Gordimer, William Trevor, and Alan Hollinghurst as well as promising newcomers Shani Mootoo, D. J. Taylor, and Giles Foden. But none of these made the shortlist, which consisted of Bainbridge's *Master Georgie*, McEwan's *Amsterdam*, Julian Barnes's *England, England*, Patrick McCabe's *Breakfast on Pluto*, Magnus Mills's *The Restraint of Beasts*, and Martin Booth's *The Industry of Souls*. Mills is not only a first-time nominee and a first-time novelist but works full-time as a London bus driver. Booth is an experienced novelist and historian, though a first-time Booker nominee. McCabe was nominated in 1992 for *The Butcher Boy*.

By recent standards this is a very conservative list. It includes no novels by authors from outside England and Ireland, though McCabe fills what has come to seem a token Celtic slot. Professor Lisa Jardine criticized the judges because, in her words, they "had not felt the need to pander to public opinion by short-listing books by Commonwealth authors—the best authors writing in English were to be found within the British Isles. Neither had they concerned themselves with special categories like women, or ethnic minorities. No, these judges had settled for the intrinsic quality of good old English novels." The nomination of women authors is always a contested issue. This year's judges in addition to Lord Hurd were Valentine Cunningham, an Oxford don; Penelope Fitzgerald, a novelist; Miriam Gross, literary editor of the *Daily Telegraph;* and Nigella Lawson, a broadcaster and columnist—thus including three women.

One need not object to the narrower-than-usual geographical and ethnic spectrum—previous Booker panelists had routinely been attacked for politically correct selections—but the six shortlisted novels can be faulted for lack of ambition. Every one is completely competent; none is dull or infuriating or inaccessible; and novelists such as Barnes, McEwan, and Bainbridge cannot write, or at least would not publish, bad books. Size is not the same as seriousness or depth, but these books, at an average length of 216 generously margined pages, strike one as less substantial than these of magisterial past winners such as Rushdie's *Midnight's Children*, A. S. Byatt's *Possession*, Barry Unsworth's *Sacred Hunger*—or, for that matter, David Caute's *Fatima's Scarf*.

Among the newcomers, Mills's *The Restraint of Beasts* displays great originality. The story of three fencing contractors, it is narrated by an unnamed Englishman whose appointment as foreman in charge of irresponsible Scots laborers Tam and Richie involves him in a series of jobs that are frustrating, almost incidentally fatal to third parties, and ultimately ominous. "The restraint of beasts" is a casual Scots phrase explaining the purpose of the fences these three erect, but it seems to apply to the men themselves, who are restrained by their diligent, fencing-obsessed boss, Donald, and who behave in a fairly bestial way. As they do their jobs with competence but with the least possible enthusiasm or compliance with orders, Tam and Richie accidentally kill several of the men who have employed them; their deadpan reaction is to bury them, standing up, in the holes dug for their gates. Their main concern is for whether it is better to bury the dead under the hanging post or the slamming post; the only repercussion is unpaid bills.

For most of the book the fencing crew is in Shropshire, building improbably large enclosures for a meat-packing firm called the Hall Brothers, followed by an ambitious scheme of electric fences twenty feet high, a set of requirements that has led some reviewers to conclude that they are helping to construct a concentration camp. The signs are mixed, though, and the mood, though dark, is black comedy rather than tragedy. Thomas Pynchon, who surprisingly contributed a blurb to this first novel, published in paperback, by an unknown novelist, called it "a demented, deadpan comic wonder," a "rude salute to the dark side of contract employment."

Mills, who has worked as a farm laborer in Scotland, writes interestingly about cultural contrasts and conflicts between the Scots and the English. His Scottish laborers are almost mute, resistant to instruction, profligate, and filthy, though not stupid. Though they live in a farming community rather than Glasgow (like the figures in James Kelman's *How Late It Was, How Late,* the 1995 Booker winner) or Edinburgh, the setting of Irvine Welsh's *Trainspotting,* Tam and Richie do little to dispel the fairly depressing picture of Scotsmen in recent fiction as obscene and shiftless drunkards.

Booth's *The Industry of Souls* takes its title from an unattributed epigraph that says it is the industry of the soul "to love and to hate; to seek after the beautiful and to recognise the ugly; to honour friends and wreak vengeance upon enemies; yet, above all, it is the work of the soul to prove it can be steadfast in these matters. . . ." This evocative passage is a good guide to the novel, but readers will discover also that it is mostly *about* industry, the work of political prisoners condemned to mine coal in a Soviet gulag, and that the nineteenth-century Russian usage of "souls" to refer to serfs is also relevant. Booth tells the story of Alexander Bayliss, a British businessman who was arrested under Stalin and sentenced to hard labor for alleged spying against the Soviet state. He spent some twenty years in the gulag. When released, he made his way to the little village of Myshkino, to the daughter of a friend from the mines, and having borne his witness, decided to stay. As he says when someone asks why he never contacted the British Embassy, "Here, once I had divested myself of my responsibility to Kirill, I discovered an intense peace such as I had never known and to leave would have been to forfeit it."

The novel begins on an auspicious day for Bayliss, who is completely assimilated and goes by the name of Shurik: it is his eightieth birthday, and it is also the day when British representatives, freed by the collapse of the Soviet state to trace and then to visit him, will appear in Myshkino. The frame tale, of the aged Shurik walking through the village and talking to his friends, is pierced by long retrospective accounts of his days in the mines, which have the

ring of authenticity and are genuinely harrowing. At the end of his birthday he must decide whether or not to return to the West; as a device for suspense this doesn't work very well. But the emotion of the book, which has been called sentimental, is justified and nuanced.

Booth is a veteran; the book is his twelfth adult novel, and he has also written children's books, poetry, a biography of Conan Doyle, and a history of opium. Nevertheless, his agent declared that *The Industry of Souls* was unpublishable and that Booth's career as a novelist was at an end. A new agent was able to place it with Dewi Lewis, a specialist publisher (mostly of photography books) located in Stockport, well out of the metropolis. Booth will be one of those authors for whom the Booker nomination assists sales and visibility.

Patrick McCabe's *Breakfast on Pluto* is the most disappointing novel on this list. He is the author of four earlier novels, at least two of which, *The Butcher Boy* and *The Dead School,* are first-rate. He specializes in an uneasy mixture of violence, Irish lowlife, pop-culture references, and surrealism. The texture of his novels is nervous and fragmented. They can be simultaneously hilarious and horrifying. In his latest book he seems to be going back over old ground, though there is an additional element in his incorporation of the Troubles and IRA bombings. The narrator and main character is Patrick "Pussy" Braden, who is the child of a priest, reared by a baby farmer in a small Irish town near the Ulster border. He has two friends. Early on he begins dressing as a girl and by his late teens is a full-blown transvestite prostitute in London. A disturbed young man, with perhaps more etiology than he really needs (one of his ideas is that he may have become a cross-dresser because his father, the priest, wears a dress), he tells his story, or at least part of it, to a psychiatrist.

McCabe never lacks audacity, and the mixture of the outrageous and casually comic in his narrative is energetic. But something has gone wrong with his style. Perhaps we are supposed to attribute the arch quality of passages such as this, with their syntactic inversions and campy slang, to Pussy Braden, who is referring to himself as "she": "As she did for all and sundry now, so sky-high giddy since she'd left Louise's she seemed to work non-stop! 'O please, please, buy me sweet Chanel!' to some hunk she now would cry, as lashings of cash upon her were laid and her kohl-rimmed eyes misted over with desire as into hipster trouser suits she slipped, blouson tops and milk-maid maxis, enough to drive her poor man wild!' 'O miaow, my darling!' she cried. 'So kind to Pussy are you that I really, truly must adore you as no lady ever did!'" At any rate, *Breakfast on Pluto* seems forced.

Julian Barnes is undoubtedly one of the best British novelists of his generation. The failure of his *Flaubert's Parrot* to win the Booker Prize, or his *A History of the World in 10 1/2 Chapters* even to interest the judges enough to make the shortlist, are offenses regularly cited by those who criticize the prize. It may be wrong to read the 1998 inclusion of *England, England* as some sort of compensation for past injustices. Nevertheless, this is not top-drawer Barnes.

The concept is extraordinarily intelligent. A tycoon called Sir Jack Pitman, who is reminiscent of the late fraudster Robert Maxwell, conceives the idea of taking control of the Isle of Wight and building there a simulacrum of England for the use of tourists. Some of the ramifications of this idea are delightful. Pitman calls on his "Concept Developer" to provide him with the "top fifty characteristics associated with the word England among prospective purchasers of Quality Leisure," and soon there is a list, predictably beginning with 1. The Royal Family, 2. Big Ben/ Houses of Parliament, and 3. Manchester United Football Club. Further down are Snobbery, Hypocrisy, Homosexuality, Whingeing, and Not Washing/ Bad Underwear. Some adjustments have to be made in the creation of the new England, called "England, England," but the Royals are moved to the island, along with Stonehenge or something like it and many other landmarks. England, England is a great success—so much so that the original thing, left on the mainland with all its tourist attractions gone, reverts to a backward agrarian form of life. Martha Cochrane, whose childhood begins the novel and who rises to the top of the Jack Pitman empire, is last seen in exile on the mainland (now called Anglia), herding ducks.

Barnes's novel satirizes many features of contemporary British life, including tabloid journalism, big business, the tourist trade, and philistinism, and it addresses big questions, such as how the real differs from reconstructions. It comes at a time when the question of what is essentially English is under urgent discussion, caused in part by the decisions of the Scots and Welsh to move toward separation from the English. It is significant that this book is *England, England,* not *Britain, Britain,* or the unimaginable *United Kingdom, United Kingdom.* The Booker Prize itself is the occasion for worrying about "the English novel." But in the end Barnes's novel falls below his own high standard: a good book, but untouched by brilliance.

The sentimental favorite and runner-up, Bainbridge's *Master Georgie,* is an historical novel, set in the early nineteenth century and concluding during the Crimean War. Like her last book, *Every Man for Himself,* which was about the sinking of the *Titanic, Master Georgie* looks at historical events out of the corner of the eye, focusing most of its attention on the relations of unfamous individuals caught up in them. Her account of the Charge of the Light Brigade, the most famous event of the war in Crimea, is typical: a somewhat obtuse man named Doctor Potter explains that "I am at least better off as far as transport is concerned; three days ago over two hundred cavalry horses of the Light Brigade stampeded into the camp, their riders having perished in a charge along the north valley."

Potter is one of the narrators, sharing his duties with a young man named Pompey Jones and a young woman named Myrtle. These two, both orphans adopted by the Hardy family, are bound together by the first sensational event in the novel, when Master Georgie finds his father, Mr. Hardy, dead in a prostitute's bed and has to return him to his own bed, with the help of Myrtle and Pompey, so that he can be discovered dead in a respectable location. As they grow up, Myrtle and Pompey assist Georgie, who is an amateur photographer as well as a doctor, in various ways; Myrtle bears children for him, as his wife has been rendered barren by a fright from a tiger rug.

The novel begins in Liverpool. It ends in Inkerman, where Georgie is a surgeon attending the British casualties and Myrtle as always is assisting. Pompey Jones becomes a combatant against his will and recounts the harrowing action: "I engaged with a boy with a pimple at the corner of his mouth. He was clumsy with terror, flicking at me with his bayonet as though warding off bees. He shouted something in a foreign tongue, and I said I was sorry but I didn't understand. I wanted to spare him, but he caught me a slash on my brow which got me cross and I jabbed him in the throat. He fell away, gurgling his reproach. I didn't know what cause I was promoting, or why it was imperative to kill, though I reckon Potter could have told me. The carnage was horrid." The fiercest fighting is in defense of the Regimental Colours, though Pompey "questioned the necessity of coming to the aid of a tattered square of silk." The closest thing to a philosophical reflection in this novel may be Myrtle's thoughts about the death of Mr. Hardy: "Everything that happens, I told myself, is the result of necessity, and therefore inevitable. It was of little comfort."

Bainbridge has written sixteen novels and for most of her career has specialized in quasi-autobiographical accounts of life in Liverpool, as in *The Dressmaker* and *An Awfully Big Adventure.* Only recently has she turned to historical fiction; her next novel is to be about Doctor Samuel Johnson. A good bit of the critical commentary on her Booker failure in 1998 assumed that she is undervalued because of her gender, or her steady sales, or her humor. One critic says that Bainbridge is dismissed as "quirky"—shorthand for a woman who isn't entirely serious, another quirky writer being poet Stevie Smith—"In England, if you write amusingly, you always run the risk of not being taken seriously."

Though there may be something in this idea, it is hard to square with McEwan's success, for *Amsterdam* is a funny book, too. Its comedy is dark and is founded on the notions that in Holland assisted suicide is legal with a doctor's note and that a clever person can assist in the death of someone who doesn't even *want* to commit suicide. The novel is constructed around the death of a remarkable woman named Molly Lane; she leaves behind a husband, thought by most to have been unworthy of her, and three former lovers. Two of them, Clive Linley, an eminent composer, and Vernon Halliday, the editor of a "quality" newspaper pursuing readers by becoming more like a tabloid, are friends; the third is Julian Garmony, a right-wing foreign secretary who seems likely to mount a successful challenge to be the next prime minister. His policies are repellent to Clive and Vernon and other *bien-pensant* members of the arts/media London world (as they are to McEwan).

The discovery of some photographs that Molly took of Garmony in women's clothing fuels a plot that raises important questions about the role of the press and the possibilities of privacy, about the responsibilities of the artist (Clive ignores a violent assault he witnesses in the Lake District in order to continue working on his new symphony), and about integrity in public life. It is, as Lord Hurd announced, "a sardonic examination of the morals and culture of our time."

McEwan, who began his career with stories of kinky sex and violence that, especially when trans- mitted in a cool, deadpan tone, earned him the nickname Ian Macabre, has settled down into one of the surest and wisest of English novelists. John Keenan in *The Guardian* remarks that "McEwan is a noted chronicler of our capacity for brutality, selfishness and cruelty. From incest to cannibalism he has left no taboo untouched in his quest to root out our darkest desires. In *Amsterdam* the tone is light, but the accent nevertheless is on discord, betrayal, selfishness and death." In the past McEwan commented that winning the Booker Prize "must be hell"—perhaps because it subjects the winner instantly to the kind of criticism of success that the Australians call the "tall poppy syndrome." Accounts of the 1998 Booker evening seemed to include novelist Will Self screaming "This stinks!" at the television, though the response by Salman Rushdie, who acclaimed the decision because *Amsterdam* "was about the world we live in rather than some other world," will relieve the hell of winning somewhat.

The Booker Prize avoids staleness by bobbing and weaving. This year's relatively quiet ceremony showed a harmonious panel choosing a popular winner from a conventional shortlist of six novels by mostly male white Britons. Observers can expect more excitement in 1999.

Shortlist for the 1998 Booker Prize:

Beryl Bainbridge, *Master Georgie* (London: Duckworth, 1998);

Julian Barnes, *England, England* (London: Cape, 1998);

Martin Booth, *The Industry of Souls* (Stockport: Dewi Lewis, 1998);

Patrick McCabe, *Breakfast on Pluto* (London: Picador, 1998);

Ian McEwan, *Amsterdam* (London: Cape, 1998);

Magnus Mills, *The Restraint of Beasts* (London: Flamingo, 1998).

Literary Societies

The number of societies devoted to the study of writers, publishers, and their works is one measure of the devotion that readers have for literary figures, even after some may no longer be as well known or highly regarded as they were among their contemporaries. Some of the more important contributions of these associations are their publications—newsletters, journals, Web pages, bibliographies, and editions of otherwise hard-to-find works by the figures whom these societies honor. Such publications, like many other activities and projects of these associations, help to place these writers and publishers in the larger perspective of literary history, maintain their reputations, and ensure that these figures will continue to have their lives and contributions reassessed.

In serving these same ends, the Yearbook *reaffirms the commitment of the* DLB *series to "make literature and its creators better understood and more accessible to students and the reading public"—and thereby to keep the study and appreciation of literature "firmly positioned at the center of a nation's life." By their nature these societies are known only among the coteries dedicated to these literary figures, and the publications of these societies would be of greater use to a wider audience of scholars and students if such prospective readers were to learn of their existence. Especially since many of the British societies are unknown in the United States, the* Dictionary of Literary Biography Yearbook *is thus pleased to present this first installment of a series of entries that will provide additional readers and students with a useful finding list of these British and American literary societies.*

The Margery Allingham Society

Roger Johnson

In January 1988 Pat Watt and Barry Pike founded The Margery Allingham Society to celebrate the life and work of a queen of crime writing. Along with Agatha Christie, Dorothy L. Sayers, and Ngaio Marsh, Margery Allingham is ranked as one of the greatest detective-story writers of the "Golden Age" from 1925 to 1965. The society quickly gained the support of Margery's younger sister Joyce, who serves as its Patron, and of other family members and friends.

Margery Allingham was born in Ealing on 20 May 1904. Shortly afterward her family moved to the former rectory at Layer Breton near Colchester, and her years spent in that part of rural Essex influenced much of her writing and thinking. Her father, Herbert Allingham, one of the most prolific authors of newspaper and magazine serials, was a son and grandson of authors, and naturally he encouraged her to write: at the age of eight she published a story in one of the magazines for which her aunt, Maud Hughes, wrote and served as editor. As Allingham's husband observed much later, in that household "no other occupation was considered orthodox, or indeed sane!"

During World War I the family moved to London, although it maintained a small house on the Essex coast. Allingham attended the Perse School in Cambridge but left at the age of sixteen to go to the school of drama and speech training at the Regent Street Polytechnic, where a year later she wrote and produced a heroic verse drama, *Dido and Aeneas.*

At the age of seventeen she wrote her first novel, *Black'erchief Dick,* after she had participated in a séance at her parents' holiday house on Mersea Island. It was published two years later with a book jacket designed by Philip "Pip" Youngman Carter, who had recently come to London to study art. The two had known of each other since childhood, and in 1927 they married and settled in a tiny flat in Holborn. There she earned her living by translating silent films into short stories for her aunt's magazine, *The Girl's Cinema,* and by writing for the newspapers.

Her first detective novel, *The White Cottage Mystery,* was serialized in *The Daily Express* (London) and later appeared in book form. During this time she also wrote the first three Albert Campion books, elevating him from a zany and rather shady adventurer in *The Crime at Black Dudley* to a true detective hero in *Mystery Mile* and *Look to the Lady.*

In 1931 she and her husband rented Viaduct Farm at Chappel, near Colchester, and she adopted the old name of the village, Pontisbright, for the Suffolk setting of *Sweet Danger,* her 1933 novel. In 1934 they bought D'Arcy House at Tolleshunt D'Arcy near Maldon, formerly the home of John Salter, the physician, traveler, and sportsman, and this became their home for the rest of their lives.

The Bottle Street Gazette
Journal of the Margery Allingham Society

Banner headline for the journal of the society devoted to the British crime writer

Allingham spent much of World War II in Tolleshunt D'Arcy, and in 1941 she wrote *The Oaken Heart,* a vivid account of village life in wartime. After the war she published two postwar novels that are among her best: *More Work for the Undertaker,* with its richness of character and setting, and *The Tiger in the Smoke,* a thriller with a palpable sense of evil.

Following her death on 30 June 1966 her fellow crime writers presented tributes such as this from Agatha Christie: "Margery Allingham stands out like a shining light. Everything she writes has a definite shape. And she has another quality, not usually associated with crime stories. Elegance. How sad it is that there are no more of her stories to which we can look forward." She left one novel unfinished, in fact, and her husband contributed the conclusion to this work, *Cargo of Eagles.* Before his own death in 1969 he wrote two additional Campion novels, *Mr. Campion's Farthing* and *Mr. Campion's Falcon.*

Barry Pike—editor of the society's journal, *The Bottle Street Gazette*—is the author of a comprehensive study of Allingham's novels, *Campion's Career* (1987), and Richard Martin contributed *Ink in Her Blood,* a study of her life and her fiction, in 1988. The standard life is *Margery Allingham: A Biography* (1991) by Julia Thorogood.

During its first seven years the society maintained an active branch in the United States, for which an American newsletter was published. Late in 1995 the society was reinvigorated under the leadership of a new committee, and, when the Maldon District Museum prepared to move into new premises, its administrators offered the society space for a Margery Allingham Room in the museum. This offer was enthusiastically accepted, and in August 1997 the museum officially opened at its new site, Promenade Lodge, Mill Road, Maldon, Essex CM9 5HX, U.K.

Through the help of Joyce Allingham on behalf of P. & M. Youngman Carter, the museum's Margery Allingham Room now houses photographs, drawings, books, and other personal belongings in addition to constabulary and criminal relics loaned by the Essex Police Museum, a life-size figure of Albert Campion, and a splendid portrait of Margery Allingham by Jean Upton. This museum is open Wednesdays, Thursdays, Saturdays, and Sundays from April through November.

The Margery Allingham Society organizes trips each year to explore the topography of places that appear in her books. Many of the sites, and sights, in her fiction are based on real places that she knew and loved—most of them within a radius of about fifteen miles—and it is thus reasonably easy for the society to arrange field trips. In addition, an annual dinner is usually held in autumn at a London restaurant. The first of these dinners was held in September 1992, when guest of honor Stephen Leadbeatter, the Home Office pathologist, presented the society with an address on forensic pathology in Allingham's books that was subsequently published in the newsletter. Now published as a biannual journal, *The Bottle Street Gazette* (named after the London street where Campion maintains his flat) contains scholarly, speculative, and frivolous articles and snippets, as well as reminiscences from friends of Allingham and her husband. In the year 2004 the society intends to celebrate her centenary.

The society welcomes enquiries and applications for membership, which should be directed to the secretary, Pamela Bruxner, at 2B Hiham Green, Winchelsea, East Sussex TN36 4HB, U.K. (phone/fax: 01797 222363).

The Arnold Bennett Society

Jean Potter

The Arnold Bennett Society was founded in 1953 in Stoke-on-Trent to promote the study and appreciation of the lives, works, and times of not only novelist Arnold Bennett but also other provincial writers associated with North Staffordshire. Its founder, Alderman Horace Barks, whose son is still a committee member of the society, was once lord mayor of the city. The year in which the society was most active was 1967, when

Sketch of the author used by the Arnold Bennett Society

the centenary year of Bennett's birth was celebrated. This centenary received national coverage, and the society participated in events such as special theatrical productions and a lecture in the city by J. B. Priestley.

British media coverage of Bennett and of the society's activities have increased during the past seven years. Following the 1970s, when the number of members dwindled to fewer than one hundred, international interest in Bennett has grown, and the society now has a membership of more than three hundred. For these members the society publishes a newsletter three times a year to share news and members' research findings related to Bennett, and it also organizes annual events, mainly for the membership but also sometimes open to the public.

These events include an annual general meeting, which is held in the Sunday school building where Bennett received his first schooling and which incorporates such activities as dramatic readings and musical performances related to Bennett's stories, slide lectures, quizzes, and private video showings of movie adaptations of his works. In commemorating the anniversary of Bennett's death on 27 March 1931, the society holds a dinner every year on a Saturday as close as possible to that date in Burslem at the George Hotel, the establishment on which Bennett based The Dragon in his Five Towns books. Past speakers at this dinner have included novelists John Wain, John Toft, Margaret Drabble, and Roy Hattersley. In recent years more than one hundred

members and guests have attended this dinner, and in 1998, the centenary of Bennett's publication of *A Man from the North,* his first novel, 156 people were present. On the day following this annual dinner a wreath is laid where Bennett's ashes are buried in Busten Cemetery.

Other events including lectures by well-known journalists are organized, as are visits to other literary societies such as those dedicated to George Eliot, Elizabeth Gaskell, Mary Webb, and H. G. Wells. The society holds Bennett seminars in conjunction with a local college, and it works closely with the city council of Stoke-on-Trent to promote interest in Arnold Bennett as a tourist attraction. For example, an Arnold Bennett room will be established in "Ceramica," a new attraction that is to be a permanent showcase of the Burslem pottery industry and that is being set up in Burslem Old Town Hall as part of the millennium celebrations. If funding permits, another major project will be that of the Bursley Sculpture Trail, a project in which a large statue of Arnold Bennett and ten life-size bronze figures of characters from his stories will be placed outside the surviving buildings associated with those characters.

The society is fortunate in having as its president Virginia Eldin, Arnold Bennett's daughter, and as a vice president, Ruth Bennett, his niece. Other notable members include Roy Hattersley, Michael Foot (both of whom are authors and former politicians), and Professor James Hepburn, editor of the Bennett letters and probably the foremost Bennett scholar today. The lord mayor of Stoke-on-Trent is asked to act as the society's patron during his/her year of office and usually attends the annual dinner.

The society has recently started to maintain a small Bennett archive linked with those larger ones nearby at Keele University and at the city reference library. Copies of materials, including audio- and videocassettes, are normally available for loan to members. Those seeking information about membership should write to the secretary of the society, Jean Potter, at 106 Scotia Road, Burslem, Stoke-on-Trent ST6 4ET, U.K., or call: 01782 816311.

The E. F. Benson Society

Allan Downend

The E. F. Benson Society was formed in 1984 and held its inaugural annual general meeting at the Royal Festival Hall, London, in March 1985. At that time there were about fifty members, but membership increased to about two hundred within the next two years and has remained near that figure ever since. Although most members are in English-speaking countries, the society has members around the world and is gratified to have them come to its meetings in the United Kingdom.

The society aims to increase public knowledge and appreciation of the Benson family and of E. F. Benson in particular—and to provide an opportunity for Benson enthusiasts to meet. To these ends the society organizes at least one literary event a year to bring members together for talks on Benson's life and work or on other members of the family, and it organizes outings to places of interest. A weekend, usually the second in July, is arranged in Rye each year for walks to visit places represented in the Mapp and Lucia books and other sights associated with Benson.

The society also publishes an annual journal, *The Dodo,* which features articles on Benson and subjects relevant to his family, and it produces quarterly newsletters announcing details of forthcoming events and reviewing books about the Benson family or others connected with them. The society annually holds at least one fund-raising event that helps finance the publication program it conducts. During the last ten years it has reprinted articles and short stories by Benson in its *Bensoniana* series, which mostly includes works that he wrote for various magazines and that have been out of print for decades. In 1994 it republished the Benson part of Betty Askwith's *Two Victorian Families* (1971), the first biography of the Benson family (along with the Strachey family), which had been out of print. In 1995 the society republished *Some Social Criminals,* a series of stories that first appeared in *On-Looker* in 1901.

The society also organized a competition in which members were asked to submit short stories using the famous Benson characters from Tilling, the fictional town based on Rye. These stories were judged by Prunella Scales and Aubrey Woods, and the winning entries appeared in *Tilling Tales,* another collection published by the society. The society has also produced a guide to Rye that recounts Benson's arrival and his life there, describes how Rye appears in his books and short stories, and gives a list of these books. The society also promotes E. F. Benson as a recognized writer of ghost stories, and the fifth issue of *The Dodo* is devoted to Benson's writings in this genre.

In 1990, for the fiftieth anniversary of Benson's death, the society organized two events to commemorate his life and work. The first was a reception at Lambeth Palace, the home of the archbishops of Canterbury and thus Benson's home while his father was archbishop. Vice President Aubrey Woods introduced the evening, which consisted of a buffet supper and Victorian and Edwardian ballads and music that Benson played. On the following Saturday the society held a memorial service at St. Mary's Church, Rye, to com-

memorate his life in the town. Readings from Benson's works were given, and the ceremonies concluded with a reading of his obituary written by Francis Yeats-Brown, a lifelong friend.

In 1998 the society held a garden party at Lamb House, Benson's Rye home, and during this year the secretary of the society organized walks around the town. These excursions have proved successful in introducing people to some of Benson's less well-known works as well as to his autobiographical works. During the next few years the society plans to continue publishing Benson works, sponsoring events, and arranging visits to places related to the lives and works of the family. In the past it has visited Marlborough College, where Benson went to school; Wellington College, where he was born and where his father, who established its reputation, was the first master; and Magdalene College, Cambridge, where A. C. Benson was master and where his diary is archived.

For membership in and other information about the society, write to Allan Downend, Secretary, The E. F. Benson Society, The Old Coach House, High Street, Rye, Sussex TN31 7AD, U.K.

The Brontë Society

Robert J. Duckett

The Brontë Society is one of the largest and oldest literary societies in the world. It was founded in 1893 to bring together readers who share an interest in the members of the Brontë family—the most famous of whom are Charlotte, who wrote *Jane Eyre* (1847), *Shirley* (1849), *Villette* (1853), and *The Professor* (1857); Emily, who wrote *Wuthering Heights* (1848); and Anne, who wrote *Agnes Grey* (1847) and *The Tenant of Wildfell Hall* (1848). Members include those whose interests are in collecting Brontë manuscripts and memorabilia, managing a Brontë museum, and encouraging understanding and appreciation of the lives and writings of the Brontës.

With more than three thousand members worldwide, the society publishes a scholarly journal, *Brontë Society Transactions,* twice a year; one newsletter, *Brontë Society Gazette,* for members; and another newsletter, *The Angrian,* for students and children. Meetings, visits, lectures, and conferences are organized by the society, and many of its international members also organize local events.

The Parsonage, the home of the Brontë family in Haworth, was purchased for the society and was opened in 1928. The Brontë Parsonage Museum and research library that the society has established there

Banner headline for the quarterly published by the Burroughs Bibliophiles

are among its major assets and responsibilities, as more than ninety thousand people visit the museum each year. Members are admitted at no charge to these facilities, which are supervised by a director and staff that includes a curator, a librarian, and an education officer.

Additional information about the society is available from: The Brontë Society, Brontë Parsonage Museum, Haworth, Keighley, West Yorkshire BD22 8DR, U.K.; telephone: 011–44–1535–642323; fax: 011–44–1535–647131.

The Burroughs Bibliophiles

George T. McWhorter
University of Louisville

SELECTED BOOKS BY EDGAR RICE BURROUGHS PUBLISHED BY THE BURROUGHS BIBLIOPHILES: *Tarzan and the Jewels of Opar,* with pictorial bibliography by Vernell Coriell (Kansas City, Mo.: House of Greystoke, 1964);

The Girl from Farris's, illustrated by Frank Frazetta (Kansas City, Mo.: House of Greystoke, 1965);

The Illustrated Tarzan Books, No. 1: Tarzan of the Apes, illustrated by Hal Foster (Kansas City, Mo.: House of Greystoke, 1967);

The Illustrated Tarzan Books, No. 2: The Return of Tarzan, illustrated by Rex Maxon (Kansas City, Mo.: House of Greystoke, 1967);

David Innes of Pellucidar, illustrated by John Coleman Burroughs (Kansas City, Mo.: House of Greystoke, 1968);

Tarzan Books, No. 23: Tarzan under Fire, illustrated by William Juhré (Kansas City, Mo.: House of Greystoke, 1968);

Two Great Adventures: "Tarzan and the Vikings" and "Sinister," illustrated by Foster (Kansas City, Mo.: House of Greystoke, 1970);

The Illustrated Tarzan Books, No. 3: The Beasts of Tarzan, illustrated by Maxon (Kansas City, Mo.: House of Greystoke, 1971);

Tarzan and D'Arnot with the Foreign Legion / Tarzan and the Jungle Goddesses / Return of Korak / Tarzan at the Elephants' Graveyard, illustrated by Foster (Kansas City, Mo.: House of Greystoke, 1971);

Tarzan and the Golden City, illustrated by Foster and Burne Hogarth (Kansas City, Mo.: House of Greystoke, 1973);

Tarzan and the Pioneers of the Veldt, illustrated by Hogarth (Kansas City, Mo.: House of Greystoke, 1974);

Illustrated Tarzan Books, No. 13: Tarzan the Ape-Man, illustrated by Maxon (Kansas City, Mo.: House of Greystoke, 1974);

The Efficiency Expert, illustrated by Frazetta (Kansas City, Mo.: House of Greystoke, 1976).

SELECTED BOOKS BY OTHERS: William Gilmour, *Tarzan and the Lightning Man* (Kansas City, Mo.: House of Greystoke, 1963);

William Gilmour, *Lost on Jupiter* (Kansas City, Mo.: House of Greystoke, 1964);

John Harwood, *The Master of Adventure* (Kansas City, Mo.: House of Greystoke, 1965);

George T. McWhorter, *Burroughs Dictionary: An Alphabetical List of Proper Names, Words, Phrases and Concepts Contained in the Published Works of Edgar Rice Burroughs* (Lanham, Md., New York & London: University Press of America, 1987);

McWhorter, *The Edgar Rice Burroughs Memorial Collection: A Catalog* (Louisville, Ky.: House of Greystoke, 1991).

Edgar Rice Burroughs dictating a novel in 1935 (photograph by Hulbert Burroughs)

In the bylaws of the Burroughs Bibliophiles the organization is identified as "a non-profit literary society dedicated to stimulating interest in and preserving the works of the great American author, Edgar Rice Burroughs." As a splinter group of the World Science Fiction Convention held at Pittsburgh in 1960, thirty charter members met and elected officers of the new society. Clarence "Bob" Hyde became president (he remains president emeritus and chairman of the board in 1998), and plans were made to adopt or initiate official publications such as the *Burroughs Bulletin* and *The Gridley Wave* as well as to hold annual conventions. As with many new societies, the Burroughs Bibliophiles learned by doing, and interest in Edgar Rice Burroughs grew as his international popularity with a new generation increased and new members were recruited.

Science-fiction newsletters and fan magazines began to proliferate in the late 1930s and early 1940s, most of them amateur publications mimeographed in purple and seeking to share enthusiasms for the emerging genre. Most of these publications were distributed gratis or with nominal fees to cover mailing costs. These works frequently referred to Burroughs as "the

Grandfather of American Science Fiction," but the first magazine devoted exclusively to the author and his work was the *Burroughs Bulletin,* founded and edited by Vernell Coriell, a circus performer and acrobat who produced his magazines on cross-country tours. Coriell published his first issue in July 1947 with the blessing of Burroughs, then in retirement at Encino, California, after having served as the oldest war correspondent in World War II.

Thirteen years later at Pittsburgh the charter members of the Burroughs Bibliophiles voted to make the *Burroughs Bulletin* their official magazine, with Coriell as editor. The board of directors of the new society also voted to publish *The Gridley Wave,* a monthly newsletter that Coriell had already begun publishing in December 1959 and that would feature news of the latest Burroughs books, films, and merchandising activity. The title of this newsletter refers to a fictional device for sending and receiving messages to and from Earth, the Earth's core, and the planet Mars—a device that Burroughs's character, Jason Gridley, discovers in *Tarzan at the Earth's Core* (1923). Using Burroughs's nomenclature for other club events, the Bibliophiles christened their

George T. McWhorter, curator of the Edgar Rice Burroughs Collection, and some items from the largest institutional archive of Burroughs materials in the world

annual conventions "Dum-Dums," after the meetings of the anthropoid apes who dance by the light of the moon in the depths of the African jungle. Dum-Dums have been held in many major American cities, with those in Los Angeles having attracted the largest crowds; two conventions, in 1988 and 1997, have been convened at Cumbria in Northern England at Greystoke Castle. In 1998 the Burroughs Bibliophiles celebrated their thirty-seventh Dum-Dum in Baltimore, Maryland, with Gabe Essoe, author of *Tarzan of the Movies* as the guest of honor.

The greatest and best-loved illustrator of the first editions of Burroughs's books was Chicago artist J. Allen St. John, who created memorable images for thirty-three first editions, beginning with simple black-and-white headpieces for *The Return of Tarzan* (1915) and ending with *Tarzan's Quest* (1936). One of his most vivid paintings that was made for *Tarzan and the Golden Lion* (1923) became the official logo of the Burroughs Bibliophiles. He also designed the masthead for the *Burroughs Bulletin,* and this has been used since 1962. St. John died in 1957, three years before the Burroughs Bibliophiles was organized, but his widow, Ellen St. John, was the club's first guest of honor at the Dum-Dum held in Chicago in 1962. An attractive blonde with delicate features, she had been the model for Jane and many other Burroughs heroines in her husband's paintings. In 1963 the Burroughs Bibliophiles honored science-fiction writers L. Sprague deCamp and Sam Moskowitz by presenting to each an engraved silver bowl adorned with St. John's "Golden Lion." The Burroughs Bibliophiles tested several different Golden Lion Award trophies before settling on the current gold engraved plaque mounted on wood, in regular use since 1978. In 1984 a second annual award, a Life Achievement Award, was designed by George T. McWhorter for long and distinguished service to the memory of Burroughs. At the 1984 Dum-Dum in Baltimore, Coriell, known as "the father of Burroughs fandom" and in terminal illness at the time, was the first recipient of this award. He died less than three years later.

A list of Dum-Dum honorees through the years reads like a Who's Who of actors, artists, writers, and publishers involved with Burroughs's works. Tarzan actors include Johnny Weissmuller, Jim Pierce, Buster Crabbe, Frank Merrill, Herman Brix, Gordon Scott, Denny Miller, and Jock Mahoney. Twenty-five years after Weissmuller's guest appearance at the Boston Dum-Dum in 1971, his costar, Maureen O'Sullivan, made her first Dum-Dum appearance in Rutland, Vermont. Other well-known Burroughs artists who have been honored are St. John, Rex Maxon, Frank E. Schoonover, Frank Frazetta, Hal Foster (who set the standard for the Tarzan comics from 1931 to 1937 before leaving the strip to create *Prince Valiant*), William Juhré, John Coleman Burroughs (son of the author and illustrator of eleven first editions), Joe Kubert, Burne Hogarth, Boris Vallejo, Michael Whelan, Bob Abbett, Gray Morrow, Thomas Yeates, and Joe Jusko. Authors, editors, and publishers who have been honored include Forest J. Ackerman, Ian Ballantine, Lester del Rey, Donald Wollheim, Richard Lupoff, Erling B. Holtsmark, and Burroughs's children.

The Burroughs Bibliophiles have done more than honor famous people at conventions and publish magazines and newsletters. Their first major project was to collect short stories that had been published only in pulp magazines and to republish them with the permission of Edgar Rice Burroughs, Inc., a family corporation that Burroughs founded in 1923 to protect his enterprises in book publishing, motion pictures and radio and television shows, syndicated newspaper Tarzan strips and comic books, and trademark merchandising of everything from Tarzan ice cream to glue, wristwatches, knives, belts, and Tinkertoys. For many years the Burroughs Bibliophile reprints of *The Girl from Farris's, The Efficiency Expert, The Scientists Revolt, Beware!, The Red Star of Tarzan,* and *The Illustrated Tarzan Books, No. 1* were the only editions available of these works.

In 1972 the Burroughs Bibliophiles began a new series of publications under the House of Greystoke imprint. This included works such as *The Battle of Hollywood by James H. Pierce, Oldest Living Tarzan* (1978), the autobiography of the fourth actor who played Tarzan and who married Burroughs's daughter, Joan. Pierce and she starred together in the 1932–1933 Tarzan radio programs sponsored by Signal Oil. The most recent House of Greystoke publication is *The Edgar Rice Burroughs Memorial Collection: A Catalog* (1991) by McWhorter, who donated his collection of 70,000 volumes to the University of Louisville Library, where he is curator.

In promoting the image of Burroughs as a master storyteller, trendsetter, and original thinker, it was necessary for the Burroughs Bibliophiles to find prominent spokesmen. Such advocates have been L. Sprague deCamp, who wrote an introduction to the 1986 Easton Press edition of Burroughs's first novel, *A Princess of Mars;* Ian Ballantine and Lester del Rey, whose reprints of Burroughs's works in Ballantine paperbacks are collectors' items; and Ray Bradbury, whose introduction to Irwin

Porges's biography *Edgar Rice Burroughs, the Man Who Created Tarzan* (1975) is a classic accolade. Sam Moskowitz–Burroughs scholar, editor, publisher, teacher, literary agent, and pulp-magazine historian–was the first to anthologize Burroughs in the mainstream press and frequently contributed scholarly articles to the *Burroughs Bulletin.* Erling B. Holtsmark, chairman of the Classics Department at the University of Iowa, is the author of two major studies of Burroughs, including *Tarzan and Tradition* (1981), which explores the classic Greek and Latin roots of Burroughs's writing. Leigh Bracket has acknowledged Burroughs's inspiration for her own Martian concepts in writing science fiction, and Henry Hardy Heins's *Golden Anniversary Bibliography of Edgar Rice Burroughs* (1964) has become a standard reference for auction houses and antiquarian bookdealer catalogues. Astronomer Carl Sagan, primatologist Jane Goodall, actor Ronald Reagan, and comedienne Carol Burnett have also been unexpected spokespeople.

In recent years members of the Burroughs Bibliophiles have brought increasing public attention to the society. They have served as authorities for interviews or as writers of articles for magazines and newspapers, and they have participated in documentaries such as *Tarzan: The Legacy of Edgar Rice Burroughs,* the 1997 television biography produced by the Arts & Entertainment network and hosted by Peter Graves, and *In Search of Tarzan,* the American Movie Classics documentary televised during AMC's film festival of thirty-two vintage Tarzan movies. Another 1997 documentary, *Moi, Tarzan,* is being shown in many European countries, where the Tarzan myth is even more popular than in the United States.

The Walt Disney Studios are producing an animated Tarzan movie due for release in theaters by late spring 1999, and the commercial success of this movie will most likely add to the merchandising of Tarzan products. In summer 1997 the Palmdale Playhouse in California staged the premiere of *You Lucky Girl!,* an unpublished play that Burroughs wrote in 1927 and in which his daughter Joan was to star. In 1998 Donald M. Grant published this play, with illustrations by Ned Dameron, along with "Marcia of the Doorstep," a story about a foundling that Burroughs wrote but could not market in 1924. McFarland published in December 1996 a much-needed update to the Heins *Golden Anniversary Bibliography* by Burroughs Bibliophile Robert Zeuschner, a professor at Pasadena City College. Publication plans for new Burroughs Bibliophiles books and catalogues, including pictorial manuals for Burroughs collectibles and a complete history of the Tarzan radio shows, have been announced.

The Burroughs Bibliophiles is an international organization with headquarters at the Burroughs Memorial Collection in Louisville, Kentucky, where the magazine and newsletter are published and where the board of directors makes plans. Active regional chapters have been established in Washington, D.C.; Los Angeles; Chicago; Atlanta; Cleveland; and Baltimore–as well as in the states of Michigan, Florida, and Arizona and in countries such as Holland, France, Germany, and Australia. Some of the chapters publish regional newletters, such as *The Panthan Newletter* of the Washington, D.C., National Capital "Panthans." During the last fifty years more than two hundred Burroughs fan magazines have appeared, also with titles incorporating recognizable Burroughs-inspired nomenclature such as *Amtorian, Barsoomian, Jasoomian, Oparian, Erbania, Tarzine, Burroughs Newsbeat,* and *Erbivore.* Some, such as *The Barsoomian Blade,* have appeared on the Internet. For more information on the Burroughs Bibliophiles or for subscriptions to the *Burroughs Bulletin,* write to George T. McWhorter, Curator, Edgar Rice Burroughs Collection, Ekstrom Library, University of Louisville, Louisville KY 40292, U.S.A.; call (502) 852-8729; or send E-mail to: gtmcwhØ1@ulkyvm.louisville.edu.

The Wilkie Collins Society

Andrew Gasson

Wilkie Collins (1824–1889) is best known for *The Moonstone* (1868) and *The Woman in White* (1860), although he wrote more than thirty major books; more than a hundred articles, short stories, and essays; and a dozen or more plays. The Wilkie Collins Society was formed in 1980 by Kirk Beetz (who acted as president) in the United States and Andrew Gasson (who acted as secretary) in the United Kingdom. The original intention of the society was to bring together those with an interest in Collins, promote research into his life and work, and foster original critical studies of the novels, stories, plays, and essays of this important author. Collins's books have attracted readers for more than a century, and 1998 marks the 150th anniversary of his first book, *Memoirs of the Life of William Collins, Esq. R.A.,* a biography of his father. His unconventional life still continues to intrigue scholars, and his life and works both challenge the skills and originality of modern researchers and delight a new generation of readers.

After a period of neglect, interest in Collins has significantly increased. Nearly all of his fiction has been republished in inexpensive and accessible editions, many with new introductions and notes by publishers such as Oxford University Press, Sutton Publishing, and Broadview Press. The short stories are also being republished in collected editions and general anthologies. Two members of the society, William Clarke and Catherine Peters, have written recent biographies of Collins, Clarke's *The Secret*

Front cover of the annual published by the Wilkie Collins Society

Life of Wilkie Collins (1988) and Peters's *The King of Inventors* (1991). Other books include Andrew Gasson's *Wilkie Collins–an Illustrated Guide* (1998) and Lillian Nayder's *Wilkie Collins* (1997). Forthcoming are a two-volume edition of Collins's letters and "Ioláni," his long-lost and previously unpublished first novel from 1844. Collins is prominent in texts on detective fiction, on the sensation novel (for example, in Nicholas Rance's 1991 study, *Wilkie Collins and Other Sensation Novelists*), in other works such as Peter Caracciolo's *The Arabian Nights in English Literature* (1988), and in television, theater, cinema, and radio productions.

In 1989 the centenary of Collins's death was marked by the international Wilkie Collins Centennial Conference in Vancouver from 29 September to 1 October, and the majority of the papers presented at this meeting have subsequently been published in *Wilkie Collins to the Forefront: Some Reassessments* (1995), edited by Nelson Smith and R. C. Terry. The preface to this volume describes how "This unique occasion in Collins studies brought together an international group of nineteenth-century scholars. . . . The Wilkie Collins Society was represented by its President from California and

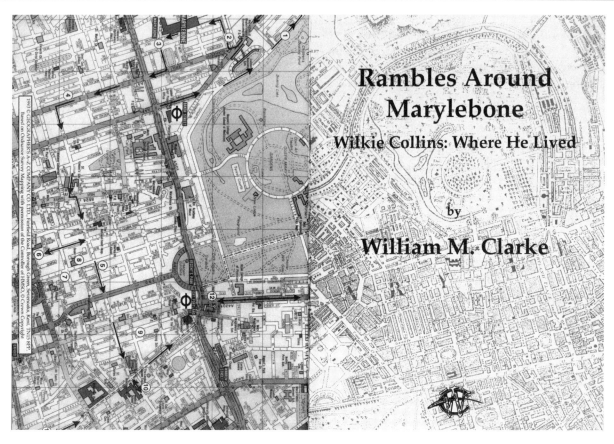

Cover for a pamphlet published by the Wilkie Collins Society

Secretary from London. The guest of honor was Mrs. Faith Clarke, great grand-daughter of Wilkie Collins." Clarke continues to be a patron of the society. Collins's centenary was also marked in the United Kingdom by a smaller meeting that the society arranged at the then Middlesex Polytechnic, together with an impressive dinner at the Reform Club in London, where guest speakers were Sir Kenneth Robinson and Benny Green.

Between 1981 and 1990 the society published eight issues of *The Wilkie Collins Society Journal* under the editorship of Kirk Beetz. Essays on Collins's full-length novels covered *Basil* (1852), *The Dead Secret* (1857), *The Woman in White, Armadale* (1866), *The Moonstone,* and *A Rogue's Life* (1879). It also published articles on Collins's private life and featured numerous book reviews. During the early 1990s the journal slipped into abeyance, but in late 1998 the first issue of a new series has been published under the joint editorship of Graham Law (professor in English Studies, Waseda University, Tokyo) and Lillian Nayder (associate professor of English at Bates College, Lewiston, Maine). In addition, the revised journal has an editorial board of well-known academics from both the United Kingdom and the United States.

The society publishes a newsletter approximately three times a year to inform members of significant events, new publications, and works in progress. It provides a forum for the exchange of information and for notes and queries, requests from members, book reviews, and other topical matters. Members are encouraged to submit for publication short contributions or longer essays of up to two thousand words. The newsletter provides a useful place for articles more speculative than those published in the journal.

During the 1990s the society has annually reprinted a series of Collins's short, lesser-known works that have not otherwise been republished since the author's lifetime. These include "The Last Stage Coachman," the first article Collins ever published (in 1843); "Reminiscences of a Storyteller," one of his rare autobiographical pieces; "Victims of Circumstances"; "A Little Fable," an unpublished, one-page short story; "A Pictorial Tour to St. George Bosherville"; and *Considerations on the Copyright Question Addressed to an American Friend* (1880).

In 1994 William Clarke wrote *Rambles around Marylebone,* a work that was specially written for the society and published in a limited edition of four hundred copies. It describes the several houses where Collins lived in London's Marylebone area, with both contemporary and modern maps provided as illustrations. Society meetings have included social events and a showing of the 1948 Sidney Greenstreet cinema version of *The Woman in White*.

The society is affiliated with the Alliance of Literary Societies in the United Kingdom and maintains close links with other organizations having related interests. Joint meetings have been held with the Dickens Fellowship, Friends of Kensal Green Cemetery (where Collins is buried), and the Pugin Society (based in Ramsgate, which Collins frequently visited late in his life).

The Wilkie Collins Society has more than one hundred members. It has always maintained an international membership, with subscribers from the United States, continental Europe, Japan, and Australia. Those interested in joining or those wanting further information should contact the membership secretary, Paul Lewis, at 47 Hereford Road, Acton, London W3 9JW, U.K.

The Stephen Crane Society

J. D. Stahl
Virginia Tech

Founded by scholar Paul Sorrentino, the Stephen Crane Society was organized in 1990 after a Crane conference hosted by Virginia Tech in Blacksburg, Virginia, the previous year. Its international membership includes specialists and nonspecialists devoted to research on, and discussion of, the life and works of Stephen Crane. The society is officially associated with the American Literature Association (ALA), and it holds its annual meeting, sponsors panels, and elects its officers at the ALA Conference in late May/early June each year in San Diego or Baltimore.

The society publishes *Stephen Crane Studies* (*SCS*), a journal of notes, queries, bibliographical material, and reviews published each spring and fall since 1992 at Virginia Tech, where both Paul Sorrentino, the editor, and J. D. Stahl, the associate editor, are faculty members in the Department of English. An annual feature of the journal is Donald Vanouse's annotated bibliography of works concerning Crane that have been published during the preceding year. In addition, *SCS* publishes a report on papers presented at the annual meetings of the society. Examples of the kinds of topics covered in the journal are suggested by those of essays such as Joseph McElrath's "Stephen Crane in San Francisco: His Reception in *The Wave*," M. Thomas Inge's "Sam Watkins: Another Source for Crane's *The Red Badge of Courage*," Zenichiro Oshitani's "Stephen Crane's Colors

Cover for the biannual journal published at Virginia Tech

in *The Red Badge of Courage*," and John Clendenning's "Crane and Hemingway: A Possible Biographical Connection." Particularly important among the articles in the journal have been James B. Colvert's essay on critical theory, "Stephen Crane and Postmodern Criticism" (spring 1992), and Stanley Wertheim's "Who Was 'Amy Leslie'?" (fall 1993), in which, as Vanouse writes, Wertheim "discusses documents concerning Amy Leslie's date of birth and her relationship to the world of prostitution in New York City. These issues are central to the complex problem of Crane's emotional involvement with Amy Leslie."

Other articles have included new information about Crane's correspondence and relationships. Of special interest is the spring 1995 issue devoted to Crane's family heritage and written by his grandnephew, Robert Kellogg Crane. This publication provides the most complete information about Crane's genealogy. It traces how Stephen Crane's family is related to other Crane families, gives a genealogical overview from the first generation of Cranes in the seventeenth and early eighteenth centuries to the seventh generation of Cranes, provides a genealogy of the Peck family (Crane's maternal lineage), lists Crane gravesites, briefly describes the Pennington School and Centenary College, and includes a section on the Cranes in the Miami valley region of Ohio.

Inquiries about membership in The Stephen Crane Society and works for publication in *Stephen Crane Studies* should be sent to Paul Sorrentino, editor, *Stephen Crane Studies,* Department of English, Virginia Tech, Blacksburg VA 24061-0112, U.S.A. E-mail should be directed to him at psorrent@vt.edu

The Gaskell Society

Joan Leach

The Gaskell Society is based in Knutsford, Cheshire, where novelist, biographer, and letter writer Elizabeth Cleghorn Gaskell (1810–1865) was brought up by her aunt following the death of her mother in 1811. Rich in Gaskell associations, the town was the basis for Cranford in Gaskell's 1853 novel of that title and for Hollingford in *Wives and Daughters* (1866): she spent her childhood there, was married in the Knutsford parish church, and is buried in the graveyard of the three-hundred-year-old Unitarian Brook Street Chapel surrounded by her ancestors' graves there. In 1832 she married the Reverend William Gaskell, who became the Unitarian minister at Cross Street Chapel in Manchester, where visits to her house, which belongs to the University of Manchester, can be arranged.

The society was organized in Knutsford following a literary luncheon and other events held on 29 September 1985 to commemorate the 175th anniversary of Gaskell's birth. It has an international membership with branches in the United States, Italy, and Japan as well as in London and South East London.

Members receive copies of the annual *The Gaskell Society Journal,* in which the society publishes scholarly articles on various aspects of Gaskell studies, in addition to *The Gaskell Society Newsletter,* which the society publishes twice a year. They may attend the annual general meeting held at The Royal George in Knutsford in September, the spring meeting held in Manchester, and a weekend residential conference held every two years at a site related to Gaskell. Such conferences have been held at Ambleside, Scarborough, Edinburgh, Oxford, and Chester. The society has also arranged visits to other places associated with Gaskell—to Heidel-

*An invitation
to join the
Gaskell Society*

Elizabeth Cleghorn GASKELL 1810-65

Cover for a brochure published by the society dedicated to the Victorian author of Cranford *(1853) and* North and South *(1855)*

berg, Germany, for example, and in 1998 to Paris—and the branches of the society regularly host programs of lectures, study sessions, and visits.

The society has a website managed by Mitsuharu Matsuoka at http://lang.nagoya-u.ac.jp/~matsuoka/EG-Society.html, and at majordomo@creighton.edu the society maintains an E-mail correspondence page. The Gaskell Society of Japan has begun a program of trans-

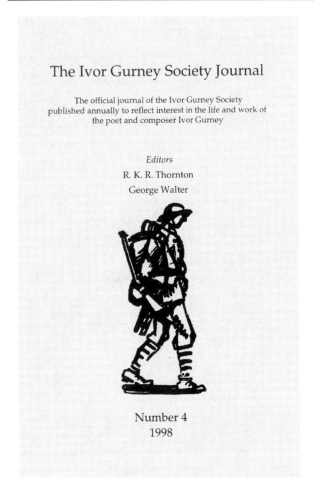

The Ivor Gurney Society Journal

The official journal of the Ivor Gurney Society published annually to reflect interest in the life and work of the poet and composer Ivor Gurney

Editors
R. K. R. Thornton
George Walter

Number 4
1998

Title page for the annual dedicated to the British poet of The Great War

lating Gaskell's works, and other translations are being considered in Spain, Norway, and China.

For information about membership in the society contact the membership secretary, Irene Wiltshire, 21 Crescent Road, Hale, Altrincham, Cheshire WA15 9NB, U.K.; telephone: 011–44–161–928–1404; E-mail: Wiltshires@aol.com.

The Ivor Gurney Society

John Phillips

The Ivor Gurney Society exists to promote interest in and enjoyment of the works of Ivor Gurney (1890–1937) by making his music and poetry available to a wider audience through performances, readings, conferences, recordings, and publications and by promoting scholarship on his life, work, and times. One particular project of the society includes preserving, cataloguing, and enhancing the Gurney archive in Glouces-

ter Library. The society has also contributed financially to the publication of *Eleven Gurney Songs* by Thames Publishing.

The society has more than two hundred members and holds an annual general meeting that members may attend. It also publishes annually *The Ivor Gurney Society Journal* and, several times a year, the *Ivor Gurney Society Newsletter*.

For membership in and information about the society write to John Phillips, Secretary, The Ivor Gurney Society, 7 Carlsgate, Hay-on-Wye, Hereford HR3 5BS, U.K., or telephone 011–44–1497–820541.

The Henty Society

Ann J. King

The Henty Society was founded in 1977 by a small group of enthusiasts led by Roy Henty, a distant relation of George Alfred Henty (1832–1902), best known as a writer of more than one hundred full-length boys' books that combine adventure with history. Most of these were published by the Glasgow-based company of Blackie, but before Henty obtained a contract with them, many other publishers, including Tinsley Brothers, produced his works. He also wrote novels, including three-deckers, one of which—*Rujub the Juggler* (1893)—was extremely successful. In addition to these he wrote many short stories and articles. For short periods Henty edited boys' magazines and other periodicals, including the *United Service Gazette,* a weekly devoted to military and naval service matters. From 1865 he was for many years special correspondent to a London daily newspaper, *The Standard,* and covered many nineteenth-century wars and other events such as the royal tour of India by the Prince of Wales, later Edward VII.

Henty was educated at Westminster School, London, and at Gonville and Caius College, Cambridge. He had a range of interests, both in business and in sport. He spent years in mining in both Italy and the United Kingdom. In the Crimea he rose to the rank of captain in the purveyors department of the British army. As a young man he had rowed for his college and was an able boxer. Also a keen yachtsman later in his life, Henty owned a splendid oceangoing yacht in which he competed in several important international events.

The Henty Society, which encourages research into Henty's life and work for the benefit of readers and collectors, has a worldwide membership. Members receive the *Bulletin,* published quarterly with articles on topics related to Henty's life and work, and at times the society publishes literary and bibliographical supplements. The society has always encouraged the compiling of bibliographical records and strongly supported Peter Newbolt's *G. A. Henty (1832–1902): A Bibliographical Study,* which was published by Scolar Press in 1996 and acclaimed for its comprehensiveness. The volume, which won a major bibliographical award, The Henry Darton Prize, covers the wide spectrum of Victorian publishing and provides a wealth of bibliographical information: it gives accounts of Henty's publishers, illustrators, and designers and includes essays on printing and binding methods.

The Henty Society continues to research American and "pirate" editions as well as those from European and Commonwealth countries. It is supporting the writing of a new biography and intends to publish a collection of Henty's lesser-known short stories. *David Sandler's Ready Reference to Henty Titles,* the provisional title for a revised guide, is to be published in 1999. Two society members also recently produced *Hugh Pruen's Henty Companion* (Kelshall, Hertfordshire, U.K.: The Henty Society, 1997), a short guide to the content of each of Henty's full-length books.

Meetings in the United Kingdom are regularly attended by members from overseas, and a strong Canadian constituency organizes its own functions. Details of membership can be obtained from Ann J. King, Secretary, The Henty Society, Fox Hall, Kelshall, Royston, Hertfordshire SG8 9SE, U.K.; telephone: 01763 287208.

WW2 HMSO Paperbacks Society

Anthony James

During World War II and the early years of the Cold War the official publisher for the British government, His Majesty's Stationery Office (HMSO), published many popular pamphlets (slim paperbacks) to explain the progress of the war and to chart its strategies. These accounts—well-written, mostly illustrated, and superbly designed—were sold at inexpensive prices and often in vast numbers. They were usually published before the outcomes of the events they recounted could be known, and Hilary St. George Saunders—a historian who wrote several of these pamphlets and who served in the British Air Ministry during World War II—has described them as "first drafts of history."

Although most of these paperbacks were published anonymously, many were written by well-known, popular, and established authors—H. E. Bates, Laurie Lee, J. B. Priestley, V. S. Pritchett, and other writers of similar stature, and HMSO used the best-possible techniques of layout and design. Thus, the series broke new

ground in content, readability, appearance, and authority. Postwar research, when the outcomes of events were known and access to the enemy's records was available, confirms and reinforces the value of the series both for the historical record and for collectors.

The WW2 HMSO Paperbacks, as the series has come to be known, is a resource too valuable to be lost. But at the time these works were published they appeared to be documents having only immediate, apparently ephemeral significance, and the materials used were nondurable. Only hindsight has shown the enduring worth of these pamphlets, and it is fortunate that many though not all of them were originally published in quantities large enough to survive the war years. But by the 1990s the passing of time in addition to many early handling and careless storage practices were threatening to make them unavailable to future generations. Some titles had already become so scarce as to be all but lost.

The WW2 HMSO Paperbacks Society was founded in 1994 with the intent of researching the series, stimulating interest in it, and saving these resources. Inquiries placed in magazines revealed that many collectors had a keen interest in these pamphlets but that no one knew either the size of the series or its bibliographic background, and inquiries at HMSO showed only that its archive material was practically nonexistent. Other research at the Imperial War Museum Library, an amazingly comprehensive resource, revealed that the series had never been documented. The British Ministry of Defence also acknowledged that it held almost no information.

It seemed that the WW2 HMSO Paperbacks Society had an almost virgin field to research. The Ministry of Information had maintained wartime responsibility for planning new publications, but that office had closed long before 1994, and its files had been deposited at the Public Record Office. As required by law, a copy of each pamphlet had been deposited with the British Library (formerly the British Museum Library) at the time it was published, but the cataloguing system involved using reference sources that, more than fifty years later, presented an apparently boundless labyrinth for exploration.

The earliest research done by the society was necessarily tentative and timid, and the first fruit was A. R. James's *A Bibliography of WW2 HMSO Paperbacks* (1993), a 48-page pamphlet that is incomplete and not entirely accurate. Nevertheless, collectors demonstrated a pent-up, unsuspected and frustrated need to know more. In responding to this need, the society began publishing its bimonthly newsletter, *WW2 HMSO PPBKS,* to stimulate research. This newsletter generated further interest and requests for more articles from magazine editors, and enough new information was soon available to enable the society to publish *WW2 HMSO Paperbacks Collectors' Guide* (1995), a follow-up pamphlet by James.

Officials of Her Majesty's Stationery Office became aware of, and interested in, this renewed search for knowledge about its publishing history, and HMSO commissioned James's *Informing the People* (1996), a book believed to be the first ever to study the wartime publishing activities the office had undertaken. This book covered some 120 wartime and early postwar pamphlets, each of which concerns some aspect of the global conflict and its consequences.

The research sponsored by the society has uncovered many surprises—unsuspected authors, forgotten titles, and new insights into other works. The main series of WW2 HMSO Paperbacks has been found to include sixty-eight works published between 1941 and 1949. Associated subseries have also been discovered, and the Ministry of Information appears to have encouraged commercial publishers to produce many similar (but nongovernmental) pamphlets during the war years.

While those commercially produced works did not benefit from the care in layout and design that HMSO lavished on its own publications, most of the commercial productions are authoritative and worth preserving alongside their official counterparts—and some are also of immense value to historians and book collectors. It now seems entirely reasonable to suppose that most of these commercially produced publications would have been lost forever had they not been rescued through the society's research into the wartime publishing conducted by HMSO.

Many important HMSO pamphlets and a few of those commercially published ones inspired by the Ministry of Information were also published in the United States, and some American government pamphlets were republished in Britain by HMSO. The whole idea was so successful that other Allied governments followed suit, and many of HMSO's pamphlets were sold internationally, often translated into local languages.

Although Joseph Goebbels, the minister of propaganda in Nazi Germany, admired the WW2 HMSO Paperbacks series and commended it to his own staff, one must recognize that the information strategy adopted by HMSO had no connection at all with propaganda. Without exception, the pamphlets in its series were serious attempts to inform with such accuracy and completeness as the need for security at the time could allow. That distinction, in particular, has brought the series lasting value and confirmed the early description of these pamphlets as being a "first draft of history."

The W. W. Jacobs Appreciation Society

Anthony James

W. W. Jacobs (1863–1943), the London-born writer of short stories and novels, published his work mainly between 1896 and 1926, although his writing career spanned a longer period. A contemporary of Sir Arthur Conan Doyle, H. G. Wells, Arnold Bennett, and Rudyard Kipling, his popularity and reputation were comparable with theirs. While the works of Wells and Doyle have remained popular, those of Bennett and Jacobs have become overlooked—although P. G. Wodehouse stated that, as a young writer, he had regarded Jacobs as a master in whose steps he should follow and that nothing had changed that high opinion. Mainly a writer of humorous stories about working-class life around the London docks or in small English country villages and minor ports, Jacobs is renowned also for some macabre works and classic horror stories including "The Monkey's Paw," a much-anthologized short story that has been produced as a play and as a motion picture at least six times.

The W. W. Jacobs Appreciation Society was founded in 1988 by a few enthusiasts determined to reverse his undeserved slide toward obscurity. Because of Jacobs's modesty and reticence, little was recorded about his life, and what had been written about his work was difficult to access. The society aimed to encourage the reading of his stories, to stimulate bibliographical research, and to track down information about his life so that a biography could be written. All of these aims were achieved by 1997.

The society's methods included placing articles in magazines aimed at book collectors, prompting responses from readers, and building a mailing list for a newsletter to be distributed for free. The newsletter aimed to encourage its readers to seek information on Jacobs's life and works and to submit papers for publication. As a result of these efforts, much information was discovered, mostly in the form of interviews, articles, and book reviews, but these were so scattered through many decades and various publications that they were inaccessible to all but dedicated researchers. Also unearthed were several archives of Jacobs's manuscripts, correspondence, and contracts, recorded but long overlooked.

Revival of interest in Jacobs and his work stimulated readers to expand their collections, and booksellers became more active in the field. Magazine and reference-book editors showed increased awareness, and the media generally picked up more snippets. Although the society does not claim credit for reestablishing this increased interest, several of Jacobs's works were republished during the most active period of the society, and some of his stories were also dramatized and broadcast by BBC World Service. The society does feel justified in claiming credit for directly stimulating and encouraging several other successful projects.

Earlier, uncompleted attempts to compile a bibliography were reexamined, and the task was undertaken by Chris Lamerton, who compiled *W. W. Jacobs— A Bibliography* (Margate, U.K.: Greystone Press, 1988), providing the first complete record of Jacobs's books and plays. A significant by-product was the building of what is almost certainly the world's largest collection of Jacobs's published works, which, together with some unpublished matter, now include more than three thousand items.

Anthony James accepted the task of writing a biography that would cover Jacobs's entire life. In 1990 he published a preliminary version, *The W. W. Jacobs Companion,* which is being enlarged for republication. James's work on this volume opened other doors, however, and he was able to interview Jacobs's family members and others who had known him well. As a result, a much more nearly complete record of Jacobs's life, probably under the title *W. W. Jacobs 1863–1943,* is to be published in 1999. The book also will cover Jacobs's career as a playwright.

John Jascoll has recovered many of Jacobs's early publications in periodicals and collected some of these in *W. W. Jacobs' Uncollected Cargoes* (Lancaster, Pa.: Hazelwood, 1996). Jascoll has also published *The W. W. Jacobs Periodical Bibliography* (Lancaster, Pa.: Hazelwood, 1996), which provides details of the first publication of 328 short stories and serial installments between 1877 and 1939 as well as other related matter. The book is comprehensively indexed. Jascoll was also able to secure the interest of David Karpeles, founder of the Karpeles Manuscript Library Museums, and collaborate with him in publishing the facsimile manuscript of Jacobs's most widely known work, the classic horror story *The Monkey's Paw* (Lancaster, Pa.: Hazelwood, 1998), which includes supplementary essays from several acknowledged Jacobs scholars.

By 1997 the society felt that it had achieved its aims, as new publications had diminished the need for its newsletter. The society therefore ceased publishing it in December 1997, when an article in this number claimed that the remaining ambition of the society would be realized by summer 1998, when on 1 July, Prince Charles, the Prince of Wales, would attend the unveiling of a commemorative Blue Plaque at 15a Gloucester Gate, Regent's Park, a former London home of Jacobs. This is a rare honor accorded annually and posthumously to only a few distinguished figures.

Information about the society is available by contacting Anthony James, The W. W. Jacobs Appreciation Society, 3 Roman Road, Southwick, West Sussex BN42 4TP, U.K. Although the newsletter is no longer published, back numbers can be ordered from the society.

The Richard Jefferies Society

Phyllis Treitel

The Richard Jefferies Society was founded in 1950 by a few citizens of Swindon, Wiltshire, where Richard Jefferies, the writer and naturalist, was born and raised. One of the founding members, Harold Adams, is still living, and the members maintain a strong feeling of continuity even though the subscription has steadily risen and most members no longer live in or near Swindon. The beauty of the land that inspired Jefferies continues to attract devoted followers: Stonehenge and Avebury are both in Wiltshire, and the ancient Ridgeway runs through it, connecting hill forts from prehistoric days.

For this reason most of the society's meetings and business is conducted in Swindon or in one of the beautiful nearby villages—such as Aldbourne, Liddington, or Chiseldon—that Jefferies knew. When anniversaries of significant dates in Jefferies's life occur, as for his centenary in 1987 or for his 150th birthday in 1998, the society makes special efforts. In August 1998 about sixty of the more than three hundred members gathered at a three-day festival in Swindon and Coate to hear talks and lectures, walk the streets that Jefferies walked, ramble through the woods he knew so intimately, and circumnavigate his beloved Coate Water. The program also included a ceremony at his birthplace in Coate, the farm of his father.

This farmhouse, together with a portion of the forty acres that once went with it, is now a museum owned by Swindon Borough Council. Admission to the museum, which is administered by volunteers from the society, is free, and it is open on two Sunday afternoons a month in summer. The museum is much as it was in Jefferies's time and houses some family keepsakes as well as books and manuscripts. It is visited by local people, who often know nothing of Jefferies or his books, and by devotees from countries such as France, Canada, Australia, and Japan.

At one side of the museum is The Sun Inn and Coate Water Country Park; to the other side is Day House Lane, leading to the farm where Jefferies's wife grew up. Beyond that are open fields, and in the distance is Liddington Hill. Another task of the members is to protect the setting of the house, and they have par-

Logo for the society honoring the British writer and naturalist

ticipated in many campaigns to prevent development of this precious stretch of open land. Their latest struggle has been to try to dissuade developers from locating a new hospital there.

As literary societies evolve and their members live farther and farther apart, the society's publications provide a means for those who cannot participate in person to continue to share their interests. In addition to spring and autumn newsletters, the society publishes a small journal, the *Richard Jefferies Society Journal,* and it has published or is preparing to publish leaflets about the places where Jefferies lived so that visitors may guide themselves on their pilgrimages. The society takes an interest in the house at Sydenham, London, where Jefferies spent several of his childhood years living with his aunt and uncle; in Surbiton, where he lived for five years as a newly married man; and in Sussex, where, loving the sea, he lived during his final years and where, after a long illness, he died at the age of thirty-eight.

Richard Jefferies's books need no advertising; they appeal to all sorts of people, to the academic and the barely educated. The society exists to bring together those who wish to know more about the man and his

books—and to protect what remains of the places that inspired him.

The Jerome K. Jerome Society

A. A. Gray

Jerome K. Jerome (1859–1927), the son of a deeply religious mother and a father who was a nonconformist minister and failed ironmonger, was a native of the East End of London. After both his parents had died by the time he was fifteen years old, Jerome became first a railway clerk at £26 per year before being drawn to the stage and leaving the security of his railway clerkship for the life of a traveling actor. For three years he pursued this theatrical career, which gave him the experiences he used in writing his first book, *On the Stage and Off* (1885). Following this, his magazine series "Idle Thoughts" provided the material for another collection of light essays, *Idle Thoughts of an Idle Fellow* (1886), and eventually Jerome became successful enough to earn his living entirely as a writer. He married, moved into a Chelsea flat overlooking the Thames River and Battersea Park, and there wrote the work that has brought him lasting fame—*Three Men in a Boat* (1889), a narrative of three young men and their dog taking a rowing holiday on the Thames.

In 1892 Jerome and other friends founded *The Idler,* a humorous magazine that published pieces by writers such as Bret Harte, Mark Twain, and W. W. Jacobs. Jerome's later works include *Three Men on the Bummel* (1900), a narrative of a tour of Germany; *Paul Kelver* (1902), an autobiographical novel; and many plays such as *The Passing of the Third Floor Back* (1907), his most famous work for the stage.

The Jerome K. Jerome Society, a registered charity, was founded in 1984 after the restoration of Jerome's birthplace, Belsize House, Bradford Street, Walsall, by architect Gordon H. Foster, the chairman of the society. The building had languished in a semi-derelict state for many years, much to the disgust of Wal-

Newsletter banner headline, the title of which is identified with the author's successful series of periodical articles

sall's literati. When the property eventually was to be sold in 1984, Foster bought it, restored it (with the help of a modest grant), and created, on the ground floor, two rooms dedicated to the memory of Jerome.

The society was founded to stimulate interest in, and public awareness of, the life and works of Jerome—and at the same time to provide financial support to the Walsall Museum and Art Gallery. Members of the society were promised that, as well as knowing that their subscriptions would be used to support these objectives, they would receive a newsletter about society activities and would be eligible to attend a dinner held annually in Walsall on or around 2 May, the anniversary of Jerome's birth. The society also has come to provide opportunities for interested people to meet, correspond, and share their enjoyment of Jerome's works, as well as to encourage research, lectures, and exhibitions concerning his life and writings.

The society has flourished and has members from all parts of the world, including the United States, Canada, Australia, Madagascar, and Italy. Its membership includes the ambassador to the Australian embassy in Vienna and a large contingent from London—which is, after all, where Jerome spent most of his life. Members of the society, while pursuing their aims of fostering and building public interest in Jerome and in his works, also manage to enjoy themselves at every opportunity.

Fortified by champagne and memories of Jerome's three holiday boat enthusiasts, they don straw boaters and stripy blazers and take boating excursions. The annual dinner has become a sparkling event and has featured many illustrious guest speakers such as Benny Green, Miles Kington, Barry Cryer, Hubert Gregg, Gabriel Woolf, and Libby Purves. The society newsletter has become a magazine, *Idle Thoughts,* that emulates the wit, humor, and general joie de vivre of Jerome. It presents a mix of serious articles with the levity and puncturing of dignity that Jerome would have enjoyed.

Information about the society is available from Tony Gray, secretary, The Jerome K. Jerome Society, c/o Fraser Wood, Mayo and Pinson, 15 Lichfield Street, Walsall, West Midlands WS1 1TS, U.K.; telephone: 01922 27686.

The T. E. Lawrence Society

Philip Kerrigan
T. E. L. S. Journal

More has been written about T. E. Lawrence than about any other twentieth-century charismatic figure apart from Winston Churchill. It would be dif-ficult to find a better example of a man who succeeded by being the right person in the right place at the right time. His involvement in the Arab Revolt of 1916–1918 made his name. In postwar years his skills as a negotiator and diplomat became evident when he acted as adviser to Prince Faisal at the Paris Peace Conference in 1919 and to Churchill at the Cairo Conference in 1921. In the years following the war he also set about writing his memoirs.

Lawrence's interest in writing was heightened through the friendship he developed with Robert Graves, whom he met at Oxford in 1919. Graves introduced him to eminent writers such as Thomas Hardy, Robert Bridges, Edmund Blunden, and John Masefield. For Lawrence the artist's creativity was of great importance, and his ambition was not merely to write a biographical record of his part in the Arab Revolt but to produce an enduring literary work of monumental significance. The standards he imposed upon himself were such that, after much revising and rewriting, when he had completed his *Seven Pillars of Wisdom* he doubted seriously whether the finished work fulfilled his aspirations. Hungry for reactions from his circle of literary friends, Lawrence sent the proofs to them. When the book was finally published in 1926 in a subscribers' edition, it received considerable attention, notwithstanding its limited circulation.

In 1922 Lawrence's decision to join the ranks of the Royal Air Force dismayed and puzzled his friends. He was discharged when his enlistment became publicly known, but he was able to persuade the authorities to allow him to join the Royal Tank Corps. After much lobbying, he managed in 1925 to rejoin the Royal Air Force as an aircraftman. During the next ten years he resumed his writing and produced *The Mint,* a record of his initiation as a recruit in 1922. Lawrence wrote this book in a clearer, freer style than that of *Seven Pillars of Wisdom.* Lawrence placed an embargo on its publication until at least the year 1950; it was in fact not published in England until 1955. Although he also wrote articles, mainly book reviews, most of his literary efforts from 1925 to 1935 were directed toward translations. Of these, Homer's *Odyssey* (1932) is the most important: the freshness of Lawrence's rendition still captivates readers. His literary success can be measured by the fact that more than a million copies of *Seven Pillars of Wisdom* have been sold, and *The Mint* has been reprinted many times by Penguin Books.

The great interest that the public showed in an Englishman who had been involved in what Lawrence called a "side-show of a side-show" in the Middle East during World War I and who subsequently spent twelve years in the ranks of the armed services still exists. The appearance of David Lean's motion picture *Lawrence of Arabia* in 1962 did much to stimulate this interest. It is therefore not surprising that in 1985, fifty years after Lawrence's death, a group of people decided to form the T. E. Lawrence Society. The modest foundations of the society were appropriately laid in the small country town of Wareham in the county of Dorset: appropriately, because in this part of England, also known as Thomas Hardy's "Wessex," Lawrence lived in his cottage, Clouds Hill, until he died in a motorcycle accident and was buried in nearby Moreton Church.

Ingrid Keith, a teacher and social worker, became involved when she heard that her local museum at Wareham planned a small exhibition to coincide with the fiftieth anniversary of Lawrence's death in 1985. Desiring to share her interest in Lawrence, she obtained permission from the museum curator to display a notice inviting others who were interested in forming a society to sign up. As a result of this initiative, a meeting was held on 29 June 1985 at the Red Lion Hotel in Wareham, where thirty founding members inaugurated the T. E. Lawrence Society. The late Roland Hammersley, DFM, was elected as chairman and Keith as secretary. As the society became better known outside Dorset, its membership increased, and when the National Portrait Gallery in London held the Lawrence of Arabia centenary exhibition during winter 1988–1989, about five hundred people were members.

The society held its first symposium in 1990 at Jesus College, Oxford, Lawrence's alma mater. One of the speakers was Jeremy Wilson, author of Lawrence's authorized biography, and he was elected chairman for the next four years. In his chairman's report for January 1990 Wilson wrote: "One of the most striking features of the Society is the sheer variety of its members' interests, which in turn reflects the diversity of Lawrence's life. He worked as archaeologist, intelligence officer, guerrilla liaison officer and leader, diplomat, writer, translator, serviceman, and marine craft expert. He was also an expert in photography, and knowledgeable about fine printing, contemporary literature, motor cycles and contemporary art. These facts and more appear among the interests declared by members."

The society is a registered educational charity. By the terms of its constitution, "the objects of the Society shall be to advance the education of the public in the life and works of T. E. Lawrence and to promote research (and to publish the useful results thereof) into his life and works." Because the myth and legend surrounding Lawrence of Arabia have provided fertile ground for many writers attracted mainly by the newsworthy and controversial nature of their subject, many publications contain inaccurate and highly speculative accounts of his career. The society therefore seeks to refute such fabrications by publishing and encouraging truthful accounts of Lawrence's life. Of the fifty or so biographies that have been published, John Mack's *A Prince of Our Disorder* (1976) and Jeremy Wilson's *Lawrence of Arabia* (1989) present the most balanced and authoritative studies available.

The society holds a symposium every two years in one of the colleges at Oxford. Speakers—experts in their particular fields—are chosen to cover a range of subjects. Members have also been encouraged to further the aims of the society by forming local groups. Two groups are now established in England, one in North America, and one in The Netherlands. The members arrange regular meetings and visit places associated with Lawrence. Such visits have included retracing Lawrence's bicycle tours in France when he was studying the construction of crusader castles for his degree thesis and trips to Syria and Jordan to see some of the sites familiar to those informed about the Arab Revolt.

Published twice a year, the journal of the society includes lectures given at its symposia, research articles, reprints of significant material about Lawrence that have been published only in obscure resources, and other information relevant to Lawrence's life. The newsletter is published four times a year and gives general information on the activities of the society. It also includes short articles on a range of subjects associated with Lawrence.

Lawrence was a prolific letter writer, and many collections of his correspondence are maintained in the United Kingdom and in the United States. The number of letters he wrote is unknown, but between five thousand and seven thousand are believed to exist. Cliff Irwin, a member who lives in Chicago, is currently compiling a worldwide catalogue and index of Lawrence's surviving correspondence. The society also has a library of books, letters, photographs, and video- and audiocassettes held on deposit by the Oxford City Library.

The society now has more than six hundred members, 67 percent of whom reside in the United Kingdom. Eighty-nine members live in the United States, and new members are welcome. Annual subscription rates covering membership, the journal, and the newsletter are currently £15 (U.K.) and £20 (overseas, which includes the dispatch of publications by air). Details may be obtained from P.O. Box 728, Oxford OX2 6YP, U.K.

International Marianne Moore Society

Elisabeth W. Joyce
Edinboro University of Pennsylvania

The International Marianne Moore Society was established in 1995 by Elisabeth Joyce with the help and support of Cristanne Miller. Because Marianne Moore's poetry in general has been critically overlooked, the organizers felt that forming a scholarly association would be an appropriate method to motivate a reevaluation of her work and her place in American modernism. They also wanted to create a community that would support academic work on Moore's poetry and foster increased communication among people devoted to projects involving her work. The society's goal of drawing greater attention to her work has been supplemented in the past three years by the sudden upsurge of books that have been published on her work. Members of the society include scholars from Great Britain, Spain, Israel, and France as well as some 150 people from the United States; among these members people are who knew Moore personally, members of her family, established scholars, and graduate students just entering the field.

Marianne Moore (1887–1972) was born in Kirkwood, Missouri, and grew up for the most part in Carlisle, Pennsylvania. She went to college at Bryn Mawr and returned to live and teach in Carlisle for the next ten years. In 1918 she moved to New York City, where she lived the rest of her life. Moore was actively involved with the arts and corresponded regularly with other poets such as William Carlos Williams, Ezra Pound, H. D., and Wallace Stevens, and she was editor of *The Dial* from 1925 to 1929.

Her poetry was published in journals and magazines such as *The Dial, The Egoist, Kenyon Review, Others,* and *Poetry.* Her books of poetry include *Poems* (1921), *Observations* (1924), *Selected Poems* (1935), *The Pangolin* (1936), *What Are Years?* (1941), *Nevertheless* (1944), *Collected Poems* (1951), *Like a Bulwark* (1956), *O to Be a Dragon* (1959), *Tell Me, Tell Me* (1966), and *Complete Poems of Marianne Moore* (1967). Among other awards for her poetry Moore won the Bollingen Prize (Yale University), the Pulitzer Prize, and the National Book Award. Her prose collections are her translation of Jean La Fontaine, *Fables* (1954); *Predilections* (1955); *A Marianne Moore Reader* (1961); and *The Complete Prose of Marianne Moore* (1986), edited by Patricia Willis.

In 1996 and 1997 the Marianne Moore Society organized panels on her work at the American Literature Association (ALA) Conference, which meets annually at the end of May. In 1997 a panel at the ALA was devoted to the work of Moore and H. D. and in 1998 the Marianne Moore panel, "H. D., and Marianne Moore: Poetics, Projections," was run jointly with the H. D.

Society. The society also runs a business meeting every year at this conference to discuss events of the past year and plan future panels.

The society also supports a listserv and a Web page, and a newsletter—which is sent electronically to all members with E-mail addresses—is published twice a year to keep members informed about important events. The listserv is run by Patricia Willis, American literature curator at the Beinecke Library, and is accessible at: MMOORE-L@LISTS.YALE.EDU. To subscribe to the list, anyone interested should send to the address: listserv@lists.yale.edu. Leave the message line blank, and type SUBSCRIBE MMOORE-L, followed by the name of the subscriber. Please send questions to Patricia Willis at willp@yalevm.cis.yale.edu.

The Web page http://www.edinboro.edu/~ejoyce/ Moore.htm is sponsored by Elisabeth Joyce of Edinboro University of Pennsylvania. The Web page includes a bibliography of recent publications on Moore's poetry, notice of upcoming events devoted to her work, and a list of manuscript repositories. In the future the society would like to post public-domain materials such as Moore's *Poems* and *Observations,* but this will need to be in a restricted format in order to conform to European copyright laws.

Those interested in joining the International Marianne Moore Society should write to Elisabeth W. Joyce, Department of English, Edinboro University of Pennsylvania, Edinboro PA 16444, U.S.A.

The Wilfred Owen Association

Helen McPhail

The Wilfred Owen Association exists to commemorate the life and work of Wilfred Owen, now perhaps the most famous of the English poets of World War I, and to encourage recognition of his influence on modern poetry. Although he was barely known at the time of his death in action only a week before the Armistice, Owen was beginning to see his poems published. From childhood he had been determined to become a poet and had spent his adolescence studying the English Romantic poets (particularly John Keats and Percy Bysshe Shelley) as well as William Shakespeare. His early education was in Birkenhead, near Liverpool, until his family moved to Shrewsbury, the rural county town where his father was assistant station manager at an important railway junction. His family was deeply devout, and after finishing school Owen considered joining the church but left to become a teacher of English in southwest France.

"Symmetry," a memorial to Wilfred Owen in Shrewsbury

Having first resisted the idea of joining the military service, he eventually enlisted and, after training, was posted to the Second Battalion of the Manchester Regiment at the end of 1916. While being treated for shell shock following his first intense experiences of the war early in 1917, he met Siegfried Sassoon, already an established poet, who recognized his talent and encouraged him. Owen, who came from an unsophisticated background and had no literary friends, quickly learned how to turn his disturbing experiences into profound poetry. As he drew on his knowledge of humanity at war, he expressed his feelings in his writing, and throughout a little more than a year before his death he worked intensively to create poems such as "Dulce et Decorum Est," "Anthem for Doomed Youth," "Strange Meeting," and "Futility." In addition to his collected poems and many anthologized selections, publications of Owen's writings include vivid letters home that were kept by his mother and, in effect, comprise his autobiography.

After a lengthy period in Scotland and England during 1917 and 1918, in hospital and then in military training camps, Owen returned late in 1918 to the front line determined to continue using his poetry to speak out for the men in his care. He was delighted to find his nerves steady, and he was awarded the Military Cross for his courage and leadership in battle as the British army liberated French villages in autumn 1918. On 4 November, however, he was killed on the bank of a canal that British forces were attempting to cross. He is buried in a British military cemetery in Ors, near Le Cateau in northwest France.

The Wilfred Owen Association organizes public events such as talks, readings, and performances, and it publishes a newsletter twice a year as part of its program of providing information on Owen's life, work, and times. Through a small memorial fund the association supports efforts to increase readers' understanding of poetry and encourages poetry writing by sponsoring students who participate in week-long courses tutored by active poets. The association originally intended to set up memorials to Owen in Oswestry, where he was born, and in Shrewsbury, where he was educated and where his family continued to live after his death. Plans were made to inaugurate public memorials for the centenary of his birth in 1993, and in 1989 the committee was officially formed to raise funds, to select artists to invite as participants, and to arrange public events to mark the occasion.

This was an ambitious program for a group of amateur enthusiasts in a quiet town where, except for attaching his name to a junior school, the poet had in general been ignored since his death; however, the three weekends of commemorative events in 1993 were attended by association members and admirers of Owen's work from all over the world. The town now maintains "Symmetry"—an abstract, silver-grey granite sculpture that stands on a circle of York stone paving in the grounds of Shrewsbury Abbey, the medieval church between the Owen home and the center of town. The site recalls the trenches and the canal where Owen was killed, and a single line of his poetry from "Strange Meeting" is engraved on this memorial: "I am the enemy you killed, my friend." In Oswestry, the Welsh border town twenty-five miles from Shrewsbury, a polished steel plaque has been engraved with the badge of the Artists Rifles, the military training unit that Owen joined after enlisting in 1915, and two sonnets— "Anthem for Doomed Youth" and "Futility." Beneath this plaque, attached to a stone wall outside the church where Owen's parents were married and where he was baptized, is a stone seat bearing Owen's initials and dates.

For the eightieth anniversary of the Armistice and of Owen's death in 1998 the association presented its first Award for Poetry. Made of gun metal and silver and specially designed by a goldsmith with an international reputation, this award is presented to a poet whose work reflects the tradition and approach underlying Owen's work. Christopher Logue, whose poetry includes a dramatic reworking of *The Iliad,* is the first recipient of the award, which demonstrates the continuing interest that the association has in celebrating poetic creativity.

The aims of the association appeal to many people initially drawn to the relatively small body of work Owen left. The facts of his early death add to the power of his writing, particularly for students who often make their first personal ventures into English literature through his poetry: his language is direct and honest, and for many people his poetry is also an introduction to the facts and atmosphere of World War I, a period of continuing historical, social, and literary significance.

Association publications—such as Ken Simcox's *Wilfred Owen–Poet of the Trenches,* an introduction to Owen's poetry that is aimed at young students who may be approaching serious poetry for the first time— help to place Owen's writing in twentieth-century literature. The ruins of Uriconium, the city established near Shrewsbury by the ancient Romans, have inspired many writers and artists through the centuries, and as a boy Owen visited it frequently and searched for remains hidden under the farmland. His poem about those Roman settlers has been published, with two others by A. E. Housman and Mary Webb, as part of an attractive leaflet produced by the three literary societies dedicated to these writers. Some of the public events sponsored by The Wilfred Owen Association—such as

talks shared with other literary societies honoring Ivor Gurney, Edward Thomas, William Blake, and Keats and Shelley—also bring together such societies, and these organizations generally share and publicize information about forthcoming activities.

Peter Owen, the poet's nephew and current president of the association, frequently travels to places connected with Wilfred Owen in England, Scotland, and France to represent both the family and the association. In addition, the vice presidents of the association include academic scholars whose work on Owen has been widely recognized. They are generous in contributing publications and correspondence and in making public appearances to illuminate Owen's life and work. Acting as a source of general information and encouragement, the association supports such academic research and publication.

Five years after Owen's centenary, most members of The Wilfred Owen Association are in Great Britain, but other countries—notably the United States and Japan—also have active members. It is one of the most active British literary societies, and it keeps subscription rates low so that membership is readily accessible. Additional information on the association is available from Helen McPhail, Chair, The Wilfred Owen Association, 17 Belmont, Shrewsbury SY1 1TE, U.K.; telephone and fax: 011–44–1743–235904.

Penguin Collectors' Society

Russell Edwards

In 1974 at a meeting in Richmond, Surrey, the Penguin Collectors' Society was founded, as the minutes record, by "a small band of enthusiasts" devoted to the productions of Penguin Books. Several of those founding members had close connections with the publishing house: Christine Lane, the daughter of Allen Lane, one of the founders of the publishing firm; Hans Schmoller, Penguin's distinguished typographer; and his wife, Tanya, who had been secretary to Lane. The timing was perhaps significant, too. Allen Lane had died in 1970, and when Penguin was taken over by the giant Longman-Pearsons conglomerate, the firm began an agonizing reappraisal in which it seemed all too likely that the distinctive character of Penguin might be lost.

But the society was not intended to be, and never has been, a pressure group. Instead, it is a gathering of those who appreciate the appearance and content of a particular line of books and who venerate those books for the influence they have held in their lives.

Logo for the society devoted to the publications of the influential paperback imprint

The first Penguin editions appeared in British bookshops on 30 July 1935. Allen Lane, who launched the new imprint with his brothers Richard and John, was the young chairman of the Bodley Head, which he had inherited from his adoptive uncle, John Lane. Once a highly respected and innovative publishing house that included *The Yellow Book* (1894–1897) among its triumphs, the Bodley Head had become moribund. The Lanes were convinced that high-quality paperback reprints, selling at sixpence, were the means to resuscitate the firm. Others in publishing thought that the Lanes were mad, a view shared by the directors of the Bodley Head, and, using their own capital, the Lanes had to pursue their plan alone.

The public proved the brothers to be triumphantly right. Readers liked the looks of the new paperbacks–compact; substantial; well printed with bright, color-coded covers bearing the penguin device; and intended to convey what Allen Lane called "a sort of dignified flippancy." They liked the selection of titles: the first ten included works by Ernest Hemingway, Compton Mackenzie, Agatha Christie, and Dorothy L. Sayers. They also liked the price; indeed, a new reading public, one that would not have dreamed of buying a hardback novel at fifteen times the cost, was born. Within the first year three million copies of Penguin paperbacks were sold. Penguin Books flourished; the Bodley Head was liquidated in early 1936.

The Lanes' vision extended well beyond the mass marketing of popular fiction, however: Penguin No. 1 was *Ariel* (1924), André Maurois's biography of Percy Bysshe Shelley. Allen Lane later proclaimed that he aimed to provide "the true everyman's library of the twentieth century." In 1937 the firm made large strides in that direction by launching the Penguin Shakespeare series, eventually completed in thirty-seven volumes, and even more significantly by publishing the first Pelican Books. George Bernard Shaw provided the opening works in that new series, which included the first original (rather than reprinted) work to be published by the

firm: Shaw enlarged his *The Intelligent Woman's Guide to Socialism and Capitalism* (1928) with new chapters in Pelican's *The Intelligent Woman's Guide to Socialism, Capitalism, Sovietism and Fascism* (1937).

Readers came to regard Pelican editions as the first places to turn for knowledge about hitherto unexplored fields of nonfiction such as astronomy or religion, medicine or music. Later in 1937 the first Penguin Specials–on contemporary world affairs–were published: books that alerted the public to events that were leading to World War II.

Through the years more than sixty Penguin series, an almost inexhaustible quarry for collectors, have been published alongside the mainstream titles. Some of these series–such as the Penguin Illustrated Classics, with their wood engravings, or the Penguin Scores, in their splendid patterned paper covers, were short-lived but are fondly remembered. Other series, such as the Penguin Classics and the Penguin Poets, triumphantly continue. Some were prestigious publishing achievements–such as the King Penguins, elegant illustrated keepsakes, and the monumental Buildings of England series. Penguin also changed children's publishing, first with the beautifully lithographed Puffin Picture Books and then with the adventuresome range of Puffin Story Books.

The Penguin Collectors' Society has more than four hundred members worldwide, including strong contingents in the United States, Canada, and Australia. The history and publications of Penguin Books (New York) are of particular interest. Allen Lane set up an organization to distribute Penguin editions in the United States in July 1939, when, on the brink of the European war, the timing of this move might have been unfortunate. It turned out to be an important one in the development of the firm, however, for Lane recruited young Ian Ballantine to run the operation on a shoestring. When the outbreak of the war made imports impracticable, Ballantine, with great initiative, turned to publishing in New York. Perhaps his greatest coup was the alliance with *Infantry Journal,* which provided the texts of books intended for the troops–*Guerrilla Warfare* and *Psychology for the Fighting Man* were typical titles–and purchased the bulk of the print run. Penguin supplied the publishing expertise and qualified for an extra paper ration as part of the war effort. The outcome was the series of Fighting Forces–Penguin Specials, now keenly sought by collectors.

Lane was perhaps less grateful than he should have been: he resented losing direct control, and friction between Lane and the New York office was constant, particularly over the design of the American Penguins. He did not understand American publishing and could not appreciate the need for illustrated covers if these books were to compete in a lively paperback market. He felt the purity of the "Penguin look" was being compromised by any pictorial cover. Even though Penguin cover art was more restrained than that of some of its American rivals (scantily clad ladies were taboo in Penguin books) Lane never recognized the delicate qualities of the now highly prized work of illustrators such as Robert Jonas.

As soon as the war was over, Lane and Ballantine parted, and Penguin Books (New York) closed down after having produced more than two hundred editions. Ballantine went on to achieve distinction with Bantam Books and other paperback imprints, but the lesson was not lost in Britain at Penguin Books, which, despite Lane's continued opposition, soon introduced pictorial covers in response to new competition from postwar publishing firms such as Pan Books.

The Penguin Collectors' Society operates informally, with volunteers serving in the offices of secretary, treasurer, and editor. An annual meeting, a most convivial occasion, is often held at a country hotel or university campus, where official business is quickly dispatched in order to allow maximum time for displaying and bartering Penguins that members bring along. Some overseas members plan their annual holidays around these gatherings, and the society has also met successfully overseas–in Amsterdam.

The most important means of communication between members of the society are its publications. *The Penguin Collector* is published twice a year, and under the direction of editor Steve Hare it has become a sixty-page illustrated magazine in mock-Penguin format, complete with colored cover. It includes research articles on Penguin series, history, and personalities; when members raise queries in it, other members can usually supply answers. Advertisements of books for sale or exchange are published, as are announcements of titles wanted. The society also publishes an annual miscellany volume commonly devoted to a significant Penguin anniversary: the volume for 1997 commemorates the sixtieth anniversary of Pelican Books, with distinguished contributors including Richard Hoggart, Asa Briggs, and J. E. Morpurgo. Additional publications of the society include *A Penguin Collector's Companion,* an alphabetical guide that indexes the whole range of material the firm has published, and a facsimile edition of the Complete Penguin Catalogue for 1935 to 1971, which is being prepared and should be an invaluable aid to collectors.

Perhaps the most remarkable publishing achievement of the society has been its production of *Life Histories.* Begun in 1956 by Paxton Chadwick, the natural-history illustrator, this volume was to have been part of the Puffin Picture Books series, and when the author

died of cancer in 1961, the book was largely completed. Publication of the series ceased, however, when booksellers were reluctant to give display space to the slender, double-size volumes, and *Life Histories* remained the only Puffin Picture Book unpublished–until the Penguin Collectors' Society took the matter in hand. To commemorate the anniversaries of both Penguin and the society as well as to honor Paxton Chadwick, a team of designers, printers, Penguin friends, the author's widow, and the society's editor collaborated in using the original plates to produce this missing Puffin, a limited edition that is already a collector's item.

While the generation that grew up with Penguins is strongly represented in the ranks of the society, many new collectors are also joining. Because Penguins were made so well and produced in such huge numbers, it is not too difficult or too expensive to start a collection, even of the earliest titles. Collecting the first thousand Penguins in first printings is a popular target; some collectors specialize in Puffins and other children's editions. Ptarmigans, Peregrines, and Peacocks from the Penguin aviary are also interests of other collectors. Relatively few secondhand bookshops have serious interests in paperbacks, but collectors are expert in rummaging through charity shops and church jumble sales, and some members compile catalogues.

Some newspapers that publish columns on collecting for investment have propagated the idea that anyone with an early Penguin edition may be holding a fortune, and the secretary of the society is regularly pestered by nonmembers who are convinced that their tattered volumes are national treasures. In fact, relatively few titles command high monetary value, but collectors are always looking for some scarce Penguins. During World War II all books were printed on inferior paper, and these copies–especially some of the green-covered crime titles–are difficult to find in pristine condition. Some of the children's series are also hard to acquire: Baby Puffins were often chewed by infants, and parts of Puffin Cut-Out Books were damaged by being cut up. Advanced collectors may try to find the privately printed Christmas Books that Lane produced in strictly limited runs for his clients and friends. In general, however, a wealth of Penguin materials is readily available for collectors to acquire.

Allen Lane was not a writer and, indeed, was not a formally educated man: he finished his undistinguished school career at the age of sixteen, and he never went to university. Nevertheless, in addition to his canny, innate business sense, he had the knack for recognizing talent when he saw it and the courage to back his judgment against that of pundits. In 1946, for instance, everyone told him that to contemplate launching a series of new translations of literary classics would be an unmitigated disaster. However, Lane backed the enthusiasm of E. V. Rieu, an obscure scholar whose *Odyssey* launched a series in which millions of copies were sold.

At Penguin Books, Lane surrounded himself with an extraordinarily talented team of editors, typographers, and designers whose devotion was remarkable—even though he could be devious and unfeeling at times. The result of their efforts, however, made Penguins not just a publisher's imprint but one of the most significant developments in the cultural life of the twentieth century.

For additional information about the society, write to Russell Edwards, secretary, Penguin Collectors' Society, 12 Harcourt Close, Henley-on-Thames, Oxon RG9 1UZ, U.K., or telephone: 011–44–1491–576748.

The Beatrix Potter Society

Marian Werner

The Beatrix Potter Society was founded in 1980 by a group of people professionally involved in the curatorship of Beatrix Potter material. It exists to promote the study and appreciation of the life and works of Beatrix Potter (1866–1943), who was not only the author and illustrator of *The Tale of Peter Rabbit* (1901) and other classics of children's literature but also a landscape and natural-history artist, diarist, farmer, and conservationist. In this last capacity she was responsible for the preservation of large areas of the Lake District through her gifts to The National Trust.

The society's membership is worldwide, and its activities include regular talks and meetings in London as well as visits to places connected with Potter. A Linder Memorial Lecture is given each spring to commemorate the contribution made to Beatrix Potter studies by Leslie Linder and his sister, Enid. Since 1984 biennial study conferences have been held in the Lake District or in Scotland and are attended by members from around the world.

In 1998 the eighth conference was held from 17 July through 24 July at the University College of St. Martin, Ambleside, Cumbria, with talks given about Potter as a writer and illustrator by speakers from the United States and the United Kingdom. Visits were scheduled to various places associated with Potter—Hill Top, Townend, Troutbeck Park, and Derwentwater—and one day was devoted to "The Ladies of the Lakes": Dorothy Wordsworth, Harriet Martineau, the Armitt sisters, and Charlotte Mason.

A quarterly newsletter, issued free to members, contains articles on various topics in addition to infor-

Emblem for the society honoring the life and work of the British children's writer and illustrator

mation about meetings and visits, reviews of books and exhibitions, members' letters, and news of Beatrix Potter collections in the United Kingdom and elsewhere. It also includes items of interest to collectors and news of Potter merchandise. The society maintains an active publishing program that includes the proceedings of its study conferences and occasional papers.

Membership details are available from The Administrator, 17 Dixon Close, Lawford Dale, Manningtree, Essex CO11 2HA, U.K.

The Powys Society

Chris Gostick

Following a small advertisement in the *Times Literary Supplement* in 1967, The Powys Society was founded by a small group of enthusiasts who felt that the quality of the Powyses' writings, particularly those of John Cowper, Theodore, and Llewelyn, was not sufficiently recognized. It declared that its aim must be "the establishment of the true literary status of the Powys family through promotion of the reading and discussion of their works."

Since then the society has expanded both its membership and its activities. It is now an international society with members in England, Wales, Scotland, Ireland, the United States, Canada, Sweden, France, The Netherlands, Italy, Belgium, Germany, Hungary, Africa, Australia, and New Zealand. Despite their geographical dispersion, members share an enthusiasm for the works of one or more members of the Powys family and their immediate circle of friends.

John Cowper Powys (1872–1963) was a prolific novelist, essayist, letter writer, poet, and philosopher—a writer of enormous complexity, profundity, and humor. After his death his books gradually went out of print, but his reputation has revived, and critics are hailing him as "a long-lost genius whose millennial themes resonate with the modern-day reader."

A powerful orator, John Cowper spent more than thirty years as an itinerant lecturer in the United States, and there he wrote his first four novels. In 1930 he retired to upstate New York, turned to full-time writing, and produced masterpieces such as *A Glastonbury Romance* (1933), *Autobiography* (1934), and *Weymouth Sands* (1934). Returning to Great Britain in 1934, he settled in 1935 in North Wales, where he wrote the historical novels *Owen Glendower* (1940) and *Porius* (1951), critical studies of François Rabelais and Fyodor Dostoyevsky, and *The Brazen Head* (1956) and other fantasies.

Other notable novels include *Wolf Solent* (1929) and *Maiden Castle* (1937), which—like all of John Cowper's fiction—are rich in psychological analysis and in their evocation of place. *The Pleasures of Literature* (1938) demonstrates the breadth of his literary interests; *The Meaning of Culture* (1929) and *In Defence of Sensuality* (1930) display the immediacy of his thought. His journal, which he kept for thirty years, is an immense work that is as yet largely unpublished, but *Petrushka and the Dancer* (1995), edited by Morine Krissdóttir, is a selection from his diaries between 1929 and 1939.

Theodore Francis Powys (1875–1953) was a man who rarely left home or traveled in a car, who claimed to love monotony, and who, as his brother Llewelyn stated, "never gave so much as a sunflower-seed for the busy, practical life." He ran his own farm, White House Farm at Sweffling, Suffolk, from 1895 to 1901 before becoming determined to write and "retiring" to Dorset. In 1904 he settled in East Chaldon, which Llewelyn Powys described as "the most hidden village in Dorset," and there he remained until 1940, when the war drove him inland to the Dorset hamlet of Mappowder. In 1905 he married Violet Rosalie Dodds, a local girl; they had two sons and an adopted daughter.

Theodore claimed that religion "is the only subject I know anything about" and that the major influence upon him was the Bible, but his unorthodox

July 1998 *The Powys Society Newsletter* No 34

Cover for the newsletter of the society dedicated to the diverse artists, philosophers, and writers in the Reverend C. F. Powys's family

Christianity reveals strands of mysticism, quietism, and pantheism. Sometimes savage, often lyrical, his novels and stories explore universal themes of love, death, good, and evil within the rural world. In spite of the apparent realism of his settings, Theodore is a symbolist and allegorist. His major works include *The Soliloquy of a Hermit* (1916), *Mr. Weston's Good Wine* (1927), and *Unclay* (1931); his *Fables* (1929) and short stories are also much admired.

Llewelyn Powys (1884–1939) was born in Dorchester, Dorset, and spent his childhood at Montacute, Somerset. He married American writer Alyse Gregory and lived for varying periods in Kenya, the United States, Dorset, and Switzerland. His twenty-six books include a biography, *Henry Hudson* (1927); a novel, *Apples be Ripe* (1930); descriptive and polemical essays; and memoirs and reminiscences. Of all the Powys brothers, Llewelyn was recognized as the most cheerful, the most at ease with existence: he was the only Powys for whom, as a writer, a title such as *Glory of Life* (1934) could hold not a shadow of the ironic. His epicurean philosophy is intimately related to the tuberculosis with which he struggled for thirty years.

Among Llewelyn's best books are *Black Laughter* (1925), about life in Africa; *Skin for Skin* (1926), a memoir of his first attack of tuberculosis and his residence in a Swiss sanatorium; *Impassioned Clay* (1931), a statement of his philosophical outlook; the essays collected in *Earth Memories* (1934), *Dorset Essays* (1935), *Somerset Essays* (1937), and *Swiss Essays* (1947); and the fictionalized autobiography *Love and Death* (1939). In their blend of the descriptive, the reminiscent, and the polemical, Llewelyn's best writings retain both their urgency of appeal and their charm of evocation.

The three brothers were members of a family of eleven children born to the Reverend C. F. Powys, vicar of Montacute for thirty-two years, and his wife, Mary Cowper Johnson. All the children were formidable individualists, but Louis Marlow writes that when they were together they became "one huge many-headed Powys." Their family identity and passionate love of nature united them; their sometimes anguished quests for separate identities drew them into a remarkable variety of careers: from schoolmaster to farmer, from poet to architect. Gertrude Powys was a painter of power and insight; Marian Powys, an authority on lace and lace-making. A. R. Powys, secretary of the Society for the Protection of Ancient Buildings, published many books on architectural subjects; Philippa Powys was a novelist and poet, as was Lucy Powys's daughter, Mary Casey.

The Powyses inevitably attracted a wide circle of friends and admirers, many of whom were also writers and artists who settled in East Chaldon in the 1930s. These included: the novelist David Garnet; the novelist and autobiographer Louis Wilkinson (Louis Marlow) and his first wife, Frances Gregg; the novelist, poet, and short-story writer Sylvia Townsend Warner; the poets Valentine Ackland and Gamel Woolsey; and the sculptors Elizabeth Muntz and Stephen Tomlin. Littleton Powys, who published two volumes of autobiography, was married twice, and his second wife was novelist Elisabeth Myers. In the United States, John Cowper Powys was friendly with novelist Theodore Dreiser and poets Edgar Lee Masters, E. A. Robinson, and Edna St. Vincent Millay; in Wales, with poet Raymond Garlick and novelist James Hanley. In all, the Powys family and their friends display an unusually wide range of social, literary, and imaginative interests.

The Powys Society holds an annual conference, organizes small gatherings and walks in areas associated with the family, and has mounted three large exhibitions. It also has an active publication program, producing three newsletters and a refereed journal that publishes scholarly articles and reviews each year. Under the imprint of the Powys Press it has published many pamphlets and books, the latest being the highly

praised *The Dorset Year: The Diary of John Cowper Powys, June 1934 – July 1935* (1998), edited and annotated by Morine Krissdóttir, former chairlady of the society, and Roger Peers, former curator of the Dorset County Museum.

The society also maintains a major archive of books, letters, typescripts, and manuscripts in the Powys Collection, which includes items by the three Powys brothers and other members of the family and its circle, at the Dorset County Museum. A fine small gallery of paintings and wood engravings by Gertrude Powys is also housed here, and the museum has a new literary gallery of Wessex writers that includes a room devoted to the Powyses and their circle of friends in East Chaldron.

Recently the society has established an Internet site at http://www.iaehv.nl/uses/tklijn/pws/powys.htm/ and an E-mail address at gostick@altavista.net. For more information contact Chris Gostick, secretary, The Powys Society, Old School House, George Green Road, George Green, Wexham, Buckinghamshire SL3 6BJ U.K.

The Dorothy L. Sayers Society

Christopher Dean

The founding of The Dorothy L. Sayers Society arose from the actions of members of the Witham community in Essex who had saved from demolition and commercial development the terrace of attractive Tudor houses with their Georgian frontage in which Dorothy Sayers had lived from 1928 until her death in 1957. The restored houses were reopened in 1976 by Ian Carmichael, who had played Lord Peter Wimsey in television productions, and a plaque reading "Dorothy L. Sayers, 1893–1957 Novelist, Theologian and Dante Scholar lived here," was placed on No. 24 Newland Street.

The aims of the society are to keep the name of Dorothy L. Sayers in the public eye by sponsoring or encouraging publication and performance of her works, to collect and preserve archival material concerning her works and her life, and to act as a center of reference and advice for scholars and researchers. For the first few years the society remained locally based in Essex and built up a solid constitution, an archive collection, and contacts with those friends of Sayers who were still alive. A close relationship with the Marion E. Wade Center at Wheaton College, Illinois, was established. In 1985 the administration of the society was passed on to Dr. Barbara Reynolds, Sayers's friend and biographer who lived in Cambridge, and Christopher Dean in Sussex, and a much wider geographical base developed for the society.

The society now has five hundred members worldwide. Half of them are in the United Kingdom, one hundred fifty in the United States (where all Sayers's papers are held, at Wheaton College) and Canada, more than seventy in Europe (with more than half of these in Germany), and the rest in the Far East. Members keep in touch through the bimonthly bulletin of the society, an annual volume of *Sidelights on Sayers* containing articles that members write on all aspects of her works and life, and the proceedings of the annual convention.

The convention is held each summer, and some half dozen additional meetings are every year. The society has met in cities such as Canterbury; Oxford; Kirkcudbright; York; Norwich; Salisbury; London; Cambridge; Lichfield; Duisburg, Germany; Wheaton, Illinois; and New York City. Lecture tours have been made in Sweden, Germany, and The Netherlands. The society has studied themes such as fungal poison, Dante, education, the Wimsey family, forensic photography, *The Emperor Constantine,* the Nicene Creed, and advertising. It has held concerts of music performed by Dorothy Sayers (who sang and studied the violin when she was young) and Lord Peter Wimsey, has sponsored performances of *The Zeal of Thy House* in Canterbury Cathedral and the Bach B Minor Mass in Oxford, and has given 50th anniversary playreadings of *The Devil To Pay, He That Should Come,* and *The Just Vengeance.*

In 1990 the society celebrated the centenary of the birth of Lord Peter Wimsey. The year opened with a full peal of Kent Treble Bob Major, rung from the church of Terrington St. Clement in Norfolk, and continued with visits to Le Saumon d'Or Hotel in Verneuil, where Wimsey had stayed in the story *A Matter of Taste,* and the Hotel Meurice, where he stayed in Paris. Meetings were held in Balliol College, Oxford, where the dean of the college gave an address on Oxford in Wimsey's day to society members, who presented a portrait of Lord Peter. A luncheon in New York City commemorated Lord Peter's early visits to the United States, and on 24 November the society celebrated his 100th birthday with a luncheon in The Park Lane Hotel in Piccadilly (110A), where the Lord Peter Wimsey Suite was officially opened by Edward Petherbridge.

In 1993 the centenary of Sayers's birth was celebrated with more than thirty events worldwide. Most notable were the publication of *Dorothy L. Sayers: Her Life and Soul,* the biography by Barbara Reynolds, and a special Oxford commemoration with a luncheon in her former college, Somerville. This event was followed by a service in Christ Church Cathedral, where she had been baptized, and by the placing of a plaque on the house where she had been born, No. 1 Brewer Street. An additional plaque was unveiled by Norma Major, the prime minister's wife, on Bluntisham Old Rectory, Sayers's childhood home in Cambridgeshire. A symposium was held at the University of Mainz, followed by a lecture tour in Germany on her life and works. A prize competition was held for creative writing among the pupils of her old school, Godolphin, in Salisbury; seminars were held in Chicago and at Wheaton College; and a Festival Evensong was held in St. James Cathedral, Chicago. Sayers's poem "The Three Kings" was set as a carol and performed and broadcast in Canterbury Cathedral.

The society has collaborated with Essex County Libraries to open The Dorothy L. Sayers Centre in the public library in Witham. This library holds a collection of her works and some of the archives of the society, and it is the site of the annual Dorothy L. Sayers Lecture, which has been given by well-known crime writers such as P. D. James, H. R. F. Keating, and Minette Walters.

The society has held joint meetings with the Inklings of Aachen, The Sherlock Holmes Society of London, and the G. K. Chesterton Society; members have also addressed the Oxford University C. S. Lewis Society. Through visits to the World War I battlefields, the Bellona Club (The Naval & Military Club in Piccadilly), and the Royal Military Academy, Sandhurst, the society has studied the history of Lord Peter Wimsey's war service. Publications by the society include the collected *Poetry of Dorothy L. Sayers, Studies in Sayers,* occasional papers, a genealogical study of her descent, and two volumes of her correspondence, *The Letters of Dorothy L. Sayers.*

The society has commissioned and erected a statue of Sayers by sculptor John Doubleday in her hometown of Witham. She is depicted standing, facing her former home with her cat, "Blitz."

In 1997 some 150 members of the society assembled at Wheaton College for its first full convention in the United States. The theme of this gathering focused on Sayers's two most popular novels, *The Nine Tailors* and *Gaudy Night,* and on her remarkable series of radio plays on the life of Christ, *The Man Born to Be King.* In addition to hearing papers on all of these works, members rehearsed readings of two of the radio plays. For 1999 the society has planned to publish a third volume of Sayers's letters–and in September to present three of the cycle of plays in *The Man Born to Be King* at The City Temple, London.

The archives of the society contain a wide range of periodical articles: reviews of her novels and of books about her, a section including all Sayers's reviews of detective fiction that she wrote for the *Sunday Times* in the 1930s, and many of her letters and articles published in the press. In all there are in excess of 1,200 items of printed material, together with sound recordings of the seminars. There are also a well-stocked working reference library and several items of stage properties that Sayers herself made for the production of *The Emperor Constantine*.

The headquarters of the society is at Rose Cottage, Malthouse Lane, Hurstpierpoint, West Sussex BN6 9JY, U.K. Its fax and answerphone number is +44 1273 835988. E-mail may be directed to jasmine@sayers.org.uk, and the society's website is http://www.sayers.org.uk.

The R. S. Surtees Society

Lady Helen Pickthorn

The R. S. Surtees Society was founded in 1979 by readers whose enthusiasm for the works of Robert Smith Surtees (1805-1864)–the sporting journalist and novelist renowned for his creation of John Jorrocks, the fox-hunting Cockney grocer–moved them to respond to an article in the *Daily Telegraph* about the author and his books. At that time not a single one of Surtees's books was in print, and these founding members felt it to be deplorable that a writer whose works are illustrated by artists such as John Leech, "Phiz," and Henry Alken, and whose powers of creating realistic dialogue and characters was not readily available or familiar to contemporary readers. To remedy this situation, members of the society adopted the aims of promoting the works of Surtees, maintaining his reputation as an author, and nurturing interest in his literary merits; pursuing these aims by republishing his works as well as

Logo for Robert Smith Surtees Society

publishing or republishing any biographical or appreciative works about him and by arranging various meetings and events; and publishing or republishing works or prints by other authors and artists, if necessary, to raise funds to achieve those aims of promoting interest in Surtees and appreciation of his work.

The society decided to reprint, in near facsimile to each first edition, all of his works by subscription. This enterprise was successful, and not only financially: members became more established as families throughout the country realized that they could acquire many old favorites from ancestral bookshelves to hand on to their children and friends, and new members from overseas joined. Many notable books that were out of print and that large commercial publishers did not wish to risk republishing have been successfully republished by the society since then: for example, Rudyard Kipling's paperback Indian Railway Series; *Some Experiences* (1899), *Further Experiences of an Irish R.M.* (1908), and *In Mr. Knox's Country* (1915) by Somerville and Ross (Edith Somerville and Violet Martin); and W. W. Jacobs's *The Lady of the Barge* (1902).

Because the chief activity of the society involves the publishing of such books, it does not publish a newsletter or journal. It holds an annual general meeting each spring and an annual dinner in London for members and guests. Anyone wishing to receive a list of titles currently published by the society or any additional information about the society should write to The R. S. Surtees Society, Manor Farm House, Nunney, Nr. Frome, Somerset BA11 4NJ, U.K.; call 011–44–1373–836937 or fax 011–44–1373–836574.

The Tilling Society

Cynthia Reavell

Edward Frederic Benson (1867–1940) was a prolific writer who published more than one hundred books, about eighty of which were fiction–ranging from *David Blaize and the Blue Door* (1918), a children's fantasy apparently inspired by Lewis Carroll, to books on physical fitness and winter sports. His biographies on people such as Charlotte Brontë, Queen Victoria, and Sir Francis Drake and memoirs such as *As We Were* (1930) and *Final Edition* (1940) are still well thought of, and he is also regarded as one of the top writers of ghost stories. He is best remembered for his six comic novels, the Mapp and Lucia series about the small-town rivalries of two middle-aged, middle-class ladies seeking social supremacy.

A Professor Getchell formed what must have been the first appreciation society dedicated to Benson

Banner headline for the newsletter of the society dedicated to the works of E. F. Benson

and his comic novels in the early 1930s. Nevertheless, Benson was neglected and largely forgotten between his death in 1940 and the reprinting of his Mapp and Lucia books in both the United States and England more than three decades later, although among the minority of readers who clamored for them to be reprinted were distinguished figures such as Sir Noël Coward, Nancy Mitford, W. H. Auden, and Edward Gorey. But not until popular paperback editions were published between the late 1970s and mid 1980s did Benson gain more readers. Midway through the 1980s his audience increased in both countries when his novel *Mapp and Lucia* (1931) was dramatized in the first of two television series starring Prunella Scales, Geraldine McEwan, and Nigel Hawthorne.

Fay Hodges, who had enjoyed the Mapp and Lucia books ever since her grandmother had introduced her to them, was responsible for setting up The Tilling Society. Hodges had felt that it would be nice to meet other people who shared her enthusiasm for Benson's works and the people and places he creates in them, and at the end of 1982 she placed an advertisement in *The Spectator*. Within a few months there was a nucleus of about a dozen members, and she began to feel that such a society should perhaps be centered in Rye, where Benson had lived and where he had set the Mapp and Lucia novels. The name "Tilling Society" was chosen because Rye was the model for the town of Tilling, named after the local River Tillingham in the novels.

At the time the society was formed, people who had fallen in love with the Mapp and Lucia novels felt isolated in their interest for Benson and his books. Either they never met other readers who had heard of Benson's works, or they lent copies of them to friends who returned them and said that they "couldn't get on with them at all." So the main function of the society was, and is, to bring together enthusiasts—no matter where they live—for the exchange of news, information, and speculation through biannual newsletters. These

newsletters are sent to around five hundred subscribers worldwide, about a third of whom live in the United States; their occupations and interests in subjects other than Benson and his works are varied.

The society through its newsletters discusses people and places that might have inspired Benson in creating the fictitious ones in his novels and shares reviews of plays, programs, translations, reprints, and other Benson-related news. The entire Benson family—including some colorful ancestors—and E. F. Benson's friends, the houses in which he lived, and details of his domestic routine are also subjects of interest among society members, and, in addition to the newsletters, The Tilling Society has published an illustrated booklet, *E. F. Benson as Mayor of Rye 1934–37: Reports from the "Sussex Express"* (1993).

The society holds an annual get-together every fall in Rye. Some members walk to Benson's grave on the hill outside Rye in the morning and then meet for lunch at a hotel restaurant. This is followed by a speaker, a reading, or a dramatization after lunch, and members then assemble for afternoon tea. In recent years some members have dressed in period outfits or as specific Tilling characters. The society has also organized visits to Lincoln, Broadway, and other places of Benson interest, and in 1990 to commemorate the fiftieth anniversary of Benson's death it held a Mapp and Lucia Ball in the Reform Club in London.

Rye, the basis for Benson's fictional Tilling, remains the center of attention for a stream of visitors, many from the United States, who come to see the town and the house where Benson lived. In September 1978 actor Aubrey Woods came to town and presented a one-man Mapp and Lucia show as part of the Rye Festival. In 1979 *Genesis and Exodus,* a biography of the Benson family, was published, and the Martello Bookshop, the headquarters of the society in Rye for more than a decade, promoted this book by hosting a party and a talk by the biographer, David Williams. That

Banner headline for the newsletter of the society honoring the life and works of the writer known for his popular novels and science fiction

summer Corgi began publishing the Mapp and Lucia books in paperback, and in 1980 *On the Edge of Paradise,* David Newsome's scholarly biography of Benson's brother, Arthur, was published.

For additional information about the society and about membership, write to The Tilling Society, 5 Friars Bank, Pett Road, Guestling, East Sussex TN35 4ET, U.K.

H. G. Wells Society

John R. Hammond

Founded in 1960, the H. G. Wells Society is an association of people interested in Herbert George Wells's life and works and eager to promote a widespread interest in his writings and ideas. Its specific aims include encouraging interest in his works among publishing, press, and broadcasting organizations; promoting a wider knowledge of his ideas and ideals; and assisting others in understanding and disseminating them. The society pursues this last aim through organizing lectures, meetings, and conferences; publishing materials; and engaging in other educational activities. It has an international membership, all of whom receive the biannual *H. G. Wells Newsletter* and an annual journal, *The Wellsian.*

The society has published a comprehensive bibliography of Wells's published fiction, nonfiction, pamphlets, and short stories—a useful reference work for scholars, collectors, and enthusiasts. It has also republished many of his works that have been out of print for years. These include: *Select Conversations with an Uncle* (1895), *The Discovery of the Future* (1902), and *The Last Books of H. G. Wells,* comprising *The Happy Turning* and *Mind at the End of Its Tether,* both first published in 1945.

Through the years the society has built a substantial collection of books and pamphlets by Wells and has also accumulated an archive of press cuttings relating to his life and work. This collection is housed in the Learning Centre of the University of North London on Holloway Road, London, where students and researchers may use it.

A weekend conference, at which members discuss Wells's life and work in a congenial atmosphere, is annually organized by the society. In recent years conference topics have included Wells's short stories, publishing and publicizing Wells, and Wells's literary friendships. The society has also arranged two major international conferences. The first, under the title "H. G. Wells Under Revision," was held in 1986 to mark the fortieth anniversary of Wells's death. In 1995 the society arranged an international symposium, "The Time Machine: Past, Present, and Future," to mark the centenary of the publication of Wells's scientific romance.

Additional information about membership or any of the society's activities is available from John R. Hammond, Secretary, H. G. Wells Society, 49 Beckingthorpe Drive, Bottesford, Nottingham NG13 0DN, U.K.

The Henry Williamson Society

Anne Williamson

The Henry Williamson Society was founded in Barnstaple in May 1980 to encourage interest in, and a deeper understanding of, the life and work of Henry Williamson (1895–1977)—soldier, naturalist, farmer, journalist, broadcaster, and author. After spending a holiday in North Devon just before World War I and becoming enamored of its scenery, the young Williamson vowed to return there. He kept this resolution, living and working there for most of his life.

His youth was spent in southeast London, in what was then the semirural suburb of Brockley, from which he had ready access to the Kent countryside that he loved. He roamed this area freely and also frequently visited maternal relatives who had been farmers in Bedfordshire. These visits nurtured his later interest in farming. In some early novels of his fifteen-volume series *A Chronicle of Ancient Sunlight* (1951–1969) he re-creates the milieu of that rural life at the turn of the century. Other early books depict the long-vanished country life of the Devon village of Georgeham. He believed in "the power of ancient sunlight" and, as a writer, sought to see the world as the sun sees it—without shadows. His detailed descriptions of nature and his ability to re-create moods aroused by natural phenomena attest to his power of total recall, and these skills have earned him recognition as a British natural-history writer. *Tarka the Otter* (1927), for example, won the Hawthornden Prize for Literature in 1928.

Several books also recount his years of service as a soldier in The Great War, and many readers consider his descriptions of life in the trenches, based on personal experience, to be the finest of such memoirs. Williamson was pleased to be a friend of T. E. Lawrence, and among others who influenced him were Richard Jefferies, W. H. Hudson, Francis Thompson, Richard Wagner, and Frederick Delius. As a farmer during the years of World War II, Williamson was resolute in his beliefs about the importance of sound agricultural practice, and on this subject he again recorded his experiences, hopes, and dreams in several books. His long, mature work—*A Chronicle of Ancient Sunlight*—remains a valuable statement on British social history and a remarkable work of fiction.

Members of The Henry Williamson Society are from all over the British Isles, and more readers overseas are becoming members. The society organizes two annual meetings, an autumn meeting in North Devon and a spring meeting held at other sites with particular connections to Williamson. Weekend programs on these occasions generally include a major presentation and supper, and these are followed by Sunday talks, discussions, displays, presentations of movies or slides, and walks or visits to nearby places associated with Williamson. Smaller local meetings of members are encouraged and have been well supported.

The society annually publishes *The Henry Williamson Society Newsletter* and *The Henry Williamson Society Journal,* the latter of which includes reviews, correspondence, reminiscences of Williamson, research articles on him, and criticism of his writing. Other projects of the society have included collecting ephemeral periodical pieces on Williamson and publishing these under the society imprint; preserving Williamson's writing hut at Ox's

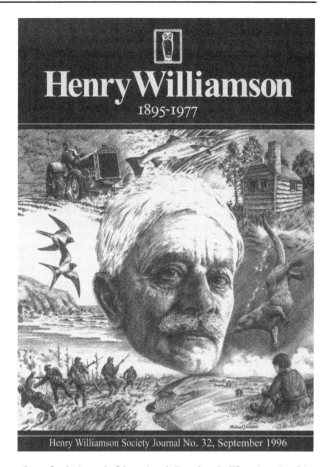

Henry Williamson Society Journal No. 32, September 1996

Cover for the journal of the society dedicated to the life and works of the British fiction and natural-history writer

Cross, Georgeham, as a memorial; and placing commemorative plaques on the house in Brockley where Williamson spent much of his childhood and youth, on Crowberry Cottage in Georgeham, and on Owl Cottage, Stiffkey.

Additional information about the society is available from Margaret Murphy, membership and general secretary, The Henry Williamson Society, 16 Doran Drive, Redhill, Surrey RH1 6AX, U.K.; telephone: 011–44–1737–763228.

Worldwide Wodehouse Societies

Marilyn MacGregor

Wodehouse societies the world over have been formed by enthusiasts of the writing of Pelham Grenville Wodehouse (1881–1975), British-born humor novelist, lyricist, and playwright. The activities of these societies range from the seriously scholarly to the light-heartedly silly: they have included placing plaques at Wodehouse-related sites, encouraging publication of research books and papers, assembling library exhibits, holding formal dinners and conventions, going on tours, attending plays and musical comedy revivals, holding dramatic readings and debates, exchanging books and collectibles, organizing songfests and kazoo choruses, sponsoring newt tanks in zoos, identifying and visiting sites mentioned in Wodehouse's works, sponsoring and participating in cricket and golf matches, reviewing audio- and videotapes, holding poetry and costume contests, competing in egg-and-spoon races and dart throwing, devising quizzes, and engaging in much browsing, sluicing, and occasional breadroll-throwing.

As the first society to be conceived, the P. G. Wodehouse Society (PGWS) of The Netherlands was started in 1973 by a group of Dutch journalists who happened to be together in Helsinki, Finland, and found common ground in their love for Wodehouse's books and plays. When they returned to Holland, they founded the PGWS after Wodehouse sent them a letter expressing his delight with the idea. Formal inauguration of the society, however, did not occur until 1981. Its membership includes about 250, and its permanent home is Mulliner's Wijnlokaal (Mulliner's Winehouse), an old pub in the center of Old Amsterdam. A specially labeled Mulliner's Port as well as a Jeeves Gin are available there. Since May 1997 in France the PGWS has also patronized its own hotel, the property of Noud Muller, owner of Mulliner's Wijnlokaal. Her Majesty, Queen Elizabeth, the Queen Mother of Great Britain is the patroness of PGWS; George de Ceuninck van Capelle is president; and honorary president is J. P. Kees van Rijswijk. The society's secretary, Rob Kooy, formerly edited the society's newsletter, *Nothing Serious,* which for years published several articles in English but recently has been published almost entirely in Dutch; Josepha Olsthoorn now edits the newletter.

The PGWS has several independent chapters in other countries, and information about it is available on the Internet (http://www.inter.NL.net/users/H.deCeuninckvanCapelle); by mail directed to Rob Kooy, secretary, PGWS, TWS at Oostergo 40, 1274 JT HUIZEN, The Netherlands; or by telephone/fax: ++31–35–525–0811.

The Wodehouse Society (TWS), which has nearly a thousand members, is also international, although it was started in the United States and most of its members reside there. In 1988 the queen mother accepted honorary membership in TWS, which was founded in 1979 by William Blood, a retired United States Air Force captain who obtained Wodehouse's written approval to do so in 1974. TWS recruited its early members primarily from participants in seminars on Wodehouse's works that Blood taught at The Cen-

ter for Learning in Retirement, Delaware Valley College, Doylestown, Pennsylvania. Blood, who served as president and edited TWS's first newsletter, *The Wodehouse Society–Comments In Passing,* in 1987 accepted an offer from members of the San Francisco Bay Area Chapter to assist with administrative chores. Volunteers from the expanded Bay Area Blandings Castle Chapter provide membership, secretarial, editorial, and accounting services for the society. The newsletter, which on 15 September 1981 was renamed *Plum Lines* in recognition of Wodehouse's nickname, Plum, is coedited by Edward Ratcliffe of the Blandings Castle Chapter and Elin Woodger of the NEWTS (a Wodehouse acronym for the New England Wodehouse Thingummy Society, located in Boston, Massachusetts).

The first TWS convention on 16 July 1982 at Delaware Valley College was such a small affair that Blood named it the Annual Gathering. After a few years, biennial weekend conventions, usually organized by a local group, were begun. These have been held twice in San Francisco and once each in Ithaca, New York; Kalamazoo, Michigan; New York City; Boston; and Chicago. The next convention is scheduled to be held in Houston, Texas, in 1999. The society has toured sites associated with Wodehouse in England, and author Norman Murphy's experience on one excursion provided the basis for his book, *A True and Faithful Account of the Amazing Adventures of the Wodehouse Society on Their Pilgrimage July 1989.*

For information about and membership in TWS, write to Marilyn MacGregor, 3215–5 Bermuda Avenue, Davis CA 95616–2758, U.S.A.; or telephone: (530) 758–6783.

Because interest in TWS has spread geographically, many society chapters that operate independently have been formed, and these are sufficiently large and active to deserve individual recognition.

The San Francisco Bay Area Chapter, formed 1 February 1981 by Pauline Blanc, has expanded east to include Sacramento and south to include Santa Cruz, California, and was the first chapter to take a Wodehousian name, the Blandings Castle Chapter, in 1992. Its newsletter, *The Argus Intelligencer & Wheat Grower's Gazette,* was edited for five years by Charles Bishop during his term as chapter president and is now edited by chapter president Jan Kaufman. Besides quarterly meetings, Blandings Castle members have taken excursions up the Oregon coast and, in November 1998, to San Simeon, California. The chapter has organized two national conventions, and the Blandings Castle Players traditionally present a dramatic reading of a Wodehouse story at each biennial convention. For information about and membership in this chapter, write to Jan

Banner headline for the newsletter of the P. G. Wodehouse Society

Kaufman, 5220 Boyd Avenue, Oakland CA 94618, U.S.A.

Maria Sensale called the first meeting of a Boston chapter for 14 December 1991, but only at the fourth meeting in early 1993 did the members adopt the acronym NEWTS for their New England–based society. The members have made excursions to Remsenburg, Long Island, to pay respects at Wodehouse's grave; to Nantucket, Massachusetts; and to New York City for the dedication of a Wodehouse plaque at the Little Church Around the Corner. On 20 October 1996 the NEWTS became the second chapter to sponsor a newt tank–at the Franklin Park Children's Zoo in Boston. *The Minewts,* edited by Elin Woodger, is the chapter's newsletter. For information and membership write to Anne Cotton, 12 Hollywood Street, South Hadley MA 01075, U.S.A.; or send E-mail to acotton@mtholyoke.edu.

In late summer 1992 William Horn organized Plum's Chums when a group of twenty-one Wodehouse enthusiasts gathered in the Foshay Tower in Minneapolis, Minnesota, for an evening of wine, cheese, dessert, and conversation. Horn's collection of books by Wodehouse was on display; the latest "Jeeves and Wooster" series on televison was discussed; and the Chums heard a passage from a sermon by their candidate in the Great Sermon Handicap. For information and membership, write to William Horn, 4511 Browndale Avenue, Minneapolis MN 55424, U.S.A.

The Clients of Adrian Mulliner, a TWS chapter of Sherlock Holmes enthusiasts, was founded in August 1992. The Clients' three founders–Jon L. Lellenberg, Susan Jewell, and Marilyn MacGregor–have claimed that they "lack serious purpose and denounce Organization as the work of Rupert Baxter." They introduce "Wodelockians and Sherhousians" to each other, promote mutual enjoyment of the two great canons, and gather during TWS biennial conventions and the Sherlock Holmes festivities each January in New York City. For information write to Marilyn MacGregor, 3215-5 Bermuda Avenue, Davis CA 95616-2758, U.S.A.

Following the summer of 1992 Jon L. Lellenberg's idea about forming a Wodehouse society chapter in Washington, D.C., was fulfilled with the first meeting of what became Capital! Capital!–the Washington D.C. Chapter–on 10 November 1992 in the Uptown Café. Meetings held every six to eight weeks have featured papers, challenges to identify quotations, and heated debates. The chapter was represented by a team that competed in the Scripture Knowledge Competition (on Wodehouse writings) at the 1997 Chicago convention. Capital! Capital!, which has been particularly active in entertaining visiting Wodehousians, now meets at The Guards, an old English pub sporting comfy wing chairs, and it is expanding its core of more than thirty members. For information and membership write to Erik R. Quick, 4505-A South 36th Street, Arlington VA 22308, U.S.A., or telephone (703) 933-0963.

The Pdrones Club (the *p* is silent, as in *pneumonia*) of St. Louis, Missouri, held its first meeting on 17 November 1992 at the Sherlock Holmes Room of the Cheshire Inn, where Eric Otten became first president by acclamation. The Pdrones have twenty-two members and meet approximately four times a year. They have a tea, an annual "typical country picnic," an anniversary dinner in November, and either a brunch or lunch. Discussion often focuses on a particular book, or members read short passages from a book of their choice. The chapter's newsletter, *The Pdrones Club,* is edited by Sandy Morris. For information and membership write to Sandy Morris, 2526 Wesglen Estates Drive, Maryland Heights MO 63043-4130, U.S.A.

For the greater Philadelphia area Daniel and Susan Cohen organized a chapter that first met on 20 January 1994 at the Dickens Inn in Philadelphia, where some two dozen enthusiasts gathered to eat shepherd's pie or toad-in-the-hole, down a few pints of the landlord's best, and talk of Wodehouse. Franklin Axe, a member of TWS in its earliest days, noted that through him this Philadelphia chapter could claim direct descent from founder William Blood's group. At the second meeting members of this Philadelphia group chose the name Chapter One to honor the memory of Blood, who founded the society, and that of Wodehouse, whose life was devoted to writing. In 1995 the chapter raised funds to sponsor a permanent newt exhibit at the Philadelphia Zoo, where a special tank in the reptile house bears a plaque acknowledging its funding by all members of The Wodehouse Society. Meetings are held approximately every two months at the Dickens Inn in Philadelphia. For information and membership write to Susan and Daniel Cohen, 877 Hand Avenue, Cape May Court House NJ 08210, U.S.A., or send E-mail to BlndgsCast@aol.com.

A Texas chapter was established on 11 March 1994 by Toni Rudersdorf. Initially known as Dronesbury following its first meeting at the River Oaks Bookstore in Houston, the chapter has become the Drone Rangers. Meetings are held every other month at a Barnes and Noble Bookstore to browse and sluice, discuss and debate, and hear papers on Wodehouse books. The chapter commemorates the date of Wodehouse's death on 14 February with a fancy-dress "Annual Remember Plum Party." Its newsletter, *Dronestar,* is edited by Toni and Bill Rudersdorf. For information and membership write to Anne Bianchi, 15906 S. Barker's Landing, Houston TX 77079, U.S.A., or send E-mail to mbianchi@worldnet.att.net.

In 1995 William and Melissa Carpenter organized the small group that became The Wuckoos of the Palace in Portland, Oregon. They held several meetings, entertained visiting Wodehouse enthusiasts, and recruited a TWS member who is now in Antarctica. For information and membership write to William Carpenter, 390 Hansen Avenue South, Salem OR 97302, U.S.A., or send E-mail to vamberry@teleport.com.

The Chicago Accident Syndicate, founded by Jon L. Lellenberg in early spring 1995, has twenty active members and another fifty-plus on the mailing list. The chapter has attended several Wodehouse plays presented by the City Lit Theater Company, and one of those plays was featured at the 1997 TWS convention organized by the Chicago chapter. Meetings frequently focus on members reading an opening paragraph of a Wodehouse novel or story, and the chapter is preparing a skit-reading for the Houston convention in 1999. For information and membership write to Daniel and Tina Garrison, 1228 Simpson Street, Evanston IL 60201, U.S.A.; telephone: (847) 475–2235; E-mail: d-garrison@nwu.edu.

The Soup & Fish Club, founded by Deborah Dillard in Virginia, has met on the first Friday of the month since late 1997. The group has watched old movies of Wodehouse novels and shared favorite quotations. For information and membership, write

to Deborah Dillard, Box 194, Clifton VA 20124, U.S.A.

The Drones Club in New York City comprises a group of loyal Wodehousians who say that they throw breadrolls at each other "in a gentlemanly fashion" at dinner, which they hold three times a year; a luncheon is also sometimes held in the Christmas season. The group has no bylaws, officers, or dues, and no minutes are kept of the proceedings. Membership is by invitation and is limited to twelve persons, although no more than eleven are elected at one time.

Sven Sahlin is president of The Wodehouse Society Sweden, which has a membership of about ninety. It was founded in spring 1984 by students led by Mikael Persson in Uppsala, and it later merged with The Drones Club of Stockholm. *Jeeves,* a journal that had been published semiannually and wholly in Swedish, has been discontinued and is to be replaced by a yearbook, also published in Swedish in mid December 1998. The society aims to hold two general meetings a year and also sponsors two golf days: in the spring a county championship open to members and nonmembers, and in autumn a President's Cup competition for members only. For information and membership write to Sven Sahlin, Katarina 22, 18451 Österskär–Sweden; telephone: +46 8540 65100; fax: +46 8540 66980; E-mail: sven.sahlin@swipnet.se.

Founded in 1989, The Drones Club (Belgium) has close ties with the Netherlands group, and the two often hold joint meetings on one side or the other of the Dutch-Belgian border. A large delegation of PGWS members attend the Drones' Annual Darts Competition and The Great Drones Balloon Hunt. *Drommelse Drones,* published largely in Dutch, is the quarterly newsletter of the Belgian chapter, which has nearly fifty members. Its meetings are held at Millfleet Hall, a country house in a rural setting of Herselt, the center of Flanders. For information and membership write to Kris Smets, Gijmelbergstraat 32A, 3201 Langdorp, Belgium, or visit the society's Web page: http://bewoner.dma.be/Jeeves36.

On 18 October 1996 Sidney Kitson founded The P. G. Wodehouse Society, India (Calcutta), with eighteen members. The society is open only to those with a "serious and insatiable" interest in Wodehouse. Its activities include regular lecture and discussion sessions, building a comprehensive collection of Wodehousiana, and publishing its newsletter, *Faute de Mieux.* For information and membership write to Sidney Kitson IPS (Ret'd), 14/2 Sudder Street, Calcutta–700 016, West Bengal, India, or telephone: 033–249–1731.

The P. G. Wodehouse Society (U.K.) was founded in March 1997 by Sir Edward Cazalet, John Fletcher, Helen Murphy, Norman Murphy, Tony Ring, and Oliver Wise. In less than two years the group has acquired an impressive array of twenty-eight patrons, including Prime Minister Tony Blair and Patrick Wodehouse, nephew of the author, and has grown to nearly four hundred members. Meetings are frequently held at the Savage Club (inside the National Liberal Club), and the society has held a Golf Day at the Tandridge Golf Club near Oxted in Surrey. PGWS (U.K.) also held a formal dinner on 15 October 1998 at the Inner Temple, London, to celebrate Wodehouse's birthday. *Wooster Sauce,* the society's quarterly, is edited by Tony Ring, who also publishes *By The Way,* an occasional newsletter. For information and membership write to Helen Murphy, 16 Herbert Street, Plaistow, London G13 8BE, U.K. The website is http://www.eclipse.co.uk/wodehouse.

The Wodehouse Society (Australia), a chapter of The Netherlands PGWS, was formed near the end of 1997, and, according to its president, Jose Van Dijk, is still in an embryonic state. For information and membership write to her at 163 Bourke Street, Wagga Wagga, 2650 New South Wales, Australia; telephone: 0061 2 69254431; fax: 0061 2 69314342.

Another chapter of The Netherlands PGWS is The Wodehouse Society of India (New Delhi), led by S. Mukherji, F 301 Lado Sarai, Quatab Mahrauli Road, 1. 110030 New Delhi, India.

On 17 October 1998 at The Netherlands society's Second Annual International Dinner in Oud-Zullen an association of Wodehouse societies was formed by the signing of the Millfleet Charter. Signatories included presidents of five societies: George de Ceuninck van Capelle for PGWS, Kris Smits for The Drones Club (Belgium), Sven Sahlin for The Wodehouse Society Sweden, Tony Ring for PGWS (U.K.), and Daniel Garrison for The Wodehouse Society. The first president of the association is Ring.

Wodehouse societies are well represented on the Internet. Moscow State University is the site of The Russian Wodehouse Society, which is also a chapter of The Netherlands PGWS. Founder and president Mikhail Aleksandrovitch Kuzmenko's home page features photos, news of the Jeeves and Wooster series shown on Russian television, places to purchase Wodehouse's books online and in Moscow, lists of other PGWS pages on the Internet, and articles about Wodehouse. For information visit the Internet address: http://mech.math.msu.su/~gmk/pgw.htm; or write to Mikhail Kuzmenko, uL Z.i.a. Kosmodemyanskikh, 35/1–142, R 125130 Moscow, Russia; or send E-mail to gmk@mech.math.msu.su.

Other World Wide Websites include:

http://www.smartnet.net/~tak/wodehouse.html
P. G. Wodehouse Appreciation Page by Tom Kreitzberg

http://www.serv.net/~camel/
The Junior Ganymede Club Book by Susan Collicott

http://www.hic.net/bssc/public_html/jeeves.html
The Jeeves and Wooster information pages by Mark Brady

http://web.egr.msu.edu/~bhurkeal/
Gussie Fink-Nottle page

http://www.crl.com/~spm/tws.html
The Wodehouse Society by Shamim Mohamed

http://weber.u.washington.edu/~mlkelley/beevor.htm
Lady Theresa "Terry" Cobbold's Home Page

http://kekux1.kek.jp/~marat/pgw.html
Pelham Grenville Wodehouse (1881–1975) by Marat Khabibullin

http://www.stichicago.com/tws.htm
The Wodehouse Society

http://www-rcf.usc.edu/~ddunn/jeeves.htm
In Appreciation of P. G. Wodehouse by Deborah Dunn

http://www.netaccess.on.ca/~erich/index.html
The Junior Drones Club by Eric Hanson

http://home.netscape.com/people/thaths/wodehouse/
P. G. Wodehouse and Songs by Sudhakar "Stephanie Bing" Chandrasekharan

The Charlotte M. Yonge Fellowship

Julia Courtney

With 145 members based mainly in the United Kingdom and North America, the Charlotte M. Yonge Fellowship owes its existence to Jean Shell of Hendon, in North London. The idea for the organization, formed to celebrate the life and works of Victorian novelist Charlotte Mary Yonge (pronounced "young"), was first proposed during a Barbara Pym Weekend at St. Hilda's College, Oxford, in August 1993. Between summer 1993 and November 1995, Shell wrote letters to likely members, arranged archive visits, and circulated handouts and application forms. As a result of her

Banner headline for the newsletter dedicated to the life and works of the Victorian novelist and children's writer

efforts, an inaugural conference on 18 November 1995 at the Friends' House, Euston, London, formally initiated the fellowship, which by this time had acquired a patron (the bishop of Basingstoke, near Yonge's home in Otterbourne) and begun publishing a newsletter twice a year.

The first annual general meeting of the fellowship was held in April 1996, when a constitution was drawn up and formally approved. According to this constitution, the aims and objectives of the fellowship are as follows:

1. To provide a forum for all those who enjoy and admire the work of Charlotte M. Yonge.

2. To offer opportunities of learning more about her life, writings, and influence.

3. To encourage publication of her works and topics relating to them.

4. To work toward restoring her reputation as a significant writer of the Victorian period.

The constitution also sets conditions of membership, which is basically "open to all in sympathy with the aims of the Fellowship," and subscription arrangements, currently £7 per year. It also provides for an annual general meeting to be held in different locations to enable as many members as possible to attend. There are also guidelines for fellowship publications—currently a newsletter covered by subscription and published twice each year, and an occasional journal, which costs £3 per issue. Administration of the fellowship is conducted by appointed officers and a committee currently chaired by Elizabeth Llewellyn Smith, principal of St. Hilda's College, Oxford; Jean Shell continues as membership secretary.

The fellowship aims to appeal to a wide range of Yonge enthusiasts, and its increasing membership suggest that it is succeeding. Meetings and activities of the fellowship appeal to general readers, book collectors, and academics, and many friendships have been formed. Several members provide links with other interest groups: Mary Shakeshaft, with the older Charlotte M. Yonge Society, and Susan McCartan, with the Jane Austen Society. Living members of the Yonge family bring geneological concerns to the fellowship, and others from the Otterbourne area are drawn by local interests: in 1994 The Hampshire Field Club and Archaeological Society published fellowship member Julia Courtney's article on Charlotte Yonge's county connections. The fellowship also attracts novelists such as Gwen Butler and Kate Saunders, and well-known actor Anne Harvey has given readings of Yonge's works.

Since 1995 members have visited Yonge's home and grave in Otterbourne, attended a lecture on the Yonge portrait held by the National Portrait Gallery, and participated in many readings, discussions, and presentations. A popular venue has been St. Alban's Church, Holborn, London, a Victorian complex of church buildings featured as "Whittingtonia" in several of Yonge's novels, and there the fellowship has enjoyed lectures from a series of speakers including Professor John Sutherland of London University.

Regular meetings provide a forum for book exchanges. With a handful of exceptions (*The Daisy Chain, The Heir of Redclyffe* and *The Clever Woman of the Family*), Yonge's works are out of print; although some, particularly the better-known historical novels, are relatively easy to obtain, others are extremely rare and sought after. Yonge's huge canon presents a challenge to the bibliographer, and few readers attempt to collect all her published work. However, there is widespread interest in collecting sets of her novels as issued by her major publisher, Macmillan, in the characteristic blue bindings with a gold CMY logo or the elegant brown-cover series. Her children's fiction was published in some new editions in the 1940s, with particularly charming illustrations. Given the current interest in publishing archives and book history, Yonge's relations with her various publishers deserve closer examination.

Also in demand are copies of various out-of-print, classic works on Yonge such as Christabel Coleridge's *Charlotte Mary Yonge: Her Life and Letters* (1903) and Margaret Mare and Alicia C. Percival's *Victorian Best-Seller: the World of Charlotte Yonge* (1947). More recent publications are also advertised and discussed at fellowship meetings, as specified in the aims of the constitution.

The scope of current scholarship indicates that Yonge continues to attract sustained academic interest. Several members have unpublished M.Phil. or Ph.D. theses of interest to other Yonge scholars, and the fellowship disseminates information about archive holdings of relevant manuscripts and letters. Barbara Dennis, June Sturrock, and honorary member Alethea Hayter have all published recent works on Yonge, and the summer 1997 issue of *Victorian Studies* included Claudia Nelson's review of *Charlotte Yonge* (1996) by Alethea Hayter and of *"Heaven and Home": Charlotte Yonge's Domestic Fiction and the Victorian Debate over Women* (1995) by June Sturrock. Chapters related to Yonge are included in Shirley Foster and Judy Simons's *What Katy Read* (1995) and in Claudia Nelson and Lynne Vallone's collection, *The Girls' Own* (1994).

The journal published by the fellowship is a forum for academic debate and the circulation of recent papers and lectures. The January 1999 issue is a good example, including the text of a talk given by Dom Andrew Johnson of Alton Abbey; papers by Hayter, Shakeshaft, and Cathy Wells-Cole; and a list of Yonge's contributions to periodicals compiled by bibliographer

Philip Drazin. Fellowship newsletters combine shorter articles and comments on Yonge's life and works, with news of members, letters, competitions, and announcements of forthcoming activities. The editor is Cecilia Bass, 32 Newland Park, Hull HU5 2DW, U.K.

The third and fourth aims set out in the fellowship constitution commit members to spread information and arouse interest in Yonge. In pursuing these aims, the fellowship has organized readings and tours at local literary festivals, particularly in Yonge's home county of Hampshire. In 1996 several members spoke about Yonge on the popular BBC daytime radio program *Woman's Hour,* and the fellowship also maintains an Internet website featuring synopses of her novels. With the centenary of Yonge's death approaching in March 2001, the fellowship is seeking a publisher for a volume of essays contributed by members on themes connected with her life and work. As Chairman Elizabeth Llewellyn Smith commented at the 1998 annual general meeting, "We cannot match the Jane Austen and Trollope societies in size, but the Fellowship, now three years old, has remained buoyant and is on course to meet its objectives."

Further information and details about membership in the fellowship are available from Jean Shell, 78 Sunningfields Road, Hendon, London NW4 4RL, U.K.

Charley

A great bookman-librarian is gone; but it is unlikely that the administrators who infest libraries are aware that their world has been diminished.

Charles Mann (1929–1998) built the superb rare books and manuscripts collections at Penn State from nothing, in an unlikely location. "Charley" was recognized throughout the bibliographical world; his surname was unnecessary. He accomplished his great work through Charleyism: an amalgam of wide knowledge (everything somehow connected), promiscuous reading, booking trips, commitment, friendships, contacts, connections, honesty, warmth, generosity, goodness, work, and work. The friends of Charley constituted a society of bookmen.

Charley was born and raised in Altoona. His family was not well-off, but he managed to surround himself with books. The existence of a Penn State branch there made it possible for him to begin college. He received a B.A. in History and Social Studies (1952) and an M.A. in English (1954), both from Penn State—where he worked all his life. While a student he began working at the Pattee Library shelving books at 50¢ an hour. He took an M.A. in so-called Library Science at Rutgers to qualify for a library appointment, but the experience did not damage him: he remained a pure bookman. In 1958 he was appointed half-time curator of the rare-books collection and formally commenced his great work with an acquisitions budget of $3,000 per year. Before that he found the ninth known copy of Marlowe's *Tamburlaine* when he was twenty-seven years old. Charley worked his budget up to $80,000, but he was not simply a buyer: donors gave their collections to Penn State because they trusted him.

All great bookmen are born that way, but Charley's passion was extraordinary. His carefully maintained high-school lists record that by 1946 he owned 312 books. A list headed "Books I Have Read For The First Time Since Sept. 6 1944" had 419 titles by 17 November 1947. Charles was a great collection builder because he knew books and loved them—really loved them.

The fields in which Charley was an expert and for which he acquired collections included Commonwealth Literature (especially Australia), the Great Exhi-

Young Charley with books (University Photo/Graphics, The Pennsylvania State University)

bition of 1851—the Crystal Palace—(about which he must have known more than anyone else), Emblem Literature, Utopian Literature, Art History (including architecture and landscaping), the History of Photography (a special specialty), the History of the Book, Ernest Hemingway, John O'Hara, Pennsylvania Imprints, nineteenth-century Gift Books and Annuals, Joseph Priestley, eighteenth-century German Literature, German Literature in Translation, Incunabula, Kenneth Burke, Theodore Roethke, Françoise Sagan, Arnold Bennett, Jean Giraudox, Paul West, and Sci Fi. Truly: all these and more. He acquired the Williamscote Library, the 2,500-volume personal collection of the eighteenth-century scholar John Loveday of Caversham. Charley arranged to have John O'Hara's study reconstructed in the Pattee Library at University Park.

Those who knew how readably Charley wrote regretted that he didn't write more. In addition to co-authoring the catalogue of the Ernest Hemingway manuscripts, Charley wrote some 200 book reviews, as well as uncounted professional reports. He didn't hoard his knowledge and discoveries; researchers from all over the world have testified to his generous and essential help. There is no accurate count of the boards, panels, and committees he served on. Charley taught English, Comparative Literature, and Bibliography courses and was promoted to a professorship in the English Department: "If you're on the University campus and don't get involved in teaching, you're in a terrible position." In 1993 he was appointed to the Dorothy Foehr Hucke Chair for Special Collections. An entertaining speaker who lectured widely, Charley was an effective ambassador for Penn State and for the book. It was said that the two most important people on campus were football coach Joe Paterno and Charley. It is unlikely that any American did more for the preservation and study of books than Charley.

Charles Mann is survived by his wife Nancy McCall, archivist for the Johns Hopkins Medical Institutions; by a daughter, Molly Ziegler; by the serious bookmen who miss him; and by the scholars who are indebted to him. Paul West stated that he was "a river to his people."

Contributions to the Charles Mann Memorial Fund should be addressed to the Dean of the University Libraries, E505 Pattee Library, The Pennsylvania State Libraries, University Park, PA 16802.

Charley and I were close friends for forty years. That isn't much for a claim: he had more close friends than anyone else I knew. We worked together on the Pittsburgh Series in bibliography, and he advised me on Bruccoli Clark Layman projects. The more I berated him, the more he laughed.

We lived far apart, and our favorite resort was the Seven Gables Bookshop at 3 West 46th Street, New York, where Charley was a great favorite. One of the gauges of his abilities was the respect he was accorded by antiquarian dealers–which was not a consequence of his purchasing power. They respected his knowledge and consulted him. Everybody who knew Charley learned from him.

When he died, Charley was searching for 1924–1926 issues of the *Pottsville Journal*–the O'Hara years. If any *Yearbook* reader knows where these issues can be acquired, I want to buy them for Charley's Library. After all, he gave me his 78 RPM record of Gene Austin's "My Blue Heaven."

– M. J. B.

Remarks Made on Behalf of Charley Mann's Students at His Funeral

Nancy asked me to say a few words on behalf of Charley's students past and present. Charley was a great mentor to us, and we would like to remind his family and friends of the impact he had upon generations of scholars here at Penn State. I was able to reach many of Charley's students from the last decade, most of whom are now faculty members at universities throughout the United States. Everyone I talked to spoke of the same defining characteristics: Charley's tremendous knowledge and love of books, his enthusiasm, and his boundless generosity.

Charley not only gave us practical advice and assistance, he infected us with his inquisitive spirit. One student admitted, "It's pretty likely that I changed the subject of my dissertation more times than any of Charley's students, but he greeted each new topic with genuine interest, enthusiasm, and, in every single case, knowledgeable advice. Not only did Charley cheerfully help me hunt down everything in the Rare Books Room that would be useful to me, he scoured catalogues and acquired many valuable titles I needed but Pattee didn't own. I don't think I could have chosen a topic that would have stumped Charley if I had actually been trying."

Charley kept looking out for his students long after they left Penn State. One old student told me, "I was amazed by his ability to remember what all his students were interested in long after they had left Penn State. I visited campus in 1996 after a more than five-year absence, and when I went to see Charley, the first thing he did was take me into the stacks to show me everything the Rare Books Room had acquired since my last visit that might possibly be of interest to me."

Another of Charley's students explained that "without his willingness to dedicate the energy and resources of the Rare Books Room to the projects of doctoral students, many dissertations–including my own–would have been a lot more difficult to produce, if not impossible. But in addition to the very real practical support he afforded me, he was also simply great fun to work with. Charley loved having people use the books he had so painstakingly acquired. Consequently, the Rare Books Room was not a stuffy place to cower under the cold eyes of suspicious librarian-wardens; it was a place where research flourished happily because Charley and his staff were always so generous with their time, their specialized knowledge, and with the collection itself. The opportunities to learn from Charley were endless."

Charley's more established students—those with the experience to appreciate how well the knowledge and skills he gave them had served in their professional lives—also spoke of the last of Charley's great qualities as a teacher: his humility. "For Charley," one of them said, "it was always about the books, never about himself. He was the humblest great man I have ever met." Indeed, I think Charley's manner—his enthusiasm, his smile, his eccentricities—sometimes disguised the fact that he was one of the country's most highly respected rare-books librarians as well as one of Penn State's greatest treasures. Because Charley rarely mentioned his own accomplishments, I shall not do so now. However, I think his reputation within the rare-books community was summarized rather elegantly last year. At that time, I was applying to one of the foremost rare-books programs in the world. My application was accepted, but the director of the school sent me a note asking if I was sure I wanted to attend: "You are, of course, welcome to come," he wrote. "But I wonder how useful you will find our program. If Charley taught you, there probably isn't much you can learn from us."

To Charley, the world of books was a world of people—friends and contacts he made during a lifetime in a profession that was really a vocation for him. Today, many of those friends are here to remember him. Fortunately for us, Charley has been busy building a functional monument to that world for the last forty years, one that will also serve as a better memorial to him than any of us could ever fashion: the Rare Books Room. I do not think I am exaggerating when I say that Penn State—indeed, the entire Commonwealth of Pennsylvania—is forever in Charley's debt. I know his students are.

– Don-John Dugas

Charley Mann

The news that Charley Mann had died suddenly in Baltimore early Friday afternoon, 17 July, spread across the Penn State campus, through State College and beyond like news of a major disaster—which it was, and is, for his friends and for Penn State. That it made the front page of the *Centre Daily Times* the next morning seemed appropriate. People reacted to the news as to a death in the family. The reaction was dramatic evidence of how many people admired Charley and of how deeply they loved and cherished him.

Small wonder, for he was a most remarkable person, and he leaves behind a remarkable achievement, the Rare Book Room of the Pattee Library.

First, the achievement. He was the first head of Rare Books. We have an account in his own words of what he was taking over:

A short survey of the Penn State Collections which are catalogued under the letter T signifying Treasure (a glowing word, suggestive of iron-bound chests, and illuminated parchments) reveals that there are a few points of strength in the collection, but in the main it presents what would be called in Madison Avenue "unrivaled for expansion." Numerically, exclusive of Pennsylvania imprint materials, the collection numbers perhaps 3500 volumes.

Today there are some 80,000 volumes. There is also the Allison-Shelley Collection of German-American materials, John O'Hara's study, Kenneth Burke's papers, the countless photographs, the maps, the medieval manuscripts and leaves, and more. If you haven't visited the Rare Book Room lately, I suggest you do so. Housed there are 77,000 items added under Charley's tenure. The words engraved in the great St. Paul's Cathedral in London honoring its architect, Sir Christopher Wren, apply well to Charles Mann: "Si monumentum requiris, circumspice" [If you need a monument, look around you].

The man was even more remarkable. He had an incredible memory, endless generosity, an insatiable appetite for knowledge, and a magical personality. His memory was prodigious. I think he knew every item in the collection, from its price to its history and its significance. He read bookseller's catalogues and remembered what they were offering. More than one scholar must have had an experience such as this. In the course of some research, I needed an out-of-print book Pattee didn't possess. I happened to mention this to Charley. Three years or so later he called me and said, "Remember that volume in the Surtees Society Publications, *Reginaldi Monachi Dunelmensis Libellus de Admirandis Beati Cuthberti Virtutibus?* I just saw it advertised in a bookseller's catalogue. Think we should buy it?"

The experience also reveals his tireless scholarly generosity. His staggering erudition was always at your disposal. Anything he knew was yours for the asking. And he wanted the Rare Book Room to serve the same function. The treasures there were to be used, not hoarded. Nothing made him happier.

He had a restless, never-to-be-satisfied appetite for learning, for knowing more, for exploring a new field of knowledge. Once he'd made his way through English Literature, for example, he moved on to Commonwealth Literature: Australian Literature, New Zealand, Indian, and taught a course in it. Bookbinding and the history of printing, Antarctic exploration, art history. One could call him a polymath, but the term is too

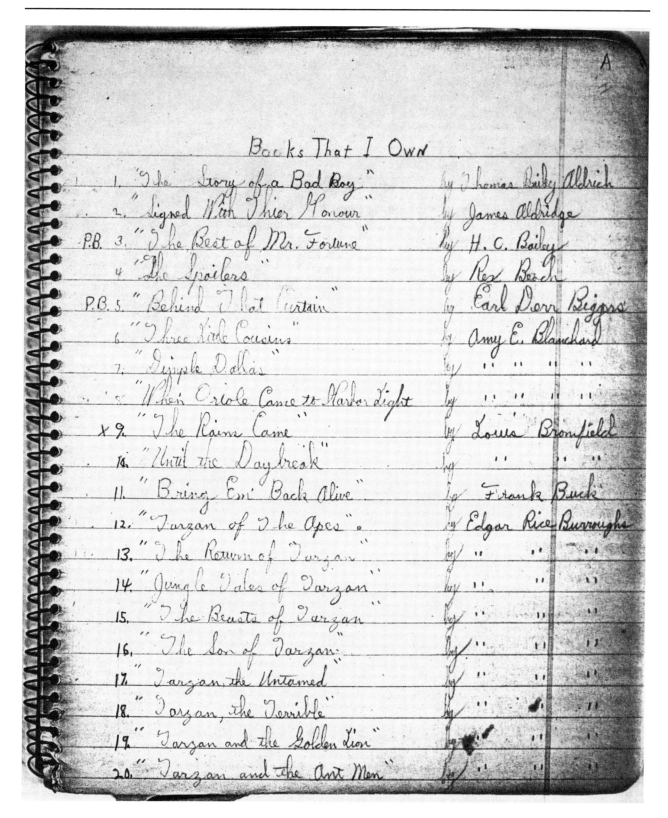

By 1946 high-school student Charles Mann owned 312 books (University Photo/Graphics, The Pennsylvania State University).

By 17 November 1947 Mann listed 419 books he had read (University Photo/Graphics, The Pennsylvania State University).

Between 1948 and 1952 Mann maintained this list, which includes 965 titles (University Photo/Graphics, The Pennsylvania State University).

stuffy. Charley carried his learning lightly, in his breast pocket as it were, to pull out whenever appropriate or needed.

With this store of information, history, and anecdotes he was a kind of walking library all by himself. He wrote well and talked well—an ideal guest for dinner or a party or traveling companion. Persons distinguished in their own field found him a fascinating associate—Kenneth Burke, the Oxford critic F. W. Bateson, the novelist Paul West, and scores of others were his friends and were willing aides in building the collection. Just yesterday someone told me Pattee's holdings in incunabula were the gift of someone who knew Charley in kindergarten. I like to think that's true. That Charley's charm began its subtle force and paid off in rare books as early as kindergarten strikes me as just right.

Charley's charm was powerful. He had personality in the best sense of the word—not *People* magazine's personality, hyped up and trendy and self-serving. I see its roots in Charley's unstudied innocence. This was not naïveté—far from it. It came from his intense focus on what was important and meaningful to him: books; his collections; his many, many friendships; his loves; his family. That intense focus washed everything else away. It was pure. He was not looking for anything extraneous or any feedback. The thing itself was all—his love for Nancy, his love for Molly, his love for Katie, his grandchild. (He was well on his way to becoming, in a field with many strong contenders, the world's most doting grandparent).

All in all, Charley gave up an enlarged sense of the possibilities in being human. He was a beautiful man. His going is an irreparable loss. But he's left us so much.

– R. W. Frank Jr.

Contribution to the 3 October 1998 Memorial Service for Charley Mann

Charley was a very special man, and to us and many others a very special friend.

Bridget and I had the privilege of meeting him soon after our arrival in State College, that is to say some thirty-five years ago, and there is no doubt in our minds that Charley contributed substantially to our pleasure of being here. His encyclopedic knowledge, his impeccable taste, his invariable courtesy saw to that, as did his generous willingness to enter into the interests and concerns of others.

Charley was the very opposite of an institutional official, in part because he was really an "institution" in his own right. He took part in our lives in so many ways, some important because intellectually potent, others important because so enjoyably whimsical. Whatever else may be said about Charley, it is a pleasure to recall that he also had a charming sense of humor.

One professional interest we shared concerned the history of photography, the celebration of photography not only as an art in its own right but for its social impact and its impact on book design and book publishing. Along those lines he was untiring in supporting our collecting activities, sometimes bringing a special morsel under his arm, sometimes pointing our noses toward exotic sources of material, sometimes complementing the university's own collection whenever attractive opportunities presented themselves.

One example of that is represented by an episode when Bridget and I found ourselves in Philadelphia with a little time to spare. We walked into an antiquarian bookstore and asked whether they had any "photographically illustrated books," that is to say nineteenth-century books published before it was feasible to reproduce photographs by letterpress. In such books, pages were left blank to which actual photographs were then glued. Yes, indeed, they had one of those, and an absolutely gorgeous example it turned out to be, a collector's dream. We were excited. How much, we asked, and were told a price, way above the resources of the B & H Henisch collection. We were very sorry, of course, but decided there and then to mention the matter to Charley upon our return. We did that, and by the following day, somehow by special overnight mail, that book was a star item in the Penn State Rare Books Room. Charley did not have to be persuaded; he instantly knew what to do, and did it.

Many years ago, we got wind of the fact that the William Darrah collection of *cartes-de-visite* photographs would come onto the market, and Charley was quick to realize before many outsiders did that this collection would be a splendid resource for researchers of nineteenth-century culture. The collection was duly purchased and has since amply proved its worth. In this way and in others, Penn State became one of the top players in the History of Photography game.

On innumerable occasions Charley, so brilliantly assisted by Sandy Stelts and her colleagues, offered the hospitality of the Rare Books Room to a variety of history-of-photography events, all of which benefited immensely from the congenial atmosphere that Charley and Sandy had created, an intellectual and aesthetic haven.

Charley in his protectorate

Even on the very last such occasion, last April, when it was alas clear that Charley was not feeling well, he acted as genial host, with unfailing courtesy and charm, and as if everything were in the best of order. Unnoticed by most of the guests, of course, it was nevertheless a heroic act. And all along, when other events in the University called for some kind of supporting exhibition and display, Charley delivered, much to the delight of outside visitors and us all.

Charley was a fine researcher in his own right, and it is a thousand pities that his plans for a book on London's Crystal Palace never came to fruition. He was probably the world's greatest expert on the subject and one of the most capable of presenting the topic to a wide body of readers. Of course, he had other interests as well. It could be that there exists here or there a book that Charley had never read, but we never came across any evidence of that sort.

Thirty-five years is a long time. Inevitably some more trivial episodes also come to mind. I recall an occasion when we sat in the lounge of the Algonquin Hotel, in full evening regalia, because we were waiting to attend a reception at the Grolier Club. A middle-aged lady, who evidently knew all about the New York scene, came up to us and said: "Hi, where are you playing tonight?" Can't recall what Charley said, but it was evidently music to her ears.

And yet, I am aware of the fact that no professional record and no anthology of amusing episodes can do justice to the whole man. Can Charley be replaced? The whole notion is absurd. With the "advancement" of science, who knows, we might all be cloned one of these days, but Charley was one of a kind and will always remain so, in the annals of academe and, above all, in our hearts.

– Heinz Henisch

Charley

Though I knew in a theoretical way that Charley was at the top of his profession, and though we were colleagues for years in the English Department and in our institute for Arts and Humanistic Studies, our relationship was not a professional one. We were friends. I knew Charley as a host, a dinner guest, a friendly presence on campus, and so even on this occasion it seems right to refer to him as Charley. He was the least pretentious of men, never standing on his dignity or angling for position. He was always simply and remarkably himself–Charley Mann.

Knowledge makes some men weighty and authoritative. They marshal their facts and review their conclusions like Major Generals of Learning, and the more learning they acquire, the weightier those conclusions become–like intellectual blitzkriegs. Charley was totally unlike that. His relationship to his won knowledge had a democratic, friendly quality. He treated his facts like friends, he never bullied them into squadrons and formations, and as if to reward him for this kind treatment, his enormous erudition, rather than weighing him down, seemed to buoy him up. Charley's learning was vast, but not formidable. He couldn't be formidable. He bore his learning lightly. It made him supple, fluid, and quick, not heavy or weighty.

But how did he get to know so much? When did he learn all that he knew? He never gave me the impression of having sweated or burnt the midnight oil. Nor did he seem to be a sedentary scholar. He was always on the move. So when did he do all that reading? He seemed to absorb books on the wing, so to speak. It was as if he were born to learning, or had picked it up with the air he breathed. Just as he exercised his learning with a light and easy touch, so it seemed to have come to him lightly and easily and naturally, like a birthright.

And what he knew! It was fantastic. He knew all about books, architecture, movies, local history, and a thousand and one other subjects. One could know Charley for years and still be surprised to discover some interest of his, some area of knowledge, some pocket of lore you had never suspected him of possessing. He had reserves almost like book reserves, not placed on open shelves yet there to be used and enjoyed by anyone interested in the subject.

What impressed me most about Charley was the pleasure he took in what he knew. It was an innocent pleasure untainted by the pride of possession. Charley enjoyed his knowledge not because it was His but because it was Knowledge, and intrinsically delightful. To talk to him, to hear him and to see him in action was to understand the difference between those who pursue knowledge for ulterior motives, and those who pursue knowledge out of sheer delight in the subject. Charley's delight in knowledge was in itself delightful. The purity of his own motives helped everyone he came in contact with. He helped to restore or to reawaken in everyone a pure love of books and knowledge untrammeled by the pressure to publish and unconstricted by the narrow confines of a research project. For Charley there was neither project nor pressure, there was only the free and open sea of knowledge in which, dolphinlike, he swam and dived and sported and snorted and flashed–too briefly–before us.

He was a rare person, and like any real rarity there was something mysterious and finally incommunicable about him. He loved to talk; he loved to impart his knowledge; he could be completely frank; yet the very richness of his knowledge, the variety of his interests, the multifariousness of his activities and personal contacts kept him apart. He was always there coming toward you on the mall or in the library with that smile on his face, yet when you parted from him you never quite knew who else, where else, or what else would come next for him as he made his lovely path through life. I think most of us had the experience of missing him when he was alive. Now we shall miss him permanently.

– Tom Rogers

The Unterberg Poetry Center of the 92nd Street Y

Kelli Rae Patton
New York, New York

In 1939 a handful of men in New York City founded an institution dedicated solely to the art of poetry. As Hitler and the Third Reich strengthened their power in Europe, a group of American Jews were laying the groundwork for a program that would eventually consist of thirty-odd literary events per year. The organization came to be known as the Poetry Center of the 92nd Street Young Men's and Young Women's Hebrew Association, and its mission is "to bring authors and audiences together for the purpose of celebrating the vital place of literature in our culture."

The 92nd Street YMHA had been founded in 1874 by a group of German American businessmen to foster fellowship among young Jewish men living in New York. Eventually, the Y expanded to include programs for young women. Along the way a formidable educational arm emerged, which included lectures, classes, and a reading series. "The Poetry Center was started to meet the needs of the very few persons in New York to whom poetry offers the theological, the ethical and the aesthetic equivalents of traditional religion," said Y Education Director and Poetry Center founder Dr. William Kolodney.

Norman MacLeod served as the first director of the Poetry Center, and the inaugural season opened with a reading by William Carlos Williams. The rest of the first season consisted of twelve readings by poets W. H. Auden, Langston Hughes, Robert Fitzgerald, and Marianne Moore. Readings began at 9 P.M. to accommodate those who worked. The series was popular, despite the admission price of fifty cents per reading. One observer commented, "The usual 'pink tea' atmosphere of such occasions is absent."

Over the course of its history, the Poetry Center has had a long line of poets as directors. Not the least of these was John Malcolm Brinnin, who succeeded in increasing the number of subscribers as well as wooing such luminaries of the literary world as E. E. Cummings, Robert Frost, and Randall Jarrell during his tenure. Welsh poet and dramatist Dylan Thomas brought his play for voices *Under Milk Wood* to the Poetry Center in 1953 for its premiere reading. This event marked the beginning of a long-standing commitment to the art of verse drama that continues to this day. When Brinnin inadvertently gave Dorothy Parker his rent bill instead of her honorarium, she quipped—so the story goes—that no matter how badly she had read she should not have been charged for it.

In 1961 Norman Mailer read poems that Kolodney deemed obscene. The curtain was pulled, and Mailer's reading was thus brought to a halt. Allen Ginsberg, who was a member of the audience, expressed his ire at what he considered censorship on the part of the Y in a letter to Kolodney. A particularly spirited portion of that letter reads, "I place my Spirit as a Poet working in an ancient prophetic tradition against yours right now and demand you apologize to Mailer for your conduct; and as Poet and member of audience I DEMAND apologies from you to me, with no more ambiguousness, for disturbing my evening. . . . Unless I hear from you . . . I will not again set foot in the Temple of the Y because it is a place of Pharisees and moneychangers."

The Poetry Center recovered from Ginsberg's attack and reconciled with him (he would go on to make several appearances on the George S. Kaufman stage, including a memorable reading with his father, Louis Ginsberg). Over the years, fiction and dramatic readings were incorporated into the schedule of poetry events, making the name Poetry Center something of a misnomer. The name stuck, however, for it was the name under which the organization had gained its renown. Because of a gift from the Greenwood family in the 1970s, the center was renamed Unterberg Poetry Center in 1991 in honor of the founder and first president of the YWHA, Bella Unterberg.

Poet Karl Kirchwey became director more than a decade ago, after serving briefly as an assis-

Cover for the diamond anniversary program of the New York organization dedicated to the celebration of poetry

tant to then-director Shelley Mason. Kirchwey has set forth four criteria for programming the Main Reading Series in an attempt to continue expanding the audience and influence of the Poetry Center: 1) diversity of genre; 2) diversity of programs; 3) diversity of racial, ethnic, geographical, and national origin; and 4) diversity of stature. Many writers have made their first appearances at the Y under his tenure, including novelist Philip Roth, playwright and actor Sam Shepard, and the English writer Muriel Spark. The famously reticent Don DeLillo gave his first public reading at the Poetry Center in 1990 at the urging of Kirchwey; DeLillo returned to the Y with a reading from his novel *Underworld* during the 1997–1998 season. American poet Stanley Kunitz has called Kaufman Concert Hall "the nerve center of American poetry."

In the fall of 1998 the Poetry Center began a yearlong celebration of its sixtieth anniversary. Irish Nobel Laureate poet Seamus Heaney opened the season on 28 September with a luminous read-

ing of both old and new work. Programming acumen and a strong membership base have enabled Kirchwey and his staff regularly to draw capacity crowds. Grace Schulman, a former Poetry Center Director and noted poet, recalls readings held in the Y's Weill Art Gallery (with a maximum capacity of 130) and marvels at the center's ability to entice such a large and dedicated audience to the nine-hundred-seat concert hall on a consistent basis. For the first half of the 1998 season, the average number of audience members was 550–nothing to sneer at in a city full of cultural opportunities. Ticket prices range from $10 to $15, depending on the event (considerably more than in that first season).

Kirchwey has made it his business to program multidisciplinary events as often as possible. Evenings of music and poetry, poets and painters, and dramatic readings comprise only a few such events. In January 1997 actress Billie Whitelaw performed the work of Samuel Beckett and spoke of her collaboration with the acclaimed playwright. That same year a handful of American poets gathered to read poems inspired by works of art; this program took its cue from an anthology edited by scholar John Hollander titled *The Gazer's Spirit*. A special interest of Kirchwey is verse drama, and he has been instrumental in seeing several verse dramas read on the Kaufman stage. In October 1993 the Poetry Center presented the first New York reading of Derek Walcott's *The Odyssey: A Stage Version*. The end of 1998 brought a revival reading of Robert Lowell's *Benito Cereno,* based on the powerful novella of race and nationalism on the high seas by Herman Melville. Actors Roscoe Lee Browne, Frank Langella, and Jack Ryland, who appeared in the original 1964 production at the now-defunct American Place Theatre, were reunited with director Jonathan Miller.

In the past several years the Poetry Center has collaborated with many other organizations to strengthen its programming base, as well as to forge a close-knit literary network across the nation. The aim of such ventures is to present high-quality literary programming on a routine basis around the country to a wide range of audiences. Since 1996 all poetry readings have been presented jointly with the Academy of American Poets, the Poetry Center's distinguished sister organization in downtown Manhattan. A lively onstage interview series, "Writers-at-Work-Live," is presented in conjunction with *The Paris Review* magazine; these interviews form the basis of interviews printed in the magazine. The first writer interviewed as part of this series was South African playwright Athol Fugard, who returned to the Poetry Center in November 1998 to read from a memoir. Playwright Arthur Miller and novelists Norman Mailer, William Styron, and Ruth Prawer Jhabvala have been the subjects of such interviews. But aside from the Main Reading Series, the Poetry Center has grown to encompass programs that appeal to a wide range of readers (and writers).

Biographers & Brunch

More than a decade ago the Poetry Center added a Sunday morning lecture series to the roster of readings. Consisting of six lectures annually, "Biographers & Brunch" presents distinguished literary biographers speaking in the Art Gallery, the small space adjacent to Kaufman Hall, about their subjects and the task of the biographer. Jean Gent, Aleksandr Solzhenitsyn, and Willa Cather were

subjects of discussion in 1993–1994. Scholar James Park Sloan considered the controversial life and work of Jerzy Kosinski a few years ago. Also among that season's offerings were lectures on Tennessee Williams, Lewis Carroll, and Paul Celan. Last season Michael Reynolds discussed the fourth volume of his biography of Ernest Hemingway. In 1998 notable English scholar Hermione Lee spoke to capacity crowds about her biography of Virginia Woolf. Future programs include a lecture by Stacy Schiff on Antoine Saint-Exupery, who wrote *The Little Prince*. The 1998–1999 season is the first to feature a discussion of a work-and-life-in-progress: James Atlas talking about his biography of novelist Saul Bellow. "Biographers & Brunch" affords metropolitan New Yorkers an intimate setting in which to discuss the lives and works of favorite authors with practicing biographers. Each lecture is followed by a lively and intellectual question-and-answer period, prompting some to call the audience of "Biographers & Brunch" the smartest in New York. In the past few seasons the cable television network C-Span has taped and broadcast several of the lectures, making "Biographers & Brunch" available to a wider range of viewers.

The Writing Program

Almost from its inception the Poetry Center offered writing workshops and literary seminars; they were often taught by the directors themselves early on, and later by scholars and writers. In recent years Harvard professor and literary critic Helen Vendler has lectured to capacity crowds on the work of John Keats, William Shakespeare, and Seamus Heaney. The Writing Program has grown steadily, offering workshops in poetry, fiction, and nonfiction. More than a dozen classes take place in fall and spring semesters. Master classes make it possible for students to work with writers appearing in the Main Reading Series on the Sunday prior to the readings. In recent years student writers have had the chance to work with playwright John Guare, poet Charles Simic, and fiction writer Robert Olen Butler.

Ancillary Programs

Important components of the Poetry Center in its current incarnation are a handful of ancillary programs. Ten years ago Kirchwey and Wendy Salinger, a teacher and writer, started the Schools Project, an outreach program for New York public high school students. Participants in the Schools Project study the work of writers appearing at the Poetry Center and attend some of readings each season. In addition, Salinger conducts a writing workshop to which the students are invited. At Union Settlement House in East Harlem, the Poetry Center established an adult literacy program in 1993. Many of the students are drawn from New York's Spanish-speaking population and are learning to read and write in English. A grant from the Lila Wallace-Reader's Digest Fund has enabled the Poetry Center to begin the two-year-long National Literary Audience Development Project. One of the many goals of the project is to foster alliances with literary organizations across the country. In addition to a guidebook (with a video companion) for literary presenters, Lila Wallace asked the director of the program, Jonathan Levi, to produce a show to tour to at least five American cities. The first full-scale stage production in the Poetry Center's history was presented in 1998: poet Robert Pinsky's acclaimed translation of Dante's *Inferno* played by four actors. Now in its twenty-fifth year, "Discovery"/*The Nation* contest is a competition cosponsored by the Poetry Center and *The Nation* magazine for poets who have not yet published a book of poems. Four winners receive a reading at the Poetry Center, publication in *The Nation,* and a small cash prize. Many past winners have gone on to distinguished careers as poets, including Lucille Clifton, Debora Greger, Marilyn Hacker, Daniel Halpern, Garrett Hongo, Larry Levis, David Mura, Katha Pollitt, Mary Jo Salter, Gary Soto, Mark Strand, Ellen Bryant Voigt, and Rosanna Warren.

Conclusion

In an effort to extend the reputation of the Poetry Center and to make its programs available to a wide-ranging public, plans are in the works to publish an anthology of poems read at the Poetry Center along with an audio companion using archival materials. WNYC, New York public radio, produced a highly successful series a few years ago called "The Poet's Voice." Thirteen programs narrated by actress Blair Brown focused on the work of poets who had appeared at the Poetry Center. The Poetry Center's audio archives, which date back to 1949, were used extensively in this project.

Testament to the growth and influence of the Poetry Center is a recent spate of fictional scrutiny and celebration. The protagonist of John Irving's 1998 novel *A Widow for One Year* reads from his work on the Kaufman stage. Kirchwey and former codirector Melissa Hammerle make cameo appearances. The playwright Donald Margulies put the spotlight on the Poetry Center in his play *Collected Stories,* which opened in New York in 1998 and starred Ute Hagen.

For many members of the literary community, a reading at the Poetry Center has served as a gauge of their literary standing. The center is a proving ground for new talent, as well as a beloved home-away-from-home for more-established writers. Cynthia Ozick, the award-winning essayist and fiction writer, has said, "The 92nd Street Y is a place of literary dreaming, a palace for poetry. I'm always overwhelmed by the chance to stand on that stage."

Martha Gellhorn

(8 November 1908 – 15 February 1998)

Tracy Simmons Bitonti

Perhaps inevitably, the obituaries for Martha Gellhorn prominently mentioned the one aspect of her life from which she most wanted to dissociate herself: the fact that she had been the third Mrs. Ernest Hemingway. Yet, as those obituaries also made clear, Gellhorn had a significant literary career as a journalist and fiction writer that was already well established before she met Hemingway and continued long after their divorce in 1945. Her journalism recorded the human side of the history she witnessed; her stories entertained readers of the magazines in which they appeared; and her novels engaged more serious readers.

Martha Ellis Gellhorn was born on 8 November 1908, in St. Louis, Missouri. Her father, George Gellhorn, was a gynecologist, obstetrician, and professor of medicine. Her mother, Edna Fischel Gellhorn, was a crusader for social and political causes ranging from pure-milk ordinances to the establishment of the League of Women Voters. Gellhorn enjoyed the best educational opportunities available; her last three years of high school were spent as one of the first students at the John Burroughs School, a progressive, private, coeducational institution. She then attended Bryn Mawr for three years, but in 1929 she left, determined to start a career as a writer and to pay her own way doing it.

Her first journalistic job was a six-month stint with the *Albany Times Union,* though her assignments were limited to the ladies' clubs and the morgue. After that, a series of travel articles she wrote for the *St. Louis Post-Dispatch* brought her to the attention of *The New Republic,* for which she wrote book reviews and, in 1929, her first signed article, "Rudy Vallee: God's Gift (1984) to Us Girls." In February 1930 she bought passage to Europe on the Holland America cruise line with an article for their trade magazine; she was intent on becoming a foreign correspondent. She spent the next two years traveling around Europe and America, taking what writing jobs she could get.

Journalism meant more to Gellhorn than a source of income. As she wrote in the introduction to *The Face*

Martha Gellhorn in 1939 (UPI/Bettmann Newsphotos)

of War (1959), a collection of her wartime reporting, in her idealistic youth she "thought of journalism as a guiding light," believing if she could help show the truth about injustices, readers would spring into action. Later she came to regard it as "a passport," a means of getting "a ringside seat at the spectacle of history in the making." Finally she saw it as a means of education, of "keeping the record straight. . . . a form of honorable behavior, involving the reporter and the reader." As she told Bernice Kert for Kert's *The Hemingway Women* (1983), however, her "real aim and ambition" was

271

always to write fiction. Her journalistic activities bought her the time to devote to fiction writing and gave her much of the raw material for it. She told Victoria Glendinning in an interview for *Vogue* (April 1988): "Fiction is much harder work than journalism, so naturally I respect it more. Fiction is mystery."

By the end of 1932 Gellhorn had finished her first novel. *What Mad Pursuit* (1934) is the story of three young women who leave the security of college to start making their own way in the world, taking as their theme the Hemingway idea from *A Farewell to Arms* that "nothing ever happens to the brave." Gellhorn had difficulty finding a publisher for this novel because of her frank treatment of sexual situations. The book was finally published in 1934 by Stokes, but Gellhorn subsequently disowned it, refusing to allow it to be listed among her works.

During this period, from 1933 to 1935 or 1936, Gellhorn was married to Marquis Bertrand de Jouvenel, a French journalist and economist. They were depicted in news articles as young, glamorous, and romantic, but the marriage did not last.

In the fall of 1934 Gellhorn returned to America, realizing the effects of the Great Depression on the country and wanting, as she wrote in *The View From the Ground* (1988), to be "enrolled in the service of the nation." A fellow journalist introduced her to Harry Hopkins, director of the Federal Emergency Relief Administration (FERA), who hired her as an investigator. She spent the next year traveling around the country, talking to the people and sending back reports about their condition and the effectiveness (or lack thereof) of the relief program. Her work gained the attention of President Franklin D. Roosevelt, and she began a warm, lifelong friendship with Eleanor Roosevelt.

After she was fired from FERA because she had incited some workers for a corrupt contractor to commit minor vandalism to call attention to their plight, she had some time to devote to fiction again, and she wrote *The Trouble I've Seen* (1936). This collection of four novellas makes the effects of the Depression undeniably concrete, showing them through vivid human characters. As Kert points out, the book was deliberately crafted to depict the spectrum of victims—the old, the middle-aged, the young, and children, in the South, East, West, and Midwest. H. G. Wells wrote a preface for the book and recommended it to Putnam in England, who published it.

Critical acclaim for *The Trouble I've Seen* poured in from England and America. Gellhorn's "sympathy" in depicting her characters was the quality that reviewers most frequently mentioned. In his review for *The Spectator* (22 May 1936) Graham Greene expressed his sur-

prise that the quality of the work did not match his expectations for the gender of the writer: "She has none of the female vices of unbalanced pity or factitious violence; her masculine characters are presented as convincingly as her female, and her writing is hard and clear." Another reviewer with strong praise for the book was Lewis Gannett, who observed in his *New York Herald Tribune* syndicated column, "Books and Things," on 25 September 1936: "Hemingway does not write more authentic American speech. Nor can Ernest Hemingway teach Martha Gellhorn anything about economy of language."

By 1937 Gellhorn's attention was drawn to the Spanish Republic, embroiled in civil war. A friend at *Collier's* gave her a letter stating that she was their correspondent, in order to help her get there; but as she recalls in *The Face of War,*

> otherwise it meant nothing. I had no connection with a newspaper or magazine, and I believed that all one did about a war was go to it, as a gesture of solidarity, and get killed, or survive if lucky until the war was over.... I had no idea you could be what I became, an unscathed tourist of wars. A knapsack and approximately fifty dollars were my equipment for Spain; anything more seemed unnecessary.

Once there, she adds, she "tagged along behind the war correspondents, experienced men who had serious work to do." One of these was Hemingway, whom Gellhorn had met in Key West in December 1936 and with whom she subsequently became involved. At his suggestion she wrote an article about life in Madrid and sent it to *Collier's;* "Only the Shells Whine" appeared in their 17 July 1937 issue, with Gellhorn's name featured on the cover. She was later added to their masthead and thus began a long association with the magazine. She spent 1937 and 1938 in Spain and America, writing and lecturing on behalf of the "Causa" and traveling to report from Czechoslovakia, England, and France about the brewing world war.

One of Gellhorn's cardinal principles was always that she earned her own money and paid her own way for whatever she wanted to do. By the end of 1938 journalism had earned her enough to buy some time to write fiction again. She was also suffering from despair over conditions in Europe, feeling that her writing was useless against the horrors of war. She settled in Cuba, locating and restoring the villa called Finca Vigía, (Watchtower Farm) where she and Hemingway lived and wrote. He worked on *For Whom the Bell Tolls* (1940), while she wrote short fiction and her next novel. *A Stricken Field* (1940) is the story of American correspondent Mary Douglas's attempts to help a young Communist couple, Rita and Peter, in the troubled times of

Prague after the Munich Pact. The first draft was completed by the fall of 1939; then Gellhorn took a Scandinavian assignment for *Collier's,* once again needing money to afford time to write. She went to Finland and Sweden as one of the first correspondents to report on the war from the Finnish front, returning to Cuba in January 1940.

A Stricken Field was published in March 1940. Critics had difficulty treating the book as a novel, because the heroine so strongly resembled Gellhorn. The reviewer for *The New York Times* (10 March 1940) commented, "Largely because it wavers so on the borderline of fiction and non-fiction, 'A Stricken Field' is a hard book to appraise. . . . 'A Stricken Field' is at its best a compelling book and a moving one, but as a novel it is weak. Miss Gellhorn has done better in her articles." In an afterword to a 1986 edition of the novel Gellhorn recalled having been offended because "*Time* magazine reviewed me, not the book." The piece to which she refers was titled "Glamor Girl" (18 March 1940), and out of eight paragraphs, only two include discussion of the novel, noting that it is "Semi-autobiographical at least." The rest details Gellhorn's activities as "a novelist with a legend," commenting about *The Trouble I've Seen* that "with Author Gellhorn's photograph and background, any publisher's publicity writer could do the rest."

Media attention to her "legend" increased in November 1940, when Gellhorn and Hemingway were married after his divorce from Pauline Pfeiffer. Gellhorn hated the spotlight; as she told Glendinning, "I do not believe that the private person has to be public property. The work, yes; the person, no."

After *A Stricken Field* Gellhorn turned to writing short stories; her next book was *The Heart of Another,* a collection published in October 1941 by Scribners, the house that published Hemingway. She worked with editor Maxwell Perkins and was friends with Charles Scribner. Before publication of *The Heart of Another,* Gellhorn expressed to Perkins her concern that critics would not treat it as serious fiction because of her reputation as a journalist, particularly with the kind of attention *Collier's* often called to her glamorous appearance. The brief notice in *Library Journal* (1 October 1941) did state that the book is "Written in journalistic style" and wondered if the stories are autobiographical, finally predicting that the book "will not be generally popular." Most of the other reviews, however, were fairly positive, though sales were relatively small.

Gellhorn spent the first part of 1942 in Cuba. As biographer Jacqueline E. Orsagh documents, Gellhorn's initial efforts to get to Europe and report the war were thwarted by restrictions against women in combat zones. She had begun working on another novel by

May but was interrupted in the summer for another *Collier's* assignment, this one in the Caribbean. In the fall she spent time in New York and Washington as well as Cuba, and by the time she visited her mother in St. Louis for Christmas she was working on the novel again. Set in the Caribbean, the contemporary story involves a triangle: Liana, a beautiful young mulatto; Marc, her rich white husband, who considers her an ornament; and Pierre, the teacher with whom she has an affair. When Pierre deserts her to fight for France, she commits suicide. *Liana* was published by Scribners in January 1944.

Reviewing *Liana* for *The Nation* (22 January 1944), Diana Trilling commented: "On the surface, or even several layers down, 'Liana' is not much more than another stereotyped, not-so-lush-as-it-could-have-been narrative of tropical miscegenation," though she admits Gellhorn had managed to achieve some effect with her "perfect blending of intellectual and emotional pitch." Other reviewers were more receptive. The review in *The New York Times* (16 January 1944) was generally positive:

> With this new novel, Martha Gellhorn (Mrs. Ernest Hemingway) establishes herself as an honest and intelligent writer who has something to say and knows how to say it well. "Liana" has certain agreeable qualities of maturity and emotional understanding which are not always to be found in even the best modern art, still a predominantly male affair.

Sales for *Liana* were quite good, and several paperback reprints appeared in the 1950s and 1960s.

While *Liana* was climbing the sales charts, Gellhorn was occupied with her journalism, having achieved her long desire to join the war effort in Europe and do what she could. As she wrote in *The Face of War,* "From November 1943, with one unavoidable break in the spring of 1944, I followed the war wherever I could reach it." The "unavoidable break" was her brief return to Cuba in March in an effort to placate Hemingway as their marriage was disintegrating. He took over as frontline correspondent for *Collier's,* and Gellhorn faced additional difficulties with army public-relations officials who did not believe that a woman should be among combat troops. But Gellhorn was determined: "I had been sent to Europe to do my job, which was not to report the rear areas or the woman's angle." She learned to use "stealth and chicanery" to get where she wanted to go; perhaps the best example was smuggling herself aboard a hospital ship that landed at Normandy on D day, when she went ashore at night to assist the stretcher bearers. Until 1946, she sneaked and wrote her way through Italy, Nijimegen, the Battle of the

Gellhorn and Ernest Hemingway in Honolulu in 1941 (John Fitzgerald Kennedy Library)

Bulge, Dachau, and Java. Gellhorn and Hemingway divorced in 1945.

In the summer of 1945 Gellhorn also worked on a play with her fellow correspondent, Virginia Cowles. The play, which someone else titled *Love Goes to Press* (a title Gellhorn hated), is set in a press camp in Poggibonsi, Italy, in 1944 and follows the adventures of Jane Mason and Annabelle Jones, war correspondents loosely based on their creators. Gellhorn emphasizes, however, in an introduction to the published version of the play in 1995 that this comedy "bears no resemblance, whatever, of any kind at all, to war and war correspondents. It is a joke. It was intended to make people laugh and make money." The play was well received during a run in London in the summer of 1946, but it ended in four days on Broadway, where American critics decided it was not funny.

By January 1947 Gellhorn was working on her next book, *The Wine of Astonishment* (1948), a contemporary war novel. *The Wine of Astonishment* centers on the experiences of Private Jacob Levy, jeep driver for the lieutenant colonel of an infantry division in Luxembourg, as he participates in the last of the fighting and in a love affair with a local girl. When he encounters

Dachau, he is so horrified that he deliberately plows his jeep through a crowd of Germans. Gellhorn was, in part, purging her own memories of the war. She explained in an afterword to a 1989 edition of the novel that she created Levy, in part, "to relieve me of the memory of Dachau. . . . If I gave Dachau to Jacob Levy, I would lose it."

One of Gellhorn's initial ideas for the title was "Point of No Return," a term used to describe the moment past which an aircraft will no longer have enough fuel to return home. This title was rejected in favor of a phrase from the Bible, but it was restored for the 1989 republication. Scribners made significant efforts to promote the book in 1948, and reviews were quite good. Some critics thought the Dachau episode problematic, but generally they praised the authenticity of Gellhorn's depiction of the effects of World War II on those who experienced it. A critic for *The Saturday Review of Literature* (9 October 1948) hailed *The Wine of Astonishment* as "a surprisingly masculine novel. Even a woman war correspondent could not be expected to see war so completely as men see it." The *New York Herald Tribune* reviewer (3 October 1948) claimed, "Because women have the greater penchant for grace, compassion and tenderness in their living and writing, they are at an initial handicap in approaching the subject of war. Martha Gellhorn has come closer to that subject than any other American woman writer." Despite the praise, the novel did not sell well.

In 1949 Gellhorn adopted a son, an Italian orphan who delighted her and kept her occupied. The two moved to Mexico. For a while, Gellhorn decided she no longer wanted to be a serious writer, and she worked on short stories for sale to popular magazines. Some of these stories were good enough to complete the collection she had contemplated since at least December 1946. She would no longer publish with the house of Scribners, however. The break was precipitated by the savage portrayal of Gellhorn in Hemingway's novel *Across the River and into the Trees,* which was being serialized in *Cosmopolitan* in 1950. She wrote to editor Wallace Meyer in April and May 1950 that she did not think the firm should be put in the position of having one of its authors attacking another one; she also wanted to sever any remaining connections to her former husband. She remained friends with Meyer and Charles Scribner, but the collection, *The Honeyed Peace,* was published by Doubleday in 1953.

In 1954 Gellhorn married T. S. Matthews, a writer who had also served as an editor of *Time.* As Orsagh points out, Gellhorn was more successful this time at keeping her private life out of the media spotlight, and once again she joined her husband's publisher. Simon and Schuster published Gellhorn's next four books: *Two By Two* (1958), four novellas about marriage; *The Face of War; His Own Man* (1961), a novel; and *Pretty Tales for Tired People* (1965), three novellas. Gellhorn and Matthews divorced in 1963.

Following *Pretty Tales for Tired People,* Gellhorn had another major war to report: Vietnam. Despite her journalistic résumé, as she explains in *The View From the Ground,* this time she was "overage for active service and without connections" until she convinced the *Manchester Guardian* to provide credentials and airfare. The series of six articles resulting from her August–September 1966 trip were printed in the *Guardian* and reprinted by the paper as a booklet titled *Vietnam: A New Kind of War.* In the five months previous to her trip, she had tried to escape her horror of the war by writing *The Lowest Trees Have Tops* (1967), a light, utopian novel about a community of expatriates in Mexico. Gellhorn then suffered what she called in *The View From the Ground* a "writer's block made of solid concrete," caused by her anguish over the war, until May 1975. She traveled around the world, engaging in a variety of nonwriting activities. As she told Glendinning, even when she did not have writer's block, "I spent a great deal of my life just living, which is why I didn't write more books."

Gellhorn spent 1975 through 1977 writing her next book, *Travels With Myself and Another* (1978), a humorous recounting of her most memorable "horror journeys," including an account of her summer 1942 travels around the Caribbean for *Collier's,* a journey across Africa, and a visit to a fellow writer in Russia. Gellhorn chronicles her adventures and mishaps without making herself the star. Instead, the focus is on the places she saw, the incidents that occurred, and the people, including Mr. Ma, the interpreter on her 1941 China trip, whose translations were frequently sprinkled with the word "whatchumcallit"; Joshua, the young African man who hired himself out as her driver but could not drive; and U. C., the Unwilling Companion on her China trip, who was, of course, Hemingway. The reviewer for *The New York Times* (23 September 1979) asserted that "gentleperson" Gellhorn deserved a medal not only for refraining from identifying (and capitalizing on the name of) U. C. but also for making him "a sympathetic as well as amusing figure, although perhaps a wee bit maddening."

Travels With Myself and Another was followed by *The Weather in Africa* (1978), a volume of three novellas. After that came *The View From the Ground,* a collection of peacetime reporting and a companion to the revised and updated *The Face of War.* Gellhorn's journalism earned high praise. When *The Face of War* first appeared, the reviewer for *The New York Times* (22 March 1959) called it "a brilliant antiwar book that is as fresh as if written for this morning," and when it was republished in 1986, a critic for the *New Statesman* (30 May 1986) claimed, "You could simply take all the articles and books written by male war correspondents and flush them down the plug hole. And, so long as you had this, you would have 90 per cent of everything worthwhile." A failed cataract operation when she was in her eighties interfered with her ability to work, but Gellhorn kept on reporting, with articles appearing in such periodicals as *Granta* and *The New Republic* in the 1980s and 1990s. She remained an active observer of contemporary events–including the American invasion of Panama and the first term of Bill Clinton's presidency–right up until her death from cancer and other complications on 15 February 1998.

Although the obituaries could not avoid discussion of Hemingway, they emphasized Gellhorn's personality and her contribution to American letters. *The Times* (London) said of her on 18 February 1998: "Her work for *Collier's* magazine had established her as a first-rate war correspondent, adept at getting to the front line and apparently impervious to the dangers once she was there." With the media attention to her personal life and her efforts to record the history of her times, Martha Gellhorn became, as the piece in *The Guardian* (17 February 1998) concluded, "part of the century's image bank."

BOOKS: *What Mad Pursuit* (New York: Stokes, 1934);
The Trouble I've Seen (London: Putnam, 1936; New York: Morrow, 1936);
A Stricken Field (New York: Duell, Sloan & Pearce, 1940; London: Cape, 1942); republished, with afterword by Gellhorn (London: Virago, 1986);
The Heart of Another (New York: Scribners, 1941; London: Home & Van Thal, 1946);
Liana (New York: Scribners, 1944; London: Home & Van Thal, 1944); republished, with afterword by Gellhorn (London: Virago, 1987);
The Wine of Astonishment (New York: Scribners, 1948); republished, with afterword by Gellhorn, as *Point of No Return* (New York: Plume/New American Library, 1989);
The Honeyed Peace: Stories (Garden City, N.Y.: Doubleday, 1953; London: Deutsch, 1954);
Two By Two (New York: Simon & Schuster, 1958; London: Longmans, Green, 1958);
The Face of War (New York: Simon & Schuster, 1959; London: Hart-Davis, 1959); expanded edition (London: Virago, 1986 / New York: Atlantic Monthly Press, 1986); expanded edition (New York: Atlantic Monthly Press, 1988);
His Own Man (New York: Simon & Schuster, 1961);
Pretty Tales for Tired People (New York: Simon & Schuster, 1965; London: M. Joseph, 1965);
Vietnam: A New Kind of War (Manchester, U.K.: Manchester Guardian & Evening News, 1966);

The Lowest Trees Have Tops (London: M. Joseph, 1967; New York: Dodd, Mead, 1969);
Travels With Myself and Another (London: Allen Lane, 1978; New York: Dodd, Mead, 1979);
The Weather in Africa (London: Allen Lane, 1978; New York: Dodd, Mead, 1980);
The View From the Ground (New York: Atlantic Monthly Press, 1988; London: Granta, in association with Penguin, 1989);
The Short Novels of Martha Gellhorn (London: Sinclair-Stevenson, 1991); republished as *The Novellas of Martha Gellhorn* (New York: Knopf, 1993)—includes *The Trouble I've Seen, Two By Two, Pretty Tales for Tired People,* and *The Weather in Africa;*
Love Goes to Press: A Comedy in Three Acts, by Gellhorn and Virginia Cowles, edited by Sandra Spanier (Lincoln: University of Nebraska Press, 1995).

PLAY PRODUCTION: *Love Goes to Press,* by Gellhorn and Virginia Cowles, Eastbourne, U.K., Devonshire Park, 10 June 1946; London, Embassy Theatre, 18 June 1946; New York, Biltmore Theater, 1 January 1947.

OTHER: "The Invasion of Panama," in *The Best of Granta Reportage* (London: Granta, 1993), pp. 267–287.

SELECTED PERIODICAL PUBLICATIONS–UNCOLLECTED: "On Apocryphism," *Paris Review,* 23 (Spring 1981): 280–301;
"A Miracle in the Caribbean," *Condé Nast Traveler,* 26 (June 1991): 82–84+;
"Cry Shame," *New Republic,* 210 (27 June 1994): 14–15.

The Digital Millennium Copyright Act: Expanding Copyright Protection in Cyberspace and Beyond

G. Spencer Lueders Jr.
University of South Carolina

Johnny Cash is mad. The Man in Black recently spied a Slovenia-based website offering illicit digital copies of his "Ring of Fire" over the Internet. Although the country-western singer no longer owns the copyrights to his works in most foreign countries, the copies he discovered are examples of electronic piracy proliferating in the digital age. Copyright owners fear that as their products increasingly become available on the Internet in digital form, pirates and criminals will make and distribute illegal copies. The manufacturers and producers of these works echo this concern; as digital works can be transmitted to millions of people around the world with a few clicks of a mouse, manufacturing costs drop to almost nothing. Pirates can appropriate the only real source of profits remaining—namely, profits that copyright has protected.

To address the copyright problems inherent in online publishing, Congress passed the Digital Millennium Copyright Act (DMCA). This legislation, which Sen. Patrick J. Leahy dubbed the year's most important bill to pass through Congress, responds to the challenges of protecting copyrighted works, performances, and sound recordings using digital technology by implementing two treaties signed in 1996 under the aegis of the World Intellectual Property Organization (WIPO), an international organization dedicated to protecting intellectual property worldwide from its headquarters in Geneva, Switzerland. The surge in congressional activity in copyright legislation reflects a rise in the importance of copyright. But how big has the copyright industry become?

In the United States, copyright industries are among the fastest-growing economic assets. In 1996 approximately $278 billion was attributed to the industries, and during the past twenty years employment in the U.S. copyright industry has grown nearly three times as fast as the annual employment rate of the entire economy. The U.S. copyright industries thus contribute more to the economy and employ more workers than do any manufacturing sectors, including those such as chemicals, industrial equipment, electronics, food processing, textiles, and aircraft. Foreign sales and exports account for approximately $60 billion, yet it is estimated that up to $20 billion is lost annually through the international piracy of copyrighted works. This loss, which has been predicted to rise with the growth of the Internet, is seen as decreasing the incentive to create new works, thereby extending the economic loss into a social loss. Because the rapid development of information technology has enabled easy duplication of copyrighted material over digital networks, a need to reanalyze existing copyright laws has sparked Congress to act.

Existing copyright law was designed to deal with the creation, distribution, and sale of protected works in tangible copies, however, and considerable challenges exist in adapting such law to intangible electronic transmissions over cyberspace, where the location or existence of a copy at any particular time is unclear. In addition, issues such as "fair use" that involve maintaining current exceptions to copyright protection and protecting on-line service providers from illegal transmissions over their networks are central to the debate. Thus, Congress spent the summer months discussing various provisions, while Cash and other copyright holders urged quick action.

By July 1998 the House and Senate had each passed its own version of the DMCA. After conflicting portions of the House and Senate bills were reconciled by a conference subcommittee in October 1998, the approved DMCA implemented the WIPO treaties while modifying current U.S. copyright laws to meet the liability obligations that those treaties impose. With the DMCA ready to be signed into law, it is expected that foreign countries waiting for the U.S. to ratify the

WIPO treaties will follow suit. But how far do the WIPO treaties go?

Signed by ninety-six countries in Geneva, Switzerland, in 1996, the WIPO treaties specifically address issues involving the protection of copyrighted material in digital form. Although these treaties contain much that is already covered in U.S. copyright law, they will strengthen international protection for U.S. performers and producers and standardize copyright practice worldwide.

Among other things, the treaties include new provisions on technological circumvention measures such as encryption, encoding, and scrambling. These provisions require all contracting countries to provide "adequate legal protection and effective legal remedies against the circumvention of effective technological measures that are used by authors in connection with the exercise of their rights under this Treaty or the Berne Convention and that restrict acts, in respect of their works, which are not authorized by the authors concerned or permitted by law." Both treaties also include provisions requiring contracting countries to protect the integrity of "copyright management information," which is defined as "information which identifies the work, the author of the work, the owner of any right in the work, or information about the terms and conditions of use of the work, and any numbers or codes that represent such information, when any of these items of information is attached to a copy of a work or appears in connection with the communication of a work to the public."

The DMCA implements these and other provisions by amending Title 17 of the United States Code, which houses the current copyright act. For example, under Section 103 of Title 1, a new chapter includes the following five sections: (1) Section 1201, which prohibits circumvention and devices used to circumvent technological measures of protection; (2) Section 1202, which protects copyright management information; (3) Section 1203, which provides civil remedies for violations of Sections 1201 and 1202; (4) Section 1204, which provides criminal remedies for violations of Sections 1201 and 1202; and (5) Section 1205, which preserves the effectiveness of federal and state laws in protecting the privacy of the individual while using the Internet.

Section 1201(a)(1) was the source of much debate concerning "fair use," a central principle of existing copyright law that allows users, without getting the consent of owners, to make copies of copyrighted works for educational and other noncommercial purposes. Congress was concerned about what might happen if copyright owners were allowed to restrict access to their works in ways that would, in effect, quickly erode the fair-use doctrine. Some members argued that prohibiting the circumvention of technological protection would create a "pay-per-use" society and allow copyright owners to exploit information that is normally accessible.

For example, a student writing a research paper may, under the fair-use doctrine, download an article from a website and even excerpt parts of it, with proper reference, in the paper. Imagine, however, that before the student can access this article, he or she has to accept the terms in a digital license agreement by clicking on its specifications that the copyrighted expression or the noncopyrightable information will not be reused in any way. Accepting the agreement and then using the article in the research paper would subject the student to a breach of contract claim for violating this licensing agreement. In such cases as this, copyright owners might greatly diminish the power of the fair use doctrine.

To ensure that libraries, universities, and consumers will continue to be able to exercise fair-use rights, Section 1201(a)(1) creates a rule-making provision excluding certain users whom the librarian of Congress determines are adversely affected by being prohibited from making fair use of a particular class of works. Waiving the prohibition in Section 1201(a)(1) for those users can prevent a reduction in the availability of a particular category of copyrighted works to such individuals and institutions. Thus, a student wishing to download a copy of an article will continue to have fair use rights and access to works under current copyright law.

Section 1201(a)(2) and (b)(1) were attacked also by makers of consumer electronic devices. These sections make it illegal to manufacture, import, or offer or provide to the public any devices, sometimes known as "black boxes," that circumvent technological measures. To distinguish black boxes from staple articles of commerce such as personal computers, VCRs, and other consumer electronics, the final versions of Sections 1201(a)(2) and (b)(1) define devices circumventing technological measures as those having "no substantial non-infringing uses" and being "expressly intended to facilitate circumvention for purposes of gaining access to or making a copy of a work."

In addition, Section 1201(c)(3) includes a "no-mandate" provision that allows manufacturers of future consumer electronics the freedom to choose designs and components, as long as Section 1201 is not otherwise violated. If this provision had not been included, the DMCA might have been interpreted to require that new digital products respond to any measure that copyright owners might choose to deploy to protect their technology. For example, a copyright owner might employ a digital protection mechanism that is compatible with a compact disk player made by Sony. If another copyright owner creates a new, different digital protection mechanism that is not compatible with the Sony compact disk player, this copyright owner may try to argue that Sony is denying consumers proper access to his new product—because the design of the Sony compact disk player is not compatible with it. Section 1201(c)(3) was added by Congress to prevent such a dispute, to ensure that a manufacturer such as Sony may design its products as it wishes (as long as it violates no other provisions in doing so)—without being required to adapt its designs to the protections that copyright owners employ.

Section 1202 aims to maintain the integrity of copyright management information in analog and digital transmissions by prohibiting its distribution with false, removed, or altered copyright information. This prohibition includes the title of the work, a notice of copyright, the name of the copyright owner, the terms and conditions for use of a work, and other identifying marks or symbols to the copyright information.

Sometimes this information is embedded in the work through a process called "digital watermarking." Computer technology in its most basic form is binary code, which consists of nothing more than a series of *1*s and *0*s that represent bits of information. When an analog song is converted into digital format, the computer converts the analog signal into binary code. The binary code cannot replicate the smooth transitions of the analog signal, however, and leaves small gaps that result in stairstep digital approximations of smooth analog curves. Although a digital approximation of a song is extremely close to its analog version, the gaps left in the digital version permit copyright protection such as "watermarking." To watermark a piece of digital music, a copyright owner may insert small bits of digital information to fill in the gaps left in the binary code that approximates the actual song.

A technique known as "dithering" provides an extremely low level of background noise that can be used to hide information used to manage copyright. Watermarking technology has become so advanced that it is possible to encrypt a code identifying the computer used to watermark a song, the computer used to download it, and even the computer used by someone who purchased a copy made from that computer used to download it. Although finding illicit copies requires copyright owners to scan the Internet in an almost needle-in-the-haystack approach, several companies are developing "spider" programs that search for copyright infringers by moving from website to website and cataloguing sound files. Once an infringer is found, the DMCA allows for civil or criminal remedies, or both.

The damages provisions begin in Section 1203, which permits any person injured by a violation of Section 1201 or 1202 to bring a civil suit in federal court. Plaintiffs may choose to be awarded damages based on the amount of the loss they have suffered as a result of the violation or may choose to receive statutory damages that provide for awards ranging from $200 to $2,500 for each violation of Section 1201 and from $2,500 to $25,000 for each violation of Section 1202. In addition, if a violator repeats any offense of either section within three years after the court has rendered its final judgment, the court may triple these amounts in its damage awards. Innocent infringers, nonprofit libraries, and educational institutions may have amounts of damages assessed against them either reduced or remitted if they are found to have been unaware and with "no reason to believe that [their] acts constituted a violation."

Under Section 1204 willful violators or those motivated by commercial advantage or financial gain may be punished by fines up to $500,000 or five years imprisonment, or both, for a first offense—and up to $1 million or ten years imprisonment, or both, for any subsequent offense. Section 1204 also creates a five-year statute of limitations and provides nonprofit libraries, archives, or educational institutions with immunity from criminal prosecution.

These sections of the DMCA provide the real power in updating copyright protection for the digital age. Photocopying the contents of an entire book or copying a videotape without permission was once illegal, but before the DMCA it was not clear whether e-mailing digital copies of a book or video to a thousand people was legal or illegal. The DMCA and WIPO treaties now firmly establish that all such actions will be illegal domestically and internationally. Writers, musicians, and artists will likely rejoice in the protections afforded by the DMCA, and copyright violators now face specific prohibitions for digital copying.

More questions remain, however. For example, does the DMCA actually prevent copying in the electronic age? The answer is no. Is it possible to completely protect an author's original work in digital format? That question remains unanswered. Development of ©-chips, which act as a tollbooth for copyrighted works at the receiving end of an electronic transmission; click-wrap licenses; and other protective measures may provide answers. But until then the Digital Millennium Copyright Act gives creators an improved measure of protection for their electronically published works.

EPILOGUE: THE BEAT GOES ON–
AT LEAST FOR TWENTY
MORE YEARS

After years of debate Congress finally enacted legislation extending U.S. copyright terms by twenty years. The Sonny Bono Copyright Extension Act (SBCEA), aptly named for the popular musician-turned-legislator who died in early 1998, responds to a 1995 directive sent by the European Union to its member countries. This directive mandated a copyright term that was twenty years longer than that which U.S. copyright law had granted.

Under the Berne Convention, an international treaty that mandates basic copyright protection rules for its member countries, a section known as "the rule of the shorter term" directed its members (including the United States and many European nations) to grant protection to foreign works only to the same extent that those works were protected in the country of their origin. So before the SBCEA was passed, European Union copyright laws were not protecting U.S. works beyond that term granted by the U.S. limit–whereas European works were receiving twenty additional years of protection and revenues in the international marketplace. The United States faced losing millions of dollars in export revenues generated from sales of its intellectual property abroad.

Signed into law in October, the SBCEA extends the term of U.S. copyright protection for works created on or after 1 January 1978 from the life of the author plus 50 years after the author's death to the life of the author plus 70 years after his or her death. In the case of works authored jointly, the act measures the "life" period from that of the longest surviving co-author. For anonymous and pseudonymous works the act extends those terms by 20 years, to a total of 95 years from publication or 120 years from creation–whichever expires first.

The three-year debate that delayed passage of the act centered on an exemption for small businesses. Owners of such businesses argued that playing a radio or television in small restaurants and bars should be exempt from paying royalties; advocates of songwriters and performers argued that any transmission of copyrighted material should be subject to royalty payments. To end the debate, the SBCEA includes a compromise: the "Fairness in Music Licensing Act," which exempts restaurants and bars smaller than 3,750 square feet and retailers smaller than 2,000 square feet from paying royalties for FCC-licensed radio and television transmissions. According to the Congressional Research Service, this provision exempts up to 70 percent of all bars and restaurants.

One question, however, may still be left unanswered by the exemption provision: what about the growth of Internet radio, which is not licensed by the FCC? One might presume that a bar failing to qualify for the exemption may nevertheless avoid royalty payments by transmitting music it receives over the Internet. Although Internet radio is still in early stages of development, it may likely reopen the debate over royalty exemptions. If so, as Internet technology becomes more advanced and accessible, Congress may have to revise the Fairness in Music Licensing Act to include such technology.

For now, the SBCEA grants U.S. copyright owners the same protections enjoyed by copyright owners in the European Union. Despite the exception provision for restaurants and bars, the SBCEA will give the U.S. economy twenty additional years of foreign sales revenue from U.S. movies, books, records, and software products sold abroad.

The Lewis Carroll Centenary

Caroline Hunt
Special Consultant: Charlie Lovett

On the hundredth anniversary of Lewis Carroll's death, Alice's influence pervaded Britain and the United States. On 27 June the British medical journal *The Lancet* referred to "Alice in Wonderland syndrome," a disorder so named for perceptual distortions with a "resemblance to the body distortions experienced by the main character in the book of that name by Lewis Carroll, the centenary of whose death is this year." The disorder, first identified in 1955, was not new, but the assumption by *The Lancet* that Carroll's centenary would interest doctors symbolized the Carroll fever that overtook much of the world in 1998.

There were church services, exhibits, symposia, dinner parties, lectures, tours, and an astonishing number of stage adaptations, ballets, and one-man shows. The Royal Mail produced Carroll stamps in its series honoring fantasy writers, and the National Portrait Gallery commissioned a Carroll card for its Postcard Biographies. Carrollians gathered in Oxford, London, New York, Seattle, and throughout the English-speaking world. Both the Lewis Carroll Society (U.K.) and the Lewis Carroll Society of North America outdid themselves to share with other enthusiasts their knowledge of the enigmatic mathematics don Charles Lutwidge Dodgson, better known by the pseudonym under which he wrote the Alice books and other delights for young readers. The North American society augmented its already fine web page (http://www.lewiscarroll.org) with a detailed schedule of centenary events, from which readers, including this one, learned of many activities both significant and obscure. The British Broadcasting Corporation also served up Carroll to the public, both over the airwaves (starting in 1997 with a broadcast of Bookworm) and on a web page in its Book Case (http//www.bbc.net.uk/education/bookcase/links.shtml). In addition, the BBC listed sites where full on-line texts of Carroll's works might be found.

The centenary really began in August 1997, with a BBC poll of the most popular books for children. *Alice in Wonderland* finished comfortably in the top ten for the sixteen-and-up age bracket, thus establishing firmly that the Alice books are not merely of antiquar-ian or scholarly interest. Officially, the first event of the centenary was a service of evensong on 10 January in Westminster Abbey, followed by laying a wreath on the Lewis Carroll memorial in Guildford. Other services followed at St. Peter's Church, Croft (Carroll's father's church) and at St. Mary's Church, Guildford, on 11 January. Dodgson had preached at St. Mary's, and a plaque was unveiled commemorating his work. Three days later, on the actual anniversary of Carroll's death, the Daresbury Lewis Carroll Society held a centenary lunch. (Carroll was born in Daresbury and baptized at All Saints Church.) Most significant of the January events was the Christ Church dinner. Charlie Lovett recounts:

> On 14 January, 1998, exactly 100 years after the death of Charles Dodgson, thirty-nine Carrollians assembled at Christ Church, Charles Dodgson's own college, for the centenary Dinner. Representatives were present from the Dodgson family, and from the Lewis Carroll Societies of North America, Japan, and Great Britain–the last society being the sponsoring organization. The formally clad group assembled in the Smoking Room of the Senior Common Room–a facility which was brought into use during non-smoking Charles Dodgson's incumbency as curator of the Common Room. Pre-dinner sherry was served, and two keepsakes distributed–a pamphlet about the Smoking Room and Dodgson's involvement in its creation, written by Dr. Catherine Richards; and a bibliography of Lewis Carroll items produced by the British illustrator Ralph Steadman, who was to be the after dinner speaker, compiled by Dr. Selwyn Goodacre.

> The guests then adjourned to the McKenna Room, where the Herkomer portrait of Charles Dodgson, which usually hangs in the Great Hall, had been specially placed for the evening. In this room, where Dodgson once gave mathematical lectures, guests were welcomed by former Christ Church librarian, John Mason.

> There followed a splendid meal, festive yet tempered with the knowledge that the gathering marked a somber event. After toasts to Her Majesty the Queen, visitor of Christ Church; the House itself; Dean Liddell; and Charles Dodgson, speakers took their turns paying tribute to Dodgson. Joel Birenbaum, president

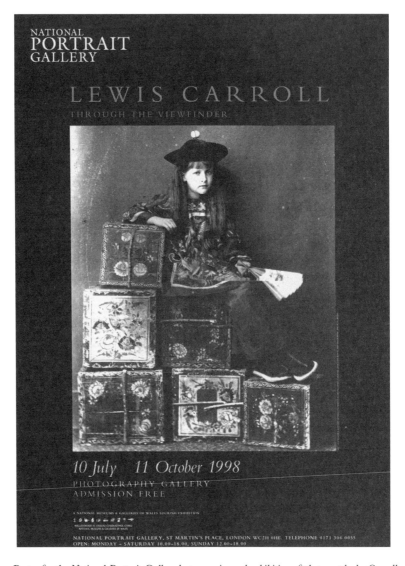

Poster for the National Portrait Gallery lecture series and exhibition of photographs by Carroll

of the Lewis Carroll Society of North America, spoke briefly and introduced Charlie Lovett, former president of that group who presented Christ Church with a copy of *In Memoriam Charles Lutwidge Dodgson,* a book of Dodgson's obituaries which he co-edited with August Imholtz Jr., and which was published for the occasion. Following a prize draw, Ralph Steadman delivered a delightful speech worthy of Lewis Carroll's own flights of fancy. This speech was later published in a small pamphlet as "My After-Dinner Speech" for the members of the British Lewis Carroll Society. After closing remarks by Anne Clark Amor, Chairman of that society, guests were presented with a packet of keepsakes, including a copy of *In Memoriam Charles Lutwidge Dodgson* specially signed by the editors. Guests dispersed through the dark arches of Christ Church and, though the hour was late, many gathered in hotel rooms and pubs, unwilling to let this special night end.

Several events early in the year recalled Alice Liddell, the original of "Alice," and her family (the Dean of Christ Church was Alice's father). Christ Church observed the centenary of Dean Liddell's death at a service of evensong on 18 January; on 6 February, the first regular 1998 meeting of the Lewis Carroll Society, at Birkbeck College in London, featured a lecture by Anne Clark Amor titled "Henry George Liddell and His Family."

THE CONTROVERSIAL CARROLL

From the beginning of the centenary year to the end, writers about Carroll could be divided into those who focused mainly on the nature of his relationships with young girls, and those who did not. Popular journalists, experts in fields other than literature, and non-Carrollians tended to dwell on the controversial; Carroll experts, generally, took a more balanced view.

The January issue of *History Today* carried an article by Ian Fitzgerald which, under the neutral heading "Death of Lewis Carroll," talked about "one of the darkest and fiercest controversies ever surrounding an author and his motivations." Conceding that the true story of Carroll's motivation "probably lies somewhere in the shady area between the innocent and the sinister," Fitzgerald concludes:

> Clearly, Dodgson's obsession with prepubescent girls cannot be discounted in any discussion of his work. At one extreme, psychologists have detected elements of cruelty, destruction and annihilation and 'oral sadistic trends of a cannibalist nature' in his work; others see it as a delightful and invigorating piece of nonsense. Whatever the truth, it is the case that most parents today would be happy for their children to listen to the story of *Alice's Adventures in Wonderland*–but they probably would not want Dodgson to be the man to read it to them.

This view was most common among critics who visited exhibitions of Carroll's photography; their accounts bore titles such as "It Won't Come Smooth" (Lindsay Duguid in *TLS*, 24 July) and "Lewis Carroll Revisited: Through a Looking Glass, Darkly" (Alan Riding in *The New York Times*, 20 August). Both men were reviewing the major exhibition of Carroll's photographs at the National Portrait Gallery in London, *Lewis Carroll: Through the Viewfinder*. Duguid's article, taking its title from a photograph of a young girl with tangled hair who despairs of brushing out its tangles, applies the phrase to Carroll's reputation. Riding's approach is unambiguous: "At the very least, his fascination for little girls is today considered dubious." He does, however, quote a rather different interpretation from the exhibit's curator:

> "I did a show of his photographs in 1974, and at the time no one asked me about pedophilia," said Colin Ford, the director of the National Museum of Wales and curator of a new exhibition of Dodgson's photographs at the National Portrait Gallery in London. "This year, the question has overshadowed everything. So a quarter of a century has totally changed our views. We see pedophilia everywhere nowadays. The world has changed quite dramatically."

Some Carroll-bashers seem not even to have seen the exhibit. Writing in *The Scotsman* on 1 July, Catherine Lockerbie noted the quadrille-like motions of scholars in the centenary year, "each bearing a new quasi-academic theory about the *extraordinary double life* of Charles

Lutwidge Dodgson" (my italics), observing, like Fitzgerald in *History Today*, "We embrace Alice but remain queasy in the extreme about her creator." The photographs of nude children, Lockerbie suggests, "would on the centenary of his death undoubtedly occasion a swift knock on his door from the vice squad."

Similarly, the British Broadcasting Corporation's *Omnibus on Carroll,* which aired on 4 January, included speculations by Jonathan Miller that, as a homosexual, Carroll preferred children too young to menstruate. (On the same program, Ralph Steadman suggested that Carroll's fantasies stemmed from drugs–specifically, perhaps, laudanum. Marina Warner's later British Council essay supported this idea at least in concept, referring to Carroll as a forerunner of Woodstock participants.) Humphrey Carpenter, in the *Sunday Times* of 4 January, countered with a withering putdown of the BBC production and its implications:

> Anyone making their first acquaintance with Dodgson via this entertaining but misleading programme is . . . likely to come away with an image of him as some sort of 1960s dropout or maharishi. . . .

However, in his riposte, "Dreamer in a Godless World," Carpenter goes on to add a new point of controversy, proposing that the Alice books may have come from another sort of impetus:

> There is an iconoclastic, mould-breaking urgency in the original Alice books that cannot be explained simply by Dodgson's mathematical cast of mind. Nor does his infatuation with Alice Liddell (if indeed he was infatuated) tell us anything about the books' real motivation. He wanted to write something to please her; but what he wrote came from a deeper level of his mind, in which (I believe) he was experiencing a profound and painful psychological conflict over the question of his religious belief, or lack of it.

Carpenter is a scholar of children's books, having edited the *Oxford Companion to Children's Literature*. Some who wrote on Carroll, however, were–like Duguid, Riding, Lockerbie, and Steadman, among others–neither Carrollians nor children's literature experts. Joe Schwartz, a Canadian chemistry teacher, pointed out in the Montreal *Gazette* (24 May) that Dodgson was familiar with M. C. Cook's *A Plain and Easy Account of British Fungi* and wondered whether he remembered "reading about the hallucinogenic properties of the Amanita muscaria" when composing the caterpillar's remarks to Alice ("One side will make you grow taller, and the other side will make you grow shorter").

Indeed, some of Alice's adventures are so reminiscent of the effects of Amanita muscaria that one won-

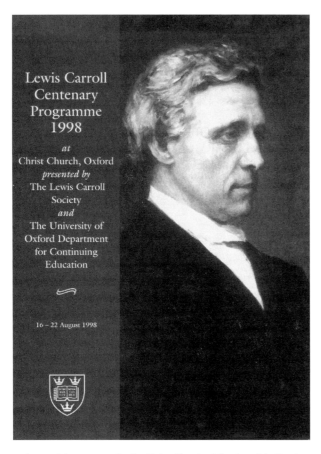

Cover of the program for the Christ Church celebration of the Lewis Carroll Centenary

ders whether Carroll had more than a literary acquaintance with the mushroom. The reddish fungus with white polka dots is readily found in England; in fact, it is the mushroom commonly depicted by the illustrators of fairy tales. Who knows how many of these delightful stories were stimulated by mushroom power?

From the beginning of the year, a few columnists took the other side. John Lanchester of *The Daily Telegraph* conceded that reading Carroll's books "is complicated by the encrustation of rumour, allegation, and outrage that has accrued around the topic of Dodgson's alleged paedophilia" but suggested that "this need not contaminate the Alice books" and highlighted the Alice books' "perfect balance of unreason and logic." Writing in *The Irish Times* on 14 January, Eileen Battersby engaged the foe more fiercely " Retrospective Freudian interpretation has a lot to answer for—particularly when applied to a long-dead individual's life and/or work."

Battersby points out some more significant features of the Alice books: Carroll's "remarkable imagination," his "adoration of childhood . . . matched with sadness at its brevity," his creation of a female character

who is "brave, clever, curious and observant . . . outspoken and ambitious," and his examination of aging.

Some writers simply focused on other aspects of Carroll. In *The Washington Post* David L. Book ran a selection of Carroll's logic puzzles as the January problems for his column, "Come to Think of It." Dismissing the whole controversy of Carroll's photographing little girls ("[t]hat curious and apparently innocent activity aside"), Book provides a detailed and lucid set of solutions for the problems.

CENTENARY EVENTS

True Carrollians generally avoided the extremes shown by writers in the popular press; celebrations in Oxford and London centered on the life of Dodgson and on the Alice books. On 13 March the Lewis Carroll Society held a joint meeting with the Children's Books History Society; the main speaker was Brian Alderson, chairman of the CBHS. Later in the same month, on 21 March, the University of Oxford Department for Continuing Education sponsored a Lewis Carroll Day School, with presentations by Mavis Batey, Karoline Leach, Edward Wakeling, and Anne Clark Amor.

Also beginning in March, transatlantic Carrollians began their centenary celebrations. Lovett, former president of the Lewis Carroll Society of North America, reports:

The Lewis Carroll Society of North America normally holds two single day meetings each year. To mark the centenary they sponsored special multi-day meetings in New York and Los Angeles. The New York gathering began on Friday, 27 March with a tour of Lewis Carroll related sights in Manhattan. Members gathered at Central Park to see two Alice monuments—the famous Delacorte Statue and the less well-known Sophie Irene Loeb Fountain. Traveling, like Alice, underground, they next stopped at the Alice terra cotta mosaic by Liliana Porter installed in the 50th Street subway station in 1994. One of several Alice murals created by artist Abram Champanier between 1935 and 1940 can be viewed in the lobby of the Gouverneur Hospital in lower Manhattan, the tour's next stop. Here Alice and her friends are depicted visiting the New York Public Library. The tour concluded with lunch, a visit to the spendid Berol collection of Carrolliana at New York University, and stops at New York shops featuring Alice merchandise.

The following day the regular spring meeting of the society featured talks by Russian scholar and translator of Alice Nina Demurova, Genevieve Smith, and Professor Donald Rackin. The meeting was held at the Fales Library of New York University.

The highlight of the New York weekend was a formal dinner that night at the Cornell Club celebrating the career of Lewis Carroll scholar Professor Morton N. Cohen, editor of Carroll's letters and author of *Lewis Carroll: A Biography*. A number of performers entertained guests, including Andrew Sellon as Lewis Carroll, and actors and singers Susan Kirkland, Anita Hollander, and R. Paul Hamilton. Many of Prof. Cohen's friends and colleagues made speeches praising his decades of diligent scholarship.

During the weekend, members of the society visited the Lewis Carroll exhibitions at the Grolier Club and Pierpont Morgan Library, where special receptions were held for the Society. The Maxine Schafer Memorial reading–an outreach program of the Society which provides an interactive reading experience for children and distributes copies of the Alice books–was delivered by Stephanie Stoffel on Sunday morning at the Donnell branch of the New York Public Library.

In the fall, the Society met in Los Angeles for two days. Our first meeting, on Saturday November 7 at UCLA, was preceded by a viewing of a special Carroll exhibit in the rare book department of the library. Speakers included Daniel Singer, Michael Welch, Anashia Plackis, and Charlie Lovett. Singer, an imagineer for the Walt Disney Corporation, hosted an evening gathering at his home in Pasadena. Sunday following the Maxine Schaefer reading at the downtown Los Angeles Public Library, the group met at the Huntington Library for presentations by Hilda Bohem, Mark Burstein, and a shadow puppet play of Alice performed by Bali and Beyond.

Throughout the year, cities on both sides of the Atlantic held notable Carroll events. An extended Carroll centenary at Cardiff included an exhibit of photographs, an exhibit of Alice illustrations, films, theater performances, and readings; there was also an academic conference (1–5 April) sponsored by the University of Wales, Cardiff, featuring Carroll biographer Morton N. Cohen and children's author Alan Garner. Ripon held an exhibit (April–May), a series of performances (July), and a Lewis Carroll flower festival (October).

Croft (Croft-on-Tees, North Yorkshire), where the Dodgson family lived for twenty-five years, celebrated the centenary in July with a flower festival, a special tea, and several outdoor performances of *Jabberwocky* adapted by Wyn Jones. At Guildford, where Dodgson died, the centenary events ran from 7 to 17 May and included "Opera through the Looking Glass," "Alice through the Camera Lens," and Jan Svankmajer's film, *Alice*. Anne Clark Amor presented "Lewis Carroll in Guildford," delivered at a meeting of the Friends of Guildford House on 18 March. There were several guided walks (one with costumed actors), a boat trip complete with a "Grand Snark Hunt," and a Mad Hatter's Tea Party. The ten-day series concluded with a church service at St. Mary's and a literary lunch.

In Oxford, summer events began in preparation for the August conference. Two-hour tours (rather steeply priced at more than twenty pounds apiece) were available each afternoon until early October. Isobel Montgomery reported on the travel page of *The Guardian* that she had arrived 11 July from London just in time and met an undergraduate guide and the head custodian of Christ Church:

> In the master's garden, which looks over Christ Church meadows, stood croquet hoops ready for a game. Still popular with students, croquet was all the rage in Oxford in 1862 when Dodgson wrote Alice. Not all in Wonderland or through the Looking Glass is fantasy, explained the guide, pointing out a cathedral window which features the treacle well mentioned at the Mad Hatter's tea party. Treacle meant cure-all in medieval English and the treacle well at Binsey is where St Frideswide cured a prince of blindness.

The tour also passed "Alice's door, just as John Tenniel drew it, which leads from the cathedral garden to the Dean's garden where flowers mentioned in the books still grow," and the Dean's lodgings. The tour concluded with tea at high table.

Cities in the United States joined the Alice frenzy. In Seattle, the Cheshire Society put on a week-long celebration with a Mad Tea and Wonderland Ball, both held at Oddfellows Hall on 4 October. *ALICE: Through the Looking Glass, Darkly,* an original stageplay by Vincent Kovar, was performed throughout the week. Alice even provided the theme for a fundraiser in Ohio in October, "The Alice Event." Held to benefit Seventh Generation, an environmental organization, the fundraiser took place at the Schoepfle Garden in the Lorain County Metro Parks. Guests could play croquet at five different levels including the White Rabbit Game (fast), the Mad Hatter Game (played on a slope), and the Queen of Hearts game (using artificial flamingoes). Correspondingly, guests could select from three different dinners at different prices, from the Queen of Hearts ($60) to the White Rabbit ($30) and the Mad Hatter ($15). Jill Sell's account in *The Plain Dealer,* 11 September, details all of this plus interviews with the actors: the White Rabbit, for instance, who hoped he had not been picked for his big ears, and the Queen of Hearts, played by "a kindergarten teacher and volleyball coach . . . who once played Aretha Franklin in a college performance."

THE OXFORD CENTENARY PROGRAM

The major event of the centenary year was a weeklong centenary program organized by Christ Church, the Lewis Carroll Society, and the University

Anne Amor, chairwoman of the Lewis Carroll Society; Matthew Alexander, curator of the Guildford Museum; the vicar of St. Mary's; and the mayor of Guildford at the dedication of a plaque honoring Carroll at St. Mary's, Guildford (photograph by Charles Lovett)

of Oxford Department for Continuing Education. Beginning with commemorative service of evensong on 16 August, the residential program gave participants a chance to see parts of Christ Church "normally hidden from the casual visitor," as one promotion put it. A visitor from the United States, Monica Edinger, offered this perspective:

A fourth grade teacher with a long time personal passion for Carroll's two Alice books, I was intrigued by the program description and ultimately quite unable to resist the chance to spend a week at Christ Church immersed in the life and times of this amazing Victorian. The conference was attended by 147 Carrollians: collectors, the current owners of Carroll's childhood home, artists, actors (from an amazing number of one-man Carroll shows), scholars, librarians, translators, teachers, and others from all over the world. Japan, Sweden, Australia, France, Italy, Canada, the Netherlands, Israel, Canada, Germany, Brazil, Slovenia, Ireland, Scotland, England, and the U.S. wererepresented.

It was a magical experience. Living at Christ Church, for a transatlantic visitor, was unique enough. It seemed as if the essentials of life in Oxford hadn't changed since Carroll's time. Tom Tower still tolls, the custodians still wear bowler hats, and tutors are still the

center of undergraduate learning. The outside stone windowsill of my Meadow Quad room had student graffiti from the middle of the nineteenth century, and my scout came daily to clean. All our meals were in the medieval Hall, with drinks at the Buttery Bar and the steward pounding a wooden mallet and announcing, "Dinner is served in the Hall!" every evening. One of my mementos is an elaborate menu from the final night's gala dinner which included toasts, speeches, a wild boar entree, and wines with each course. The last page is for autographs; on my copy is "Lewis Carroll," inscribed by an attendee who had studied Carroll's signature and put it there for fun.

Every morning we listened to a lecture by one of the members of the Lewis Carroll Society. In the afternoons were special tours of Lewis Carroll's Christ Church, guided walks around Oxford, the libraries, and even a boat trip. Evening activities included rare films, Carrollian games, and panels on translation and collecting. There truly was a ghostly feeling visiting Carroll's old rooms, now metamorphosed into the Graduate Common Room, seeing the Cheshire Cat tree in the Deanery garden (Christina Bjork, Swedish author of *The Other Alice,* and I chased the current Dean's cat around that tree trying to get it onto a limb for a photo,) and Alice Liddell's nursery, looking out from the Library into the garden as Carroll must have done, and lazing along the river as he and the Liddell girls had done that famous day when he first told the story. We were captivated by such rarely screened films as Jonathan Miller's BBC Alice and an early Betty Boop in Wonderland. Best of all was just being together–all of us connected with a passion for Lewis Carroll and his unique vision.

Edinger's passion for the Alice books dates from her childhood, bolstered by visits to the British Library, children's literature seminars, and an extended comparison of Alice illustrators. Her book, *Fantasy Literature in the Elementary Classroom,* was published by Scholastic in 1996; she has consistently incorporated the Alice books in her own classroom. Edinger and Roxanne Hsu Feldman have a website (http://www.dalton.org/ms/alice), "Many Faces of Alice," describing Edinger's Alice applications and listing useful resources (especially for illustrations). Feldman, a children's literature specialist formerly at the New York Public Library is now, like Edinger, at the Dalton School. "Many Faces of Alice" is unique among Carroll websites in featuring both scholarly materials and original student artwork.

COLLECTING

The centenary, predictably, boosted sales of Carrolliana. As early as 24 January, *The Times* carried a feature article, "Alice at the Auction House," in which the auctioneer David Park was interviewed ("Good Lewis Carroll memorabilia is a buoyant market") and typical Carrolliana market prices described. In March, Christie's, London, offered Sophie Anderson's watercolor "Girl with Lilacs," a portrait of Elizabeth Turnbull (a young girl who was employed by the artist). Dodgson bought the portrait, which he described as "a little picture . . . of a child's head in profile," in July 1865 and placed it on his mantel in Christ Church. Also at Christie's, six of Millicent Sowerby's twelve watercolors for the 1907 edition of *Alice* came up for sale in April.

Most of the centenary excitement for collectors, of course, concerned books. The copious Carroll offerings at the ABA fair occasioned a detailed article by Jim McCue in *The Times* on 2 June; McCue cited editions of *Doublets: A Word Puzzle* (£10,750), *Phantasmagoria* (£2,300), and various copies of *The Hunting of the Snark* (one for £750, one for £13,000, and one for £32,975). Copies of the English first edition of *Alice* were available at £2,750 and at £3,250. The real excitement came at the end of the year, as recounted by Charlie Lovett, who attended:

The 10 November sale at Sotheby's London included 31 lots of Carroll material, including several important association copies, but the highlight of the year for Lewis Carroll collectors came on 9 December,

when the private collection of Justin G. Schiller was auctioned at Christie's, New York. Schiller, an antiquarian bookseller and a pioneer in the field of collecting and selling rare and early children's books, had acquired a number of important Carroll items over the years, several of which he bought from the stock of his own New York bookshop. Christie's produced a superb illustrated catalogue for the sale of thirty-eight lots which culminated in Schiller's copy of the rare first edition of *Alice's Adventures in Wonderland.* One of only five copies in private hands, this copy included ten original pencil drawings by John Tenniel, his preliminary sketches for illustrations in the book as well as marginal markings made by Charles Dodgson himself in preparation for *The Nursery Alice.* The impending sale of the book was publicized in *The New York Times,* on CNBC, and elsewhere, and the press area was packed for the midday sale. Fine copies of the 1866 Appleton *Alice* and the 1866 London edition brought strong prices, as did two books with the rare inscription "'Lewis Carroll' alias Charles Lutwidge Dodgson." Dodgson's own copy of *The Hunting of the Snark* was hammered down at $18,000, below its estimate, and a few other bargains were found by bidders. The final lot, the 1865 *Alice,* opened at $800,000 and quickly rose to $1.4 million, with most of the bids coming from the telephones. When the hammer fell, it had fetched the highest price ever paid for a children's book or for a work of 19th-century literature–$1.54 million, including buyers premium. The book was sold to an anonymous American collector.

PUBLICATIONS

Commercial publishers on both sides of the Atlantic hastened to catch the momentum in Carroll's centenary year. Editions and translations abounded, from Puffin's centenary edition of the Alice books to a "new abridgment," from Dover, of the 1898 American edition from Macmillan. Alice's adventures appeared as *Alice Harikalar Ülkesinde,* adapted into modern Turkish (from an older Turkish version), and as *'Alisah Be-erets Ha-pela'ot* in modern Hebrew. The same translator, Rinah Litvin, also rendered *The Annotated Alice* for the centenary as *Harpatka'ot Alis be-erets ha-pela'ot : ha-sefer ha-mu'ar.* In March, Macmillan (U.K.) brought out *The Alice Companion*: *A Guide to Lewis Carroll's Alice Books,* by Jo Elwyn Jones and J. Francis Gladstone; later (August), New York University Press published a U.S. edition. (Charlie Lovett reviewed *The Alice Companion* witheringly, commenting on its obsessive focus on a political interpretation and on its many factual inaccuracies.) Less pretentious but more reliable, Mavis Batey's *The World of Alice* appeared in the Pitkin Guides (U.K.) series, updating her earlier *Alice's Adventures in Oxford,* in the same series. Karoline Leach's *In the Shadow of the Dreamchild* (Peter Owen) was described by its publisher as "an important study that challenges all the accepted thinking" (though many Carrollians would agree with Leach that the little-girl controversy was overstated at best).

Some publications targeted a more specialized audience. Smithmark Publishers, New York, offered Stephanie Lovett Stoffel's *The Art of Alice in Wonderland,* and Oak Knoll Press of Delaware prepared to launch a significant new bibliographical contribution in early 1999: Charles C. Lovett's *Lewis Carroll and the Press: An Annotated Bibliography of Charles Dodgson's Contributions to Periodicals.* Continental publishers followed suit, with translations of Cohen's biography into French (Editions Autremont) and Spanish (Anagrama). In Venice, Marsilio published Guido Almansi's *La Nuova Alice,* and in Paris, Editions Autremont brought out *Alice,* by Jean-Jacques Lecercle. Stephanie Bolster's *White Stone: The Alice Poems,* featured on the Lewis Carroll Society's web page, was published by Véhicule Press and promoted by a reading tour; the volume received the Governor General's Literary Award for Poetry. In Germany, Thorofon Classics rushed to release a compact disc of the Radio-Philharmonie Hannover's recording of *Alice in Wonderland Balletmusik'* performed on 12 January.

Timing its publication in the month of the Oxford conference, the Lewis Carroll Society brought out Charles Lovett's book *Lewis Carroll's England.* A less comprehensive guide was *Lewis Carroll's Ripon* (Maurice H. Taylor). In Wales, *Alice in Llechweddland* (Llechwedd Slate Caverns) by Ivor Wynne Jones was presented as "A contribution to the international centennial commemoration of the death of Lewis Carroll, author of *Alice in Wonderland."* In the United States, Lovett and August A. Imholtz edited *In Memoriam, Charles Lutwidge Dodgson, 1832–1898: Obituaries of Lewis Carroll and Related Pieces,* for the Lewis Carroll Society of North America.

Among other notable Carroll centenary books, *Reflections in a Looking Glass: A Centennial Celebration of Lewis Carroll, Photographer* (Aperture), meticulously edited by Morton N. Cohen and originally prepared to accompany an exhibit at the University of Texas, was reviewed by Martin Gardner in the *Los Angeles Times* on 6 December. Gardner gives an evenhanded account of the Carroll-as-pornographer question, an inevitable issue since all four of the nude photographs that survive are reproduced in the volume. He also cites at length Cohen's comment:

> They see a dour, bleak, unhealthy world in these photographs, a repressed sexuality writ large. One wonders if they are not bringing their own neuroses to these works, twisting and despoiling their beauty. . . . Carroll was as successful in sublimating his emotional desires as he was in achieving his distinction as a photographic artist, and, certainly the two are related. But he was aware of himself and his unconventional desires,

and he was honest and open with his child sitters and with their elders. . . .

The question of Carroll's interpreters and their motives generated an M.A. thesis at the University of Kentucky, Amy Lynn Jackson's "The One Hundred Year Love Affair between Lewis Carroll and Psychoanalytic Critics."

EXHIBITS

Exhibits of many kinds studded the centenary, beginning with the Christ Church display of Carroll's photographs. Also in Oxford, "For Alice," with works by Brian Partridge, Jean Stockdale, and Rossina Conroy, ran from 9 June to 4 July at the Museum of Oxford. A separate Carroll exhibition ran at the same museum from 11 July to 5 September. The Hertford Museum offered "Alice in Wonderland," from Alan White's collection, from 14 January to 7 March. The Daresbury Lewis Carroll Society presented a combination of exhibits with a children's book fair on 29 March, and in early April "Alice: the Wonderful World of Lewis Carroll" opened at the Bethnal Green Museum of Childhood in London. There were exhibits at Swale House, where young Dodgson lodged while attending Richmond Grammar School, and at Rugby, where he prepared for Oxford. A traveling exhibit from the British Council, "Tweedledum and Tweedledee: An Exhibition of the Life and Works of Lewis Carroll," with a companion essay by Marina Warner, toured from January through May. And, as always, Carroll's manuscript "Alice's Adventures Underground," with his own illustrations, remained on permanent display at the British Library.

In the United States and Canada, major exhibits included the Grolier Club's (1 April–29 May), from Jon Lindseth's collection, and the Pierpont Morgan Library's "a k a Lewis Carroll" (22 May–30 August), from the Arthur Houghton collection. Anna Lou Ashby, curator of printed books, assembled the exhibition, which included Dodgson's microscope and pocket watch, some of his photographs, and many original drawings by Tenniel. A ring and purse that once belonged to Alice Liddell were there, and so were games and toys associated with Alice, and memorabilia from the 1933 Paramount film and the 1951 Disney animated feature. The library also sponsored a Family Day on 30 May, billed as a highly varied afternoon: a mask-making workshop, a tea party, Paul Peabody's marionette show, and an improvisatory theater session. The Harry Ransom Humanities Research Center at the University of Texas, Austin, mounted "Reflections in a Looking-Glass: A Centenary Exhibition of Lewis Carroll," with

Carroll's memorial stone in The Poet's Corner, Westminster Abbey (photograph by Charles Lovett)

materials from the center's two Carrolliana collections (Weaver and Sewell), augmented by photographs from the Gernsheim History of Photography collection.

Other exhibits occurred all over the world–some traditional, some distinctly iconoclastic. The Osborne Collection of Early Children's Books at the Toronto Public Library displayed many of its holdings from 17 April to 4 July in "We're All Mad Here." A highlight was the 1988 Canadian *Alice,* a deluxe folio edition with George Walker's woodcuts. (A companion edition of *Through the Looking Glass* was announced for summer publication.) The Eltham Wiregrass Gallery in Melbourne hosted an exhibit of contemporary works by Kay Steventon and Kim Tarpey called "Looking for Alice," in which the artists explored, in a number of different media, their responses to the Alice books. In Tel Aviv, an exhibit of paintings by Eliaz Slonim, "Alice in Wonderland," opened on 8 January; Slonim's Alice, "portrayed as a sexually aware young woman," struck Angela Levine of *The Jerusalem Post* as "in line with contemporary opinion about Carroll, whose hobby-career of photographing young girls, preferably naked, is generally regarded with suspicion." Turin's center for children's books, Liber et Imago, sponsored a display of

Alice books in Italian (16–30 December). In Spain, "Alice in Wonderland," by Carmela Llobet, appeared from 14 November 1997 to 8 January 1998 in Barcelona, and "Lewis Carroll and His Work" appeared at the Leather Museum of Vic, near Barcelona, from 3 May 1997 to 4 April 1998.

Internet tourists could see some exhibits on the World Wide Web; the Lewis Carroll page had excerpts from the Barcelona exhibit's catalogue, as well as several images. Sophie Anderson's painting could also be seen (and Carroll's mantel, where it hung). More than a dozen photographs of ceramics by Graham Piggott also appeared on the Carroll Society's page.

PERFORMANCES

Throughout the centenary year, Alice and other Carroll creations appeared on stage in various adaptations, some carefully faithful to Carroll's books and others allied only thematically. Kevin Moore played Carroll in *Crocodiles in Cream,* using excerpts from Carroll's books and letters; the critical hit of the season, *Crocodiles* played in various locales around Britain. On 3, 4, and 5 April, Gorilla Rep presented Alison McGonigal's adaptation *Alice* at the Harry du Jur Playhouse of the Henry Street Settlement in Manhattan. The production, which featured contemporary costumes and an audience situated in the middle of the performers, followed Carroll's plot. In August, on the opposite coast, Susan Marx designed and directed an *Alice in Wonderland* for La Habra Depot Theatre in California. Like the Manhattan show, it was geared specifically for children. Youthful "telegrammers" greeted the audience, urging them to "buy" messages to send to the actors, who ranged from elementary through high school age. In February, the Little General Playhouse in Marietta, Georgia, also presented a fairly traditional *Alice* but with a different gimmick: for five dollars, youngsters in the audience could dress up and have their pictures taken with the Wonderland characters. Shaler High School in Pennsylvania staged an adaptation by Bruce Schrum in January.

Another production with a young cast was Ojai's Flying H Group's ambitious musical presentation *Alice in Wonderland* in Ventura County, California, in July. Todd Everett, from the *Los Angeles Times,* ranked the set and costumes higher than the script—"a quick tour through the highlights of Lewis Carroll's book"—and music—"Steven Moore's songs are (at best) forgettable"—but gave several of the main performances high marks. Everett pointed out a common problem in children's theater, the gap between the experienced few (usually Alice and a few others) and the uneven remainder of the cast ("sometimes 'movement' consists of standing in one spot and staring blankly at the audience").

Some productions took more liberties with the text. Debra Wise and Wes Sanders "adapted" Carroll's Alice books into a two-act play for the Underground Railway Theater in Boston. Staged in early June at the Boston Center for the Arts, *Alice Underground* made Alice (played by Wise) a grown woman who is balancing motherhood with a career and has a child (played by Wise's eight-year-old daughter)—named "Carol." (Wise's other daughter, age six, had a smaller part.) Alice enters Wonderland as a return to her childhood but retains much of her adult perspective. Quoted by Patti Hartigan of *The Boston Globe* (29 May), Wise observed, "It's a metaphor for adult life. It's like an existential creep show. The mother finds herself in the Wonderland books, and all these children follow her around like little Bosch figures."

In Scotland, Tall Stories Theatre Company put on *Alice and Mr. Dodgson,* a play which, in the words of reviewer Sarah Rutherford (*The Scotsman,* 12 August) "avoids speculation [about the real relationship between the two] by ingeniously using only words from the Alice books to re-create an enchanting and poignant meeting between Dodgson and the grown-up Alice in which they travel back to Wonderland together."

Several Alice productions took the form of dance. The Anglo-American Ballet's world premiere of *Alice in Wonderland,* with music by Mala Aprahamian and choreography and costumes by Catherine Kingsley, took place at Queens Theatre in the Park on 14 March. Reviewing the production for *Newsday* (16 March), Steve Parks found "way too much talk" and too little action ("Christina Marie Ryan makes a languid Alice, drifting aimlessly on stage to the moody, classically oriented original score by Mala Aprahamian")—a score he judged "beautiful, if a bit somber." Parks identified a common problem with children's productions, condescension:

> while artistic director Kingsley's narration is indispensable, it also talks down to the audience, seeming to assume a less than "Sesame Street" sophistication. The monologue pointing out each of the characters represented on the painted backdrop, for instance, is an insulting waste of time. And here's the White Rabbit, duh.
>
> Give the kids more credit, please. It's OK to leave something to the ballet imagination.

At the Kentucky Center for the Arts on 23 April, the Louisville Ballet premiered a new work by Dale Brannon, *Alice in Wonderland,* using Carroll's story and a 1953 score by Joseph Horovitz. Not technically "new" but far more startling was a rendition by Michael Uthoff, originally designed in the 1980s and first presented in 1995. Uthoff's version gives the Cheshire Cat in-line skates and the Mad Hatter a skateboard, for starters; interviewed by Kenneth La Fave for *The Arizona Republic,* Uthoff justified his meld of Bach with rock and his substitution of projections (by Jerome Sirlin) for conventional scenery. The Arizona Ballet reprised Uthoff's 1885 production in April.

New Zealand actor Warwick Broadhead rendered *The Hunting of the Snark* as a recital augmented with puppets, to be performed before small audiences (twenty or fewer) in home settings. After more than two hundred performances, he traveled to Britain for the centenary; audiences, paying £300 per show, ranged from Royal Shakespeare Company actors to a Carrollian whose wife arranged a solo viewing as a birthday gift.

As the centenary year drew to a close, Alice productions continued. The Dallas Theater Center announced a new adaptation by Karen Hartman, *Alice: Tales of a Curious Girl,* scheduled for its world premiere in early 1999.

CONCLUSIONS

It would be difficult to live through 1998 without meeting Carroll at every turn. Two February newspaper stories illustrate how pervasive the Alice phenomenon was. In New York, Parks Commissioner Henry Stern was notified that the Alice in Wonderland statue had a misquotation on its base: "All mimsy were the borogroves" (instead of "borogoves"). Before the centenary, apparently no one had noticed the error–which, in any event, proved too costly to fix. In England, *The Daily Telegraph* (11 February) used Carroll's appeal (as well as Beatrix Potter's) to emphasize the plight of almost a hundred captive dormice. Evacuated from the woods near a proposed rail link to the Channel Tunnel, the dormice were to be relocated elsewhere. ("Amid widespread public concern, the dormice were transported to temporary addresses in Somerset with the intention . . . of preparing them to return to the wild in counties where they have become extinct.") The rail link was never built, and the rail company did not fund the dormouse project. Volunteers offered garages and sheds, but Paul Bright, "who is running the national dormice recovery programme for English Nature, said their plight was serious"–partly because they kept waking up prematurely in captivity, and partly because reintroducing them to the wild would be so complex and expensive. Meanwhile, new colonies of dormice moved into the evacuated area, presumably multiplying the problem should a future rail link be built by a different company.

There were even reminders–fewer than one might have wished–of Carroll's full complexity. The British journal *Nature* reprinted an abridged version of its 1898 obituary notice, which listed several mathematical accomplishments before summing up:

> Mr. Dodgson's mind was essentially logical, in spite of the whimsical humour which as endeared "Lewis Carroll" to every boy and girl–nay, every adult–in the kingdom. A shy and retiring man, he was to his friends a most charming companion, overflowing with the quaintest of humour, and one whose love for children was typical of himself, and whom to know was to love.

And Mavis Batey, writing in *Oxford Today* (Trinity issue), echoed this emphasis on the logical quality of Carroll's mind–with a host of splendid anecdotes about his teaching of logic. (Critics who claim that Carroll could not communicate with girls past puberty might be startled to learn of his success in teaching logic to female high school and college students.) Batey's resounding conclusion suits the events of 1998 all too well:

> Today we may need more than a game of logic to clear our minds, but it would be most appropriate if the Oxford High School, where Carroll propounded his theories, were to start the ball rolling in this centenary year of his death by having lessons on how to tear media fallacies and political spin-doctoring to pieces. Alice, with her sturdy independence of thought, would have known how to cope. "I know they're talking nonsense," she would have said loudly, as she checked her facts and resisted all their attempts to manipulate her.

Robert Pinsky Reappointed Poet Laureate

Ernest Suarez
The Catholic University of America

In his second term as poet laureate of the United States, Robert Pinsky expanded "The Favorite Poem Project," which he had started the previous year. Pinsky first thought the project would include 100 people, some of them well known but most of them coming from a cross section of the American public. Individuals would be audio- and video-taped reading their favorite poems, with the project becoming part of the bicentennial celebration of the Library of Congress. The program has ballooned into Pinsky's major undertaking as laureate. Pinsky now plans to choose 1,200 people to read their favorite poems on audio- and videotape. The two hundred video recordings are to represent the nation's bicentennial in the year 2000, and the one thousand audio tapes are to commemorate the millennium. Pinsky feels that the recordings will form "a record, at the end of the century, of what we choose, and what we do with our voices and faces, when asked to say aloud a poem that we love."

In contrast to the Library's Archive of Recorded Poetry and Literature, Pinsky's project is not centered on professional poets. Pinsky claims that people's bodies instinctively react when reading a poem aloud. The act of reading the poem "engages the mind and the body in a genetically primary sensation that involves a column of air in the trunk and the production of syllables. The sensation causes comfort and alertness. Thus the individual body, not necessarily even the individual artist, can be a medium for art." He is "convinced that this video and audio record of many Americans reading aloud poems they love will have a lot of value for our country: as a record of where we stand, as a model for education in the future, and as testimony to the possibly neglected state of the culture we already have."

The poet laureate is appointed by the librarian of Congress annually, with the term running from October to May. The position—which was called consultant in poetry to the Library of Congress until 1986—was founded in 1936, when Archer M. Huntington endowed the Chair of Poetry at the Library of Congress. Archibald MacLeish, who then served as librarian of Congress, made the consultant a yearly appointment, with the provision that it was possible to serve more than one term.

Pinsky is the thirty-seventh poet to serve as laureate:

Robert Pinsky in 1996, at the time his book The Figured Wheel *was published (photograph © by Sigrid Estrada)*

Allen Tate	1943–1944
Robert Penn Warren	1944–1945
Louise Bogan	1945–1946
Karl Shapiro	1946–1947
Robert Lowell	1947–1948
Leonie Adams	1948–1949
Elizabeth Bishop	1949–1950
Conrad Aiken	1950–1952
William Carlos Williams	(Appointed but did not serve)
Randall Jarrell	1956–1958
Robert Frost	1958–1959
Richard Eberhart	1959–1961
Louis Untermyer	1961–1963
Howard Nemerov	1963–1964
Reed Whittemore	1964–1965
Stephen Spender	1965–1966
James Dickey	1966–1968
William Jay Smith	1968–1970

Joseph Auslander   1937–1941

William Stafford	1970–1971
Josephine Jacobsen	1971–1973
Daniel Hoffman	1973–1974
Stanley Kunitz	1974–1976
Robert Hayden	1976–1978
William Meredith	1978–1980
Maxine Kumin	1981–1982
Anthony Hecht	1982–1984
Robert Fitzgerald	1984–1985 (Appointed but served in a health-limited capacity)
Reed Whittemore	1984–1985 (Interim consultant in poetry)
Gwendolyn Brooks	1985–1986
Robert Penn Warren	1986–1987 (First designated poet laureate)
Richard Wilbur	1987–1988
Howard Nemerov	1988–1990
Mark Strand	1990–1991
Joseph Brodsky	1991–1992
Mona Van Duyn	1992–1993
Rita Dove	1993–1995
Robert Hass	1995–1997
Robert Pinsky	1997–present

As laureate, Pinsky receives a $35,000 annual stipend. The laureateship is intended to provide the appointee with the freedom to create a special project. The previous laureate, Robert Hass, created the "Watershed" conference, uniting novelists, poets, and storytellers to speak about the relationship between writing, community, and nature. James Dickey videotaped noted poets reading their work. Joseph Brodsky championed placing poetry in hotels, supermarkets, and airports. Gwendolyn Brooks started poetry workshops for elementary school children.

The laureate also gives a reading of his or her verse and presents an annual lecture, which the library publishes. Through the annual reading series, laureates collectively have brought more than two thousand writers to read for the Archive of Recorded Poetry and Literature. In 1997 Pinsky delivered a lecture titled "On Digital Culture and the Individual Soul" at the library. For his inaugural lecture, which was held in the Montpelier Room on 9 October, Pinsky claimed that "The first and main thing about digital culture is that it is a part of history. It smells of us. It is human. We made it. It is an outcome." He wants to approach the "new cultural developments through the lens of poetry," stressing that the "computer is an extension of poetry. Poetry is a technique developed by this animal, the human—a fairly useless animal. It has no claws, no hide, no real teeth and it doesn't run fast, but it is clever and it looks around a lot. For survival it developed forms of communication evolved for the purposes of memory, for the effective storage of important information

and the transmission of that information accurately and effectively from one person to that person's peers."

Pinsky, who was the poetry editor for *The New Republic* in the 1980s, currently edits poetry for *Slate,* a weekly Internet magazine. He believes that computers can convey information much as storytelling bards once did through poems. Computers can convey mass art and culture, because "an image of Michael Jackson singing with brilliant cinematography is reproduced and duplicated tens of thousands of times and it can spread all over the globe very rapidly. . . . The medium for mass art is by its nature highly duplicable. I do not deplore or applaud it, but I am trying to understand it. My idea of body piercing is that it is not a revolt against parents, it is a revolt against one's own childhood, the Electra winky-gahinky action figure. American 12-and-13-year-olds hunger for something that's not likely to be in the Sears Roebuck catalog. The individual soul loves mass art but we become jaded. Sometimes I just turn off the TV and reach for a copy of *The Complete Poems of Emily Dickinson.*" He relishes the opportunity to deliver his message because "It is appropriate for a poet to be attached to a place of memory because poetry is an ancient way of enhancing memory, a means that predates writing. . . . The Library of Congress is the greatest house of memory in the world. There is more human striving recorded and cataloged in this institution than there has ever been anywhere."

A professor of creative writing at Boston University, Pinsky was awarded the Leonore Marshall Prize in 1997 for *The Figured Wheel: New and Collected Poems, 1966–1996.* His other volumes of verse include *Sadness and Happiness* (1975), *An Explanation of America* (1979), *History of My Heart* (1984), and *The Want Bone* (1990). The Academy of American Poets gave Pinsky's verse translation *Inferno of Dante* (1994) the Harold Morton Landon Translation Award, and in 1996 he received the Poetry Society of America's Shelley Memorial Award. His essays are collected in *Landor's Poetry* (1968), *The Situation of Poetry* (1977), and *Poetry and the World* (1988). His new book is *A Brief Guide to the Sounds of Poetry* (1998).

On 26 June 1998 I met with Pinsky in his suite of offices at the Library of Congress, where we discussed his recent work:

Suarez: Your essay "Poetry and the World" addresses poems that deal with the court, things having to do with the world. But in that essay worldly things imply the metaphysical.

Pinsky: I was reacting to the weary, worn-out idea of poetry and politics. I was trying to come at the same material in a different way. And one of the ways you would define the distinction between the worldly and the political is that the worldly encompasses and implies the metaphysical realm as well as the realm of interaction of power and people.

Suarez: How does this operate within your own poetry?

Pinsky: To put it as simply as possible, for a long time I have tried to look around me. At a certain point early in my career, I realized I had actually made more than one attempt at writing about the personal things that had concerned me from my childhood on. Introspection is an important part of a work of art for me. But my next ambition as an artist was to look around me and to try and think what things seemed important and manifest in my life and the lives of other people who had not yet made their ways into poems. So, I try to absorb what I think and see and feel a great deal that does not immediately remind me of something by Rimbaud, or Allen Ginsberg, or John Donne, but seems significant.

Suarez: How does this concept operate within recent poems of yours, such as "The City Dark," "Ginza Samba," and "Avenue"?

Pinsky: "Avenue" is an attempt to include details of retail, of the life of the agora. Very often the word "marketplace" is entirely pejorative, when in fact the marketplace or the agora is the common place where we come together and meet one another. And "Avenue" is an attempt to find a suitably flexible and complex way to see that marketplace, rather than sentimentalize it and ignore the capitalistic nature of it. I did not want to denounce it in a stock or stereotypical way, but rather try and approach it without egotism. The poem uses a lot of hovering pronouns, so it is not me on the avenue, but me trying to catch the life of the avenue. "Ginza Samba" is horizontal in space. I suppose you can say it is vertical in time. It tries to look again at all the transactions between souls and the worldly historical world—enslavement, sale of a human being, abortion, marriage, mastery of a musical instrument—and see them in their ugliness and beauty and all the other qualities they have. "The City Dark" is probably the most traditional of the three poems. It is an attempt to write something that does what those two poems do, but with more of the familiar rhetoric of a nature poem. I'm trying to look at the city as you would a mountain or a lake and to feel the bars, the glitter of the mica in the concrete pavement, and to feel the city the way you might feel natural beauty.

Suarez: You mention the hovering pronouns in "Avenue." Were you trying to interject a Whitmanian consciousness into the poem?

Pinsky: I think that is a fair description of the poem. And, shifting rapidly amongst "he," "we," "I," and "you" was a way to get there by a different route, to see if you could discover a different reality by using a different path to get there.

Suarez: Why that particular decision?

Pinsky: It's hard to say. A lot of these things are intuitive, but one gets impatient with structures: the structure of I do this or I did that. That is a familiar structure. It's like tapping the kaleidoscope. The kaleidoscope is quite interesting at one stage, but if you look at it a long time, sooner or later you want to tap it. Or if you play a tune at one tempo, you might suddenly decide to try it in another tempo. I believe that musicians sometimes just transpose the tune in order to make it sound a little different. Most musicians even improvise so the music can take a different form.

Suarez: Are you saying that the decision was a sonic one?

Pinsky: All decisions in poetry are sonic. All poetry comes through either the ear or the voice.

Suarez: As you are saying, all poetry is sonic, but at the same time, you are applying language which is rational in one way or another.

Pinsky: Yes, you are making a decision with your voice; you are writing with your voice. You're trying it out to see how it sounds. And you can rationalize music too. You can say the harmonic structure indicates that certain notes would be played in certain ways in order to remind you of where you are. You can rationalize all those things. You can look at a tune, or some great chorus in the tune, and make up a reason why there is a flat nine. There is a rational explanation for it all, but you have to try it out with your ear.

Suarez: What's the relationship between the sound and the subject matter?

Pinsky: In a word, the relationship between sound and subject matter is art. That is the whole art: managing to get the emotions to be expressed by the actual sounds you are making. Sometimes, sounds like "ah" are there, but in the right context, an "ah" or "oh" can mean quite a lot. It can sound stupid or it can sound great.

Benjamin Anastas Interview

Lauren MacIntyre
The New Yorker

Benjamin Anastas's novella, An Underachiever's Diary, *was published in 1998 by The Dial Press. He is now at work on his second book.*

DLB: Your narrator, William—whose twin brother bounces from one triumph to the next as they grow up—opts for obscurity. In college, he writes a paper on underachieving, stating that instead of saying "yes, yes," to life, the underachiever says "no, thank you." He goes on: "Underachievers are not to be confused with younger, slower brothers of southern presidents, like Billy Carter and Roger Clinton. These gentlemen do the best with whatever genetic leftovers they've been given, while the underachiever is entrusted with a master key to opportunity's home office, and misplaces it." Was this idea of underachieving the genesis of your book, or did it work itself into the book later?

BA: I wanted to write about twins. I'm a fraternal twin—I have a twin sister. It's a subject that I had always wanted to write about but was never sure how to approach. The book isn't autobiographical in the sense that I didn't have the childhood that's described in the book. I grew up in Cambridge, Massachusetts, and I saw other people having that kind of childhood and it always sort of fascinated me.

DLB: How did your twin take to the book?

BA: She liked it. I have more trouble showing what I write to people who are very close to me than I do showing it to total strangers. I remember during the book tour, I was reading at a bookstore in Boston. I read some sections of the book that touched on the family life, and afterwards my mother, who was there, said to a friend that was with her, "Having a son as a writer is a mixed blessing." My mother is the director of the doctoral program at the Smith College School for Social Work. She's a pretty serious taskmaster, and after the book came out, her students started passing it around, thinking that they're finding all this stuff out about her.

Benjamin Anastas (photograph © by Marion Ettlinger)

DLB: Did she find that she had to defend herself to people?

BA: I think the line she gave to people who asked her about it was, "My son says the book is fiction, and it is fiction."

DLB: Did you have any similar experiences yourself?

BA: Oh, sure. And I think it has a lot to do with what's happening in the culture right now. Memoirs are so popular. Everyone assumes that if you write something, it's about you–even if it's fiction. Publishers use personality to sell their books. There's always an author photo. They send you out on tour if they can afford it. It's easy for people to confuse the book with the author when they're that closely associated. But the connection between book and author is much more complicated. Maybe even more so in memoir, where you have an author who's claiming what he's written is true. Of course, it's not: it's narrative. How could the writing convey something *exactly* the way it was? There's experience and there's artifice. They're related, but there's no direct correlation.

DLB: Were you uncomfortable with the process you're describing–the book tour, the readings?

BA: I'm not that good at readings. Performing is a different skill, I think, than writing. One of the reasons I like to write is that you can do it by yourself in your apartment and you don't have to be public about it. I think most writers feel that way. I didn't resent the readings so much as I knew that I wasn't that good at them.

DLB: The book is essentially a monologue, though, and the voice is strong and funny. It seems like the perfect material for a reading.

BA: Not the way I read it, though. I get nervous. I look really morose and I start reading too slowly. At one of my first readings, I made the mistake of not saying, "Hello, my name is Ben Anastas, I wrote this novel, blah blah blah . . . ." Everyone assumed it was a memoir. I got questions afterwards, like "Where is your brother now?"

DLB: Was it coincidence that you chose to write a fictional diary at the same time all these memoirs are coming out?

BA: Well, it wasn't a coincidence. I wanted to write an anti-memoir, really, because most of the autobiographies coming out now are really recovery narratives: somebody is recovering from a trauma, and they're writing about it from a later perspective, so there's this nice little moral victory for everybody. I wanted to write a book where the narrator hasn't recovered from anything. As a matter of fact, he's just gone deeper into his trauma and there's not necessarily any lesson to be gleaned from what he's gone through.

DLB: Are you happy with how the book was received?

BA: There were good reviews and it's coming out in paperback. It was optioned for a film and good stuff like that. But I don't think you can . . . [pauses]. I think you need to publish three or four books before you can attach any significance. . . . I remember being an MFA and thinking, once I sell my first book I'm going to be set. It's going to be perfect. But the checks take seven months to come. . . . It's a nightmare. When the book came out last March, I was in the worst financial state of my life. Everyone kept asking me why I wasn't happy. "You look so upset," they'd say. I'm upset because my landlady hates me.

DLB: How do you feel about the book being optioned for film?

BA: When I first found out about it, people would ask me who I thought should be in it. But even now after I've had time to think about it, I just can't imagine the book as a film. Not that I think it's above being filmed–not at all–I just can't see it. I guess that's why I write books and not screenplays.

DLB: Were you involved in the process at all?

BA: My agent handled it. They didn't ask me to write the screenplay because they wanted someone experienced. That's just as well because I'd like to put my energy elsewhere. The less I know about the process the better, because these things famously take forever to happen–if they happen at all. I can't get wrapped up in it.

DLB: On the copyright page, the book is listed as being catalogued as a novella, but it feels larger than that somehow.

BA: I feel like it alludes to a whole book. It alludes to a novel, but it doesn't represent one thematically.

DLB: You read enough James Michener novels, though, and you find that it's nice to pick up a book that's more pared down . . . .

BA: That goes back to one of my crackpot theories about authorship.

DLB: Which is what?

BA: I feel like there are a lot of writers working today who are more interested in the romance of authorship. It's like they feel they should fit every observation they can think of into their book because that's what writers do, and it's such a bore. Writers are

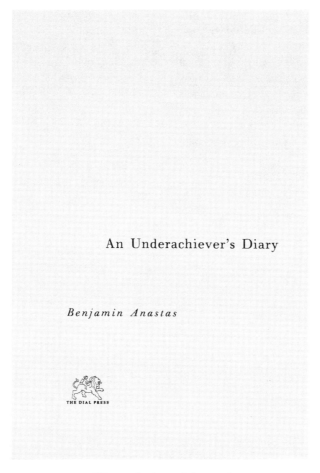

An Underachiever's Diary

Benjamin Anastas

THE DIAL PRESS

Title page for Anastas's first novel

no different or no better than anybody else. It's just that we have this weird compulsion to put things out on paper. The only thing that really matters in the end, it seems to me, are books–not writers. Hopefully, you're making something that's going to mean something to someone in five minutes, or five years, or whenever. Books last and writers don't.

DLB: What was the hardest part of the book-writing process for you?

BA: Seeing the book through to publishing form and seeing it published. I was lucky in that I had the contract before I started the rewrite. But it was still difficult to know something might be happening once the book was written and having to sit and wait. Waiting to get a book contract is much harder, of course. I've been through that. I'd had stuff sent around for me before that didn't stick. You put all your energy into a book and then an agent tells you she'll take you on, and you think, Great, an agent's going to take me on. Fantastic. And then three or four people see the manuscript and

they don't want it and your agent tells you, "Well, I'm not sure what's going to happen. You're on your own."

DLB: It's hard when that happens once, to sit down and write another book. You have to be very headstrong.

BA: It's also difficult because everyone in New York is so spineless. They make judgments that are based more on reputation than on actual work. If enough people see you as a rejected writer . . . it doesn't matter if you send two projects around and they don't hit, and then you write a brilliant novel the third time around. People are going to say, "I've seen this guy before."

DLB: There are agents who'll stop sending a manuscript around to all the different houses once it's been rejected by a handful for that very reason.

BA: It shouldn't be that way. Editors don't want to be the first person to discover you. They want to be the second or the third or the fourth. It seems like you

297

really have to have an agent. And it helps to have published short stories. Not that it's all that important, but it helps. And an MFA program helps. But it's still very, very hard for a regular person to break in. Whereas, if you're represented by Andrew Wylie–well, you know *that* person's going to make it. It doesn't seem like it was always this way. Not that things were ever bright and rosy–publishing has always been a commercial enterprise. But it seems to me that book publishing is starting to follow the Hollywood model, which is dangerous. As hard as publishing my book was, I was just so happy that somebody took it. And I was happy that it was published with The Dial Press, which is a very small operation. I mean, it's part of Random House, Inc., yes, but there are just three editors there.

DLB: How was the editing experience?

BA: It was good. Nobody likes criticism. I guess I'm not alone in that. But in the end, if I were to take out the draft that I handed in and the finished book and put them side by side, it'd be pretty indisputable that the finished book was much better.

DLB: Did it change dramatically?

BA: No, no. Nothing dramatic, but I have my ticks like any writer. I like to write really long sentences and sometimes there's really no need for it.

DLB: How did you feel about the critics likening your narrator's voice to Holden Caulfield's?

BA: [Laughs]. I don't know. I'm not really sure how valid a comparison it is. I really like Salinger. I hadn't read Salinger for a really long time. When the first couple of proofs came in with J.D. Salinger references, I thought, Jesus, I've gotta see if this is true or not. I reread *Seymour: An Introduction* and *Frannie and Zooey*. I think they gave Salinger a try with the hardcover, actually, but nothing ever happened. Now since it's due out in paperback, they're going to send it back to him. The *Times* said that the book reminded them of Exley's *A Fan's Notes,* so they put that on the cover, but I don't think my book bears any similarity to his whatso-

ever. *A Fan's Notes* is a hefty autobiographical novel about a middle-aged football fan who's into Frank Gifford. My book is more of an anti-autobiography, a false autobiography. Maybe it's because I was chosen for a Frederick Exley Award a while back. People just assume he was a big influence on me.

DLB: Do you have influences?

BA: Totally. I try to read as much as I can. I was influenced by *Notes from the Underground* when I wrote *An Underachiever's Diary.* Nabokov's *Speak, Memory* is one of my absolute most favorite books. I just love it.

DLB: After the book came out, could you take a breath and enjoy it?

BA: No, I was worried about the whole thing. Worried, worried, worried. For three months before it came out and three months afterwards I couldn't even think. It wasn't like I was obsessed with how it was doing, but it was my first book. I knew it was out there. I was worried that there were mistakes in the galleys and that reviewers were going to see the mistakes. I think back to when I was in grad school, how I thought the whole process was going to be so different than it actually is. I wonder now what the faculty members thought, looking out at all of us kids who had these thoughts about how fantastic it was going to be.

DLB: Even if they were to have warned you, though . . .

BA: None of us would have listened. A friend of mine told me a great story. We both had a fantastic teacher at Iowa, Deborah Eisenberg. A few years after we graduated, he ran into Deborah in the street and she asked him how he was doing. He said, "Well, it's really hard. I'm having trouble with the book I'm writing and my agents are giving me all this bizarre feedback and I'm not really sure what to do." And Deborah looked at him, and said–not in a mean way–just, nice, cheerfully: "Well, that's good, Alex. Why should it be any different for you?"

Second International Hemingway Colloquium: Cuba

John Unrue

University of Nevada, Las Vegas

The Ernest Hemingway Museum of Cuba held the Second International Colloquium at the Villa Pan-Americana Hotel, located between Cojimar and central Havana, from 19 July to 25 July 1997. The colloquium was chaired by Gladys Rodriquez Ferraro, director of the museum. The North American coordinator was Prof. Bickford Sylvester (University of British Columbia). On the evening of 19 July, conference attendees were hosted at the Finca Vigía, where most of the North American guests had a first opportunity to visit Hemingway's Cuban home. The evening was enlivened by Cuban music and daiquiris.

The theme of the colloquium was "The International Scope of Hemingway's Works." From 20 July through 24 July, Cuban and North American scholars, writers, and journalists presented papers and participated in seminars while interpreters provided simultaneous translations of each conference session. Many papers focused on Hemingway's years in Cuba and on works set in Cuba and the Gulf Stream area: *To Have and Have Not* (1937), *The Old Man and the Sea* (1952), and *Islands in the Stream* (1970). Among those treating movies of Hemingway's works were Ruth Prigozy (Hofstra University), who presented "*Islands in the Stream* as Novel and Film"; John Weser (Santa Rosa Junior College), whose paper was "Hemingway vs. Howard Hawks: *To Have and Have Not*"; and Mark Ott (University of Hawaii), who presented "Creating the Caribbean in Hawaii: The Filming of *Islands in the Stream.*" Marsha Belvance (Ketchum, Idaho) traced the consistency between Hemingway's life and literary works, as revealed by photos, letters, and selections from those works, and Roberto Núñez Juama (Cuban National Archive) discussed the photographic collection at the Ernest Hemingway Museum. Ann Putnam (Puget Sound University) pointed out tragic foreshadowings of *The Old Man and the Sea* in "The Undefeated." John Unrue (University of Nevada, Las Vegas) demonstrated Hemingway's "process of knowing" in the evolution of his art. In "Hemingway's Triangular Soul" Ned Quevedo Arnaiz (Jose Martí Higher Pedagodical Institute, Cuba) illustrated patterns of threes through-

out Hemingway's life and art and argued that Spain, the United States, and Cuba were ultimately the three places where Hemingway's greatest art flourished.

Several papers focused on Hemingway and politics. Douglas E. La Prade (University of Texas-Pan American) discussed suppression, distortion, and propaganda concerning Hemingway in "Francoist Censorship of Hemingway in Spain," and Armando Cristóbal Pérez (director of Ciencias Sociales Publishing House and deputy editor of *Marx Ahora,* Cuba) examined Hemingway's maturing social conscience in "*To Have and Have Not:* The Discovery of Transcendence." Masvidal Saavedra (Higher Arts Institute, Cuba) spoke of the role of myth in Hemingway's fiction and of the importance of myth and literature in understanding history. Lazaro Martinez and Enrique Sanchez Michel (Jose Martí Higher Pedagogical Institute, Cuba) pointed out Hemingway's humanistic philosophy reflected in his short stories of the 1930s. Two other papers, "Hemingway and War" by Romelia Santana Álvarez (Jose Martí Higher Pedagogical Institute, Cuba) and "Ernest Hemingway and His War Literature" by Javier Vidal Vega and Liván Leyva Filgueras (both of the University of Havana), also emphasized Hemingway's political sensitivies and compassion for common people. Enrique Cirules (Jose Martí Publishing House) discussed "Hemingway on the 60th Anniversary of the publication of *To Have and Have Not.*" In "Why Maria is Pregnant: The Irony of Hispanic Linguistics and Anti-Fascist Satire in *For Whom the Bell Tolls,*" Wolfgang Rudat (University of Houston) discussed themes of politics and sexuality as developed through language.

Eliza Pérez Fernández (Ernest Hemingway Museum) presented "Ernest Hemingway's Culinary Preferences," and Robin Bourke (Grand Prairie College, Alberta, Canada) noted the importance of food and wine for topicality in Hemingway's fiction. In "The Treatment of Feminine Characters in Ernest Hemingway's Works" María del Carmen Fournier (Enrique J. Varona Higher Pedagogical Institute, Cuba) discussed women in Hemingway's art, and two scholars gave papers focusing on Afro-Cuban culture in his work.

Hemingway's living room at La Finca Vigía (photograph by John Unrue)

María Caridad Valdés Fernández (Ernest Hemingway Museum) pointed out Afro-Cuban elements in *The Old Man and the Sea* and *Islands in the Stream* and suggested their relationships to museum pieces at La Vigía. Larry Grimes (Bethany College) presented "Spanish Mysticism, Religious Syncretism and Afro-Cuban Culture in Hemingway." The evolution and impact of the Hemingway fishing tournament was the subject of a paper by Cuban journalist León Almeida. Gerald Lochlin (California State University, Long Beach) discussed Hemingway's sensitivities to and protection of the environment.

Ileana Ortega Cerra and Carmen Zita Quirantes Hernández (Jose Martí National Library, Cuba) demonstrated the role of the written media in defining and establishing Hemingway's presence, and William Diebler (*Pittsburgh Post-Gazette*) discussed Hemingway's transition from journalism to art in "Hemingway Reached for the Right Star." Neftalí Pernas Abreu and journalist Jorge Santos Cabellero offered personal portraits of Hemingway based on recollections of relatives and friends who had known him in Spain and Cuba. Ruth Hawkins, William Stafford (Arkansas State University), and journalist John Trout informed the confer-

ence about the establishment of the Pigott Hemingway Museum and the Pfeiffer Library Conference Center and gave a slide presentation illustrating the restoration of the Pfeiffer home. Bickford Sylvester concluded the paper presentations by reflecting on the approaching Hemingway Centenary.

Two seminar sessions and an interpretive reading of "First Poem to Mary" by Mary Cruz followed the paper sessions. The first seminar, "Writing to Read, Reading to Write: Teaching Hemingway in the Writing Classroom," was moderated by Larry Grimes (Bethany College). The following were speakers and topics: Beverly Connor (University of Puget Sound), "Writing and Remembrance: Hemingway's Use of Longing"; Barbara Sylvester (Western Washington University), "The Lion, the Marlin, and the Man: Literature and Cross-Curriculum Writing in an Age of Ecological Consciousness"; Joe Haldeman (MIT), "Hemingway as Bridge between Writing as Technique and the Technical Writer"; and Mary Haldeman (MIT), "Hemingway's Work as Common Ground in the ESL Classroom." The second seminar was moderated by Harvard Knowles (Phillips Exeter Academy), who read "The Innocent Reader and Ernest Hemingway." The follow-

La Floridita, "The Cradle of the Daiquiri" (photograph by John Unrue)

ing were speakers and topics: Manuel Zenick (Chevy Chase, Maryland), "Across the River and into My Life: Hemingway as Non Traditional Students Re-Member Him" and Richard Raleigh (St. Thomas University), "Martinis at the Palace: Teaching Hemingway on Location."

On the evening of 21 July 1997, Hemingway's birthday, Hotels Horizontes hosted the II Colegio International "Ernest Hemingway" at a buffet dinner at one of Hemingway's favorite places, Restaurant La Terraza, located on a cove in Cojimar, the site of the fishing village that became the fictional home of Santiago in *The Old Man and the Sea*. Those who looked down from La Terraza on the cove got a sense of the place from which the old fisherman began rowing on his journey "too far"; their perspective was that of the fictional tourists who, as outsiders looking down from the terrace, mistook his giant fish carcass for that of a shark. The walls of the Restaurant La Terraza are lined with photographs of Hemingway that commemorate the novel and the movie.

A special moment for North American conference members was a private tour of Finca Vigía arranged by Gladys Rodriquez Ferraro. Small groups of conference

participants were bused to the Finca Vigía and permitted to walk through the house—an opportunity not afforded to visiting tourists, who must view the interior of Hemingway's former home only through open windows. Every room in the Finca Vigía was available to view and to photograph, although flash photos were not permitted. The curators of the house were generous, helpful, and notably protective of the contents, especially of Hemingway's large library: no one was permitted to examine any books or papers. The guest house, or cottage, was not open; however, the tower, where Hemingway escaped to write, was accessible and was filled with photographs.

Conference participants were also entertained for an evening at La Floridita, which Hemingway made famous and which is now an upscale bar and restaurant. All were treated to what is said to be the Hemingway daiquiri. To visitors, La Floridita, which celebrated its 180th anniversary in 1997, appears much like a Hemingway shrine. His old bar stool and reserved place at the far-left corner when facing the bar are protected by a cordon ensuring that no other person will sit there. Above the bar stool and around the room on the wall are photographs of Hemingway and celebrities, including several photos of Hemingway and Fidel Castro holding fishing tournament trophies.

Interpreters and tours of Old Havana were available to conference participants, and many persons took the opportunity to visit Hotel Ambos Mundos, where Hemingway stayed in spring 1932, and La Bodeguita del Medio, another bar associated with Hemingway. Some participants accepted invitations to El Viejo y el Mar Hotel (The Old Man and the Sea Hotel) at the Marina Hemingway to see a water ballet based on *The Old Man and the Sea*. Others were guests of the mayor of Havana and were treated to a buffet dinner, *mojitos,* beer, and Cuban music at his home.

Following the official close of the colloquium by Francisco Lópex Sacha, chairman of the Writers Association of the Writers and Artists' Union of Cuba, some conference participants chose to take part in a post-session event: a trip to Camaguay Province to retrace the course of Thomas Hudson during the final episodes of *Islands in the Stream*. Cuban novelist Enrique Cirules, a native of the area, was the guide for this overnight event on 25–26 July. Heavy rains, however, prevented travel that had been planned throughout the area.

Those who attended the Second International Colloquium agreed that it provided rich literary and cultural experiences and gave them a sense of the spirit of the place that inspired and informed much of Hemingway's fiction. Although relationships between the governments of the United States and Cuba remain poor, it is possible for scholars, writers, and journalists to travel to Cuba in order to retrace the paths Hemingway followed in his life and art and to engage in discussions with Cuban scholars and journalists. However, it has not yet become possible for North American scholars to gain access to Hemingway's books, manuscripts, or papers that remain in Cuba. Stephen Plotkin, curator of the Hemingway Collection at the Kennedy Library and one of those who attended the colloquium, estimates that there are approximately three thousand photographs (some with annotations), two thousand letters (largely to Hemingway), and between five hundred and one thousand pages of manuscripts. Estimates of the number of books in Hemingway's collection range from seven thousand to nine thousand. These materials are deteriorating and are in serious need of professional attention if they are to be preserved.

U.S. citizens seeking to travel to Cuba must be licensed by the Office of Foreign Assets Control (OFAC) of the U.S. Treasury Department, Washington, D.C., 20220. Licenses for participants in the Hemingway Colloquium were obtained by Marazul Tours, Inc., Tower Plaza, 4100 Park Avenue, Weehawken, N.J., 07087. At present no direct flights from the United States to Cuba are available, and anyone wishing to visit Cuba is urged to take advantage of the experience and expertise of a good travel agency. Connecting flights to Jose Martí Airport, Cuba, are available from Nassau in the Bahamas and from Cancún, Mexico. Communication between U.S. and Cuban scholars is also possible by e-mail.

The Making of Americans Contract

Contact *Editions*

including the Publications of the

THREE MOUNTAINS PRESS

29, Quai d'Anjou, *Ile Saint-Louis*, Paris

R. C. SEINE 280.434

Memorandum of agreement between Contact Editions, publishers of Paris, and Miss Gertrude Stein, of Paris, author of The Making of Americans, for the publication of said book.

The publishers agree to publish the book in an edition of 500 copies, to be sold at a retail price or prices to be fixed by the publishers. They further agree to give the author ten copies of the book.

The author shall receive as royalties 10 per cent of the retail price of all copies sold, the first payment to be made however only after there has been a sale of three hundred and fifty (350) copies, and quarterly thereafter. The first statement of sales is to be made November 1st, 1925, and later statements shall be made each quarter year.

It is agreed that the author shall retain sole ownership of the copyright.

In case of subsequent editions published by Contact Editions, it is agreed that the author's royalties, under the same proviso as above, shall be twenty-five instead of ten per cent. In case Contact editions act as agent in procuring a later publisher for the re-edition of the work, they agree to consult with the author to the end that she establishes her own terms with the new publisher. Should Contact Editions under-

Contract for Gertrude Stein's The Making of Americans *(Robert McAlmon Papers, Beinecke Library, Yale University)*

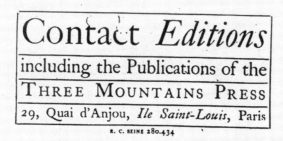

34

take the sale of sheets to another publisher it shall be only after consultation with the author, so that further dealings, about the book, and the copyright ownership shall be between the author and the new publishers.

Alterations in the text, after the manuscript has been put in type, shall be at the charge of the author, as shall any expense due to delay in approving proofs on the part of the author.

dated this   day   of May 1925   Paris.

The Making of Americans, the only Gertrude Stein work published by Robert McAlmon's Contact Editions, led to Stein's falling-out with McAlmon. McAlmon at first planned to print 1,000 copies of the 925-page novel at an estimated cost of $3,000, but he then reduced the printing by half. Extensive revisions had to be made in the galley proofs because the French printer, Maurice Darantière, could not understand that the repetitions in the text were intentional. Stein believed that the mistakes would not have been made if McAlmon—who had left for a visit to America—had supervised the typesetting. While the book was being printed, Stein attempted to sell sheets of the edition to a British publisher, and McAlmon believed this attempt to be a violation of their agreement. By December 1926 only 103 copies had been sold—mostly, McAlmon claimed, to Stein's family and friends.

–Robert Trogden

Ernest Hemingway's Reaction to James Gould Cozzens

The 30 September 1957 letter to *Time* editor Robert Manning, in which Ernest Hemingway reacts to the *Time* cover story (2 September 1957) on James Gould Cozzens, has been acquired by the Thomas Cooper Library at the University of South Carolina. Manning had told Hemingway about the article while it was being prepared and sent him takes from the *Time* research on Cozzens.

The *Time* article quotes Cozzens as stating: " *The Old Man and the Sea* could have run in *Little Folks* magazine. Under the rough exterior of Hemingway, he's just

a great big bleeding heart." Hemingway's letter describes *Guard of Honor* (1948) as synthetic and *By Love Possessed* (1957) as a soap opera and calls Cozzens a fascist; nonetheless, Hemingway claims that "Reading the personal things he said about me did not make me angry." Manning believes that "The letter to me was simply his response to the research (and of course the *Time* story). He sent it simply for my amusement; didn't ask for anything or even expect a response" (to Matthew J. Bruccoli, 3 April 1998).

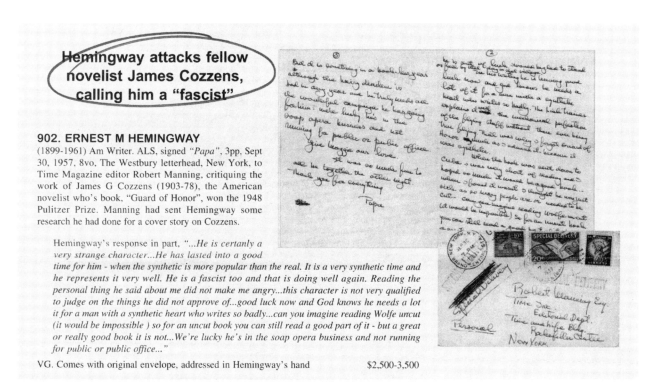

Hemingway attacks fellow novelist James Cozzens, calling him a "fascist"

902. ERNEST M HEMINGWAY
(1899-1961) Am Writer. ALS, signed *"Papa"*, 3pp, Sept 30, 1957, 8vo, The Westbury letterhead, New York, to Time Magazine editor Robert Manning, critiquing the work of James G Cozzens (1903-78), the American novelist who's book, "Guard of Honor", won the 1948 Pulitzer Prize. Manning had sent Hemingway some research he had done for a cover story on Cozzens.

Hemingway's response in part, *"...He is certanly a very strange character...He has lasted into a good time for him - when the synthetic is more popular than the real. It is a very synthetic time and he represents it very well. He is a fascist too and that is doing well again. Reading the personal thing he said about me did not make me angry...this character is not very qualified to judge on the things he did not approve of...good luck now and God knows he needs a lot it for a man with a synthetic heart who writes so badly...can you imagine reading Wolfe uncut (it would be impossible) so for an uncut book you can still read a good part of it - but a great or really good book it is not...We're lucky he's in the soap opera business and not running for public or public office..."*

VG. Comes with original envelope, addressed in Hemingway's hand $2,500-3,500

RWA Inc. auction catalogue, number 43

Melissa Bank Interview

Lauren MacIntyre
The New Yorker

Melissa Bank (photograph © by Marion Ettlinger)

Melissa Bank's collection of stories, "A Girl's Guide to Hunting and Fishing," is to be published by Viking in June 1999.

DLB: The title story in your collection appeared last winter in *Zoetrope: All Story,* a quarterly founded by Francis Ford Coppola that made news when it launched two years ago. In each issue, in addition to publishing stories from newer writers, *Zoetrope* includes a classic reprint of a story that went on to become a movie (Mary Orr's "The Wisdom of Eve," which sparked off *All About Eve* [1950],

appeared in the first issue). They also commission a story. "A Girl's Guide to Hunting and Fishing" was commissioned, is that right?

MB: Yes. They called me in and told me the idea. Francis had heard about *The Rules*—that how-to-marry-a-man guide that came out a few years ago—and he had an idea for a story in which a woman follows the rules and discovers that love doesn't go by them.

DLB: Did he give you the ending?

MB: Basically, he wanted the story to be about that one idea: that love doesn't follow any rules. The story description was maybe two sentences. But it was a story that I'd tried before to write on my own, and when they approached me about it, I was thrilled, because it was the kind of story I was hoping to write anyway, to conclude my collection.

DLB: Did you enjoy working with them?

MB: Absolutely. They were wonderful. They handled everything so well. I'd never worked on a commission before. Other times, when I'd published stories in magazines or wherever, there was very little–if any–editing that went on. At *Zoetrope* I was really involved with Adrienne Brodeur, my editor. We really scrutinized the story together. There were a lot of issues that came up, and I really respected the way Adrienne handled them. She is a great editor. Really smart. And a lovely person, besides.

DLB: You worked in publishing yourself for a while?

MB: I did. I worked for Molly Friedrich, who is now my agent. It was my second job in publishing. I was bad at it. I always felt behind. I couldn't read fast enough. But I loved working for Molly. She was the exact same kind of agent then that she is now–only now she's famous. She took care of her authors. She was fast. She handled everything with real integrity.

DLB: Has she always been your agent?

MB: Oh, no. In fact, I never thought she'd take me on. I had another agent for a long time, and then when the *Zoetrope* story came out there were agents who started approaching me. I'd always stayed in touch with Molly, just because I love her, but, I never thought. . . . First of all, Molly isn't really a short-story person. She told me that early on.

DLB: Did you decide to try your luck, anyway, after the *Zoetrope* story came out?

MB: Well, I was approached by another agent, and in our meeting she asked me what I was looking for in an agent, and I said, "Well, to tell you truth, in my mind, the fantasy agent is Molly Friedrich." She asked me why Molly wasn't representing me and I told her that Molly had never read my work. She said, "Why don't you call Molly and ask her what she thinks of me and my reputation?" So I went to Molly and, sure enough, she told me that the agent I'd talked to was wonderful and energetic, et cetera, et cetera. And I said, "The only problem, Molly, is that she isn't you." And that's when I decided to show her my manuscript.

DLB: Were you nervous because you knew her so well?

MB: I honestly didn't think she would take me on. I felt like I was too small. No other agent could really have competed with her, though, in terms of trust and respect. I've known her now for fifteen years.

DLB: That's a real testament to her. Often, when you work for someone and see what they're like behind the scenes, you can feel just the opposite.

MB: I think it is unusual. I felt like I'd won the lottery when she told me she wanted to represent me.

DLB: When did all this happen?

MB: On Martin Luther King Day–January 1998. Molly became my agent on a Tuesday. That Tuesday afternoon she submitted my manuscript to twelve publishers. On Wednesday morning, ten of them called back and said they wanted to buy the book. It was amazing. Then there was an auction.

DLB: What was the auction process like?

MB: Molly set it up so I had the right to refuse any offer–meaning I could go with the editor that I wanted. So I went around town and met the editors.

DLB: What was that like?

MB: The funny thing was, I had spent so many years just scrambling and being supplicant that at first I just didn't really get it that they wanted me. I remember talking to a very nice editor at Little, Brown and in the middle of our meeting being overwhelmed with the feeling that I was back interviewing for a publishing job again. I was thinking, "OK, after this, I'll go down to Personnel and take that typing test. . . ." I'm so glad I did it, though. I met some really wonderful people. Robin

Desser. Lee Haber at Hyperion. I met a lot of terrific editors.

DLB: Did you feel at all like the tables had been turned? Like it was their turn to impress you?

MB: No, no, no. If anything, the attention felt weird—to have people talking directly to you, saying things like "You're *so* talented." How do you handle someone saying that? Your head gets carbonated. I really understood how success could ruin somebody—especially a younger writer. If I sort of wasn't as old as I am—I'm thirty-eight—and if I hadn't gone through what I've gone through, I think it would've ruined me. It's too noisy. It's the opposite of writing. It's all wrong.

DLB: What made you decide to go with Viking?

MB: Everybody there seemed to be totally behind the book. There were probably ten people at that meeting, all of whom had read it. The editorial director was there. The publisher came in at one point. I just got the sense that people were behind it. And, of course, the main thing for me was that I loved Carol DeSanti, who became my editor. She's incredible.

DLB: Did you feel a shift in how you approached your work once you got the contract?

MB: It was strange because I'd spent years working on these stories, getting them right. And then, all of a sudden, I had a deadline. It was like working for fifteen years and suddenly being told you have to make the three 'o clock Federal Express truck. I worked very closely with Carol. For a long time I'd been the sole judge of my work. I think that's something that just sort of happens over the years. I can remember being an MFA and showing my work to other people. They'd say, "This is good," or, "This isn't good," and then in my head it would become Good or Not Good. Or *The New Yorker* would reject a story and it would then become Not That Good. But after a while—maybe it's a survival thing, or maybe it's just what happens naturally after years of reading your own work—you know what works. When I finished "My Old Man," I knew it was a good story. I said, "I just wrote my best story." And I remember a friend of mine telling me, "I just don't think it's that good." And I thought, I know it's good.

DLB: It must have been nice to have an editor to work with after you'd spent that kind of time with the stories on your own.

MB: [Laughs] I called her my adolescent boyfriend because I was just dying to hear her voice. There was a time when we were calling and faxing back and forth and I'd just *jump* for the phone when I knew she was on the other end of the line. I valued her opinion that much. She approaches stories from their center, not from the outside. She's right there in the heart of the story with you. There was something slightly disconcerting about going back to valuing someone's opinion that much, after I'd gotten to the point where I thought I knew if something was good or bad. But she was always right. We were under some deadline pressure, and I remember she cut some funny stuff out of a rewrite I'd done—material I found hard to give up. She said, "This doesn't belong in the first story of this collection." And she was right.

DLB: You mentioned earlier that you consider yourself an older writer, when in fact most people would probably lump you in the younger writer category—including the people at *Granta,* who've been composing that "Best Younger Writers" list. Do you associate yourself that way? Do you feel like you had one big break, or was it more of a gradual breaking in?

MB: I would say this: I worked so hard for what felt like many years. I wouldn't have done it any other way, but it wasn't easy: I held a job in advertising, which was excruciating. I feel like I got really lucky in terms of having Molly as an agent. She knew the editors that the book would appeal to, and she found them, and that's lucky. I don't imagine that all agents are as intuitive, or know editors as well in terms of their taste. She's very smart about who will like what. That's one of the best reasons to have an agent. She knew that Carol DeSanti was someone who would get my humor, which was very fortunate for me. It is a huge break and a huge piece of luck, and there are plenty of talented people who never get it. But I don't feel like it came easily. I was always worried that my endurance would run out before the book was finished.

DLB: Was the job in advertising draining you, or were you just getting tired of writing itself?

MB: I think it's true when people say that succeeding as a writer is less a talent contest than a test of endurance. How many times can you be rejected and stand up again and go back for more? That's a lot of it. It's hard to keep going—especially as you get older—when everything else in your life has an immediate, or at least some kind of measurable, success. I think you have to try to find a way to keep loving what you're doing, because most writers experience what I do, I think, which is a lot of bad nights where you write total dreck. You have to learn how not to hate your own guts if you're not writing well—or at least to accept that as part of writing. And you can't get downed by failure.

DLB: Your book is a collection of stories about the same young woman at various points in her life. The same characters appear and reappear. Tim O'Brien did something similar in *The Things They Carried.*

MB: I love *The Things They Carried.* It's one of my favorite books.

DLB: Your collection reads a lot like a novel because the stories follow a chronological order.

MB: It is like a novel in some ways, although it doesn't conform to the structural conventions of one. I remember reading *Nine Stories* and being so excited when a character would reappear. I guess the book *is* novelistic in that the stories really build on one another.

DLB: Most of the stories are about love, although they seem to cover a lot of other territory, too. Do you think of them as love stories?

MB: Every one of them is a love story, I think. Love is what interests me most: how people find it; how they make it stay; what's good for them when they're with another person versus what isn't. Somehow love always ends up being the most important thing—the thing people care the most about. I think of my stories as love stories, but maybe not in the conventional sense. I'm interested in the realism of how we live our lives, so while they're love stories, I wouldn't say they're particularly romantic.

DLB: What do you think are your strengths as a writer?

MB: Dialogue. I hear people talking in my head when I'm writing.

DLB: What other writers do you find particularly inspiring?

MB: I've been reading a lot of Nick Hornby lately. I feel like I try to do a lot of the same things he's doing. I love Salinger, and Tolstoy. . . . *Anna Karenina* is one of my favorite books. Right now I'm reading Arthur Golden's *Memoirs of Geisha,* which I like. *The Remains of the Day* was a wonderful book. [Pauses.] For years I didn't read any contemporary fiction. I found myself too influenced. I just read the classics. I needed to get my I.Q. up: it was horrible, advertising.

DLB: Were there any ways in which you think it helped you as a writer?

MB: It's tough, because in advertising, you're basically like a vacuum salesman, trying to get in the door. If I walked into a meeting and read copy that was fun or interesting, but didn't sell the product, people would just stare at me. It wouldn't fly. And in a way, that part of it was good. It curbed my self-indulgence as a writer. I'd think about the stories I was writing and think, OK, there's somebody on the other end of this story who wants to know what's going to happen next. They're more concerned about what's going to happen to the character than about whether or not you're a good writer. Don't let anything get in the way of your story and the reader, including really good, beautiful language. If you're writing an ad or you're writing for TV, you have to make every word work hard. And that's a good discipline to learn. People are busy. Don't waste their time. I'm not saying don't go on for three pages about a death if that death is what you're writing about. But don't talk about yourself when you should be talking about your character. Sometimes I think that really beautiful writing is sort of like spending a little too long looking in the mirror and primping. OK. You look good. Move on.

Octavio Paz

(31 March 1914 – 19 April 1998)

Luis Leal
University of California, Santa Barbara

Poet, essayist, critic, and diplomat, Octavio Paz was one of the most brilliant men of letters not only in the Hispanic world but internationally as well. His books have been translated into many languages, and in 1990 he received the Nobel Prize in Literature in recognition of the excellence of his prose and poetry. In his many essays he is able to portray the Mexican people and their culture in a convincing manner, and as a poet he expresses with deep feeling his vision of humanity and his own place in the cosmos. His ideas are always expressed in a terse, clear style elaborated with striking figures of speech.

Octavio Paz, the son of Octavio Paz and Josefina Lozano, was born 31 March 1914 in Mexico City. His paternal grandfather, Ireneo Paz (1836–1924) from Guadalajara, Jalisco, is remembered for the many historical novels he wrote. Paz said that his grandfather was a well-known journalist and writer who fought against the French during their intervention in Mexico from 1862 to 1867 and who, although he first supported Porfirio Díaz, later opposed the old dictator. Octavio Paz's father, who died in a railroad accident in 1934, was also a journalist—in addition to being a diplomat and an attorney. He represented Emiliano Zapata in the United States in 1916 and was one of the initiators of agrarian reform. Born in Mexico, Paz's mother was of Andalusian parents. Except for a short time in Los Angeles, California, where his father was in exile, Paz spent his childhood and youth in Mixcoac, one of the southern suburbs of Mexico City that has become an integral part of the metropolis. "As in all Mexican houses at that time," Paz says in Rita Guibert's article in *Seven Voices* (1973), "the men of my house weren't very good Catholics, but rather freethinkers, Masons, or liberals. Whereas, the women were devout Catholics."

Paz's first studies were all in Mexico City, first in a French school of Marist Brothers, from which he went to Williams English School, where he learned to write clearly and concisely. Among the first books he read were works by three French writers—the political

theorist Jean Jacques Rousseau, the historian Jules Michelet, and the novelist Victor Hugo—authors recommended by Amalia, his father's sister, who taught him French. He was also reading other books that he found in the library of his grandfather, who had collected a fine library to which Paz had free access in his childhood. The library was rich in French literature and in the works of poets, nineteenth-century

Spanish novelists, and modernist and Mexican writers. Another book that impressed him was *The Golden Ass* (ca. A.D. 124–170), the narrative romance of Apuleius, the Latin satirist.

Paz's secondary studies were in the Escuela Secundaria Número 5, to which he had to take the streetcar for a forty-five minute ride from Mixcoac to the Colonia Juárez, where the school was located on Marsella Street. There in 1929 he met José Bosh, a Spanish student who later died in the Spanish Civil War and to whom Paz dedicated "Elegía a un compañero muerto en el frente de Aragón" (Elegy to a friend who died at the Aragon front). Bosh, according to Paz, had influenced the formation of his political ideas and attitudes toward totalitarian governments and institutions.

At age seventeen Paz began studying at the National Preparatory School (San Ildefoso), and during his second year (1932) he published his first poems in *Barandal* (Balustrade), a review that he founded and directed along with other poets of his generation. In 1933 he published his first book of poems, *Luna silvestre* (Wild Moon), and directed *Cuadernos del Valle de México* (Valley of Mexico Notebooks), a review that lasted for only four numbers. The following year Spanish poet Rafael Alberti gave a series of conferences in Mexico that Paz stated were for him a great revelation. Other poets who influenced him during those early years included the Chileans Pablo Neruda and Vicente Huidobro and the Spaniard Luis Cernuda.

Paz's next two works of poetry, *¡No pasarán!* (They Shall Not Pass!, 1936) and *Raíz del hombre* (Root of Man, 1937), were important to him—the first because it earned him an invitation to visit Europe, the second because it marked his development as a poet. In 1937 he went to Yucatán in order to establish a school for the children of the workers and peasants. Although he remained there only four months, his experiences with nature in Yucatán, the ancient Mayan culture, and the plight of the workers inspired him to write the poems collected in 1941 in *Entre la piedra y la flor* (Between the Stone and the Flower). Years later Paz said that the subject matter of those poems was "el hombre mexicano del Sur, de Yucatán, en su paisaje" (the Mexican man of the South, of Yucatán, in his landscape).

The year 1937 was one of great activity for Paz. That year he married writer Elena Garro, with whom he had a daughter, Elena, but this marriage ended in divorce years later. In 1937 he also published "Sonetos," a collection of five sonnets that appeared in *Taller Poético* (Poetry Workshop), a literary review that he, Rafael Solana, and Miguel N. Lira published from

1936 to 1938. Having published *¡No pasarán!* and having been recommended by Neruda, Paz was invited to attend the Second Writers Congress of Anti-fascist Writers meeting in Paris, Barcelona, and Valencia in 1937. In Paris he met Neruda, Louis Aragon, and César Vallejo, and, accompanied by Elena, Paz proceeded to Barcelona and then to Valencia, where he became acquainted with other writers such as Vicente Huidobro, Miguel Hernández, Manuel Altolaguirre, Antonio Machado, and Alejo Carpentier, who were also attending the meeting.

In Valencia, Altolaguirre published Paz's collection *Bajo tu clara sombra y otros poemas de España* (Under Your Transparent Shade and Other Poems of Spain, 1937). Paz's 1990 book *Pequeña crónica de grandes días* (Small Chronicle of Great Days) includes the essay "El lugar de la prueba (Valencia, 1937–1987)," which recounts that he was invited to Valencia to give the inaugural speech celebrating the fiftieth anniversary of the meeting. He writes that his

> deepest and most permanent impressions of that summer of 1937 were not from my association with writers. . . . I was moved by my encounter with Spain and its people: to see with my own eyes and touch with my own hands the landscape, the monuments, and the stones that since childhood I knew through my reading and my grandparent's stories.

After returning to Mexico in 1938 Paz began to write his first essays on international politics for the workers' newspaper *El Popular*. He also published the monthly literary periodical *Taller* (Shop, 1938–1941), where he printed the first Spanish anthology of T. S. Eliot's. He had already published *Raíz del hombre*. Henceforward, universal themes attracted his attention, even though he remained preoccupied with the nature of language and its function in the development of cultures and literatures. In 1941 he edited the influential anthology *Laurel,* in which he included the internationally known work of poets such as John Donne.

Influenced by the writers he had met, Paz in 1943 was instrumental in establishing, with the help of Octavio G. Barreda, the first vanguard literary review in Mexico, *El Hijo Pródigo* (The Prodigal Son). The following year he received a Guggenheim Fellowship that liberated him from his job that he had held since the early 1940s as a bank clerk in the Central Bank of Mexico. Paz spent that year in the United States, principally in San Francisco, Los Angeles, and New York. In Middlebury, Vermont, where he taught one summer, he met poets Robert Frost and Jorge Guillén; from Middlebury he went to Washington, D.C., where he met Juan Ramón Jiménez. During his entire stay in the United States, Paz took notes about life and customs of the people, and he used these in his *El laberinto de la soledad* (1950; translated as *The Labyrinth of Solitude,* 1961). In New York, Francisco Castillo Nájera, a friend of his father and the Mexican ambassador, invited Paz to join the diplomatic service in 1945. The poet José Gorostiza, chief of the service, sent him to Paris, where he started a new career that he abandoned only in 1968, when he resigned in protest over the massacre of students in Tlatelolco by the Mexican government on 2 October that year.

During his visit to Paris, Paz met André Breton; the two established a friendship that strengthened Paz's interest in the surrealist movement and that continued through Breton's later return visit to Mexico. By 1949 Paz had written many poems that he collected that year in *Libertad bajo palabra* (Freedom under Oath), which gave him international recognition as a first-rank poet.

The 1950s was one of the more productive decades in Paz's life. In 1950 he published *The Labyrinth of Solitude,* a seminal book that brought him recognition as a perceptive critic of cultural, historical, and political processes. This collection of essays was followed in 1951 by another masterpiece, *¿Águila o sol?* (translated as *Águila a sol/Eagle or Sun?,* 1970), and in that year Paz made his first trip to the Far East, an experience that influenced him for the rest of his life. In New Dehli, Paz met the artist Maria José Tramini, whom he married in 1964.

In Mexico he continued his literary activities, publishing additional books of poems *Piedra de sol* (Sunstone, 1957) and *La estación violenta* (Violent Season, 1958)—while collaborating in 1956 with the group "Poesía en Voz Alta" (Poetry Readings) and staging his only known dramatic production, *La hija de Rappaccini* (Rappaccini's Daughter), a one-act piece inspired by Nathaniel Hawthorne's short story of that same title. This drama was published first in the *Revista de Literatura Mexicana* (1955–1957), a literary review that Paz, Carlos Fuentes, and Emmanuel Carballo founded.

In 1967 Paz became a member of the prestigious Colegio Nacional de México, whose members are appointed for life by the president of the republic. After 1968 Paz devoted himself to writing and lecturing, offering seminars in several American and European academic institutions: the University of Pittsburgh, the University of Texas at Austin, Cornell University, Harvard University, and Cambridge University. In October 1971 he established the magazine *Plural,* and in 1977 he founded *Vuelta* (Return), which was published until the year of his death.

In an essay in *The Siren and the Seashell, and Other Essays on Poets and Poetry* (1976) Paz observes that "poetry continues to be a force capable of revealing to man his dreams and of inviting him to live those dreams in the light of day." This force is in Paz's own poems, and especially in his books *Entre la piedra y la flor, A la orilla del mundo* (At the Ear of the World, 1942), and *Libertad bajo palabra* (Freedom under Word [of Honor], 1949), three works in which he collected his best poems of that period. The idea of freedom is fundamental in Paz's work; it never disappears from his writings, and it is interesting that he incorporates themes of freedom as well as love and rebellion in his surrealistic poetry. In 1959 he told interviewer Claude Couffon that the effects of the civil war he had seen in Spain in 1937 made him question the possibility of transforming the human condition. This sentiment he expressed in the poems he had collected in *Raíz del hombre.*

His collections of poems published since *Semillas para un himno* in 1954 develop in depth the theme of man's freedom, but they do so without giving up his cosmic vision of reality, which includes universal problems that confront modern man and those intrinsic to his human nature. This vision is expressed in Paz's search for new images, since for him the image is the heart of the poem. His poetic works—and his essays—are efforts to synthesize reason and beauty as manifested in our time.

The poetic form that Paz gave to his experiences can best be observed in *La estación violenta,* a book in which he collected nine poems written between 1946 and 1957. In "El cántaro roto" (The Broken Jug) the poet confronts problems such as the arid nature of the land, hunger, lack of social progress, and discontinuity with the past as these are manifested through the history of Mexico. "Piedra de sol" (Sunstone), another poem of 584 endecasyllabic verses distributed in irregular strophes, has a circular structure that mimetically represents the circularity of time. Repetition of the same images and traditional symbols (tree, water, and wind), as reflected in a mirror, gives the poem a surreal feeling. To emphasize the circular nature of time the last six verses are identical to the first six, and this closure returns the reader to the beginning and thus completes a circle, as does the sunstone of the Aztec calendar.

To give the form greater continuity, capital letters and closing periods are omitted, a technique that contributes to what Paz calls *poesía en movimiento* (poetry in motion). He expanded this concept of poetry in motion, applied it to poetry in general, and used the phrase as the title of an anthology of Mexican verse that he and others published in 1966. The

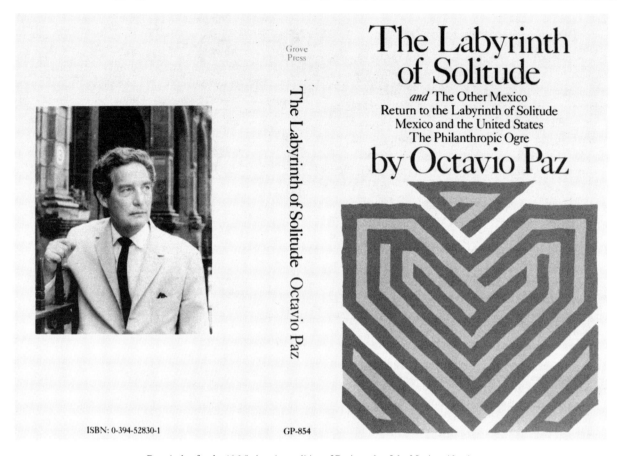

Grove Press

The Labyrinth of Solitude

and The Other Mexico
Return to the Labyrinth of Solitude
Mexico and the United States
The Philanthropic Ogre

by Octavio Paz

ISBN: 0-394-52830-1   GP-854

Dust jacket for the 1985 American edition of Paz's study of the Mexican identity

term also characterizes Paz's own poetry, which is constantly in search of new forms.

In his poetry published after *Salamandra (1958–1961)* (1962), a new feature appears in the introduction of Eastern ideas, concepts, and images in collections such as *Viento entero* (Total Wind, 1965), *Blanco* (White, 1967), and *Ladera este (1962–1968)* (East Slope, 1969). In these books Paz integrates Eastern philosophy and imagery into his verse without letting it supplant his well-defined attitude toward reality, and they add an exotic quality to his poetry. In "Total Wind" Paz expresses an Eastern theme, "the present is perpetual," by using universal images such as "wind without edges" and "light beyond time." *Blanco* contains a single poem printed with black and red ink in a long strip, as in the prehispanic codices, and in *Poemas (1935–1975)* (1979) Paz writes of *Blanco:*

> As the reading advances, the page unfolds into a space whose movement allows the text to appear and, in a certain way, creates it. . . . The typography and binding of the first edition of *Blanco* were meant to give emphasis not so much to the presence of the text as to that of the space containing it, which is what makes possible writing and reading.
>
> [translated by Luis Leal]

The subject matter of the poem, nevertheless, is as important as its form, for the poem presents the poet's confrontation with reality–and Paz finds reality in *la palabra* (the word) rather than in the senses or thought. For him, words reflect sensorial impressions and therefore constitute reality, as expressed in the following verses from *Blanco:*

> the flower
> not seen nor imagined:
>   heard,
>   appears,
>   a yellow chalice
>   of consonants and vowels,
> I   burning.

His work always in evolution, Paz published concrete poetry collections in *Discos visuales* (Visual Disks) in 1968 and *Topoemas* and *Renga* (translated as *Renga: A*

313

Chain of Poems, 1972); with Edoardo Sanguinetti, Charles Tomlinson, and Jacques Roubaud, in 1971.

Since 1950, the year he published *The Labyrinth of Solitude,* Paz was also recognized as a brilliant prose writer, thinker, and cultural historian. With that book translated into the main languages of the world, Paz was accepted abroad as the principal interpreter of Mexican culture. In addition to the clear style of the work, Paz's book is valuable for its interpretation of Mexican history and culture, an interpretation that invalidated all previous ones, such as that offered by Samuel Ramos in his *El perfil del hombre y las cultura en México* (1934; translated as *Profile of Man and Culture in Mexico,* 1972). In an article in the *Los Angeles Times* on 12 October 1990, the day that Paz received the Nobel Prize, Juanita Darling states that the Swedish Academy of Letters praised Paz's "exquisite love poetry" as well as his social and literary essays, especially his *The Labyrinth of Solitude,* which members of the committee called "an exploration of Mexican identity that has become a standard test in courses on Mexican history and political science since its publication in 1950."

Perhaps most significant about *The Labyrinth of Solitude* is the fact that Paz thought many critics had misinterpreted it. As early as 1970, the year he published *Posdata* (translated as *The Other Mexico: Critique of the Pyramid,* 1972), Paz wrote:

> Perhaps it would be worth the trouble to explain (once again) that *The Labyrinth of Solitude* was an exercise of the critical imagination: a vision and, simultaneously, a revision—something very different from an essay on Mexican-ness or a search for our supposed being. The Mexican is not an essence but a history. Neither ontology nor psychology. I was and am intrigued not so much by the "national character" as by what that character conceals; by what is behind the mask.

That the method Paz used in analyzing Mexico and the Mexican in 1950 had not changed in twenty years can be deduced from his words in *The Other Mexico:*

> In *The Labyrinth of Solitude* I tried hard (without wholly succeeding, of course) to avoid both the pitfalls of abstract humanism and the illusions of a philosophy of Mexican-ness. . . . In those days I was not interested in a definition of Mexican-ness but rather, *as now,* in criticism: that activity which consists not only in knowing ourselves but, just as much or more, in freeing ourselves. Criticism unfolds the possibility of freedom and is thus an invitation to action.

Criticism is inherent in all of Paz's essays, and his deep belief in criticism and freedom kept *The Labyrinth of Solitude* alive. Features other than its ideological content have kept it in the canon: its external form, its clear and terse style, and in general Paz's skillful use of poetic imagery to express ideas. The work represents a conjunction of Paz the poet and Paz the essayist.

The Labyrinth of Solitude stimulated the thinking of prominent writers. Carlos Fuentes, in his *Myself with Others,* writes that when he went to Europe to study international law in 1950, "Octavio Paz had just published two books that had changed the face of Mexican literature, *Libertad bajo palabra* and *El laberinto de la soledad.* My friends and I had read those books aloud in Mexico, dazzled by a poetics that managed simultaneously to renew our language from within and to connect it to the language of the world." This seminal book by Paz will continue to shape Mexican thought and international concepts about Mexico and its people.

In 1956 Paz began to publish a series of books on literature, art, and aesthetics that made him well known in all these fields. In *El arco y la lira* (1956; translated as *The Bow and the Lyre,* 1973), he elaborated a brilliant theory of poetics that he continued to expand in *Los hijos del limo: Del romanticismo a la vanguardia* (1974), translated that same year as *Children of the Mire: Poetry from Romanticism to the Avant-Garde; The Siren and the Seashell, and Other Essays on Poets and Poetry* (1976); *On Poets and Others* (1986); and *Convergences: Essays on Art and Literature* (1987). He also expressed ideas on translation and other literary topics in *Traducción: literatura y literalidad* (1971) and wrote and collected critical essays about Latin American literature in *Las peras del olmo* (The Pears of the Elm, 1957), *Cuadrivio* (Quartet, 1965), and *Corriente alterna* (1967; translated as *Alternating Current,* 1973).

Not content with having achieved world recognition as a poet and essayist, Paz also expressed opinions about world politics in his *El ogro filantrópico: Historia y política, 1971–1978* (The Philanthropic Ogre: History and Politics, 1971–1978, 1978) and *Tiempo nublado* (1983; translated as *One Earth, Four or Five Worlds: Reflections on Contemporary History,* 1985). In the foreword of *Tiempo nublado,* a collection of essays he published in *Vuelta* and other periodicals between 1980 and 1983, Paz writes: "I am not a historian. My passion is poetry and my occupation literature; and neither the one nor the other gives me the authority to express my opinions about the convulsions and agitations of our time." However, he examines contemporary world problems such as terrorism, totalitarianism, and poverty with great skill and understanding.

Not less important are Paz's books of poetic prose, including *¿Aguila o sol?*, which refers to the two sides of a Mexican coin and which he uses to refer to the uncertainties of life. Eliot Weinberger calls this collection one of the most important books of Spanish prose poetry. Another collection is *El mono gramatíco* (1974; translated as *The Monkey Grammarian,* 1981), which, with *¿Aguila o sol?*, was included in *Poemas (1935–1975).*

In 1982 Paz published an important book of literary criticism, an exhaustive study of the life, works, and times of Sor Juana Inés de la Cruz, the great seventeenth-century poet. In 1971 Paz had been invited by Harvard University to give a series of lectures, one of which dealt with Sor Juana, and in 1973 he repeated the series. Armed with all the notes he had taken, Paz addressed a series of conferences on Sor Juana's life and works in 1974. The following year he decided to write a book about this famous Mexican nun and intellectual, and the first three parts were completed in 1976. He wrote no more of this book until 1980, when, moved by some remorse, he finished and published the volume in 1981. Enriched by his interpretation of seventeenth-century life in Mexico, to which he dedicates the first three parts of this study before offering his insightful analysis of Sor Juana's great poetry, Paz's book will be hard to surpass. In it Paz finds new meaning in Sor Juana's tragic last years of her life in the convent when Church dignitaries forced her to give up secular writing at the height of her creative period, when she was forty-five years old. Fearful of the Inquisition, she signed a declaration of faith with her own blood. Paz finds that her censors' actions do not diminish the value of her works and that the writer should not fear the consequences of censorship: "Her writings, especially her *Repuesta* and *Primero sueño,* are the best remedy against the moral intoxication which wants to make her end and humiliation an edifying lesson."

Although famous as a writer of lucid prose, Octavio Paz was essentially a poet. By reading his many books of poetry, one can trace the development not only of Hispanic poetry but also of contemporary Western poetry. His work is a *poesía en movimiento,* a constantly changing poetic expression that has served as a model to other poets since 1937. His poetry can be seen as a search for a perfect form for expressing transcendental themes—but without losing its Mexican identity.

As a poet, essayist, and critic of art and literature, Paz was one of the more brilliant Hispanic figures of the twentieth century. His many books, principally those in poetry and in literary and cultural criticism, merited the prizes he received: the Gran Premio Internacional de Poesía in 1963, both the Premio Cervantes and the International Prize for Literature in 1982, the Premio Internacional Menéndes Pelayo in 1987, and the Nobel Prize in Literature in 1990. As a representative of Latin America's thinkers and men of letters, Paz also earned international recognition for his intellectual independence and his defense of the rights of the writer. As a poet he had great sensibility, and as a thinker he had both profound vision and a strong belief in liberty and justice. With his death in 1998, Mexico lost one of its most respected spokesmen.

BOOKS: *Luna silvestre* (Mexico City: Fábula, 1933);

¡No pasarán! (Mexico City: Simbad, 1936);

Raíz del hombre (Mexico City: Simbad, 1937);

Bajo tu clara sombra y otros poemas Ediciones España (Valencia: Españolas, 1937; revised edition, Mexico City: Tierra Nueva, 1941);

Entre la piedra y la flor (Mexico City: Nueva Voz, 1941);

A la orilla del mundo y Primer día; Bajo tu clara sombra; Raíz del hombre; Noche de resurrecciones (Mexico City: ARS, 1942);

Libertad bajo palabra (Mexico City: Tezontle, 1949);

El laberinto de la soledad (Mexico City: Cuadernos Americanos, 1950; revised edition, Mexico City: Fondo de Cultura Económica, 1959); translated by Lysander Kemp as *The Labyrinth of Solitude: Life and Thought in Mexico* (New York: Grove, 1961);

¿Águila o sol? (Mexico City: Fondo de Cultura Económica, 1951); published in a bilingual edition, translated by Eliot Weinberger as *Águila o sol / Eagle or Sun?* (New York: October House, 1970; revised edition, New York: New Directions, 1976);

Semillas para un himno (Mexico City: Fondo de Cultura Económica, 1954);

El arco y la lira: El poema; La revelación poética; Poesía e historia (Mexico City: Fondo de Cultura Económica, 1956); translated by Ruth L. C. Simms as *The Bow and the Lyre: The Poem, Poetic Revelation, and Poetry and History* (Austin: University of Texas Press, 1973);

Piedra de sol (Mexico City: Tezontle, 1957); bilingual editions, translated by Muriel Rukeyser as *Sun Stone / Piedra de sol* (New York: New Directions, 1962); translated by Peter Miller as *Sun-Stone* (Toronto: Contact, 1963); translated by Donald Gardner as *Piedra de sol / The Sun Stone* (York, U.K.: Cosmos, 1969); translated by Weinberger as *Sunstone / Piedra de sol* (New York: New Directions, 1991);

Las peras del olmo (Mexico City: Universidad Nacional Autónoma de México, 1957; revised edition, Barcelona: Seix Barral, 1971);

La estación violenta (Mexico City: Fondo de Cultura Económica, 1958);

Agua y viento (Bogotá: Ediciones Mito, 1959); translated by Weinberger as *Viento, Wind, Agua, Water, Piedra, Stone* (Isla Vista, Cal.: Turkey, 1990);

Tamayo en la pintura mexicana (Mexico City: Universidad Nacional Autónoma de México, Dirección General de Publicaciones, 1959);

Libertad bajo palabra: Obra poética, 1935–1958 (Mexico City: Fondo de Cultura Económica, 1960; revised edition, 1968);

Dos y uno tres (Palma de Mallorca: Eds. Papeles de Son Armadans, 1961);

Salamandra (1958–1961) (Mexico City: Mortiz, 1962);

Selected Poems of Octavio Paz, bilingual edition, translated by Rukeyser (Bloomington: Indiana University Press, 1963);

Viento entero (Delhi: The Caxton Press, 1965);

Cuadrivio (Mexico City: Mortiz, 1965);

Los signos en rotación (Buenos Aires: Sur, 1965);

Puertas al campo (Mexico City: Universidad Nacional Autónoma de México, 1966);

Blanco (Mexico City: Mortiz, 1967); translated by Weinberger as *Blanco* (New York: The Press, 1974);

Corriente alterna (Mexico City: Siglo Veintiuno Editores, 1967); translated by Helen R. Lane as *Alternating Current* (New York: Viking, 1973);

Claude Lévi-Strauss o el festín de Esopo (Mexico City: Mortiz, 1967); translated by J. S. Bernstein and Maxine Bernstein as *Claude Lévi-Strauss: An Introduction* (Ithaca, N.Y.: Cornell University Press, 1970); translation republished as *On Lévi-Strauss* (London: Cape, 1970);

Discos visuales (Mexico City: Ediciones Era, 1968);

Marcel Duchamp (Mexico City: Ediciones Era, 1968); translated by Gardner as *Marcel Duchamp; or, The Castle of Purity* (London: Cape Goliard, 1970);

Ladera este (1962–1968) (Mexico City: Mortiz, 1969);

Conjunciones y disyunciones (Mexico City: Mortiz, 1969); translated by Lane as *Conjunctions and Disjunctions* (New York: Viking, 1974);

La centena (Poemas 1935–1968) (Barcelona: Seix Barral, 1969);

México: La última década (Austin: Institute of Latin American Studies, University of Texas, 1969);

Posdata (Mexico City: Siglo Veintiuno, 1970); translated by Kemp as *The Other Mexico: Critique of the Pyramid* (New York: Grove, 1972);

Topoemas (Mexico City: Era, 1971);

Las cosas en su sitio: Sobre la literatura española del siglo XX, by Paz and Juan Marichal (Mexico City: Finisterre, 1971);

Los signos en rotación y otros ensayos, edited by Carlos Fuentes (Madrid: Alianza Editorial, 1971);

Traducción: literatura y literalidad (Barcelona: Tusquets, 1971);

Vuelta (Mexico City: El Mendrugo, 1971);

Renga, by Paz, Jacques Roubaud, Edoardo Sanguineti, and Charles Tomlinson (Paris: Gallimard, 1971; Mexico City: Mortiz, 1972); translated by Tomlinson as *Renga: A Chain of Poems* (New York: Braziller, 1972);

Apariencia desnuda: La obra de Marcel Duchamp (Mexico City: Era, 1973; enlarged, 1979); translated by Gardner and Rachel Phillips as *Marcel Duchamp: Appearance Stripped Bare* (New York: Viking, 1978);

Early Poems, 1935–1955, translated by Rukeyser and others (New York: New Directions, 1973);

El signo y el garabato (Mexico City: Mortiz, 1973);

Solo a dos voces, by Paz and Julián Ríos (Barcelona: Lumen, 1973);

El mono gramático (Barcelona: Seix Barral, 1974); translated by Lane as *The Monkey Grammarian* (New York: Seaver, 1981);

Los hijos del limo: Del romanticismo a la vanguardia (Barcelona: Seix Barral, 1974; corrected and enlarged, 1981); translated by Phillips as *Children of the Mire: Poetry from Romanticism to the Avant-Garde* (Cambridge, Mass.: Harvard University Press, 1974);

La búsqueda del comienzo: Escritos sobre el surrealismo (Madrid: Fundamentos, 1974);

Teatro de signos / Transparencias (Madrid: Fundamentos, 1974);

Pasado en claro (Mexico City: Fondo de Cultura Económica, 1975; revised edition, 1978);

The Siren and the Seashell, and Other Essays on Poets and Poetry, translated by Kemp and Margaret Sayers Peden (Austin: University of Texas Press, 1976);

Xavier Villaurrutia en persona y en obra (Mexico City: Fondo de Cultura Económica, 1978);

El ogro filantrópico: Historia y política, 1971–1978 (Mexico City: Mortiz, 1978);

In / Mediaciones (Barcelona: Seix Barral, 1979);

A Draft of Shadows, and Other Poems, edited and translated by Weinberger, Elizabeth Bishop, and Mark Strand (New York: New Directions, 1979);

Air Born / Hijos del aire, by Paz and Tomlinson (Mexico City: Pescador, 1979);

Poemas (1935–1975) (Barcelona: Seix Barral, 1979);

Rufino Tamayo, by Paz and Jacques Lassaigne (Barcelona: Ediciones Poligrafia, 1982); translated by Kenneth Lyons (New York: Rizzoli, 1982);

Sor Juana Inés de la Cruz; o, Las trampas de la fe (Barcelona: Seix Barral, 1982); translated by Peden as *Sor Juana; or, The Traps of Faith* (Cambridge, Mass.: Harvard University Press, 1988);

Sombras de obras: Arte y literatura (Barcelona: Seix Barral, 1983);

Tiempo nublado (Barcelona: Seix Barral, 1983); translated by Lane as *One Earth, Four or Five Worlds: Reflections on Contemporary History* (San Diego: Harcourt Brace Jovanovich, 1985);

Hombres en su siglo y otros ensayos (Barcelona: Seix Barral, 1984);

Cuatro chopos / The Four Poplars, bilingual edition, translated by Weinberger (New York: Center for Edition Words, 1985);

The Labyrinth of Solitude; The Other Mexico; Return to the Labyrinth of Solitude; Mexico and the United States; The Philanthropic Ogre, translated by Kemp, Yara Milos, and Rachel Phillips Belash (New York: Grove, 1985; enlarged edition, London & New York: Penguin, 1990);

On Poets and Others, translated by Michael Schmidt (New York: Seaver, 1986; Manchester U.K.: Carcanet, 1987);

Carta de creencia (Mexico City: Ediciones Papeles Privados, 1987);

Arbol adentro (Barcelona: Seix Barral, 1987); translated by Weinberger as *A Tree Within* (New York: New Directions, 1988);

The Collected Poems of Octavio Paz, 1957–1987, edited by Weinberger and translated by Weinberger, Bishop, and others (New York: New Directions, 1987); republished as *The Collected Poems 1957–1987* (Manchester: Carcanet, 1988);

Convergences: Essays on Art and Literature, translated by Lane (San Diego: Harcourt Brace Jovanovich, 1987; London: Bloomsbury, 1987);

Primeras letras, 1931–1943, edited by Enrico Mario Santí (Barcelona: Seix Barral, 1988);

Poesía, mito, revolución (Mexico City: Vuelta, 1989);

Lo mejor de Octavio Paz: El fuego de cada día (Barcelona: Seix Barral, 1989; Mexico City: Fascículos Planeta, 1989);

Hombres en su siglo (Barcelona: Seix Barral, 1990);

Pequeña crónica de grandes días (Mexico City: Fondo de Cultura Económica, 1990);

In Search of the Present / La búsqueda del presente: 1990 Nobel Lecture, bilingual edition, translated by Anthony Stanton (San Diego: Harcourt Brace Jovanovich, 1990);

La otra voz: poesía y fin de siglo (Barcelona: Seix Barral, 1990); republished as *The Other Voice: Essays on Modern Poetry,* translated by Lane (New York: Harcourt Brace Jovanovich, 1991; Manchester: Carcanet, 1992);

Obras completas, 14 volumes (Barcelona: Círculo de Lectores, 1991);

Itinerario (Mexico City: Fondo de Cultura Económica, 1993);

La llama doble: amor y erotismo (Barcelona: Seix Barral, 1993); translated by Lane as *The Double Flame: Love and Eroticism* (New York: Harcourt Brace, 1995);

Essays on Mexican Art, translated by Lane (New York: Harcourt Brace, 1993);

Vislumbres de la India (Barcelona: Seix Barral, 1995); translated by Weinberger as *In Light of India* (New York: Harcourt Brace, 1997);

An Erotic Beyond: Sade, translated by Weinberger (New York: Harcourt Brace, 1998).

PLAY PRODUCTION: *La hija de Rappaccini,* Mexico City, Teatro Caballito, 30 July 1956.

OTHER: *Voces de España: Breve antología de poetas españoles contemporáneos,* edited by Paz (Mexico City: Ediciones Letras de México, 1938);

Laurel: Antología de la poesía moderna en lengua española, edited by Paz and others (Mexico City: Séneca, 1941);

Anthologie de la poésie mexicaine, edited by Paz, translated by Guy Levis Mano (Paris: Editions Nagel-UNESCO, 1952);

Matsuo Basho, *Sendas de Oku,* translated by Paz and E. Hayashiya (Mexico City: UNAM, 1957);

Anthology of Mexican Poetry, introduction by Paz, translation by Samuel Beckett (London: Thomas & Hudson, 1958; Bloomington: Indiana University Press, 1958);

Poesía en movimiento (1925–1966), edited by Paz and others (Mexico City: Siglo XXI, 1966);

William Carlos Williams, *Veinte poemas,* edited and translated, with an introduction, by Paz (Mexico City: Ediciones Era, 1973);

Versiones y diversiones, translated by Paz (Mexico City: Mortiz, 1974);

Xavier Villaurrutia: antología, edited by Paz (Mexico City: Fondo de Cultura Económica, 1980).

The Electronic Text Center and the Electronic Archive of Early American Fiction at the University of Virginia Library

David Seaman and Kendon Stubbs
Alderman Library, University of Virginia

A version of this article was presented by David Seaman and Kendon Stubbs at the Digital Library Workshop, University of Library and Information Studies, Tsukuba Science City, Japan, 5 March 1997.

I: THE ELECTRONIC TEXT CENTER

In 1992 the University of Virginia Library committed space, equipment, and staff to create a center that provides on-line access to commercial, full-text databases; makes equipment available for creating and analyzing electronic text; teaches how to use these new tools and techniques; and directs the development of Standard Generalized Markup Language (SGML) and humanities computing at the university. After seven years of operation, the Electronic Text Center at the University of Virginia continues both to develop its on-line collections and to encourage the use of electronic texts.

HOLDINGS

The Internet-accessible holdings include thousands of texts and related digital images. Some of the holdings at the center are commercially available, and their use is contractually limited to the University of Virginia or to the thirty-nine VIVA (Virtual Library of Virginia) sites. The center has always bought large, commercially available electronic text collections in the form of SGML data files rather than CD-ROMs so that these can be loaded onto a Unix server and users across the Internet may have on-line access to them. Among these items are the following:

The Oxford English Dictionary (25 volumes)
English Poetry Database (4,500 works)
American Poetry Database (1,288 works)
African-American Poetry Database (2,500 poems)

The Patrologia Latina (221 volumes)
The Old English Corpus (3,000 items)
English Verse Drama Database (1,500 titles)
English Prose Drama Database (1,500 titles)
British philosophy: 1600–1900
American Civil War newspapers
The Pennsylvania Gazette

Approximately two thousand other literary, historical, philosophical, and religious materials in various languages also can be accessed by any Internet user; on its Web site the electronic archive currently receives more than one million hits per month from all over the world. The selection of materials available to the public includes many eighteenth- and nineteenth-century English literary and historical works (often with illustrations) and some French, German, Latin, Japanese, Chinese, Cyrillic, and medieval English titles. Among the English language holdings are texts and images taken from the University of Virginia Special Collections, including letters of Thomas Jefferson, Mark Twain material, and nineteenth-century African-American historical documents.

All of the on-line texts are encoded with SGML and are converted automatically "on the fly" to Hypertext Markup Language (HTML) for use through the World Wide Web. The staff of the center tags those texts that it creates or marks up according to the *Text Encoding Initiative Guidelines,* and with increasing frequency the staff works with students and faculty at the University of Virginia and other schools to create new electronic texts and images. A good example of a product of one such collaboration is the *Japanese Text Initiative,* a growing collection of SGML-encoded and searchable Japanese literature prepared by Kendon Stubbs (University of Virginia) and Sachie Noguchi (University of Pittsburgh) and published on the Inter-

Mark Twain in His Times

The Electronic Text Center, University of Virginia

Written and Directed by Stephen Railton,
Department of English, University of Virginia

Produced by David Seaman, Virginia Cope, Lisa Goldberg, Tom Lukas,
Catherine Tousignant and David Gants; Electronic Text Center, University of
Virginia

Filmed almost entirely on location at
the Special Collections Department, University of Virginia

*This interpretive archive, drawn largely from the resources of the Barrett Collection, focuses on how
"Mark Twain" and his works were created and defined, marketed and performed, reviewed and
appreciated. The goal is to allow readers, scholars, students and teachers to see what Mark Twain and
His Times said about each other, in a way that can speak to us today.*
*Contained here are dozens of texts and manuscripts, scores of contemporary reviews and newspaper
articles, hundreds of graphic images, and many different kinds of interactive exhibits. If you'd like help
navigating the site, start with "Piloting Lessons" in "About This Site."*

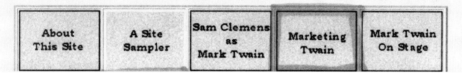

*Home page for Mark Twain documents available through the Electonic Text Center (©1996 by Stephen Railton and The University
of Virginia Library)*

net by the University of Virginia Library Electronic
Text Center.

Faculty and students who use the Electronic Text
Center are advancing from being consumers of on-line
information to being producers of it, as they reshape
and supplement these holdings into clusters of web documents suited to particular purposes. Professor Stephen
Railton's *Mark Twain in His Times,* a tool for teaching the
work of the nineteenth-century American novelist, is a
good example of how faculty is using the electronic
medium.

ACCESS

Because most of the electronic texts in the archive
are available on-line, the center can provide the same
search software for all its collections and can use a web
browser such as Netscape as a common and familiar
interface. The center has developed its own suite of
Common Gateway Interface (CGI) scripts, including
web forms and SGML-to-HTML filters, to allow users
to search and browse the texts. The benefits to the user
are obvious: having been taught to use one database, a

user knows how to search any of the on-line holdings at
the center and thus overcomes the frustrations borne by
having to use CD-ROMs—each disk with a different
interface.

USERS

One principal aim of the center is to build a broad
community of people who use humanities-related electronic resources at the University of Virginia. To this
end the center runs regular training sessions, including
classes on scanning, TEI, HTML, and other aspects of
using and creating electronic texts and images. For
seven years the staff has worked daily with users ranging from first-year undergraduates in composition
classes to graduate students studying Anglo-Saxon literature, American Studies, rabbinical responsa, medieval
French, and other teaching and research subjects.

The center is continuing to build relationships
with university presses, publishers of academic books
and scholarly journals, and other digital libraries that
are developing. The server at the center supports two
journals edited and produced at the University of Vir-

ginia—*The Visual Anthropology Review* and *Essays in History*—and the center has produced searchable e-texts of two works published by the University Press of Virginia: Timothy D. Pyatt's *Guide to African-American Documentary Resources in North Carolina* (1996) and Michael Plunkett's *Afro-American Sources in Virginia: A Guide to Manuscripts* (1995). As part of an ambitious publication program by the Bibliographical Society of the University of Virginia, the center has taken text printed in volumes of *Studies in Bibliography* through fifty years and converted it into SGML files, and these are now distributed on the Internet.

The center has also been successful in attracting grant money to help underwrite the cost of two ambitious projects: *The American Heritage Virtual Archive Project* and *The Electronic Archive of Early American Fiction*. The first grant, made to the universities of Virginia, Duke, Stanford, and California (Berkeley) by the National Endowment for the Humanities (NEH), is to support the coding of thousands of pages of archival finding aids into SGML by using the Encoded Archival Descriptions tags. The second grant is from the Andrew W. Mellon Foundation and is the most ambitious project undertaken to date by the center.

II. EARLY AMERICAN FICTION: 1775–1850

The University of Virginia Library is fortunate to have one of the major collections of rare first editions of American fiction in its Clifton Waller Barrett Library of American Literature, supplemented by the Taylor Collection of Popular American Fiction. These collections include many of the first editions in the two standard bibliographies of American fiction: Lyle Wright's *American Fiction 1774–1850* and the *Bibliography of American Literature* (BAL). *The Electronic Archive of Early American Fiction* will include digital representations of first editions from the special collections at the University of Virginia Library that are listed in these two bibliographies: 420 works in 560 volumes by 81 authors (circa 118,000 pages) from the first seventy-five years of a distinctly American literature.

This period includes masterpieces such as James Fenimore Cooper's *The Last of the Mohicans* (1826), Edgar Allan Poe's *Tales of the Grotesque and Arabesque* (1840), and Nathaniel Hawthorne's *The Scarlet Letter* (1850) as well as many works popular in that time but now forgotten and largely unavailable to teachers, readers, and scholars. *The Electronic Archive of Early American Fiction* will make these works available again and in doing so will illuminate the historical and cultural milieus in which the great works of this period can be read and studied. Moreover, it will ensure that every word of every work can be indexed and searched: it is

possible in an on-line collection to find in seconds every occurrence of a word or concept, and the combination of searchable text and high-resolution color images provides a detailed, flexible view of the material. Three major tasks are required in creating *The Electronic Archive of Early American Fiction*: creating color digital images of every page of the 560 volumes, converting these images to SGML-tagged text, and combining the text and images into a database that students and scholars from the high school to the postgraduate level can use.

POSSIBILITIES

Through high-quality color facsimiles and searchable texts, the World Wide Web makes it possible for many more readers to use these texts. *The Electronic Archive of Early American Fiction* also affords opportunities to study scholarly use of original rare books and of their computer simulacra and to determine how electronic texts of rare books can serve scholars and teachers. A critical part of the project involves assessing the costs and uses of the electronic texts in comparison with those of the original rare books. The staff of the center plans to test the hypothesis that for some uses of rare books, high-quality electronic texts and digital images are adequate substitutes. In order to survey users, the center will put on the World Wide Web a form to collect demographic information on the knowledge, attitudes, and behaviors of those who use American fiction on-line. Questions will elicit information, for example, on how easy the users find it is to use on-line texts in comparison to using original paper texts. Answers to such questions will be compared with data collected in a survey of those who have used the original rare books.

THE PRODUCTION PROCESS: IMAGING

Since one goal of *The Electronic Archive of Early American Fiction* is to test whether some patrons can use digital versions of rare books rather than the original editions, the staff of the center is methodically making images of all parts of every book—the spines, endpapers, front and rear covers, and all pages of the book. For color comparisons involving each book the staff records a test sheet including a ruler and Kodak gray-scale and color strips. From the digital facsimile one can get an idea of the appearance of every part of the book, and with Virtual Reality Modeling Language (VRML) one can see the book in a three-dimensional representation on the screen.

Through the use of high-resolution Phase One digital cameras (5,000 x 7,000 pixels), the page images are being scanned as TIFF files in 24-bit color at a reso-

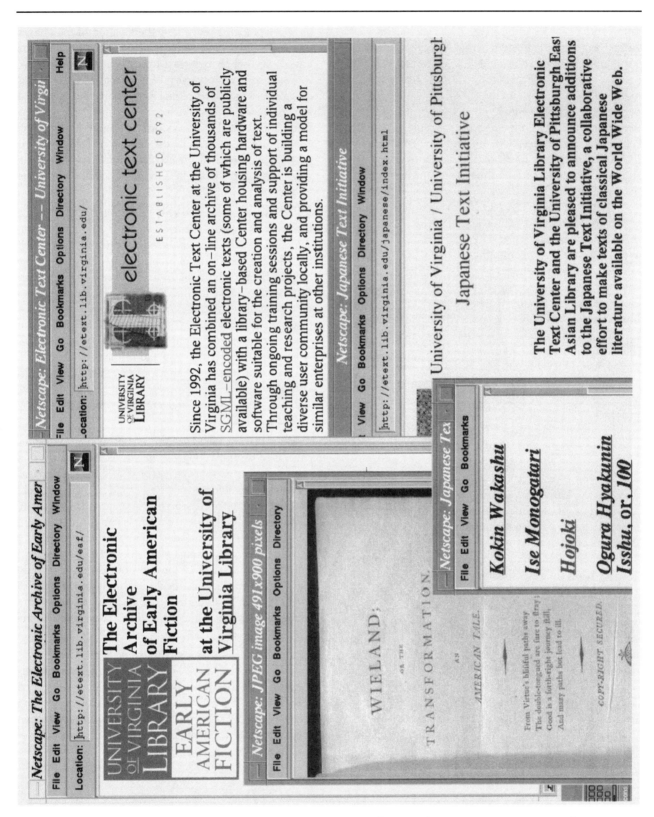

Several Web pages illustrating the range of materials accessible to users of the Electronic Text Center (© 1996 by Stephen Railton and The University of Virginia Library)

lution of circa five hundred dots per inch. Each 220-page book requires ten writable CD-ROMs, each costing $3, to store off-line the 5.5 GB of archival page images. Each TIFF image is also converted to a high-quality and low-quality JPEG derivative for display on the World Wide Web. Although the bulk and the storage costs of these images are significant, the text center decided to capture high-quality color images instead of grayscale or bitonal black-and-white images so that it would not have to make page images of these books again.

These color images are proving to be popular with early users, who value the sense of the original that such images provide. They are striking on screen and allow users to enlarge them a good degree; early tests made of these images on 1,400-dot-per-inch inkjet color printers are stunning. In order to recover some of the expenses of creating these e-texts–and to provide funds for creating additional e-texts, probably of American fiction published after 1850–the center has contracted to publish *The Electronic Archive of Early American Fiction* on CD-ROM and to make this collection available on-line as part of the Literature Online (LION) Web service that the publisher, Chadwyck-Healey Inc., provides.

THE PRODUCTION PROCESS: SGML TEXTS

A commercial service uses the page images produced at the University of Virginia as the source for the text it transcribes. This method is much cheaper and faster than it would be for the text center to transcribe the documents because of both the nature of the source material and its bulk. Optical character recognition (OCR) works well with modern typefaces and often accords reasonably well with late nineteenth-century printed matter, but it works less effectively with earlier materials. Printing flaws such as uneven inking and broken type–typical features of material printed before the late nineteenth century–disrupt the integrity of the letter form and thereby frustrate the ability of the software to recognize letters.

As a text is created, SGML tagging is added to record physical and structural characteristics such as title-page layouts, pagination, paragraphs, verse lines, italics, and diacritical marks. Images from each page of

the electronic text must have the location of the images that correspond to them marked so that the two can be linked together in hypertext form. When the works are returned to the University of Virginia, the text center completes a standard bibliographical header to record all the details of the print source and the electronic version and to include keyword information that will enable users to search the items. A standardized description is created for each pictorial illustration in a work, and the final text is indexed and put on the World Wide Web.

Though the initial cost of creating an e-text of a rare book is high, that e-text can be distributed for considerably more uses than the book, and the cost of each use of the e-text is thus much lower than that of the book. The availability of an on-line version of *The Scarlet Letter* may make it unnecessary for library patrons to secure funding for travel to the University of Virginia to see the first edition of *The Scarlet Letter,* and having an on-line edition may accommodate many other users for whom the cost of accessing the original text might be too high. It is significant that 70 percent of the books to be put on-line in *The Electronic Archive of Early American Fiction* are not in print and are available in only a few university libraries.

In the next four years the staff of the text center expects to see the same tremendous pace of change that has marked its first seven years as a library service, as emerging technologies such as VRML, image searching, and Internet-wide search tools become increasingly useful to the humanities scholar. Users of the text center become more sophisticated in their ambitions and needs with each passing semester, and the amount of full-text and image data coming from commercial publishers is growing dramatically. Moreover, the abilities of the center to undertake the creation of large data projects has increased along with its recognition of the benefits of doing so.

The needs that the Electronic Text Center was founded to meet have continued throughout all this growth. The data must be maintained in standardized forms such as SGML that can survive in a time of rapid change, and the role and facilities of the library remain central to the development and long-term viability of on-line services.

Fellowship of Southern Writers

George Garrett
The University of Virginia

The idea of the Fellowship came from the late Cleanth Brooks, who had been thinking of the need for some sort of organization aimed at encouraging Southern literature in general and, especially, offering some kind of formal recognition to young Southern writers. In 1987 while Brooks was visiting Chapel Hill, he talked about the idea at some length with scholar Louis D. Rubin Jr., and together they decided to begin. On 18 September 1987 Brooks sent out a letter to a varied group of Southern writers, saying: "For some time several of us have been discussing the need for, and the possibility of founding, a society of fellowship of Southern writers." The writers were invited "to meet and establish an organization to encourage and recognize distinction in Southern writing." The meeting was scheduled for and held on 30–31 October in Chattanooga.

Why Chattanooga? First of all, because it already had a highly successful Biennial Conference on Southern Literature, created by the Arts & Education Council there, one that had already been built up the widespread support of the local community. Rubin, who, together with George Core, editor of *The Sewanee Review,* joined Brooks in arranging the first meeting, says that Chattanooga and its conference seemed especially appropriate because of "the fact that it was a civic and not an academic undertaking and equally that it was not identified with any one school group or coterie or a particular kind of Southern writing." This latter goal, literary neutrality, was more important than one might have imagined. "The two universities most active in contemporary Southern letters, Vanderbilt University and the University of North Carolina at Chapel Hill, were good possibilities for a home. But each of them was associated with a particular group of writers, and we did not want the Fellowship to fall under the aegis–no matter how benevolent–of any one group." On 22 June, Rubin, Brooks, and Core met with Chattanooga community leaders at the offices of the Lyndhurst Foundation, from whom the Fellowship received both an organizational grant and, later, a development grant. The organizational meeting of the Fellowship took place in October 1987. Those present included Brooks, Fred Chappell, Core, Shelby Foote, George Garrett, Blyden Jackson, Andrew Lytle, Lewis P. Simpson, Elizabeth Spencer, Walter Sullivan, C. Vann Woodward, and Rubin.

Not present at the meeting but already committed to the support of the Fellowship were Eudora Welty, Robert Penn Warren, Peter Taylor, Walker Percy, Ernest J. Gaines, and John Hope Franklin. Said Rubin: "We wanted to encourage and stimulate good writing in the South. While we didn't think of our group as competing with any of the national academies and institutes–to which many of our group already belonged–we wanted the work of young Southern authors to be read and evaluated and recognized by other Southern writers for whom the region and the subject matter would not seem 'quaint' or 'exotic.' But at the same time we wanted to recognize and encourage only work of the highest quality, free from insularity and localism. And we wanted our members to include not only novelists, poets, dramatists and critics, but writers of history and other genres whose work displayed literary excellence." Brooks was chosen to be the first chancellor of the Fellowship; Rubin was named chairman of the executive committee; Core was chosen to be secretary-treasurer; and Garrett became vice chancellor. In addition to the eighteen writers already committed, James Dickey, Ralph Ellison, Reynolds Price, and William Styron joined the others as founding members of the Fellowship.

At the outset the Fellowship agreed to hold a meeting and an awards convocation in conjunction with the regular Biennial Chattanooga Conference on Southern Literature. The University of Tennessee at Chattanooga offered to house the archives of the Fellowship at the Lupton Library. The Fellowship set out to secure endowments from which prizes would be awarded to younger Southern writers. One form of recognition of distinction would be membership in the Fellowship, and the highest award, given for a lifetime of achievement in letters, would be a medal that the original membership, without consulting its first chancellor, named the Cleanth Brooks Medal.

Soon the Fellowship was incorporated under the law. It received a development grant from the Lyndhurst Foundation to cover operating expenses and such incidental costs as the casting of bronze medallions for the individual Fellows. Photographer Curt Richter was commissioned to photograph each Fellow, and the photographs are on display in the Fellowship's Archive Room, renamed in 1997

The Fellowship of Southern Writers, 1997: Sally Robinson, William Hoffman, Madison Jones, Fred Chappell, Shelby Foote, Richard Bausch, Ernest J. Gaines, Dave Smith, Wendell Berry, John Hope Franklin, Clyde Edgerton, Louis D. Rubin Jr.; seated, Ellen Douglas, Walter Sullivan, Elizabeth Spencer, George Garrett, Doris Betts, George Core, C. Eric Lincoln (photograph courtesy of George Garrett)

the Arlie Herron Room in honor of the professor of Southern literature at the University of Tennessee at Chattanooga. In the months prior to the first full-scale meeting and convocation of the Fellowship, endowments for the various awards were secured. The Hillsdale Foundation created the Hillsdale Prize for Fiction. The James G. Hanes Foundation offered a Hanes Prize in Poetry. Chubb Life supported the Robert Penn Warren Award in Fiction, and the Bryan Family Foundation financed an award in drama. The Fellows contributed funds for an award in nonfiction and for the Fellowship's New Writing Award.

After two terms of two years as chancellor, Brooks was followed in turn by Rubin, Garrett, and Doris Betts. Spencer is now vice chancellor. The full membership of the Fellowship now includes A. R. Ammons, James Applewhite, Richard Bausch, Wendell Berry, Betts, Chappell, Core, Ellen Douglas, Clyde Edgerton, Horton Foote, Shelby Foote, Franklin, Gaines, Garrett, Gail Godwin, William Hoffman, Jackson, Madison Jones, Donald Justice, C. Eric Lincoln, Romulus Linney, Marsha Norman, Price, Rubin, Mary Lee Settle, Simpson, Dave Smith, Lee Smith, Spencer, Styron, Sullivan, Welty, Woodward, and Charles Wright. In the decade since its beginning some Fellows have died: Brooks, Dickey, Ellison, Lytle, Percy, Monroe K. Spears, Taylor, and Warren.

Beginning with the first formal convocation of the Fellowship in 1989, awards have been presented to the following Southern writers: Hillsdale Prize for Fiction–Ellen Douglas (1989), Richard Bausch (1991), Josephine Humphreys (1993), William Hoffman (1995), Lewis Nordan (1997), Bobbie Ann Mason (1999); Hanes Prize for Poetry–Kelly Cherry (1989), Robert Morgan (1991), Ellen Bryant

Voigt (1993), Andrew Hudgens (1995), Yusef Komunyakaa (1997), T. R. Hummer (1999); Chubb Award for Fiction in Honor of Robert Penn Warren–Lee Smith (1991), Cormac McCarthy (1993), Madison Smartt Bell (1995), Allen Wier (1997), Barry Hannah (1999); Bryan Family Foundation Award for Drama–Jim Grimsley (1991), Pearl Cleage (1995), Naomi Wallace (1997), Margaret Edson (1999); Fellowship Award for Non-Fiction–Samuel F. Pickering Jr. (1991), John Shelton Reed (1995), Bailey White (1997), James Kibler (1999); Fellowships New Writing Award–William Henry Lewis (1997), Michael Knight (1999); Special Achievement Award–Andrew Lytle (1995), James Still (1997); James Still Award–Charles Frazier (1999); Cleanth Brooks Medal for Distinguished Achievement in Southern Letters–John Hope Franklin (1989), Eudora Welty (1991), C. Vann Woodward (1993), Lewis P. Simpson (1995), Louis D. Rubin Jr. (1997), and Shelby Foote (1999).

In addition to their biennial meeting and the public awards convocation, the Fellows are active participants in the Chattanooga Conference on Southern Literature. They join in panel discussions, readings, and lectures, and the keynote address for the conference is given by a member of the Fellowship. In 1997 the speaker was novelist Ernest J. Gaines. Prizewinners visit local and area high schools and meet with students.

The Fellowship has now been in existence and active for ten years. "We are beginning our second decade in excellent shape," Rubin says. "We are now firmly linked to the Chattanooga Conference and we have high hopes that we can play an ever more active part in recognizing and honoring achievement and encouraging excellence in Southern letters."

The Year in Texas Literature

Paul Ruffin
The Texas Review

Novelist Clay Reynolds, who has probably followed the evolution of Texas literature as closely as anyone, doesn't feel so good these days about the state of Texas letters. When he penned his guardedly optimistic essay "Texas Fiction in the Nineties" about ten years ago, our writers were on a roll. "For nearly ten years," he says, "Texas writers crawled over the Lone Star landscape like a plague of scorpions, searching under every cactus, rock, and palmetto for a story, a character, an event, a happening, a legend, a myth, almost anything that could be cobbled into a song, story, or poem. When 'telling it like it was' became passé, writers began telling it like it should have been, altering history and fact to fit sensibilities more in tune with the nonsmoking section, low-fat, and bottled water generation."

Reynolds argues that we wore ourselves out—"instead of beating our own drum, we were beating a dead horse"–that we "have sat idly by and watched the quality of what we were doing slip right on by us. We allowed our standards to slide in order to accommodate lesser lights that never had the potential for either illumination or warmth. Sadly, we responded to a national mood, a national temper, one informed by a narrowness of mind and humorlessness of spirit."

He blames our decline on many influences, not the least of which were the creeping tentacles of political correctness and the infusion of "foreign" elements that "arrived with Birkenstocks and cable knit, Range Rovers and gas-powered log fireplaces, low-fat salad dressings and bagels, Ben and Jerry's ice cream and Coors beer." And, he continues, "we've claimed them as our own, some even before their carpetbags were fully unpacked."

"The lode's played out," says Reynolds.

And yet, and yet. . . . Hope does spring eternal, as 1998 has shown, with the venerable Texas luminaries Larry McMurtry, Cormac McCarthy, and Elmer Kelton managing at least a book a year, always popular and always Texan in focus. The Great Triumvirate recently scored heavily with sequels.

One could argue the relative importance of McMurtry in American literature, but only a fool would deny his output or his significance in Texas literature. None of our recent writers have devoted so much effort to bringing to life legendary Old West figures such as Calamity Jane and Billy the Kid. In 1998 his *Crazy Horse* lengthens the list with a biographical treatment of the enigmatic Sioux chief who joined forces with Sitting Bull to defeat General Armstrong Custer at the Little Bighorn. Only 160 pages, it is a relatively thin book for McMurtry, but it is a valuable contribution to American history.

In 1998 Pocket Books brought out a paperback version of McMurtry's *Comanche Moon* (published in hardback in 1997), putting us back in the saddle again with Augustus McCrae and Woodrow Call, now in their last years of Indian fighting. It is a powerfully long (nearly a thousand pages) and sometimes tedious book, but for fans of Augustus and Woodrow, it is worth the ride. This book, by the way, won a Spur award: Best Novel of the West—not exactly a Pulitzer here, but certainly prestigious.

A bit less well known nationally than McMurtry, but with a reputation in Texas of equal luster (and winner of more Spur awards than I have room to list), Elmer Kelton continued his line of Westerns (over forty books in all) with the reprint paperback release of *Hot Iron*, published by Forge. Set in the Texas Panhandle with the usual mix of cowboys and rustlers and cattle, this is one of Kelton's least appealing books, as sales indicate. *The Smiling Country,* though, published by Forge in 1998, brings back Hewey Calloway, a character in Kelton's *Good Old Boys,* a highly successful book and popular movie. Calloway is facing an all too typical dilemma: an aging cowboy tries to come to terms with the modern world—well, as modern as 1910 Texas. As he grows long in the tooth, he looks back with regret and forward with fear, as most men do if they live long enough. Having been a fan of Elmer's for a long time, I must say that he is losing nothing of his edge. *The Smiling Country* is perhaps the best book he has written. If he could just win the Pulitzer, my bet is that Kelton would bump McMurtry into the shadows. In many respects he

Dust jacket for a biography of the Sioux chief whose life continues to provoke differing opinions from historians of the American West

is the better writer, and he knows when a story should end.

The sizzlingly popular Cormac McCarthy completed his Border Trilogy in 1998 with the publication of *Cities of the Plain: A Novel* (as if we expected a play), which brings together John Grady Cole (*All the Pretty Horses*) and Billy Parham (*The Crossing*) in the early 1950s on a ranch in New Mexico. It's the aging cowboys story again, only this time told by a writer whose prose is at times the best I've read since Faulkner. Readers approaching *Cities of the Plain* with the notion that they are going to be entertained by breathless, nonstop violence will come away disappointed, because this is a book more of reflection and dialogue, a far cry from the bloody trails of the earlier books. (There's action enough, mind you.) Universally acknowledged the least impressive of the Trilogy, *Cities of the Plain* is nonetheless a powerful book, one that completes an enduring epic that American literature may never witness the likes of again.

Collectively these three men are keeping Texas on the literary map and probably will for some time to come. It remains to be seen whether either of them will ever be taught in the universities as major figures in American literature—the work of all three is the focus of most courses in Southwestern or Texas literature presently—but given the burgeoning scholarship on McCarthy, the bet is that he stands a good chance.

There was a fair amount of fiction activity among the lesser lights in Texas fiction during 1998. A. C. Greene, whose name anyone familiar with Texas literature will immediately recognize, published his first novel in 1998; at 150 pages *They Are Ruining Ibiza* (University of North Texas Press) may be more accurately described as a novella. Clay Reynolds calls the book "superb, stunning. . . . There is a Hemingwayesque quality about it; it's haunting and marvelously in tune with the present time." Author of over twenty books, Greene, formerly book editor and columnist for the *Dallas Times-Herald,* currently writes a column for the *Dallas Morning News.*

Naemm Murr (University of Houston) received positive reviews for *The Boy,* a new novel from Houghton Mifflin. In *The New York Times Book Review* Margot Livesey says, "While reading *The Boy,* I intently turned the pages, carried along by Murr's dark energy, his sharply intelligent prose, his genius for the unexpected, his keen sense of atmosphere," and Hans Johnson in *The Washington Post World* suggests that Murr's language "may cast a spell over some readers." *Kirkus* was not so kind: "Technically a capable debut, though the unreality both of its Mephistophelean central figure and of his beneficiaries and victims makes it, finally, unconvincing." And it certainly isn't Texas literature.

C. W. Smith's *Understanding Women* (Texas Christian University Press) is a wonderfully written initiation story of a boy's coming to awareness of the mysteries of the female body during the mid 1950s, when the only way most kids under seventeen discovered women was through secretive glimpses of mothers, sisters, or cousins or through studying the lingerie section of the Sears catalogue and imagining what was under those bastion-like corsets and brassieres. John Nichols (*Milagro Beanfield War*) calls it a "loving and courageous novel, rich in humor, savvy, sex and a social conscience. There's a sweet sorrow in it like *Tender Mercies,* and a wonderful adolescent's yearning that shapes the prose, helping it to soar." If this book, pretty hefty at 400 pages, doesn't score well, it won't be Smith's fault: *Understanding Women* is a fine examination of a young male's slow (and very memorable) discovery of the mysteries of the female. You're not likely to get a better spread of Tex-Sex.

El Camino Del Rio, Jim Sanderson's first novel, won the University of New Mexico Press 1997 [Frank] Waters Award. Marilyn Stasio of *The New York Times Book Review* calls this a "lean and lyrical first novel," and in a *Washington Post Book World* review Paul Skenazy writes, "Sanderson makes the gritty, thankless landscape of the border come alive, from the relentless heat to the failed hopes." This story of a Texas Border Patrol agent is a fine first novel for Sanderson, who teaches English at Lamar University.

Rolando Hinojosa's *Ask a Policeman* is likewise set on the Mexican border, where Rafe Buenrostro, a Texas policeman, joins forces with Mexican police to deal with super villain Lee Gomez. This novel, released by Arte Publico Press in June, has enjoyed brisk sales.

A Literary Guild and Mystery Guild selection, *All the Dead Lie Down* is sure to do nothing but enhance Mary Willis Walker's reputation—she has won six mystery-writer awards for her last three novels: *Zero at the Bone, The Red Scream,* and *Under the Beetle's Cellar.* Walker is already regarded as one of the state's leading mystery writers.

Grolier published two children's books by Judy Alter this year: *The Santa Fe Trail* and *Cissie Palmer.* Alter, who directs TCU Press, has been a highly prolific fiction writer over the years, and she writes well for all ages. Joan Lowery Nixon added two more juvenile books to her canon in 1998 with *Lucy's Wish* and *Will's Choice,* both published by Bantam/Doubleday/Dell; these two books are the first of her Orphan Train Children Series.

There was a dearth of short-story collections by Texans in 1998. One enjoying widespread attention and impressive sales is Peter LaSalle's *Hockey Sur Glace,* published in paperback (after its 1996 introduction in cloth) by Breakaway Books in August. This unique blend of seven short stories and four poems, written in what *Kirkus* refers to as "elegantly poetic prose," bridges the gap between sports and literature, doing for hockey what W. P. Kinsella and Paul Hemphill have done for baseball. The book has earned positive responses from all quarters, from *The Village Voice Literary Supplement* to *Sports Illustrated.* It has absolutely nothing to do with Texas, though.

Taking advantage of the continued popularity of the genre, Texans published many significant memoirs in 1998. The thinnest of them, one of the best-selling of the lot, and arguably the most memorable is by Texas high school English teacher Ron Rozelle, whose *Into That Good Night* was an across-the-transom miracle book for Farrar, Straus, and Giroux. Alternating chapters chronicle Rozelle's childhood in the small town of Oakwood, Texas, and the experience of watching his father suffer an agonizing decline from Alzheimer's. GraceAnne

DeCandido writes of *Into That Good Night* in *Booklist*: "Like a stone washed smooth by the sea, Rozelle's language glows in the light and feels good in the hand"; a reviewer in *Publishers Weekly* observes, "Rozelle splices together two eras in a potentially tricky structure that ultimately yields a spare, beautifully written memoir. . . ." This little book is Rozelle's first, though he has a couple of others in the works.

Ballantine brought out Pat Mora's *House of Houses* in paperback this year. Unlike the conventional memoir, *House of Houses* uses the narrative structure of a house (in El Paso) through which the generations of her family, dead and living, move and tell their stories, which Mora refers to as "recipes for living." *Kirkus* calls it an "ingenious structure" and praises Mora's prose style as "a language deftly mingling the natural cadences of speech and precise, poetic imagery."

In his new book from TCU Press, *In Jewish Texas,* Stanley Ely traces his Jewish ancestry from the turn of the century, when his family arrived in Galveston, to his expatriation to New York, where he could live more comfortably with his homosexuality, which had driven a deep wedge between him and his family. *Library Journal* calls it a "charming and honest memoir," and *Booklist* refers to it as a "fascinating saga."

The University of North Texas recently reissued A. C. Greene's *A Personal Country,* the story of his childhood in West Texas. *The New Yorker* refers to it as "a book that has strength, character, and personality." It is yet another fine publication by one of the major figures in Texas literature.

Garbrielle Fraser Hale, who runs Winedale Publishing, released in September Laura Furman's *Ordinary Paradise,* only the second book published by the press. The first, husband Leon Hale's *Home Spun,* was quite well received, especially in the Houston area, where Hale writes a column for the *Houston Chronicle.* Like Rozelle, Furman deals with the loss of a parent and the emotional stress of disease in her memoir, though apparently not quite so successfully. In *Booklist* DeCandido says of the book, "Some of the vignettes along the way . . . are a bit too small, or recounted too narrowly, to resonate widely," and from *Kirkus*: "May be of interest to others who've lost loved ones to this disease [ovarian cancer], but too prosaic in the telling to sustain most readers' engagement." Though Furman teaches at the University of Texas, there's not much Texas here.

Jim Sanderson's *A West Texas Soapbox* (Texas A & M University Press) is a series of "darkly humorous essays" (as described by the publisher). Sales are weak, though, and this book is not likely to add much impetus to Sanderson's reputation, which seems to be well on the rise since the publication of his book of stories

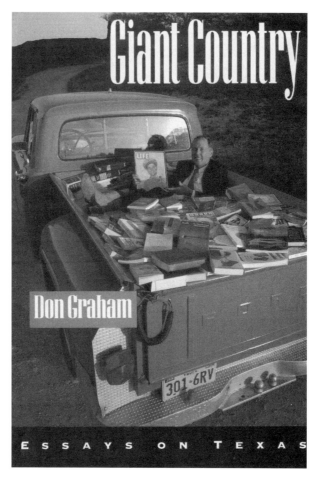

Dust jacket for the collection of essays about the author's fellow Texas writers

Semi-Private Rooms, which won the 1992 Kenneth Patchen Prize, and *El Camino Del Rio*.

Many other prose works, neither fiction nor memoir, deserve mention here. Mike Cox, whose *Texas Ranger Tales: Stories That Need Telling* appeared in 1997 from Republic of Texas Press (not quite what it sounds like) followed up in 1998 with *Texas Ranger Tales II*, also from RTP, and *Stand-Off in Texas* (Eakin Press). This last book covers three recent exciting events in Texas history: the Branch Davidian fiasco at Waco, the killing spree by a lone gunman at Luby's Cafeteria in Killeen, and the standoff with members of the Republic of Texas (what it sounds like). Cox is head of media relations for the Texas Rangers and the Texas Department of Public Safety.

In August, Texas A & M University Press released an unusual book by Deborah Douglas called *Stirring Prose: Cooking with Texas Authors,* in which she blends essays, memoirs, and recipes by such well-known Texas writers as Liz Carpenter, Molly Ivins, Kinky Friedman, and Clay Reynolds. It's doing quite well on the market.

A. C. Greene pops up in this category too, with his *Sketches from the Five States of Texas* (Texas A & M University Press), a delightful and insightful introduction to five clearly distinctive areas of the state. Most of this book is taken from columns Greene wrote for the *Dallas Morning News*. One reviewer has written, "They [these pieces] represent A. C. Greene at his best and most engaging." That's saying a lot, given the literature this man has produced in his lifetime.

Dale Walker's *The Boys of '98: Theodore Roosevelt and the Rough Riders,* published by Forge in May, just might be the best treatment of the Battle of San Juan Hill in existence. *Kirkus* calls it a "lively and carefully detailed narrative." Walker does a fine job of blending fact and narrative, the way a good history teacher does. Readers will find the interviews with surviving Rough Riders especially interesting.

"If you like boots, brawls and drawls, you're going to love this book," Laura Bush, wife of Texas Governor George W. Bush, says of Don Graham's *Giant Country,* published in April by TCU Press, who's doing more than any other press in the nation to keep Texas literature alive and well. A compilation of essays written by Graham over the past twenty years or so, *Giant Country* is a humorous, though essentially accurate, treatment of major Texas writers (Dobie, Webb, Bedichek, Porter, Perry, Graves, and McMurtry) and an introduction to one of the state's finest minds. Readers will be especially entertained by the interview Graham conducts with himself at the beginning of the book and the essay titled "Anything for Larry," in which he calculates how much money he has made for McMurtry over the years and what he himself has enjoyed in "pilot-fish" earnings in the process (one entry reading *1974: "Is Dallas Burning? Notes on Recent Texas Writing," Texas Historical Association, Waco, $00. Net loss: $250 air fare, $200 hotel, $100 bar bill, fine for drunk & disorderly conduct, $75*). Graham, J. Frank Dobie Regents Professor of American and English Literature at the University of Texas, is also the author of *Cowboys and Cadillacs: How Hollywood Looks at Texas, No Name on the Bullet: A Biography of Audie Murphy,* and *Texas, a Literary Portrait.*

Tom Pilkington's *State of Mind: Texas Literature & Culture* (Texas A & M Press) is a thorough treatment of the evolution of Texas literature from its origins (he goes back as far as Cabeza de Vaca) through current superstars McMurtry and McCarthy. This series of highly intelligent essays treats the definition and distinctive characteristics of the Texas writer and suggests where the state may be headed in literature. I was fortunate enough to have been one of the manuscript readers for *State of Mind* (I gave it an enthusiastic endorsement), and I say fervently that for anyone interested in Texas literature the book is a must.

The year 1998 was a good one for Texas poets. The perennial Walt McDonald's sixteenth collection of poems, *Blessings the Body Gave,* won the Ohio State University Press/*The Journal* Award. Vintage McDonald, these poems deal with war and family and the Southwestern landscape those of us familiar with his work so delight in. It is quite likely that McDonald, who has won a host of prestigious awards for his work, will ultimately be the most productive poet of our generation.

Moreover, it will be said of him that he was the first major American poet in a long time to bring poetry back to the level of the general reader through his choice of subject matter and theme, clarity of vision, and excellence of craft. McDonald's poetry puts to shame most of the effete, convoluted collections being released today.

The University of Houston poets certainly scored well in 1998, with books by Mark Doty (*Sweet Dreams,* Harper), Adam Zagajewski (*Mysticism for Beginners,* Farrar, Straus and Giroux), Tony Diaz (*The Aztec Love God,* Black Ice Books), Patty Seyburn (*Diasporadic,* Helicon Nine Editions), and Edward Hirsch (*On Love,* Knopf), recent recipient of a MacArthur Fellowship. Significant figures though they be in American poetry, these poets actually have little to do with Texas literature.

Naomi Shihab Nye, one of the most recognizable names in Texas poetry, had a new collection out in 1998, *Fuel* (BOA Editions). This attractive book, fairly hefty at 136 pages, has garnered a few scattered reviews. "Bill's Beans," Nye's tribute to mentor William Stafford, is my favorite of these poems, perhaps because I too fell under his spell. "We'll thank him forever for our breath," she writes.

One of the state's brightest rising stars in poetry, Michael Lieberman, Chair of Pathology at the Baylor College of Medicine in Houston, was a bit late breaking onto the scene. His first full-length book, *A History of the Sweetness of the World,* won the 1995 *Texas Review* Southern and Southwestern Poetry Breakthrough competition and enjoyed very positive reviews across the country. His newest collection, *Sojourn at Elmhurst,* recently released by New Rivers Press, is likewise being well received. Lieberman's future looks very bright indeed.

In spite of Clay Reynolds's bleak assessment, Texas literature appears for the moment not to be losing its identity, not to be sliding into oblivion. Tom Pilkington cautions at the end of *State of Mind,* though: "Thus the future of literature in Texas appears bright. The future of Texas literature . . . is somewhat less certain."

Letter from Japan

Kiyohiko Tsuboi
Kobe Women's University, Seto College

and

Nobuko Tsuboi
Tsuyama Higashi High School

FICTION

In the past decade or so the interest that readers had held for Japanese fiction seems to be declining, as these readers have shifted their interest from literature that examines serious social and spiritual problems to light, popular writing. Although the Nobel Prize was awarded to Kenzaburo Oe years ago and thousands of copies of Haruki Murakami's *Norwegian Wood* (1962) are still being sold, writers are paying attention more to a present society full of turmoil and irresponsible people than to what critics have called the interior life.

Because of recent moral deterioration in Japan, some young girls engage in *enjo-kosai*–literally, "financial-aid friendship," in which high-school girls receive monetary aid from middle-aged friends for dating or prostituting for them–and boys commit violent crimes without cause. In 1997 a junior-high student in Kobe killed a twelve-year-old handicapped boy, cut off his head, and hung it on the school gate. Many such crimes by *kireru* or "conscience-snapped" boys and girls using knives and other weapons have occurred.

Japanese adults do not understand that the childhood that their children are experiencing differs from that which those adults recall having, and the adults avoid the task of understanding their children. Some writers, however, think that these children are different from ordinary, respectable citizens and try hard to write about them. In June 1996 Miri Yu published "Boys Club," in which she examines the violence that contemporary young people display: threatened by other delinquent bullies, a group of boys oppressed by strict curfews and extra studies after school suddenly attacks a girl whom they see at a local station. Yu reveals the current social milieu that encourages young people to act violently.

Ryu Murakami's documentary novel *Love and Pop* (1996) explores *enjo-kosai*. A sixteen-year-old girl goes shopping at Shibuya, a popular entertainment site in Tokyo, with three other girls. She finds a jewel that she likes very much, but, being short of money, she and the other girls befriend a middle-aged man and go to a karaoke singing spot. Although the four girls together have been given enough money to buy the jewel that the sixteen-year-old wants, she is willing to take only her share–and she tries to earn the rest of the amount she needs by selling her body. Murakami does not dictate a lesson but simply tries to understand the girl by showing how the individual's moral choices are shaped by social influences.

In 1997 Murakami wrote *In the Misosoup,* a newspaper serial published at the time the twelve-year-old boy was killed in Kobe. In this serial Frank, an American whose frontal lobe is supposed to have been surgically removed, visits a red-light district and massacres men at a "match-making pub" in Shinjuku, Tokyo. Frank claims that a child has no more of a motive to commit murder than it has to get lost, and Murakami has commented that in creating this character's confession at the end of the novel, he was writing about the massacre Frank commits when the real murder occurred in Kobe. Murakami had to struggle with his moral aversion in writing about Frank's desire to kill.

POETRY

More people are showing interest in composing tanka and haiku, traditional short poems, in recent decades. There is no way to count these enthusiasts, but some guess that perhaps one million are interested in tanka and an equal or greater number in haiku. Hundreds of professional poets and their many disciples write poems, read and criticize the work of each other, and publish their work in magazines and anthologies. Newspapers carry columns of poems, and broadcasts of tanka and haiku programs appear almost weekly on television.

Tanka

The early Japanese poems are found in *Kojiki* (Record of Ancient Matters, 719), *Nihon shoki* (Chronicles of Japan, 720) and *Man'yoshu* (Collection of Ten Thousand Leaves), a late eighth-century anthology. The oldest poems show few regular meters, but subsequent poems have five and seven syllables per line. As the Japanese language has no stresses, meter depends on the number of syllables per line, and the pattern of alternating five- and seven-syllable lines sounds as natural to Japanese ears as the pentameter line does to English. From the mid seventh century the tanka, which in its classical form takes its subject matter from nature, appears to have been dominant, but until the middle of the eighth century courtiers ended the *choka* (long poem), consisting of an indefinite number of pairs of five- and seven-syllable lines, with tanka consisting of five lines in a syllable pattern of 5–7–5–7–7. Readers praised the beauty and elegance of these courtiers' works most highly, but the formal conventions prevented poets from using even natural images freely. For instance, in the case of insects only the cicada and the cricket can be employed—not the butterfly, the bee, or the firefly—because contemporary Japanese appreciate the sounds, rather than the shapes, of insects. Thus tanka poets concentrated on a limited number of subjects—primarily on the beauty of nature, seasonal changes, and human affairs (marriage celebrations, separations, grief, and love)—and avoided subjects such as war, physical suffering, death, and all that is dark and ugly.

Following *Man'yoshu,* the next major collection of tanka is the *Kokin wakashu* (Collection from Ancient and Modern Times, 905), the first of twenty-one imperial anthologies. These collections varied in size and quality, but each was considered the most important literary achievement of that day. The tanka of *Kokin wakashu* were much influenced by the mannered elegance and conceits of classical Chinese poetry but also display a strong native Japanese poetics. In ancient Japan courtiers and intellectuals read and wrote Chinese and tried to follow the style of Chinese classics in composing sophisticated poems, while women wrote Japanese tanka. As writers could express their own emotions better in vernacular Japanese, tanka gradually became popular even among males.

In the eighth imperial anthology, *Shin kokin wakashu* (New Collection from Ancient and Modern Times, 1205), poets used association to structure their works. Adjacent poems were linked by similar images and common allusions to ancient poetry, and in the anthology all the poems of the major divisions, such as those devoted to each season or to love, were arranged on the basis of the appearance of seasonal changes or the progress of a love relationship. The last imperial anthology, *Shin shoku kokin wakashu* (New Collection from Ancient and Modern Times, Continued), was completed in 1439.

Following *Shin kokin wakashu,* imperial anthologies displayed an increasingly sterile style with respect to the traditions of the Heian period (794–1192), but by the Edo period (1600–1868) the center of tanka composition had passed gradually from the court to warriors, merchants, and commoners. Early in the Meiji period (1867–1912) the influential poet-critics Tekkan Yosano and Shiki Masaoka called for a break with the elegant past of the courtiers' tradition and named their poetry of thirty-one syllables tanka rather than *waka* (Japanese poems):

> ka me ni sa su
> fu ji no ha na bu sa
> ha na ta re te
> ya ma hi no to ko ni
> ha ru ku re n to su

> [With tassels of wisteria flower
> Hanging and falling down
> from a big vase
> In my sick bed
> I can see the spring is coming to the end]

> —Shiki Masaoka.

In 1899 Tekkan founded the Shinshisha (New Poetry Society) and in 1900 began publishing *Myojo* (Bright Star), a literary magazine. One of the leading contributors was his wife, Akiko Yosano, whose passionate lyricism brought a new romantic vigor to the modern tanka:

> ya wa ha da no
> at tsu ki chi shi o ni
> fu re mo se de
> sa mi si ka ra zu ya
> mi chi o to ku ki mi

> [Thou hast never touched
> The soft female skin
> Under which the young, hot blood runs.
> Art thou not lonely?
> Thou, the cold moralist].

Even since World War II the tanka has been a popular verse form among writers. Today hundreds of societies (*kessha,* or groups with masters) with a million practitioners carry on the tradition. Composing tanka has been a traditional activity in the court, and the imperial family continues annually to hold a tanka meeting to which poets from all over Japan are invited.

Haiku

While courtiers, warriors, and those of high rank typically enjoy tanka, the common Japanese reader enjoys haiku poems—those composed of lines having a syllable pattern of 5-7-5 with one syllable consisting of one vowel, or one vowel and one diphthong, and expressing concisely an emotion or idea. Because haiku is composed in a more limited space (seventeen syllables) than tanka (thirty-one syllables), readers generally find it to be more powerful, and because it is easier for laymen with little knowledge of the rules to compose haiku than to write tanka, haiku has become the most popular verse form. Having originated in the first three lines of the traditional thirty-one-syllable tanka, haiku began to rival that older form during the Tokugawa feudal governments (1603–1867), when the haiku master Basho Matsuo elevated it to a highly refined verse form.

At first the subject matter of the haiku was restricted to objective descriptions of nature and seasonal conditions in evoking a definite though unstated emotional response, but in its seventeen syllables it became an art form that states little and suggests much. In general the haiku presents a collage of images, and the lines feature joyful humor and sharp irony. Ezra Pound and other Imagists in Europe noticed and took up the haiku technique of collage, pasting together independent yet associated images, and Paul Eluard wrote poems in the haiku style in France. It has become one of the most important forms of traditional Japanese poetry, and its popularity has spread to other countries.

There has been much confusion over the meanings of the three terms *haiku, hokku,* and *haikai. Hokku* literally denotes the "starting" link of a much longer chain of verses known as *haikai no renga* (a linked verse with humor and irony), or simply *haikai,* a verse that has lines with syllables in a 5-7-5 pattern with a pair of 7-7 syllables added. A light haikai poem was originally considered a diversion through which poets could relax from composing serious waka poetry. By the time of the renga master Sogi (1421–1502), however, it had become a serious art form with complex rules and high aesthetic standards. In the seventeenth century Teitoku Matsunaga succeeded in establishing a conservative haikai school with strict formal rules, and he sought to incorporate in haikai the elegance and aesthetic elevation of tanka and serious renga. After Teitoku's death his formal style was challenged by the more freewheeling Danrin school of haikai led by Soin Nishiyama, who emphasized the comic aspects of this verse.

Basho Matsuo was the greatest of haikai poets and was instrumental in establishing this poetry as an art form. Having been instructed in both the Teitoku and Danrin styles of haikai, he gradually developed a new style of his own in the late seventeenth century. His work transcended the conflict between serious renga and comic haikai in expressing humor, irony, humanity, and religious insight all within the space of a single seventeen-syllable hokku. His representative work is Oku no hosomichi (The Narrow Road to the Deep North, 1694), and the following are examples of his well-known haiku:

fu ru i ke ya
ka wa zu to bi ko mu
ni zu no o to

[The old pond
A frog jumped into
Splash]

si zu ke sa ya
i wa ni si mi i ru
se mi no ko e

[In the quietude
The voice of a cicada
Seeps into rocks].

Mainly under the influence of the painter-poet Buson Yosano in the late eighteenth century, a movement with the theme "Return to Basho!" began to restore haiku to the high aesthetic standards Basho had embraced. Buson possessed both a romantic imagination and a painter's eye for pictorial scenes:

U re i tsu tsu
o ka o no bo re ba
ha na i ba ra

[Immersed in the melancholic mood
I climbed the hill
And there the flowered briers].

More poets became writers of haikai in the early nineteenth century, and the quality of the poetry written in this form diminished as its popularity grew. The poems of a writer such as Issa Kobayashi, however, who wrote about poverty and about his love of small animals and insects, are pathetic but memorable. His best-known work is the anthology *Oraga haru* (The Year of My Life, 1820), and the following is one of his well-known haiku:

wa re to ki te
a so be ya o ya no
na i su zu me

[Come and play with me
Thou, poor orphaned sparrow.
I have no parents either].

Modern Haiku

Largely through the efforts of Shiki Masaoka and through the development of haiku, hokku gradually acquired an independent character in the 1890s. Haiku was a new verse form similar to the traditional hokku but different in that it was to be written, read, and understood as an independent poem, rather than as a part of a longer poem. *Hototogisu,* the magazine that Shiki started in 1897, became the most influential source of haiku published. As early as 1892 Shiki had come to feel that a new literary spirit was needed to free poetry from centuries-old rules prescribing topics and vocabulary.

In "Jojibun" (Narration), an essay published in the newspaper *Nihon* in 1900, Shiki introduced the essential method–that of *shasei,* or sketching, making a direct description from nature–to explain his theory. He believed that a poet should present things as they really are and should write in the language of his own speech. He wrote frequently of his tuberculosis in both his poems and essays such as "Byosho rokushaku" (The Six-foot Sickbed, 1902), but his work is almost entirely lacking in self-pity:

o to to hi no
he chi ma no mi zu mo
to ra za ri ki

[The day before yesterday
I was not able to take water
From a gourd].

In 1912 Kyoshi Takahama published in *Hototogisu* his apologia for the strict seventeen-syllable form, the seasonal theme, and the realism of the sketch that Shiki had advocated. Through his friend Hekigodo Kawahigashi he became acquainted with Shiki and began to write haiku poems. In 1898 Kyoshi became editor of *Hototogisu,* and he and Hekigodo, two of Shiki's disciples, broke with each other after Shiki died. Hekigodo became the leader of a new style of haiku, one that disregarded the traditional rules; for a time Kyoshi was preoccupied with writing novels in a sketchy, realistic style, but he eventually returned to writing haiku. In "Susumu beki haiku no michi" (The Proper Direction for Haiku, 1918) he opposed Hekigodo's new movement, advocated realism in haiku, and stressed that haiku poets should contemplate nature as it is.

By 1920 a second generation of poets–including Shuoshi Mizuhara, Seishi Yamaguchi, and Suju Tankano–clustered about *Hototogisu* and created many fresh haiku:

shun shu no
ka gi ri wo tu tu ji
mo e ni ke ri

[In Spring melancholy
Azalea fully bloomed
Flamingly].

–Shuoshi Mizuhara.

no ni de re ba
hi to mi na ya sa si
mo mo no ha na

[Picnicking afield
Everybody's so kindly
Under the peach blossoms].

–Suju Takano.

Mizuhara broke away from the *Hototogisu* school in 1931, two years after he assumed editorship of the magazine *Ashibi.*

Even after World War II the traditional haiku poets, as Kyoshi Takahama had advocated, appreciated and praised the natural beauty of flowers, birds, the moon, and breezes, and above all they rigidly followed the 5–7–5 form in presenting themes involving the natural seasons. However, in 1947 critic Takeo Kuwabara criticized such postwar haiku as "second-rate art" since it followed the old conventions and embraced *wabi* and *sabi* (the simplicity and quietude peculiar to Japanese taste), rather than attempting to incorporate any innovations such as those which were appearing in the rest of the radically changing society. The young poets have protested, however, and tried to find avant-garde ways to express themselves in the haiku form, as in this poem by Tota Kaneko:

man ju sha ge
do re mo
ha ra da shi
chi chi bu no ko

[Crimson cluster-amaryllises amass
Belly-bared children play
In the Chichibu mountains].

(All translations are by Kiyohiko Tsuboi.)

John Hawkes: A Tribute

(17 August 1925 – 15 May 1998)

Donald J. Greiner
University of South Carolina

When John Hawkes died on 15 May 1998, three months short of his seventy-third birthday, he left a void in the long line of innovative novelists who changed American fiction after 1950. Membership in this elite group is always fluid and, depending on the tastes of the reader, includes major writers such as Joseph Heller, Kurt Vonnegut, Robert Coover, William Gaddis, and William Gass. Hawkes, along with John Barth and Thomas Pynchon, was one of the most admired creators of what later became known as post-modern fiction.

It was not always that way. Although he published his first novel, *The Cannibal,* in 1949, he did not find a consistent readership until 1961, when *The Lime Twig* earned widespread praise. Three years later *Second Skin,* his most celebrated novel, was a finalist for the National Book Award. By that time Barth had published *The Sot-Weed Factor* (1960); Pynchon had published *V.* (1963); and, with Hawkes, the three giants of contemporary innovative American fiction were established. When Hawkes died at Rhode Island Hospital in Providence during heart bypass surgery, his legacy was secure and readily apparent: sixteen novels, four plays, and two miscellanies of short fiction and novellas. His most recent novel, *An Irish Eye,* was published in 1997.

Hawkes was born in Stamford, Connecticut, on 17 August 1925. He spent much of his boyhood in Alaska, served with the American Field Service during World War II, married Sophie Tazewell in 1947, and graduated from Harvard University in 1949. While a student at Harvard, he wrote *The Cannibal* under the tutelage of Albert Guerard, who helped him find a publisher in James Laughlin. Laughlin's New Directions remained Hawkes's publisher for thirty years until Harper and Row published *The Passion Artist* in 1979. His fiction was particularly esteemed in the United States, where he was elected to the American Academy and Institute of Arts and Letters, and in France, where he was awarded the prestigious Prix du Meilleur Livre Etranger and Le Prix Medicis Etranger. Hawkes taught literature and creative writing at Harvard from 1955 to

John Hawkes (photograph by Jerry Bauer)

1958 and at Brown University from 1958 until he retired in 1988.

Sustained discussion of Hawkes's novels began in the 1960s and lasted throughout the rest of his career. The direct catalyst for the commentary was the publication of *The Lime Twig* and *Second Skin.* The indirect catalyst was a remark Hawkes made in 1965 to an interviewer for *Wisconsin Studies in Contemporary Literature,* a remark that became both widely disseminated and

Dust jacket for the author's 1979 novel about a middle-aged protagonist who is ignorant of women but obsessed by them

consistently misinterpreted: "I began to write fiction on the assumption that the true enemies of the novel were plot, character, setting, and theme, and having once abandoned these familiar ways of thinking about fiction, totality of fiction or structure was really all that remained. And structure–verbal and psychological coherence–is still my largest concern as a writer." Hawkes's provocative comment was misread as an arbitrary rejection of plot, character, setting, and theme in fiction, but such was not the case. Voicing his opinion before Jacques Derrida proclaimed in 1967 that reality is a construct and that there is nothing but the text, before Pynchon published *Gravity's Rainbow* in 1973, and before postmodernism was broadly defined as a concept or accepted as a label, Hawkes all but declared that realistic fiction was outmoded and that Realism was nothing more than another literary convention like Romanticism or Neoclassicism.

Hawkes did not mean that his novels lack the conventional staples of fiction, but he did insist that round characters, the logic of cause and effect, easily recognizable locales, and the kind of exposition that provides details are no longer the primary means of structuring a novel. His unsettling combination of comedy and terror and his dismissal of traditional realism made his novels both new and difficult for the unprepared reader. His general goal throughout his career was to free the novel from the limitations of reader expectation, to demonstrate to passive readers that the writer has no obligation to fill in the story or round out the characters.

Hawkes's emphasis was always language, what he called "verbal coherence." At his lyrical best, as in *Second Skin* or *The Blood Oranges* (1971), he offers flights of language that lure the reader into an imaginary world. Committed to creating a setting rather than re-creating one in his fiction, he structured his novels on the intricate play of verbal patterns, parallel images, and cross references. *The Cannibal,* for example, requires a patient and active reader who accepts the deliberate rejection of

335

chronological sequence and explicit motive and follows recurring patterns of imagery sustained not by action but by words. William Gaddis's observation that Hawkes's "sentences are themselves 'events'" is on the mark.

Hawkes also created characters who are remarkable, but not in the Dickensian sense illustrated by the first line of *David Copperfield* (1849–1850), "I am born." Rather, his most memorable characters are typically first-person narrators who are usually unreliable and who come alive on the page not because of the reader's identification with them but because of their voices. The reader may not know what they look like, or where they come from, or what they wear, but the reader is always aware of how they manipulate language to explain their actions. Charging into the novels without traditional exposition or explanatory detail, Hawkes's characters make up their tales to stress that their narratives are fiction as opposed to "real" and that their tapestries of words are nearly always concerned with threats to love conjured by those who would limit the freedom of the imagination. Zizendorf in his hallucinatory, war-torn Germany (*The Cannibal*), Skipper on his wandering island (*Second Skin*), Cyril in his Illyria (*The Blood Oranges*), and Michael in his photography studio (*Whistlejacket*, 1988) create their worlds as they tell their stories.

The Cannibal was Hawkes's first important attempt to free both the reader and the genre of fiction from the constraints of conventional realism. It was also my initial venture into the imagination of John Hawkes. I met him in early 1967 when I was a student at the University of Virginia and he was invited to Charlottesville for a reading. Committed then to the literary masters of the day, to William Faulkner and Ernest Hemingway, Robert Frost and T. S. Eliot, I had not heard of Hawkes. Upon receiving an invitation to a postreading buffet, I decided that I had better read one of his books before joining him for a meal. By the time I got to the Hawkes shelf in the Alderman Library, the only novel available was *The Cannibal*. Being a mere two hundred pages long and a book not on the syllabus of required reading in any of my classes, *The Cannibal* was the kind of volume I thought I could read in three hours. I was wrong. It took me three days.

At first baffled and then mesmerized by Hawkes's cascading language, I found myself drawn to a terrifyingly comic account of Germany in the throes of defeat after World War II. During the next few years I read every Hawkes novel I could locate. I agreed with the commentators who named *Second Skin* one of the ten most important American novels written since 1950, and I published my first book on Hawkes in 1973. Yet Hawkes and I did not become friends in the sense of exchanging phone calls and letters until 1976, when we met twice: the first time in February, when he gave a reading at the University of South Carolina, where I teach; the second in April, when I was invited to participate in the John Hawkes Symposium held at Muhlenberg College, Allentown, Pennsylvania. Before 1976 we had corresponded only once. On that occasion he wrote to request a signed copy of my book on his work in exchange for a first edition of *Second Skin,* which he inscribed, "For Donald Greiner as part of our trade with thanks and best wishes, John Hawkes." When we met on Valentine's Day 1976 at the University of South Carolina, the first book I asked him to inscribe was *The Cannibal.* He obliged: "To Don and Ellen for your hospitality, your friendship, and the elegance of your fictive empire–Much love to you both, Jack." For the next twenty-two years we exchanged phone calls, letters, or inscribed books at least twice a year. He was always generous with his time.

In April 1996 Hawkes and I spoke for two hours on the telephone at his request while I conducted an interview about *The Frog* (1996), an interview published later that fall in *Critique: Studies in Contemporary Fiction*. In December 1997 he sent a copy of *An Irish Eye,* his last novel, with the inscription: "For Don and Ellen, all these years wonderful friends, most sustaining readers (writer), Best of holidays, Love Jack." Five months later he died.

Of the thousands of American novelists who began their careers after World War II, John Hawkes was one of the dozen or so who revitalized fiction. To the high spots of his canon–*The Cannibal, The Lime Twig, Second Skin, The Blood Oranges, Adventures in the Alaskan Skin Trade* (1985), and *Whistlejacket*–he brought a lyrical language, a venturesome imagination, and a leap beyond realism. He was a gentle man who loved horses, white wine, a sustained laugh, and the French countryside. Most of all, he was a writer who mattered.

Winning an Edgar

Carol McGinnis Kay
University of South Carolina

Sue Grafton said, "Holt agreed to let me be the one to call you and tell you the news. You're nominated for an Edgar! Congratulations!"

This was February, so I didn't think the call was an April Fool's joke, but I couldn't think of a single thing to say. For months I had known that *"G" Is For Grafton: The World of Kinsey Millhone,* a book I cowrote with Natalie Hevener Kaufman, had been submitted by our publisher, Henry Holt, for an Edgar Award in the critical/biographical category for 1997. These prizes in detective fiction have been given annually by the Mystery Writers of America (MWA) since 1953, and they are greatly coveted by mystery writers and critics of mysteries. Neither of us, however, had indulged in much hope for the book to be among the five finalists for an Edgar. It wasn't that we were overly modest about out book—we had worked hard and produced what we considered a reliable and engaging study of one of the most popular detectives in contemporary fiction—but we had moved into a realm in which neither of us had any experience. We simply had no idea about what to expect in the world of big commercial publishing.

We are both academics, faculty members at the University of South Carolina. Natalie is a professor of political science, specializing in international law and gender issues, while I am a professor of English, whose doctoral training was in Shakespeare. To make the mental shift from writing for a few experts in the field—we joke in academe that if more than ten people in the world can understand your book, it's not very good—to writing for the general reading public required conscious readjustments on our part. For me, the readjustment required more than just awareness of audience. At that time I was returning to the faculty after almost twenty years as a college administrator. During those two decades I had relied on detective fiction for nighttime reading to keep me relatively sane; it was very reassuring to read about a world where the wicked are always caught and the good usually survive—a world quite unlike my daily experience as a dean. Returning to full-time teaching, I made a conscious decision to redirect my research agenda from Shakespeare to American detective fiction. Since I've always considered professors of English

Natalie Hevener Kaufman and Carol McGinnis Kay with their Edgars

to be detectives of words and literature, using the lens of criticism in much the same way regardless of the subject under scrutiny, this did not strike me as quite the odd redirection it did some of my colleagues. I discussed the change with Natalie, a friend in political science with whom I had often talked about detective fiction because we tend to like the same authors and we both teach detective novels; she typically includes one or two in her political science courses, and I frequently teach an undergraduate English course on the development of American detective fiction. With her interest in the social issues, my interest in the literary quality, and our mutual interest in the genre's place in the history of ideas and culture, I suppose it was inevitable that one day over lunch we came up with the happy idea of writing a book together. Because we both loved the humor, toughness, and complexity of Kinsey Millhone, the choice of writing about Grafton was easy and immediate.

Our "shift" to writing about a popular contemporary author proved to be easier than we anticipated. Even doing the research and preparation prior to the writing process had been pleasant. Granted, we had worked hard; my humanist soul still cringes at the memory of the elabo-

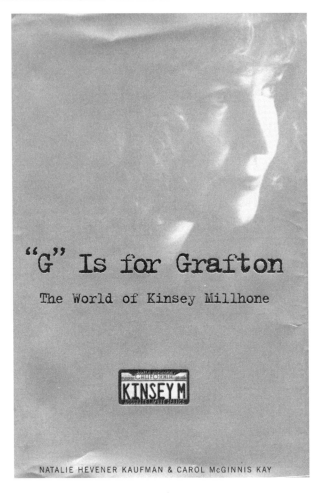

Dust jacket for Kay and Kaufman's award-winning book

rate social science forms that Natalie insisted we complete for every Grafton novel (although I can now admit those forms gave us amazing control over a wealth of material). At the same time, we enjoyed doing the research and developing a breezier style of writing than we normally use for scholarly writing. Because our academic training complemented, rather than duplicated, each other, discussing the thirteen novels together was intellectually exciting. Above all, it was rewarding to get to know Sue Grafton. She and her husband, Steven Humphrey, welcomed us to their St. Louis home and their permanent home in Santa Barbara for days of talk about Kinsey and Grafton's own life. Her openness and warmth were unexpected bonuses to the writing process.

From our first visit, it was as if we were old friends with this amalgam of Sue Grafton/Kinsey Millhone. And now here was Sue on the phone, wanting to be the first to congratulate us for an Edgar nomination. I still don't remember what I said to Sue that day. I just hope that I was more coherent than I felt. After Sue's call, I phoned Natalie, and the numbness wore off as we talked. Within a

couple of hours, our editor at Holt and the publicist had called with more details, and suddenly the two of us were making plans to fly to New York and attend the annual Edgar Allan Poe Awards Dinner on 30 April 1998.

As all the information from MWA began arriving during the next few months, I kept asking Natalie if she had prepared any remarks for an acceptance speech, just in case *"G"* actually won. She refused to consider the idea. I agreed that our competition was formidable, and we knew that one of the other authors had already won an Edgar in this category, but I pushed, "We have one chance in five. What are you going to do if lightning strikes and they call our names?"

"I'll just let you speak, and then I'll say, 'Me too.'"

Natalie remained adamant; she insisted she was happy to leave preparing an acceptance speech to me since I was the only one nursing any optimism. I wouldn't have called my perspective optimistic. I ran into John Jakes at Hilton Head shortly after Sue's call. When I told him about the nomination, he was generous with his congratulations, but also very cautionary about the politics of the process. Again, I realized how little we knew about the inside workings of such an organization and award selection. Thus, my dogged preparation of remarks was prompted less by a hope of winning than by a former academic administrator's mania for never being caught off guard.

Our formal invitations from MWA had told us to be at a VIP Reception at 5:30 for the fifty-five Edgar nominees, committee members judging the awards, and the press. Each of us was given a name tag with a colored border to identify the category for which we were nominated or judging. Having secured our green-trimmed tags, thus signaling that we were in the critical/biographical family, Natalie and I accepted drinks from the passing waiter and began to circulate through the room. The event was a lovely idea, but awkward in actuality. Here was a roomful of nominees allegedly gathered for a pleasant social hour but in fact developing eyestrain from surreptitiously checking name tags to see if this person or that person was the competition. We did not meet any judge for our category until the last minute, when the chairperson was checking to be sure we had all received our certificates of nomination. The press wanted to talk only with nominees for the film and television categories, especially the script writers for *L.A. Confidential* and *Law and Order*. In spite of the pleasure of meeting some writers I admire, such as Diane Mott Davidson and Laura Lippman, and seeing others from a distance, such as James Lee Burke, I was actually relieved when we could leave to join our editor, Marian Wood, for the general cocktail hour.

More than forty round tables filled the enormous room, leaving space against one wall for a large platform with a podium. In front of the platform was a dance floor where a band was playing. Everyone at our table, which was near the podium, was either a nominee, a spouse of a nominee, or an employee of Holt associated with one of their three nominated books. At each place was a handsome *Mystery Writers Annual,* which included lists of all the nominees and excerpts from the first page of each nominated book, as well as articles by mystery writers and congratulatory ads from publishers of nominated books. We were pleased to see that the suspense would be over soon for us: the critical/biographical category was third in the listing of awards.

The award ceremony began promptly with the arrival of dessert course at nine o'clock. Margaret Maron, general chair for the awards and moderator for the evening, introduced the chair of each committee to present the Edgars. There were welcoming remarks and salutes to dignitaries, but all I remember are the announcements of awards. First was the category of best children's mystery, won by Barbara Brooks Wallace for *Sparrows in the Scullery;* next was best mystery play with only one nominee, *A Red Death,* adapted for the stage by David Barr. Our category

was next, and I was convinced that the room was about to explode from pent-up suspense. People become more than a little self-centered in this kind of situation.

Carolyn Wheat read the five nominees for best critical/biographical work of 1997. We two sat poised for action: either jumping up to rush to the podium, or clapping our hands as if we were genuinely delighted that someone else had won.

"And the winner is *"G" Is for Grafton* by Natalie Hevener Kaufman and Carol McGinnis Kay!"

As our table erupted into cheers, Natalie and I leapt to our feet and hurried up to the podium, where Carolyn handed us each an award—a ceramic bust of Edgar Allan Poe with each of our names and the year on the pedestal. Clutching Edgar, I gave my much-prepared remarks, opening with a paraphrase of Helen Hunt at this year's Oscars: "We'd like to thank every mystery writer we've ever read." I was mindful of the need for brevity, but this was our moment in the spotlight, and there were people we wanted to thank, Sue Grafton above all, because her novels made the book both necessary and possible. Natalie did just what she had threatened: she added, "Thanks, Sue," and we fled back to our table to hug a very happy Marian Wood and relinquish Edgar for a few minutes to our tablemates, who wanted to see what he looked like.

The rest of the night is a confused whirl of other awards, with hugs and congratulations for all the winners and admirable stiff upper lips from the other nominees. The only downside to winning your award early is that you have to sit there politely for the rest of the ceremony, when you are dying to get to a telephone and start calling family and friends. We were pleased, however, to see that Laura Lippman won in best original paperback category for *Charm City,* because we both like her fiction. And we were extremely impressed by seeing our new Japanese publisher, Hiroshi Hayakawa, win the Ellery Queen award for lifetime contributions to publishing detective fiction. As the incoming MWA president, Stuart Kaminisky accepted his future responsibilities with a light touch that generated laughs and knowing nods from his fellow writers. The only lengthy remarks were from Barbara Mertz, grand master, and James Lee Burke, winner in the best mystery category for *Cimarron Rose*. In spite of my eagerness to get to a phone, I remember enjoying listening to them talk about their experiences as writers, and I understood what they meant about treasuring the joy of this night.

Marian did finally have the chance after the ceremony to introduce us to Hiroshi Hayakawa, who, in turn, introduced us to his friend, Michael Crichton. When Michael Crichton stood up and up and up, he looked down at me, nodded toward the Edgar I held, smiled warmly, and said, "Isn't he a handsome fellow?"

Annual Awards for
Dictionary of Literary Biography
Editors and Contributors

In 1998 the *Dictionary of Literary Biography* inaugurated two annual awards. One, a $1,000 award, will be presented to the editor(s) of the book that the Bruccoli Clark Layman staff editors select as the most distinguished *DLB* volume published during the year. The other award, of $500, will be presented to the contributor who has written the entry that the BCL editors select as the most distinguished example of reference writing published in a *DLB* volume that year. These awards will be announced in the *DLB Yearbook,* in *Library Journal,* and on GaleNet, the on-line library service of the Gale Group.

The editorial prize in 1998 was awarded to Professor Carla J. Mulford, Pennsylvania State University, for her work on *DLB 200: American Women Prose Writers to 1820*. The contributor's prize was awarded to Professor Amy Schrager Lang, Emory University, for her entry on Mary Rowlandson, which was published in *DLB 200*.

Editorial

My husband was consulted some years ago by a man doing his homework in preparation for the hereafter. As a good Catholic, he expected to be spending time with F. Scott Fitzgerald in Heaven, and he wanted conversational guidance. My husband provided a reading list and refrained from pointing out that, a less good Catholic, Fitzgerald might not yet have cleared Purgatory. (He had been some decades waiting admission into a Catholic cemetery.)

To attain Heaven only to be subjected to the humiliation of social rejection is impossible, so presumably Fitzgerald will be constrained to courtesy. But even the best-researched and most enlightened conversational gambit palls when one has heard it five or ten thousand times before. It occurs to me that one man's Heaven *is* another man's Purgatory: that for a writer elevation comes only after there is not another fan left on Earth. (Well, not another *pious* fan.) Is it possible that literary genius is punished to the degree that it was bestowed? Alas, poor Shakespeare! No—surely by now he is permitted five-minute appearances on a balcony every hundred years or so; it will be understood that his presence is required at the Celestial Globe.

Questions of this kind crowd the mind as one ages. Fifty-five years ago, when I was ten, I asked my mother, in a panic of discovery, "What will it be like to be dead?" and she said, "It will be the way it was before you were born." Her words were not entirely reassuring, but they had for me then a convincing probability, and they still do. However, mothers can be wrong.

If I find, to my surprise, that consciousness goes on, that I am in a kind of extension of life on Earth without the disagreeable bits (thereby demonstrating that Heaven is attained not by denomination, faith, or charity but by a variation of Calvinist election, like winning the lottery without buying a ticket), I will not take a place at the end of the line of patient souls waiting their turns for fifteen minutes to entertain Jane Austen. I will head for the reading room of the Pearly Library, where I will settle down with a copy of the author's completed and perfected text of *Sanditon*, moving on eventually to the other novels she has written since 1817. I will find out how *The Mystery of Edwin Drood* is solved. I will read the completed text of *The Love of the Last Tycoon*, having taken three minutes with *The Great Gatsby* to see if Fitzgerald accepted the emendation of "Astoria" to "Long Island City" and "retinas" to "irises."

If a sudden restlessness in the room makes me look up, and I see Jane Austen, or Charles Dickens, or F. Scott Fitzgerald at the door (and why not?), I will be ready with my greeting:

"Shhhhh. . . ."

– A.F.B.

Literary Awards and Honors Announced in 1998

ACADEMY OF AMERICAN POETS LITERARY AWARDS

FELLOWSHIP
Charles Simic.
HAROLD MORTON LANDON TRANSLATION AWARD
Louis Simpson, *Modern Poets of France: A Bilingual Anthology* (Story Line).
JAMES LAUGHLIN AWARD
Sandra Alcosser, *Except by Nature* (Graywolf).
LENORE MARSHALL–*NATION* MAGAZINE PRIZE FOR POETRY
Mark Jarman, *Questions for Ecclesiastes* (Story Line).
RAIZISS/DE PALCHI TRANSLATION AWARD
Geoffrey Brock, *Poesie del disamore,* by Cesare Pavese.
TANNING PRIZE
A. R. Ammons.
WALT WHITMAN AWARD
Jan Heller Levi, *Once I Gazed at You in Wonder* (Louisiana State University Press).

THE AGATHA AWARDS

BEST NOVEL
Kate Ross, *The Devil in Music* (Penguin).
BEST FIRST MYSTERY NOVEL
Sujata Massey, *The Salaryman's Wife* (Harper Mass Market Paperbacks).
BEST SHORT STORY
M. D. Lake, "Tea for Two," in *Funny Bones: 15 New Tales of Murder and Mayhem,* edited by Joan Hess (Signet).
BEST NONFICTION WORK
Willetta L. Heising, *Detecting Men* (Purple Moon).

AMERICAN ACADEMY OF ARTS AND LETTERS AWARDS

ACADEMY AWARDS IN LITERATURE
Annie Dillard, Albert Guerard, Edward Hirsch, Bradford Morrow, Robert D. Richardson Jr., Mary Ruefle, Gjertrud Schnackenberg, Edward Snow.

AWARD OF MERIT FOR POETRY
Thom Gunn.
GOLD MEDAL FOR DRAMA
Horton Foote.
WITTER BYNNER PRIZE FOR POETRY
Elizabeth Spires.
E. M. FORSTER AWARD IN LITERATURE
Kate Atkinson.
ADDISON METCALF AWARD IN LITERATURE
Rick Moody.
SUE KAUFMAN PRIZE FOR FIRST FICTION
Charles Frazier, *Cold Mountain* (Atlantic Monthly).
ROME FELLOWSHIP IN LITERATURE
Eli Gottlieb.
RICHARD AND HILDA ROSENTHAL FOUNDATION AWARD IN LITERATURE
Joseph Skibell, *A Blessing on the Moon* (Algonquin).
MILDRED AND HAROLD STRAUSS LIVING IN LITERATURE AWARDS
Marilynne Robinson, W. D. Wetherell.
HAROLD D. VURSELL MEMORIAL AWARD IN LITERATURE
Howard Bahr.
MORTON DAUWEN ZABEL AWARD IN LITERATURE
Yusef Komunyakaa.

AMERICAN BOOK AWARDS

Jim Barnes, *On Native Ground: Memoirs and Impressions* (University of Oklahoma Press); Sandra Benítez, *Bitter Grounds* (Hyperion); Allison Adelle Hedge Coke, *Dog Road Woman* (Coffee House); Angela Y. Davis, *Blues Legacies and Black Feminism* (Pantheon); Don DeLillo, *Underworld* (Scribners); Scott DeVeaux, *The Birth of Bebop* (University of California); Nora Okja Keller, *Comfort Woman* (Viking); Thomas Lynch, *The Undertaking* (Norton); Brenda Marie Osbey, *All Saints* (Louisiana State University Press); Nancy Rawles, *Love Like Gumbo* (Fjord); John A. Williams, *Safari West* (Hochelaga).
EDITOR/PUBLISHER AWARD
Douglas Messerli (Sun & Moon Press).

LIFETIME ACHIEVEMENT AWARDS
Paul Metcalf, Vivian Gussin Paley, A. Lavonne Brown Ruoff.

AMERICAN LIBRARY ASSOCIATION AWARDS

JOHN NEWBERY MEDAL
Karen Hesse, *Out of the Dust* (Scholastic).
RANDOLPH CALDECOTT MEDAL
Paul O. Zelinsky, *Rapunzel* (Dutton).
MARGARET R. EDWARDS AWARD FOR OUTSTANDING LITERATURE FOR YOUNG ADULTS
Madeleine L'Engle.
CORETTA SCOTT KING AUTHOR AWARD
Sharon M. Draper, *Forged by Fire* (Atheneum).
CORETTA SCOTT KING ILLUSTRATOR AWARD
Javaka Steptoe, *In Daddy's Arms I Am Tall: African Americans Celebrating Fathers* (Lee & Low).
MILDRED L. BATCHELDER AWARD
Josef Holub, *The Robber and Me* (Holt).
PURA BELPRÉ AWARDS
Victor Martinez, *Parrot in the Oven* (HarperCollins); Stephanie Garcia, illustration for Gary Soto, *Snapshots from the Wedding* (Putnam).
DARTMOUTH MEDAL
Paula E. Hyman and Deborah Dash Moore, eds., *Jewish Women in America: An Historical Encyclopedia* (Routledge).

ANTHONY AWARDS

BEST NOVEL
S. J. Rozan, *No Colder Place* (St. Martin's Press).
BEST FIRST NOVEL
Lee Child, *Killing Floor* (Jove).
BEST PAPERBACK ORIGINAL
Rick Riordan, *Big Red Tequila* (Bantam).

BLACK CAUCUS OF THE AMERICAN LIBRARY ASSOCIATION LITERARY AWARDS

FICTION
Sandra Jackson-Opoku, *The River Where Blood Is Born* (One World).
FIRST NOVEL
Brian Keith Jackson, *The View from Here* (Pocket Books).
NONFICTION
Toi Derricotte, *The Black Notebooks: An Interior Journey* (Norton).

OUTSTANDING CONTRIBUTION TO AFRICAN AMERICAN LITERATURE
Black Classic Press.

BOOKER PRIZE

Ian McEwan, *Amsterdam* (Cape).

BOSTON BOOK REVIEW LITERARY PRIZES

BINGHAM POETRY PRIZE
John Ashbery, *The Mooring of Starting Out: The First Five Books of Poetry* (Ecco); Frank Bidart, *Desire* (Farrar, Straus &Giroux).
FISK FICTION PRIZE
Bernhard Schlink, *The Reader: A Novel* (Pantheon).
THE REA NON-FICTION PRIZE
Anne Fadiman, *The Spirit Catches You and You Fall Down: A Hmong Child, Her American Doctors, and the Collision of Two Cultures* (Farrar, Straus & Giroux).

BRAM STOKER AWARDS

NOVEL
Janet Berliner and George Guthridge, *Children of the Dusk* (White Wolf).
FIRST NOVEL
Kirsten Bakis, *Lives of the Monster Dogs* (Farrar, Straus & Giroux).
NOVELETTE
Joe R. Lansdale, "The Big Blow," in *Revelations*, edited by Douglas E. Winter (HarperPrism).
SHORT STORY
Edo van Belkom and David Nickle, "Rat Food."
FICTION COLLECTION
Karl Edward Wagner, *Exorcisms and Ecstasies* (Fedogan & Bremer).
NONFICTION
Stanley Wiater, *Dark Thoughts: On Writing* (Underwood).
LIFE ACHIEVEMENT AWARDS
William Peter Blatty, Jack Williamson.
SPECIALTY PRESS AWARD
Richard Chizmar (Cemetery Dance).
HAMMER AWARD
Sheldon Jaffery.

CALDECOTT AWARD

Paul O. Zelinsky, Jacob W. Grimm, and Wilhelm K. Grimm, eds., *Rapunzel* (Dutton).

DARTMOUTH MEDAL

E. Paula Hyman, Deborah Dash Moore, and Paula Hyman, eds., *Jewish Women in America: An Historical Encyclopedia* (Routledge).

FIRECRACKER ALTERNATIVE BOOK AWARDS

FICTION
Scott Heim, *In Awe* (Harper Flamingo).

NONFICTION
Carolyn Lei-Lanilau, *Ono Ono Girl's Hula* (University of Wisconsin Press).

POETRY
Gerry Gomez Perlberg, ed., *Queer Dog: Homo/Pup/Poetry* (Cleis).

POLITICS
Howard Zinn, *The Zinn Reader: Writings on Disobedience and Democracy* (Seven Stories).

SEX
Tristan Taormino, *The Ultimate Guide to Anal Sex for Women* (Cleis).

MUSIC
Laurent de Wilde, ed., *Monk* (Marlowe).

ART/PHOTO
Isabel Samaras, ed., *Devil Babe's Big Book of Fun* (Manic D).

GRAPHIC NOVEL
Bob Fingerman, *Minimum Wage: Book 2 – The Tales of Hoffman* (Seven Hills).

KIDS
Javaka Steptoe, *In Daddy's Arms I Am Tall: African Americans Celebrating Fathers* (Lee & Low).

OUTSTANDING INDEPENDENT PRESS OF THE YEAR
2.13.61 Publications.

GAY, LESBIAN, AND BISEXUAL TASK FORCE OF THE AMERICAN LIBRARY ASSOCIATION LITERARY AWARDS

LITERATURE
Lucy Jane Bledsoe, *Working Parts* (Seal).

NONFICTION
Adam Mastoon, *The Shared Heart: Portraits and Stories Celebrating Lesbian, Gay, and Bisexual Young People* (William Morrow/Lothrop, Lee & Shepard).

GILLER PRIZE

Alice Munro, *The Love of a Good Woman* (McClelland & Stewart).

GOVERNOR GENERAL'S LITERARY AWARDS

CHILDREN'S LITERATURE–ILLUSTRATION
Kady MacDonald Denton, *A Child's Treasury of Nursery Rhymes* (Kids Can Press).

CHILDREN'S LITERATURE–TEXT
Janet Lunn, *The Hollow Tree* (Knopf Canada).

DRAMA
Djanet Sears, *Harlem Duet* (Scirocco Drama/Gordon Shillingford).

FICTION
Diane Schoemperlen, *Forms of Devotion* (Phyllis Bruce/HarperCollins).

NONFICTION
David Adams Richards, *Lines on the Water: A Fisherman's Life on the Miramichi* (Doubleday Canada).

POETRY
Stephanie Bolster, *White Stone* (Signal/Véhicule).

TRANSLATION (FROM FRENCH TO ENGLISH)
Michel Tremblay, *Bambi & Me* (Talonbooks).

GUARDIAN FICTION PRIZE

Jackie Kay, *Trumpet* (Picador).

THE CALVIN & ROSE G. HOFFMAN PRIZE FOR DISTINGUISHED PUBLICATION ON CHRISTOPHER MARLOWE

David Riggs.

HUGO AWARDS

BEST NOVEL
Joe Haldeman, *Forever Peace* (Berkley).

BEST NOVELLA
Allen Steele, ". . . Where Angels Fear to Tread."

BEST NOVELETTE
Bill Johnson, "We Will Drink a Fish Together."

BEST SHORT STORY
Mike Resnick, "The 43 Antarean Dynasties."

BEST RELATED BOOK
John Clute and John Grant, eds., *The Encyclopedia of Fantasy* (St. Martin's Press).

IMPAC DUBLIN LITERARY AWARD

Herta Müller, *The Land of Green Plums* (Metropolitan).

INTERNATIONAL BOARD ON BOOKS FOR YOUNG PEOPLE

ANDERSON AWARDS
Katherine Paterson (author); Tomi Ungerer (illustrator).

Dust jacket for the collection that won the 1998 Governor General's Award for Poetry, and the author, Stephanie Bolster

THE KIRIYAMA PACIFIC RIM BOOK PRIZE

Ruth L. Ozeki, *My Year of Meats* (Viking).

LAMBDA LITERARY AWARDS

LESBIAN FICTION
    Elana Dykewomon, *Beyond the Pale* (Press Gang).
GAY MEN'S FICTION
    Aryeh Lev Stollman, *The Far Euphrates* (Riverhead).
LESBIAN STUDIES
    Lisa C. Moore, ed., *Does Your Mama Know?* (Red-Bone).
GAY MEN'S STUDIES
    Charles Kaiser, ed., *The Gay Metropolis: 1940–1996* (Houghton Mifflin).
LESBIAN POETRY
    Joan Larkin, *Cold River* (Painted Leaf); Eileen Myles, *School of Fish* (Black Sparrow).
GAY MEN'S POETRY
    Cyrus Cassells, *Beautiful Signor* (Copper Canyon).
LESBIAN MYSTERY
    Randye Lordon, *Father Forgive Me* (Avon).

GAY MEN'S MYSTERY
    David Hunt, *The Magician's Tale* (Putnam).
LESBIAN BIOGRAPHY/AUTOBIOGRAPHY
    Barbara Wilson, *Blue Windows: A Christian Science Childhood* (Picador USA).
GAY MEN'S BIOGRAPHY/AUTOBIOGRAPHY
    Rafael Campo, *The Poetry of Healing* (Norton).
ANTHOLOGIES/FICTION
    Robert Drake and Terry Wolverton, eds., *His 2* (Faber & Faber).
ANTHOLOGIES/NONFICTION
    Gordon Brent Ingram, Anne-Marie Bouthillette, and Yolanda Retter, eds., *Queers in Space: Communities, Public Places, Sites of Resistance* (Bay).
PHOTOGRAPHY/VISUAL ARTS
    David Leddick, *Naked Men: Pioneering Male Nudes, 1935–1955* (Universe); Robert Giard, *Particular Voices: Portraits of Gay and Lesbian Writers* (MIT Press).
HUMOR
    Bob Smith, *Openly Bob* (Rob Weisbach).
SPIRITUALITY
    Rebecca Alpert, *Like Bread on the Seder Plate* (Columbia University Press).

SCIENCE FICTION/FANTASY
Nicola Griffith and Stephen Pagel, *Bending the Landscape* (Overlook).
DRAMA
Moises Kaufman, *Gross Indecency: The Three Trials of Oscar Wilde* (Vintage).
CHILDREN/YOUNG ADULT
Jacqueline Woodson, *The House You Pass on the Way* (Delacorte-Seymour Lawrence).
TRANSGENDER
Carol Queen and Lawrence Schimel, eds., *PoMo-Sexuals: Challenging Assumptions about Gender and Sexuality* (Cleis).
SMALL PRESS
Lisa C. Moore, *Does Your Mama Know?* (Red-Bone).

LANNAN LITERARY AWARDS

LIFETIME ACHIEVEMENT
John Barth.
FICTION
J. M. Coetzee, Lydia Davis, Stuart Dybek, and Lois-Ann Yamanaka.
NONFICTION
Chet Raymo, Lawrence Weschler, and Howard Zinn.
POETRY
Frank Bidart, John Davis, and Mary Oliver.

LEEWAY FOUNDATION GRANTS

CREATIVE NONFICTION
Karen Rile, Beth Kephart.

LILLIAN SMITH BOOK AWARDS

FICTION
Elizabeth Cox, *Night Talk* (Graywolf).
NONFICTION
John Lewis and Michael D'Orso, *Walking with the Wind: A Memoir of the Movement* (Simon & Schuster).

LINCOLN PRIZE

James M. McPherson, *For Cause and Comrades: Why Men Fought the Civil War* (Oxford University Press).

THE JOHN D. AND CATHERINE T. MACARTHUR FOUNDATION FELLOWS

Linda Bierds, Edward Hirsch, Ayesha Jalal, Charles Johnson, Don Mitchell, Ishmael Reed.

Dust jacket for the volume that won the 1998 Governor General's Award as the best-illustrated children's book

MINNESOTA BOOK AWARDS

AUTOBIOGRAPHY AND BIOGRAPHY
Paul C. Nagel, *John Quincey Adams: A Public Life, a Private Life* (Knopf).
CHILDREN'S NONFICTION
Dan Buettner, *Africatrek: A Journey by Bicycle through Africa* (Lerner).
COLLECTED WORKS
Kathleen Coskran and C. W. Truesdale, eds., *Tanzania on Tuesday: Writing by American Women Abroad* (New Rivers).
CREATIVE NONFICTION
Jan Zita Grover, *North Enough: AIDS and Other Clear-Cuts* (Graywolf).
FANTASY AND SCIENCE FICTION
John M. Ford, *From the End of the Twentieth Century* (Nesfa).
HELP AND GUIDANCE
Gladys Folkers and Jeanne Engelmann, *Taking Charge of My Mind and Body: A Girl's Guide to Outsmarting Alcohol, Drugs, Smoking, and Eating Problems* (Free Spirit).

HISTORY
 Paul Clifford, *Icy Pleasures: Minnesota Celebrates Winter* (Afton Historical Society).
ILLUSTRATED BOOKS
 Catherine Koemptgen, *Connections & Reflections: Mothers & Daughters in Their Own Light, in Their Own Words* (Pfeifer-Hamilton).
INFORMATION
 John Farmer, *Minnesota Business Almanac* (MSP Books).
FUN AND HUMOR
 Janet Letnes, *Growing Up Lutheran: What Does This Mean?* (Caragana).
MYSTERY AND DETECTIVE
 Vince Flynn, *Term Limits* (Pocket Books).
NATURE
 John Henricksson, *A Wild Neighborhood* (University of Minnesota Press).
NONFICTION
 David Lebedoff, *Cleaning Up: The Story behind the Biggest Legal Bonanza of Our Time* (Free Press).
NOVELS
 George Rabasa, *Floating Kingdom* (Coffee House).
PERSONAL PAPERS
 Elizabeth Taylor, *The Far Islands and Other Cold Places: Travel Essays of a Victorian Lady,* edited by James Taylor Dunn (Pogo).
PICTURE BOOKS:
AUTHOR
 Marion Dane Bauer, *If You Were Born a Kitten* (Simon & Schuster).
ILLUSTRATOR
 Stephen Gammell, *Is That You, Winter?* (Harcourt Brace).
POETRY
 Michael Dennis Browne, *Selected Poems, 1965–1995* (Carnegie-Mellon University Press).
SHORT STORIES
 Beth Weatherby, *Small Invasions* (Plains).
YOUNG ADULT FICTION
 William Durbin, *The Broken Blade* (Yearling).
THE FLANAGAN PRIZE
 Paul Gruchow, *Boundary Waters: The Grace of the Wild* (Milkweed).

MYSTERY WRITERS OF AMERICA EDGAR ALLAN POE AWARDS

GRAND MASTER AWARD
 Barbara Mertz, a.k.a. Elizabeth Peters and Barbara Michaels.
BEST MYSTERY NOVEL
 James Lee Burke, *Cimarron Rose* (Hyperion).

BEST FIRST MYSTERY NOVEL BY AN AMERICAN AUTHOR
 Joseph Kanon, *Los Alamos* (Broadway Books).
BEST ORIGINAL PAPERBACK MYSTERY NOVEL
 Laura Lippman, *Charm City* (Avon).
BEST FACT CRIME BOOK
 Richard Firstman and Jamie Talan, *The Death of Innocents* (Bantam).
BEST CRITICAL/BIOGRAPHICAL WORK
 Natalie Hevener Kaufman and Carol McGinnis Kay, *"G" Is for Grafton: The World of Kinsey Millhone* (Holt).
BEST YOUNG ADULT MYSTERY
 Will Hobbs, *Ghost Canoe* (Morrow Junior Books).
BEST JUVENILE MYSTERY
 Barbara Brooks Wallace, *Sparrows in the Scullery* (Atheneum).
BEST MYSTERY SHORT STORY
 Lawrence Block, "Keller on the Spot."

NATIONAL BOOK AWARDS

FICTION
 Alice McDermott, *Charming Billy* (Farrar, Straus & Giroux).
NONFICTION
 Edward Ball, *Slaves in the Family* (Farrar, Straus & Giroux).
POETRY
 Gerald Stern, *This Time: New and Selected Poems* (Norton).
YOUNG PEOPLE'S LITERATURE
 Louis Sachar, *Holes* (Farrar, Straus & Giroux).
MEDAL FOR DISTINGUISHED CONTRIBUTION TO AMERICAN LETTERS
 John Updike.

NATIONAL BOOK CRITICS CIRCLE AWARDS

FICTION
 Alice Munro, *The Love of a Good Woman* (Knopf).
NONFICTION
 Philip Gourevitch, *We Wish to Inform You That Tomorrow We Will Be Killed with Our Families: Stories from Rwanda* (Farrar, Straus & Giroux)
BIOGRAPHY/AUTOBIOGRAPHY
 Sylvia Nasar, *A Beautiful Mind: A Biography of John Forbes Nash, Jr.* (Simon & Schuster).
POETRY
 Marie Ponsot, *The Bird Catcher* (Knopf).
CRITICISM
 Gary Giddons, *Visions of Jazz: The First Century* (Oxford University Press).

NATIONAL COUNCIL OF TEACHERS OF ENGLISH

CHRISTOPHER AWARD
David Parker, *Stolen Dreams: Portraits of Working Children* (Lerner).
ORBIS PICTUS AWARD
Laurence Pringle, *An Extraordinary Life: The Story of a Monarch Butterfly* (Orchard).

NATIONAL HUMANITIES MEDAL

Henry Louis Gates Jr.

JOHN NEWBERY MEDAL

Karen Hesse, *Out of the Dust* (Scholastic).

NOBEL PRIZE FOR LITERATURE

José Saramago.

SCOTT O'DELL AWARD FOR HISTORICAL FICTION

Karen Hesse, *Out of the Dust* (Scholastic).

ORANGE PRIZE

Carol Shields, *Larry's Party* (Viking).

THE PARIS REVIEW PRIZES

THE AGA KHAN PRIZE FOR FICTION
David Foster Wallace, "Brief Interviews with Hideous Men #6."
THE B. F. CONNERS PRIZE FOR POETRY
John Drury, "Burning the Aspern Papers."
THE PARIS REVIEW DISCOVERY PRIZE
Martin McDonagh, "The Cripple of Inishmaan."

PEN AMERICAN CENTER LITERARY AWARDS

ERNEST HEMINGWAY FOUNDATION/PEN AWARD FOR FIRST FICTION
Charlotte Bacon, *A Private State* (University of Massachusetts Press).
PEN/FAULKNER AWARD
Rafi Zabor, *The Bear Comes Home* (Norton).
PEN/VOELCKER AWARD FOR POETRY AND THE BERLIN PRIZE FELLOWSHIP
C. K. Williams, *The Vigil* (Farrar, Straus & Giroux).

Katy MacDonald Denton, whose illustrations for A Child's Treasury of Nursery Rhymes *won a 1998 Governor General's Award for children's literature (photograph by Peter Adamo)*

PULITZER PRIZES

BIOGRAPHY
Katharine Graham, *Personal History* (Knopf).
CRITICISM
Michiko Kakutani, *The New York Times*.
DRAMA
Paula Vogel, *How I Learned to Drive* (Dramatists Play Service).
FICTION
Philip Roth, *American Pastoral* (Houghton Mifflin).
GENERAL NONFICTION
Jared Diamond, *Guns, Germs and Steel: The Fates of Human Societies* (Norton).
HISTORY
Edward J. Larson, *Summer for the Gods: The Scopes Trial and America's Continuing Debate over Science and Religion* (Basic Books).
POETRY
Charles Wright, *Black Zodiac* (Farrar, Straus & Giroux).

REA AWARD FOR THE SHORT STORY

John Edgar Wideman.

REFERENCE AND USER SERVICE ASSOCIATION AWARDS

FICTION

Julia Alvarez, *Yo!* (Algonquin); Margaret Atwood, *Alias Grace* (Nan A. Talese); Wayson Choy, *The Jade Peony* (Vancouver, B.C.: Douglas & McIntyre; New York: Picador); Seamus Deane, *Reading in the Dark* (Knopf); Charles Frazier, *Cold Mountain* (Atlantic Monthly); Cristina Garcia, *The Aguero Sisters* (Knopf); Haruki Murakami, *The Wind-Up Bird Chronicle* (Knopf); Tom Perrotta, *The Wishbones* (Putnam); Lee Smith, *News of the Spirit* (Putnam); Aryeh Lev Stollman, *The Far Euphrates* (Riverhead); Lois-Ann Yamanaka, *Blu's Hanging* (Farrar, Straus & Giroux).

NONFICTION

Walter Alvarez, *T. Rex and the Crater of Doom* (Princeton University Press); Rick Bragg, *All Over But the Shoutin'* (Pantheon); Barbara Ehrenreich, *Blood Rites: Origins & History of the Passions of War* (Metropolitan); Orlando Figes, *A People's Tragedy: The Russian Revolution, 1891–1924* (Viking); Roger Fouts with Stephen Tukel Mills, *Next of Kin: What Chimpanzees Have Taught Me about Who We Are* (Morrow); Kennedy Frazier, *Ornament and Silence: Essays on Women's Lives* (Knopf); Sebastian Junger, *The Perfect Storm* (Norton); Jon Krakauer, *Into Thin Air* (Villard); Pauline Maier, *American Scripture: Making the Declaration of Independence* (Knopf); Jonathan Raban, *Bad Land: An American Romance* (Pantheon); Deborah Solomon, *Utopian Parkway: The Life and Work of Joseph Cornell* (Farrar, Straus & Giroux); Simon Winchester, *The River at the Center of the World: A Journey Up the Yangtze and Back in Chinese Time* (Holt).

POETRY

Sarah Lindsay, *Primate Behavior* (Grove); Marge Piercy, *What Are Big Girls Made Of?* (Knopf); Derek Walcott, *The Bounty* (Farrar, Straus & Giroux).

THE RITA AWARDS

BEST TRADITIONAL ROMANCE

Lucy Gordon, *His Brother's Child* (Thorndike).

BEST SHORT CONTEMPORARY ROMANCE

Jennifer Greene, *Nobody's Princess* (Harlequin).

BEST LONG CONTEMPORARY ROMANCE

Ruth Wind, *Reckless* (Silhouette).

BEST CONTEMPORARY SINGLE TITLE

Susan Elizabeth Phillips, *Nobody's Baby But Mine* (Avon).

BEST SHORT HISTORICAL ROMANCE

Barbara Samuel, *Heart of a Knight* (Harper Paperbacks).

BEST LONG HISTORICAL ROMANCE

Maggie Osborne, *The Promise of Jenny Jones* (Warner).

BEST REGENCY ROMANCE

Jean Ross Ewing, *Love's Reward* (Kensington).

BEST ROMANTIC SUSPENSE/GOTHIC

Ingrid Weaver, *On the Way to a Wedding* (Silhouette).

BEST PARANORMAL ROMANCE

Justine Dare, *Fire Hawk* (Topaz).

BEST INSPIRATIONAL ROMANCE

Melody Carlson, *Homeward* (Multnomah).

BEST FIRST BOOK

Elizabeth Boyle, *Brazen Angel* (Island).

THE EDWARD E. SMITH MEMORIAL AWARD (SKYLARK AWARD) FOR IMAGINATIVE FICTION

James White.

SOCIETY OF AUTHORS

THE BETTY TRASK PRIZE

Kiran Desai, *Hullabaloo in the Guava Orchard* (Faber & Faber).

THE BETTY TRASK AWARDS

Nick Earls, *Zigzag Street* (Macmillan); Phil Whitaker, *Eclipse of the Sun* (Phoenix House); Gail Anderson-Dargatz, *The Cure for Death by Lightning* (Virago); Tobias Hill, *Underground* (unpublished).

THE CHOLMONDELEY AWARDS

Roger McGough, Robert Minhinnick, Anne Ridler, Ken Smith.

THE ERIC GREGORY AWARDS

Mark Goodwin, Joanne Limburg, Patrick McGuinness, Kona Macphee, Esther Morgan, Christiania Whitehead, Frances Williams.

THE MCKITTERICK PRIZE

Eli Gottlieb, *The Boy Who Went Away* (Cape).

THE RICHARD IMISON MEMORIAL AWARD

Katie Hims, *The Earthquake Girl*.

THE SAGITTARIUS PRIZE

A. Sivanandan, *When Memory Dies* (Arcadia Books).

THE SOMERSET MAUGHAM AWARDS

Rachel Cusk, *The Country Life* (Picador Macmillan); Jonathan Rendall, *This Bloody Mary Is the Last Thing I Own* (Faber & Faber); Kate Summerscale, *The Queen of Whale Cay* (Fourth

Estate); Robert Twigger, *Angry White Pyjamas* (Indigo).

THE TRAVELLING SCHOLARSHIPS
Dorothy Nimmo, Dilys Rose, Paul Sayer.

THOMAS COOK / *DAILY TELEGRAPH* TRAVEL BOOK AWARD

Tim Mackintosh-Smith, *Yemen: Travels in Dictionary Land* (Murray).

T. S. ELIOT AWARD

Madison Jones.

WHITBREAD PRIZES

BOOK OF THE YEAR
Ted Hughes, *Birthday Letters* (Farrar, Straus & Giroux).
NOVEL
Justin Cartwright, *Leading the Cheers* (Sceptre).
FIRST NOVEL
Giles Foden, *The Last King of Scotland* (Knopf).
CHILDREN'S NOVEL
David Almond, *Skellig* (Delacorte-Seymour Lawrence).

POETRY
Ted Hughes, *Birthday Letters* (Farrar, Straus & Giroux).
BIOGRAPHY
Amanda Foreman, *Georgiana, Duchess of Devonshire* (HarperCollins).

WHITING WRITERS' AWARDS

Michael Byers, *The Coast of Good Intentions* (Houghton Mifflin); Nancy Elmers, *No Moon* (Purdue University Press); Daniel Hall, *Hermit with Landscape* (Yale University Press); W. David Hancock, *The Convention of Cartography;* James Kimbrell, *The Gatehouse Heaven* (Sarabande Books); Ralph Lombreglia, *Make Me Work* (Farrar, Straus & Giroux); D. J. Waldie, *Holy Land: A Suburban Memoir* (Norton); Anthony Walton, *Mississippi* (Knopf); Charles Harper Webb, *Reading the Water* (Northeastern University Press); Greg Williamson, *The Silent Partner* (Story Line).

YOUNG READER'S CHOICE AWARDS

YOUTH
Louis Sachar, *Wayside School Gets a Little Stranger* (Morrow).
SENIOR
Karen Cushman, *Midwife's Apprentice* (Clarion).

Necrology

Alexander, Margaret Walker – 30 November 1998
Ambler, Eric – 22 October 1998
Amory, Cleveland – 14 October 1998
Andrieu, René – 26 March 1998
Apstein, Theodore – 26 July 1998
Auerbach, Arnold M. – 19 October 1998
Baker, Augusta Braxston – 23 February 1998
Barkham, John – 15 April 1998
Batchelder, Mildred – 25 August 1998
Behn, Noel – 27 July 1998
Bettmann, Otto L. – 1 May 1998
Biblo, Jack – 5 June 1998
Bosquet, Alain – 17 March 1998
Briley, Dorothy – 25 May 1998
Brinnin, John Malcolm – 26 June 1998
Brown, Ralph S. – 17 June 1998
Butler, Francelia – 18 September 1998
Carlile, Clancy – 4 June 1998
Carter, Randolph – 12 October 1998
Castaneda, Carlos – 27 April 1998
Commager, Henry Steele – 2 March 1998
Cookson, Dame Catherine – 11 June 1998
Crewe, Quentin – 14 November 1998
Cross, Beverley – 20 March 1998
Davis, Robert Gorham – 16 July 1998
de Kay, Ormonde – 2 October 1998
Delgado, Louis Jr. – 1 December 1998
Dent, Tom – 6 June 1998
Donnelly, Honoria Murphy – 22 December 1998
Drury, Allen – 2 September 1998
Dudintsev, Vladimir – 23 July 1998
Durbridge, Francis – 11 April 1998
Edmonds, Walter D. – 24 January 1998
Ellis, Edward Robb – 7 September 1998
Farris, Jack – 26 November 1998
Fickling, Forrest E. – 3 April 1998
Finn, Richard Boswell – 16 August 1998
Fowlie, Wallace – 16 August 1998
Frank, Gerold – 17 September 1998
Friend, Robert – 12 January 1998
Gaddis, William – 16 December 1998
Garro, Elena – 22 August 1998
Gellhorn, Martha – 15 February 1998
Gitlin, Paul – 16 December 1998

Glyn, Sir Anthony – 20 January 1998
Godden, Rumer – 8 November 1998
Goldman, James – 28 October 1998
Green, Julian – 13 August 1998
Hawkes, John – 15 May 1998
Herbert, Zbigniew – 28 July 1998
Hindus, Milton – 28 May 1998
Hoban, Lillian – 17 July 1998
Hogan, Ray – 14 July 1998
Holub, Miroslav – 14 July 1998
Hopkins, John R. – 23 July 1998
Huddleston, Trevor – 20 April 1998
Hughes, Ted – 28 October 1998
Hymes, James Lee Jr. – 6 March 1998
Innes, Hammond – 10 June 1998
Irwin, Annabelle – 13 September 1998
Johnson, Albert – 17 October 1998
Johnson, Ronald – 4 March 1998
Kazin, Alfred – 5 June 1998
Kendrick, Walter – 25 October 1998
Lardner, Rex – 27 July 1998
Laxness, Halldor – 8 February 1998
Lenz, Hermann – 12 May 1998
Lewis, Janet – 30 November 1998
Link, Arthur Stanley – 26 March 1998
Locke, Sam – 18 September 1998
Main, Mary – 8 November 1998
Mangione, Jerre – 16 August 1998
Mankowitz, Wolf – 20 May 1998
Mann, Charles Jr. – 17 July 1998
Marasco, Robert – 6 December 1998
McEnroe, Robert E. – 6 February 1998
Merrill, Bob – 17 February 1998
Micheline, Jack – 27 February 1998
Miller, Vassar – 31 October 1998
Morley, Hilda – 23 March 1998
Morris, Wright – 25 April 1998
Murray, Jim – 16 August 1998
Myers, Andrew Breen – 12 October 1998
Narcejac, Thomas – 7 June 1998
Newman, Ralph G. – 23 July 1998
O'Brien, Darcy – 2 March 1998
O'Connor, Philip – 29 May 1998
Okoye, Mokwugo – 21 September 1998

Parker, Maynard – 16 October 1998

Paz, Octavio – 19 April 1998

Peterson, Don – 25 April 1998

Peterson, Louis – 27 April 1998

Qabbani, Nizar – 1 May 1998

Rawley, Donald – 3 May 1998

Reich, Cary – 3 March 1998

Rybakov, Anatoly – 23 December 1998

Rycroft, Charles – 24 May 1998

Sagoff, Maurice – 18 March 1998

Sanders, Lawrence – 7 February 1998

Schwann, William – 7 June 1998

Seymour-Smith, Martin – 1 July 1998

Shepard, Richard F. – 6 March 1998

Smith, Warren Hunting – 22 November 1998

Snow, Vernon F. – 25 June 1998

Southgate, Patsy – 18 July 1998

Spears, Monroe K. – 23 May 1998

Spies, Adrian – 2 October 1998

Stevens, Leslie – 24 April 1998

Strigler, Mordechai – 10 May 1998

Suall, Irwin J. – 17 August 1998

Tanner, Tony – 5 December 1998

Thompson, Kay – 2 July 1998

Treat, Lawrence – 7 January 1998

van Buren, Paul Matthews – 18 June 1998

Vlasto, Solon G. – 24 August 1998

von Rezzori, Gregor – 23 April 1998

Walker, Mildred – 27 May 1998

Walter, Eugene – 29 March 1998

Weidman, Jerome – 6 October 1998

West, Dorothy – 16 August 1998

Wharton, Don – 6 May 1998

Wolseley, Roland – 31 May 1998

Worth, Marvin – 22 April 1998

Wyden, Peter – 27 June 1998

Wynd, Oswald – 21 July 1998

Checklist: Contributions to Literary History and Biography

This list is a selection of new books on various aspects of literary and cultural history, including biographies, memoirs, correspondence, diaries, notebooks, and journals of literary people and their associates.

Abbott, Shirley. *Love's Apprentice*. Boston: Houghton Mifflin, 1998.

Adler, Laure. *Marguerite Duras*. Paris: Gallimard, 1998.

Alexander, Edward. *Irving Howe: Socialist, Critic, Jew*. Bloomington: Indiana University Press, 1998.

Amburn, Ellis. *Subterranean Kerouac: The Hidden Life of Jack Kerouac*. New York: St. Martin's Press, 1998.

Arico, Santo L. *Oriana Fallaci: The Woman and the Myth*. Carbondale: Southern Illinois University Press, 1998.

Bakewell, Michael. *Lewis Carroll: A Biography*. New York: Norton, 1998.

Barker, Juliet R. V. *The Brontës: A Life in Letters*. New York: Overlook Press, 1998.

Bayley, John. *Iris: A Memoir of Iris Murdoch*. London: Duckworth, 1998.

Bethea, David M. *Realizing Metaphors: Alexander Pushkin and the Life of the Poet*. Madison: University of Wisconsin Press, 1998.

Blondel, Nathalie. *Mary Butts: Scenes from the Life. A Biography*. Kingston, N.Y.: McPherson, 1998.

Brooks, Cleanth, and Robert Penn Warren. *Cleanth Brooks and Robert Penn Warren: A Literary Correspondence,* edited by James A. Grimshaw Jr. Columbia: University of Missouri Press, 1998.

Cagle, William R. and Matthew J. Bruccoli. *150 Years of the American Short Story: An Exhibition*. Bloomington: The Lilly Library, Indiana University, 1998.

Callahan, John. *Will the Real John Callahan Please Stand Up?: A Quasi Memoir*. New York: Morrow, 1998.

Callow, Philip. *Chekhov, the Hidden Ground: A Biography*. Chicago: Ivan R. Dee, 1998.

Cantwell, Mary. *Speaking with Strangers*. Boston: Houghton Mifflin, 1998.

Caveney, Graham. *Gentleman Junkie: The Life and Legacy of William S. Burroughs*. Boston: Little, Brown, 1998.

Chambers, Colin. *Peggy: The Life of Margaret Ramsay, Play Agent*. New York: St. Martin's Press, 1998.

Cline, Sally. *Radclyffe Hall: A Woman Called John*. New York: Overlook Press, 1998.

Cockburn, Leslie. *Looking for Trouble*. New York: Doubleday, 1998.

Cole, Phyllis Blum. *Mary Moody Emerson and the Origins of Transcendentalism: A Family History*. New York: Oxford University Press, 1998.

Cuthbertson, Ken. *Nobody Said Not to Go: The Remarkable Life of Emily Hahn*. Boston: Faber & Faber, 1998.

Davies, James A. *A Reference Companion to Dylan Thomas*. Westport, Conn.: Greenwood Press, 1998.

Davis, Linda H. *Badge of Courage: The Life of Stephen Crane*. Boston: Houghton Mifflin, 1998.

Dickey, Christopher. *Summer of Deliverance*. New York: Simon & Schuster, 1998.

Dillon, Millicent. *You Are Not I: A Portrait of Paul Bowles*. Berkeley: University of California Press, 1998.

Diski, Jenny. *Skating to Antarctica: A Memoir*. Hopewell, N. J.: Ecco, 1998.

Dubus, Andre. *Meditations from a Movable Chair: Essays*. New York: Knopf, 1998.

Dunn, Richard M. *Geoffrey Scott and the Berenson Circle: Literary and Aesthetic Life in the Early 20th Century*. Lewiston, Idaho: Mellen, 1998.

Ellis, David. *D. H. Lawrence: Dying Game, 1922–1930*. Cambridge: Cambridge University Press, 1998.

Fetherling, Doug. *The Gentle Anarchist: A Life of George Woodcock*. Vancouver, B.C.: Douglas & McIntyre / Seattle: University of Washington Press, 1998.

Fryer, Jonathan. *André & Oscar: The Literary Friendship of André Gide and Oscar Wilde*. New York: St. Martin's Press, 1998.

Galbraith, John Kenneth. *Letters to Kennedy,* edited by James Goodman. Boston: Harvard University Press, 1998.

Gelbart, Larry. *Laughing Matters: On Writing M*A*S*H, Tootsie, Oh, God!, and a Few Other Funny Things*. New York: Random House, 1998.

Gilmore, Lyman. *Don't Touch the Poet: The Life and Times of Joel Oppenheimer*. Jersey City, N.J.: Talisman House, 1998.

Goodman, Susan. *Ellen Glasgow: A Biography*. Baltimore: Johns Hopkins University Press, 1998.

Greenfield, George. *Enid Blyton*. Thrupp, Stroud, Gloucestershire, U.K.: Sutton, 1998.

Haefele, Fred. *Rebuilding the Indian: A Memoir*. New York: Riverhead Books, 1998.

Healy, Dermot. *The Bend for Home*. New York: Harcourt Brace, 1998.

Heller, Joseph L. *Now and Then: From Coney Island to Here*. New York: Knopf, 1998.

Herrick, William, and Paul Berman. *Jumping the Line: The Adventures and Misadventures of an American Radical*. Madison: University of Wisconsin Press, 1998.

Holland, Merlin. *The Wide Album*. New York: Holt, 1998.

Houston, James. *Zigzag*. Toronto: McClelland & Stewart, 1998.

Hutchinson, G. O. *Cicero's Correspondence: A Literary Study*. Oxford: Oxford University Press, 1998.

Inchausti, Robert. *Thomas Merton's American Prophecy*. Albany: State University of New York Press, 1998.

Jacobs, Eric. *Kingsley Amis: A Biography*. New York: St. Martin's Press, 1998.

Johnson, Greg. *Invisible Writer: A Biography of Joyce Carol Oates*. New York: Dutton, 1998.

Johnston, Kenneth R. *Hidden Wordsworth: Poet, Lover, Rebel, Spy*. New York: Norton, 1998.

Kercheval, Jesse Lee. *Space: A Memoir*. Chapel Hill, N.C.: Algonquin Books, 1998.

Kershaw, Alex. *Jack London: A Life*. New York: St. Martin's Press, 1998.

Kuusisto, Stephen. *Planet of the Blind*. New York: Dial, 1998.

Leaska, Mitchell Alexander. *Granite and Rainbow: The Life of Virginia Woolf*. New York: Farrar, Straus & Giroux, 1998.

Levi, Peter. *Horace: A Life*. New York: Routledge, 1998.

MacHann, Clinton. *Matthew Arnold: A Literary Life*. New York: St. Martin's Press, 1998.

MacNiven, Ian. *Lawrence Durrell: A Biography*. London: Faber & Faber, 1998.

Makoto Ueda. *The Path of Flowering Thorn: The Life and Poetry of Yosa Buson*. Stanford, Cal.: Stanford University Press, 1998.

Mann, Thomas, and Heinrich Mann. *Letters of Heinrich and Thomas Mann, 1900–1949,* edited by Hans Wysling. Berkeley: University of California Press, 1998.

Mason, Gregory. *Arrows of Longing: The Correspondence between Anaïs Nin and Felix Pollak, 1952–1976*. Athens, Ohio: Swallow Press, 1998.

Maynard, Joyce. *At Home in the World: A Memoir*. New York: Picador USA, 1998.

McPherson, James Alan. *Crabcakes*. New York: Simon & Schuster, 1998.

Michaelis, David. *N. C. Wyeth: A Biography*. New York: Knopf, 1998.

Miller, John E. *Becoming Laura Ingalls Wilder: The Woman behind the Legend*. Columbia: University of Missouri Press, 1998.

Minta, Stephen. *On a Voiceless Shore: Byron in Greece*. New York: Holt, 1998.

Moore, Sam. *American by Choice: The Remarkable Fulfillment of an Immigrant's Dreams*. Nashville, Tenn.: Thomas Nelson, 1998.

Motion, Andrew. *Keats*. New York: Farrar, Straus & Giroux, 1998.

Myerson, Joel, ed. *The Selected Letters of Ralph Waldo Emerson*. New York: Columbia University Press, 1998.

Nelson, Bobby Jack. *Keepers: A Memoir*. New York: Norton, 1998.

Nicolson, Nigel. *Long Life*. New York: Putnam, 1998.

Nordstrom, Ursula. *Dear Genius: The Letters of Ursula Nordstrom,* edited by Leonard S. Marcus. New York: HarperCollins, 1998.

Page, Tim. *Dawn Powell*. New York: Holt, 1998.

Pagliaro, Harold E. *Henry Fielding: A Literary Life*. New York: St. Martin's Press, 1998.

Paley, Grace. *Just as I Thought*. New York: Farrar, Straus & Giroux, 1998.

Patey, Douglas Lane. *The Life of Evelyn Waugh: A Critical Biography*. Cambridge, Mass.: Blackwell, 1998.

Paxton, Michael. *Ayn Rand: A Sense of Life*. Salt Lake City, Utah: Gibbs Smith, 1998.

Peacock, Molly. *Paradise, Piece by Piece*. New York: Putnam, 1998.

Price, Reynolds. *Clear Pictures: First Loves, First Guides*. New York: Simon & Schuster, 1998.

Rayfield, Donald. *Anton Chekhov: A Life*. New York: Holt, 1998.

Reynolds, Barbara, ed. *The Letters of Dorothy L. Sayers: 1937–1943, from Novelist to Playwright*. New York: St. Martin's Press, 1998.

Robb, Graham. *Victor Hugo: A Biography*. New York: Norton, 1998.

Rodis-Lewis, Genevieve. *Descartes: A Biography,* translated by Jane Marie Todd. Ithaca, N.Y.: Cornell University Press, 1998.

Ross, Lillian. *Here but Not Here: A Love Story*. New York: Random House, 1998.

Rubenfeld, Florence. *Clement Greenberg: A Life*. New York: Scribner, 1998.

Sante, Luc. *The Factory of Facts*. New York: Pantheon, 1998.

Schofield, Robert E. *The Enlightenment of Joseph Priestly: A Study of His Life and Work from 1733 to 1773*. University Park, Penn.: Pennsylvania State University Press, 1998.

Scott, Patrick, comp. *"The Biographical Part of Literature": An Exhibition in Celebration of Literary Biography from the Collections of Thomas Cooper Library*. Columbia, S.C.: Thomas Cooper Society, 1998.

Secrest, Meryle. *Stephen Sondheim: A Life*. New York: Knopf, 1998.

Settle, Mary Lee. *Addie: A Memoir*. Columbia: University of South Carolina Press, 1998.

Simon, Linda. *Genuine Reality: A Life of William James*. New York: Harcourt Brace, 1998.

Spencer, Elizabeth. *Landscapes of the Heart: A Memoir*. New York: Random House, 1998.

Stebbins, Chad. *All the News Is Fit to Print: Profile of a Country Editor*. Columbia: University of Missouri Press, 1998.

Steiner, George. *Errata: An Examined Life*. New Haven, Conn.: Yale University Press, 1998.

Stevenson, Robert Louis. *Selected Letters of Robert Louis Stevenson,* edited by Ernest Mehew. New Haven, Conn.: Yale University Press, 1998.

Theroux, Paul. *Sir Vidia's Shadow*. London: Hamilton, 1998.

Thomas, D. M. *Alexander Solzhenitsyn: A Century in His Life*. New York: St. Martin's Press, 1998.

Toth, Emily, Per Seyersted, and Marilyn Bonnell, eds. *Kate Chopin's Private Papers*. Bloomington: Indiana University Press, 1998.

Trillin, Calvin. *Family Man*. New York: Farrar, Straus & Giroux, 1998.

Turner, Paul D. L. *The Life of Thomas Hardy: A Critical Biography*. Malden, Mass.: Blackwell, 1998.

Tynan, Kenneth. *Kenneth Tynan: Letters*. New York: Random House, 1998.

Vitale, Serena, and Ann Goldstein. *Pushkin's Button*. New York: Farrar, Straus & Giroux, 1998.

Volkov, Solomon. *Conversations with Joseph Brodsky: A Poet's Journey through the Twentieth Century,* translated by Marian Schwartz. New York: Free Press, 1998.

Waldron, Ann. *Eudora Welty: A Writer's Life*. New York: Doubleday, 1998.

Watts, Steven. *The Magic Kingdom: Walt Disney and the American Way of Life*. Boston: Houghton Mifflin, 1998.

Waugh, Auberon. *Will This Do?: The First Fifty Years of Auberon Waugh; An Autobiography*. New York: Carroll & Graf, 1998.

West, James L. W. *William Styron: A Life*. New York: Random House, 1998.

West, Richard. *Daniel Defoe: The Life and Strange and Surprising Adventures*. New York: Carroll & Graf, 1998.

West, W. J. *The Quest for Graham Greene*. New York: St. Martin's Press, 1998.

White, Edmond. *Marcel Proust*. New York: Viking, 1998.

Williams, John R. *The Life of Goethe: A Critical Biography*. Oxford & Malden, Mass.: Blackwell, 1998.

Winchester, Simon. *The Professor and the Madman*. New York: HarperCollins, 1998.

Woodhouse, Jayne. *Beatrix Potter*. Des Plaines, Ill.: Heinemann Interactive Library, 1998.

Wright, Thomas E. *Growing Up with Legends: A Literary Memoir*. Westport, Conn.: Praeger, 1998.

Zagorin, Perez. *Francis Bacon*. Princeton, N.J.: Princeton University Press, 1998.

Contributors

Tracy Simmons Bitonti . . . . *Columbia, South Carolina*

William R. Cagle. . . . . *Director Emeritus, The Lilly Library*

Richard Curtis. . . . . *New York, New York*

Susan Thach Dean . . . . *University of Colorado at Boulder*

Charles L. Egleston . . . . *Pierpont Morgan Library*

George Garrett . . . . *University of Virginia*

Amy S. Green . . . . *John Jay College of Criminal Justice*

Donald J. Greiner . . . . *University of South Carolina*

Henry Hart . . . . *College of William and Mary*

Caroline Hunt . . . . *College of Charleston*

Carol McGinnis Kay . . . . *University of South Carolina*

John E. Lane . . . . *Wofford College*

Michael L. Lazare . . . . *New Milford, Connecticut*

Luis Leal . . . . *University of California, Santa Barbara*

G. Spencer Lueders Jr.. . . . . *University of South Carolina*

Lauren MacIntyre . . . . The New Yorker

Tom McCormack . . . . *New York, New York*

Ted Mitchell . . . . *Thomas Wolfe Memorial*

Merritt Moseley. . . . . *University of North Carolina at Asheville*

Celso Lemos de Oliveira . . . . *University of South Carolina*

Kelli Rae Patton. . . . . *New York, New York*

Stacey Peebles . . . . *Austin, Texas*

Paul Ruffin . . . . The Texas Review

David Seaman . . . . *Alderman Library, University of Virginia*

James R. Simmons Jr. . . . . *Louisiana Tech University*

Kendon Stubbs . . . . *Alderman Library, University of Virginia*

Ernest Suarez. . . . . *Catholic University of America*

Kiyohiko Tsuboi. . . . . *Kobe Women's University, Seto College*

Nobuko Tsuboi . . . . *Tsuyama Higashi High School*

John Unrue . . . . *University of Nevada, Las Vegas*

Thomas J. Wood. . . . . *University of Illinois at Springfield*

Fred M. Woodward . . . . *University Press of Kansas*

Cumulative Index

Dictionary of Literary Biography, Volumes 1-206
Dictionary of Literary Biography Yearbook, 1980-1998
Dictionary of Literary Biography Documentary Series, Volumes 1-19

Cumulative Index

DLB before number: *Dictionary of Literary Biography,* Volumes 1-206
Y before number: *Dictionary of Literary Biography Yearbook,* 1980-1998
DS before number: *Dictionary of Literary Biography Documentary Series,* Volumes 1-19

B

G

Cumulative Index

K

Locke, Richard Adams 1800-1871 . . . . DLB-43

Locker-Lampson, Frederick
1821-1895 . . . . DLB-35, 184

Lockhart, John Gibson
1794-1854 . . . . DLB-110, 116 144

Lockridge, Ross, Jr. 1914-1948 . . . . .DLB-143; Y-80

Locrine and Selimus DLB-62

Lodge, David 1935- DLB-14, 194

Lodge, George Cabot 1873-1909 . . . . DLB-54

Lodge, Henry Cabot 1850-1924 . . . . DLB-47

Lodge, Thomas 1558-1625 . . . . .DLB-172

Loeb, Harold 1891-1974 . . . . DLB-4

Loeb, William 1905-1981 . . . . DLB-127

Lofting, Hugh 1886-1947 . . . . DLB-160

Logan, Deborah Norris 1761-1839 . . . . . . DLB-200

Logan, James 1674-1751 . . . . DLB-24, 140

Logan, John 1923- DLB-5

Logan, Martha Daniell 1704?-1779 . . . . . . DLB-200

Logan, William 1950- DLB-120

Logau, Friedrich von 1605-1655 . . . . DLB-164

Logue, Christopher 1926- DLB-27

Lohenstein, Daniel Casper von
1635-1683 . . . . DLB-168

Lomonosov, Mikhail Vasil'evich
1711-1765 . . . . DLB-150

London, Jack 1876-1916 . . . . .DLB-8, 12, 78

The London Magazine 1820-1829 . . . . DLB-110

Long, Haniel 1888-1956 . . . . DLB-45

Long, Ray 1878-1935 . . . . DLB-137

Long, H., and Brother DLB-49

Longfellow, Henry Wadsworth
1807-1882 . . . . DLB-1, 59

Longfellow, Samuel 1819-1892 . . . . DLB-1

Longford, Elizabeth 1906- DLB-155

Longinus circa first century DLB-176

Longley, Michael 1939- DLB-40

Longman, T. [publishing house] DLB-154

Longmans, Green and Company DLB-49

Longmore, George 1793?-1867 . . . . DLB-99

Longstreet, Augustus Baldwin
1790-1870 . . . . .DLB-3, 11, 74

Longworth, D. [publishing house] DLB-49

Lonsdale, Frederick 1881-1954 . . . . DLB-10

A Look at the Contemporary Black Theatre
Movement DLB-38

Loos, Anita 1893-1981 . . . . .DLB-11, 26; Y-81

Lopate, Phillip 1943- Y-80

López, Diana (see Isabella, Ríos)

Loranger, Jean-Aubert 1896-1942 . . . . DLB-92

Lorca, Federico García 1898-1936 . . . . . . DLB-108

Lord, John Keast 1818-1872 . . . . DLB-99

The Lord Chamberlain's Office and Stage
Censorship in England DLB-10

Lorde, Audre 1934-1992 . . . . DLB-41

Lorimer, George Horace 1867-1939 . . . . . DLB-91

Loring, A. K. [publishing house] DLB-49

Loring and Mussey DLB-46

Lossing, Benson J. 1813-1891 . . . . DLB-30

Lothar, Ernst 1890-1974 . . . . DLB-81

Lothrop, Harriet M. 1844-1924 . . . . DLB-42

Lothrop, D., and Company DLB-49

Loti, Pierre 1850-1923 . . . . DLB-123

Lotichius Secundus, Petrus 1528-1560 . . . .DLB-179

Lott, Emeline ?-? DLB-166

The Lounger, no. 20 (1785), by Henry
Mackenzie DLB-39

Louisiana State University Press Y-97

Lounsbury, Thomas R. 1838-1915 . . . . DLB-71

Louÿs, Pierre 1870-1925 . . . . DLB-123

Lovelace, Earl 1935- DLB-125

Lovelace, Richard 1618-1657 . . . . DLB-131

Lovell, Coryell and Company DLB-49

Lovell, John W., Company DLB-49

Lover, Samuel 1797-1868 . . . . DLB-159, 190

Lovesey, Peter 1936- DLB-87

Lovingood, Sut (see Harris, George Washington)

Low, Samuel 1765-? DLB-37

Lowell, Amy 1874-1925 . . . . DLB-54, 140

Lowell, James Russell
1819-1891 . . . . .DLB-1, 11, 64, 79, 189

Lowell, Robert 1917-1977 . . . . DLB-5, 169

Lowenfels, Walter 1897-1976 . . . . DLB-4

Lowndes, Marie Belloc 1868-1947 . . . . DLB-70

Lowndes, William Thomas 1798-1843 . . . DLB-184

Lownes, Humphrey [publishing house] . . .DLB-170

Lowry, Lois 1937- DLB-52

Lowry, Malcolm 1909-1957 . . . . DLB-15

Lowther, Pat 1935-1975 . . . . DLB-53

Loy, Mina 1882-1966 . . . . DLB-4, 54

Lozeau, Albert 1878-1924 . . . . DLB-92

Lubbock, Percy 1879-1965 . . . . DLB-149

Lucas, E. V. 1868-1938 . . . . . . DLB-98, 149, 153

Lucas, Fielding, Jr. [publishing house] DLB-49

Luce, Henry R. 1898-1967 . . . . DLB-91

Luce, John W., and Company DLB-46

Lucian circa 120-180 . . . . .DLB-176

Lucie-Smith, Edward 1933- DLB-40

Lucini, Gian Pietro 1867-1914 . . . . DLB-114

Luder, Peter circa 1415-1472 . . . . .DLB-179

Ludlum, Robert 1927- Y-82

Ludus de Antichristo circa 1160 . . . . . . DLB-148

Ludvigson, Susan 1942- DLB-120

Ludwig, Jack 1922- DLB-60

Ludwig, Otto 1813-1865 . . . . DLB-129

Ludwigslied 881 or 882 . . . . DLB-148

Luera, Yolanda 1953- DLB-122

Luft, Lya 1938- DLB-145

Lugansky, Kazak Vladimir (see
Dal', Vladimir Ivanovich)

Luke, Peter 1919- DLB-13

Lummis, Charles F. 1859-1928 . . . . DLB-186

Lupton, F. M., Company DLB-49

Lupus of Ferrières circa 805-circa 862 . . . DLB-148

Lurie, Alison 1926- DLB-2

Luther, Martin 1483-1546 . . . . .DLB-179

Luzi, Mario 1914- DLB-128

L'vov, Nikolai Aleksandrovich
1751-1803 . . . . DLB-150

Lyall, Gavin 1932- DLB-87

Lydgate, John circa 1370-1450 . . . . DLB-146

Lyly, John circa 1554-1606 . . . . .DLB-62, 167

Lynch, Patricia 1898-1972 . . . . DLB-160

Lynch, Richard flourished 1596-1601 . . . .DLB-172

Lynd, Robert 1879-1949 . . . . DLB-98

Lyon, Matthew 1749-1822 . . . . DLB-43

Lysias circa 459 B.C.-circa 380 B.C. DLB-176

Lytle, Andrew 1902-1995 . . . . .DLB-6; Y-95

Lytton, Edward (see Bulwer-Lytton, Edward)

Lytton, Edward Robert Bulwer
1831-1891 . . . . DLB-32

M

Maass, Joachim 1901-1972 . . . . DLB-69

Mabie, Hamilton Wright 1845-1916 . . . . . DLB-71

Mac A'Ghobhainn, Iain (see Smith, Iain Crichton)

MacArthur, Charles 1895-1956 . . . . .DLB-7, 25, 44

Macaulay, Catherine 1731-1791 . . . . DLB-104

Macaulay, David 1945- DLB-61

Macaulay, Rose 1881-1958 . . . . DLB-36

Macaulay, Thomas Babington
1800-1859 . . . . DLB-32, 55

Macaulay Company DLB-46

MacBeth, George 1932- DLB-40

Macbeth, Madge 1880-1965 . . . . DLB-92

MacCaig, Norman 1910- DLB-27

MacDiarmid, Hugh 1892-1978 . . . . DLB-20

MacDonald, Cynthia 1928- DLB-105

MacDonald, George
1824-1905 . . . . .DLB-18, 163, 178

MacDonald, John D.
1916-1986 . . . . .DLB-8; Y-86

MacDonald, Philip 1899?-1980 . . . . DLB-77

Macdonald, Ross (see Millar, Kenneth)

MacDonald, Wilson 1880-1967 . . . . DLB-92

Macdonald and Company (Publishers) . . DLB-112

MacEwen, Gwendolyn 1941- DLB-53

Macfadden, Bernarr 1868-1955 . . . . . . DLB-25, 91

MacGregor, John 1825-1892 . . . . DLB-166

MacGregor, Mary Esther (see Keith, Marian)

Machado, Antonio 1875-1939 . . . . DLB-108

Machado, Manuel 1874-1947 . . . . DLB-108

Machar, Agnes Maule 1837-1927 . . . . DLB-92

Machen, Arthur Llewelyn Jones
1863-1947 . . . . .DLB-36, 156, 178

MacInnes, Colin 1914-1976 . . . . DLB-14

MacInnes, Helen 1907-1985 . . . . DLB-87

Mack, Maynard 1909- DLB-111

Mackall, Leonard L. 1879-1937 . . . . DLB-140

Cumulative Index

ISBN 0-7876-2520-5

90000

9 780787 625207

ISBN 0-7876-2520-5

90000

9 780787 625207